Second Edition

CRIMINAL JUSTICE

in the community

Charles P. McDowell, Ph.D.

anderson publishing co.
2035 reading road
cincinnati, ohio 45202
(513) 421-4142

since 1887

Criminal Justice in the Community, Second Edition

Copyright © 1993 by Anderson Publishing Co./Cincinnati, OH

ISBN 0-87084-559-4
Library of Congress Catalog Number 92-70235

Ellen S. Boyne *Project Editor*　　　　　　　*Managing Editor*　Kelly Humble

Cover illustration and design by Sharpe Grafik Works

TABLE OF CONTENTS

(Chapter 2, continued)

Chapter 3

COMMUNITIES IN TRANSITION:

THE EVOLVING ENVIRONMENT OF CRIMINAL JUSTICE   57

Chapter 8

THE POLICE CULTURE

AND THE CHALLENGE OF THE TWENTY-FIRST CENTURY   **229**

Chapter 11

JUVENILE JUSTICE _____ **339**

Photo Credit: Bill Powers, Frost Publishing Group, Ltd.

Chapter 1

INTRODUCTION

Our system of criminal justice is enormously complex. In one way or another it touches the lives of all of us. Contact with the criminal justice system can take a variety of forms: serving on a jury, getting a traffic ticket, hiring an ex-offender, being robbed or getting directions from a police officer—to name but a few. Some contacts are personal and direct while others are vicarious (for instance, what we experience through television or movies). Other contacts are secondhand, consisting of what we have been told and believe to be true. These are not really "contacts" at all, but anticipations. Examples include the elderly citizen who is afraid to go out after dark for fear of being attacked, the rape victim who refuses to report the crime because she thinks she will be humiliated at the hands of the authorities, and the young boy who is frightened of the police because an overly zealous parent has told him that if he misbehaves, "the cops will take him away and put him in jail."

Contact with the criminal justice system (real or imagined) can make a strong impression and leave long-term residual feelings. These feelings shape attitudes and provide much of the basis on which individuals view the system as a whole. Because of this, people develop divergent and sometimes conflicting attitudes toward the same things. Adding to the confusion, the system itself is often characterized by diversity, internal contradictions and fragmentation. How can the average person be expected to make sense out of such chaos? How is the criminal justice system itself supposed to respond to the wide range of

1

feelings and expectations held by the people it nominally serves? These are not simple questions, and there are no easy answers to them. Perhaps the best way to understand the system, especially as it functions within the total community, is to look at it from several different perspectives.

THE ADMINISTRATION OF JUSTICE
AS A PUBLIC ENTERPRISE

The administration of justice is a public enterprise: it is a function of government. Criminal justice agencies are public agencies. This simple fact has profound significance. Only certain kinds of activities can or should be carried out by the government. Moreover, knowing that an activity is a public function offers considerable insight into how it is organized and administered. Public activities differ from those in the private sector in some fundamental ways. Consider the following:

COLLECTIVE GOODS

Economists sometimes use the term "collective goods" to describe indivisible benefits. An indivisible benefit is something that benefits all members of society regardless of whether a given individual chooses to use it or even wants it. For example, most homeowners pay school taxes whether or not they have children in the public schools. They do so because public education is a collective good that benefits all citizens and is something from which society as a whole derives a benefit. The administration of justice is another indivisible benefit. Theoretically, the police are as close as the nearest telephone, and in an emergency they can marshal enormous resources for the benefit of an individual. To see this in action, one need only watch the procedure at a serious traffic accident.

The caption, *"City Man Injured in Motorcycle Accident,"* appeared in a local newspaper. The article that followed took up less than two inches and simply stated that a local resident was seriously injured when he struck an automobile that was making an improper turn into a shopping center. The article noted that the man was in stable condition in a local hospital and that the driver of the car had been charged in the accident. Most people would skim the article without giving it a second thought; few would realize the high drama that was involved. Let's take a look at what happened.

The driver of the car made a sharp left turn without first signaling, because on an impulse he decided to go into a store in a shopping center he was passing. He said he did not see the motorcycle approaching in the traffic lane he crossed.

The motorcycle struck the front fender of the car at about 35 miles per hour. The driver was thrown from the motorcycle face-first into the windshield. When the vehicles came to a stop the driver of the motorcycle was critically injured.

The county emergency medical transportation service received a number of calls simultaneously, each reporting the accident. The dispatcher gave the call to the nearest mobile intensive care unit, instructing it to respond on an emergency basis. The dispatcher then notified the fire and police departments by direct line. The fire department dispatched an engine company along with a rescue squad from a fire station located a few blocks away. The police dispatcher sent two patrol units and a supervisor, all of whom responded with lights and sirens.

In less than five minutes all the units were at the scene of the accident. The victim had obvious multiple compound fractures of the extremities and it appeared that his neck might have been broken. He was bleeding heavily, was in respiratory distress, and was quickly going into shock. Emergency first aid was started by the fire department personnel while the paramedics set up their equipment. The police assisted with the victim, re-routed traffic and began their investigation of the accident. Because of the seriousness of the victim's injuries, it took about 30 minutes to stabilize and "package" him for transportation. During the entire time, the paramedics were in direct radio contact with the emergency room where there was a specialist in emergency medicine. They were able to control the bleeding, relieve the respiratory distress and immobilize the broken bones. The victim's neck was also immobilized and he was secured to a "backboard" so he could be moved without aggravating his injuries. He was finally placed in a police helicopter, which had landed in the playground of a nearby school, and rushed to the hospital. The police controlled the crowd of bystanders, interviewed witnesses, photographed and measured the accident scene and took the driver of the car into custody for further questioning after having his car impounded. Fire department personnel cleaned up the accident scene, washed away the gasoline from the motorcycle and swept up the glass and other debris from the wreck before departing. Within an hour from the moment the accident happened, everything was back to normal at the scene. The victim, although critically injured, was responding well at the hospital. The fire fighters were back in their station. The driver of the car was in the process of making a statement to the police. The bystanders had departed. What did this utilization of the city and county's resources cost the victim? Nothing. They are collective goods available to all of us.

Although in theory the administration of justice produces a collective good, it is somewhat selective in how it is actually used, paid for and perceived. The poor, even though they pay fewer taxes, tend to receive a disproportionate share of criminal justice services. Even so, many of them resent the quality of the service they receive, alleging that a dual standard in the administration of justice operates to their detriment. The affluent pay more taxes but seem to receive little direct benefit from the money spent. They are especially annoyed by actions of the courts and prisons that they perceive as foolish, if not actually dangerous. Neither group understands the perspective of the other.

If the criminal justice system operated in a market economy and users paid for what they got, many who need police assistance would not be able to afford it. If there were a charge for a district attorney's services, how many victims could afford to pay for the prosecution of those who harmed them? Who would pay for the prisons? The administration of justice, by its very nature, must be a public undertaking. At least in theory, this assures all citizens of equality before the law and makes the services of the entire criminal justice system available to everyone. Public agencies, however, do not always seem to function in support of the interest of their clientele. Why is this?

INSTRUMENTS VS. INSTITUTIONS

Downs has noted that "bureaus" come into existence in four ways. First, they can emerge through what Max Weber called the "routinization of charisma."[1] This kind of organization typically grows out of the teachings or philosophy of some charismatic leader. Many religions and social movements are formed this way. Second, a bureau may be created in order to carry out a specific function that is either not being met at all or is being met inadequately. This happened when municipalities took over fire fighting from the insurance companies. Third, a new agency can split off from a parent organization, such as the Air Force did from the Army after World War II. Fourth, a new organization can be created through "entrepreneurship." This occurs when a group of advocates promotes a particular policy and gains enough support to establish an organization for carrying out that policy.[2]

When concern for a particular problem on the part of a segment of society is brought to the attention of the authorities, action of some type is likely to result. If the appropriate public agency has the authority to act on the problem, it will probably do so. If there is no authority to act, then legislation may be introduced to give some public agency the authority it needs. The police, courts, correctional systems and prosecutors are all authorized by law to deal with some aspects of a public problem (i.e., crime), and each of these agencies acts in response to its perception of what the public needs or demands.

To the extent that a public agency effectively fulfills the purpose for which it was created, it may be regarded as an instrument for achieving some goal or objective. However, Carroll Quigley has rather dryly noted that "instruments" invariably become "institutions." He said that an institution is an instrument that has taken on activities and purposes of its own, separate and different from the purposes for which it was formed. As a consequence, institutions tend to achieve their original purposes with decreasing effectiveness.[3] He gives three reasons for this. First, "instruments" are composed of people, and over time people tend to substitute their own goals for those of the institutions of which they are a part. Second, the rules essential for the efficient management of an organization tend to become more important to the organization than its original objectives. Finally, many organizations are reluctant to change and therefore fall behind the times through simple inertia. For these reasons many public agencies tend to become institutions more concerned with advancing their own interests than with achieving the purposes for which they were created.

Peter has noted that most things do not work very well. "In time," he said, "every post tends to be occupied by an employee who is incompetent to carry out its duties...[W]ork is accomplished by those employees who have not yet reached their level of incompetence."[4] This so-called Peter Principle clearly has merit; we all can find examples of people who have been promoted beyond their level of competence. However, the problem is not simply a matter of public organizations filled with people who are incompetent. More often the problem is that the organization no longer does what it was formed to do in the first place, either because it has been captured by tradition or because it has redirected its resources in favor of protecting the personal interests of its members. In some cases the organization simply has not kept pace with change. Kharasch has embodied this idea in his concept of the *institutional imperative*, which states: "Every action or decision of an institution must be intended to keep the institutional machinery working."[5] He continues, "To speak of any goal or purpose of an institution other than keeping the institutional machinery running is no more meaningful than to speak of the goal of an automobile exhaust or the purpose of the hum of a sewing machine."[6] This substitution of personal for organizational goals is known as "goal displacement."

Problems of goal displacement (and even incompetence) are not unusual in any organization, but why do they seem to be so common and so difficult to deal with in public agencies? If the quality of service provided by a private company diminishes over time, its consumers will look to other, better sources. This will eventually cut into the profits of the company and give it a clear message: shape up or go out of business. The private-sector economy is very sensitive to this kind of message. The formula by which private businesses evaluate their performance is very basic: they measure the value of their outputs by their profits. If the public will not buy a given product or service, it is usually because the commodity is either not wanted in the first place or because it can be obtained better or cheaper elsewhere. This, however, does not generally apply to government and is certainly not the case with the criminal justice system.

Police departments do not compete with one another any more than courts or prisons do. Moreover, public agencies do not usually have to justify their existence or their actions once they have been created. Unfortunately, agencies like police departments and courts are not directly accountable to the public in any realistic way, and there are no reliable means for measuring the quality of their outputs. This is one reason why there are such tremendous differences among public agencies with similar responsibilities. Understanding disparities in the administration of justice requires an appreciation of the fact that its processes are carried out by public agencies, many of which are as responsive to their own "institutional imperatives" as they are to the needs of the community. The general lack of direct accountability on the part of these agencies, combined with their inability to accurately measure the value of their outputs, creates many opportunities for consumer discontent.

To counter this, it is not unusual for a government agency to engage in a public relations effort to polish a tarnished image. However, if the basic problem is that the agency is not responsive to the needs of its clientele, then public relations alone will not solve it. Criminal justice agencies are by no means exempt from the problems that beset all organizations, and it is important for the system to be alert to the subtle changes that can transform it from being an effective instrument into a sluggish, unresponsive institution. This means, among other things, that they must continually remind themselves that they operate within the broader context of society. This calls for a dual awareness. On the one hand, each agency must carefully monitor its external environment: it must know who and what its clients are, and how it can meet their needs as efficiently and effectively as possible. A sensitivity to change and a willingness to adapt to new requirements are essential. On the other hand, it must also keep a watchful eye on internal issues. Since criminal justice agencies are composed of people, "people problems" can be a major source of trouble. Coping with human resources is one of the most important tasks of management, yet it is a responsibility too often overlooked or given insufficient attention. The rapid rise of unions in the public sector (particularly among police) is clear evidence that such problems have been ignored or mishandled.

POWER SETTINGS [7]

A second frame of reference deals with power. Power is the ability to act. Perhaps more importantly, it is the ability to make others act. The state is vested with considerable power. It has the authority to compel its citizens to do certain things (such as stop at red lights) and not to do others (such as steal or commit murder). Of course, there are people who disregard laws and do as they wish. In such cases the state may apply its coercive powers in apprehending and punishing them. However, power is far more subtle than the foregoing suggests, for it is not always based on law and administered with an even hand. Organizations and individuals attempt to obtain power for a variety of reasons: to carry out a mission, to increase the amount of control exercised over the immediate environment and to enhance the position of individuals within the organization. In fact, a great deal of what people do involves getting and exercising power—often for its own sake, and sometimes to the detriment of the public.

From the perspective of a public agency, it is important to remember that organizations, like people, are not isolated from the rest of society. What an organization becomes and how it fulfills its social functions are determined in large measure by its relationships with other people and organizations. The cluster of people and organizations vital to the interests of an agency may be described as its "power setting." This power setting is composed of a number of major elements: the executive, rivals, beneficiaries, "regulatees" and allies.

THE EXECUTIVE

The "executive" is the person who has ultimate authority over the organization, such as the chief of police, the district attorney or the warden of a prison. These people are not sovereign: they do not wield absolute power, but instead have their powers limited by law, custom or the bodies that control their funding (such as city councils or state legislatures). The executive is the person within the organization who is supposed to shape its policies into operational realities. The power of an executive may show itself in his or her degree of accomplishment or lack thereof. The executive's decisions will be influenced by the kinds of things that influence the decisions of all others. The fact that someone occupies a position of executive authority by no means proves that he or she is the best person for that particular position; some executives are clearly incompetent. To the extent that an executive is incapable of discharging his duties, the entire organization and its clientele will suffer to some degree.

RIVALS

Any organization that competes with another organization is a rival. Competition may be *functional* (competition for like tasks) or *allocational* (competition for resources). In general, there is very little functional rivalry among criminal justice agencies—there is usually just one police department in town. This lack of functional competition may be a major factor in the relatively low quality of the output of some agencies. On the other hand, criminal justice agencies have many allocational rivals. The police department must normally compete with all other municipal departments for its budget, just as the department of corrections must compete with other state agencies for its funds. There may even be fierce competition for funds *within* an organization. If there is an ample supply of money for everyone, allocational conflicts tend to be insignificant. However, when the competition for funds becomes acute, the resulting rivalries can get intense and even unpleasant. Voter initiatives based on citizen dissatisfaction with government taxation, inflation and economic depression have created a serious financial crunch for all levels of government. As a result, not all agencies (or bureaus within agencies) will survive during periods of economic hardship and one can expect to see shifts in the delivery of public services, including criminal justice services. Money needed for expensive programs will be much harder to get. For many agencies, an inability to maintain current levels of service in the face of greater demands and shrinking budgets will ultimately produce clientele dissatisfaction in areas where services must be cut or otherwise modified. Indeed, it appears that the last decade of the century will face major challenges at all levels of government; many changes can be anticipated.

BENEFICIARIES

Some people clearly benefit from the services of government agencies. For example, the resident of a burning house benefits directly from the services of the fire department, just as a welfare recipient is a direct beneficiary of the welfare department. Direct beneficiaries are likely to take an active supporting interest in the affairs of the agencies that provide them with benefits. They often exert a collective influence on advancing the interests of the agencies they utilize.

Other people are indirect beneficiaries; they generally give little thought to the indirect benefits they receive. For example, although prisons do help the public by keeping dangerous offenders out of circulation, few of us give any thought to this benefit or to the people who provide it. Indirect beneficiaries more or less ignore the agencies that serve them, allowing them to manage themselves somewhat unfettered.

Criminal justice agencies have relatively few direct beneficiaries. However, as a collective good, "justice" is not supposed to favor any particular group. For this reason the criminal justice system does not openly seek to benefit specific segments of the public. Perhaps the most obvious direct beneficiaries of the criminal justice system are those who supply such resources as radios, cars, weapons, supplies, equipment, facilities and consulting services. Another major category includes attorneys and others in the legal system who make their livings dealing with people within the criminal justice system. However, since most people only indirectly benefit from the system, they generally do not expend much personal effort in understanding how it works. It is presumed by most members of the community that those who work within the system do what they should; their goals and methods are rarely questioned. Some criminal justice professionals decry this apathy and urge citizens to take a more active interest; however, without some means for making people see themselves as direct beneficiaries, their appeals are likely to meet with little success. On the other hand, some criminal justice agencies abhor public scrutiny, believing their work is none of the public's business.

SUFFERERS

Just as some people benefit from government action, others may suffer from it. Very few agencies of government take direct action against individuals—the criminal justice system being the major exception. People suspected of having committed crimes are arrested by the police, prosecuted in the courts and incarcerated in prisons. As direct sufferers they have an immediate and direct interest in what the criminal justice system does.

There are also *indirect* sufferers. This category includes minorities, young people, the elderly and business owners. Some minorities may justifiably feel that they have been singled out for special negative attention. Young people may believe they are discriminated against, just as the elderly may believe they are inadequately protected. Those involved in business may believe that the system does not give them adequate protection, making it too easy for criminals to prey upon them. The validity of these feelings is secondary; what is important is that some people perceive their relationship with the criminal justice system as subjective and "unfair." If one believes one is a sufferer, then one is in actuality a sufferer; or, as W.I. Thomas said, "What is real in perception is real in its consequences." It should be noted in passing, however, that the criminal justice system is designed with the notion that some people ought to suffer as a consequence of violating the law or being disorderly; however, no person should be punished on the basis of age, race, sex or national origin. As we will see later, this is easier said than done.

"REGULATEES"*

Ours is a highly complex society, and in order to achieve overall harmony among competing interests there must be a variety of regulations governing behavior. People simply cannot be allowed to do as they please in all circum-

---

* The term *regulatee* is used by Downs in *Inside Bureaucracy*. See references at the conclusion of this chapter.

stances. Therefore, regulations exist, and many are enforced by the criminal justice system. The same police officer who is expected to protect you from serious criminals is also expected to maintain order. This is done through the regulation of such activities as traffic, alcohol consumption, the use of drugs, the ownership and use of dangerous weapons, and so on. Often such regulation is achieved by requiring licenses for such things as driving, owning or carrying guns, or permission to practice certain occupations. This is a necessary and proper function of government. Although most people accept these regulations, some become unhappy when they personally encounter their enforcement. The simple matter of getting a traffic ticket illustrates the point clearly. Nearly all veteran police officers have been confronted with the verbal abuse of the motorist who is unhappy because the officer is "harassing" him instead of "catching crooks." In addition, in recent years the police and courts have come under heavy criticism for enforcing laws that regulate morals, particularly those dealing with recreational drugs or sexual behavior among consenting adults.

On the other hand, some people object when police refuse to regulate the behavior of others. For example, it is not uncommon for a person to insist that the police take action against someone who has been bothering them. However, when informed that it is not within the scope of police authority to do so, a complainant may become angry or hostile if he or she feels like a rejected beneficiary, i.e., a sufferer. When citizens have expectations that are uninformed or unrealistic, they are likely to be disappointed with the outcome.

ALLIES

People or groups who are willing to support an agency in the event of conflict are its *allies*. Alliances can be formed for peculiar reasons, and in the criminal justice system it is possible to become an adversary of one element of the system simply by becoming the ally of another. For example, public defenders (and defense lawyers in general) have different goals than police and prosecutors. Even police and prosecutors may find themselves on opposing sides of some issues. Perhaps more important is the emergence of the public as an ally of the system. Some criminal justice agencies, especially the police, want the general public as an ally; others, such as the courts, are indifferent. The police need allies for a number of reasons. They need the public to help in reporting crimes and in acting as witnesses. They may also need political support, especially when budgets are at stake. The courts do not require the same kind of voluntary citizen assistance: members of the public who are needed at a trial can be subpoenaed. There is very little that citizens can do to assist the prison system, although citizen assistance may be important in the case of community-based corrections. It is important to remember that alliances are not usually made for their own sake; allies are courted and recruited for specific purposes.

Downs has noted that different bureaus may have radically different power settings.[8] If we are to understand the criminal justice system, we must examine each of its major components in light of its own unique power setting. We also need to realize that power settings can vary considerably from one community to the next. Finally, if we are concerned with the pattern of relationships between the community and the criminal justice system, it is important that we see how the community contributes to the power settings of the various parts of the criminal justice system. By taking this approach we can identify sources of conflict and attempt to correct them.

Understanding the nature of power settings can aid members of the community in influencing the quality of justice. By the same token, members of criminal justice agencies can use their understanding of power settings to establish a more effective outreach to the community. Community leaders (including those within the criminal justice system) can make use of the multitude of power settings within the community to improve the quality and scope of their respective roles.

COMMUNITY ECOLOGY

Studying the criminal justice system in a college course is a lot like dissecting frogs in biology. One cuts up the frog and looks at its parts. We do much the same thing with the criminal justice system in most courses: we divide it into its major elements and look at the parts. Just as the frog in biology lab is not quite the same creature it was when it was alive, neither is the criminal justice system the same in the classroom as it is in actuality. The "live" criminal justice system is an organic part of the larger community and is deeply entwined in the full range of community structures and processes. One cannot hope to fully understand the criminal justice system without looking at it "alive" in its ecological context.

The word "community" is a term used to describe a broad array of human groupings, some of which have little in common with one another. It is clear that communities vary on the basis of size, location, degree of urbanization, social composition and economic base. It is less clear that they also vary on the basis of what they provide to—and expect from—their residents. Some communities are close-knit and supportive while others are cold and impersonal. The quality of the administration of justice as a community process also varies from place to place. Some places have higher expectations of the system than others, some are more willing to invest resources in the system than others, and so on.

To better understand community ecology, let us take a brief look at some of its elements.   The combination of factors discussed below (the list is by no means complete) is what gives a particular community its own unique criminal justice system and explains why there is so much variation from one place to another.   It is the combination of many factors that produces the flavor of any given community.   Obviously the factors can combine in many different ways.

THE IDEA OF "CITY"

When we speak of community, most of us think of the specific towns in which we live.   The idea of "community" is closely identified with the concept of "city."   A city, in its simplest sense, is an aggregate of people within common geographic boundaries.   Unfortunately, reality is not quite that simple.   Cities change over time and have life cycles.   Where a city is in terms of its life cycle says a great deal about the place and its inhabitants.   Perhaps one of the best-known classifications of cities using this approach was by Lewis Mumford, who set forth a six-stage cycle of the growth and decline of the city.

The Life Cycle of a City [9]

The Eopolis (Stage 1):   This is the village community, which by contemporary standards we would consider to be both primitive and quaint.   The *eopolis* represents the first permanent (as distinguished from nomadic) settlement of an area.   People have made the place their home and have begun the domestication of animals.   The hallmark of this stage of community development is the generation of surplus.   In this primitive kind of community, social associations are based on blood ties, that is, on kinship.   The villages tend to be composed of clans or tribes of people related to one another.   At least initially, this kind of community has very little contact with "outsiders."

The Polis (Stage 2):   The association of villages or kinship groups into a somewhat larger grouping, perhaps in order to provide for mutual defense, leads to the development of the *polis*.   The bringing together of these various groups soon produces a division of labor that ultimately leads to the development of trades and crafts.   The *polis*, according to Mumford, remained a collection of families whose way of life remained basically homogenous.   Considerable control could still be exercised over the individual by his family and associates, and the roles each person was expected to perform were still largely determined for him.

The Metropolis (Stage 3):   The *metropolis* is a regional center that usually is strategically located along some major transportation route (the older ones were usually located along water routes). The metropolis is somewhat of a "mother" city, attracting residents from other, smaller communities. People are attracted to the *metropolis* because of its commercial and mercantile functions. Trade between the *metropolis* and other cities along its transportation routes provides a cultural cross-fertilization, further enhancing the division of labor and the specialization of trades and crafts. Of course, all of this produces a new set of social relationships that include a much broader range of associations than the family or kinship group. It is in the *metropolis* that we see the first signs of a beginning class struggle, for it is there that the "ties that bind" loosen and the inequalities of society become patterned and obvious. The *metropolis* is characterized (at least in the Western world) by mass literacy, a relatively fluid class system and the use of inanimate energy (the latter was in fact the basis of the industrial revolution—a major factor in producing the modern industrial state). It is now possible for a *metropolis* to form in geographic areas that were not previously suitable, as we are no longer dependent on navigable waterways for transportation. The combined use of air routes, railways and motor transport has given a new meaning to geography. In the *metropolis* we find people as individuals rather than as members of families or clans, and this means that the kinds of controls that must be placed on them must come from sources outside the family; hence, the need for extensive laws and ordinances, and for agencies to enforce and adjudicate them.

The Megalopolis (Stage 4):   Mumford says that this stage marks the beginning of the decline of the city. The utopian view that growth in technology can cure social ills begins to be offset by the dystopian view suggesting that technological growth almost certainly either generates or intensifies more social evils than it reduces or cures. In the *megalopolis*, the city concentrates on bigness and power—on economies of scale, and the owners of the instruments of production and distribution subordinate every other fact of life to the achievement of riches and the display of wealth.   Standardization and mechanization prevail; the *megalopolis* ushers in an age of cultural aggrandizement: scholarship and science by tabulation; sterile research; elaborate fact-finding with no reference to rational intellectual purpose or any ultimate possibility of social use. It would seem that at this point the community no longer supports the needs of its residents, but virtually consumes them as a kind of fuel needed to stroke a huge social machine gone wild. Rigidity and ossification take place, and the citizen becomes an appendage to his own institutions.

The Tyrannopolis (Stage 5):   In this stage Mumford sees parasitism and exploitation as pervading all aspects of social, economic and political life. Placehunting, privilege-seeking, bonus-collecting, favor-currying, nepotism, grafting and tribute-exacting become rife in both government and business, and are accompanied by widespread moral apathy and a general failure of civic responsibility. Each group and each individual takes what it can get away with; the motto becomes: "Me first!" Wars, disease and starvation emerge, and productive work in the arts and sciences ceases.

The Necropolis (Stage 6):   This is Mumford's final stage, and in it he paints a picture that is harrowing and bleak: war, famine and disease plague both city and countryside. The cities themselves become mere shells. *Necropolis* is the city of the dead, where flesh is turned to ashes and life is turned into a meaningless pillar of salt. Mumford described the *necropolis* in *The Culture of Cities*, written in 1938. That was less than a decade before the devastation of World War II and the rise of the modern post-industrial state.

Although Mumford's life cycle of cities presents an interesting overview of their historical, social, political and technological growth, it is also important because it reminds us that cities serve different functions. Although the basic functions of the police are the same in all cities, there are apt to be significant differences in how departments discharge their responsibilities. Although the residents of most cities expect similar results from their police departments, the kind of organization and procedures that work in one kind of city might not be as effective in another. One cannot conclude that one department is necessarily better or worse than the other. Different kinds of cities have their own pressures, problems and needs. The administration of justice within a given city can only be fully understood in the light of the needs and makeup of that particular place. As a result, it would be inappropriate to compare criminal justice agencies in one city with those in another unless the two cities were comparable in all major respects.

POPULATION

The size of a community's population is important. Typically, the more populous the city, the greater its diversity. As we saw in Mumford's classification, people in smaller communities tend to be bound together by somewhat closer ties of kinship, occupation and social convention. In larger communities, they tend to be bound together by interdependent economic needs and political interests. Other factors, such as racial composition and population density, also play important roles in defining the community. For example, members of minority groups who come to cities in search of opportunity often find only further disappointment and a new definition of poverty. Many seek the comfortable familiarity of ethnic or racial enclaves and in the process contribute to the cleavages already evident in most cities.

Density, the number of persons per square mile of land area, is a subtle but important factor. Population density links numbers of people with the space they occupy. Some cities have been able to expand their boundaries to accommodate growing populations while other cities have been locked into fixed boundaries surrounded by incorporated areas that block expansion. When this happens, a "central city" may find itself surrounded by other, smaller incorporated cities. These suburban cities might then provide much of the labor force used by the central city while contributing little to its tax base (almost half of local taxes are based on resident property values). When this happens, population figures for the central city do not accurately reflect the total number of people who impact on it. Any actual growth within the central city automatically increases its density.

The relationship between crime and population density has been widely debated. It has been shown that crime rates tend to be highest in the central city and diminish as one moves out toward the suburbs. It has also been shown that population density tends to follow the same pattern. However, the relationship between the two is not as simple as it looks. High density alone would no doubt provide more opportunity for many kinds of crime, but the key is the quality of the density. As Harries points out, "It would seem that conventional measures of population density (persons per acre or persons per acre of residential land) are quite inadequate as predictors of criminal environments. A crowding index, such as persons per room, is apparently a much better measure since it approximates human reactions to space and is more likely to help us predict areas of social pathology."[10] When large numbers of people are crowded together under conditions that strain the human capacity for effective adjustment, there may indeed be good grounds for anticipating conflict, disorder and violence.

THE TECHNOLOGICAL ENVIRONMENT

Technology has been described variably as a blessing and as a curse; in reality, it is a combination of both.[11] Technology has brought about tremendous social change, solving old problems and creating new ones. Technology is closely related to the nature of the labor force and plays a major role in determining the economic base of the community. For example, some cities depend essentially on manufacturing, whereas others may be characterized by a mill, college or university, military establishment or service occupation. Advances in technology and changes in the economy can have a dramatic impact on each type. The rapid increase in foreign car imports and recessions in the automotive industry, for example, has created enormous difficulties for Detroit and other "car cities." The development of the microelectronics industry resulted in the emergence of high technology corridors outside Los Angeles and Boston and the rapid growth of cities like Richardson, Texas (home of Texas Instruments).

The kinds of industries that develop in a given area help shape the work force and define the nature of the community. Clearly, technology is changing many cities—not always for the better. Some older, traditional cities have been plagued with problems. As one writer has noted, "The inner-city has changed. Middle-class whites have abandoned the city for the suburbs, leaving behind growing percentages (often large majorities) of lower-class blacks, the elderly and the poor. This is the new clientele who are the objects of urban bureaucracies, and it should be no surprise to find these bureaucracies under attack in the inner cities...."[12]

As communities change, the criminal justice systems within them also undergo rapid change. Driven by advances in technology, criminal justice is employing more sophisticated equipment and processes that are bringing about some fundamental changes in the way the police and courts perform. This in turn has produced a need for different kinds of employees than those hired in the past. The technological environment is a constantly changing and often confusing component of the community ecology. It cannot be ignored in any serious attempt to understand the criminal justice system.

Social Structure

We live in a stratified society in which people group together according to their levels of income, education and social values. These groupings reflect social class. However, as there are no definite rules for assigning class position (except at the uppermost levels of society), one's social class is not always easy to determine. A combination of factors must be considered: occupation; prestige within the community; possessions, wealth and residence; patterns of social interaction; degree of class consciousness; value orientations; and the amount of power wielded within the community.

Moreover, communities can differ considerably in their distribution of social classes. There are very wealthy communities that contain primarily upper-class and upper middle-class residents, just as there are very poor communities with large numbers of working-class people. Since each social class has its own value orientations and outlook (especially with respect to the criminal justice system), the class composition of the community will play a major role in the nature and quality of the criminal justice system expected and supported by the community.

POLITICAL ECONOMY

McKinney and Howard note that, "Ecology produces demands; culture determines the type and quality of responses that government will make; and political economy identifies the strategy—that is, how, when, and in what manner these demands will be satisfied. The political economy perspective allows us to view public organizations in terms of the power government officials exercise."[13] This is a synthesizing perspective; it allows us to tie together a number of the points that have already been mentioned.

Government has limited resources. Although in theory it may be legally capable of doing a great many things, as a matter of practical reality it actually does very few of them. Put another way, government must make some rational decisions about how it will allocate and spend its resources. The limitation is based on its ability or lack of ability to pay for those things. A given community can only raise so much revenue and its expenditures must roughly equal those revenues. This is why many government agencies operate at less than desirable levels of effectiveness. If it were possible to hire as many employees as were needed, and to purchase all the equipment required, then providing effective public services probably would not be a problem. Very few communities have this luxury.

How, then, does government decide what services it will provide and determine what the precise extent of those services will be? First, government provides what it considers to be "essential services," which include public safety and education; beyond that, it looks for a balance that provides the greatest number of social benefits for the largest number of people at the lowest possible cost. Second, the services provided result from a public policy process. This process is influenced by a wide range of considerations, including (but not limited to) the power setting of government agencies, citizen expectations and tolerances, pressure group activities, class structure of the community and political expediency. For example, in a mid-sized North Carolina community, a woman decided that a shelter was needed for battered women. She believed the community needed a refuge for women with means who faced physical violence in their own homes. While staying in the home they could be counseled and given information concerning their legal rights. At the time, there was no such refuge. Public policy dictated that women who were being abused should either call the police and secure criminal charges against their abusers or seek civil remedy in the appropriate court. This woman wanted the city to fund the "women's shelter"; that is, she wanted to alter the public policy concerning the plight of abused women. In order to achieve this objective, she went to a number of politically active sources: the Council on the Status of Women, several other women's organizations and the local media. Contact was made with female members of the city council and the county commission. Pressure was placed on key political officials (including the local state representative and state senator, the mayor and city manager, and even the governor's office). After an intensive and well-orchestrated campaign, the city and county jointly appropriated money to fund the women's shelter. This example illustrates how public policy and the provision of services can be shaped by individuals and special interest groups.

Two facts are evident: (1) the closing years of the current century are going to require considerable imagination and innovation in dealing with the social problems that plague the cities, and (2) city governments are going to be faced with major problems in funding public programs. The political economy of the community will become a focal point in the debate over solutions to these problems in the allocation of scarce resources. The entire criminal justice system will feel the consequences.

SUMMARY

We now have three major frames of reference to use in exploring the relationship between the community and the criminal justice system. At this point it is fair to ask, "Exactly how will these broad frames of reference help us understand community/criminal justice system relations?" In the first place, by looking at the full range of criminal justice services and practices as public enterprises, we can see the basis for many of the strengths and weaknesses of the system. The concept of collective goods tells us that criminal justice is designed for everyone's benefit, yet experience shows that in reality it is selectively distributed—and not everyone "benefits" from it in the same ways. We also see how the problem of goal displacement can convert an instrument into an institution, watering down the overall effectiveness of its operations. That this has happened to the criminal justice system will be made clear.

In the second place, by looking at the criminal justice system from the perspective of power and power settings, we will be able to see some of the subtle (and not so subtle) forces that work on both individuals and groups in the shaping of policies and operations. The idea of an agency's executive gives us a device for examining how individual responsibility "at the top" influences what an agency does—or fails to do. The idea of the executive is also important because it represents a point where subjective and objective factors cross in the development and implementation of policy. The concepts of functional and allocational rivalry enable us to understand the kinds of competition that force decisions, determining not only what will be done but also how it will be accomplished. It also shows why a great deal of an agency's resources are consumed in "playing politics" instead of "delivering the goods." The concept of power is vitally important because it is based on the premise that give-and-take relationships are part of a zero-sum game in which winners can win only at the expense of losers.

The third frame of reference—community ecology—underscores the fact that criminal justice can only be understood in context, specifically, in the context of the community of which it is a part. The elements that make up the ecology of a community are staggering in their complexity. Likewise, the size of a community and its composition in terms of its structure, population density and level of technology are critical variables in the larger equation.

The criminal justice system draws upon the community and reflects its composition in various ways. Gross inequalities in power relationships almost always result in an inequitable distribution of services. Factors associated with class affect the full range of criminal justice practices, from hiring police officers to determining which offenders will be given active time for their crimes and who will be placed on probation. These same class factors also influence community expectations of criminal justice agencies, including the kinds of services that will be tolerated and/or demanded.

The whole issue of criminal justice and community relations would be simple and problem-free if there were one set of rules which could be applied with equal effectiveness to all communities. Unfortunately, this is not the case. Just as communities vary dramatically, so does the quality of the administration of justice within them. Thus, the study of one is actually the study of the other.

DISCUSSION QUESTIONS

1. What are some of the ways to determine whether an "instrument" has become an "institution"?

2. Are most people direct or indirect beneficiaries of the criminal justice system? What are the consequences of this?

3. Why do you think so many people support the efforts of government to regulate the behavior of citizens—but at the same time resist being regulated themselves?

4. How would you describe the kind of community in which you live? How does the kind of community you live in influence the quality of criminal justice?

5. Do you think social class makes a difference in how people are treated by the criminal justice system? If so, give some specific examples.

6. Is social policy made "fairly"? Do you think that special interest groups demand too much?

7. Describe the "collective goods" provided by government in your community. Do they really benefit everyone? Would we be better off without some of them?

8. How can you have "allocational rivals" in a government agency? Give an example.

9. Do you think it is possible for the criminal justice system to convince citizens that they are direct beneficiaries? If so, how?

10. How has technology made city life more complex in recent years? Has this hurt the quality of justice?

11. Have recent trends in society limited the impact of class on the freedom of the individual?

12. To what extent is a person's access to "justice" determined by the status he or she enjoys in the community? What particular status-related factors are likely to be the most important?

REFERENCES

[1] Anthony Downs, *Inside Bureaucracy*. (Boston: Little, Brown and Company, 1967), 5; see also Max Weber, *The Theory of Social and Economic Organization*, trans. A.M. Henderson and Talcott Parsons (New York: The Free Press of Glencoe, 1947), 363.

[2] Downs, *Inside Bureaucracy*, 5.

[3] Carroll Quigley, *The Evolution of Civilization* (Indianapolis: Liberty Press, 1979), 101-102.

[4] Lawrence J. Peter and Raymond Hall, *The Peter Principle* (New York: William Morrow & Co., 1969), 27.

[5] Robert N. Kharasch, *The Institutional Imperative* (New York: Charterhouse Books, 1973), 24.

[6] Kharasch, *Institutional Imperative*, 24.

[7] Downs, *Inside Bureaucracy*, 44-47.

[8] Downs, *Inside Bureaucracy*, 44-47.

[9] Lewis Mumford, *The Culture of Cities* (New York: Harcourt, Brace and Co., 1938).

[10] Keith D. Harries, *The Geography of Crime and Justice* (New York: McGraw-Hill Book Company, 1974), 83.

[11] Emmanuel G. Mesthene, "The Role of Technology in Society," in *Technology and Man's Future*, ed. Albert H. Leich (New York: St. Martin's Press, 1977), 159-160.

[12] Jerome B. McKinney and Lawrence C. Howard, *Public Administration: Power and Accountability* (Oak Parks, IL: Moore Publishing Co., 1979), 104-105.

[13] McKinney and Howard, *Public Administration*, 106-110.

Photo Credit: Clark County School District

Chapter 2

SOCIAL CONTROL

Although their residents may seem to have a lot in common, most communities are quite diverse. Because of this diversity a certain amount of conflict is inevitable. It arises because differences in such things as income, social status, race, ethnicity, religion and education foster different perspectives. The result is that people will behave in ways that others may find strange or even "socially unacceptable." It is necessary to establish a common ground where individual and group differences give way to consensus. In short, there is a need for social control.

Some of the most effective forms of social control consist of the internalized values learned from one's "reference group." The process of socialization teaches people how to act among their peers and represents a powerful system of social control. Beyond this there is a formal system of social control based on law. In theory, the law does not recognize individual or group differences, but provides a set of expectations common to all. It is impossible in the narrow scope of a single chapter to describe in detail the origins and structure of law and the legal system; however, without at least some overview it would be virtually impossible to explore the relationship between the criminal justice system and the community.

LAW AND SOCIAL CONTROL

Without law there would be no criminal justice system. In fact, there would be no cities—at least as we know them. Business, industry, science, the arts—if they were to exist at all—would be radically different. Thomas Hobbes acknowledged this when he said that in a land without laws there would be "no arts, no letters, no society, and which is worst of all, continual fear and danger of violent death, and the life of man solitary, poor, nasty, brutish, and short."[1] The role of law in society—especially in light of the relationships between the criminal justice system and law, and between the community and law—is important to consider because the concept of law is the cornerstone upon which everything else is built.

THE FUNCTIONS OF LAW

Law, like all other social institutions, serves specific purposes. Before we determine how well the law serves its purposes, we need to understand what those purposes are. If they are clear, easily understood and logical, then we would expect the processes of formal legal institutions to follow suit. If, on the other hand, the purposes of law are complex, contradictory and illogical, we would expect to find its institutions and processes embroiled in controversy and conflict. Fundamentally, the law serves two broad purposes which are closely interrelated: the need for order and the need for justice. It is sometimes difficult to separate the two, and each is highly complex in its own right. Taken together, they have been topics of discussion among legal scholars for centuries.

The Need For Order

If people could do whatever they wanted, the result would be anarchy. Or, as Bodenheimer points out, "Where anarchy reigns, there are no obligatory rules which each person is bound to recognize and obey. Everybody is free to follow his own impulses and to do whatever comes to his mind."[2] If we were all hermits, anarchy might be acceptable or even appropriate. However, we are not hermits: we live in close association with one another and have mutual responsibilities, whether we recognize them or not.

Each group within society serves some purpose, undertakes action to benefit its members, and should be able to exist in harmony with all other groups. If this is to occur, there has to be some means for establishing order so behavior can be predicted, passions controlled and reasonable predictability assured. For this reason, each group recognizes a set of norms or rules that governs the conduct of its members. Since society itself is the overriding group, law is the system of norms that applies to all and assures order among its members. Law allows individuals and groups to organize their lives and affairs. Because of this, legal norms are considered so important that their compliance is backed by the threat of state-imposed force. Although the need for order reduces individual liberty, it also reduces many of the threats an individual would otherwise face. In its most basic sense, "order" is a trade-off in which the individual makes certain personal sacrifices in return for collective social benefits. It is clear that the sacrifices should be necessary and the benefits proportionate. If they are not, the trade-off would be "unjust."

The Need for Justice

Order by itself is no guarantee of justice. There can be order under tyranny in which a despotic government ruthlessly regulates every aspect of a person's life. However, most would consider such a society "unjust"; Americans expect their laws to prevent injustice. The second major function of law, therefore, is to achieve justice. "Justice" is clearly a much more complex issue than "order," because there is no universally accepted definition for it.

Justice has been defined in terms of its goals; for example, "To coordinate the diversified efforts and activities of the members of the community and to allocate rights, powers, and duties among them in a manner which will satisfy the reasonable needs and aspirations of individuals and at the same time promote maximum productive effort and social cohesion."[3] Exactly what does this mean? The answer is not clear. Bodenheimer noted that "when we delve into the problem of justice and try to unravel its perplexing secrets, discouragement and despair are likely to befall us."[4] Is justice, as Plato suggested, the obligation of people to tend to their own business and not meddle in the affairs of others? Or, is equality its goal, as Aristotle suggested?[5] Or is justice, as Herbert Spencer proposed, the freedom of every person to reap whatever benefits his talents would allow, impeded only by the obligation of not infringing on the equal freedom of another? Legal scholars have debated these questions throughout recorded history. The answer is as elusive today as it always has been.

In its most basic sense, justice seems to require an accommodation or synthesis between the rights of the individual (however those rights are defined) and the needs of society (whatever those needs might be). "Justice demands that freedom, equality, and other basic rights be accorded and secured to human beings to the greatest extent consistent with the common good."[6] The most perplexing question remains: who is to decide what those rights are, or what constitutes the common good? Difficulty in deciding what is "just" and to what extent trade-offs and compromises must be made is at the root of many of the problems within the criminal justice system and the community itself.

141394

THE SOURCES OF LAW

Although based on moral and philosophical issues, the law as a formal institution is pragmatic. Laws are formal rules—but where do they come from? We know that statutes are enacted by legislatures and that courts create law by their decisions, but these formal processes must be based on something more fundamental. To find the answer we must look at both the informal and formal sources of law.

Informal Sources of Law

Laws are based on shared values, experiences, sentiments and subjective interpretations of what is "right." Societies existed before there were formal laws. In fact, laws represent the formalization of the norms that preceded them. Norms that governed early societies grew out of beliefs about the environment and mankind's place within it. Spiritual beliefs were particularly influential. It should come as no surprise that a great deal of man's early norms arose from superstition and religion.

Among the earliest and most important laws are those embodied in the Torah—the first five books of the Hebrew Bible: Genesis, Exodus, Leviticus, Numbers and Deuteronomy. The Torah is believed to be canonical; in other words, it is considered divinely inspired. It is the keystone of three of the world's major faiths: Judaism, Christianity and Islam. Of the three, Judaism holds it in the highest esteem. Originally called the Law of Moses, by the second century B.C. it was called the *Torah* (Hebrew for *law*). Since about the third century A.D. it has also been called the *Pentateuch* ("five books," from the Greek *pente teuchos*). The Torah is not solely law; it also includes songs, oracles, prayers, miracles and history. This book of sacred writings has given the world not only some of its richest and most poignant literature, it is also the very wellspring of law itself. Consider, for example, the Decalogue (Ten Commandments) as a source of moral/legal guidance, or the terrible threat in Leviticus to those who would break the covenant ("I will even appoint over you terror...") as the basis for the legitimacy of retribution.[7]

For many generations religion *was* law. It was the responsibility of religion to define morality according to revelation or inspiration and to codify behavior accordingly. There were several reasons why this could be done with little difficulty. Early religion regulated highly homogeneous communities which were not nearly as diverse and complex as they are now. In the absence of science, human knowledge was minimal at best. So little was known that mastery of all but the most esoteric forms of knowledge was within the grasp of nearly everyone. In other words, people were equally ignorant.

Custom also influenced the ideology that ultimately became embodied in law. Forms of social organization, the distribution of land and other property, as well as various rights, duties and obligations arose out of the community. In this context the division of labor produced different rights and responsibilities that ultimately came to be seen as "proper" in their own right. Much of this "proper" conduct eventually shifted from custom to law.[8] It was not until the time of Henry II (1154-1189) that the ancient tribal system based on religion and custom began to give way to a system of formal law. It is significant that during the reign of Henry II the church and the state were formally separated. Thereafter, a system of writs, procedures and common law began to emerge. After establishment of the political state, *formal* sources of law emerged. However, the earlier *informal* sources continued (as they still do) to exert a major influence on the nature of the law.

Formal Sources of Law

The most important formal source of law is legislation. In the United States at the federal level, laws are passed by the Congress. State legislatures perform the same function at the state level, while local laws (ordinances) are passed by city councils, boards of aldermen or county supervisors. In each case the intent is the same: to formalize a norm. The authority of a state to pass laws for its internal regulation and to provide for government is called its *police power*. A state must have such power in order to preserve the health, safety, morals and welfare of its residents. The state is responsible for the protection of its citizens; it accomplishes this by ensuring public safety and order. States have very few limitations on this power: they must conform to the requirements of their own constitution and may not enact laws that violate or contradict federal law or the United States Constitution.[9] In general, local governments are considered elements of state government and are subordinate to them.

Legislatures enact many laws that merely formalize earlier custom or sentiment. For example, laws that prohibit *malum in se* crimes—acts considered evil in and of themselves, such as murder, rape and robbery—simply codify ancient sentiment. Legislatures also enact *malum prohibitum* legislation—laws that prohibit (or require) some act, not because the act (or failure to act) is inherently evil, but because the existence of such a law will operate to benefit society or some specific group. Examples include laws that prohibit the sale of guns to minors or felons; establish age, safety and compensation requirements; and regulate the safe and orderly flow of traffic.

As Chambliss and Seidman note, "Regardless of how homogeneous a society may at first glance appear, behind the cloud of consensus and unanimity there always lurks the fact of widespread disagreement on what constitutes the 'right and proper' thing to do."[10] This means that legislation frequently results from interest group activity in which some group seeks the passage of laws that reflect its own particular interests—often in opposition to the interests of other groups. Examples include laws that assure profitable returns to specific industries (such as milk, insurance and tobacco) and those that require a percentage of construction contracts to be given to minority contractors (so-called *set-aside contracts*). Chambliss and Seidman point out that "every detailed study of the emergence of legal norms has consistently shown the immense importance of interest group activity, not the 'public interest' as the critical variable in determining the content of legislation."[11] Thus, the output of legislation can mean rags or riches, servility or power, or weakness or strength to every interest group in the country.[12] If laws reflect special interests, and if legislation is more "available" to some members of the community than others, then laws may actually contribute to social inequities and foster, rather than resolve, conflict.

Another source of law comes in the form of *delegated* or *autonomic* legislation by which administrative agencies are created and vested with rule-making authority. For all practical purposes, the rules they make carry the weight of law. These agencies flourish under a wide variety of names: commissions, bureaus, boards, authorities, administrations and so on. Though their rule-making powers are checked both by judicial review and by the legislatures that created them, many of these agencies are extremely powerful and have the authority to regulate some very important aspects of our lives.

A final major source of law resides within the courts. "It is today the prevailing opinion in the Anglo-American legal world that a decision of a court of law—especially a court of last resort—which explicitly or implicitly lays down a legal proposition constitutes a general and formal source of law."[13] When a court renders a holding, that decision carries the impact of law. In general, courts seek to avoid creating new laws, preferring to follow precedent. However, in the case of some controversies, either no precedent has been set, or existing precedent is inadequate. In such cases the courts make "new law" by their decisions. Law generated by the courts tends to favor certain groups over others: "On the whole, courts have been particularly active in rule-making in those areas of law which affect litigants who are sufficiently wealthy to be able to activate legal processes."[14] Although there are many legal problems affecting the poor that never reach the courts (in spite of the fact that the number of people who might be affected is very large), this is changing. Legal advocacy for the poor, minorities and others has increased dramatically within the past two decades. In recent years the courts have been used with great frequency to hear disputes in the area of criminal justice and have rendered landmark decisions, especially in the areas of rights of the accused and the imprisoned.

It is important to remember that the major formal sources of the law employ formal organizations, such as legislatures, courts and administrative agencies, which operate in their own unique power settings. Moreover, membership in these organizations is very much a function of class and status. One does not become an attorney, judge or legislator effortlessly; the process of becoming a functionary within these institutions nearly always involves a socialization process of its own, a process that operates to produce order and predictability—the same end sought by the law itself.

TYPES OF LAW

There are many kinds of law: constitutional law, case law, statute law, treaties, regulations of administrative agencies, executive orders and local ordinances, to name but a few. However, it is convenient to divide law into two major classes: *civil* and *criminal*. Before looking at these two areas, it is important to distinguish between *substantive* and *procedural* law.

Substantive law is "that part of the law which creates, defines, and regulates rights."[15] It specifically defines the legal relationship between citizens and the state as well as among citizens themselves. The bulk of substantive law comes to us from the legislative branch of government. A simple way to remember what substantive law means is to think of it as the *substance* of what our lawmakers require of us. When we say something is "against the law," we are usually referring to substantive law.

Procedural law, on the other hand, sets forth the "methods and means of enforcing substantive legal rights. It provides the machinery to maintain suits to enforce these rights or to obtain redress for their invasion."[16] Perhaps it is easiest to think of procedural law as the body of regulations providing the mechanisms for bringing substantive law into practice. Both civil and criminal law have substantive and procedural components. All of this simply underscores the fact that the law is not a random, chaotic application of rules of convenience. The law not only regulates and imposes order; it is itself ordered and well-regulated.

Civil Law

Historically, people have engaged in behaviors such as marrying (and often divorcing), striking bargains and entering into obligations, selling goods or giving them away, borrowing and repaying money, asserting the right to enjoy the use of certain chattels, leaving money to heirs, and claiming (or renouncing) citizenship. Although these are essentially private or personal matters, the state has an interest in how they are conducted. Collectively these kinds of transactions have a major impact on all of us. In some cases, misconduct in these areas is a crime (e.g., bigamy, theft and fraud). For the most part, however, these kinds of transactions are regulated not by criminal law but by *civil* law.

Civil law has both substantive and procedural components. It is designed to assist in the regulation of private affairs and to provide means for settling disputes when conflicts arise. In general, conflicts arise when there is a dispute between parties over either a breach of agreement or a failure to perform some duty imposed by law. In these cases, the state does not prosecute as it does in criminal matters. The private parties themselves contest the controversy, using the courts to do so.

A controversy between private parties that is heard in the courts is a civil suit. It is an adversarial proceeding and must follow certain procedural rules. The party bringing the complaint is the *plaintiff*. The plaintiff must allege some wrong and ask the court to provide a remedy. These remedies can take a wide range of forms, such as:

- *Mandatory Injunction*—an order by the court that specifically directs some person to do something

- *Prohibitory Injunction*—an order by the court that prohibits some person from performing some specific activity

- *Reformation*—a court order that changes a written instrument in order to reflect the actual agreement which had been entered into by two or more parties (where the instrument either inaccurately reflects such agreements or omits them)

- *Restitution*—where the court attempts to restore a person to a previous position or status

- *Declaratory Judgment*—in which the court makes a determination of what the parties' legal rights are

- *Compensatory Damages*—money awarded to compensate for losses sustained because of the wrongful actions of another

- *Punitive Damages*—money awarded in addition to compensatory damages in order to punish the person who did the original harm or deter others from doing the same

- *Nominal Damages*—a small sum of money awarded (in cases where no actual loss resulted as a consequence of the wrongful behavior of another)

- *Liquidated Damages*—money awarded according to a previous agreement made by the parties involved

The kind of remedy sought depends on the kind of conflict that is brought before the court. It is also very important to remember that many (perhaps most) conflicts *do not* come before a civil court. In most instances an out-of-court settlement is reached by the parties involved, ending the matter without an actual trial.

Most private controversies arise as a result of a breach of an agreement (breach of contract) or when someone suffers a harm because another person has failed to perform a duty imposed by law (tort).

A *contract* is nothing more than an agreement between two or more parties that creates some kind of obligation. Contracts are voluntarily entered into, but once entered into they become enforceable by law. A person failing to uphold an obligation created by contract may be sued for the breach, and appropriate remedies may be sought. Thus, if Waldo agrees to build a house and sell it to Ambrose for a certain sum of money, he has entered into a contract and is bound by its terms. Let us assume Waldo agreed to build the house and sell it to Ambrose for $50,000. However, by the time the house is finished, the price of housing in the area has gone up and Leonard offers to buy the house from Waldo for $75,000. If Waldo then tells Ambrose he will not sell him the house (or will not sell it at the price previously agreed upon), Ambrose then has a *cause of action* and can sue Waldo for breach of contract.

Torts are wrongful acts (not involving a breach of contract) that arise as the result of the tortfeasor's failure to abide by some lawful duty. A tort duty is imposed by law. "Tort law establishes standards of conduct which all citizens must meet. It creates social duties among all members of society."[17] An unintentional tort arises when one accidentally breaches a duty imposed by law. Most unintentional torts are based on negligence—the failure to use reasonable care. Most tort cases in this country are automobile collision suits in which the plaintiff argues that the defendant was negligent in the operation of a vehicle (i.e., was in violation of duties imposed by traffic law). Intentional torts, on the other hand, are based on willful misconduct where a wrongful act was intended. This includes such things as libel, slander and false imprisonment.

Theoretically, every citizen has the right to prosecute a civil wrong. However, that right is severely limited. Because most people lack the legal knowledge and ability to bring suits before the courts, they must rely on an attorney to handle the case. As a result, legal fees can effectively bar those with meager resources from bringing suits. In some cases lawyers will accept a *contingency fee*—a fee based on the percentage of a favorable judgment. Such fees can run as high as 40 percent. Even when attorneys are willing to accept cases on contingency, the client may still be required to pay for all actual costs. Although legal remedies exist for virtually all legitimate civil wrongs, access to them tends to be limited to those who have money. This is another example of how class, status and power affect how various members of the community are able to influence their environment—or how they are prevented from doing so.

Criminal Law

A crime is an offense against the state; it is a public rather than a private wrong. An act is not a crime unless it is made a crime by law. There are no "secret" crimes (at least not in the United States). Crimes have traditionally been classified as *treasons, felonies* and *misdemeanors*. A treason, previously known as *lese majesty*, is an offense against the duty of allegiance. It consists of levying war against the government or giving aid and comfort to its enemies.[18] Felonies are serious crimes for which the state may inflict the death penalty or impose a lengthy term of imprisonment (usually in excess of a year). All other crimes are misdemeanors and may be punished by a fine, a relatively short term of imprisonment or both.

The substantive law of crimes defines what acts are prohibited; criminal procedure governs the actual administration of justice from the initial investigation through release from prison and into parole and aftercare. The guarantees that deal with criminal procedure are defined primarily in the Fourth, Fifth, Sixth, Eighth and Fourteenth Amendments to the Constitution. These procedural rules define what the state may and may not do in pursuing a criminal action against a private person. We are now ready for a specific definition of crime. *A crime is a legal wrong for which the offender is liable to be prosecuted and, if convicted by a court of competent jurisdiction, punished by the state.*[19] A crime is not simply a violation of moral sensibilities (although that may be involved); it violates a specific law that carries with it a specific punishment. Such laws are passed for a number of reasons. For one, criminal law seeks to protect the public from violent or dangerous conduct such as assaults, murders and arson. Criminal laws also seek to protect public health through such devices as pure food and drug laws and other statutes that regulate such things as the practice of medicine and pharmacy. Some criminal laws are designed to maintain order (e.g., traffic laws). Other criminal laws protect the right of privacy (e.g., laws making it a crime to unlawfully intercept private communications) or seek to protect public morality (e.g., laws regulating or prohibiting such things as prostitution, pornography and the consumption of alcohol by minors). In some cases, criminal law is enacted to advance some kind of public policy, as in the case of backing civil rights legislation with criminal sanctions.

The forbidden act or omission (*actus reus*) that is the basis of the crime must be spelled out in clear detail. In order to convict a person for violating the law, each element of the offense must be proven beyond a reasonable doubt. All crimes are composed of such elements. When the police investigate an allegation of criminal misconduct, they try to determine whether each of the elements of a crime took place. Their goal is to obtain evidence proving each element so the prosecutor can convince a jury of the defendant's guilt. If any of the elements of the crime are missing or cannot be demonstrated, then the "crime" does not exist (even though the demonstrable elements may support conviction on another, closely related crime). In some cases it is also necessary to show criminal intent or *mens rea* (from *actus non facit reum, nisi mens sit rea*, or "an act does not make the doer of it guilty unless he intended the act"). Criminal intent is a vague concept, and the courts have generally found that it exists along a gradient extending from negligence to recklessness to that which was done "knowingly," and finally to conduct that was intentionally committed in spite of knowledge that it was illegal. In the case of strict liability crimes there is no need to show intent; proof of the act itself is sufficient to sustain a conviction. Statutory rape cases are strict liability crimes: all the state needs to prove is that the accused had sexual intercourse with a female below the age of consent. What the accused thought is irrelevant; all that matters is what he did. This raises an interesting side issue—the difference between motive and intent. A person's reasons for committing a crime are of no consequence to the state; all that counts is establishing that the offender intended to commit the crime.

There are, of course, many defenses a person can offer when accused of a crime. If a defense is consistent with those allowed by law, and if the accused can establish the credibility of his defense, a successful prosecution might be avoided. However, no defendant is required to offer a defense; it is the job of the state to convict him. All defendants are presumed innocent until proven guilty. However, there is an important difference between factual and legal guilt. A person can be factually guilty without being legally guilty. Just because a person is not prosecuted or has been prosecuted and acquitted does not mean he is "innocent"; it only means he is not legally guilty of a crime even though he may have committed the act.

THE CRIMINAL JUSTICE SYSTEM

In order to make the laws work, the state has established an elaborate network of agencies to ensure that laws are obeyed. The police, among other things, try to learn exactly what crimes have been committed and who committed them. They use their authority to investigate and develop this information. After establishing that a crime has been committed, the police identify the offender and gather evidence. After doing so, they turn the case over to a prosecutor so a formal accusation can be made against the suspected offender. The case is heard by a court and the accused, if convicted, is liable to some kind of lawful punishment. Each aspect of the administration of justice is carefully regulated by procedural law, custom, administrative guidelines and precedent. The state is limited in how it may go about this process. Hopefully, it ultimately results in "order" tempered by "justice." Even so, there are many ways in which inequities can creep into the administration of justice.

A criminal justice agency may be negligent in its duties: the police may either fail to investigate a crime or overlook it, depending on the nature of the crime and the status of those who are involved. Some criminal defendants may fare better than others because they can afford better legal counsel. Public policy in a given community can produce an uneven enforcement of the law, favoring some groups over others. Another potential problem is that criminal justice agencies may perform their duties improperly, as when police "beat a confession out of" a suspect or otherwise improperly and illegally obtain evidence. A prosecutor might be "bought" and refuse to prosecute certain offenders—or a court may be biased in favor of (or against) a defendant. Defense lawyers may literally extort their clients or fail to provide them with an adequate defense. Citizens themselves can subvert the administration of justice by failing to report crimes, refusing to cooperate with authorities during an investigation, withholding evidence or concealing crimes. In short, there are many ways the administration of justice can fail. When this happens, the system fails to provide the benefits promised by the rule of law, and society moves closer to the grim picture painted by Hobbes.

Another problem is that many people do not understand the administration of justice. They do not understand the distinctions between civil and criminal law. Some people have too much faith in the law and think it can do more than is actually allowed, while others have absolutely no faith in the law. The law itself has not always been "fair." Though court decisions continually change the meaning of law in an effort to keep it abreast of the times, it often seems to lag behind, producing resentment and hostility. There are many ways the administration of justice can contribute to poor community relations. This will be discussed in the following chapters.

PUBLIC CONTROL

Criminal law, as administered by the criminal justice system, may be regarded as part of the *public control system*. Criminal laws are intended for the benefit of the public as a whole, even though a given crime may have a direct impact only on the parties immediately involved. For this reason justice is supposed to be "blindfolded"—seeing neither race nor creed, wealth nor poverty, high nor low status. Although criminal laws may incorporate moral judgments, theoretically they are still applied across society as a whole.

The criminal justice system is the mechanism of the public control system. The work of the various criminal justice agencies should be seen as a collective good intended to benefit all. Of course, if these agencies fail in their responsibilities they reduce the actual worth of the collective goods they are supposed to produce.

PRIVATE CONTROL

Not all conflict is sufficiently serious to require government intervention. Social control actually extends along a continuum. At the "mild" end, control is simple, personal and "corrective" in nature. At the opposite end, it is complex, formal and punitive. At some point along this continuum—as misbehavior becomes relatively serious—the private control system becomes ineffective and the public control system must enter the picture.

The private control system is composed of institutions that are intended to shape, nurture and support the individual. They are *socializing* institutions. Their processes are carried out in personal, face-to-face settings and their relationship with the individual is usually intimate and long-lasting. The ultimate goal of the private control system is to produce a "proper" person—one who is able and willing to function in an acceptable manner according to the standards of his or her peer group and the larger community. In American society, the private control system is composed of five major elements: family, school, religion, the work setting and the individual's immediate social environment.

THE FAMILY

The family is probably the single most influential force in a person's life. The family in which a person is reared is the wellspring from which nearly everything else flows. The first and most basic function of the family is to nurture the infant physically and mentally. This is fundamental to the child's development, and much of his or her personality will be shaped through this process. Child rearing is also the means by which the individual is taught the basic roles that will be expected of him or her through life, and is the process through which basic values are transmitted from one generation to the next.[20]

The development of the child is an enormously complex process. It involves not only the development of motor skills and self-awareness, but also the foundations of sex-role identification and moral beliefs. Ideally, the individual emerges from childhood with a conscience, a sense of personal worth and a willingness to accept the basic conventions of society. The individual's conscience is perhaps the most important and long-lasting control mechanism of all.

It is the gate through which most behavior passes and the yardstick by which the individual judges what is proper and what is not. The development of the conscience takes place after a child bonds with his parents and has certain controls imposed upon him. The controls that are accepted and integrated into the personality are then used to moderate behavior. These controls generally take the form of rewards and punishments linked to the child's actions. A smile, a frown, a strongly worded "NO!" or a pat on the head can each be a powerful instrument for shaping behavior. Of course, the behavior that the child is rewarded or punished for is also important; these form the basis for his or her values. Different groups have different child-rearing practices that reflect that particular group's norms. Even when groups share the same basic values, they may have different ways of expressing or reinforcing them. This is one reason why pluralistic societies are so complex.

The American family has undergone profound changes over the past generation, many of which have weakened the traditional family unit. For example, the number of single-parent families increased from 12.9 percent of all families with children in 1970 to 27.3 percent in 1988. In 1988, single-parent families made up 21.7 percent of white families with children, compared with 59.4 percent of black families with children and 33.6 percent of Hispanic families with children.[21] Impacting significantly on these numbers is a rapidly accelerating divorce rate. In 1960, for every married couple living together, there were 35 couples who were divorced; by 1988 there were 133. However, the trend toward single-parent families probably has been influenced more by children born out of wedlock than by parents who divorce. In 1989, childbearing among unmarried women was at the highest level ever recorded in the United States, with rates of 80.9 per 1,000 unmarried black women and 23.2 per 1,000 white women between the ages of 15 and 44.[22] The full consequences of this trend are difficult to assess at this point but will undoubtedly have a significant impact in the near future.

Many of these households are economically and emotionally impoverished. In the center cities the problem is compounded by the scourge of drugs, especially crack cocaine. A big part of the problem is that crack, unlike heroin, is widely used by women. That fact alone seems to strengthen the stranglehold of poverty on many families: "If single-parent households have contributed to the intractability of poverty in the past, no-parent households may be poverty's appalling future."[23] Crack addiction by women has also resulted in an explosive increase in birth defects, child abuse and parental neglect, and "has bankrupted parental authority and...is destroying the fraying social fabric of inner-city neighborhoods all over the United States."[24] The following comments of an inner-city youth support this contention:

"My generation, what we were instilled on was morals, values and respect," Sam says. "If I disrespected your mother, she would beat me, and when I got home my mother would beat me, too. Respect played a bigger part. Now the new generation—what's being cool to them is being a hustler. It's got a lot to do with T.V., parents, babies having babies. When you're young, you're gonna do what your parents do, [and] if your mother is on the pipe, you're going to be on the pipe." He hobbles away on crutches—Sam got his leg broken recently in some mysterious street-corner dispute—heading for the shooting gallery....[25]

SCHOOL

At approximately the age of five, most children move beyond the narrow world of the family and into the second most important institution of their lives: school. Schools impose control through *what* they teach and *how* they teach it. Ideally, schools reinforce and expand upon the values imparted by the family. Schools actually do far more than teach "subjects" to students; they impart social and behavioral expectations and teach students to interact with others. Schools also mediate the plurality of our society. Children of different races, ethnic backgrounds and social classes are brought together and given common instruction in academic and social skills. In fact, one of the missions of the schools is to prepare young people for responsible citizenship by encouraging them to:

- Show concern for the welfare and dignity of others;
- Support the rights and freedoms of all individuals;
- Help maintain law and order;
- Know the main structure and functions of government;
- Seek community improvement through participation;
- Understand the problems of international relations;
- Support rationality in dealing with social problems;
- Take responsibility for one's own obligations; and to
- Help respect their own families.[26]

Schools reward children for conforming and punish them for misbehaving. Good grades and peer approval push the student in the direction of academic and social achievement; bad grades and punitive measures signal the child and his or her parents that the child's performance is lacking. Children who exhibit serious problems may be referred to school psychologists or counselors, or if the problem is serious enough, to public mental health programs for treatment. All of this is done in an effort to impose social control over children as they move toward maturity.

Education begins in preschool and extends all the way through graduate school, each step building on the progress of that which preceded it. The process itself is enormously complex and calls for a great deal of coordinated effort. In the early years of the Republic, the principle educational emphasis was on literacy. During the seventeenth and eighteenth centuries, literacy in America was spread primarily through church-controlled schools, parents teaching their own children and masters teaching their apprentices.[27] With the rapid development of compulsory public education in the United States, the task shifted to the schools and extended well beyond the traditional "three Rs." With the explosion of technology in the last half of the twentieth century, there has been a corresponding growth in the number and complexity of schools and a much greater emphasis on higher education. The new literacy is not measured so much in one's ability to read as in competence in the information sciences—including the ability to use computers.

Unfortunately, schools can and sometimes do fail in teaching these skills. In fact, the American educational process has come under heavy criticism on a number of fronts. American students have been compared with students in other countries with discouraging results. For example, during the 1960s and 1970s the International Association for the Evaluation of Educational Achievement administered exams to elementary and secondary school students in 17 developed countries. About 30,000 American students took a total of 19 exams in subjects ranging from math to literature. As a group, they finished *last* in seven categories and they did not rank either first or second on *any* of the exams.[28]

Student performance is not the only problem: "Of the students who score in the bottom 20 percent on standardized college entrance exams, 40 percent become education majors. Or, as a recent Carnegie Corporation report concluded, 'the problem with teacher education is that the wrong people are studying the wrong things in the wrong places.'"[29] An 87-question examination given to a representative sample of 696 seniors at 67 colleges yielded some dismaying results: "sixty percent thought the Korean War began during the Roosevelt, Eisenhower or Kennedy administrations, or shrugged in bafflement. One-third confused Reconstruction with the Marshall Plan, and one in four college seniors thought that 'from each according to his abilities, to each according to his needs'—Marx's daydream—was from the U.S. Constitution."[30] As one commentator pointed out, "Only 2 percent of the 3,000 institutions of higher education have core curricula. Students can graduate from 38 percent of America's colleges and universities without having taken a single history course, as at the university where the humanities requirement can be satisfied with a course on interior decorating."[31] In some cases curricula are designed to meet purely political agendas. A dispute at the University of Texas in Austin is but one example. There, thousands of students take English 306, which is the only required course on composition. As reported in *The Washington Post*, "[in the summer of 1990] an attempt was made to give a uniform political topic and text to all sections of E306. It was decided that all sections would read *Racism and Sexism*, an anthology with a pronounced left-wing slant."[32] Although that particular text was not adopted after some faculty members complained that instruction was being subordinated to political indoctrination, the controversy continues at the University of Texas as well as on many other campuses.

Some problems in public education seem to defy solution. For example, efforts to place students who display high levels of ability together in enriched classes has produced so-called "gifted and talented" programs. Although these programs provide an enormous benefit for students who participate in them, they also automatically label the students who are not in them as "second class." Schools that do not use these enriched programs also come under criticism. According to at least one educator, they were essentially being "asked to accept a watered-down curriculum and double standards of discipline for the sake of social engineering or racial politics."[33] Average students feel cheated and some educators see the tracking system (or the use of "ability groups") as a deliberate attempt to counter the legal gains won by the civil rights movement.

Though over-involvement of parents in the schools can be a problem, their *under-involvement* is an even bigger problem. As one teacher lamented, "You're the parent, the nurse, the policeman, the social worker, and very last, you are the teacher."[34] Many parents put their own careers or interests ahead of their children and essentially abandon them to the schools. In the United States nearly 73 percent of mothers with school-age children work outside the home, nearly 25 percent of all children under age 18 live with a single parent and only 7 percent of school-age children live in a two-parent household where there is only one wage earner.[35]

Even when schools are willing, that is no guarantee that they will have the *ability* to provide quality education. Since public education is funded largely by property taxes, community wealth has a major impact on educational opportunity:

> The Texas Supreme Court noted last October that despite overall increases, the state's 100 wealthiest districts were spending an average of $7,233 per student while the 100 poorest districts were spending $2,978. In San Antonio, those statistics translate into Alamo Heights students learning on up-to-date computers while across town in Edgewood, pupils study computer science by 'typing' on a keyboard sketched on paper. Patricia Rodriguez recalls trying to do classwork in an un-air-conditioned building in 98-degree heat. The richer district has swimming pools and tennis courts; at one Edgewood elementary school this spring, students played basketball with a plastic bucket for a goal.[36]

Moreover, what is the cost of crime associated with inadequate education? There does appear to be a clear relationship between low levels of educational attainment and prison incarceration. For example, the number of high school dropouts who were inmates in Texas prisons in 1988 was more than 90 percent.[37] It is not possible to determine the cost of educational failure in terms of criminal outcomes, but it is safe to say that the cost is considerable.

RELIGION

Religion has played a powerful role in the history of mankind. It answers some difficult questions and provides a framework for living. For many people religion provides meaning that allows them to make sense out of an otherwise capricious world. Most important for this discussion, religion is closely related to the whole realm of ethics and morality.[38] Moral laws (as interpreted by religion) assume the weight of divine commandments, and ethical duties become personal obligations to those who practice religion. Thus, religion not only explains life to its members, it also compels ethical behavior and fosters a sense of community. Religion provides rituals for our most significant personal events: birth, marriage and death—making faith an important vehicle for traveling through life.

The standards of behavior expected by most religions represent a direct form of social control. In earlier times the church was able to physically enforce its standards of behavior; however, because sacred and secular courts have been separate since the time of Henry II, the church may no longer inflict direct punishment on moral offenders. When the ethics and morality fostered by religion complement what is taught at home and in the schools, the individual is presented with a relatively consistent set of expectations. A violation of those expectations will result in punishment by these private agencies through a variety of informal and extralegal means. Such punishments are intended to coerce the person back to correct behavior and to prevent recurrences of the unacceptable behavior.

Religion in the United States has played a much more important social role than most people realize. Because America was an English colony, the bulk of its colonists were from a Protestant background, but as Hudson points out,

> ...it was an English Protestantism with a difference. At home the great majority of the people were Anglicans, members of the Church of England; and the "Dissenting" interest composed of Presbyterians, Congregationalists, Baptists, and Quakers was relatively small. In the colonies this situation was reversed. By the end of the colonial period the Congregationalists and the Presbyterians were the two largest American denominations. The Baptists and the Anglicans were roughly equal in size, and the Quakers—widely dispersed through-

out all the colonies—ranked fifth in number of adherents. It was this difference in the religious [makeup] of the population that Edmund Burke had in mind when he noted in his speech *On Conciliation with the American Colonies* (1775) that "the people [of the colonies] are Protestants, and of that kind which is the most adverse to all implicit subjection of mind and opinion."[39]

The transplanting of a variety of Protestant faiths to the New World assured a great diversity in religious perspectives. Moreover, the congregations in the colonies were not generally established on the parish system, in which individuals were more or less assigned to a church based on where they lived. Instead, congregations formed into "gathered" churches in which membership and support were based on purely voluntary participation. Thus, from the outset, religion in America supported and maintained diversity within the community.

Religion and education fit hand-in-glove in the New World. For example, even though the Northwest Ordinance of 1785 set aside land for public schools in every township, there was a lapse of time before the schools were actually built and staffed. In the meantime, ministers often served as schoolmasters.[40] The impact of religion on higher education was even more profound. As Hudson notes, "For the greater part of the nineteenth century, most secondary and collegiate education was carried on under denominational auspices. Of the 516 colleges and universities founded before the Civil War, only a few had no religious affiliation."[41]

After a century and a half of growth, the liberal Protestant churches began a period of declining membership in the 1960s. Some of the decline was based on members dropping out because of changes in liturgy, the ordination of women and homosexuals, and political activism by members of the clergy. The so-called "sexual revolution" of the 1960s, led by the advent of the birth control pill and followed by the highly divisive issue of a woman's right to have abortions on demand, altered traditional perspectives on morality. The removal of prayers from the public schools certainly severed a long-standing link between religion and education. Although religion continues to be important for many Americans, its influence appears to be in decline.[42] Moral issues seem less important and more remote from urban populations than in times past, and the extent to which religion shapes behavior is more open to question than it was in the past.

THE WORK SETTING

When the person leaves school and enters the labor force, the norms of the work setting act as a control over behavior. Those who conform are rewarded with privileges, promotions, raises and other benefits. Those who do not are likely to find themselves looking for a new work setting. Few people fully realize the actual extent to which the work setting imposes control on the individual. Some jobs require specific kinds of clothing; most set the exact hours and place where the employee is to work; and some even extend control into more private aspects of a person's life. Some employers pressure their employees to involve themselves in civic or professional activities within the community and others specify where the individual should live.[43] As people adapt to the requirements of their work settings, their lives take on a degree of predictability and stability they in turn demand of others.[44]

THE SOCIAL ENVIRONMENT

A person's social environment is composed of associations, place of residence, work and play. People who have similar family backgrounds, levels of education and occupations tend to cluster together. An individual's social environment is a composite of all these individual factors—plus many more—and serves as a major source of private control. Our social environment is our "place" from which we can become "out of place"—where we do not belong. One result of being out of place is that we quickly become confused as to what is expected of us. The cues and behavioral signals are different or unfamiliar, and our inability to predict just what will happen next is unsettling. We see this, for example, when we go as a guest into the home of a person whose social standing is quite different from our own or when we visit unfamiliar enclaves in the city.

The components of the private control system work together to influence behavior. They collectively function to keep the individual within the confines of an orderly and predictable environment. For the most part, the private control system shapes the person with an emphasis on preventing misbehavior. The sanctions imposed by the private control system are informal and personal, centering around the acceptance or rejection of the individual as a person.

The private control system can fail in two ways. First, some or all of its elements may simply fail to fulfill their responsibilities. This can happen when children are abused or neglected by families, when they are ignored or rejected by the schools, when they do not come under the influence of a religion or when they find their attitudes out of harmony with the non-deviant work environment. The second kind of failure occurs when a person comes under the influence of a family or other primary setting that actually teaches or encourages deviant values.

Most people are "controlled" in their day-to-day activities by an acceptance of moral and ethical values and a willingness to do what is expected. From time to time, conflicts occur—most of which can be solved through informal processes. Sometimes conflicts require more formal mediation, for which an individual may seek recourse in the civil courts. In more serious cases, an individual will behave in a way that the private control system either cannot resolve or in which private intervention would be inappropriate. In such cases the criminal justice system may be called upon to invoke formal sanctions. Were it not for the existence of conflict and the need for control, there would be no need for a criminal justice system—and no concern about how well it relates to the community.

CRIME AND DISORDER:
THE POLITICS OF BEING HUMAN

The criminal justice system is society's major formal response to problems of crime and disorder. It is the means by which the state exercises its police power to provide for the common good and assure justice for its citizens. We have already noted that the criminal justice system must operate within the framework of substantive law and procedural due process. It must also function in a manner consistent with community sentiment. Difficulty with this arises partly from the fact that the criminal justice system must perform its tasks in a continually changing environment and must satisfy substantial numbers of people with widely varying notions of what "law and order" is (or ought to be). Dealing with crime has been particularly difficult because it means so many things to so many people.

Until approximately 1969 most academic research on crime was done by sociologists.[45] Their basic premise was that criminals were somehow different from noncriminals, and major research efforts consisted of looking for the ways criminals and noncriminals differed.[46] To be sure, sociologists and criminologists have added to our knowledge of crime and criminals. Their theories of crime causation provide insight into the structure and functioning of criminal subcultures and the impact of social culture on crime. However, in 1968 a number of articles by economists began to appear, and these works have provided an important new perspective.[47] Economists argue that criminals are much the same as anyone else: they are rational people who seek to maximize their own self-interest, and their decisions are made in light of rational considerations. The basic question, according to this viewpoint, is simply whether or not the individual sees criminal conduct as being in his best interests. This underscores the thesis that all behavior is meaningful, although its meaning may not always be clear to outside observers (some psychologists argue that the true meaning of a person's behavior might not be clear to the individual himself). Unfortunately, when we talk about the "meaning" of behavior we run the risk of using definitions that have limited value. Legal definitions by themselves, for example, tend to be sterile and out of context because they discount motive. Sociological definitions, on the other hand, tend to be repetitious and self-fulfilling. Perhaps what we need is a model that allows us to see criminal behavior in context and permits us to examine the relationships among criminals, victims and the criminal justice system. The use of economic theory is helpful in providing us with such a perspective.

CATEGORIES OF CRIME

From an economic viewpoint, criminal offenses may be divided into three categories: (1) crimes against the person; (2) crimes against property; and (3) "victimless" crimes.[48] The first two are predatory or coercive crimes. Crimes against property, moreover, are nothing more than a transfer of income or assets. So-called victimless crimes involve the production and consumption of illegal goods. This classification is not inconsistent with the traditional categories of crime used by law enforcement agencies.

At the root of the economic perspective is the concept of "getting and giving." A person tries to get what he or she wants and in return something must be given. In the legitimate marketplace there is usually a close relationship between the value of the two. For example, if you want a stereo system worth $1,000, that is what you would expect to pay for it. You might be able to get the same stereo through some kind of barter; in that case, the person trading the stereo would want something worth approximately the same in return. You might swap a used car for the stereo, and if you really did not want the car anymore (or if you saw the continued ownership of it as a liability), you might feel you made a "good deal" even though the car might have been worth more than the stereo in objective terms.

However, in looking at criminal transactions we must avoid being seduced by monetary value. Money is, after all, only one medium of exchange, and there are many others. It is fairly obvious that in any given transaction it is important for the individual to get what is desired, in return for no more than it is worth—preferably less. A final, important point is that in the usual business context both buyer and seller have a common means for assigning value (usually monetary worth). In the case of crime, however, this relationship becomes distorted. The objective worth of an object or service is replaced by the idiosyncratic value attached to it by the criminal. In other words, the value of a stereo is not necessarily its "fair market value" or any other value its rightful owner might place on it, but might be measured instead in terms of the risk involved in stealing it or by how much the thief wants the stereo himself.

Some transactions involve little more than the exchange of items of tangible value, such as money for merchandise. In other transactions the exchange may involve intangibles such as reputation, esteem, honor, convenience or power. A transaction may involve all of these elements, under various circumstances. Different circumstances determine the values placed on the elements of a transaction.

OPPORTUNITY COST

Not only does crime have a great deal to do with values, it is strongly related to opportunity and to factors that correlate with opportunity. *Opportunity cost* is what one must give up in order to get something. The decision to spend a dollar on something is also the simultaneous decision not to spend that same dollar on other things. Part of the cost of what you get for your money is what you are willing to forego in favor of what you buy. Questions of value can be very important when considering opportunity cost. Someone who places a high value on his own honesty may not be willing to sacrifice self-esteem in favor of getting something by cheating. In that case, cheating would not be "economical" even though it might result in a significant financial gain. An action that one person considers rational under the circumstances might be repugnant to a different person under the same circumstances. This is why some people are almost never honest, others are honest most of the time, and yet others are almost never dishonest.

In the case of crime, although the "transaction" is illegal, legality may or may not have much to do with the actual situation—at least as it is perceived by the people involved. Gordon points out this difference in perceptions:

> Only rarely, it appears, can ghetto criminals be regarded as raving, irrational, antisocial lunatics. The "legitimate" jobs open to many ghetto residents, especially to young black males, typically pay low wages, offer relatively demeaning assignments, and carry the constant risk of layoff. In contrast, many kinds of crime "available" in the ghetto often bring higher monetary return, offer even higher social status, and—at least in [some] cases...carry relatively low risk of arrest and punishment.[49]

Seen in this light, people with low incomes may give up little or nothing by participating in crime; in fact, they may actually stand to gain a great deal. "If all factors were equal, we would predict that people with low opportunity cost (low educational attainment and lack of job experience) would have a greater propensity to engage in crime. Examples would be the young, the poor, and members of minority groups."[50] Available data on crime, especially on illicit narcotics networks, clearly supports this hypothesis.

The most prevalent of all crimes are those committed against property: various forms of larceny and theft. A theft devoid of its moral-legal value is merely an involuntary transfer of assets from a rightful owner to someone else.

A professional thief may rationalize the act by claiming that it is a way to make a living and that the "investment" made in what is stolen is the risk taken in stealing it. Many thefts are committed by "honest" people as well, or at least by people who do not see themselves as criminals or thieves. However, since generally "honest" people place a value on their reputations, they must reconcile their values with their actions. One way of doing this is to manipulate the moral meaning of illegal acts. This allows them to violate their principles without having to abandon them.[51] This manipulation may be accomplished through the use of techniques of neutralization (psychological devices used to create justification for what would otherwise be unacceptable behavior). These techniques help one to protect oneself from the voice of a guilty conscience and the criticism of the larger society.[52] Sykes and Matza discuss five major techniques:

1. **Denial of Responsibility:** "I couldn't help it; that's just the way things are done around here."

2. **Denial of Injury:** "It doesn't make any difference: they have insurance." "So what? No one got hurt."

3. **Denial of Victim:** "He had it coming." "He should not have been there in the first place."

4. **Condemnation of the Condemners:** "Who are they to say it's wrong to smoke grass? They get high on liquor."

5. **Appeal to Higher Loyalties:** "I didn't do it for myself."

Techniques of neutralization allow an individual to manipulate moral meanings so that broad social definitions of right and wrong can be accepted at the same time the behavior is self-gratifying. This kind of manipulation can make an illegitimate transaction "economical" to a person by removing from consideration a moral standard he or she may not wish to surrender.

One of the reasons that nearly all citizens engage in some kind of criminal conduct from time to time is that the "transfer" may be based not on an actual exchange (e.g., dollars for a stereo), but on the assumption that the wrongdoer will not get caught and therefore will not have to answer for his actions. A person may "take a chance" on something under the assumption that the chance of getting caught is slim, and that the punishment upon discovery would be tolerable. Traffic violations are a good case in point. Suppose Waldo is following Ambrose in a no-passing zone on an isolated country road. Waldo is in a hurry but Ambrose is not; he is driving 35 m.p.h. in a 45 m.p.h. zone and there is little traffic. Waldo might reason that if he passes Ambrose illegally he might have a head-on collision with another car or might get caught by the police. Since the volume of traffic is low and the odds of a police car being just out of sight are slim, Waldo decides to "go for it." He succeeds in passing Ambrose and is pleased: his "gain" (being able to go faster) was purchased at what seemed to be a minimal risk. Moreover, he is able to neutralize his act by making excuses: "It's not like I'm driving while drunk, and anyway, it's the fault of the idiot in front of me: I had to pass him before he caused an accident." Nominally honest citizens—at least those who value having an honest reputation—can keep their reputation and still steal; however, they must do so in a way that offers little risk of getting caught and at the same time preserves their public reputation. There are many ways of doing this, ranging from padding expense accounts and cheating on income taxes to stealing supplies from the workplace and embezzling funds through computer manipulations.

Based on an economic perspective, a great deal of criminal behavior can be seen as being relative to the context in which it occurs as well as a function of the values and desires of those involved. The majority of people elect to commit crimes from time to time. In most cases the crimes are not serious. Why do some people elect to commit crimes—including serious crimes—while others do not? Much of the answer is found in class and power relationships, for those are the variables that probably correlate the closest with the opportunities and incentives to commit crimes.

CLASS, OPPORTUNITY COST AND CRIME

If the economics of crime are based on "getting and giving," then it is important to know just how resources are distributed in the first place. As Gordon noted, "the character of crime in America flows almost inevitably from the structure of our social and economic institutions."[53] He says that what a person has is a function of his class and status. A person with high or upper-class status presumably would have more than those in the lower classes, at least in terms of economic resources.

Not only do the affluent have more economic advantages than the poor, they also have the opportunity to maintain the political and economic institutions that produce and protect their wealth. For this reason, those with high status tend to be politically conservative. They also place a high value on their reputation and status within the community, and typically disavow violence as a means for settling conflict (their lives are closely regulated by negotiations and agreements). Not only do they espouse the virtues important to their own lives, they measure the worth of others on the basis of those same virtues. Crimes of violence are inconsistent with their lifestyle, and traditional crimes against property are not only unnecessary but carry a significant threat to their reputations and community standing. Members of the middle and upper classes are, however, by no means exempt from criminal behavior.

The types of crimes committed by middle- and upper-class people flow logically from their occupations and outlook on life. For example, economic crime is a very rational response to the expectations of a materialistic society. If the task of the corporation is to augment and protect the capital of its owners, and if those who manage corporations are rewarded economically and socially for success in doing so, then the goals of getting and protecting capital carry a high value in their own right. The affluent perform these tasks not only on behalf of their corporations, they do so on their own behalf as well—all quite legally. However, if a corporation finds it difficult to function successfully in a harshly competitive marketplace, it may look for ways of "helping things along."

These kinds of crimes are not executed for monetary gain alone; other goals include power (i.e., within the business community), personal prestige, a sense of accomplishment, or even idealistic ends such as keeping people employed and contributing to the local economy. Perhaps in most cases the risk is low, the chance of success high and the circumstances ideal. People who do not understand the power of nonmonetary motives shake their heads and say, "I just don't see why he did it. He seemed to have everything!" They fail to understand the "economics" of crime by not seeing all that was given in return for what was received.

Of course, this process operates at personal as well as corporate levels. Indeed, it might be reasonable to ask if it is possible to separate people from their businesses. If a corporate executive wants to conduct business with a foreign firm, and if the cost of doing so calls for bribes, how long does it take before the businessman sees bribery as just another necessary form of business? Should businessmen who provide hotel accommodations and prostitutes for buyers in town for a convention be considered pimps, or are they merely doing what has to be done to stay competitive in the market? It is easy for affluent people to rationalize their conduct while at the same time deploring the depravation of "criminals." Techniques of neutralization can soften unethical or illegal behavior in the minds of those who commit them, enabling them to continue their activities with a relatively clear conscience. This is made easier when people selectively define both crimes and criminals in a way that excludes themselves. Thus, white-collar criminals are more likely to see as "criminals" people who commit street crimes, seeing those criminals as different from themselves in kind rather than degree.

The poor, on the other hand, are faced with an entirely different set of circumstances. For one thing, they play virtually no role in "making the rules." Although they have likes and dislikes as all people do, and have the same kinds of need for survival and self-esteem, they must look for these things in a substantially different environment than middle- and upper-class people. Again, the situation that confronts them calls for choices. Accepting conventional social values such as honesty, nonviolence, the Protestant work ethic and the need to delay gratification implies an exchange—suggesting that subscribing to those values will ensure that immediate needs will be met and life will be at least tolerable, if not pleasant. The reality of urban slums clearly contradicts this. Where unemployment is more the norm than the exception and where a sense of personal worth is difficult to sustain, the "exchange" seems foolish. That is, the opportunity cost of crime is so low that for many people the choice is virtually made for them. There is so little to be lost and so much to be gained that crime not only does not seem wrong, it appears necessary. Again, techniques of neutralization play a powerful role. Since 1981 there has been a rapidly expanding commerce in crack cocaine, which is most frequently encountered in inner-city areas. It is sold almost exclusively by low-level retail dealers.[54] According to a Drug Enforcement Administration profile, the majority of crack users spend over $100 a week on the drug, which is considered highly addictive.[55] The rapid rise of crack addiction has created new economic opportunities in inner cities, and large numbers of young people are actively involved in its manufacture and distribution. From an economic perspective, it is simply the production of a product (and delivery of a service) for money. However, in a larger sense the sale of crack also provides nonmonetary incentives: power and prestige. It provides these benefits at a "cost" of foregoing income, remaining powerless and being without prestige. What is the opportunity cost of selling crack? Many in the trade would probably argue that it would be foolish *not* to be involved. Interestingly enough, however, few of them would be likely to accept responsibility for the enormous violence and social disruption caused by crack.

Even crimes of violence can be understood when viewed in context. We noted earlier that civil law provides a means for correcting private wrongs. Civil processes also consume time, are expensive and require a certain amount of sophistication to use. In addition, many problems do not lend themselves to such solutions. This is especially the case among the poor, where disputes are seen as personal matters and solutions are considered best when they are quick. Thus, many homicides are nothing more than overly successful assaults that escalated from "killing and cutting" talk. A fistfight can be a matter of honor; avoiding a fight in favor of a civil suit is not only inappropriate in some settings, it is absurd.

Some crimes of violence represent a complex interplay of social and psychological factors. For many who commit crimes of violence, the act is not undertaken for its own sake, but rather to advance some other end or to solve what the offender perceives as a problem.[56] Even when attention is shifted to professional criminals, we find that they are people who make choices that appear to be highly rational. In studying burglars, car thieves, loan sharks, hit men, fences and other "professionals" in crime, Plate has observed that they tend to have a variety of similar characteristics. Most of them:

- Prefer anonymity;
- May be on speaking terms with local police;
- Are not necessarily members of organized crime;
- In all likelihood are not drug addicts;
- Tend to take arrests and even imprisonment in stride;
- Do not generally leave fingerprints;
- Make practice runs before committing their crimes;
- May be prudent in spending their illegal incomes;
- May be "family men."[57]

People are, of course, far too complex to be reduced to any single formula, economic or otherwise. However, by looking at criminal conduct as an economic transaction, we can see a great deal of the "logic" behind much of it. It also brings into stark relief much of what the sociologists and psychologists tell us about poverty, emotional deprivation, differential association, alienation, anomie and collective behavior. It makes it easier to understand why values cherished by some seem to have limited meaning to others. Finally, it makes it possible to understand why the kinds of crimes committed by the poor are incomprehensible to the affluent (and vice versa).

As long as criminal behavior is personal and meaningful to the person who commits it, *crime* is not seen as a problem; however, when crimes are committed by *others* for reasons that are not clear to those who hear of it, then the crime *per se* is seen as the problem. This perspective will be made clearer in the next chapter.

SUMMARY

The diversity of human associations inevitably leads to conflict, and any orderly society must develop mechanisms for preventing or resolving conflict. The formal approach to dealing with conflict is through law, which sets forth the rights and duties of all citizens and the means by which the laws themselves are to be administered. One of the basic functions of law is to establish order, and another is to secure justice. Although these concepts are mutually reinforcing, they also contain some inherent contradictions. One problem is that "justice" itself is very difficult to define.

Many of our ideas of justice arise from informal sources of law, tradition, religion and sentiment. The formal sources of law stem from the legislative and judicial functions of government, which are not completely free of external influences like interest groups and even the socialization processes of legislators and judges that can influence the kinds of decisions they make.

The law itself may be divided into criminal and civil categories. Criminal law concerns itself with the positive rights and duties of all citizens and enforces those obligations by invoking the criminal justice process. Civil law, on the other hand, deals with the realm of private wrongs and provides a legal forum in which the contesting parties may have their cases heard. Civil wrongs generally fall under one of two headings: breaches of contract and torts. Although all citizens have the right to use the civil courts, many cannot do so because of the expense of legal counsel. The criminal justice system (the police, courts and corrections) administers the criminal law, and may be regarded as the *public control system*. Obviously, it concerns itself with the more serious cases of conflict.

Along with the public control system there is an informal *private control system* composed of nurturing and socializing agencies: family, religion, the work setting and the individual's primary social associations. The private control system has the task of nurturing the individual and instilling basic values. Ideally, each of the components of the private control system are mutually supportive and collectively serve to prevent the kinds of conflicts which must be handled by the public control system.

Law itself is rather sterile because it does not give much consideration to *why* people commit the acts which have been labeled as crimes. To better understand that, it is important to look at the economic functions of crime. Viewed from this perspective, crime is seen as rational behavior in which the individual engages in certain transactions. Criminal behavior has purpose and meaning to the person who commits it, even though it may seem senseless and inappropriate to an outside observer. In some cases, crime may be accepted by the criminal as an illegal necessity, but more often it is rationalized or justified—allowing the offender to see himself as a noncriminal while enjoying the benefits of the crime.

A great deal of criminal activity is related to the socioeconomic status of the offender; class and status play a major role in determining opportunity cost. Crime itself is often a highly complex combination of legal, social, psychological and economic variables closely related to the individual's perception of himself and his needs. This is one reason the crimes of the poor make so little sense to the affluent, and vice versa.

DISCUSSION QUESTIONS

1. Do the goals of order and justice actually represent conflicting expectations of the law?

2. If sentiment is an informal source of law, can law be objective in a diverse community?

3. Does the police power of the state authorize or justify unpopular laws? Can you cite any examples?

4. How do special interest groups influence legislation to the detriment of the "public interest"?

5. What kinds of acts may be both torts and crimes?

6. In what major ways does civil law differ from criminal law?

7. How can one's social class influence the ability of an individual to secure justice through civil courts?

8. Can an act be a crime if the law does not provide a punishment?

9. Why is the private control system essentially a crime prevention system?

10. Do you think the family of today is as important a factor in shaping the individual as the text implies?

11. Does religion really have a role in contemporary society?

12. How can a person's work environment control his behavior?

13. Can justice ever be completely blind (objective)?

14. What is the relationship between the private and public control systems?

15. It has been said that a given community gets the kind of justice it deserves. What does this mean? Is it true?

16. How do nontangibles play a role in the economics of crime?

17. How could a community go about altering the "opportunity cost" of crime in low-income areas?

18. Why do you think low-income people frequently see business as having the objective of exploiting them?

19. Why can crime almost never be viewed objectively?

20. If the criminal justice system provides for an administration of *criminal* justice, should we support the development of a *civil* justice system?

REFERENCES

1 Thomas Hobbes, *Leviathan*, I, 13.

2 Edgar Bodenheimer, *Jurisprudence: The Philosophy and Method of the Law* (Cambridge, MA: Harvard University Press, 1962), 166.

3 Bodenheimer, *Jurisprudence*, 177.

4 Bodenheimer, *Jurisprudence*, 178-179.

5 Aristotle's concept of equality is quite different from contemporary definitions. He apparently believed that equal things should go to equal people, but not that all people were equal. He believed the just distribution of society's benefits should be according to merit, and the people who exhibited the greatest civic excellence should receive the greatest rewards. His concept of justice also included a retributive component in which those who violated his notion of distributive justice would be punished according to the nature and magnitude of their offense. Both Plato and Aristotle were well aware of both the value and the drawbacks of law. Laws, because of their rigidity, could also cause hardships. They knew that general, universal rules designed to control complex human behavior had a great potential for being counterproductive and that some means of establishing equity where the law was defective was required. (This concept subsequently became embodied in English law and was carried over to American jurisprudence.)

6 Bodenheimer, *Jurisprudence*, 207.

7 Exodus 20; Leviticus 26.

8 See, for example, William F. Walsh, *Outlines of the History of English and American Law* (New York: New York University Press, 1926).

9 See, for example, *United States Constitution*, Article VI.

10 William J. Chambliss and Robert B. Siedman, *Law, Order, and Power* (Reading, MA: Addison-Wesley Publishing Company, 1971), 59.

11 Chambliss and Siedman, *Law, Order, and Power*, 73.

12 Chambliss and Siedman, *Law, Order, and Power*, 73.

13 Bodenheimer, *Jurisprudence*, 286.

14 Chambliss and Siedman, *Law, Order, and Power*, 90.

15 Harold J. Grilliot, *Introduction to Law and the Legal System* (Boston: Houghton Mifflin Company, 1979), 13.

16 Grilliot, *Introduction to Law and the Legal System*, 14.

17 Grilliot, *Introduction to Law and the Legal System*, 36.

18 See, for example, *United States Constitution*, Article III, Section III.

19 Thomas J. Gardner and Victor Manian, *Criminal Law: Principles, Cases and Readings* (St. Paul: West Publishing Company, 1980), 7.

[20] See, for example, Muriel Jones and Dorothy Jongeward, *Born to Win: Transactional Analysis With Gestalt Experiments* (Reading, MA: Addison-Wesley Publishing Company, 1971), 65.

[21] Spencer Rich, "A Generation Alters Notion of U.S. Family," *The Washington Post*, 5 September 1989, A12.

[22] Rich, "A Generation Alters Notion of U.S. Family," A12.

[23] Vern E. Smith, Howard Manly and David L. Gonzales, "Children of the Underclass," *Newsweek*, 11 September 1989, 18.

[24] Smith et al., "Children of the Underclass," 18.

[25] Smith et al., "Children of the Underclass," 20.

[26] Ronald A. Gerlach and Lynne W. Lamprecht, *Teaching About the Law* (Cincinnati: Anderson Publishing Co., 1971), 65.

[27] David Harman, "Keeping Up in America," *Wilson Quarterly* (Spring 1986), 117.

[28] Val D. Rust, "What Can We Learn From Others?," *Wilson Quarterly* 8 (New Year's 1984), 80.

[29] "The Failure of Teacher Ed," *Newsweek*, 1 October 1990, 58.

[30] George F. Will, "Colleges Don't Require Learning," *Houston Chronicle*, 13 October 1989, 14B.

[31] Will, "Colleges Don't Require Learning," 14B.

[32] George F. Will, "Radical English," *The Washington Post*, 16 September 1990, B7.

[33] Patrick Welsh, "Fast-Track Trap: How 'Ability Grouping' Hurts Our Schools, Kids and Families," *The Washington Post*, 16 September 1990, B1.

[34] John McCormick, "Where Are The Parents?," in "Education: A Consumer's Handbook," *Newsweek*, Fall/Winter 1990 special ed., 54.

[35] McCormick, "Where Are The Parents?," 58.

[36] Ginny Carroll, "Who Foots the Bill?," in "Education: A Consumer's Handbook," *Newsweek*, Fall/Winter 1990 special ed., 54.

[37] Texas Department of Commerce, press release, 11 July 1988.

[38] See, for example, Kenneth E. Boulding, *Beyond Economics: Essays on Society, Religion, and Ethics* (Ann Arbor, MI: University of Michigan Press, 1968).

[39] Winthrop S. Hudson, *Religion in America*, 3rd ed. (New York: Charles Scribner's Sons, 1981), 7.

[40] Hudson, *Religion in America*, 154.

[41] Hudson, *Religion in America*, 154.

[42] Barry Sussman, *What Americans Really Think* (New York: Pantheon Books, 1988), 198-199.

[43] William H. Whyte, Jr., *Organization Man* (New York: Simon and Schuster, 1956).

[44] Other interesting perspectives on work and its influence on behavior may be found in the following sources: James O'Toole, ed., *Work and the Quality of Life: Resource Papers for Work in America* (Boston: MIT Press, 1974); Louis B. Shaw, *The Bonds of Work: Work in Mind, Time, and Tradition* (San Francisco: Jossey-Bass, 1968); and Studs Terkel, *Working* (New York: Avon Books, 1975).

[45] Howard Abadinsky, *Social Service in Criminal Justice* (Englewood Cliffs, NJ: Prentice-Hall, Inc., 1979), 1-35.

[46] Ralph Andreano and John Siegfried, eds., *The Economics of Crime* (New York: John Wiley and Sons, 1980), 13.

[47] See, for example, Gary S. Becker, "Crime and Punishment: An Economic Approach," *Journal of Political Economy* (March 1968), 169-217; Gordon Tullock, "An Economic Approach to Crime," *Social Science Quarterly* (June 1969), 59-71; Gary S. Becker and William M. Landes, eds., *Essays in the Economics of Crime and Punishment* (New York: National Bureau of Economics Research, 1974); Lee R. McPheters and William B. Stronge, eds., *The Economics of Crime and Law Enforcement* (Springfield, IL: Charles C Thomas, Publishers, 1976); Simon Rottenberg, ed., *The Economics of Crime and Punishment* (Washington, DC: American Enterprise Institute, 1973); and Isaac Ehrlich, "Participation in Illegitimate Activities: A Theoretical and Empirical Investigation," *Journal of Political Economy* (May 1973), 521-565.

[48] Morgan O. Reynolds, "The Economics of Criminal Activity," in *The Economics of Crime*, ed. Ralph Andreano and John J. Siegfried (New York: John Wiley and Sons, 1980), 27-69.

[49] David M. Gordon, "Capitalism, Class, and Crime in America," in *The Economics of Crime*, ed. Ralph Andreano and John J. Siegfried (New York: John Wiley and Sons, 1980), 103.

[50] Reynolds, "The Economics of Criminal Activity," 35.

[51] Gresham M. Sykes, *Criminology* (New York: Harcourt, Brace, Jovanovich, Inc., 1978), 308.

[52] See especially Gresham M. Sykes and David Matza, "Techniques of Neutralization: A Theory of Delinquency," *American Sociological Review* (December 1957), 664-670.

[53] Gordon, ""Capitalism, Class, and Crime in America," 93.

[54] Drug Enforcement Administration, "Drug Alert—Crack," *The NarcOfficer* (November/December 1986), 15, 49.

[55] David L. Westrate, "The Crack Problem," *The NarcOfficer* (November/December 1986), 15, 17-18.

[56] For a valuable perspective on the relationship between psychiatry and crime, see Seymour L. Halleck, *Psychiatry and the Dilemmas of Crime* (Berkeley, CA: University of California Press, 1967).

[57] Thomas Plate, *Crime Pays!* (New York: Simon and Schuster, 1975), 17-21.

Photo Credit: Ford Foundation

Chapter 3

COMMUNITIES IN TRANSITION

The Evolving Environment of Criminal Justice

Ideally the public and private control systems should complement one another, but sometimes they do not. Their inability to do so can indicate failure in either or both of the systems or a lack of harmony between them. In smaller and more closely knit communities, they are much more likely to reinforce one another and thereby effectively control behavior. However, American society has become increasingly diverse, resulting in tension and conflict among its different groups—especially in the larger urban areas. Two broad categories of change underlie much of this conflict. First, in recent decades, many of the traditional rules governing behavior have changed dramatically. Second, the communities themselves have changed. As a result, the larger and more urban communities have become virtual battlegrounds of conflicting interests and values. This has had a profound impact on society as a whole, as well as on all aspects of the criminal justice system.

Competing segments within a community come into conflict over a variety of issues—including how their conflicts should be solved. Within this broader framework, the private control system is in growing turmoil as traditional guides to behavior are challenged, modified or discarded. Moreover, many of the "services" it used to provide are shifting to the public sector. Examples include the provision of day care for children, health care for the poor and elderly, and support for the homeless, unemployed and disabled. Special interest groups are also making demands for change. These tensions are reflected in popular cliches like the generation gap (age-based differences); the sexual revolution (challenges to traditional morality); the feminist movement (gender-based conflict); the civil rights movement (race-based differences), and so on. The criminal justice system is caught up in this turmoil and must somehow respond to its often conflicting demands.

In reality, it is impossible to separate the people from the criminal justice system. With the exception of traditional custodial prisons (which are closed, isolated institutions), criminal justice agencies are in constant contact with the public, either directly or indirectly. In fact, without close and continuing support from the public, the criminal justice system simply could not function. Just as the community depends on the criminal justice system, the system depends on the community. Although criminal justice is fundamentally an individual responsibility, most of its actual processes are carried out by professionals hired for that purpose, and different parts of the community have different expectations of how that should be done. It is the work of criminal justice professionals that makes the system's operation a reality. Although private individuals can make arrests and initiate prosecutions, most prefer that these tasks be carried out by the police and prosecutors. In a very real sense, we delegate our individual responsibilities to the system. It is clear that there is not always a consensus on what should be done, who should do it or even what its results ought to be.

There ought to be an easy, open flow of information and cooperation between the public and the criminal justice system; unfortunately, this is seldom the case. As many as one-half or more of all crimes are never reported to the police. A great many people actively seek to avoid jury duty or having to act as a witness. There is widespread distrust of lawyers, courts, the police and prosecutors. While most people want "justice"—however they choose to define it—many of them prefer not to play a direct, personal role in the process.

Conversely, many criminal justice agencies (and their employees) hold the public in contempt and have little regard for how people feel. Some services are delivered poorly or with indifference—or sometimes even with outright hostility. In some communities, the relationship between the criminal justice system and the people is rich with misunderstanding, stress and dissatisfaction—a situation that is expensive in both psychological and operational costs. When people lose confidence in government, they withhold their support. This can result in crimes remaining unsolved, criminals going unpunished and fear replacing reason. When this happens, morale and effectiveness within the system also suffer, evidenced by poor performance and bad attitudes which produce a self-perpetuating cycle. In some communities, even police and court officials themselves have become criminals. The point where the public and the criminal justice system meet is important because that is where conflict must be identified and community expectations understood, acknowledged and served.

PUBLIC EXPECTATIONS: THE COMMUNITY AS A WHOLE

Even though groups may have differing expectations of the system, the community as a whole has certain expectations that generally transcend individual or group goals. These community-wide expectations form a framework within which individual and group perspectives can be negotiated. Community expectations are broad-based and exist in spite of individual or group differences. These expectations are not always realistic nor are they always met, but they still represent at least a loose consensus that the criminal justice system should control crime, maintain order, help the public and prevent crime.

CONTROL OF CRIME

Regardless of sex, age, race or income, people want to be secure in their persons and places—free from victimization by criminals. They want to go about their business without getting hurt or being exploited and therefore expect the criminal justice system to keep crime under control. Is this a valid expectation? In fact, crime is a serious problem. The risk of being the victim of a violent crime is greater than the risk of death resulting from cancer, injury or fire.[1] Fully one-fourth of the 95 million households in the United States were victimized by a crime of violence or theft in 1989.[2] More specifically, almost 3 out of every 100 people over the age of 12 were victims of a violent crime, and almost 7 out of every 100 were victims of property crimes.[3] Crime imposes severe personal and financial hardships and the public feels strongly that one of the principle tasks of the criminal justice system should be its control. Unfortunately, although the consequences of crime are clear, the meaning of "crime control" is not. Questions of how crime should be controlled and how effective the system is in controlling it will be dealt with in subsequent chapters. For now it will suffice to say that, as seen by the public, one of the most important tasks of the system is the control of crime.

An interesting paradox is that—despite the actual volume of crime and an often unreasonable fear of it—the public does not see it as a particularly urgent problem compared with others. According to a 1989 Gallup Poll, only 6 percent of the respondents indicated crime was the most important problem facing the nation. They were much more concerned about economic issues and drugs (34 percent and 27 percent, respectively).[4] This may be misleading, however; economic pressures are a very real and daily part of the lives of most Americans while crime is not—and drug-related problems have become a media staple. Even so, in 1989 a nationwide sample of high school seniors revealed that 86.3 percent worried about crime and violence "often" or "sometimes,"[5] and more than 8 out of 10 Americans apparently feel both that the level of crime has increased nationwide and that the situation is going to get worse during the next 10 years.[6]

The results of numerous public surveys suggest that although the public is concerned about crime, its attitudes are complex and sometimes contradictory. For example, though 8 out of 10 people believed crime increased nationwide in the preceding year or two, only 5 out of 10 thought it increased in their own neighborhood during the same period.[7] In terms of fear of crime in their own neighborhood, only 40 percent indicated they would be afraid to walk alone at night.[8] Women were much more concerned about their safety than men, regardless of the time of day. Interestingly enough, although there was a great deal of concern about safety in one's neighborhood, most of those who expressed concern did not translate their fear into a desire to move. In fact, the majority (about 60 percent) of all respondents of each age and race group had no complaints about their own particular neighborhood, and those who did were more worried about trash, noise and overcrowding than about crime. Another interesting result was that respondents showed a tendency to rate their own neighborhoods as less dangerous than other neighborhoods in the metropolitan area.

The general public is also ambivalent in its attitudes about the best way to control crime. The largest single proportion (25 percent) believe that the most important thing that can be done is to cut the drug supply; another 24 percent call for harsher punishments; while 12 percent think that teaching values and respect for the law is the most important strategy. Ten percent rated the reduction of unemployment as the most important strategy, while only 5 percent said they believed that hiring more police is the most important thing that can be done.[9] Almost twice as many people (61 percent) believe the best way to lower the crime rate is by attacking social problems than believe it is by improving law enforcement (32 percent).[10]

Although the public is generally satisfied with the police, the same cannot be said for its attitude toward the courts. In a 1989 Gallup poll, 83 percent of the respondents thought the courts were not harsh enough in dealing with criminals, and 79 percent thought criminals were being let off too easy.[11] As an interesting sidebar, in a 1990 survey 31 percent of the respondents rated the honesty and ethical standards of lawyers as low or very low, whereas only 9 percent gave the same rating to police officers.[12]

MAINTENANCE OF ORDER

Crimes, especially felonies, are typically thought of as the more serious instances of deviance. Other acts, including minor crimes, often arise out of relatively ordinary contexts. In general, the community expects the system to maintain order so routine activities can be conducted without interference. Much of the ordinary activity within a community requires intervention simply to keep routine problems to a minimum (and to keep them from becoming major problems). We see this most readily in the regulation of traffic; however, that is only one example of how communities try to prevent problems or limit their scope. All communities have various ways of protecting health and safety and of regulating the pursuit of commerce and pleasure. For example, food products are inspected; medical and dental practices are licensed; restaurants (and their employees) are inspected; the sale of alcohol and tobacco is restricted, and so on. In the case of public safety, building and fire codes are established and enforced; plumbing and electrical contractors are licensed and their work is inspected; the ownership and use of firearms are restricted; and standards for the safe flow of traffic are established and enforced. Public well-being is advanced through the regulation of utilities, the licensing of occupations, and regulations and restrictions on the manufacture, sale and distribution of dangerous or toxic substances. All of these are part of the broad "police powers" of government.

For years communities have expected the police to control such neighborhood "disorders" as public intoxication, panhandling, prostitution, juvenile misconduct and disorderly conduct. The goal has not been so much to punish offenders as to minimize the misconduct. Even though the police have been expected to deal with these issues, they often have encountered hostility when they tried to do so. As Kelling notes, "Citizens in neighborhoods plagued by crime and disorder were disaffected because they simply would not have police they neither knew nor authorized whizzing in and out of their neighborhoods 'takin' names and kickin' ass.'"[13] Police involvement in domestic disorders is a good example. This kind of order maintenance has been frustrating to both the police and their clients; "But, given the routine of police work, officers have had no alternative to their typical response: Go to a call, pacify things, and leave to get ready for another call."[14] As will be seen later, a new and potent revolution in policing is intimately concerned with these issues, promising vastly improved results. In the meantime, the public still expects the criminal justice system to maintain order.

PUBLIC ASSISTANCE

The criminal justice system also provides assistance to people in need of help. For the most part this is done by the police because of their ready availability. People who become lost, hurt, confused, frightened or desperate call the police for assistance even though their immediate problem may have nothing to do with crimes or law-breaking. In fact, responding to these kinds of calls constitutes the bulk of a police officer's duty time in many places. Rendering first aid, locating missing persons and recovering lost or stolen property are typical examples of how the police assist people.

Some prosecutors operate consumer fraud units that provide legal advice or assistance to people who think they have been mistreated by unscrupulous merchants. Small claims courts provide an easy and inexpensive way for people to settle disputes, and public defenders provide valuable assistance to those who are charged with crimes but cannot afford private counsel. All in all, the criminal justice system provides a tremendous amount of assistance to people, although that fact is seldom recognized as such.

Providing assistance is nothing new. As Kelling and Moore note, "In the late 19th Century, municipal police departments ran soup lines; provided temporary lodging for newly arrived immigrant workers in station houses; and assisted ward leaders in finding work for immigrants, both in police and other forms of work."[15] There is a longstanding tradition of using the criminal justice system to deal with problems, and many people expect the system to be both able and willing to help them directly.

CRIME PREVENTION

Finally, the community expects the criminal justice system not only to control crime but to prevent it as well. This is an expectation embedded in historical tradition. When the Metropolitan Police was established in London in 1829, the objective behind its institution was the concept of a "preventive police." This idea was clearly articulated by Patrick Colquhoun who, when describing the power of the police, said that it was to be based "...upon the broad scale of general prevention—Mild in its operations, —Effective in its results; having justice and humanity for its basis, and the general security of the State and Individuals for its ultimate object."[16] This is an important point, for a police force based on prevention is quite different from one based on repression.[17] There is a compelling logic to the belief that an ounce of prevention is worth a pound of cure, and crime prevention is regarded as a legitimate community objective. The problem, of course, lies in how it is to be accomplished. Since everything is a trade-off, preventing crime invariably comes at the expense of at least some degree of individual liberty. Because of this, civil libertarians have objected to such preventive measures as police conducting highway sobriety checkpoints, periodic drug and alcohol tests of transportation personnel and airport screening for bombs. Their reservations are based on the grounds that these preventive law enforcement measures constitute an unwarranted invasion of personal privacy.[18] Although the public wants crime prevented, it is often reluctant to surrender individual liberty to get it, and this is one of the continuing dilemmas within the criminal justice system.

PUBLIC POLICY:
DEALING WITH EXPECTATIONS

In theory, government can deal with almost any problem; but in reality there are limits to what can actually be accomplished. Figuring out what can and should be done is a matter of establishing public policy and setting priorities. In addition to being part of the management function, establishing public policy and setting priorities are also part of the larger political process that often pits segments of the community against one another and contributes to the institutional conflict so characteristic of American politics.

POLICY

Policy is made at two levels. At the so-called "policy level," it is made by senior elected and administrative officials. At the municipal level, this normally consists of the city council and city manager (or those who perform similar functions). Policies made at this level represent a commitment to deal with some problem or issue; they may be regarded as general goals of government.[19] Although public policies establish or prioritize programs, they do not normally specify how they are to be carried out. That is done by specific units of government (like the police or health department), which must develop specific operational policies to achieve these larger goals. Thus, policy at the operational level is the plan of action that directly supports government objectives. For example, a community with a high rate of homelessness might develop a policy of providing public shelters for them. This might be done at the policy level by passing a local ordinance authorizing the expenditure of public funds to temporarily house certain people. At the operational level, a number of departments might be specifically responsible for converting this goal into actual practice. Various responsibilities might be assigned to the health department, the police department, the public works department and so on. These departments must then determine how they are going to use their resources to support the public policy of providing shelter to the homeless.

Many cities short-circuit the policy process by delegating policy-making to the operational departments, by making public policy only in response to some specific crisis, or by voicing policies they have no intention of actually supporting (we see this most often in the promises politicians make to gain support from potential voters). Perhaps the most noteworthy shortcoming of public policy-makers is their failure to correlate the full resources of government in trying to deal with public problems. In some cases, the operational departments offer policies that are nothing more than cliches or platitudes (i.e., painting "To Protect and Serve" on police cars). The failure to develop public policy adequately supported by departmental efforts is especially conspicuous in the criminal justice system. Because public policy in most cities is a broad commitment, and since the actual provision of services is left to the imagination of individual departments, the results often demonstrate a failure of policy formation at all levels. The high homicide rate in Washington, DC is an example.

The number and rate of homicides in the District of Columbia began a precipitous rise in 1987.[20] Many of these killings involve young black males and many of them are drug-related, as the following example illustrates:

> On Saturday night, someone walked up to Anthony Stewart's car and opened fire. He was in a car at a stoplight at First Street and Rhode Island Avenue NW, an intersection known for its brisk narcotics trade. Police found Stewart lying in the street, hit four times. Numerous bullet holes pocked the body of the brown car. From witnesses and evidence, police believe a passenger jumped from the car and ran away as Stewart, the driver, moved across the front seat and out of the passenger door. A second burst of bullets caught him there. Stewart died a short time later at the Washington Hospital Center.[21]

The response to this homicide was a routine (and proper) police investigation. Unfortunately, their response only dealt with that specific homicide. This is essentially what the police do: they respond to each incident as they are notified and like the Metropolitan (Washington, DC) Police, seldom take a systems approach to the problem. Yet, a careful look at the people involved in these kinds of violent episodes clearly shows consistent patterns of misbehavior including substance abuse, spouse and child abuse, accidents, truancy from school and work, and sexual promiscuity.[22] A rational public policy to reduce homicides would attack all of these things in an integrated fashion rather than simply focusing police resources on individual murders. It would be a policy that seeks to correlate the efforts of all of the community's resources. Thus, any public policy attempting to reduce homicides in the District of Columbia also needs to take into consideration the explosive narcotics problem, educational policies, family support and so on—and these issues have to be seen as interrelated. Saddling the police department alone with responsibility for the problem is unrealistic and unfair, especially if the police are poorly trained and organized. To be fair, other agencies must also deal with these problems, but they must do so on an integrated basis. Consider the following case:

> In a night filled with despair, Medic 9 got a radio call for a pregnant woman about to deliver—a new life was to begin. Paramedic Jones, 22, moved quickly in the medic van to find sheets for the delivery. The medics rushed up the stairs of a home at 57th Street SE. But instead of finding the hopeful scene they expected, they found a prenatal nightmare. A dazed woman, nearly naked, was sitting on the toilet hemorrhaging. It had been happening for two hours, she told the medics. She also said she had syphilis and a PCP and heroin problem.[23]

To be sure, the District of Columbia (like other cities) has a variety of agencies that can deal with various aspects of this woman's chaotic life—public health, welfare and police departments (to name but a few), but each department only deals with its piece of the problem and does so largely independently of every other department. This is what happens when public policy is left primarily to individual departments, and this is one reason why so many public services seem so ineffective.

Departments that routinely deal with recurring activities or problems usually establish guidelines to carry out their work. These guidelines take the form of operational policies based on corporate memory and past experience. Rational operational policies are supported by clearly articulated principles and employ specific methods of action. For example, if a police department has a policy of strict law enforcement based on the principle of the rule of law, then it must establish guidelines on such things as the use of force and arrest procedures that are responsive to procedural law. It must also prohibit illegal conduct by police officers. If a department espouses a set of principles but lacks operational guidelines to carry them out, then its policies will be hypocritical and pointless.

The use of rational operational policy benefits an organization in several ways. First, by establishing guidelines everyone is obliged to follow, operational policies keep individuals (as members of the organization) from acting in an arbitrary fashion. Because of this, they make it possible to predict the behavior of members of the organization. This is important because it fosters decentralization, allowing senior executives to concentrate on matters involving exceptions to the policy. It also provides a basis for evaluating performance and thereby strengthens accountability.

Even so, operational policies are not always rational. Many departments function on the basis of tradition and their policies are based on "the way things have always been done (and if you don't like it, you can go somewhere else!)" This results in rigid, static organizations. Yet other departments are governed by autocratic chiefs who simply impose their will on their subordinates. This produces departments that are likely to be out of touch with the needs of their own members as well as those of the community.

Perhaps the biggest problem arises from the fact that so many government entities operate in isolation from one another, sometimes producing results that border on the bizarre. For example, on November 11, 1989, a woman in a major urban city was notified by a police detective that her 31-year-old son was dead and that his body was at the morgue—where it had been for eight months. He apparently was taken to the hospital on March 15, 1989, where he died from a drug overdose. After his death, the body was taken to the morgue at the Medical Examiner's Office where it was received with full identification. Between the date of his death and the day (eight months later) when the police notified his mother that his body was in the morgue, probation officials obtained a warrant for his arrest, fire department and hospital officials sent her a bill for medical services, and the police department came to her house seeking information on his whereabouts. After being notified that he was in the morgue, she went there but "...let other family members identify the body because they'd been told that, during the eight months, even under refrigeration the body had decomposed." The deceased's brother said, "I just can't believe the incompetence of the government, the hospital, the police...."[24] Rather than being incompetent, it is much more likely that each of the agencies involved simply did what it normally does without regard for the responsibilities of other agencies or departments that might be involved.

On a less bizarre note, many police departments routinely auction off stolen or recovered property that goes unclaimed. The sad part is that many of these departments make no effort to contact the people from whom this property was stolen (and who reported the thefts to the police). The operational policy is to recover stolen property and hold it for disposition. If not disposed of by some other means (i.e., court order or some other legal requirement), the property is sold. There is no policy requiring the people having custody of the property to coordinate with the patrol or detective divisions in identifying owners (or, if their identities are known, notifying them that their property is available).

What kinds of problems become policy issues? This is essentially a political issue. The homicide rate in Washington, DC, as noted above, reached an all-time high in 1990—prompting numerous television reports and newspaper articles. The city government came under intense public pressure to "do something about it." Unfortunately, the timing could not have been worse. In that same year, after a long, bitter and racially divisive trial, the mayor was convicted on a misdemeanor cocaine charge. After his conviction, rather than run for another term as mayor, he ran for an at-large seat on the city council. He lost, and the incoming administration found itself faced with a huge budget deficit, a bloated and very expensive bureaucracy, and a host of serious social problems. The fire department was under regular criticism for its apparent inability to provide timely ambulance responses; the school superintendent was fired; and a study commission made extensive recommendations on the restructuring of the city's government (including a recommendation to terminate the employment of a large number of public employees). With so many pressures from various directions, how could a sensible, coordinated policy be formulated to deal with the homicide problem? Although the police department beefed up its homicide unit, no carefully integrated, systematic effort was designed to deal with the problem. In short, because there was no genuine public policy, the problem continued. In the final analysis, it was easier to blame the problem on drugs than to try to solve it through the development of rational public policy.

SETTING PRIORITIES

It should be clear that limitations on manpower and money have a significant impact on what government can do. We noted earlier that bureaucracies face both functional and allocational conflicts in which scarce resources are typically allocated on a competitive basis. This calls for setting priorities. Since government cannot do everything, it must chose from among its options and select the things it will do. There are certain baseline services that must be provided: public safety, education, public works and administrative support functions (i.e., tax collection, city administration, etc.). Additional services also may be provided, depending on the availability of funds and a constituency to demand them. However, not all constituencies are equal in the power they exert, and therein lies the political aspect of setting public priorities.

The political process is one of power relationships (hence, the importance of the power setting discussed earlier). Having an agenda is one thing; having the clout to convert it into a public policy is a different matter. This is precisely why many special interest groups have sought "empowerment" (i.e., the clout it takes to become a serious player in the political arena). Homosexuals, for example, have historically been without clout because of widespread social disapproval of their sexual preference. However, in many urban areas they have formed coalitions with other special interest groups and thereby influenced electoral outcomes through classical political methods. As a result, they have come to be taken seriously by politicians. This has catalyzed the development of public policies that prohibit discrimination on the basis of sexual preference and the appointment of homosexuals to boards and commissions that make and oversee public policy.

Priorities invariably represent individual or group agendas. In some cases priorities can be set in a "win-win" context, that is, a constituency can seek a benefit that (at least in theory) does not operate to the detriment of any other constituency and benefits all. Public education is a case in point. Educating children is an indivisible benefit. Other agendas are by their very nature "zero-sum" games in which there are winners and losers; when one party wins, all other parties lose. For example, there is a movement in a number of urban school systems to adopt an "Afrocentric" curriculum, essentially renouncing the older curriculum based on the history, philosophy and social science of "dead white European males."[25] Ultimately, the question of priorities is not so much which agenda is "right," but which one is supported by the constituency with the most clout. This is why groups form coalitions with other groups: doing so strengthens their collective positions and thereby increases their clout. When this happens, special interest agendas can be successfully negotiated to result in a shifting of both policies and priorities.

PUBLIC FINANCE:
PAYING FOR WHAT THE PUBLIC WANTS

Although the politics and sociology of public policy are complex, the bottom line is very basic: who pays and who benefits? Decisions by government to provide any benefit (to the community as a whole or to any part of it) are policy decisions as well as economic decisions involving the expenditure of public funds. Everything has to be paid for, and those who do the paying usually want something in return. As we have seen, the decision to spend a dollar on one thing is also the simultaneous decision not to spend that same dollar on something else. If a community has enough money to fund all of its policy goals, there will be little or no allocational conflict. If there is not enough money for competing expenditures, something has to give. Either income has to be increased or expenses have to be lowered. Financing public policies occurs at three levels with a great deal of overlap: federal, state and local governments all play a role. The financial relationship among these levels of government is often complex and frustrating.

WHERE THE MONEY COMES FROM AND WHERE IT GOES
—THE FEDERAL GOVERNMENT

The so-called "Tax Freedom Day" is the date in any given year when the average worker's total tax obligation is paid, assuming all of his or her earnings (starting on January 1) went to the payment of federal, state and local taxes. It falls sometime in May. Of all taxes collected, the most immediate and visible are probably the income and social security taxes collected by the federal government. Governments, like people, have expenses. The federal government spends a great deal of money each year (the 1993 budget exceeded $1.5 billion). That money has to come from somewhere, and most of it comes from the earnings of individuals. Approximately 34 percent of the 1993 federal budget came from individual income taxes, 29 percent came from social security taxes, 7 percent came from corporate income taxes, and 3 percent came from excise taxes. Much of the rest is "borrowed" from the public. In terms of expenditure, the largest portion (55 percent) was spent on medicare, health and education, income security and veterans benefits. The next largest amount (19 percent) went to national defense.[26]

The fairness of the federal tax structure has been hotly debated for many years. It is a debate that will continue well into the foreseeable future. In simple terms, the public wants as much as it can get from the federal government while paying as little for it as possible. Politicians spend money because it strengthens their position with the voters who benefit from these expenditures. As a result, there is a constant tug of war over what the federal government spends its money on and how it taxes the public for that purpose. In recent years there has been considerable upheaval in the federal tax system and its consequences are now being felt at all levels of government. President Reagan's Economic Recovery Tax Act of 1981 was the largest tax-reduction act in American history: it lowered individual tax rates by 25 percent and cut the top rate on investment (so-called "unearned") income from 70 to 50 percent. Then, in 1986 Congress passed the Tax Reform Act, which did away with the old system of tax brackets, replacing them with a lower two-bracket formula, and eliminated a number of the traditional exemptions and exclusions. However, the federal budget tripled during the Reagan years, causing the public debt to skyrocket. The federal deficit now stands at over $3.6 billion. In fiscal 1993 the government must pay about $217 billion in interest to the public on its debt. The total interest on gross federal debt is about $294 billion, including $77 billion paid to trust funds.[27] As the income tax structure was being modified, so was the Social Security tax system. In 1983 Congress raised Social Security taxes, increasing both the tax itself and the maximum amount of earnings subject to Social Security taxes. Questions of how much and what kinds of income should be taxed, and at what rates they should be taxed, are subject to constant debate—as is the issue of how federal revenues should be spent. (Some of it is spent on "national" items such as defense, but more is spent on local problems of national importance, such as health care and transportation.)

WHERE THE MONEY COMES FROM AND WHERE IT GOES —STATE AND LOCAL GOVERNMENT

Although state governments tend to rely on sales and excise taxes (on such commodities as gasoline and cigarettes), most have some form of income tax.[28] In the past, a substantial amount of revenue has come to the states from the federal government through a variety of grants-in-aid, revenue sharing, entitlement and special purpose programs designed to help states meet regional and local needs. With the increasing national debt, the federal government began to cut back on these programs. For example, a phasing down of revenue sharing was initiated under the Nixon administration as part of the president's "New Federalism." State governments were removed from the revenue-sharing program in 1980; in 1987 it was discontinued for local governments. A number of entitlement programs have been cut or eliminated as well. In addition, the Persian Gulf War against Iraq (which broke out in January of 1991) added to the federal expenditures in ways that will be felt for many years.

The income provided by state and federal governments is actually a financial incentive for local governments to achieve state or federal policy objectives. Sometimes referred to as "strings" attached to the money, substantial federal and state funding is provided to local governments in support of public transportation, education, employment, social services, health and income security. These contributions are significant: in 1987 federal contributions to state and local governments amounted to $123.6 million.[29] Federal contributions are considered extremely important because of the limits on local governments with regard to financing their operations. To meet the loss of federal funds, many municipalities have had to raise their own tax rates and reduce nonessential services.

Some local income is raised within the community itself through various taxes (e.g., personal property, income, business, sales and gross receipts taxes), but there are limits on the extent to which a community can tax its citizens. Other income is generated by charging users of utilities, sewerage and sanitation services, and parks and recreation facilities. However, income from these sources is typically used to support the services themselves—not to raise general revenue. The combination of increased demands for services and shrinking revenues at all levels of government has left many communities facing serious financial problems. Cuts in federal programs upon which local governments have become overly dependent have been especially painful. Existing programs have had to be trimmed or eliminated and new ones delayed or cancelled, usually to the displeasure of their beneficiaries.

CHANGING COMMUNITIES
AND CHANGING EXPECTATIONS

Why are so many communities financially strapped? There are three basic reasons: the communities themselves have changed; the people in them have changed, and changes in technology have modified the community's economic base. These factors have significantly altered the financial viability of many cities. In nearly every case they have had a major impact on local government's perception of its ability to finance the kind and quality of services they wish to provide.

Most communities were founded when America was still a very young country, and their purposes were quite different from what they are today. Some were ports or hubs along transportation lines; others grew up during the industrial revolution and served industries that are now defunct; yet others grew up supporting a unique function such as a military base, college or particular religion. Advances in transportation and the development of suburbs caused important shifts to take place. Businesses began moving to outlying areas to take advantage of lower costs, taking many of the more affluent residents of the city with them.

Population changes continue to redefine where Americans live. The fastest growing cities are in the Southwest, which has grown dramatically as the population shifted from the Northeast and Midwest. Whereas in the past a great deal of the movement was from cities to suburbs, now it is from suburbs to "exurbs"—communities 30 to 50 miles away from the major urban centers. Many people are attracted to medium-sized cities near major metropolitan areas—believing they can have the best of both worlds. In some cases, growth in smaller communities comes about as a result of an inability on the part of the larger city to accommodate more growth (perhaps because of fixed boundaries); in other cases, suburban and exurban growth represents a desire to escape from the problems of the major urban area.

At the same time people began moving from cities to suburbs, the American economy began a steady shift from manufactured goods toward the provision of services. The development of the so-called "service economy" was the result. In 1920 service industries (e.g., transportation, communications, wholesale and retail trade, and professional and business services) employed 39 percent of all workers; today they employ 75 percent of all non-agricultural workers. Between 1960 and 1989, 86 percent of all new jobs were a part of the service economy. Such jobs call for well-educated or highly trained people: accountants, nurses, business executives, engineers, mechanics, and so on. Contributing to this shift were advances in communications and computer technology, which allowed many businesses to move from cities to suburban areas.[30]

After large numbers of people and industries moved out of the cities, shopping centers soon appeared. To facilitate access they were usually built at the intersection of two major thoroughfares. Originally, these shopping centers consisted of a cluster of buildings sharing a common parking lot; in the past two decades, however, they have evolved into air-conditioned malls with a great array of amenities. Shopping malls in turn attracted mid-rise office buildings and even industrial parks, further drawing people from cities to suburbs. By 1973 suburban employment in the United States had become greater than downtown employment. The trend has continued.

As technology lowered the number of labor-intensive jobs, people with limited job skills found it increasingly more difficult to earn enough to meet the cost of living. Those with limited or marginal job skills tended to remain in (or migrate into) urban areas—either in the hope of finding employment, because of the availability of welfare, or both. The social makeup of many cities changed as a result. As economically depressed areas within cities expand, there is a decline in tax revenues and an increase in welfare and social service costs. When the inward migration of the poor is rapid, it is common for the more affluent members of the community to move further out into the suburbs (and often out of the community altogether)—taking an important part of the tax base with them. A familiar pattern in the second half of this century, this has culminated in the concentration of large numbers of poor and dependent people in urban areas which are no longer able to provide employment or finance their housing, health and education needs. The remaining city is often called the "inner city," and as its proportion of poor residents increases, so do social service costs. The increased costs are usually met at the expense of the city's infrastructure, which begins to decline. As this happens, crime rates rise—making the inner cities even less desirable as business sites or residential areas.[31]

Because the federal government has provided support (in one way or another) since the New Deal of the 1930s, it is logical for cities to look to it for help.[32] Historically it has sponsored various programs to eliminate poverty, reduce illiteracy, improve health, control crime and ensure economic opportunity for the disadvantaged. Since such programs have channelled federal funds to the local level, local governments have become heavily dependent on them over the years. This trend has continued to the present, and federal involvement has grown considerably over the years. As Kantor pointed out,

> In 1960, there were 44 federal grant programs for cities spending $3.9 billion annually. By 1968, there were over 500 grant programs expending $14 billion in cities, a figure that grew to $26.8 billion by 1974. Unlike the previous two decades when federal policy focused on the physical development of urban areas, most of these new programs sought to promote redistributive social reforms of the cities.[33]

The federal government created the Department of Housing and Urban Development (HUD) in 1965. One of HUD's earliest efforts was a Model Cities Program using federal funds to stimulate the development of deteriorating inner cities. The Model Cities Program was eventually dropped in favor of revenue sharing plans and Community Development Block Grants, in which the federal government provided money to state and local governments, letting them determine their own priorities and solutions.

During the Carter administration, federal funds were narrowly focused on cities suffering from severe economic and physical deterioration, shrinking populations and declining tax bases. The Reagan administration cut urban programs, ended general revenue sharing and reduced Community Development Block Grants. The federal government was forced to recognize that in light of the soaring national debt it could not continue providing funding for local problems on such an elaborate scale. However, in spite of the cutbacks, the federal government continues to support local governments in their efforts to deal with their problems, utilizing both new proposals—such as the movement to create federally subsidized "enterprise zones," and established programs—such as Aid to Families with Dependent Children (created in 1953), the federal food stamp program (created in 1964) and Medicaid and Medicare (established in 1965).

The continuing decline of federal funding has left cities with the prospect of having to find other or better ways of dealing with their own problems. This can be especially difficult. For example, communities with weak economies must not only import goods and services, but also must bear the burden of greater welfare and human services needs. Providing heavy subsidies to support these needs invests money in programs that fail to return wealth to the community. Such efforts then become "...transactions of decline, and once adopted the need for them grows greater with time, and the wherewithal for supplying them grows less."[34] Ultimately, the communities with the greatest social needs become the ones least able to afford them.

It should be noted that federal programs are also closely linked to partisan and special interest politics. Advocates of selected federal subsidies typically decry subsidies that do not benefit them, and call for their elimination or reduction in favor of their own "pet programs." This is why advocates for social programs at the local level have made a steady demand for cuts in defense spending. They argue that cutting defense spending will result in a "peace dividend" that can then be spent on social programs.

Financially pressed communities, particularly those undergoing rapid change, face another closely related problem because a significant proportion of local government income comes from property taxes. These taxes are threatened by property values that are subject to rapid change (as in declining neighborhoods) and are seriously eroded by exemptions and other relief measures.[35] Thus, though providing large numbers of people with subsidized housing may benefit those who live in them, it hurts local government by committing economic resources to capital expenditures that not only have to be built and maintained but which also reduce property tax revenues. However, "fixing" the problem can sometimes create other problems. For example, during the Reagan administration the federal government phased out aid for the construction or rehabilitation of low-income housing, shifting to the assistance of individuals through rent vouchers or certificates.[36] The result was a decline in the number of housing units, because local governments already faced with tight budgets were reluctant to fund new construction or undertake major rehabilitation projects. As the number of units available declined, the number of poor people using vouchers increased. Since the poor's housing costs rose because of increased demand, they were forced to pay a larger portion of their already limited income for housing. The end result is that they have become more dependent on government for such things as health care (the most expensive category of transfer payments).

In recent decades another major change in communities has come about through a process called "empowerment." This refers to the development of political power by groups who were previously disenfranchised—including the poor, minorities and special interest groups (e.g., gender activists, homosexual rights advocates, etc.). The Kennedy administration began the first major effort in this direction in what ultimately took shape as President Johnson's "War on Poverty." This was a broad assault on economic, political and racial inequality. As Hodge and Lagerfeld note, "Ambitious programs designed to enhance the upward mobility of the poor, especially blacks—Head Start, Upward Bound, Job Corps—had been linked to the Community Action Program, an ill-fated effort to increase the political power of the poor in cities and elsewhere."[37] Previously powerless groups have come to realize that if they want policy changed (or funded) to their benefit, they have to play a serious role in community politics. As such awareness has increased, these groups have become surprisingly successful, sometimes with results that dismay the majority. Consider, for example, the case of a woman raped by a man she fears has AIDS. Her attacker was caught and arrested and she wanted him tested for the virus. However, "...advocates of personal rights, including the American Civil Liberties Union, argue that nobody should be tested for AIDS against his or her will, even in the situation where the victim fears she has been infected by her convicted rapist. These advocates of personal rights want to block involuntary testing because of massive job and other discrimination against persons with AIDS."[38] This is an example of public policy being shaped by a rather strong gay rights lobby which is concerned that any AIDS-testing policy will ultimately result in an infringement on their rights. Indeed, the issue of individual rights and individual responsibility to the community is at the heart of public policies dealing with AIDS. Many people believe that what consenting adults do in private is no one else's business; however, some states have enacted laws that require people who test positive for the HIV virus to notify past sexual partners.

To some, these new laws seem an obvious, elementary response to a killing disease that imposes enormous economic and human costs on the community. To others, however, such laws must be vigorously opposed. The ACLU, for one, argues that since there is no known cure for AIDS, such disclosures do not help those already infected and are therefore unreasonable. Communitarians respond that disclosure does save the lives of those not yet infected, and thus helps the community. Civil libertarians argue that HIV carriers who are identified are liable to lose their jobs, housing and insurance and hence oppose all but the most voluntary disclosure. Here, communitarians concur; but their response is to favor accompanying disclosure with measures to thwart discrimination against HIV carriers.[39]

Consider also the following:

A Minnesota law providing for a four-year sentence for first-time crack users and probation for first-time users of powdered cocaine is racially biased and thus unconstitutional, a judge has ruled. Hennepin County District Judge Pamela Alexander said there is no reason why people convicted for possessing crack should be treated any differently from those convicted of possessing any other form of cocaine. Attorneys for the five suspects who challenged the crack law said 92 percent of people arrested on charges of possession of crack in 1988 were black, while 85 percent of people arrested on charges of possessing powdered cocaine were white. Crack is cocaine in the form of highly purified, pebble-like nuggets that can be smoked.[40]

The conflict is not new. Thomas Jefferson, in his First Inaugural address, said that "the will of the majority is in all cases to prevail." However, he added an important proviso: The will of the majority, "to be rightful must be reasonable [because] the minority possess their equal rights, which equal law must protect, and to violate [them] would be oppression."[41] The problem, of course, is the definition of "reasonable." The question has been argued ever since with regard to equality issues involving women, racial and ethnic minorities, the handicapped, the elderly, homosexuals, and so on. The concern has always been that a numeric majority could use its weight to impose its will on society's minorities, resulting in the suppression of their liberty. A variety of laws and court rulings since the Civil Rights Act of 1964 and the Voting Rights Act of 1965 have made it clear that people cannot be discriminated against on the basis of such things as age, sex, race, national origin or sexual preference. Members of these groups claim that past practices have in fact denied them opportunity. They have sought remedies for that through both formal and informal means that have taken the form of various "affirmative action" plans and consent decrees, many of which have a direct impact on public policy and public finance. Minority programs in publicly funded construction projects have required federal contractors to establish hiring quotas for blacks; agreements have been made to accelerate the hiring and promotion of "target groups" to achieve "balance," and informal understandings to replace key public officials with those of another race or gender at the earliest practical date have been reached.

Whether or not these practices are fair or proper—a subject of much debate—is outside the scope of this book, but it is important to note that such practices have a major impact on community politics, including the setting of public policy and the delivery of services. They contribute to the diversity of the American community and are intimately involved in the entire criminal justice process. As we will see, some of the most vexing problems facing the criminal justice systems involve satisfying segments of the community that have different expectations and goals. Some of the most intransigent problems facing the system are in reality problems of race, ethnicity, gender, health status, income distribution, education and economics.

THE CONTEMPORARY DILEMMA

The social, demographic and economic forces described above have left us with cities that range from extremely wealthy to desperately poor. As they vary considerably in their needs and resources, there is no single formula that can satisfy them all. Each community must set its own policies and priorities, and each must deal with its own problems as best as it can. Neither the federal nor state governments can solve local problems, although to a certain extent they can help financially. However, it seems probable that severe fiscal limitations at all levels of government make outside funding increasingly unlikely.

The money shortage is just one part of the problem. Community perceptions of what its problems are will continue to be shaped by partisan issues based on race, gender, sexual preference and socioeconomic status. The diversity of the American community has long been one of its greatest strengths, but in the coming century it may well prove to be one of its biggest problems. The criminal justice system is likely to be torn by conflicting goals and community objectives, and may well change dramatically within the next three decades —shaped by forces not even anticipated three decades ago.

SUMMARY

Although the public and private control systems are the primary vehicles for social control, they are only partially effective. Ambiguity within the public control system limits its effectiveness, while changing social values and cultural diversity limit the private control system. Since the criminal justice system draws its support from diverse elements of society, and since different components within the community have different expectations, the system is faced with conflicting demands and expectations. Even so, the community has certain expectations of the system that transcend the wishes of its various elements: the control of crime, maintenance of order, provision of assistance to the public and crime prevention. How these things are to be done is another matter: although there is a general consensus that these things ought to be done, there is little agreement as to how they should be accomplished.

Government carries out it goals by setting public policies and then arranging them in a system of priorities. Public policies are set by the political leadership of the community and are translated into operation realities by specific agencies of government. Unfortunately, the policy process is not always well understood or utilized. Some communities delegate the policy-making process to their operating departments or establish policy only in response to specific crises or emergencies. In some communities policy statements are little more than propaganda and represent no real commitment to meeting goals. In most communities the value of public policy is diluted because of a failure to integrate the policy into the full resources of the community.

The kinds of problems that become policy issues are not limited to problems of community-wide interest. Since policy-making is a political process, it is subject to political pressures. Elements within society that have previously been "powerless" have come to recognize this and have asserted themselves in the political arena—either as single-issue advocacy groups or as part of a larger coalition—and thereby have been able to influence the policy-making process. Undoubtedly this will continue and probably will add to the cultural and political diversity of the American community.

Making policy is one thing; carrying it out is another matter. Government programs, regardless of their nature, cost money. The single largest source of government's revenue is from taxes on individual earnings or property. Although revenues are raised at all levels of government, social problems are essentially local issues. In the past, the federal government has provided significant funding to state and local governments to help them meet their needs. However, a rising federal deficit and increased costs of government at all levels have resulted in diminished support from the federal government. This has meant that many local programs have had to be curtailed, eliminated or modified simply because there has not been enough money to pay for everything the government wants to do.

This fiscal austerity has been complicated by the changing nature of many communities. Population redistributions, advances in technology and the shift to a service economy have all had a major impact on American communities. The older, larger cities have experienced a rapid decline in their tax base, accompanied by a rapid increase in the size and cost of social programs. Some of our most serious social problems are now concentrating in urban areas that are increasingly unable to deal with them. Crime and disorder are closely related to urban decline and economic dependence; they pose a particularly difficult challenge for local government. As communities shift in their racial, economic and political makeup, their priorities change accordingly. As a result, we are seeing greater emphasis on such things as race and gender politics that promise to make the coming decades a period of great change. The criminal justice system itself will be an important part of this change.

DISCUSSION QUESTIONS

1. How does cultural diversity influence the private control system?

2. Although most people expect government to control crime, many disagree on how it should be done. Why is this the case?

3. Why does the public expect the criminal justice system to maintain order but criticize it for doing so?

4. What does the term "police power of the state" mean? What does it have to do with the police as a specific institution?

5. Is it realistic to expect the criminal justice system to provide public assistance? Why or why not?

6. Why does crime prevention invariably call for some degree of surrender of personal liberty? Is it a fair expectation?

7. Setting public policy is described as a "political process." What does this mean?

8. What is the difference between public policy and operational policy, and how are the two related?

9. How does the use of rational policy actually benefit an agency of government?

10. What is the relationship between power settings within the community and the process of setting public policy priorities?

11. Should the federal government carry a larger part of the financial burden for meeting social problems at the local level? Why or why not?

12. How do federal and state governments create public policy at the local level?

13. How does public support for the poor contribute to declining tax revenues?

14. Why does the emergence of a service economy have such a negative impact on the poor?

15. What are "exurbs," and what do they have to do with economic changes in the larger metropolitan areas?

16. What are the key demographic elements in creating the so-called "inner cities"?

17. What does "empowerment" mean, and what does it have to do with community politics?

18. Are programs such as Affirmative Action fair? Should they be?

19. Should poor communities be provided with financial remedies by neighboring wealthy communities? Why or why not?

20. How do you expect communities to look in the next two or three decades? Will they be much the same, or will they be different? If they are different, how will those differences be reflected?

REFERENCES

1 Marianne W. Zawitz, ed., *Report to the Nation on Crime and Justice*, 2nd ed. (Washington, DC: U.S. Department of Justice, Bureau of Justice Statistics, March 1988), 24.

2 Bureau of Justice Statistics, "Crime and the Nation's Households, 1989." *Bureau of Justice Statistics Bulletin* (September 1990).

3 Timothy J. Flanagan and Kathleen Maguire, eds., *Sourcebook of Criminal Justice Statistics 1989* (Washington, DC: U.S. Department of Justice, Bureau of Justice Statistics, U.S. Government Printing Office). See Tables 3.1 (p. 220) and 3.20 (p. 235).

4 George Gallup, Jr., *The Gallup Report*, Report No. 285 (Princeton, NJ: The Gallup Poll, June 1989), 4, 5.

5 Flanagan and Maguire, *Sourcebook of Criminal Justice Statistics 1989*, Table 2.61, 182.

6 Flanagan and Maguire, *Sourcebook of Criminal Justice Statistics 1989*, Tables 2.21 (p. 142) and 2.22 (p. 143).

7 Flanagan and Maguire, *Sourcebook of Criminal Justice Statistics 1989*, Tables 2.21 (p. 142) and 2.19 (p. 141).

8 Flanagan and Maguire, *Sourcebook of Criminal Justice Statistics 1989*, Table 2.33 (p. 155).

9 Flanagan and Maguire, *Sourcebook of Criminal Justice Statistics 1989*, Table 2.26 (p. 145).

10 Flanagan and Maguire, *Sourcebook of Criminal Justice Statistics 1989*, Table 2.35 (p. 158).

11 Flanagan and Maguire, *Sourcebook of Criminal Justice Statistics 1989*, Tables 2.36 and 2.37 (p. 159).

[12] Flanagan and Maguire, *Sourcebook of Criminal Justice Statistics 1989*, Tables 2.14 (p. 138) and 2.16 (p. 139).

[13] George L. Kelling, "Police and Communities: The Quiet Revolution," *Perspectives on Policing* 1 (June 1988), 3.

[14] Kelling, "Police and Communities: The Quiet Revolution," 3.

[15] George L. Kelling and Mark H. Moore, "The Evolving Strategy of Policing," *Perspectives on Policing* 4 (November 1988), 5.

[16] Patrick Colquhoun, *A Treatise on the Commerce and Police of the River Thames* (1800; reprint, Montclair, NJ: Patterson Smith, 1969), 38.

[17] William H. Hewitt, *British Police Administration* (Springfield, IL: Charles C Thomas, Publisher, 1965), 130.

[18] Spencer Rich, "Balancing Community and Individual Rights," *The Washington Post*, 25 December 1990, A17.

[19] "A policy is a deliberate choice to follow a course of action made between various alternatives by officials responsible for establishing formal policy." *Molton v. City of Cleveland, Ohio*, 839 F. 2d 240 (1988).

[20] Office of Criminal Justice Plan and Analysis, *1988 Crime and Justice Report*. (Washington, DC: District of Columbia Government, June 1989), 8.

[21] "Over 42 Hours, D.C. Streets Throb With Fear," *The Washington Post*, 28 August 1989, A1, A8-A9.

[22] Michael Gottfredson and Travis Hirschi, "Criminal Behavior: Why We're Losing the War on Crime," *The Washington Post*, 10 September 1989, C3.

[23] "Over 42 Hours, D.C. Streets Throb With Fear," A1, A8-A9.

[24] Eric Charles May, "D.C. Woman Sues Over Death Notice That Arrived Late," *The Washington Post*, 23 December 1990, B1, B2.

[25] See for example, Molefi Kete Asante, *The Afrocentric Idea* (Philadelphia: Temple University Press, 1987).

[26] Executive Office of the President, *Budget of the United States Government, Fiscal Year 1993* (Washington, DC: U.S. Government Printing Office, 1992).

[27] Executive Office of the President, *Budget of the United States Government, Fiscal Year 1993*.

[28] Nine states do not have broad-based income tax. They are Alaska, Florida, Nevada, New Hampshire, South Dakota, Tennessee, Texas, Washington and Wyoming.

[29] U.S. Bureau of the Census, *Statistical Abstract of the United States: 1990*, 110th ed. (Washington, DC: U.S. Government Printing Office, 1990), Table 460, 276.

[30] U.S. Bureau of the Census, *Statistical Abstract of the United States: 1990*.

31 See especially James Q. Wilson and George L. Kelling, "Broken Windows," *The Atlantic Monthly*, March 1982, 29-36, 38; and its rebuttal, Samuel Walker, "'Broken Windows' and Fractured History" in *Critical Issues in Policing: Contemporary Readings*, ed. Roger G. Dunham and Geoffrey P. Alpert (Prospect Heights, IL: Waveland Press, Inc., 1989), 382-394.

32 See especially, Robert W. Hodge and Steven Lagerfeld, "The Politics of Opportunity," *Wilson Quarterly* (Winter 1987), 109-127.

33 Paul Kantor, *The Dependent City* (Glenview, IL: Scott Foresman, 1988).

34 Jane Jacobs, *Cities and the Wealth of Nations* (New York: Random House, 1984), 193.

35 Lowell Harriss, "The Property Tax and Local Finance." *Proceedings of the Academy of Political Science* 35:1 (1983), 3.

36 "The Decade by the Numbers: Housing," *The Washington Post*, 12 December 1989, A18.

37 Hodge and Lagerfeld, "The Politics of Opportunity," 109-127.

38 "Balancing Community and Individual Rights," 109-127.

39 Amatai Etzioni, "The New Rugged Communitarianism," *The Washington Post*, 20 January 1991, B1, B2.

40 "Drug Law Found Biased," *The Washington Post*, 29 December 1990, A4.

41 Jefferson, Thomas A., First Inaugural Address (delivered Washington, DC, March 4, 1801), cited in *Speeches of the American Presidents*, ed. Janet Podell and Steven Anzovin (New York: The H.W. Wilson Company, 1988), 38-40.

Photo Credit: Tony O'Brien, Frost Publishing Group, Ltd.

Chapter 4

RACE AND
COMMUNITY EXPECTATIONS

Approximately three out of four Americans live in a metropolitan area. These people have different economic, social and cultural backgrounds, and although they live close to one another and share a great deal in common, many remain widely separated by their differences. Urban areas have become highly heterogeneous because of the ways in which their populations are distributed socially and economically. As we saw in the last chapter, cities are complex environments and their residents have been caught up in an accelerating rate of change, throwing both the cities and their populations off balance.[1]

Cities and their inhabitants experience numerous problems. However, it is important to remember that a problem always arises from the relationship between two or more factors. For example, traffic is a problem not just because there are too many cars, but also because the roadways cannot adequately handle the volume of traffic. Not only do problems have multiple "sides," people tend to see them relative to their own perceptions. If their perceptions are one-sided, overly simplistic or in error, both their perceptions of the problems and their preferred solutions are apt to be flawed.

People within groups often share common perceptions and believe some of their problems are the consequence of policies and practices of other groups. For instance, many middle-class citizens blame their high taxes on the "lower class," claiming that welfare supports the lazy at the expense of those who work.

Many of the chronically poor believe they are trapped in a state of dependence created and maintained by those who "control the system" specifically for the purpose of exploiting them. The young feel exploited by the old, and the old feel exploited by the young; educators blame their failures on parents, while parents blame government in general—and the schools in particular—for the decline of the educational system. Those who have been hit hard by inflation blame oil companies for the poor economy, who in turn blame the Arabs, who then blame the consumers. Society's significant economic and social problems often divide and polarize groups who view the same problems from different, conflicting perspectives. However, the causes and cures for these problems are usually far more complex than most critics realize.

It is difficult for the diverse components of a community to unite against their common problems when so many view their neighbors as being responsible for the problems in the first place. The criminal justice system is not exempt from these passions, either within its own institutions or in its relationships with the public, but in spite of this, it must do the best it can to serve the public as a whole. Unfortunately, a good deal of the criticism of the system comes from people who feel their needs are not being met. In recent years we have seen the development of the single-issue interest group that proclaims its interests to the exclusion of all others.

Racial diversity is probably the most obvious divisive factor in our society. This is especially so in the larger urban areas that have undergone major economic and demographic shifts in recent decades. However, before discussing race, we need to first examine the nature of poverty. This is important because the two issues are closely related and a great deal of misunderstanding has arisen from a failure to appreciate the consequences of poverty on race relations.

POVERTY

When people speak of "the poor," they usually are referring to those who have little or no money. While this is correct, it is by no means inclusive. The poor lack a great deal more than money; they are also deficient in power, status, material goods and influence. Typically, they are ill-educated, live in undesirable locations, work at demeaning jobs (when they are employed) and often suffer the contempt of those who are more fortunate. As Radelet has noted, "Poverty is mean, it is brutal, it is frustrating, it is painful, and it blights the spirit. There are few things in this world that are worse than being caught in the grip of poverty."[2]

Poverty has never been the exclusive domain of any particular group. It ignores differences of race, sex, ethnicity, age and geographic location. Poverty is an especially persistent social ill because it feeds upon itself—poor education leads to diminished work opportunities, unemployment or underemployment. The low income resulting from underemployment restricts social advancement and fuels the cycle of poverty. The relationship between education and income is reflected in the following statistics. People with only an elementary school education earned an average of $11,730 per year in 1987 compared with $23,382 for those with a high school diploma and $38,337 for those with college degrees.[3] Poverty is often regarded as a trap from which escape is extremely difficult. It is closely tied to class and status; those who comprise the poorest segment of the community usually enjoy the least status.

It is widely believed that poverty produces its own "culture." This proposition was first set forth by the sociologist Oscar Lewis.[4] He contended that a "culture of poverty" exists because it provides rewards that enable the poor to adjust to their chronic poverty, and that these attitudes and responses are passed from one generation of poor to the next. Perhaps the culture of poverty with its peculiar social, psychological and economic facets is in part responsible for the ambivalent attitude many people have toward poverty. Although most realize the conditions that produce poverty are beyond the control of the poor, they are nevertheless inclined to blame them for their poverty, ascribing it to laziness, reluctance to work or even "God's will." In a sense, many people subconsciously equate affluence with "goodness" and poverty with "badness," although this relationship is seldom openly expressed in such blunt terms. The affluent typically expect the poor to show them the deference and gratitude they feel they deserve. At the same time, they deny any responsibility for the plight of the poor, even though a great deal of the problem is a direct function of our economic system—the same system that rewards the affluent for not being poor![5] There is, of course, a long social heritage behind this attitude. It is firmly rooted in the rigid class systems of Europe (from which we derive much of our cultural heritage) and in legal precedents like the Elizabethan poor laws and subsequent vagrancy laws that virtually made it a crime to be poor.

The poor are placed in an extremely difficult position. They are expected to accept and live by the rules imposed by the larger society—to be honest, hard-working and responsive citizens and to suffer with patience and a positive attitude. However, many of the poor feel caught in a web of humiliation, self-denigration and dependency, and find their situation difficult to accept with grace. In economic terms, there is no significant *opportunity cost* for rejecting the values of the dominant society in favor of activities that are illegal but more profitable. When the poor see the dominant society as being responsible for their poverty or willing to take advantage of it, their despair can turn to resentment or even hatred.

An important aspect of poverty is the involvement of minorities. Poverty is often equated with minority status, which is a significant error. The fact that some minorities may be heavily represented in the ranks of the poor by no means indicates that all members of a given group are poor. There are some aspects of minority status that make poverty more likely, however, and that make escape from poverty more difficult. Before looking at minorities *per se*, it is important to note that ours is a harshly competitive society in which the ability to compete never has been equally distributed. This is not the result of historical accident, for the history of American social and economic relations has been based on carefully enforced patterns of economic and social dominance fostering the submission of some groups to the will of others. In its most basic form, it is a question of power. The uneven distribution of power is clearly reflected in our system of social stratification, which has traditionally hindered the advancement of some while facilitating that of others.

From colonial days until well into the twentieth century, this process has reflected racial and ethnic differences. White Anglo-Saxon protestants historically have been the dominant group. The white settlers regarded Native Americans as savages unworthy of their property, while Asians were brutally exploited for cheap labor. Blacks were seen as property to be used at the pleasure of their owners. Inequality was institutionalized, respected and even protected by law. Although legally enforced discrimination is a thing of the past, we are now living with its long-term consequences, which have given us of our most difficult and enduring contemporary social problems. Nowhere is this clearer than in the relationship between poverty and race.

Although the sociology and history of race and ethnic relations are far too complex to summarize here, it is important to remember that contemporary minority problems are firmly rooted in the nation's history. As a result, the problems are too complex to be cured by simple solutions. Although attempts have been made to bring minorities into full participation in the mainstream of society, for many the change has come too late and offers too little. Residual effects, hardened attitudes, alienation and generations of institutionalized poverty continue to play a major role in contemporary society.[6]

BLACKS IN AMERICA *

Race is one of the most persistent issues affecting American justice. Accusations, charges and counter-charges abound on both sides and passions run high. The troubled relationship between the police and the black community is only the tip of a much larger iceberg. As Silberman noted, "At its core, the urban problem is a problem of race; so is the welfare problem, the migrant and farm labor problem, the school busing problem—and, to a degree that few

---

* Although the term *African American* has gained acceptance among some groups as a descriptor of Americans of African descent, the term *black* will be used throughout this text to avoid an unwieldiness of word flow.

people have been willing to acknowledge openly, the crime problem."[7] The contemporary situation has evolved out of a specific historical context and it is important to review some of its milestones to appreciate where we stand today.

Blacks were brought to this country as slaves, and that fact alone distinguishes them from any other group. While other groups have experienced dislocation and poverty, only blacks have had the additional experience of slavery. The status of *slave* was not just economic; it was a status that had a profound effect on the individual as well as the group. When a race is subjected to slavery, it is not only condemned to do work others will not do, it is also forced to repress the richness of personality inherent in all humans. Slavery denied freedom of expression. Although it could not completely suppress self-expression, it forced expression into culturally acceptable forms. Among Southern blacks of the last century, this expression emerged in the form of "folk songs" —melancholy spirituals that allowed blacks to share their grief, express emotions and affirm hope in the future. Later it gave way to the blues—songs which conveyed much of the same feeling, but with less emphasis on the spiritual. Few white, middle-class Americans fully appreciate how much of our musical heritage we owe to black musicians, including the "perfessers," who composed and played in New Orleans whorehouses to entertain waiting customers with improvised music—music that became known as jazz.

Black slaves could not strike out against injustices; to do so was to invite harsh punishment or death. In fact, they were expected to show servility, deference and an exaggerated politeness—to know and remain "in their place" and to avoid being "uppity." Their frustration produced aggression that had to be channeled into either passive or symbolic forms, but even that had to be done with great caution. Silberman noted that there developed a side of black culture that remains largely unknown to other cultures:

> The overwhelming majority of black Americans have had to stay in the dark without power and influence, and without contact with powerful and influential people. Hence they have had to find their own sources of dignity and pride—their own ways of investing their lives with meaning and significance, and their own outlets for their anger. One way has been through an elaborate fantasy life of heroism and triumph over the rich and powerful. Nowhere is this fantasy life revealed or celebrated more clearly than in black folklore and narrative poetry....[8]

Best known in black folklore are the Uncle Remus stories. Although "Uncle Remus" was the literary creation of a white journalist, Joel Chandler Harris, the stories came straight from black folklore. At first glance they seem to be amusing fairy tales about animals who find themselves in various kinds of predicaments. In a very real sense they are like fairy tales, for they mask a much harsher and malevolent theme: "...a biting parody of white society, as well as an outlet for black fantasies about the day when the weak would triumph over the strong."[9]

After the Civil War the state of the black community worsened considerably, despite the fact that they had been legally emancipated. At the beginning of the Reconstruction, the family was a relatively stable institution within the culture, but that changed during the last three decades of the nineteenth century with the advent of deteriorating social and economic conditions. Blacks working in many skilled areas (construction trades, railroad firefighting, brickmasonry, etc.) were quickly forced out of these occupations by Jim Crow legislation. These laws regulated the lives of blacks as strictly as slavery had. Frustration began to manifest itself in a new form, a type of narrative poetry known as "toasts." The toasts were part of an oral tradition that gave structure to blacks' feelings as well as an opportunity to express those feelings. They consist for the most part of an exchange of tall tales, jokes and insults.[10] Closely related to them are "the dozens," which are highly structured, rapid exchanges of obscene, rhymed insults typically directed against the participants' mothers or other female relatives. They are games of verbal skill in which frustration, hostility and aggression are sublimated and used in a physically non-threatening way, bringing peer approval and respect to skilled practitioners. Not only do they provide practical training in the use of wit and self-discipline, they also allow for the discharge of hostility without recourse to actual violence.

One of the most popular toasts dealt with Stacker Lee, a "badman" whose violent and wild nature gets him into trouble with everyone and eventually leads to his undoing. In fact, his attributes are extensions of stereotypes about blacks:

> Because black Americans, and especially black men, have been imprisoned by white stereotypes of them—because they have found it so difficult, if not impossible, to escape those stereotypes—they have fought back, in part, by accepting the stereotypes and turning them upside down. Through the medium of folklore, black men have converted their supposed exaggerated sexuality, physical prowess, and animal-like or (child-like) inability to control their impulses from negative to positive attributes.[11]

Thus, Stacker Lee became the badman who stood up to authority in a suicidal gesture of defiance. The badman of the toasts merged into and finally became embodied in the "bad nigger." In slave folklore, he was "the docile fieldhand who suddenly goes berserk" and posed a threat to both blacks and whites.[12] Because the bad nigger is not afraid of death or anything else, he cannot be threatened—he is completely free. Silberman points out that the bad nigger image was cultivated by Malcolm X:

> Until the last year or two of his life, when he was struggling to develop a more goal-oriented approach, Malcolm X deliberately cultivated a "bad nigger" image, and black Americans in every walk of life loved him for it. "That Mal-

colm ain't afraid to tell Mr. Charlie, the FBI or the cops or nobody where to get off," a New York cabdriver observed. "You don't see him pussyfootin' 'round the whites like he's scared of them." "Malcolm says things you or I would not say," a civil rights leader remarked. "When he says those things, when he talks about the white man, even those of us who are repelled by his philosophy secretly cheer a little inside ourselves, because Malcolm X really does tell 'em, and we know he frightens the white man. We clap."[13]

The bad nigger image has been reinforced in songs and movies and the ethos it represents is a stand from which many young blacks will not retreat. This new attitude is reflected in "rap" music, which is a manifestation of the expression of black frustration and anger in music and lyrics. This form of expression is popular among the young who believe that rap's often harsh lyrics simply reflect the world around them. As one commentator noted, "As much as grown-ups might wish otherwise, youngsters listen hard to rap lyrics. Even halfhearted fans of rap can recite 42 consecutive lines at twice the speed of light. The staccato street poetry can be so raw that it almost commands youngsters to confront their feelings about the world it portrays: a sometimes violent world that seethes with racial and sexual tension."[14]

One result is that the long-standing fabric of servility, exaggerated politeness and a willingness to accept abuse is giving way to a fearsome violence. The blues, toasts, dozens, rap and other devices for converting rage into play have ceased to function and the bad nigger is moving from myth to reality—"from toasting, signifying, and playing the dozens to committing robbery, murder, rape, and assault." This may be one of the major factors that "underlies the explosive increase in criminal violence on the part of black offenders."[15]

> Equally important, black men have new and more effective ways of deadening the pain; as narcotics, toasts and the dozens cannot compete with heroin, cocaine, or the increasingly popular (and potent) combination of methadone and wine. Drugs not only kill the pain, they provide a euphoric high as well. Nor can toasts or the dozens provide as much (or as satisfying) "action" as a mugging, robbery, or burglary, or as much evidence of an individual's manhood.[16]

The current status of blacks in America is the product of a dramatic and complex fabric of interrelated events. It began with enforced transportation to America as slaves and was shaped by events leading up to and extending beyond the Civil War. Around the time of World War I the migration of a large part of the black population resulted in profound economic, social and political consequences that continue to shape the situation of America's black communities. A brief overview of this process and its outcomes will help bring the current status of blacks into focus and will illuminate the relationship between blacks and the criminal justice system.

DEMOGRAPHY:
THE GREAT EXODUS

At the beginning of the twentieth century, America was a country of enormous potential wealth; however, much of its population—both black and white—was poor. Even though the nation's industrial base had developed rapidly since the Civil War, 60 percent of the population still lived in rural areas and 41 percent depended on agriculture for their livelihood.[17] Almost 80 percent of the black population lived in rural areas (compared to 57 percent of the white population), and they were among the poorest of the poor. At the turn of the century, the majority of blacks worked in agriculture (for the most part as tenant farmers or sharecroppers) or as domestic servants. Although able to survive on what was essentially a subsistence economy, few had any real opportunity for educational, economic or social improvement.

When the United States entered World War I in 1917, immigration from Europe was reduced while the industrial base expanded to meet wartime requirements. The need for industrial labor triggered a major movement of blacks from the rural South to the industrial Northeast. However, 10 years after the war ended, the depression began. As the economy came to a standstill, black migration slowed due to a lack of new opportunity in urban areas. With the outbreak of World War II the depression ended and the economy accelerated at a rapid rate (and continued to do so for two decades after the war ended). The wartime economy again produced major labor shortages resulting in new opportunities for blacks; and once again, many left for a new life in the cities. Between 1940 and 1970 about 1.5 million blacks migrated from the rural South into industrialized urban areas. This movement was often tentative—taken in steps—going first from a Southern farm to a Southern city, and finally to a Northern city such as New York, Chicago or Philadelphia. This massive migration ultimately transformed the racial composition of many urban areas. On the average, blacks comprised 10 percent of the population of the 20 largest American cities in 1940. By 1960 they comprised 22 percent and by 1980, 36 percent.[18] Viewed in other terms, just prior to the World War II approximately 49 percent of the black population lived in urban areas, but by the beginning of the 1990s the proportion had risen to 81 percent.[19]

Blacks moving into the cities were forced into compact areas that were rigidly segregated. Because of low levels of income, most were renters whose options were limited to what was available. As a result, residential areas tended to be exclusively black and were characterized by poverty, low levels of income, minimal social services, underemployment, declining physical conditions and inadequate educational resources. These neighborhoods took on a character of their own, embodied in the "subculture of poverty," and growing up in them has had a profound impact on subsequent generations.

Residential segregation by race has been driven by three important forces. First, because blacks moved into the neighborhoods that were open to them, there was an inward migration of blacks that served to concentrate their presence. Neighborhood selection was both a matter of choice (people wishing to live close to those who shared a common social circumstance) and necessity. Second, whites exhibited a desire to avoid living in racially mixed neighborhoods, based on beliefs that such neighborhoods were unstable and that they were likely to have lower property values and higher crime rates. Third, the actions of local government and the financial and real estate industries enforced a pattern of residential segregation based on race.[20]

The result is that poor blacks are now more likely to be concentrated in inner-city neighborhoods. This means that they "...to a much greater degree than poor whites, interact mainly with other disadvantaged people. Black poor children attend schools with other poor children, go to churches with impoverished congregations, and deal with merchants geared to do business with a poor clientele. Racial segregation in residence reinforces the effects of economic separation."[21] The problem was compounded by the flight of whites from urban neighborhoods as blacks moved in, and was further (and more seriously) aggravated by the flight of middle-class blacks to more affluent suburbs. This has resulted in more than just a concentration of blacks in inner cities; it has produced a distilled residue of people who are poor, powerless, dependent and angry. This is the population that is most heavily dependent on welfare and other support programs and most involved in crime and urban disorder.

ECONOMIC ISSUES

Power and status are closely related to wealth. Personal wealth and income determine where, how well, and often how long one will live. It is impossible to separate the quality of life from income and wealth. For some (those who inherit money) wealth is an accident of birth, but for most it is a function of working, saving and investing. Success in the labor force requires varying degrees of education, skill and access. Some jobs lead nowhere, enabling the wage-earner to put bread on the table, but little else. Other jobs are linked to upward mobility and provide a wide array of rewards—both financial and social.

The upward mobility of blacks has been a slow and laborious process. Just before the outbreak of the World War II, 87 percent of all black families were believed to have been below the poverty level (compared to 48 percent of white families).[22] The movement of Southern blacks into Northern cities required a shift in patterns of work. Without education or job skills, many were hired as laborers or machine operators, or worked in menial jobs. Their wages were low, and the rewards of their labor were typically minimal. Even so, blacks made major economic gains and became a significant component of the non-agricultural labor force. Although the 1960s marked the end of black economic gain based on migration, the decade was extremely important in ushering in the civil rights movement. Among the most significant advances was the Civil Rights Act of 1964, which made the practice of job discrimination on the basis of race illegal. As a result, blacks began entering the economic mainstream, and significant advances were made in education and the reduction of discrimination. At this point the physical shift of the black population began to take second place to the issue of qualitative advancement in all aspects of American life.

Much has been written about the disparity of income between blacks and whites. The median income of black households in 1987 was slightly more than half the median income of white households. In the same year, 33 percent of blacks were below the poverty level as compared to only 11 percent of whites.[23] Such comparisons, however, mask an economic miracle: the emergence of blacks from economic destitution to economic viability—mostly within the span of two generations.

THE FAMILY

At the same time the black community began to develop wealth and economic influence, a trend emerged that has had a profound influence on the black economy: the rise of the poor, single female-headed family. As Jaynes and Williams point out, "...the two most numerically important components of the black class structure have become a lower class dominated by single female-headed families and a middle class largely composed of families headed by a husband and a wife."[24] These groups seem to be moving further apart in most respects, with the former comprising the core of the economically depressed and the latter becoming the economical mainstream.

Changes in the structure of the black family have been profound and represent a radical departure from the past. As Gutman noted,

> At all moments in time between 1880 and 1925—that is, from an adult generation born in slavery to an adult generation about to be devastated by the Great Depression of the 1930s and the modernization of southern agriculture afterward—the typical Afro-American family was lower class in status and headed by two parents.... This was so in the urban and rural south in 1880 and 1900 and in New York City in 1905 and 1925.[25]

Historically, approximately three-quarters of all black families have been headed by both parents. This pattern persisted through the depression and the migration to the cities during and after World War II. However, this began to change in the 1980s when 49 percent of black families with children under 18 were headed by single women. Unlike white families headed by a single female (which usually result from the breakup of a marriage), single black females who head households are increasingly never married.[26] In fact, marriage as an institution is no longer the norm for young blacks; just 30 percent of all black men and women between 15 and 44 were married in 1988, down from 50 percent in 1960.[27] An important footnote to this difference is that white single female-headed households are likely to become poor as a consequence of their failed marriages while black single female-headed households are likely to be poor from the start.[28]

In 1960 only 6 percent of households were headed by never-married black women, but by 1984 almost 25 percent of them were. We should note that the proportion heading households is not the same as the proportion having children out of wedlock: in 1988 the black out-of-wedlock rate had reached 63.5 percent (up from 18 percent in 1950), but many of these women and their children remained in the mother's parental household. By the same token, in 1960 approximately 40 percent of divorced or separated black women headed a household but by 1984 the proportion had reached 66 percent. The significance of this becomes apparent when we see that by combining estimates of the proportion of children born to unmarried women with those who will be raised by divorced or separated parents, over 85 percent of all black children are likely to spend some time in a single-parent home before their eighteenth birthday, and most will do so in a single female-headed household.[29]

Single-parent families, especially those headed by never-married women, are likely to be poor. In fact, bearing a child out of wedlock appears to be almost a guarantee of long-term poverty. These families only have one wage earner, and not only do these women earn less than men, many of them cannot earn enough money after paying for child care to justify working. Consequently, they slide into welfare and dependency. This problem forms the core of urban poverty out of which many of black America's most serious social and economic problems have emerged. If the trend continues, an increasingly large proportion of black children will be raised in poverty. In 1969, 58 percent of all poor black children were in single female-headed households but by 1984 the proportion had risen to 75 percent. This has been referred to as the "feminization of poverty," which when combined with demographic factors produces a dense population of poor children who are increasingly isolated from non-poor and non-black children.

EDUCATION

It is hard to overestimate the importance of education: it imparts values, develops skills, transmits culture, socializes the individual, instills expectations and opens the door to opportunity. The formal part of education—going to school—is also a community process. Public schools are essentially locally funded and are an integral part of the local culture and political process. For years they have been at the center of controversies ranging from curriculum design to teacher salaries to race-related matters.[30] Public education is central to the American dream and for that reason has been the focus of considerable attention in recent decades.

Education is particularly important for black Americans because it facilitates entry into the economic and social mainstream. Although blacks have historically fallen far behind whites in educational attainment, the gap has narrowed significantly since the 1960s. In 1940 the median number of years of school for black males was 6.5 (compared to 10.9 for white males), and nearly two-thirds of all black adults had less than nine years of schooling. Improvements have been dramatic: by the mid-1980s nearly 80 percent of all blacks completed high school. However, although more are graduating from high school, the rate of black enrollment in colleges appears to be declining. It rose from about 39 percent in 1973 to 48 percent in 1977, but dropped to about 37 percent in 1986. Moreover, historically black colleges account for a disproportionate percentage of black degree recipients, suggesting that black participation in mainstream higher education may be a matter of immediate concern. In addition to declining undergraduate enrollment, there has also been a decline in blacks entering graduate school.[31]

Within this larger framework, blacks have had to deal first with the basic availability of education and then with the quality of what was available. Prior to 1954 school segregation based on race was a legally accepted fact under which states typically spent less on education for blacks than for whites. For example, the average per-pupil expenditure in 11 Southern states was 211 percent greater for whites than for blacks.[32] The turning point came in 1954 when the United States Supreme Court handed down its landmark decision in *Brown v. Board of Education of Topeka*, holding that segregation of public schools based on race violated the constitutional rights of black children. School desegregation was slow and did not make significant progress until the federal government linked aid for local education to compliance with desegregation requirements. Although school desegregation has been implemented to varying degrees depending on jurisdiction, perhaps the main thing that keeps black children segregated from white children in schools has more to do with racial concentration than with segregation. School integration, especially when it was based on forced busing, often led to white parents withdrawing their children from public schools and enrolling them in private schools. It also contributed to the "white flight" to suburban areas. In many parts of the country (particularly in the South) school districts are county-wide and it has been possible (although not popular) to achieve racial balance through busing. However, in other jurisdictions (particularly in the North) central cities have their own school districts. In such areas, busing for integration purposes precludes the crossing of school district lines. Thus, as whites migrated to the suburbs and cities become increasingly black, the proportion of black students in the public schools soared. In some urban school districts (such as Washington, DC, Atlanta, Newark and Detroit) the student population is overwhelmingly black, and for all practical purposes there is no one with whom to integrate.

Desegregation has also produced a particularly difficult problem commonly referred to as *resegregation.* This happens when students in an integrated school are separated for what seem to be perfectly valid reasons. Although there is no intent to separate races *per se*, the results are often the same. This usually comes about through efforts to separate students on the basis of ability grouping or academic tracking. It also results from attempts to establish compensatory or special education programs or to enforce disciplinary actions. The overall result has been that blacks are under-represented in academically enriched classes (such as gifted and talented programs) but are over-represented in disciplinary actions and remedial education programs. This has produced conflicting viewpoints, charges and countercharges. It is a problem yet to be resolved.

The most recent and potentially divisive race-related controversy in public education has to do with curriculum. Its consequences could have a long-lasting impact on those involved. One result of the civil rights movement has been an increased awareness of the multicultural richness of American society. Led by California, a number of school systems have tried to emphasize the multicultural nature of American society, especially in history and social sciences texts. American history traditionally has been taught from the perspective of politics and government, placing relatively little emphasis on the social or cultural aspects of history. Traditional curricula, which emphasize the contributions of white Europeans, have come under criticism for their lack of attention to women and minorities. In an effort to develop curricula that present American society as pluralistic and multicultural, textbooks have been modified to include the contributions of blacks, women and others.

It is within this context that a new concept, known as *Afrocentric education*, has emerged.[33] One of its leading proponents is Dr. Leonard Jeffries, Jr., former chair of the black studies department at City College in New York City. Jeffries divides humanity into the "ice people" (those of European ancestry) and the "sun people" (those of African descent). He claims the latter are superior to the former because they are essentially "humanistic and communal" whereas the former are fundamentally "materialistic, greedy and intent on domination." In materials passed out to his students, Jeffries suggests that an abundance of the skin pigment *melanin* gives blacks an intellectual advantage over whites.[34] He believes than an Afrocentric perspective in the public schools would help children learn "the larger truth, which cannot be seen from a white perspective."[35] The Afrocentric perspective claims that Egypt was the cradle of Western civilization. The ancient Egyptians, according to this perspective, were black and it was they who developed mathematics and philosophy.

Advocates of the Afrocentric curriculum claim it can be used to overcome low self-esteem and low performance levels among black school children by giving them a mythology that will motivate and inspire them. As one educator has noted, since "...nothing else works, maybe, in order to counteract a mythology that says that blacks are of no value, [a solution] is to give them a mythology that says blacks are of supreme value. Maybe this will keep [some black youths] in school long enough to have them be something other than a crack dealer."[36] Where this movement will lead is unclear; however, it is controversial, it has strong proponents and it is being adopted by a number of school districts.

THE BLACK MALE

The black male is often spoken of as an "endangered species." There can be little doubt that black males, as a group, are in the throes of a crisis. Nearly one in four is behind bars, on parole or on probation.[37] Although they make up approximately 3.5 percent of the college population, black males account for 46 percent of the prison population. A black male has a one out of 23 chance of being murdered before his twenty-fifth birthday. In 1986 only 35 percent of black males aged 18 to 29 were employed full time year-round. The problem is pervasive:

The crisis among black men is measurable. In nearly every category, black males score badly. Compared to males of other ethnic groups, black males have higher unemployment rates, lower labor force participation rates, and lower high school graduation and college enrollment rates. But they rank first in areas detrimental to themselves or the community, such as in incarceration and homicide. Black male youth earnings have plunged over the past 15 years. For example, in 1987, roughly 33% of black male high school dropouts between the ages of 20 and 29 had no reported earnings.[38]

The impact of this reaches into all aspects of black community life. For example, while 50 percent of black Americans between 15 and 44 were married in 1960, only 30 percent were in 1988. Today, for black males under 25 marriage is practically non-existent, the immediate consequence of which is that increasingly large numbers of black children are being raised in single female-headed households. One educator has noted that the crisis of the black male is the crisis of the black community: "It is the source of the rage and despair of black women who have been left to raise families alone, of the anger of children who have learned to hate their fathers. It will soon be the biggest crisis in America."[39]

What produces this tragic outcome? Perhaps much of the problem is exemplified in the biography of a black man who became part of the problem and is now part of the solution. His introspective analysis of what led to his own downfall may be representative of many others. He is a highly articulate journalist who was raised in a black middle-class neighborhood. In looking back on his own experiences he said:

> ... I and the others in our loosely-knit gang started out like most other kids. Ebullient and naive, we played sandlot football, mowed neighbors' lawns for spending change and went to the movies. We devoured comic books, exchanged baseball cards and attended church. Yet somewhere between adolescence and adulthood, something inside us changed. Our optimism faded. Our hearts hardened, and many of us went on to share the same fates as the so-called disadvantaged.[40]

He said that he perceived his chances as being severely limited. It began with an assessment of what happened to his own parents, who "managed to exceed the accomplishments of their forbearers, but...lagged behind their white contemporaries." Although his parents tried to shield him from the kinds of racism they had experienced, he still chaffed at "...the look of white storekeepers' eyes when you enter; the 'click' of door locks when you walk past whites sitting in their cars." In developing his own sense of self-identity, he concluded:

> Our parents...had learned to swallow pride for survival's sake. But my more militant generation seemed less inclined to make that compromise. In a curious way, we saw *anything* that brought us into the mainstream as a cop-out. We came to regard the establishment as the ubiquitous, all powerful 'white man' who controlled our parents' lives and, we believed, determined our fates as well. I think once we resigned ourselves to that notion, we became a lost and angry lot.[41]

He found it difficult to "think about a future in which we were wholly subject to the whims of whites." Education did not seem to be the answer, as he saw no relationship between school and "reality." He and his friends did not like the role models in his community: "...[T]hey were unappealing to us as hero[e]s. They couldn't stand up to the white man. They didn't fulfill our notions of manhood." Others were more appealing: "...[W]e revered the guys on the streets, the thugs who were brazen and belligerent. They wore their hats backwards, left their belt buckles unfastened and shoelaces untied. They shunned the white establishment and worshipped violence. In our eyes, they were real men." Although admitting that his defiance may have stemmed from youthful rebellion, he said it came mostly from "rage at a world we sensed did not welcome us."[42]

The workplace was also threatening: "All of us knew that working in the system carried a price: humiliation on some level. Among us was the lingering fear that the racially integrated work world, with its relentless psychological assaults, was in some ways more perilous than life in the rough-and-tumble streets. At least in the streets, the playing field is level and the rules don't change." He slid into street crime and a few months after shooting a man was arrested at the age of 20 for robbing a McDonald's restaurant. It was in prison that he came to the conclusion that he could "pull his life out of the toilet." He reflected on his status: "My new life is still a struggle, harsher in some ways than the one I left. At times I feel suspended in a kind of netherworld, belonging fully to neither the streets nor the establishment."[43]

The alienation of the black male fosters some very harsh and potentially destructive attitudes. Consider the case of Mike McGee, a former alderman from Milwaukee's 10th Ward. In February of 1990 McGee "...announced formation of a Black Panther Militia that he said would direct violence against white elites in five years unless $100 million was invested in Milwaukee's black community."[44] One of his supporters, the owner of the *Milwaukee Courier* and a local radio station, noted that, "No black man in America should be held physically or morally responsible for anything that he does in the United States...." McGee was asked if he lived by a moral code and he replied:

> My moral code is that I don't feel there are any laws that the United States has made that I'm bound to respect because I consider myself to be at a state of war. I live by a set of codes that are accepted and condoned by my community. I call them black laws. There are white laws, and there are black laws. The black code is set by black society and has standards passed down to me through generations that have been able to make it despite all the oppression. In other words, it's a survival code.[45]

In the black community there is widespread belief that malice against blacks by whites is deliberate, direct and highly destructive. Many believe, for example, that white government leaders play a pivotal role in the drug crisis by deliberately making drugs easily available in black neighborhoods, and that white prosecutors conspire to bring groundless charges against black elected officials. Some believe AIDS is a weapon of racial warfare. A *New York Times*/WCBS-TV News poll in New York City found that 10 percent of blacks said the AIDS virus was "deliberately created in a laboratory in order to infect black people." Another 19 percent said the theory *might* be true.[46]

CRIME

The principle sources of information on crime in America are the *Uniform Crime Reports* published by the Federal Bureau of Investigation and the reports issued by the Bureau of Justice Statistics as part of the National Crime Survey. These sources complement each other and provide information that permits analysis of crime by race and other characteristics. The *Uniform Crime Reports* compile data from local law enforcement agencies and represent the "official" statistics of crimes known to the police. The National Crime Survey provides data from an ongoing survey of approximately 100,000 persons aged 12 or older, interviewed twice a year in about 50,000 households. Although both sources are subject to error, they represent the best information available on crime in America.

Crime is one of the single most serious issues facing the black community. Blacks commit crimes at a rate dramatically disproportionate to their representation in the general population. Although blacks comprise approximately 13 percent of the total population, between 1985 and 1989 they accounted for approximately 47 percent of all arrests for violent crimes (murder, forcible rape, robbery and aggravated assault).[47] Blacks also accounted for approximately 32 percent of the arrests for property crimes (burglary, larceny-theft, motor vehicle theft and arson).[48] For the years 1985 through 1989 blacks accounted for an average of 62 percent of all persons arrested for robbery, 52 percent of all persons arrested for murder and non-negligent manslaughter, 46 percent of all persons arrested for forcible rape, 40 percent of all persons arrested for aggravated assault, 41 percent of all persons arrested for prostitution and commercialized vice, and 38 percent of all persons arrested for motor vehicle theft.[49]

The majority of crimes committed *by* blacks are committed *against* blacks, a circumstance that has held constant for generations.[50] This places the black community at greater risk for both criminal victimization and intervention by the criminal justice system, a relationship that has resulted in great bitterness between blacks and the larger social system—particularly the criminal justice system. In central cities blacks have higher robbery and household burglary rates than whites, regardless of the age or family income of the victim or household head.[51] The high crime rate in central city black neighborhoods has other costs as well: many small businesses "...survive by adopting protective measures that add to the 'armed camp' mentality that often pervades inner-city black communities. These measures, though needed to ensure the survival of the businesses, convey strong messages about the quality of life in such environments."[52]

Many violent crimes are as senseless as they are tragic, including murders that arise from arguments over clothing or a failure to show respect.[53] Reports of seemingly senseless acts of black-on-black violence are commonplace: "One week it's a stabbing over a bag of chips, the next it's a shooting to avenge a wrong look or warn a group of junior high students to avoid a certain street corner."[54] Much of this violence appears to be extremely cold and calculated. As Isaac Fulwood, Jr., police chief in Washington, DC, noted, "In my personal conversations with young people who have been involved in violence, there is no remorse, there is not the first tear, there is no sense that this is wrong."[55] The magnitude of the problem is illustrated by the fact that homicide by another black is the leading cause of death for black males between the ages of 15 and 34. To put it in perspective, the young black males in the armed forces who served on the front line during the war against Iraq (Operation Desert Storm, 1990-1991) were less likely to be killed in action than their counterparts in the central cities were to be murdered on the streets of their own neighborhoods.

RELATIONSHIPS WITH THE POLICE

Over the years it has been widely reported that racial prejudice has resulted in blacks being both mistreated and ignored by the police. Although there is a great deal of truth to both claims, they are oversimplified to the point of being misleading. Police departments are agencies of local government and generally draw their manpower from the communities they serve. Therefore, police attitudes have historically reflected local sentiment. Moreover, since policing generally has been regarded as a blue-collar occupation, it is logical that police attitudes have been shaped by peer expectations and class values of the police officers themselves. This traditional picture started to change in the 1960s as police departments themselves changed, and the process has continued through to the 1990s. Most police departments (especially those in urban areas) carefully screen police applicants in an attempt to function more along a professional law enforcement model than according to the expectations of the lowest common denominator of the community. Though this by no means assures that racial prejudice does not exist within police departments, it does mean that when racially motivated misconduct occurs it is more likely to reflect individual perspectives than departmental policy.

However, it is worth remembering that police officers are neither historians nor sociologists. White police officers generally do not know a great deal about the cultural heritage of blacks, nor do they understand the psychological mechanisms blacks have employed to deal with their common problems. What they *do* know is that blacks constitute the bulk of their work (at least in areas where there are large concentrations of blacks). Moreover, most do not have much contact with responsible, middle-class blacks and therefore have little opportunity to see the positive side of black society. Worse yet, many white police officers do not distinguish between different strata of blacks and therefore tend to treat them all alike—something deeply resented by the black citizens they serve. Perhaps because they witness so much violence and brutality among blacks, white police officers typically insulate themselves from the larger black community, a process encouraged within the ranks of the police.

Over time many officers associate violence and brutality not with *individuals* but with *race*. As a result they come to view blacks as violent and distasteful people. This is reinforced by contact with young males who play the "bad nigger" role. The police generally do not know anything about the role-playing significance of this behavior, but see it as a challenge to their authority not to be taken lightly. The situations become especially problematic when police encounters with young black males are played out before a bystander audience. When the social and psychological needs of the black male come into conflict with the professional responsibilities of the police, the black male usually loses. Viewed in these terms it is not hard to see that much of the problem between blacks and the police is not a matter of natural enmity or even mutual hostility, but the product of mistaken perceptions and a lack of communication.

The police play a prominent role in the lives of many black people, especially in the inner cities where crime rates and social disorganization are highest. Police interventions, though often necessary and proper, are frequently regarded as intrusive and unwelcome (even when initiated by citizen complaints). When police interventions are carried out by white officers they may be seen by blacks as motivated by racial prejudice. Most white police officers are familiar with what some call the "broken record" ("The only reason you are stopping/ arresting/questioning me is because I'm black"). Resentment flows both ways. Police officers resent being accused of racism when they are simply doing their job; black citizens resent being confronted by white police officers when they feel it is unwarranted. Rancor over the gap between police performance and community expectations originally focused on the lack of means by which the black community could redress grievances against the police. The current focus is on empowerment and a drive to increase participation in police departments and their management.

Up until the 1960s blacks were essentially excluded from serving in police departments, and the token black police officers who *were* hired typically had limitations placed on what they were allowed to do and how far they could advance. All of that changed with the urban riots of the 1960s, the civil rights legislation of the 1970s, affirmative action programs designed to increase black participation in police departments and the use of consent decrees to guide police hiring and promotion practices. The rise in the number of cities with black mayors and police chiefs has also had an impact on the entry of blacks into police departments and their subsequent advancement through the ranks. One researcher discovered that the most significant variables associated with black representation in police ranks in 1975 were the proportion of blacks in a city's labor force and the presence of black mayors. By 1985 the presence of black police chiefs and affirmative action consent decrees also emerged as significant variables in increasing the number of black police officers.[56]

Unfortunately, these efforts have created friction within the ranks of police. Exemplifying this is the situation of the Maryland State Police. The Coalition of Black Maryland State Troopers, Inc. filed a promotion discrimination suit against the 84-percent-white Maryland State Police, resulting in a consent decree in which the state agreed to pay more than $89,000 to the Coalition and $275,000 for attorney's fees. The consent decree allocates cash settlements ranging from $2,000 to $115,000 for more than 50 black troopers and imposes a five-year timetable for increasing the department's black representation through the rank of first sergeant to 22 percent. In addition, the decree calls for black representation in all ranks through lieutenant colonel. The predominantly white Maryland Troopers Association responded by saying that the $45 million lawsuit is unconstitutional and asking the court to throw out what it termed "racial quotas" for promotions.[57] The Maryland consent decree is typical of many others. In its wake it is liable to leave a simmering resentment by white troopers who feel their black colleagues have been given an unfair advantage based on race—just as many black troopers will resent their white colleagues for subscribing to what they believe is a pattern of institutional racism. There is no simple solution to this problem—if there is a solution at all.

HISPANICS

Another significant minority group in the United States consists of Spanish-speaking people. Hispanics are an extremely diverse group and represent many different cultural and ethnic backgrounds. The current Hispanic population of approximately 18.8 million comprises about 8 percent of the total United States population. As a group they are expanding rapidly, having grown by 30 percent between 1980 and 1988—a rate four times greater than the American population as a whole. Much of this growth is fueled by illegal aliens, who represent 23 percent of that growth.[58] Although the Hispanic population is concentrated in nine states (California, Texas, New York, Florida, Illinois, Arizona, New Jersey, New Mexico and Colorado), three-quarters of them live in the South or the West.[59]

Although the crime rate of Hispanics does not come close to that of blacks, it has been a problem. In addition, Hispanics have long complained of discriminatory treatment at the hands of law enforcement officials who they see as representative of the interests of the dominant power structure. Much crime involving Hispanics may be considered a natural consequence of the poverty in which they live, the economic system that exploits them for cheap labor, and the virtual absence of effective legal remedies for the problems they have faced. All of this has been exacerbated by the conflicting expectations of two cultures operating in the same environment, language difficulties and long-standing patterns of discrimination.

MEXICANS

Perhaps the largest group of Hispanics in the United States is composed of Mexicans, who represent well over 12 million. Americans of Mexican origin represent 63 percent of all Hispanics in the United States. Many are descended from families who occupied their land before it was acquired by the United States and who were annexed along with the land they owned.[60] Most, however, either migrated to the United States during the present century or are descendants of those who did. Mexican Americans have the largest families of all Hispanics but the second lowest level of family income (Puerto Ricans have the lowest level of family income of all Hispanic groups).[61] One reason for the low level of family income among Mexicans is that a large proportion of their population consists of illegal aliens who earn poverty-level wages.

Mexicans, like Hispanics as a whole, do not represent one single cultural, ethnic or historical background. Many who live in the West and Southwest differ not only from the Anglo society in culture, language and ethnicity, but among themselves as well.[62] As a group, they have not fared well economically. Many work as laborers and a substantial number work in seasonal agricultural industries, often under harsh conditions. Many agricultural workers are nomadic and follow the various growing seasons. This means that they must live in migrant labor camps, which have been criticized for their dehumanizing conditions:

> ...[T]he camps in which the farm laborers were put up were often horrible collections of unshaded tents and shacks, inadequately supplied with water and open-ditch latrines. Moving from one such camp to another in boxcars, trucks, or rusted jalopies piled high with bedsprings, chicken coops, and children, the Mexicans knew they were in no promised land.[63]

The permanent settlements in the cities—the *barrios*—are likewise typically substandard in the quality of housing, although in recent years substantial progress has been made. However, like blacks, Mexicans have had to endure prejudice and animosity for generations:

> Race prejudice was circulated as scientific dogma in the early decades of the century; R.L. Adams of the University of California, in his text *Farm Management* stated that Mexicans were "childish, lazy and unambitious." He argued that as farm laborers they should be segregated from the Japanese who were "tricky" and both should be kept separate from Negroes given that they were "notorious prevaricators...constantly annexing to themselves such minor things as chickens, lines from harnesses, axes and shovels."[64]

Long considered an "invisible minority," Mexican Americans are now a highly visible component of many American cities. Their problems are matters of legitimate and proper concern to state and local governments. For example, many schools are beginning to offer bilingual instruction. A cultural blending seems to be taking place, which was eloquently summed up by Dr. Manuel Guerra, an educator of Mexican descent:

> We do not want to give up the Spanish language, pray to God in English, substitute mashed potatoes for frijoles or "junk" our piñatas. Rather we want to bring all of these values to American society as our contribution to the diversity and wealth of our country. Rather than the melting pot, we believe in the heterogeneity of American society, including the give and take with other peoples and other cultures.[65]

PUERTO RICANS

The 2.3 million Puerto Ricans in America comprise about 12 percent of the total Hispanic population. The United States acquired Puerto Rico in the aftermath of the Spanish-American War (1898). During World War I the residents of Puerto Rico were granted American citizenship. At the beginning of the twentieth century there was already some migration of Puerto Ricans from the islands to New York City (the ultimate destination of most emigrating Puerto Ricans), but it was not very consequential. By 1910 New York City had only about 500 people of Puerto Rican birth. In 1924 the Immigration Act shut off the influx of immigrant labor from Europe, creating the demand for a new source of labor—a need that was quickly filled by Puerto Ricans. By 1930 there were about 45,000 Puerto Ricans in New York City; after World War II the number of Puerto Rican immigrants reached 50,000 per year. By 1970 the Puerto Rican population of New York City had reached over one million.[66]

Puerto Ricans came to New York City in search of opportunity as well as to escape the crowded conditions and economic pressures of the islands, which stifled any hope for the future. They encountered resentment, hostility and prejudice, as has virtually every large group that moved into the city. Perhaps one of the reasons Puerto Ricans have faced so much hostility is because they are the first group of newcomers to bring a cultural practice of widespread intermingling and intermarriage of peoples of many different ethnic backgrounds.[67] In addition, Puerto Ricans have been seen as an economic threat by the already hard-pressed blacks in New York City (which has the highest black population of any city in the world). Puerto Ricans have had great difficulty entering skilled-labor unions and relatively few have been able to move into white-collar occupations.

Puerto Ricans crowded into Morrisania in the Bronx and into East Harlem (also known as *Spanish Harlem* or *El Barrio*), living in run-down tenements and entering into their own subculture of poverty. The Puerto Ricans, like the Mexican Americans of the Southwest, have had to face a multitude of problems ranging from questions of self-identity to basic survival. They are slowly changing the face of New York City and are beginning to develop the political and economic participation necessary for entering the mainstream of American life.

CUBANS

Another major component of the Hispanic population consists of Cubans. The first major wave of Cuban Americans fled the Castro regime in the years following 1959. When the first batch of Cubans fled their homeland they were allowed to take with them only five pesos, one watch, one ring and the clothes on their backs. About 300,000 Cubans arrived in the United States, most of whom settled in the Miami-Dade County area of southern Florida. These refugees have been described as "the cream of a nation in exile" because so many of them were middle- and upper-class men and women who brought with them a great many skills and a strong sense of pride and dedication.

> By the end of Castroism's first decade, the Cuban community in Miami showed a respectable top layer of affluence. Many of the Cubans still eagerly awaited the day when Castro would be overthrown and they could return to their rightful homeland. But thousands were discovering that children born in the house of strangers create blood ties to those strangers and their house. Increasingly, Cubans who had children enrolled in American schools were applying for citizenship papers and settling in for good.[68]

Cuban Americans are the most successful component of the Hispanic ethnic group. They have the highest median family income of all Hispanic groups and have the highest proportion of individuals aged 25 and older who have completed four or more years of college. The Cuban Americans have the smallest family size of all Hispanics and the largest proportion of families who are married couples. Since there are two or more earners in 58 percent of Cuban families, their economic strength is greater than that of any other Hispanic group. Unfortunately, this success does not seem to have been repeated with the refugees who fled Cuba during the summer of 1980. Between April 21 and September 26, 1980, approximately 125,000 Cuban refugees came to the United States in the so-called "Freedom Flotilla." Many came without job skills, some were mentally ill, and it was rumored that others had been cast out of prisons and jails. Almost 2,000 were detained in federal jails awaiting deportation. They are often referred to as *Marielas* because they departed from the harbor at Mariel in Cuba.

Finally, a substantial number of Hispanics are entering the United States from Central and South American countries. They number approximately 2.1 million and represent about 11 percent of all Hispanics. Many have fled from political and economic chaos in their homelands and have sought refuge in American cities. They are too diverse a group to characterize, but like other ethnic minorities they face problems of assimilation.

ASIANS

Like Hispanics, Asians in American are an extremely diverse and rapidly growing group. Between 1970 and 1980 the number of persons of Asian background in the United States more than doubled. By 1987 almost 43 percent of all immigrants who entered the United States came from Asia; by 1989 they were estimated at 2.8 percent of the population—an increase of nearly 80 percent since 1980.[69]

Asians include many nationalities and ethnic groups with different languages, customs and cultural legacies. Although they are a small part of the total population, they tend to concentrate in selected geographic and urban areas, and their presence will have an extremely important impact on American life in coming generations. For this reason it is important to understand their backgrounds, contributions and problems.

THE CHINESE

The first major migration of Chinese came to the United States in the decades following the Civil War. This migration probably peaked in the 1880s. Most came from the southern province of Kwangtung. They came as laborers and were the men who "...tunneled through mountains, cleared forests, built rail-roads, worked in the mines, reclaimed swamps, fished along the California coast, gathered wheat and cash crops, and helped open up the great American West for settlement."[70] Most were young men whose goal was to work hard, save money and return to China. Chinese society in late nineteenth-century America was highly artificial, consisting primarily of transient males who lived in ethnic enclaves. Because they worked as laborers, they did not have to master English nor did they have any incentive to adopt American customs. They remained segregated from the mainstream. Moreover, because they were willing to work hard for little money, they became ready targets of racial hatred. To make matters worse, in 1900 the United States participated in an international military expedition to relieve the foreign legations in Peking that had been taken under siege by the so-called "Boxers." Shortly thereafter, anti-Chinese sentiment began to take the form of legislation designed to bar Chinese laborers from entering the country. As a result, the Chinese population in America diminished rapidly.

Public sentiment changed dramatically during World War II, when the anti-Chinese immigration laws were repealed. Following the war, Chinese immigrants entered the country in record numbers. By 1980 the Chinese population in America exceeded 800,000 and was concentrated in the New York/New Jersey metropolitan and San Francisco Bay areas.

The Chinese who have come to America have had extremely low participation rates in public welfare programs and very low crime and delinquency rates. Indeed, they represent a disproportionate number of the top achievers in higher education, particularly in math and the sciences. Although on a whole the Chinese are seldom involved with the criminal justice system, the expansion of American-based Chinese gangs has resulted in efforts by law enforcement agencies to learn more about their operations. *Triads* and *Tongs*, Chinese gangs that often are listed as social organizations, frequently are involved in organized illegal activities.[71] One estimate indicates that there are more than 30 Tongs operating in the United States.[72]

THE JAPANESE

Like the Chinese, early Japanese immigrants were mostly males who came as sojourners looking for quick wealth so they could return home and enjoy economic security and high status. After the Chinese Exclusion Act of 1882 curtailed the inward migration of Chinese laborers, Japanese immigrants quickly took their place. Young Japanese males came to the west coast where they worked as laborers. However, their sense of entrepreneurship quickly led many into small business. As they settled in as farmers and tradesmen, the Japanese quite literally imported wives (who were available through catalogues as "picture brides"). With wives, families soon emerged and the original desire to return to Japan was replaced by an even greater desire to find success in America. However, their success soon became a source of hostility toward them, and like the Chinese before them, they became targets of racial hatred. The Asiatic Exclusion League was formed in San Francisco in 1905, and its primary goal was to halt Japanese immigration. In 1913 the California legislature passed the Alien Land Act, which prohibited land ownership by aliens ineligible for citizenship. In 1924 Congress passed the Immigration Act, which specifically barred aliens who were ineligible for citizenship. This measure was designed to restrict the inward migration of Asians.

The first generation of Japanese in America—the *Issei*—came to this country with a different language and alien customs. It was only natural that they preferred to remain apart from the larger society. As a result they "...developed an unusually active and highly organized community life. Entrepreneurs evolved a self-sufficient ethnic economy that served virtually all needs."[73] How this would have evolved will never be known, as the onset of World War II completely altered the Japanese-American community. Japan attacked Pearl Harbor on December 7, 1941 and on February 19, 1942 the President issued Executive Order 9066 authorizing military commanders to designate areas from which individuals and groups could be excluded for national security reasons. Shortly thereafter, the commander of the Western Defense Command designated a major portion of the west coast as an area from which people of Japanese ancestry were to be excluded. As a result, over 110,000 Japanese Americans were rounded up and placed in camps. In the process they lost their homes, businesses and even their very communities. The complex ethnic community established by the *Issei* was gone forever.

A new pattern emerged after the war. Many second-generation Japanese Americans (the *Nisei*) had served in the army during the war, mostly in the all-*Nisei* 442nd Regimental Combat Team, which was one of the most highly decorated units in the history of the United States Army. Their extraordinary performance made it abundantly clear that Japanese-American loyalty and courage were beyond question. The old prejudices, which had been fed by the pre-war hysteria, were gone and the *Nisei* moved quickly into the mainstream of American life. Among the third generation (the *Sansei*), intermarriage with Caucasians is common and Japanese are no longer strangers in an alien land: they are highly productive members of the American community. Like the Chinese, the Japanese in America have an extremely low crime rate and have little contact with the criminal justice system.

KOREANS

Koreans first came to the United States in 1903 when a group arrived in Hawaii to work on the sugar plantations. They differed from the Chinese and Japanese immigrants in several important ways. For one thing, they came from various parts of Korea and not from a single province or area. Many more of them were literate and a lot of them were true immigrants with no intentions of returning to their homeland. Finally, many of these early Korean immigrants were Christians. Their assimilation into a predominantly Christian culture was thus made easier.

The Koreans organized themselves around their churches and village councils, which largely regulated their lives. However, as Korea was a Japanese colony until after World War II, the Japanese government began to suppress the immigration of Koreans to the United States. Because of this, relatively few Koreans came to this country until after World War II. Larger numbers came after the Korean War. Many of the post-war immigrants were either students or Korean women who married American servicemen who had been sent to Korea. The 1965 Immigration Act eliminated an old quota system, thereby allowing many more Koreans into the United States. Many of the post-1965 Korean immigrants have come not as students or brides but as true immigrants. Like nearly all other immigrants, they have moved into the urban areas where they have attempted to find their way into the mainstream.

However, recent Korean immigrants have found themselves in a new and particularly difficult position. Many of them moved into predominantly black areas, where they started small businesses such as convenience stores, food markets, dry cleaners and restaurants. The operation of such businesses does not require great fluency in English. They buy stores in depressed areas because they can afford them. They run them as family businesses and work hard to make them succeed—often working long hours, seven days a week. This has given them little time to develop fluency in English or to participate in community activities. Moreover, as family businesses they do not usually hire "outsiders," if in fact they could find anyone willing to work the hours they impose on themselves or to accept the salaries they themselves are willing to take out of the business. As a result, some blacks in these areas see them as foreigners who have come into their neighborhoods to extract wealth without making contributions to the community. The relationship between Korean merchants and their black neighbors has been marked by episodes of considerable hostility. Sadly, many of these incidents are based more on language problems than substance. However, as cultural differences have been overcome the relationship between the Koreans and the black community has improved.[74]

SOUTHEAST ASIANS

Another ethnic group among the Asians in America is also the most recent. It consists of Southeast Asians from Vietnam, Cambodia and Laos. In April of 1975 Saigon fell, ending the lengthy and disastrous Vietnam War. In the immediate aftermath, approximately 130,000 Vietnamese refugees came to this country as part of an official resettlement program. A second wave came between 1975 and 1977 and consisted largely of so-called "boat people" who fled their homes in fear of political and ethnic reprisal, traveling either in small boats or over land against overwhelming odds. Those who succeeded left behind many more who were murdered by pirates or who died of illness or other causes during their flight. Even larger numbers remain confined in refugee camps where they live in limbo, unwanted by any country. After 1978 a third wave —consisting of ethnic Chinese expelled from Vietnam—followed.

The first-wave refugees were well-educated. They fled because of their pre-existing ties to the United States. Most were Catholics who had lived in urban areas. Their major shortcoming was a lack of fluency in English. The second- and third-wave refugees were much different: they were not as well-educated and did not come from urban areas; many of them were simply not prepared for life in an urban, industrialized nation. The United States wanted a resettlement policy that would keep these people from grouping together in ethnic enclaves and "...although resettlement was delegated to voluntary agencies, the U.S. government urged these agencies to disperse refugees throughout the United States and prevent the development of large ethnic communities which might create political tensions between state, local, and national governments or put undue strain on local communities."[75] Unfortunately, the effort did not succeed; many of these refugees have concentrated in urban areas, the largest being in Los Angeles and New Orleans.

For many refugees the move to America resulted in lower status, underemployment and the need to receive welfare benefits. Even though most of these refugees have found employment, it typically has been in low-paying occupations below what they had in the past, particularly in the case of Vietnamese refugees. To make matters worse, the economy has not been able to absorb these refugees. In addition to the impact of their poor language skills, the fact that they came at a time of relatively high unemployment has made their adjustment difficult and painful. To make matters worse, the unpopularity of the Vietnam war left many Americans wary of accepting large numbers of Vietnamese refugees—particularly at a time when the public seemed mostly interested in forgetting the war.

Dependence on welfare on the part of many Southeast Asians has brought them into conflict with other minorities—particularly blacks and Hispanics—who have viewed them as allocational rivals. Thus, the assimilation of

Southeast Asians has been difficult and the entry of some into crime was a predictable outcome. Some Vietnamese immigrants have been linked to Chinese criminal organizations or Vietnamese gangs (thought to be made up largely of former members of Vietnamese armed forces). Vietnamese youth gangs also have begun to emerge in several cities.[76] Perhaps the most unique type of crime committed by Southeast Asians is the "home invasion," in which a gang of youths forces its way into a residence, coercing the residents to surrender their valuables. The victims of these crimes typically have been other Vietnamese people, many of whom have been reluctant to report their victimization to the police.

DIVERSITY OR TRIBALISM?

Is the American community (or even society) a single entity with a rich variety of manifestations, or is it a loosely confederated coalition of tribes in economic and social competition with one another? In truth, it is both. Some segments of the community are separated by gaps that are simply too wide to bridge. Others are much closer together. The predominant social metaphor for many generations was the "melting pot," which suggests the assimilation of ethnic diversity into a larger, harmonious society. For many, the melting pot metaphor has become a reality. First-generation immigrants tended to cluster together for mutual support; many had great difficulty mastering a new language and customs, and giving up the old. It was easier and psychologically safer to live and work together, thereby creating ethnic islands in their communities; hence, the Chinatowns, Little Italys, *barrios*, and so on. The second generation of immigrants, however, was educated in the public schools along with the children of the larger society. In the process they learned the language and customs. Most were assimilated into the larger society, although there always has been a residual of those who could not make the transition.

The notion of "community" has changed dramatically. As one commentator points out, "Most Americans no longer live in traditional communities. They live in suburban subdivisions bordered by highways and sprinkled with shopping malls, or in tony condominiums and residential clusters, or in ramshackle apartment buildings and housing projects. Most of them commute to work and socialize on some basis other than geographic proximity. And most people pick up and move to a different neighborhood every five years or so."[77] Perhaps the most important divisive factor in the community is income. As Reich notes, "Eighty-five percent of the richest families in the greater Philadelphia area live outside the city limits, and 80 percent of the region's poorest live inside."[78] This is true in other urban areas as well. The outcome is that public services are splintered, with different kinds of services expected by different groups depending on their economic status. What they actually receive is a function of the ability of the community to pay. Wealthy communities cannot only offer their residents more, they offer kinds of services that poor communities do not have. More money is spent on education, libraries, parks and recreation, and the arts. Poor communities with less to spend allocate a larger proportion to public safety, welfare and human services. These differences often are seen by the poor not as economic issues, but rather as conflicts over power, discrimination and autonomy.

The emerging consequences are clear. According to one observer, "Our great national achievement—fashioning a common citizenship and identity for a multi-ethnic, multi-lingual, multi-racial people—is now threatened by a process of relentless, deliberate Balkanization. The great engines of social life—the law, the schools, the arts—are systematically encouraging the division of America into racial, ethnic and gender separateness."[79] Those who stand to benefit from this process in the short term support it wholeheartedly. Increasingly, those who reject the process are denounced as racists, sexists or homophobes. The concept of *empowerment* fosters the strengthening "diversity," often in a zero-sum (win-lose) way. What are the consequences for the criminal justice system?

The criminal justice system does not merely react to this larger process—it is a part of it. For example, affirmative action is a very real issue in the hiring and promotion of police officers. *Who* shall police the "community" and *how* they are to do it is likewise an emerging issue of great concern in many cities. The criminal justice system does not operate separate from the community of which it is a part but reflects its social divisions and conflicts. To the extent that the community is in conflict, especially over racial and ethnic issues, the police will be faced with conflicting demands they may be powerless to reconcile.

SUMMARY

The United States is an increasingly urban nation with cities heavily populated by racial minorities. Since these racial and ethnic groups often have differing perspectives on economic and social issues, and since their expectations are frequently in conflict with one another and with the larger community, it is important to understand the basis for their differences.

Poverty and race are closely related. Minorities historically have been economically disadvantaged. However, poverty is more than financial insolvency; it also involves a diminished status, an absence of power and a reduction of opportunity. People who live in poverty must adapt to it, resulting in what some have called a "culture of poverty." The uneven distribution of wealth and power has made it especially difficult for minorities to move into full social participation. This has been particularly true in the case of blacks.

The current black population emerged from a history of slavery and segregation that fostered a unique ethnic culture. During the twentieth century there has been a massive migration of blacks from the rural South to the urban North. The result has concentrated large numbers of blacks into urban areas where they have had to adapt to an entirely new lifestyle. Forced into segregated areas, blacks often became tightly concentrated in areas poorly served by local government. As a result of the civil rights movement, blacks have made significant economic and social gains, but the historical legacy of their poverty remains and in some respects has worsened. The black family has undergone considerable change, much of it resulting in further destabilization and the "feminization of poverty" through the rise of the never-married female-headed household. Although blacks have made great strides in education, problems remain. The school districts serving the largest urban areas are becoming increasingly black, thus further segregating black and white children not because of race but because of geography. Even within integrated schools the practices of ability grouping and tracking have frequently had the result of *resegregating* students on the basis of race (despite the fact that such an outcome was not intended). The development of Afrocentric education in predominantly black school districts is intended to provide black children with an educational model that will enhance self-esteem and improve their education, but it may also have the effect of further isolating black children from white children.

Black males have become the subject of considerable attention because of high rates of crime participation and low achievement—so much so, in fact, that they are regarded by some as an "endangered species." Social disorganization and high crime rates within the black community have had a significantly negative impact on the quality of life for many. Moreover, it has brought many black males into adversarial contact with the police. The problem is exacerbated by the fact that up until the 1960s blacks were largely excluded from employment as police officers. Only in recent years has the number of black police officers increased significantly—the product of falling barriers, affirmative action, the use of consent decrees in civil litigation and conscientious efforts by public administrators to integrate the police service. Even so, some of these efforts have themselves been the source of friction.

Hispanics in America also have gone through troublesome times. The majority of Hispanics in America are of Mexican descent, many of whom came to this country illegally or are descended from those who did. Because of this, many have been forced into low-paying agricultural labor from which it has been all but impossible to build a better life. Other Hispanics include Puerto Ricans, who migrated mostly to New York City, where they now form a large part of the urban population. Cubans fleeing from Castro have had a major impact on the Miami, Florida area. The first refugees—those who fled in 1959-1960—were affluent and literate, and able to adapt quickly and successfully. Those who followed have been quite different and have had more problems adapting.

Asians in America constitute a diverse group, for the most part consisting of Chinese, Japanese, Koreans and Southeast Asians. Early Chinese and Japanese immigrants came with the expectation of finding their fortune and returning to their homelands. Although they made a major contribution to the development of the nation, they faced racial hatred and public hostility. Their numbers were curtailed by restrictive legislation that made it difficult for them to either enter the country or gain citizenship. Much of this changed during World War II; since then their assimilation has been smooth and productive. Koreans emigrating to this country have tended to move into depressed urban areas where they have come into conflict with blacks and Hispanics. Much of their difficulty has arisen through language problems and the nature of their work ethic (i.e., working long hours for low pay in family-run businesses). These problems appear to be fading as the Koreans are becoming an increasingly welcome part of the urban landscape.

The most recent Asian immigrants are the Southeast Asians who have come to this country in the aftermath of the Vietnam War. Although the first refugees were well-educated and urban in background, those who followed them have not been and have thus had difficulty in finding their way. In addition to problems related to coming in the aftermath of an unpopular war, they have had difficulty learning English and finding worthwhile employment. Like other immigrants in this situation, some have been involved in criminal activity (primarily against other Southeast Asians).

Racial minorities make up a significant proportion of the overall population. Because of their unique situations many have developed political and economic agendas that sometimes go against the mainstream. The question at this point is whether fostering diversity in favor of minority perspectives is preferable to the goal of assimilation—or following previous groups into the melting pot. The process of seeking answers to this will involve the criminal justice system and have a major impact on how that system is staffed, whose needs it serves and how it will be done.

DISCUSSION QUESTIONS

1. Why is poverty seen as a trap, and why is it so hard to escape from it?

2. Why is it inaccurate to equate poverty with minority status?

3. List and explain three factors that resulted in the concentration of urban blacks into segregated enclaves.

4. What are the consequences of the rapidly expanding proportion of black families headed by never-married females?

5. What is the key difference between poor white families headed by single women and poor black families headed by single women? Why is this difference important?

6. Why is education particularly important for blacks?

7. Why is it so difficult for urban schools to integrate on the basis of race?

8. What is Afrocentric education and what is the controversy surrounding it? Do you think it is a good idea?

9. Why is the black male spoken of as "an endangered species"?

10. How does black-on-black crime create greater race-related problems for the police? Can anything be done about it?

11. How does the high crime rate among blacks contribute to an "armed camp" mentality in black neighborhoods?

12. What is the consequence of white police officers having limited contact with middle-class blacks?

13. In what ways do the various Hispanic ethnic groups differ from one another? What do they have in common?

14. Why have Mexican Americans been considered an "invisible" minority?

15. How do the most recent Cuban refugees differ from those who fled Cuba in 1959?

16. How did World War II impact on the social organization of Japanese Americans?

17. How has their work ethic brought Korean immigrants into conflict with their black and Hispanic neighbors?

18. Why has it been particularly difficult for the most recent Southeast Asian immigrants to assimilate into American culture?

19. How has the United States succeeded or failed as a "melting pot"?

20. Is there any danger in advocating "diversity"? If so, what is the danger?

REFERENCES

[1] See, for example, Alvin Toffler, *The Third Wave* (New York: William Morrow and Company, Inc., 1980). Toffler argues that much of what appears to be chaos belies a "startling and potentially hopeful pattern" that he sees as part of the rise of a new civilization.

[2] Louis A. Radelet, *The Police and the Community* (Beverly Hills: Glencoe Press, 1973), 217.

[3] U.S. Bureau of the Census, *Statistical Abstract of the United States: 1990*, 110th ed. (Washington, DC: U.S. Government Printing Office, 1990). See Table 718 (p. 445).

[4] Oscar Lewis, *Five Families: Mexican Case Studies in the Culture of Poverty* (New York: Basic Books, 1959).

[5] See, for example, Herbert J. Gans, "The Uses of Poverty: The Poor Pay All," *Social Policy* 2 (July-August 1971), 20-24.

[6] See especially William Julius Wilson, *The Truly Disadvantaged: The Inner City, The Underclass, and Public Policy.* (Chicago: The University of Chicago Press, 1987).

[7] Charles E. Silberman, *Criminal Violence, Criminal Justice* (New York: Vintage Books, 1978), 160.

[8] Silberman, *Criminal Violence, Criminal Justice*, 189.

[9] Silberman, *Criminal Violence, Criminal Justice*, 191.

[10] Silberman, *Criminal Violence, Criminal Justice*, 194.

[11] Silberman, *Criminal Violence, Criminal Justice*, 202.

[12] Silberman, *Criminal Violence, Criminal Justice*, 204.

[13] Silberman, *Criminal Violence, Criminal Justice*, 204.

[14] Laura Sessions Stepp, "Rap's Message Is Their Medium," *The Washington Post* (August 23, 1992), B1, B5. See also David Gates, et al., "The Rap Attitude," *Newsweek* (March 19, 1990), 56-63.

[15] Silberman, *Criminal Violence, Criminal Justice*, 206.

[16] Silberman, *Criminal Violence, Criminal Justice*, 211.

[17] U.S. Bureau of the Census, *Historical Statistics of the United States, Colonial Times to 1970*, Bicentennial Issue, Part 1 (Washington, DC: U.S. Government Printing Office, 1976). See Series A 73-81, "Population by Type of Residence, Sex and Race: 1880-1970, 12, and Series D 1-10, "Labor Force and Its Components: 1900 to 1947," 147.

[18] Gerald D. Jaynes and Robin M. Williams, Jr., eds., *Blacks and American Society* (Washington, DC: National Academy Press, 1989), 62.

[19] For an especially interesting treatment of this topic, see Nicholas Lemann, *The Promised Land* (New York: Random House, 1991).

[20] Jaynes and Williams, *Blacks and American Society*, 140-144.

21 Jaynes and Williams, *Blacks and American Society*, 283-284.

22 Jaynes and Williams, *Blacks and American Society*, 271.

23 U.S. Bureau of the Census, *Statistical Abstract of the United States: 1990*, Tables 720 ("Household Type, By Median Income and Income Level, 1987," p. 446) and 744 ("Persons Below Poverty Level, By Race of Householder and Family Status: 1979 to 1987", p. 461).

24 Jaynes and Williams, *Blacks and American Society*, 275-276.

25 Herbert G. Gutman, *The Black Family in Slavery and Freedom, 1750-1925* (New York: Vintage/Random House, 1976).

26 See especially Irwin Garfinkel and Sara S. McLanahan, *Single Mothers and Their Children: A New American Dilemma* (Washington, DC: The Urban Institute, 1986).

27 Paul Taylor, "Nonmarital Births: As Rates Soar, Theories Abound," *The Washington Post*, 22 January 1991, A3.

28 Taylor, "Nonmarital Births: As Rates Soar, Theories Abound," A3.

29 Larry L. Bumpass, "Children and Marital Disruption: A Replication and Update," *Demography* 21:1 (February 1984), 71-81.

30 See, for example, "How to Teach Our Kids," in "Education: A Consumer's Handbook," *Newsweek*, Fall/Winter 1990 special ed., 54.

31 William T. Trent, "Equity Considerations in Higher Education: Race and Sex Differences in Degree Attainment and Major Field From 1976 Through 1981," *American Journal of Education* 41 (May 1984), 280-305.

32 Jaynes and Williams, *Blacks and American Society*, 59. (See also chapter 7, "The Schooling of Black Americans," 329-389.)

33 See, for example, Molefi Kete Asante, *The Afrocentric Idea* (Philadelphia: Temple University Press, 1987).

34 Joseph Berger, "Professors' Theories on Race Stir Turmoil at City College," *The New York Times*, 20 April 1990, B1.

35 Leonard Jeffries, Jr., "Review of the New York State Curricular Materials K-12, Focus: African American Culture," Appendix 4 to *A Curriculum of Inclusion*, New York State Education Commissioner's Task Force on Minorities: Equity and Excellence (July 189).

36 John H. Bracy, "Facing Africa: The Price of Our History," *African Commentary* (November 1989), 12-14.

37 Bill McAllister, "Study: 1 in 4 Young Black Men Is in Jail or Court-Supervised," *The Washington Post*, 27 February 1990, A3.

38 Margaret C. Simms, "Wanted: A Few Good Men," *Black Enterprise*, February 1991, 41.

39 Patrick Welsh, "Young, Black, Male, and Trapped," *The Washington Post*, 24 September 1989, B1, B4.

[40] Nathan McCall, "Dispatches from a Dying Generation," *The Washington Post*, 13 January 1991, C1, C4.

[41] McCall, "Dispatches from a Dying Generation."

[42] McCall, "Dispatches from a Dying Generation."

[43] McCall, "Dispatches from a Dying Generation."

[44] David Maraniss, "Midwest Alderman With A Militia Threatens to 'Disrupt White Life,'" *The Washington Post*, 18 July 1990, A11.

[45] Maraniss, "Midwest Alderman With A Militia Threatens to 'Disrupt White Life,'" A11.

[46] Jason DeParle, "New Weapons of Racial Warfare?," *Dayton Daily News*, 2 November 1990, 1C.

[47] Based on *Uniform Crime Reports* data for the years 1985 through 1989.

[48] *Uniform Crime Reports*, 1985 through 1989.

[49] *Uniform Crime Reports*, 1985 through 1989.

[50] See, for example, Howard A. Palley and Dana A. Robinson, "Black on Black Crime," *Society* 24:5 (July-August 1988), 59-62.

[51] Catherine J. Whitaker, "Black Victims," *Bureau of Justice Statistics Special Report* (Washington, DC: U.S. Department of Justice, April 1990), 1.

[52] Jaynes and Williams, *Blacks and American Society*, 466-467.

[53] Tom Watson, "From Mom's Grief, Crusade Emerges Against Black-on-Black Violence," *The Washington Post*, 11 February 1991, A5.

[54] Rene Sanchez, "A Generation Born of Violence Creating a Brutal Legacy," *The Washington Post*, 27 January 1991, B1.

[55] Gabriel Escobar, "Washington Area's 703 Homicides in 1990 Set A Record; Police Say Disrespect for Life, Especially Among Youths, Is Fueling Violence," *The Washington Post*, 2 January 1991, A1, A6.

[56] William G. Lewis, "Toward Representative Bureaucracy: An Assessment of Black Representation in Police Bureaucracies," *Public Administration Review* 49 (1987), 257-268.

[57] "Black Troopers Settle Bias Suit," *The Washington Post*, 5 January 1991, B5.

[58] Joe Schwartz, "Hispanics in the Eighties," *American Demographics* (January 1988), 43-45.

[59] Lisa D. Bastian, "Hispanic Victims," *Bureau of Justice Statistics Special Report*, January 1990, 2.

[60] See John R. Howard, "Mexican Americans: The Road to Huelga," in *Awakening Minorities* (Chicago: Aldine Publishing Co., 1970), 89-104.

[61] U.S. Bureau of the Census, "The Hispanic Population in the United States: March 1986 and 1987 (Advance Report)." *Current Population Reports*, Series P-20, No. 416.

[62] Manuel P. Servin, *An Awakening Minority: The Mexican Americans*, 2nd ed. (Beverly Hills: Glencoe Press, 1974), 45.

[63] Bernard A. Weisberger, *The American People* (New York: American Heritage Publishing Co., Inc., 1971), 351.

[64] Howard, "Mexican Americans," 94.

[65] Cited in Weisberger, *The American People*, 353.

[66] Stephan Thernstrom, ed., *Harvard Encyclopedia of American Ethnic Groups* (Cambridge, MA: The Belknap Press of the Harvard University Press, 1988), see especially "Puerto Ricans," 858-867.

[67] Joseph R. Fitzpatrick, *Puerto Rican Americans: The Meaning of Migration to the Mainland* (Englewood Cliffs, NJ: Prentice-Hall, Inc., 1986), 3-6.

[68] Weisberger, *The American People*, 364.

[69] U.S Bureau of the Census, *Statistical Abstract of the United States: 1992*, 112th ed. (Washington DC: U.S. Government Printing Office, 1992). See especially Table 8, p. 11.

[70] Shih-Shan Henry Tsai, "Chinese in the United States," in Hyung-Chan Kim, *Dictionary of Asian American History* (New York: Greenwood Press, 1986), 3-6.

[71] James W. Osterburg and Richard H. Ward, *Criminal Investigation: A Method for Reconstructing the Past* (Cincinnati: Anderson Publishing Co., 1992), 760-761.

[72] *Nontraditional Organized Crime: Law Enforcement Officers' Perspectives on Five Criminal Groups* (Washington, DC: U.S. General Accounting Office, September 1989), 3.

[73] S. Frank Miyamoto, "Japanese in the United States," in Hyung-Chan Kim, *Dictionary of Asian American History*, 7-12.

[74] For one perspective on the relationship between the Korean and black communities in Los Angeles after the 1992 riots, see Edward Norden, "South-Central Korea: Post-Riot L.A.," *The American Spectator*, September 1992, 33-40.

[75] Gail P. Kelly, "Southeast Asians in the United States," in Hyung-Chan Kim, *Dictionary of Asian American History*, 39-47.

[76] James W. Osterburg and Richard H. Ward, *Criminal Investigation: A Method for Reconstructing the Past* (Cincinnati: Anderson Publishing Co., 1992), 761-762.

[77] Robert B. Reich, "Secession of the Successful," *New York Times Magazine*, 20 January 1991, Section 6, 15, 17, 42-45.

[78] Reich, "Secession of the Successful," *New York Times Magazine*, 15, 17, 42-45.

[79] Charles Krauthammer, "The Tribalization of America," *The Washington Post*, 6 August 1990, A11.

Photo Credit: Bill Powers, Frost Publishing Group, Ltd.

Chapter 5

COMMUNITY PROBLEMS

As the twentieth century enters its final decade, many communities are faced with a variety of increasingly serious problems. Some are basically economic (e.g., finding adequate revenues to meet the demand for services), while others combine social, technological and economic issues (e.g., drug abuse and homelessness). Such problems are interrelated, and each in its own way threatens the very fabric of the community. They will have a profound impact on the criminal justice system as a whole and on the police in particular. Dealing with these issues will require a great deal of imagination and commitment, and it is possible that existing approaches and resources will not be sufficient. The following problem areas probably will be among the toughest issues to face the American community in the near term.

DRUGS

Throughout history humankind has used pharmacological substances for healing, recreation and pain reduction, and for bringing about desired physiological and psychological changes. Seers and spiritualists have used drugs to induce trances during which (they claim) it is possible to enter into closer communion with the gods or to understand the mysteries of life. Drugs have been valuable to society in easing physical suffering. The use of anesthetics has made possible the development of surgical techniques that otherwise would be inconceivable. Unfortunately, though, drugs also have a less salubrious side. Their abuse can be a serious problem to both the individual and the community. The consequences of drug abuse extend far beyond the immediate impact on the individual to influence the community in many ways. Some effects are subtle (e.g., the loss of respect for conventional social institutions), while others are more direct (e.g., the cost of maintaining addicted "boarder babies" in public hospitals).

Although the use of drugs goes back to antiquity, drug abuse as we understand the term actually started in the nineteenth century and was made possible by advances in chemistry, technology and transportation. For example, after morphine was first isolated in 1805 by a German chemist, its value as a painkiller was quickly exploited. However, its subsequent widespread abuse could not have happened without the invention of the hypodermic needle in 1853. Heralded as a scientific breakthrough, the needle permitted the administration of drugs directly into body tissues, causing a faster onset of action and a greater rate of absorption. Nine years later the Civil War erupted, resulting in enormous casualties. Over 618,000 men perished and an even larger number were wounded. Morphine was so widely used in the treatment of the wounded that morphine dependence became known as "the soldier's disease."

Since the consequences of drug addiction were not understood during the nineteenth century, narcotics were not controlled until the early years of the present century. They have since become the center of a major illicit economy and are linked to a number of other serious social problems. The sale of illicit narcotics fuels an extremely lucrative financial infrastructure that operates outside the legitimate economy. This has produced a unique market economy that has proven extremely difficult to battle and has offered quick wealth to those willing to assume the risks. Even so, the problem could not have reached its current proportions without a potentially receptive population of users. Two factors in the 1960s set the stage: widespread alienation among middle-class whites arising from disenchantment with the Vietnam War, and the emergence of inner cities as places of despair and frustration. The counterculture of the 1960s supported drug use. Stories of drug use by entertainers and sports figures seemed to legitimize its glamor, thereby encouraging its recreational use. At the same time, the economic desperation and social disorganization of the inner cities was waiting for a "solution." Drug abuse now touches all parts of American society and is a serious problem. According to a 1988 analysis by the National Institute on Drug Abuse, 72.4 million Americans aged 12 or older (37 percent of the population) had tried marijuana, cocaine or other illicit drugs at least once in their lifetime.[1]

Although there are many kinds of drugs, the sections that follow will deal only with the drugs most frequently abused and those which present the most serious current problems. Others, such as hallucinogens and depressants, will not be covered, even though they may cause significant problems in their own right. The important thing to keep in mind is that illicit drugs have an impact on society that goes far beyond individual drug dependence. It is a problem that is not going to go away on its own and may even become one of the single most important issues in population centers, both large and small.

NARCOTICS

The term *narcotic* refers to opium and its derivatives or synthetic substitutes. The opium poppy (*Papaver somniferum*) is its primary nonsynthetic source. Opium and its derivatives have numerous legitimate medicinal uses, including the relief of intense pain. One of its most important alkaloid constituents is morphine, an extremely effective painkiller. Interestingly enough, in its early years morphine was marketed as a cure for opium addiction. By the turn of the century, opium was used in many patent medicines, without restrictions or warning to the consumer, resulting in widespread dependence.

In 1874 two English chemists developed the chemical compound *diacetylmorphine* by chemically altering the morphine alkaloid. In 1898 the Friedrich Bayer Company, a German pharmaceutical firm, marketed the drug under the name *Heroin* and sold it as a cure for both opium and morphine addiction, with the claim that it was absolutely non-addictive.[2] Heroin was outlawed in 1914 with the passage of the Harrison Narcotic Act and is currently listed under the Comprehensive Drug Abuse Prevention Act of 1970 as a Schedule I drug. This category includes drugs that have a high potential for abuse, have no currently accepted medical use and lack accepted safeguards for use under medical supervision.

Heroin can be taken in many ways: orally, or through inhalation, injection or smoking (referred to as "chasing the dragon"). It is used by some drug users to "come down" from the effects of cocaine use. Heroin is a strong central nervous system depressant and the body reacts to it very quickly. Because of its tremendous potency, heroin can be marketed in very small quantities at a considerable profit. According to the Drug Enforcement Administration's Domestic Monitoring Program (which monitors the retail marketing of heroin), the average price per milligram in the United States in 1988 was three dollars and its average purity was 23.6 percent. This purity rate is a significant increase over 10 years ago, when the average purity was in the single digit range.[3]

Although heroin use in the United States appears to be declining overall, it remains a serious problem. Heroin overdose deaths from 1985 to 1988 gradually increased, and the number of heroin-related hospital emergency room admissions increased by almost 30 percent during this same period.[4] The National Institute on Drug Abuse estimated in 1989 that a total of 1.9 million people aged 12 or older have used heroin.[5]

MARIJUANA

Marijuana is derived from *cannabis sativa*, a hemp plant that grows widely throughout the world in temperate and tropical regions. It is obtained by drying the leaves and flowering top of the cannabis plant and is processed and consumed much like tobacco. Its potency varies by how much tetrahydrocannabinol (THC) is present in the plant. Marijuana grown in the United States is generally of inferior quality, usually with less than .5 percent THC potency. The most potent marijuana is found in the so-called *sinsemilla* (Spanish for "without seeds"), which comes from the unpollinated female cannabis plant and contains up to 20 percent THC.

Although marijuana is a Schedule I drug, it continues to be the most commonly used illicit drug in the United States. Almost 66 million Americans (33 percent) have tried it at least once in their lives. In 1988 17 percent of youths and 56 percent of young adults had used marijuana. These rates have steadily declined since 1979, when they were 31 percent and 68 percent, respectively. In 1988, 31 percent of adults 26 and older had used it. This number has steadily increased since 1972, a phenomenon largely explained by the aging of individuals who began using drugs in previous years.[6] In the 1988 survey of high school seniors, 49.8 percent of the males and 44.5 percent of the females admitted to having used marijuana.[7] By comparison, only 12.1 percent of the same sample admitted to using cocaine and 1.1 percent admitted to using heroin.[8] The reported use of marijuana among high school seniors has consistently declined over the past 12 years. Fifty percent of the class of 1978 admitted to marijuana use; by 1989 the figure had dropped to 29.6 percent.[9]

COCAINE

Cocaine is a stimulant extracted from the leaves of the coca plant. The first step in producing cocaine is to make coca paste, which is used to produce cocaine base. The base is dissolved in ethyl ether, acetone or a mixture of both and then filtered to remove any impurities. A mixture of acetone and concentrated hydrochloric acid is then added to precipitate cocaine hydrochloride, which is filtered and carefully dried to produce a white, crystalline powder known as cocaine hydrochloride. This is the product most commonly found on the street and is usually sold at 30 to 40 percent purity. Although it is usually inhaled through the nose, it also can be injected into the bloodstream. Cocaine, like marijuana, is a popular recreational drug and is incorrectly believed by many of its users to be harmless. In the past, because of its relatively high cost, cocaine was typically associated with the affluent; however, in recent years its price has dropped and it has become much more popular among the poor. It produces an intense pleasurable effect that lasts less than an half an hour and can result in both physiological and psychological dependence. Since cocaine decomposes if smoked directly, it must be converted back to a relatively pure base ("freebase") before it is suitable for smoking. *Freebasing*, which emerged in the 1970s, is a process by which the active drug is removed from its salt base by mixing the cocaine with baking soda or ammonia and then with water and ether. The ether evaporates, leaving a powdery cocaine base which can be smoked. The freebase is heated in a pipe until it vaporizes, and the product is inhaled directly into the lungs. Freebasing is dangerous because ether is extremely volatile and heating freebase that is not dry can result in an explosion and severe burns. In 1981 a new process was first noted in Los Angeles, San Diego and Houston. It produced a residue called *crack*, which has spread rapidly throughout the country. To make crack, cocaine powder is processed by using ammonia or baking soda and heating it to remove the hydrochloride, which is safer than using the highly volatile ether. This produces a cocaine base in the form of chunks or chips, which can be vaporized in a pipe or smoked with marijuana.

When ordinary cocaine is snorted, it takes about eight minutes to penetrate the mucous membranes and produces a mild high that lasts a little less than a half hour. Crack reaches the brain within a few seconds and its high is much more intense but only lasts from five to 10 minutes. Following a "hit" of crack, the user generally experiences a restless irritability accompanied by severe depression and an almost insatiable craving for more. Apparently, cocaine overstimulates the "reward center" of the brain by influencing dopamine, a chemical found naturally in the brain. Cocaine causes dopamine to remain active longer than normal, signaling an intense craving for more of the drug—causing the user to take more cocaine or crack just to feel normal. Addiction to crack can occur very quickly, and unfortunately, there are few, if any, effective treatment models for cocaine addiction.

The 1988 National Household Survey on Drug Abuse found that the number of "current" cocaine users dropped by 50 percent (from 5.8 million in 1985 to 2.9 million in 1988). However, the same survey also found that within the cocaine-using population, its use is intense. Some 862,000 people reported using it once a week or more, compared with 647,000 in 1985; and some 292,000 used the drug daily or almost daily, compared with 246,000 in 1985.[10] Cocaine use appears to be highest among the unemployed and those aged 18 to 25 and is rapidly becoming the scourge of the inner cities.

DRUGS AND CRIME

There are two broad perspectives on the relationship between drugs and crime. The first holds that drugs are a direct cause of crime. Advocates of this position claim that drug use encourages criminal behavior by reducing inhibitions, stimulating aggression and interfering with the ability to earn a legitimate income. In addition, laws that control drugs can be viewed as conducive to crime because they create a black market in which drug-dependent people need a substantial income to support their habit.[11] A rival perspective holds that, although drug use does not necessarily cause criminal behavior, the same circumstances that lead a person into crime may also encourage drug abuse. This perspective suggests that drug abuse might not even occur until *after* the person begins committing crimes and could therefore only be part of a larger lifestyle that includes criminal activity.[12] However, one thing is clear: there *is* a relationship between drugs and crime.

This relationship seems to occur in three overlapping ways.[13] First, crimes may be committed by people under the influence of drugs because of the ways the drugs can alter one's mood, perception or physiological functions. In the early decades of this century, those concerned with drug abuse focused primarily on heroin. At that time, it was widely believed that drugs in general—and heroin in particular—were a direct cause of violent crimes. "Drug fiends" were often presented in the media as extremely dangerous people. In truth, drug addicts were generally a pathetic group more likely to commit crimes of acquisition to support their habit. Drug-induced violence can occur, but is most likely to involve strong hallucinogenic drugs such as PCP (*phencyclidine*) and LSD (*lysergic acid diethylamide*); however, even this relationship is open to question as not all users are affected in the same way. Moreover, hallucinogen use is relatively rare even within the drug-using population. Thus, we cannot say that using drugs necessarily *causes* a person to commit crimes (much less crimes of violence). Some people who intentionally commit crimes do so under the influence of drugs, perhaps because their chemically altered state reduces their inhibitions or otherwise facilitates their illicit behavior in some way.

Some insight into this problem has been gained through the use of "drug forecasting," a program begun by the National Institute of Justice in 1987 in New York City. By 1989, 22 cities had entered the program, which is designed to provide each city with estimates of drug use among arrestees and information for detecting changes in drug use trends. Information under this program is collected in the central booking facilities of the participating cities. For about 14 consecutive evenings each quarter, trained local staff members obtain voluntary and anonymous urine specimens and interviews from a new sample of arrestees. More than 90 percent of the arrestees agreed to be interviewed and about 80 percent agreed to provide a urine specimen. The specimens are analyzed for 10 drugs, including cocaine, opiates, marijuana, PCP, methadone, Valium, methaqualone, Darvon, barbiturates and amphetamines. In 1989 the percentage of males testing positive for a drug at the time of arrest ranged from 53 percent in San Antonio to 82 percent in San Diego. Positive drug-testing results for female arrestees ranged from 45 percent in Indianapolis to 83 percent in Washington, DC. In eight of the 17 cities participating in the program, 70 percent or more of the female arrestees tested positive for a drug.[14] The survey also indicated that cocaine was the most prevalent drug for the majority of male and female arrestees during 1989. In an earlier study (1986), more than one-third of the inmates sampled in a survey of state prisons reported that they were under the influence of a drug when they committed the offenses for which they were incarcerated.[15]

Even though a person might not necessarily commit a crime because he or she has taken drugs, the drugs' effects can influence the nature of the crimes committed by a person under their influence. Experienced homicide investigators know that murders committed under the influence of drugs tend to be more disorganized, violent and pointless than those committed by people not under the influence of drugs at the time they kill. For example, on the morning of April 9, 1988, a Washington, DC housewife drove her husband to work. On the way they discussed her plans to get the oil in the car changed. On her way back, she stopped to buy some crack, which she smoked after returning home. She then made breakfast for her children. After the children dressed and while they were watching television, she smoked more crack. At some point she "got real jittery," after which she strangled her four-year-old son and eight-year-old daughter with a clothesline and unsuccessfully attempted to murder her two-year-old daughter. When asked by the police why she killed her children, she said, "I hadn't planned on it. I hadn't even thought about it."[16]

The second relationship between crime and drugs manifests itself when crimes are committed to obtain drugs. In a sample of state prisoners sentenced for robbery, burglary, larceny or a drug offense, half admitted to being daily drug users and about 40 percent admitted to being under the influence of an illegal drug at the time they committed the crime for which they were incarcerated. These proportions were higher than those reported by inmates convicted of other crimes.[17] Heavy users of drugs are less able to function as effective employees and are more likely to be outside the mainstream labor force. Thus, 48 percent of a sample of state prison inmates who had been users of major drugs reported that they received income from illegal activities during the time they were last free, as compared to only 10 reported by nonusers.[18]

Finally, the drug culture itself is essentially a criminal enterprise and many crimes are committed as part of how that culture operates.[19] This has been abundantly clear in the spread of crack, which has not happened by accident. Dominican immigrants in New York City have been credited with first developing a mass market for the drug.[20] They established drug distribution networks that quickly and efficiently exploited inner city neighborhoods. However, Jamaican drug dealers have probably been even more efficient in expanding the market for crack. Organized into small groups commonly known as *posses*, they have been involved in a broad range of mutually supportive criminal activities, including trafficking in narcotics and firearms, money laundering, fraud, kidnapping, home invasion, robbery and murder.[21] There may be as many as 20 Jamaican posses involving several thousand members and associates operating in the United States and Canada. So far they seem to be operating on the eastern seaboard, in parts of the Midwest and in the Southwest.

The original posses were formed in Jamaica and were based on local geographic and political ties. Many of those who are now operating in the United States are comprised of illegal aliens with criminal histories. Up until 1988 Jamaicans involved in drugs trafficked almost exclusively in marijuana; however, the current trend is to deal predominantly in cocaine. Much of it is oriented toward setting up and operating crack houses. They have traveled throughout the country to establish a network of crack dealerships and are believed to control up to 40 percent of the crack distribution system. The Jamaican posses also have brought considerable violence with them, and according to the Treasury's Bureau of Alcohol, Tobacco and Firearms (BATF), have been "...responsible for approximately 1,000 murders since 1985. Washington, Philadelphia, Dallas, Houston, Kansas City, Denver—all have suffered Jamaican invasions. In New York, [they] have succeeded in taking over much of Brooklyn and Harlem, establishing themselves as the city's second largest traffickers, after the Dominicans."[22] They have shown a willingness to use extreme violence to force out competition, protect their territories from rival gangs and enforce discipline against thefts. This violence sometimes shows up in chilling ways: in several areas when purchasing narcotics, they hold a gun next to the customer's head until the transaction is completed or the drugs are passed through a slot in the door. West coast gangs, most notably the Bloods and the Crips, have followed suit and are spreading eastward. The important point is that specific criminal organizations are intentionally exploiting inner-city populations through a highly profitable enterprise that is accelerating the destruction of the communities themselves.

Homicides growing out of drug transactions have become a serious problem in many cities and the rate appears to be increasing. In 1985, for example, 21 percent of the homicides reported in the District of Columbia were identified as drug-related. This proportion increased steadily to 34 percent in 1986, 51 percent in 1987, and as much as 80 percent in 1988.[23] According to a 1989 report on urban violence, police departments confirmed that urban areas with "combat-like conditions" could be found in New York, Boston, Philadelphia, Baltimore, Washington (DC), Miami, Cleveland, East St. Louis, Detroit,

Chicago, Atlanta, New Orleans, Houston, Dallas, Oakland and Los Angeles.[24] These areas have been described as "...places where the level of concentrated violence has risen so high that city services barely function, not simply because workers and administrators blatantly redline the areas as in the past or for lack of resources, but also out of well-grounded fear for their lives."[25] Much of this is attributed to the influence of crack.

DRUG ABUSE:
THE HUMAN SIDE OF THE EQUATION

At the beginning of this century, America was essentially a rural and agricultural nation. Most of the drug problem at that time seems to have been concentrated in working and middle-class populations because the drugs that were abused were legal and their effects touted as beneficial. Many of them were taken as medicinal preparations. By 1900, every bottle of Coca-Cola® contained one-third to one-half a line of cocaine, and a competing beverage also manufactured in Atlanta (hometown of Coca-Cola®) was aptly called *dope*.[26] As the government adopted policies designed to protect the public from impure foods and dangerous drugs, all of that changed. The legal control of drugs started with the Harrison Act (1914) and was followed by the Marijuana Tax Act (1937). These legislative efforts were combined with a lurid if inaccurate portrayal of drug use that successfully sought to distance "respectable" people from drug abuse. It created what amounts to a high-risk protective tariff for those who deal in drugs—artificially inflating their cost and separating drug abusers from much of "ordinary America." This ultimately brought about a shift in the drug-abusing population so that by the 1990s serious drug abuse involving opiates is identified as occurring almost exclusively in the rapidly growing urban inner-city neighborhoods. Thus, while young whites in the suburbs "experiment" with marijuana, inner-city blacks are increasingly involved in heavy use of crack cocaine. Middle- and upper-class America has been largely able to absorb its drug problem, but the same has not been true of the urban poor. While members of the more affluent segment of society merely consume the drugs they take, the drugs taken by the poor have begun to consume *them*.

The relatively rapid development of the minority-dominated inner cities created a fertile opportunity for drug exploitation. When crack cocaine emerged in the inner cities it fell into a receptive environment, and its consequences are just now being fully appreciated. As one major newsweekly reported in 1988,

Crack is more than just the latest drug to hit the American underclass. Since its appearance on inner-city streets three to five years ago, it has proven to be an illicit bonanza for those who sell it and a curse on those who use it. Unlike

heroin, crack is widely used by women. That fact alone has disastrous consequences for low-income families. If single-parent households have contributed to the intractability of poverty in the past, no-parent households may
be poverty's appalling future. And crack is a catastrophe for the young. It has
touched off an explosive increase in birth defects and an epidemic of child
abuse and parental neglect. Its profits, in neighborhoods where the standard of
living is very low, have led or forced thousands of inner-city youngsters into
hard-core crime, and many others into addictions from which they may never
recover. It has bankrupted parental authority and it is destroying the fraying
social fabric of inner-city neighborhoods all over the United States.[27]

The crack problem goes even further. Many health professionals believe
that crack is a significant factor in the transmission of sexually transmitted diseases (including AIDS) because it promotes high-risk sexual behavior. Some
women, for example, stay in crack houses for long periods of time smoking and
having sex with many partners—some of them exchanging sex for crack.[28] A
recent study found that 96 percent of teenage crack users between 13 and 19
years of age were sexually active, and about 50 percent of them reported that
they combined their crack use with sexual activity. Not surprisingly, the study
also found that a history of sexually transmitted diseases was more common
among teens who combine sex with crack use.[29]

Unlike other drug epidemics, crack cocaine has had a significant effect on
women of childbearing age. Infants in the womb who are exposed to crack are
more likely to need more medical services than those whose mothers did not use
drugs when they were pregnant. In addition, drug-exposed infants are more frequently born prematurely and have low birth weights. Many of these children
may also have long-term learning and developmental deficiencies that can have
a profound impact on their lives. Some of these babies are abandoned by their
mothers and become "boarder babies," living in public hospitals. As *The Washington Post* reported in 1989, "...there is an increasing number of babies, some
of them as old as nine months, who have never seen the sun or felt the wind,
who have never slept in a darkened room, whose only form of human bonding is
with a changing sea of doctors and nurses."[30] Even though hospital staff do
their best to enrich the lives of these "throwaway" children, they cannot win:
"Hospital officials say the longer the babies remain in the hospital, the more
withdrawn they become. At first, the babies eagerly reach out to the daily parade of doctors and nurses who tend to them. But when the sea of faces continues to change and the staff dashes away to take care of the sick children, some
boarder babies sense rejection and begin to withdraw."[31] Perhaps even more
frightening is what happens to the ones who go home with crack-addicted mothers. As one physician pointed out, "We are coming to see that it is not being
born to a crack mother that dictates a poor outcome for a child. What damages
these children is the situation they go home to where they are not cared for,

where they are ignored, where they are left alone and don't get love. That is what cripples these children."[32]

Although the full impact of prenatal crack addiction is yet to be fully realized, the emerging picture is frightening. At the economic level, the Department of Health and Human Services estimates that it may cost more than $500 million in state and federal money to pay for the hospital delivery, postpartum care, physical therapy and foster care placement through age eight (about $11,000 per year per child). This money must come from already tightly stretched tax dollars and must compete with funding for other social programs. Crack-impaired babies are almost certain to experience major problems when they enter public education because of neurological damage that will take the form of language delays, memory deficits, perceptual problems and an inability to control impulses and emotions—all of which is likely to lead to significant behavioral problems.

The damage done to a community (particularly an urban community) by drugs is pervasive and systemic. The illicit drug economy denies government at all levels the tax revenues it needs to provide essential services. In addition, it encourages the disadvantaged to believe that conforming to traditional economic values is counterproductive. An oft-heard question asks, "How can you expect a disadvantaged youth to be willing to work in a fast food restaurant for minimum wages when he can make hundreds of dollars a day selling drugs?" The tremendous wealth generated by the illicit sale of drugs allows some dealers to pay cash for expensive cars, wear heavy gold jewelry and otherwise conspicuously display their wealth. This breeds contempt for honest work and ethical conduct. It makes a mockery out of education, diminishes the value of religion and fosters jealousy. Moreover, the illicit drug economy produces a loss of legitimate productivity by siphoning off talent into illegitimate enterprises.

The illicit drug economy also corrupts legitimate institutions. The corruption of police officers is a matter of intense and continuing concern, especially in cities with serious drug problems (e.g., New York City, Chicago, Miami, Washington, DC, etc.). At the individual level, police officers who use drugs themselves may be less willing to aggressively enforce drug violations. At the institutional level, some of the kinds of corruption experienced by police departments include:

- Accepting bribes from drug dealers or traffickers in exchange for "tips" regarding drug investigations, the identity of undercover officers, details of drug interdiction strategies, the names of informants, etc.;

- Accepting bribes from drug dealers or traffickers in exchange for interference in the justice process such as non-arrest, evidence tampering, perjury, etc.;

- Theft of drugs by police officers from property rooms or crime labs for either personal consumption or sale to others;

- The seizure of drugs from users or traffickers without an accompanying arrest based on police officers' intent to keep the drugs for personal use;

- Robbing drug dealers of their profits and/or their drugs;

- Extorting drug traffickers for money (and sometimes property) in exchange for non-arrest or non-seizure of drugs.[33]

The rapid rise of drug-related violence has transformed the pattern of firearms use in the cities. Not only is gratuitous violence beginning to be seen as appropriate, it is carried out with increasingly robust firepower. Legislation banning cheap handguns, combined with the growing status of sophisticated and expensive firearms, has ushered in an escalation in the use of more lethal weapons. The police are now encountering military-type assault weapons, automatic and semi-automatic rifles and pistols, and even such weapons of mass destruction as hand grenades and high explosives. These weapons have taken on a status of their own; their use has become more prevalent and their consequences more lethal. Not only are these weapons carried by drug dealers, they also are carried by large numbers of urban youth who feel they need them to "protect themselves." As a result, arguments that at one time would have ended with a black eye or split lip now end up with a body in the morgue.

Neighborhoods in which illicit drug trafficking is common develop mean characteristics. The sense of community diminishes and residents feel increasingly isolated, as if they are caught up in a storm they are powerless to control. This sense of isolation estranges them from the rest of the community and diminishes their respect for the police (who do not seem to be able to protect them). The eventual acceptance of blighted neighborhoods by those who cannot escape from them undermines confidence in local government and saps the willingness to work in support of a wholesome community. In the end, the community becomes a battleground.

DRUGS AND THE POLICE

The drug problem has thus far seemed to defy solution. At the national level, the federal government is faced with the question of whether the best approach is by attacking the *supply* side or the *demand* side. Advocates for attacking the supply side advocate policies that will either encourage producer nations to quit producing drugs or help the United States interdict them. Unfortunately, the producer nations tend to have poorly developed legitimate economies and the production of drugs is simply too economically rewarding. The international cocaine trade, for example, may well "...be the most significant transfer of wealth between affluent and less economically developed countries in the world today."[34] These countries simply have no other product that comes close to the value of the drugs they export. Even where the producer nations have expressed a willingness to work with the United States on crop substitution or drug interdiction programs, the actual drug producers have obtained so much capital that they have become powerful enough to challenge their governments. Corruption, intimidation and tremendous gaps between the official government and local economies are major problems in these countries. There is also the matter of national pride. The citizens of drug-producing countries have no reason to be particularly sympathetic to the United States. American efforts to control their production of drugs are seen by many as unwarranted and unwanted interference in their own internal affairs.

Fighting drugs at the demand side of the equation calls for law enforcement efforts at the federal, state and local levels that are targeted at manufacturers, distributors and those who sell and use drugs. Federal efforts are carried out by the Drug Enforcement Administration, the Federal Bureau of Investigation, the U.S. Customs Service and others. However, in most communities, the lion's share of the burden falls on local law enforcement agencies: the police. Local police departments must use limited resources to deal with drug-related violence, halt the spread of drug use and control drug-related crime. All of this must be done while protecting the integrity of their own organizations and the legal system itself.[35] The police simply cannot do it by themselves, and traditional law enforcement techniques have not proven effective. As a result of the absence of complaining victims and the reluctance of witnesses to testify, drug arrests and prosecutions are difficult to accomplish. This usually forces the police to engage in proactive operations such as buy-busts, stings, undercover operations, and so on. Even though their efforts may be aggressive and well planned, in most places they are simply not enough to solve the problem.

In any given community, the police must make a determination about how they are going to approach the problem based on the relationship between the community's resources and the nature and extent of its drug problem. Each department must ask how its resources are going to be applied so they can deal with such as gang-related violence associated with drug trafficking, controlling "street crimes" committed by drug users (e.g., robbery, burglary, theft), preventing drug abuse by minors and protecting the integrity of the criminal justice system. They must also concern themselves with community confidence in their efforts. Without public support the police cannot hope to win the drug war. A variety of strategies are available. What will work in one place may not work in another. There is no "magic formula."

Because the police are the law *enforcement* component of local government, their authority is itself limited by the law. Historically this has meant that the police approach must involve strategies that ultimately result in the identification and arrest of lawbreakers. New perspectives on policing are challenging that assumption. Community policing and problem-oriented policing (to be discussed more fully in Chapter 7) offer refreshing new perspectives that may prove to be quite valuable in dealing with the drug problem. Unfortunately, these techniques are only in their infancy. Although they have generated a great deal of excitement in police circles, they have not yet been widely adopted—and there are significant obstacles to be overcome before they can be adopted.

Since law enforcement is a selective process, the tactics employed by the local police department need to take a number of factors into consideration. For example, what enforcement strategies are most likely to produce the best results? What aspect of the overall drug problem should receive the greatest concentration of law enforcement efforts? How can the police measure their success, and how can they tell if their efforts are cost-effective? How can the police department take advantage of existing community sentiment to combat drugs? These are some of the most difficult and challenging problems facing American cities in the near future.

THE AIDS EPIDEMIC [36]

In 1981 Dr. Michael Gottlieb was puzzled by five patients he was treating at the University of California Medical Center. All of them suffered from a particularly virulent form of pneumonia; all five also had Kaposi's sarcoma, a disease affecting the blood vessel tissue in the skin or internal organs that is normally associated with older men of Mediterranean descent. However, what was most puzzling was that the immune system in all of these patients had failed. All five were homosexuals. Gottlieb did not know it at the time, but he was treating some of the nation's earliest AIDS cases. By 1982 the disease had been reported in 15 states, the District of Columbia and two foreign countries. By late September of 1988, more than 74,000 cases of AIDS had been reported in the United States, and almost 42,000 persons were known to have died. In 1988 the U.S. Public Health Service estimated that the United States had a population of approximately 1.5 million infected individuals, and that by 1992 the cumulative number of diagnosed AIDS cases would total 365,000, with 263,000 cumulative deaths.[37]

Acquired Immunodeficiency Syndrome (AIDS) is caused by the Human Immunodeficiency Virus (HIV), which basically destroys the body's immune system. People infected with HIV may not have any symptoms of AIDS; in fact, the virus can remain dormant in an infected person for as long as 10 years. Even though the virus is dormant, those who are infected can still transmit it to others. At some point—for reasons that are not well understood—the virus becomes active and reproduces. This can result in a disease known as AIDS Related Complex (ARC), in which some of the symptoms of AIDS appear. It also can result in a full-blown case of AIDS, in which the person's immune system is completely destroyed. Most victims of active AIDS die within two years of the disease's onset, usually from opportunistic infections.

Although the AIDS virus can be found in a wide range of body fluids (including blood, semen, vaginal and cervical secretions, saliva, human milk, urine, tears and a variety of body tissues), concentrations appear to be greatest in blood and semen. Until recently, the AIDS virus was most commonly passed through homosexual contact, although it could also be transmitted through heterosexual intercourse. By 1992, only 50 percent of all new AIDS cases involved homosexual males. The second most common means of transmission was intravenous (IV) drug use and the sharing of contaminated needles. The proportion of AIDS victims who are IV drug users steadily increased from 17 percent in the mid-1980s to 24 percent in 1989 and is projected to reach 30 percent by 1993. However, as a leading researcher has pointed out, "AIDS is not a disease of homosexuals or drug addicts or indeed of any particular risk group. The virus is spread by intimate contact, and the form of contact seems to be less important than the contact itself."[38]

AIDS AND MINORITIES

Current trends indicate that AIDS is now an epidemic moving rapidly and with great devastation among minorities, particularly in impoverished urban areas. Its rates are increasing among women and children, particularly among poor blacks and Hispanics.[39] Although blacks and Hispanics represent about 12 and 7 percent of the population, they account for 24 and 7 percent of the AIDS cases, respectively. The proportion of AIDS cases among blacks and Hispanics is twice their proportion in the population. The intensity of this problem becomes even more stark when the rates among women and children are examined. Minority children are hit especially hard: among children with AIDS, 53 percent are black, 22 percent are Hispanic and 24 percent are white. Black women represent 52 percent of all cases among women and Hispanic women account for another 19 percent. Thus, AIDS is a new, devastating and extremely expensive addition to the problems and pressures that already burden the poor.[40]

AIDS AND INTRAVENOUS DRUG ABUSERS

Intravenous (IV) drug abuse is a major risk factor in the spread of AIDS. There are an estimated 1.2 million IV drug users in the United States. Although most of them are addicted to heroin or other opiates, many take cocaine intravenously. Moreover, IV drug abuse is closely associated with impoverished social conditions and is concentrated in the inner cities where blacks and Hispanics are overrepresented. It is particularly hard to reach these drug abusers with public health information because so many are poorly educated, unskilled, distrustful of authority and alienated from the mainstream of society. Among IV drug abusers HIV infection is spread for the most part by needle sharing.

Needle sharing is apparently part of the sociological context of IV drug abuse. Essentially all IV drug users report needle sharing during some period of their drug-use careers.[41] Since newcomers to the world of IV drug abuse are unlikely to have the necessary equipment, they must rely on more experienced associates. This means that initial IV drug abuse is likely to occur in the presence of another IV drug abuser who shares his or her needle with the initiate. Once initiated, the IV drug abuser may continue to share needles as part of the social context of drug abuse—common use of paraphernalia being part of the drug abusers' social bonding process.[42] The use of so-called "shooting galleries" as communal injection sites also facilitates the sharing of needles, especially where the shooting gallery is run by an operator who charges a fee for the use of the facility and rental of injection equipment.

Some communities and activist groups favor making sterile needles available to IV drug abusers. The results of this highly controversial measure, where it has been applied, are not clear. It seems apparent that as long as they are drug-dependent, IV drug abusers are likely to continue sharing needles. Efforts to slow the spread of AIDS by making sterile needles available may only serve to facilitate existing drug dependence without eliminating the added risk of spreading AIDS.

Only about one out of every seven drug abusers is currently in a treatment program, and drug dependence is seldom changed without the drug-dependent person going through treatment. The federal government is actively exploring ways of expanding its outreach to drug abusers and finding ways of helping them reduce the risk of HIV infection.

The problem of prostitution is closely related to the spread of AIDS by female IV drug abusers. Since many female drug abusers turn to prostitution to support their addiction, they have become an especially efficient vector for transmission of the disease.[43] The Centers for Disease Control and Prevention collaborates with a number of other agencies in an ongoing study of prostitutes in Atlanta, Colorado Springs, Las Vegas, Los Angeles, Miami, Newark/Patterson and San Francisco in an effort to track the spread of disease by prostitutes. In the research areas, black and Hispanic women show higher rates of AIDS than white women. Half of the prostitutes interviewed had histories of IV drug abuse and over three-quarters of those who tested positive for the HIV antibody admitted to being IV drug users.[44]

There is a related but inadequately researched adjunct to the problem of prostitution and AIDS. Increasingly large numbers of drug-dependent females have turned to sexual promiscuity in return for crack. Though they are not prostitutes in the classic sense, they may add to the problem by offering sex for drugs as an immediate transaction at the crack houses they patronize. In addition, the issue of bisexual men has yet to be fully explored. It may be yet another vehicle by which AIDS is transferred from one victim population to another.[45] For example, married bisexual males who live in middle-class suburbs commonly seek homosexual contact in the central cities, often with male runaways who have turned to male prostitution for economic reasons. The young male prostitutes are at high risk for infection, and they share this risk with their "customers," who in turn may share it with their wives (or other contacts).

AIDS AND THE HEALTH CARE SYSTEM: THE PROBLEM OF COST

AIDS is probably the single most important health care issue facing the American community. In addition to the potential human tragedy involved, the sheer cost of dealing with the problem is overwhelming. Based on an estimate of $60,000 per patient, holding constant between 1988 and 1992, the cumulative lifetime medical care costs of treating all AIDS patients is estimated at $2.6 billion in 1988, $3.5 billion in 1989, $4.7 billion in 1990, $6.0 billion in 1991 and $7.5 billion in 1992.[46] These figures do not include nonmedical costs such as loss of earnings by AIDS victims, transportation and housekeeping costs, or social support services for AIDS victims. Programs that provide care and treatment for AIDS victims must compete for money with other programs and needs; it is highly unlikely that all competing requirements can be funded. The result is usually the creation of allocational rivalries that produce a general underfunding of most public needs and a serious underfunding of selected programs. AIDS treatment is likely to be seriously underfunded if treatment costs continue to rise. Public sentiment is unlikely to support unrestricted public expenditures for the treatment of victims who are viewed negatively by many. As Inciardi has noted, public attitudes toward AIDS victims are not universally positive: "...to many...AIDS has become like syphilis, leprosy, and plague—the contemporary metaphor for corruption, decay, and consummate evil."[47] If forced to decide which public programs will receive funding, many citizens are apt to feel that

AIDS victims should have a low priority, especially since the disease is virtually always fatal. Public funding has already leveled off: Congress, which promised $850 million to local AIDS groups in 1990, has only delivered $235 million. As one commentator noted, "The danger is that people will throw up their hands and say this is another insoluble problem of the underclass like crack and lousy schools."[48]

THE GEOGRAPHY OF AIDS

The nature of the AIDS epidemic also differs by geographic area. New York and California have been particularly hard hit by the disease (representing 48 percent of the reported cases in 1988). However, there are significant differences between AIDS victims in those states. In California homosexual and bisexual men have accounted for the bulk of the AIDS cases. As a group they have tended to be relatively affluent, educated, white, middle-class people who function largely within the mainstream of the community. In New York, on the other hand, AIDS victims have been much more likely to be poor, inner-city minorities—IV drug users, or the sexual partners or children of IV drug users. In 1987 the number of AIDS-related deaths among drug users in New York City surpassed that of homosexual males. Public health officials in New York estimate that one-half of the city's IV drug users are infected with the AIDS virus, compared with 5 percent of users in most other American cities.[49]

AIDS AND THE POLICE

Police officers probably have more contact with AIDS-infected people than any other occupational group except health care workers. They are in frequent contact with people who have been injured through accidents, crimes or domestic violence. As a result they are at risk of making contact with contaminated blood. In addition, the police are in frequent contact with prostitutes and IV drug offenders and are at risk from these people. The risk ranges from being bitten, cut or scratched to being stuck accidentally by needles while searching suspects. The problem is even more acute in poor neighborhoods, and the police are fully aware of the health consequences involved.

In 1982 the National Institute of Justice urged police departments to develop policies for dealing with AIDS-infected people. Law enforcement agencies have responded and there is a growing body of literature oriented specifically toward law enforcement personnel.[50] Policies typically call for using glove and mask protection under certain circumstances (e.g., incidents likely to bring the hands into contact with blood or body fluids, certain kinds of crime scenes, etc.). One problem the police face in some jurisdictions is that confidentiality laws prohibit medical personnel from telling the police whether or not a suspect tests positive for the AIDS virus. This means that a police officer assaulted by a person suspected of having AIDS or who has come into contact with blood or body fluids suspected to be HIV-positive may have information withheld on whether the suspect has AIDS. In one such case, the police were called to the scene of a suicide where they found a young man who had hanged himself. The responding officers cut him down and administered cardiopulmonary resuscitation during which they came into direct contact with a large quantity of the victim's blood. The officers were not successful in reviving him and the victim was declared dead upon arrival at the hospital. Meanwhile, other officers processing the scene found a suicide note in which the victim stated he had taken his life because he believed he had AIDS. At the request of the police the victim was tested for the AIDS virus—but based on confidentiality laws in the state where this incident took place—the police were told they could not be informed of the results.

RELATED LEGAL ISSUES

The AIDS issue constitutes two kinds of problems at the same time: it is a public health issue as well as a civil rights issue. Although the courts have upheld government's right to undertake measures to support public health, that right is not unlimited. For example, Section 504 of the Rehabilitation Act of 1973 (29 U.S.C., Section 794) prohibits any program receiving federal funding from discriminating against anyone on the basis of a handicap. It is not clear whether Section 504 applies to people with AIDS, although such individuals would appear to fall under its protection. This view is supported in the outcome of *School Board of Nassau County v. Arline* [55 U.S.L.W. 4245 (1987)], in which the plaintiff, a public school teacher, was fired from her job because she had tuberculosis. She sued the school board, claiming that she was protected under Section 504. The Supreme Court ruled 7-2 in her favor, clearly stating that Section 504 protects people with contagious diseases. The *Arline* decision does not mean that a person suffering from a contagious disease cannot be dismissed; if they are incapable of performing their duties or if there is a clear risk of transmitting the disease, they *can* be dismissed. The decision to terminate a person's employment must rest on specific evidence that a risk does exist and that the employer cannot provide the infected employee with a reasonable work alternative.

Screening populations at risk has proven to be a volatile issue. Although all prisoners in the federal system are screened for AIDS upon entry into the system (and at six-month intervals thereafter), state penal systems do not have a standardized approach to inmate screening. Homosexuals as a group have offered the greatest resistance to widespread screening; they have also been strongly in favor of legislation restricting access to data on those infected with the HIV virus. Their concern has been that they are likely to be discriminated against because of their sexual preference, and widespread screening would have a disproportionate impact on their civil liberties. There has been strong legislative support for this position.

The future of the AIDS issue is uncertain. A serious disease with no cure in sight, it cannot be dismissed as either a disease belonging only to gays or IV drug abusers. If it finds a more efficient vector for transmission, it could infect a much larger proportion of the population than current projections suggest. There is no cure for the disease. If efforts to develop a vaccine are successful, it will only diminish the rate of infection—not cure those already diagnosed as HIV-positive. It is likely that AIDS will continue to be a social problem with significant impact on the community well into the foreseeable future. The costs of dealing with it will almost certainly diminish the amount of money available for other social problems, while remaining inadequate for effectively treating the needs of AIDS victims. AIDS is an issue especially prone to exploitation on the basis of emotion and prejudice. Police are likely to find themselves in the middle of the controversy. Already, many police officers are unwilling to engage in resuscitative efforts on strangers out of fear of getting AIDS. This may indicate that the disease is likely to become another issue that will separate the police from the public—at least the portion of the public they fear may have AIDS.

If AIDS becomes identified as a disease of the poor, racial and ethnic minorities, and those whose sexual identity and lifestyle differ from that of the majority, it is highly probable that the larger community will turn its back on it. It is possible that the rejection will take the form of accelerated "white flight" from ethnic areas, increasing the economic and social isolation of high-risk populations.

THE HOMELESS

"Street people" are a diverse group often referred to by terms that describe either their appearance or behavior: bums, bag ladies, panhandlers, winos, runaways, and so on. There always have been street people of one kind or another, and public policy toward them has generally ranged from indifference to hostility. As a group, homeless people are an increasingly common sight in many communities. In recent years their problems have received widespread attention in the media, and they have become much more prominent in the social consciousness. The homeless are one of the most underrated but significant problems facing the police, because in many jurisdictions the police are forced to formulate public policy on how they will be treated.

Many people are disturbed at the sight of disheveled men in tattered clothing sleeping on steam grates and crazy-looking women pushing shopping carts filled with junk. Even more disturbing are reports of children living on the streets with their homeless mothers, indigent people sleeping in cardboard packing boxes or living under bridges, and teenage runaways targeted by "chickenhawks" or others who seek to exploit them for economic or sexual purposes. Although "homeless derelicts, broken-down alcoholics and skid row bums have existed in most times and places throughout our history, the seemingly sudden appearances of homeless young men, women, children, and whole families on the streets and in the shelters [is a] clear signal that something has gone very seriously wrong."[51]

Who are the homeless? How many of them are there? And why are they homeless? Many believe that the majority of the homeless are crazy people turned loose from mental hospitals, alcoholics who have bottomed out or deadbeats living on the charity of others (or on money from government programs). The working public is particularly offended when confronted by them in parks, libraries, subways and other public facilities (especially when the people are intoxicated, incontinent or boisterous). Many people are offended at the sight of panhandlers, especially those who appear capable of working. These "affronts to common decency" no doubt underscore a negative public opinion of the homeless.

The homeless have always been with us, but their composition has varied as social circumstances have changed. In the early years of the country, some of the poor were accepted within the community because their poverty stemmed from acceptable circumstances (e.g., widows and orphans whose behavior was consistent with community expectations). On the other hand, individuals depending on public charity as a result of their own "moral weakness" were seen as undeserving—especially if their behavior was inconsistent with community standards. The "undeserving" poor were encouraged to go elsewhere. Perhaps the most important era of homelessness in America was during the Great Depression of the 1930s, when large numbers of people (both individuals and families) wandered the country in search of jobs or opportunity. World War II ended the depression and fostered an economic boom that lasted until the 1960s. During that period, homelessness—at least the kind seen during the depression—disappeared from public view. The continued urbanization of America during the 1970s and 1980s, combined with inflation and unemployment, led to a rapidly increasing poverty rate. As poverty increased, so did homelessness—eventually taking on a new visibility.

Part of the problem has been in defining who the homeless really are. Much of how homelessness is defined is a function of choice; therefore, people who choose to live on the streets or in inadequate facilities are not homeless, regardless of how inadequate their housing is. On the other hand, those who live in makeshift quarters, flophouses or shelters because they do not have the resources to do otherwise *would* be considered homeless under most definitions.[52] Homelessness is closely linked to poverty, and since poverty is a matter of degree, homelessness is also a matter of degree. Thus one may distinguish between the *literally homeless* and the *marginally housed*.[53] The literally homeless have no place to go and must find some kind of shelter or sleep on the streets. The marginally housed, on the other hand, live close to the edge but are still able to find "more or less stable" housing—at least most of the time. Based on research in Chicago, Wright estimates the ratio of poor persons to the marginally housed to the literally homeless to be on the order of 600 to 50 to 3 at any given point in time.[54] He contends that because of the precarious situation of many of the poor, "the number of homeless in the span of a year exceeds the number homeless on any given night approximately by a factor of three."[55] In commenting on the magnitude of the problem, he states that, "As a rule of thumb, we can speak of a half million homeless people in America at any one time. And if the ratio of one-night homelessness to annual homelessness estimated for the city of Chicago...is generally true, then the annual homeless population of the nation is on the order of one-and-a-half million."[56]

HOW ARE THE HOMELESS DISTRIBUTED?

Based on the results of research in the National Health Care for the Homeless Program (HCH), Wright has created a representative model of 1,000 homeless people which distributes as follows:[57]

- Homeless families. 220
  - children 99
  - adult women. . . 83
  - adult men 38
- Homeless children 19 or less. . . . 47
- Homeless adult women 156
- Homeless adult men. 577
- TOTAL. 1,000

Homeless Families

The most typical "homeless family" is an adult female with one or more children. Lacking financial resources or job skills, these families are dependent on charity, welfare and/or their own ingenuity. A minority of homeless families consist of two-parent, nuclear families displaced by unemployment or other economic misfortune. For example, the author is familiar with the plight of a number of homeless families living out of trucks and cars camped in public parks. These families are from economically devastated areas in West Virginia and have come to Fairfax County, Virginia (an affluent suburban county adjacent to Washington, DC) to look for day labor, usually in the building trades. They are basically hard-working people displaced by economic misfortune, who are trying to maintain themselves until they can get back on their feet.

Homeless Women

Homeless women are more likely to be psychiatrically impaired but less likely to be dependent on drugs or alcohol. Perhaps the most conspicuous homeless women are the so-called "bag ladies"—women bundled up in tattered clothing carrying possessions in paper bags in shopping carts. Although this stereotype certainly exists (and does so in large numbers), it is not an adequate description of the female homeless. Coston's research among New York's bag ladies sheds light on their motives and lifestyle, and offers a fascinating glimpse into this world.[58] Homeless women tend to be slightly younger than homeless men. Coston found their average age to be 47 and the average time they had lived on the streets to be five years. About half of her sample of 35 women were black; the other half, white. Most of them said they lived on the streets because they had no other choice. Coston found that about one-third of her sample consisted of permanent street people. They are perhaps the most visible bag ladies: "bizarrely-dressed women talking to themselves and pushing carts piled high with the bags that have become their distinctive feature are not an uncommon sight for women in this class, since everything they own must travel with them."[59] Another one-third consisted of "part-time" bag ladies. These are women who live on the edge of a precarious social existence. The theft of a welfare check may be all it took to get them evicted from their marginal residences. They tend to drift back and forth from the streets to rooming houses and cheap hotels, and typically eat at soup kitchens or shelters. They usually do not dress in an odd manner or act crazy and are likely to be overlooked by the public. The final third consists of "situational" bag ladies who find themselves on the streets in the aftermath of a disastrous divorce or to escape from some personal problem that exceeded their ability to cope. These women are likely to recover and reintegrate at some point; their period on the street usually represents the low point in their lives.

Coston's study does not claim to be completely representative and almost certainly it is not. She approached 104 women for interviews, and about two-thirds declined. Those who declined were probably the most psychiatrically impaired, leaving her with an unrepresentative sample. Even so, it appears clear that the most important need of most homeless women is community-based mental health services. They are infrequently involved in crime and are more likely to be victims than offenders.

Homeless Men

Homeless men represent the largest category of street people, but only by a slender margin. Only a small percentage (perhaps no more than 3 percent) are over 65 years of age. The median age reported in Wright's study was 34 years.[60] About one-third of them are veterans of the Armed Forces who tend to be slightly older. This segment of the homeless population has a higher percentage of whites than does the segment of homeless non-veterans. For many of the Vietnam-era veterans, post-traumatic stress disorder (PTSD) is a common psychiatric disorder. However, it is not at all clear whether these men actually sustained traumatic experiences or if this is a general classification of convenience. Many of them are alcohol- or drug-dependent. The remainder of the non-veteran, homeless males consists of those who have fallen through the cracks of the community mental health system. Most do not pose any immediate danger to themselves or others and lead lives that are largely unproductive.

Homeless Children

A small but important minority of the homeless consists of children under 19. According to Wright, "many of these homeless teenagers are runaway or throwaway children fleeing abusive family situations: 9 percent of the girls ages thirteen to fifteen, and 24 percent of the girls ages sixteen to nineteen, were pregnant at or since their first contact with [the] HCH clinic system; the rate for sixteen-to-nineteen-year-olds is the highest observed in any age-group."[61] Drug and alcohol abuse is common among these children, and there is well-founded speculation that many are sexually exploited—thereby placing them at elevated risk for HIV infection.

Wright's analysis of the problem of homelessness estimates that about 40 percent are alcohol abusers and another 10 percent are abusers of other drugs, one-third are mentally ill, many have long-term chronic employment problems, and most are estranged from their families and disaffiliated from the larger society.[62] He sees homelessness as "...a housing problem, an employment problem, a problem of social disaffiliation, a mental health problem, a substance abuse problem, a family violence problem, a problem created by cutbacks in social welfare spending, a problem resulting from the decay of the traditional nuclear family, and a problem intimately connected to the recent increase in persons living below the poverty level, as well as others."[63]

THE HOMELESS AND PUBLIC POLICY

Part of the problem of public policy with regard to the homeless is that, for the most part, there is none. Involuntary forms of institutionalization (hospitals, shelters or jails) are not viable options. Although many of the homeless are ignored, a policy of "looking the other way" is also no longer possible. Though most agree that something needs to be done, none of the rational solutions seem feasible for one reason or another. Developing community-based mental health clinics, shelters for the literally homeless and detoxification centers for alcoholics all require money. Even where funding is available, there is often an unwillingness in many neighborhoods to accept these treatment facilities.

Communities are generally willing to overlook street people as long as they are essentially out of sight. However, when they move into business districts, parks, public facilities and residential neighborhoods, their presence becomes more problematic. It is impractical and unconstitutional to enact laws that punish people for their *status*. "Poor laws," which were common throughout most of our history, are no longer an option. Instead, communities must deal with specific issues that are related to homelessness—including unemployment, housing, mental health, and so on. Even if communities are willing to confront these issues, how do they match resources with people in need of them? Presumably, many street people would take advantage of various community resources, but should those who do not want to do so be free to simply live on the fringe? Should their presence be tolerated when their lifestyle is clearly at odds with community standards? The policy issue therefore divides into two related components: providing social services and dealing with those who refuse to use them. Both issues invariably fall most squarely on the shoulders of the police.

THE POLICE AND THE HOMELESS

There is a gnawing suspicion on the part of some parties that the homeless are somehow part of a larger pool of criminals and miscreants that threaten the social fabric. However, upon closer inspection a more benign picture emerges. For example, a Baltimore study compared arrests of homeless people with arrests in the general population and produced some interesting results.[64] Homeless arrestees tended to be older and were more likely to be white than arrestees in the general population. They were typically arrested for disorderly conduct.

When arrested for more serious crimes, the charges tended to be based on relatively trivial incidents. For example, burglary was often charged when homeless people were found occupying vacant buildings and larceny charges were often based on shoplifting food. These data support other findings that the homeless who come to the attention of the police are "...primarily single males, often with drinking or drug problems, who appear to *prefer* to live on the streets and to survive by begging or petty theft."[65]

However, the police are drawn into dealing with the homeless not so much in response to *crime* as in response to *disorder*. Order maintenance has been a police function for generations and often employs informal, unofficial methods. Even though these methods may not always be legal, they have generally been accepted by the portion of the community that has benefited from them. In the past these "unofficial" techniques included such things as driving homeless people to the city limits and telling them to leave and not come back. When the police take "official" action against someone, it must be based on law. Historically, it has been most convenient for them to "criminalize" disorder so offenders could be arrested and processed by the system. This was done through a variety of vagrancy statutes and laws prohibiting "disorderly conduct." The use of vagrancy laws was severely limited in 1972 when the United States Supreme Court struck down a Florida vagrancy law because of its vagueness.[66] That law read:

> Rogues and vagabonds, or dissolute persons who go about begging, common gamblers, persons who use juggling or unlawful games or plays, common drunkards, common night walkers, thieves, pilferers or pickpockets, traders in stolen property, lewd, wanton and lascivious persons, keepers of gambling places, common railers and brawlers, persons wandering or strolling around from place to place without any lawful purpose or object, habitual loafers, disorderly persons, persons neglecting all lawful business and habitually spending their time by frequenting houses of ill fame, gaming houses, or places where alcoholic beverages are sold or served, persons able to work but habitually living upon the earnings of their wives or minor children shall be deemed vagrants and, upon conviction, shall be punished [by a maximum of ninety days in jail and a $500 fine, or both].[67]

As vagrancy laws were eliminated because of their vagueness, they were replaced by laws prohibiting "disorderly conduct," which sought to criminalize much the same kind of conduct but focused on specific behaviors rather than status. Perhaps the most commonly used grounds for arrest of homeless people have been disorderly conduct, assault and battery on a police officer, and resisting arrest—charges that "...are regularly filed as a package by police officers involved in controlling street people...."[68] However, criminalizing homelessness has not helped solve the problem; if anything, it has only made it more complex.

Homeless people who are arrested may spend a few hours or days in jail, but when released they return to the same environment from which they came.

If the police are to help the homeless, they need resources not commonly available in many communities. As things presently stand, the police have few alternatives to incarceration. This is not a small problem. As one police executive has noted,

> The dimensions of the problem are national in scope, but local in impact. Every jurisdiction in the Nation will have to deal with the homeless in some form during the remainder of this century. Until such time as public policy decisions have been made at the local, State and national levels with respect to mental health facilities and detoxification centers, the problem will continue to fall largely on the shoulders of local law enforcement. Cooperation between city authorities and the police department, as well as the implementation of [internally designed police] programs...are ways of confronting an issue that is affecting more and more of our Nation's cities and towns every day.[69]

Things are not likely to get better any time soon. There are a large number of problems facing the cities, many of which exacerbate one another. For example, the drug problem is producing an entirely new generation of children who are likely to have trouble succeeding in school and who may wind up dependent on the resources of government. Such a contingency would swell the ranks of the homeless and make that problem even more difficult to resolve. AIDS and related health care issues will siphon off a great deal of money that could otherwise be used in social programs that will therefore either go or underfunded or completely unfunded. The criminal justice system will have to deal with all of these issues on a daily basis—but will have to do so with inadequate resources. The challenges of the next century will call for responses far beyond what has been available in the past. The question is whether the system can or will meet those challenges.

SUMMARY

The American community is challenged by complex and often interrelated problems. Some of these problems threaten the overall quality of community life and all of them have a direct impact on the police. Unfortunately, the police do not have the resources to solve these problems and can only attempt to deal with their immediate consequences. Law enforcement agencies develop policies that enable them to deal with social problems, but the tactics used by the police are quite different from those needed to solve the causes of these problems. Many of our most serious social problems arise from a larger context that local government has been either unwilling or unable to address. Problems such as drug abuse, AIDS and the homeless are changing the complexion of the community. The criminal justice system has a responsibility to come to grips with these issues to the best of its ability.

Drug abuse has occurred throughout recorded history, but is in its present form an entirely new problem that has grown out of advances in technology and transportation. Advances in chemistry and pharmacology have made new and much more potent drugs available, and modern transportation has converted the world into a global marketplace for them. The enormous profits in drug trafficking have created a shadow economy that not only threatens legitimate economies but also underwrites the large-scale corruption of individuals and institutions.

Patterns of drug abuse have shifted and new, more serious problems arising from these changes can be found in virtually every community. For a long time, the recreational drug of choice was marijuana. Even though its usage rates are dropping, marijuana has been so widely consumed in the United States that its use and possession are not regarded as serious problems by large segments of the public. Perhaps the most significant recent trend in drug abuse has been the emergence of cocaine—particularly crack cocaine—as a drug of preference. Crack is much more addictive than marijuana and its use is spreading rapidly among the poor, where it is having a disproportionate impact on all aspects of life. It has been linked with violent crime and has become an important issue in prenatal and infant health care as increasing numbers of babies are born drug-dependent and/or abandoned by their parents. In addition, the drug problem deprives communities of productive labor and tax revenues while breeding a contempt for authority and a rejection of conventional social norms. The scope of the problem is so large that law enforcement has barely been able to keep abreast of it.

AIDS is a relatively new problem, dating back only one decade. However, since its discovery it has become the single most important public health issue in America. Although initially identified with homosexual activity, it is now also associated with intravenous drug use. Like the drug problem, AIDS is having a disproportionate impact on minority communities, further aggravating existing problems. The economic and human cost of AIDS is likely to become a major issue in the near future. The police come into frequent contact with HIV-positive individuals and must develop policies for dealing with them. Their policies must take into consideration the rights of those who are infected but must also protect the safety of the police.

The problem of the homeless has re-emerged and presents a significant challenge to many communities. As the needs of the homeless vary according to individual circumstances, an overall solution seems beyond reach. As the police move away from their earlier practice of "criminalizing poverty," new solutions must be found for meeting the needs of the homeless while maintaining public order. This is an important issue because much of the conflict between the police (and the larger community) and the homeless has been based on disorderly conduct on the part of the homeless rather than serious crimes committed by them. As the focus of the problem shifts from the police to the larger community, new solutions need to be identified and implemented.

DISCUSSION QUESTIONS

1. Why is drug abuse a uniquely "modern" problem?
2. How do high drug profits make it especially difficult for society to deal with the drug problem?
3. Is the casual use of marijuana as a recreational drug a "real" problem? Explain your position.
4. Why is crack cocaine such a problem?
5. If the government "decriminalized" drugs, would the problem go away? What do you think would happen?
6. Do drugs "cause" crime? If so, how?
7. What is the relationship between the economics of drug distribution and violent crime in the cities?
8. How are the police corrupted by the illicit drug economy?
9. Why is crack a "significant factor" in the spread of sexually transmitted diseases and AIDS?
10. How has the "crack epidemic" differed from other drug epidemics?
11. Does drug abuse really damage the community, or is that claim a hysteria tactic?
12. How are the police limited in their efforts to deal with drug abuse? Can (and should) these limitations be lifted?
13. What is the relationship between AIDS and drug abuse?
14. Would the development of an AIDS vaccine solve the problem? If not, why not?
15. Why do minority children comprise a disproportionately large share of AIDS victims?
16. Is AIDS related to other public health issues? If so, what are they?
17. How can the problem of prostitution and AIDS be dealt with?
18. Do you think the public will be willing to support health care for large numbers of AIDS victims? If not, what will happen to them?

19. How does the pattern of AIDS vary by geographic area?

20. Is it ethical to withhold from doctors and police information on whether a person has AIDS?

21. Should communities be required to provide facilities (such as shelters and public rest rooms) for the homeless? Why or why not?

22. Why isn't the proportion of elderly homeless people larger than it is?

23. What is the difference between the "literally homeless" and the "marginally housed"?

24. Should the homeless be forced to use shelters or take advantage of other programs designed for their safety?

25. What should the police do about homeless people who make a nuisance out of themselves?

REFERENCES

[1] U.S. Department of Health and Human Services, Public Health Service, "Highlights of the 1988 National Household Survey on Drug Abuse" (Rockville, MD: National Institute on Drug Abuse, August 1989).

[2] U.S. Department of Justice, Drug Enforcement Administration, *Drug Enforcement Handbook* (Washington, DC: U.S. Government Printing Office, 1988), 161.

[3] U.S. Department of Justice, Drug Enforcement Administration, *Worldwide Heroin Situation Report* (Washington, DC: U.S. Government Printing Office, January 1990), 38.

[4] U.S. Department of Justice, Drug Enforcement Administration, *Worldwide Heroin Situation Report*, 38.

[5] U.S. Department of Health and Human Services, Public Health Service, "Highlights of the 1988 National Household Survey on Drug Abuse," C-84-3.

[6] U.S. Department of Health and Human Services, Public Health Service, "Highlights of the 1988 National Household Survey on Drug Abuse," 3.

[7] Lloyd D. Johnson, Patrick M. O'Malley and Jerald G. Bachman, U.S. Department of Health and Human Services, National Institute on Drug Abuse, *Illicit Drug Use, Smoking, and Drinking by America's High School Students, College Students, and Young Adults, 1975-1988* (Washington, DC: U.S. Government Printing Office, 1989), 42, 44, 46.

[8] Johnson, O'Malley and Bachman, *Illicit Drug Use, Smoking, and Drinking by America's High School Students, College Students, and Young Adults, 1975-1988*, 42, 44, 46.

[9] Timothy J. Flanagan and Kathleen Maguire, eds., U.S. Department of Justice, Bureau of Justice Statistics, *Sourcebook of Criminal Justice Statistics 1989* (Washington, DC:

U.S. Government Printing Office, 1990). See Table 3.91, "Reported Drug Use, Alcohol Use, and Cigarette Use Within Last 12 Months Among High School Seniors," (p. 310).

[10] U.S. Department of Health and Human Services, news release, embargoed for release at 10:00 A.M., EST, Monday July 31, 1989.

[11] Christopher A. Innes, U.S. Department of Justice, Office of Justice Programs, Bureau of Justice Statistics, "Drug Use and Crime" (Washington, DC: U.S. Government Printing Office, July 1988), 2.

[12] Innes, "Drug Use and Crime," 2.

[13] P.J. Goldstein, "The Drugs/Violence Nexus: A Tripartite Conceptual Framework," *Journal of Drug Issues* 13 (1985), 493-506.

[14] U.S. Department of Justice, Office of Justice Programs, "1989 Drug Use Forecasting Annual Report" (Washington, DC: U.S. Government Printing Office, June 1990), 2.

[15] Innes, "Drug Use and Crime," 1.

[16] Saundra Torry, "She Smoked Crack, Then Killed Her Children." *The Washington Post,* 6 January 1990, A1, A7.

[17] Innes, "Drug Use and Crime," 1.

[18] Innes, "Drug Use and Crime," 2.

[19] U.S. Department of Justice, Office of Justice Programs, Bureau of Justice Statistics, *Violent Crime in the United States* (Washington, DC: U.S. Government Printing Office, March 1991), 17.

[20] Michael Massing, "Crack's Destructive Sprint Across America," *New York Time Magazine,* 1 October 1989, 38-41.

[21] United States Treasury (Bureau of Alcohol, Tobacco and Firearms), untitled intelligence report, 1988.

[22] Ibid.

[23] U.S. Department of Justice, *Violent Crime in the United States,* 17.

[24] "Dead Zones," *U.S. News and World Report,* 10 April 1989, 20-32.

[25] "Dead Zones," 20-32.

[26] David Musto, as quoted in *A Yale Historian Sniffs Something Familiar in Today's Cocaine Craze,* interview by Maria Wilhelm, in *People,* 24 November 1986, about his book *The American Disease* (Oxford, England: Oxford University Press, 1987).

[27] Tom Morganthau, "Children of the Underclass," *Newsweek,* 11 September 1989, 18.

[28] United States General Accounting Office, *Drug Abuse—The Crack Cocaine Epidemic: Health Consequences and Treatment* (Washington, DC: U.S. Government Printing Office, January 1991), 20.

[29] M.T. Fullilove and Robert E. Fullilove, "Intersecting Epidemics: Black Teen Crack Use and Sexually Transmitted Disease," *Journal of the American Medical Women's Association* 44 (September/October 1989), 147, 151.

30 Marcia Slacum Greene, "Boarder Babies Linger in Hospitals," *The Washington Post*, 11 September 1989, A1, A7.

31 Greene, "Boarder Babies Linger in Hospitals," A1, A7.

32 Juan Williams, "The Real Tragedy of Crack Babies," *The Washington Post*, 30 December 1990, C5.

33 David L. Carter, "An Overview of Drug-Related Misconduct of Police Officers: Drug Abuse and Narcotics Corruption," in *Drugs, Crime and the Criminal Justice System*, ed. Ralph Weisheit (Cincinnati: Anderson Publishing Co., 1990), 79-109.

34 Duane C. McBride and James A. Swartz, "Drugs and Violence in the Age of Crack Cocaine," in *Drugs, Crime and the Criminal Justice System*, ed. Ralph Weisheit (Cincinnati: Anderson Publishing Co., 1990), 158.

35 Mark H. Moore and Mark A.R. Kleiman, "The Police and Drugs," *Perspectives on Policing* (September 1989).

36 For an excellent discussion of the early history of AIDS in America, see Randy Shilts, *And the Band Played On: Politics, People and the AIDS Epidemic* (New York: St. Martin's Press, 1987).

37 "Report of the Second Public Health Service AIDS Prevention and Control Conference," *Public Health Reports* 103, Supp. 1 (1988), 3.

38 Robert C. Gallo, "The AIDS Virus," *Scientific American* 256: 1 (1987), 56.

39 Malcolm Gladwell, "After 10 Years, AIDS Epidemic Shifting to Poor and Dispossessed, *The Washington Post*, 5 June 1991, A3.

40 Donald Hopkins, "AIDS in Minority Populations in the United States," *Public Health Reports* 102, Supp. 6 (November-December 1987), 446-447.

41 J.L. Black, M.P. Dolan, H.A. DeFord, J.A. Rubenstein, W.E. Penk, R. Robinowitz and J.R. Skinner, "Sharing of Needles Among Users of IV Drugs," letter to the *New England Journal of Medicine* 314 (1986), 446-447.

42 D.C. Des Jarlais, S.R. Friedman and D. Strug, "AIDS and Needle Sharing Within the IV-Drug Use Subculture," in *The Social Dimensions of AIDS: Methodology and Theory*, ed. D.A. Feldman and T.M. Johnson (New York: Praeger, 1986); and D.C. Des Jarlais and S.R. Friedman, "HIV Infection and Intravenous Drug Use: Critical Issues in Transmission Dynamics, Infection Outcomes, and Prevention," *Reviews of Infectious Diseases* 10 (1988), 155.

43 See, for example, K.G. Castro, S. Lieb, H.W. Jaffe, J.P. Narkunas, C. Calisher, T. Bush and J.J. Witte, "Transmission of HIV in Belle Glade, Florida: Lessons for Other Communities in the United States," *Science*, 8 January 1988, 193-197; and P.J. Goldstein, *Prostitution and Drugs* (Lexington, MA: Lexington Books, 1981).

44 Charles F. Turner, Heather G. Miller and Lincoln E. Moses, eds., *AIDS—Sexual Behavior and Intravenous Drug Use* (Washington, DC: National Academy Press, 1989), see especially 142-147.

45 Turner et al., *AIDS—Sexual Behavior and Intravenous Drug Use*, 150-153.

[46] Fred J. Hellinger, "National Forecasts of the Medical Care Costs of AIDS: 1988-1992," *Inquiry* 25 (Winter 1988), 469-484.

[47] James A. Inciardi, "AIDS and Drug Use: Implications for Criminal Justice Policy," in *Drugs, Crime and the Criminal Justice System* (Cincinnati: Anderson Publishing Co., 1990), 303.

[48] Gladwell, "After 10 Years, AIDS Epidemic Shifting to Poor and Dispossessed."

[49] Patricia Gadsby, "Mapping the Epidemic: Geography as Destiny," *Discover*, April 1988.

[50] See, for example, David Bigbee, *The Law Enforcement Officer and AIDS*, 3rd ed. (Washington, DC: Federal Bureau of Investigation, U.S. Department of Justice, 1 September 1989).

[51] James D. Wright, "Address Unknown: Homelessness in Contemporary America," *Society* 26:6 (September-October 1989), 45.

[52] Wright, "Address Unknown: Homelessness in Contemporary America," 46-47.

[53] Wright, "Address Unknown: Homelessness in Contemporary America," 47.

[54] Wright, "Address Unknown: Homelessness in Contemporary America," 47.

[55] Wright, "Address Unknown: Homelessness in Contemporary America," 47.

[56] Wright, "Address Unknown: Homelessness in Contemporary America," 47.

[57] For an excellent analysis of this topic, see James D. Wright "The Worthy and Unworthy Homeless," *Society*, July-August 1988, 64-69. The data cited in this section are taken from that source.

[58] Charisse Tia Maria Coston, "The Original Designer Label: Prototypes of New York City's Shopping-Bag Ladies," *Deviant Behavior* 10 (1989), 157-172.

[59] Coston, "The Original Designer Label," 167.

[60] Wright "The Worthy and Unworthy Homeless," 67.

[61] Wright "The Worthy and Unworthy Homeless," 66.

[62] Wright "The Worthy and Unworthy Homeless," 69.

[63] Wright "The Worthy and Unworthy Homeless," 69.

[64] Pamela J. Fischer, "Criminal Activity Among the Homeless: A Study of Arrests in Baltimore," *Hospital and Community Psychiatry* 39:1 (January 1988), 46-51.

[65] Peter Finn, "Dealing With Street People: The Social Service System *Can* Help," *Police Chief* 2 (1988), 47-51.

[66] *Papachristou v. Jacksonville*, 405 U.S. 156 (1972).

[67] Cited in Candace McCoy, "Enforcement Workshop: Policing the Homeless," *Criminal Law Bulletin* 22:3 (1986), 263-274.

[68] McCoy, "Enforcement Workshop," 272.

[69] Barney Melekian, "Police and the Homeless," *FBI Law Enforcement Bulletin* 59:11 (1990), 1-7.

Photo Credit: Frost Publishing Group, Ltd.

Chapter 6

THE POLICE

A Historical Perspective

The police in America are an institutional contradiction. Although uniquely modern, in many ways they are clearly a product of their past. Although they are unlike the police of any other country, their roots are firmly embedded in the history of other nations, including England, Italy and Greece.[1] Because police history is in some ways also the history of government, the distinctive style of government in America has played a major role in shaping our police forces. Since our most direct link to government is at the community level, American police forces have been primarily local institutions and therefore have been most responsive to community pressures and local politics. As the community changes, the police must change with it, and this process has been clearly evident in recent decades.

The word "police" comes from *polis*, a Greek word that refers to both the "city" as a physical place and the "state" as its government. Historically, the main responsibilities of government have been to protect the citizens and provide a safe environment. In its most basic sense, *to police* means *to provide civil government*. Doing so, however, involves a great deal more than simply passing and enforcing laws. To fully understand this we need to look again at the concepts of private and public control.

Until recent times the public control system had relatively little to do with regulating the behavior of individuals. Prior to the industrial revolution, most

155

communities were small and their residents were bound together by common sentiment and shared religious beliefs. Government provided a larger framework by maintaining the prevailing social class system, defending the faith and dealing with foreign affairs. The behavior of individuals was basically regulated by the private control system.

Until the Age of Enlightenment (roughly the eighteenth century), everyday life was heavily influenced by two especially important belief systems: astrology and religion. Indeed, the two were often difficult to separate. Astrologers studied the movements and positions of heavenly bodies and interpreted them in terms of their significance to events on earth. The ability to predict events such as eclipses and floods gave astrologers great power; they were widely respected not only in Europe but in Asia as well. Astrologers divided the heavens into 12 sections corresponding to the 12 constellations along the path the sun appeared to follow. These 12 sections (or "houses") became the zodiac, and each house was seen as having power over some aspect of life.

Astrology was a major influence on man's intellectual development. It is the mother of both astronomy and medicine (the astrological sign of Jupiter, $\, 2\!\!\!\downarrow \,$, is *still* placed at the beginning of a physician's prescriptions). Because they did not have the scientific knowledge commonly taken for granted today, people thought their lives were controlled by external forces. Astrology was seen as a means for understanding those forces.

Religion, which complemented astrology, was the second major belief system that regulated community life. Religion embodies the belief in one or more supreme beings who not only created the world and all of the other heavenly bodies, but who also control the destinies of humankind. The distinction between religion and astrology was that religion dealt with things that were unseen—things that had to be accepted *on faith*. Philosophy is closely related to religion but is based on reason rather than either faith or observable phenomena. The practice of religion is regulated by creeds and rituals that serve to explain the human being's role with respect to all other things. Religion, therefore, defines *morality*, or what is right and wrong in God's scheme of things. The individual's role in a theologically-oriented society is not to decide for himself what is right or wrong, but to accept the church's teachings and live accordingly. Things not understood are not to be questioned, but rather taken on faith.

The interplay between astrology and religion is evident in the explanations given for the plague which swept Europe in the late 1340s. The medical faculty at the University of Paris claimed the plague was caused by a triple conjunction of Saturn, Jupiter and Mars in the fortieth degree of Aquarius (which was supposed to have taken place on March 20, 1345).[2] The common man saw only one explanation: the wrath of God. As historian Barbara Tuchman noted, "Planets might satisfy the learned doctors, but God was closer to the average man." She further noted that some people genuinely thought the plague might even be "God's terminal disappointment with his creature" because of the sins of humankind.[3] It took another 500 years before man, "the sinner," learned that the plague was caused by the bacillus *Pasteurella pestis* and conveyed by fleas carried by rats.

The Protestant Reformation of the seventeenth century, the rise of mercantile capitalism, the age of Political Revolution and the Industrial Revolution changed the foundations upon which these belief systems rested. Ultimately, as man moved into new and challenging forms of social organization, he was freed from the bondage of superstition, ignorance and feudalism. The *polis*—the city—changed in size, scope and function, as well as in complexity. Government shifted to secular leadership as religion, medicine, science and astrology began to go their separate ways. The basis for the authority by which the polis was governed increasingly became that of law rather than custom, superstition or dogma. The use of law to regulate human affairs required three major domains of government. The first consisted of bodies that *made* the laws: parliaments and legislatures. The second consisted of those who *interpreted* the laws: courts and legal tribunals. Finally, the use of law in government required administrators or executives to *discharge* the mandates provided for by the laws. It was not until the emergence of secular law that policing in its most rudimentary form could emerge.

EVOLUTION OF THE POLICE: THE BRITISH HERITAGE

The administration of civil affairs and the enforcement of laws were originally quite synonymous—the responsibilities were carried out by the same officials. One of the earliest of these officials was the "Reeve" or "Shire-reeve," or "Sheriff" as the position came to be called. In England the sheriff was the executive authority of his county and as such was a very important official. He had a number of duties, including attending judges at court, executing writs issued by the courts (and prisoners condemned by them), caring for prisoners awaiting trial or execution, and in some jurisdictions, collecting taxes. The sheriff thus *administered* justice according to the customs of his time, but was not a law enforcement officer by today's definition. Another interesting official was the *coroner*, who, among other things, served as a check on the sheriff. Under certain circumstances, a deceased person's property had to be forfeited to the crown, and it was the coroner's job to determine the cause of death so a proper disposition could be made of property. However, the most important forerunner to the police was the *constable*. In medieval England, a number of officers were elected to serve the local lord in the administration of the affairs of the community. These officials included such colorful characters as the ale-taster, the bread-weigher and the swine-ringer; however, the most important of all was the constable.[4] By the end of the thirteenth century, the constable was recognized by the crown as having a special responsibility for keeping the peace. Actually, the constable was more of what we would consider a district attorney than a police officer because his basic job was to bring complaints before the courts. Critchley sums up early "policing" in England—after the passage of the Statute of Winchester (1285)—in terms of the following basic principles:

> First, it was the duty of everyone to maintain the King's peace, and it was open to any citizen to arrest an offender. Second, the unpaid, part-time constable had a special duty to do so, and in the towns he was assisted in this duty by an inferior officer, the watchman. Third, if the offender was not caught red-handed, hue and cry was to be raised. Fourth, everyone was obliged to keep arms with which to follow the cry when required. Finally, the constable had a duty to present the offender...at court...[5]

Thus, the community was actually "policed" by all of its citizens, with the constable playing more or less an organizing and officiating role. The constable, however, was supposed to ensure that violations would be brought before the court for proper adjudication if they took place. Viewed in this light, he was more an officer of the court than a police officer.

As might be imagined, the job was not a popular one; many sought to avoid having to serve as constable. Over time, the office fell into disrepute, being considered fit only for the inept, incompetent or elderly. Since individual behavior was directed more by the private control system, the constable was needed only in unusual or extraordinary circumstances. The system of parish constables was known in England as the "old police" and is widely regarded as having been very inefficient. It was allowed to persist for over 500 years, until cities began to grow in size and complexity. As this happened, crime and social disorder likewise increased until it reached proportions that could no longer be tolerated. Even such "police" as did exist were quite different in their approach to crime than are the police of today. Police in those days were not public servants in the modern sense; "They were members of a liberal profession who operated on the principle of fee for service. If a man had been robbed, he could go to a magistrate's court like that at Bow Street and hire a police officer to try to get his property back."[6] These police officers worked independently of one another—essentially for fees from clients or rewards from the government. By 1821 the situation in England had reached the following state, as described by a magistrate of the times: "The manner in which hordes of thieves are suffered to prowl about the Metropolis and its neighborhood and rob and maltreat passengers when a crowd is assembled, is a disgrace to our police system. Yet while these things are going on, officers in abundance are loitering about the police offices, waiting for hire. Protection is reserved for individuals who will individually pay for it."[7]

The absence of effective civil police combined with increasingly frequent public riots forced public officials to rely on the military to suppress public disorder. This alarmed many influential thinkers of the time. People such as Patrick Colquhoun, Jeremy Bentham and brothers Henry and John Fielding favored the creation of a civil police to deal with urban disorder. Their recommendations were repeatedly rejected, based on the fear that such a police force would violate English liberty. Ultimately, the fear of riots and recognition of the need for moral reform created a responsive political climate. The result was passage of the Metropolitan Police Act on July 19, 1829, largely through the efforts of the Home Secretary, Sir Robert Peel. The Act created a metropolitan police for London, which was to be divided into 17 police divisions, each under the command of a police superintendent. Each police division had four inspectors and 16 sergeants, and each sergeant was to supervise nine police constables. Each constable was to be armed with a rattle with which he could summon aid and a short "truncheon" which was to be carried concealed beneath the constable's coat. The police were unarmed because their founders wanted them to earn support through respect rather than through force. The English police are (for the most part) still unarmed, although that is likely to change in the near future.[8]

The men recruited for the new police force were required to be under 35 years of age and in good physical condition. Other prerequisites included a height of at least five feet, seven inches, and the ability to read and write. Each applicant had to produce two letters of reference from previous employers. Former watchmen were not accepted into the new police. The pay was low: 19 shillings a week, and almost total control was imposed over the lives of the new policemen. There was also a deliberate policy of not hiring men who had "the rank, habits, or station of gentlemen," thus excluding former military officers or members of the aristocracy.[9] The founders of the Metropolitan Police were Richard Mayne and Charles Rowan, who also served as its first commissioners. They sought to avoid political corruption of the police by keeping its members restricted to the "working class." Although this tactic worked, it had the simultaneous effect of locking police work into the status of a blue-collar occupation, a pattern that has persisted to the present. Finally, at 6:00 p.m. on Tuesday evening, September 29, 1829 the first "new police" marched out of their stations and into the streets of London. On that evening, the police as we know them came into being.

Unfortunately, the new police were not well received. They were widely denounced throughout London as an "outrage and an insult" to the people. Police constables who tried to control traffic were run down and lashed with whips; many others were subjected to unremitting hostility in the form of jeers, insults and taunts. In August of 1830 the first London police constable to be killed in the line of duty met his fate when he was stabbed to death. In 1833 a constable was killed when he charged into a group of rioters; his death was ruled a justifiable homicide (later overturned). The London police persevered; in the words of one historian, "Such were the intolerable conditions in which the Metropolitan Police forged the reputation which, within a few years, was to make the force world-famous. Their imperturbability, courage, good humor, and sense of fair-play won first the admiration of Londoners and then their affection."[10]

It is interesting to note that much of our culture derives from our colonial relationship to England. However, the American colonies declared their independence some 50 years before the Metropolitan Police was established. One can only speculate on how the American police would have developed if the Peelian reform had taken place before America's independence.

POLICE IN AMERICA:
THE POLITICAL ERA (1845-1914)

Even though the colonies severed their political ties with England, Europe's influence on America was felt for many generations. The new nation was composed primarily of small agricultural communities and a few large cities. Few communities had police forces; those that did copied the English constable-watchman system. As in England, these rudimentary police forces were at best only marginally effective. Conditions in the two countries were quite different, and as a result their respective police forces evolved differently.

Unlike England, America was a frontier country. People could move about as they wished, and the new nation—blessed with rich natural resources and a constantly expanding frontier—offered both land and opportunity. In addition, social conventions were different. The American rejection of a class system based on aristocracy opened the door to opportunity for generations of newcomers. However, economic opportunity also provided conditions that bred violence and disorder. The new frontier was not handed over freely by its previous tenants. The new cities became places of diversity, reflecting the whole panorama of immigration in which there were "divisions not only between classes, but also between whites and blacks, Irish and native born, Protestant and Catholic, and beer drinkers and prohibitionists." And as Richardson notes, "These political and social cleavages profoundly affected the development of urban police in the United States."[11]

As the urban population expanded, these "political and social cleavages" were aggravated by inadequate housing, crowding, poverty, discrimination and other social ills. Slums emerged and became breeding grounds for crime and disorder. By the middle of the nineteenth century it became apparent that some kind of formal police agency was essential if cities were to cope with the increasing disorder. The old watch-and-ward systems were obviously inadequate. Something new had to be done. State legislatures met the problem by authorizing cities to create municipal police departments. (During the nineteenth century, American cities were considered to be instrumentalities of state legislatures; the idea of home rule charters was not yet popular.) This allowed state governments to impose political control over how cities were to police themselves without having to pay the cost (which was met out of local revenues). The first unified, 24-hour municipal police department was created in 1845 when New York City merged its separate day and night watches into a single police department. Philadelphia did the same in 1848, as did Boston in 1854. Within a few years police departments appeared in most major cities.

Early police departments were quite different from those of today. At first, police officers did not wear uniforms, although uniforms became the rule rather than the exception by the 1860s. In order to identify themselves, New York City police officers were supposed to wear a small badge in the shape of a star, and for this reason they were sometimes called "star police."[12] Since the shaping of police departments was profoundly influenced by local politics, it should come as no surprise that politics quickly became a part of all aspects of the fledgling departments. Political influence played a role in determining who was hired, the type of assignment an officer received, and whether he would be selected for promotion. Fogelson pointed this out clearly when he wrote:

> ...[W]hat set the American police apart from the French, German, and British police was not so much their commitment to local control, a civilian orientation, and a responsive style *as their relationship with the political machine.* The machine was urban America's outstanding contribution to the art of municipal government. Exemplified by Tammany Hall, it emerged in New York, Philadelphia, and other eastern cities in the early and middle nineteenth century and in Chicago, Kansas City, San Francisco, and other western cities not long after [emphasis added].[13]

Although American police were armed and had a ranked structure, they were organized with a distinctively civilian orientation. Few would have mistaken them for military personnel. At first the police had only a vague idea of what it was they were supposed to do. The maintenance of order was probably the most important task of the police officer. The individual officer did it by physically walking a "beat" and keeping a watchful eye. They were not used for fire suppression or for the administration of prisons, nor were they given any judicial duties (all of which are common police functions in other countries). They were, however, used for a wide range of public duties:

In the absence of other specialized public bureaucracies, the authorities found
the temptation almost irresistible to transform the police departments into
catchall health, welfare, and law enforcement agencies. Hence the police
cleaned streets and inspected boilers in New York, distributed supplies to the
poor in Baltimore, accommodated the homeless in Philadelphia, investigated
vegetable markets in St. Louis, operated emergency ambulances in Boston,
and attempted to curb crime in all these cities. By the end of the century most
departments engaged in a wide range of activities other than keeping the
peace.[14]

The police kept close contact with the people of the city—and so did the
politicians. Today most of us only see politicians on television or hear from
them at election time. In the nineteenth century politicians were in much closer
contact with their constituents. Ward leaders made it their business to know
who needed what and to help them get it. After all, this was how one got
elected. Since the job of police officer had become desirable because it provided a relatively good income and a fair amount of job security, local politicians played a key role in helping would-be police officers land their jobs. Once
appointed, they were expected to remember their benefactors, especially at election time: "Empowered to preserve order at the polls, the patrolmen decided
whether or not to eject repeaters from the lines, protect voters from the thugs,
and respond to complaints by poll watchers and ballot clerks. If the officers
abused their authority, the citizens had little or no recourse...."[15] Naturally, the
police became closely entwined with politicians, creating problems that would
take decades to change.

Another problem soon developed. In the late nineteenth century, moralistic
civic leaders introduced legislation that sought to control behavior—particularly
with respect to the regulation of drinking, gambling and sex. The police were
responsible for enforcing these laws, pitting them against politicians who tried
to influence police discretion. Worse yet, entrepreneurs operating on the wrong
side of the law were more than willing to bribe the police directly. The problem
of corruption emerged and has never been completely eradicated.

The police were gradually shaped by the nature of their cities and the conditions of their work. They learned that the highly moralistic laws they were
expected to enforce demanded more than they could give. It also became clear
that although they were people of the community, they grew apart from it in the
course of their duties. By the end of the nineteenth century, police departments
had become highly inbred. New members entered at the lowest level and had to
work their way up through the ranks before attaining command positions (just as
they do now). In the process they were shaped by the organizational culture of
the department. Over time police departments became *instruments* for their officers—providing them security, acceptance and a place in life. At the same
time, police departments also became *institutions*, developing a number of

characteristics that have persisted over time and have become part of the legacy of contemporary police departments.

During the political era, police operations and administration reflected the political context of the times. As might be expected, the principal roles of the police included a combination of crime control, order maintenance and social services. Since they were established and operated at the community level, American police forces were decentralized and geographically dispersed. As an agency of local government, the police maintained close, personal contact with members of the community. Demands for police services came primarily from two sources: politicians interested in meeting constituent needs, and individuals who wanted the police to take some action on their behalf. The approach to policing was simple: officers worked foot patrols and dealt with problems as they encountered them. In some cases the police also provided basic investigative services. Their organizational structure and methods of operation were accepted with little criticism as long as they satisfied political and community leaders. Unfortunately, this grass-roots intimacy with the community and the necessity of appeasing politicians made the police vulnerable to corruption. Although they were relatively effective during the political era, a number of important factors forced reform.

POLICE IN AMERICA:
THE REFORM ERA (1914-1968)

Decisions produce consequences, some of which are unintended and sometimes these unintended consequences have a greater influence on future events than would be expected. This has been especially true of the police in America. Their organization, administration and performance of duties produced consequences that remain with us to the present. They also produced unintended consequences that forced reform. The police departments that emerged during the political era were products of the conditions of the times. Not only were the police driven by political and community pressures, they were also severely limited by the technology available to them. In spite of these limitations they had considerable freedom in how they could perform their duties. As the United States entered the twentieth century, all of this changed.

Before looking at the major events that drove police reform, a word of caution is in order. It is difficult to separate oneself from the present when looking at the past. It is tempting to look at the police of a century ago in light of today's expectations and to be highly critical of what we find. However, we are talking about two very different worlds. Police officers who walked foot beats in the reform era did so in cities still lighted by gas. They knew virtually nothing about things we take for granted, including fingerprinting, ballistics, the forensic sciences, telecommunications or even squad cars. The procedural law that governed their methods was far less restrictive. Although they were ill-educated and poorly led, they were tough and pragmatic. They also tended to be white males from predominantly Anglo-Saxon backgrounds—men who embraced the prejudices and stereotypes readily accepted by their contemporaries. These prejudices became an integral part of the police culture and were reflected in who was let into (or kept out of) the police forces, as well as how police services were delivered and who received them. Some departments, including New York and Boston, became ethnic enclaves (for the Irish) and were the vehicle by which immigrants and sons of immigrants found their place in America. They were men of their times, and as times changed so did the circumstances that defined police work. Those changes produced a reform era which extended into the very recent past.

The reform era was the product of three major forces. It was ushered in by the courts and the increasingly important role played by their decisions. Second, changes in local government (which have been considerable in the present century) likewise have had a profound impact on how the police are administered and managed. The rise of professional public administration and the emergence of management as a discipline are seldom fully appreciated for the important role they have played in the era of police reform. Third, advances in technology have had a dramatic impact on the tools available to the police and have extended their capabilities beyond anything that could have been imagined in the political era.

REFORM AND THE LAW: THE ROLE OF THE COURTS [16]

During the political era, most crimes were reported directly to the police officer on the beat. Before the age of telephones and radios it was necessary for individual police officers to physically walk their beats. This allowed them to see what was going on and made them available to citizens who wished to report crimes or other problems.[17] Moreover, police officers had to deal with problems as they encountered them. Prior to the reform era, police work typically involved dealing with problems at their source. This often amounted to a well-placed rap with a nightstick, a swift kick in the pants or a stern "talking-to," replete with warnings and threats. It also included taking drunks and vagrants to the city limits and warning them not to return. Police officers viewed this kind of "corrective action" as a good way of maintaining order without having to tie the system up unnecessarily. Although the police still have a great deal of discretionary latitude, legal reforms have dramatically reduced their ability to take the law into their own hands.

In the "old days," developing suspects was usually easy. Gathering evidence, however, was a different matter. The best source of evidence was the suspect himself, and the most frequently used law enforcement techniques were search, seizure and interrogation. The limitations on search and seizure were extremely lax by today's standards, and suspects who confessed made it easy to secure a conviction. The police had to rely on interrogations in the early years because physical evidence was limited. Forensic science was in its earliest stages and its application was seldom seen on the streets; indeed, police photography at the turn of the century was an innovative and exciting advancement. The police did not routinely collect blood samples, tool marks or trace evidence for comparison in a laboratory. What passed for evidence in those days was much less sophisticated: a gun, a knife or perhaps an article of clothing left at the crime scene. Therefore, the best means of obtaining evidence was to interrogate suspects, and some of those interrogations were severe indeed. Consider the following comment (made in 1910 by the Chief of the Memphis Police Department at a meeting of police chiefs) concerning an incident that had taken place several years earlier:

> ...[H]e began questioning the man, who refused to divulge his name, where he was from, where he roomed, or who is confederate was....He was very abusive to Captain O'Haver, so I was informed the next day, and that officer finally concluded that the Police Station proper was too public a place for him to further question the thief, and took him downstairs into the cellar. What followed I don't know, but Captain O'Haver reported the next day that he succeeded in getting from him where he roomed, the description of his partner....They were convicted and each sentenced to ten years in the Tennessee Penitentiary. Now I don't know what Captain O'Haver did to secure the information he desired....[As] I said to Captain O'Haver the next morning; whatever you did was right. You may call it whatever you please, the 'Third Degree' or any other kind of degree, but it had the desired effect. No innocent man suffered and the guilty parties were punished.[18]

We will never know the number of cases solved during the early years of this century as a result of torture, "third-degree" methods or illegal arrests perpetrated by the police. It is not even possible to speculate on what proportion of successful convictions involved tactics of this type, although it was probably much higher than most people would like to believe. Rampant abuse of police authority to secure evidence led to a series of court rulings that limited the methods the police could use. Ultimately, one of the most significant developments in law enforcement was the strengthening of individual rights through the application of constitutional law. This has been done by the appellate courts through the review of cases in which the conduct of the police has been challenged on constitutional grounds.

Because American police departments are decentralized, only the courts have been in a position to bring about wide-scale changes in police conduct. This is especially true of the Supreme Court, whose role of judicial review was established in the historic case of *Marbury v. Madison* in 1803. The Supreme Court's application of the concept of judicial review to the acts of state legislatures and the decisions of state courts has made it the highest court in the land. During the reform era, police tactics were dramatically redefined by court rulings dealing with due process and individual protection, the right to counsel, unreasonable searches and seizures, and compulsory self-incrimination. The application of constitutional law by the Supreme Court has probably been the single most important factor in police reform during this century.

The first 10 amendments to the Constitution are known as the Bill of Rights. They were adopted in 1791 as a limitation on the United States government. When they were ratified, they did not (and were not intended to) apply to the states. One of the most important amendments in the Bill of Rights is the Fifth Amendment, which provides safeguards for persons accused of crimes. Among other things, it states that no person shall be compelled in any criminal case to be a witness against himself, nor shall any person be deprived of life, liberty or property without due process of law. However, in 1833 the Supreme Court held that the Fifth Amendment was a restraint on the federal government only, and not on the states.[19] It was not until 1868 (when the Fourteenth Amendment was passed) that a federal constitutional provision concerning due process became applicable to the states. The Fourteenth Amendment provides, in part: "...nor shall any state deprive any person of life, liberty, or property, without due process of law." The definition of "due process of law" was never defined and has been the source of much litigation since the passage of the amendment.

The relationship between the Fifth and Fourteenth Amendments is of fundamental importance to the criminal justice system. When the Fourteenth Amendment was ratified, it did not embrace the rights spelled out in the Fifth Amendment, and the Supreme Court was quickly faced with having to determine whether the due process clause of the Fourteenth Amendment protected those individual rights against the *state* in the same manner that the Bill of Rights protected them against the *federal* government. At first the Supreme Court was reluctant to apply federal standards in state cases; however, through a series of decisions it has reversed its earlier position. By the 1960s the trend was unmistakably clear. In *Mapp v. Ohio* the Supreme Court extended the protection of the Fourth Amendment (prohibiting unreasonable searches and seizures) to the states and made it clear that federal courts would establish minimum standards in determining the legality of searches and seizures;[20] in *Gideon v. Wainwright* the Sixth Amendment right to counsel was made binding on the states;[21] and the Fifth Amendment prohibition against self-incrimination was likewise applied to the states in *Malloy v. Hogan*.[22] Thus, today most of the protections in the Bill of Rights apply to the states by virtue of the Fourteenth Amendment.

One of the most significant legal shifts affecting law enforcement has been this "absorption" of the Bill of Rights. The continuing legal scrutiny of the police by both federal and state courts has thus limited what the police can do. Some claim that this has "handcuffed" them; others claim that it has reduced serious abuse of police authority. It has certainly made law enforcement a much more legally demanding job and placed a greater burden on individual police officers. Many of these court decisions have resulted in the release of people convicted or accused of serious crimes, and this has appalled and angered many private citizens. But these same decisions have also forced the police to be more circumspect in their tactics and to place a much greater emphasis on training and supervision. Although it may be more difficult to arrest suspects or to obtain evidence, the use of sweat-boxes, the third degree, unlawful searches and seizures, and other gross violations of individual rights have gone the way of the gaslight. Now suspects are advised of their rights, legal counsel is made available and strong basic safeguards of individual liberties protect *all* citizens. When police abuses do occur, they tend to be the exception rather than the rule. The fact that they generate considerable publicity is evidence of their rejection by both the public and the police. The following widely publicized episode illustrates the point:

> It began with wailing police cars chasing a motorist through the night, cornering his car in a Los Angeles suburb and surrounding the driver as he stepped into the street. A sergeant fired a 50,000-volt Taser stun gun at the unarmed black man, then three officers took turns kicking him and smashing him in the head, neck, kidneys and legs with their truncheons. A hovering helicopter bathed the scene in a floodlight as 11 other policemen looked on. When the beating was over, Rodney King, 25, an unemployed construction worker, had suffered 11 fractures in his skull, a crushed cheekbone, a broken ankle, internal injuries, a burn on his chest and some brain damage.[23]

What made this event so notorious was that a bystander videotaped two minutes of the beating. The video was widely shown on national television and produced a thunderous outrage. The conduct of the offending police officers was criticized by police officers and private citizens alike. The fury provoked by the beating was minor, however, compared to the public's reaction to the subsequent acquittal of the police officers after trial on a variety of charges relating to the assault. In a poll taken after the acquittal, 92 percent of the blacks and 73 percent of the whites questioned did not think that the verdict was justified.[24] The public's anger rested on the premise that the police are supposed to be enforcers of the law, not a force above it. It is thus evident that, even though abuse of authority by the police still occurs, it is no longer accepted by the public as part of the cost of doing business.

MUNICIPAL REFORM:
THE RISE OF PUBLIC ADMINISTRATION

Police services in America historically have been provided by *municipal* departments. Although the number of federal and state law enforcement agencies has grown tremendously in this century, the focal point of police work remains at the local level. As of 1990 approximately 12,400 police agencies employed 523,262 officers and 190,998 civilians, and provided law enforcement services to over 233 million Americans.[25]

To fully understand police reform, it is important to appreciate the relationship between police departments and the municipal governments of which they are a part. The process of local government itself has evolved over the years, going from government by political elites in George Washington's time through the system of spoils to the current management by professional public administrators.[26] The police were established during the turbulent years of the "spoils system," which began with Andrew Jackson's inauguration as president in 1829 and lasted until the turn of the century.

The rise of cities in America began in earnest after the Civil War, when the mechanization of agriculture increased the nation's food supply while freeing large numbers of people for the burgeoning urban industries. This was the age of the Industrial Revolution, when steam was harnessed and factories quickly took advantage of a labor pool consisting of both immigrants and native-born Americans. The railroads vitalized transportation, enabling goods to be shipped across the country. They acted as two-way lifelines between the cities and the rest of the country, and reduced dependency on the traditional port cities. The population of New York City quadrupled from 1860 to 1910, while Philadelphia's population tripled during the same period. Urbanization was not limited to the older seaport cities. Fueled by more than 200,000 immigrants each year between 1866 and 1917, cities and towns across the country blossomed and were connected with one another by railroads.[27]

In this "rough-and-tumble" period, public service was synonymous with politics. The cities were firmly controlled by the parties in power and the public purse was in the hands of politicians, who elevated to a fine art the use of graft, bribery and outright theft. Indeed, political corruption was the hallmark of local government—especially in the larger cities. As cities swelled with recent arrivals, the need for public services grew rapidly, and the spoils system enabled corrupt politicians to profit enormously. Politicians conspired with business groups to defraud taxpayers through building contracts, civil engineering construction projects and the purchase of supplies and commodities. Utility franchises were obtained through bribes and kickbacks, and illegal vice was protected by the police at the behest of either politicians (to whom they owed loyalty for their jobs) or criminals (who simply paid them for protection). Countless numbers of inept and unqualified people were put on the public payroll in return for political support. The political "machine" controlled city hall; as they gained ill-gotten fortunes, they delivered jobs and services to their constituents. Although there were numerous attempts at reform—and corrupt politicians were regularly lampooned in the press—the problem persisted.

One of the most important initial reform efforts came at the federal level, but eventually had a significant impact on the cities. The question of civil service reform had been an important issue since the 1870s, but no substantive action was taken until President Garfield was assassinated in 1881. Spurred by the exposure of frauds in the Post Office Department and Garfield's assassination by a would-be office holder, Congress passed the Civil Service (Pendleton) Act in 1883. This Act created a Civil Service Commission consisting of three commissioners who were required to draw up rules for competitive examinations for certain federal positions. The rules were, among other things, to exclude "drunkards" and give military veterans preference in hiring. They also had to apportion government jobs in the District of Columbia fairly among citizens of various states and were required to provide civil servants with certain protections. It was an important step because it marked the beginning of a movement away from the spoils system by emphasizing *merit* over *connections* in the granting of government employment.

Four years later (in 1887), Woodrow Wilson wrote an article now considered to be one of the classics in public administration.[28] In it he noted that, "It is getting harder to run a constitution than to frame one." He called for "...a science of administration which shall seek to straighten the paths of government, to make its business less unbusinesslike, [and] to strengthen and purify its organization...." Wilson's central thesis was that public administration should be "outside the proper sphere of politics." It was his belief that ours had been a history of legislative oversight and not "of progress in governmental organization." This was the beginning of a movement to remove politics from administration and to establish professional public administration.

The field of public administration, in its infancy at the turn of the century, looked to business for conceptual guidance. Public administrators quickly adopted the principles of "scientific management" as the best way of doing the job with the least resources. The emphasis on efficiency was both a tacit rejection of political corruption and an effort to establish accountability in local government. The movement was led by the New York Bureau of Municipal Research, which was founded in 1906. This organization, like others that copied it, sought ways of applying scientific management to the public sector to increase efficiency and reduce political abuse. It was during this period that the concept of the "city manager" emerged and the profession of public administration was first defined.

As municipalities struggled to move away from the spoils system and toward professional public administration, the police were likewise forced to change, although their reforms were much slower in developing. Early voices included August Vollmer, the Chief of Police of Berkeley, California, and his protégé, Orlando W. Wilson. Perhaps the most important reformer was J. Edgar Hoover, who took over the Justice Department's inefficient and discredited Bureau of Investigation and transformed it into a model law enforcement agency: the Federal Bureau of Investigation. Hoover emphasized high standards in recruiting and training, and encouraged the use of the most advanced scientific techniques available in the fight against crime. He cultivated a public image of integrity and competence for his agency and offered a wide range of technical assistance to local law enforcement agencies. Hoover's efforts had a direct impact on local police departments. "Struggling as they were with reputations for corruption, brutality, unfairness, and downright incompetence, municipal police reformers found Hoover's path a compelling one. Instructed by O.W. Wilson's texts on police administration, they began to shape an organizational strategy for urban police analogous to the one pursued by the FBI."[29]

Reformers sought to break the ties between police and politicians by implementing civil service reforms that eliminated patronage. In many cities police chiefs were given considerable autonomy to eliminate their dependence on political pressures. These police reforms fit hand-in-glove with the reform movement in public administration. They were readily accepted because they were seen as improving police efficiency and reducing corruption. As the police became more autonomous, they sought to professionalize their role by basing their operations on the narrow enforcement of criminal law. Although these efforts achieved their intended goals, they also resulted in some unintended consequences. For one thing, the police became much more isolated from both citizens and mainstream public administration. Attempts to influence how they operated were quickly criticized as unwarranted interference. They were seen either as interventions by those not knowing what they were doing or as efforts to bring the police back under the control of politicians. Police departments became more and more insular, not only defining their own operations but providing their own administration as well. As a result, police departments became almost totally autonomous.[30] Police administrators were selected from those who had come up through the ranks and few were educated beyond high school. Although some had administrative talent, most did not—and their generally conservative style of administration served as a damper on change. This did not change until the urban riots of the 1960s and the passage of the Omnibus Crime Control and Safe Streets Act of 1968 (which arbitrarily marked the end of the reform era of American police). The emphasis on *law enforcement* as the pinnacle of police work lead departments away from many of the services they had previously performed and further isolated them from much of the community.

REFORM AND TECHNOLOGY:
A RENAISSANCE FOR THE POLICE

Technology has been the driving force behind the development of modern society. From the harnessing of steam to the development of nuclear energy, technology has shaped our lives in ways too numerous to count. Technology not only has created entirely new kinds of work (e.g., computer programming), it also has altered how more traditional kinds of work are accomplished. This is especially true of the police. They have undergone a technological renaissance during the present century; it has been particularly evident in three areas: transportation, communications and forensic science.

Transportation

Most of the major developments in the history of transportation have occurred in the last 200 years. Prior to the invention of the steam engine by James Watt in 1765, land transportation depended on animal power while water transportation relied on favorable winds and currents. Both land and water transportation were slow, inefficient and often fraught with danger. The harnessing of steam in the nineteenth century dramatically altered the technology of transportation. Initially it facilitated the development of steamships and railroads that shortened travel time and increased the volume of goods that could be shipped. It also enabled travel between points previously inaccessible to one another. Moreover, the use of steam was a catalyst for further technological advances. For example, it quickly produced a need for vessels better suited to accommodate steam boilers and other machinery. The outcome was a revolution in marine and naval engineering, with rapid advances in hull design that resulted in a transition from wooden ships to ironclads and finally to ships made of steel. Experimentation in engine technology led to the development of the compound reciprocating steam engine, and eventually the steam turbine. By the end of the last century, the diesel engine was perfected. Just as sailing ships were replaced first by steamships and then by vessels powered by diesel engines, steam locomotives were also replaced by diesel engines, thereby increasing their efficiency and lowering their operating cost. The world very quickly became a much smaller place.

Although ships and trains moved large numbers of people and massive quantities of goods, individuals continued to rely on shoe leather and animals for short-distance, local transportation until the development of the automobile. In 1887 Gottlieb Daimler developed a gasoline engine for a motor vehicle; eight years later Charles and Frank Duryea established the first American automobile company. Automobiles were largely novelties until 1914, when Henry Ford introduced the assembly line to manufacture his Model T, the car that brought the automobile to the "great multitude." The automobile changed America in profound ways, including how the police operated and the circumstances under which they came into contact with their communities.

When police departments first emerged during the political era, officers walked foot beats. They did so for obvious reasons: it was the easiest way to get around, it did not cost anything, and it was just about the only way to bring the officers into contact with their clientele. The easily identifiable police officer was available to the residents of his "beat" and was expected to deal with most of the problems brought to his attention. Although some officers rode bicycles or horses, the "neighborhood cop" was typically the one who walked the beat. an officer's beat was determined by the amount of physical space he could reasonably be expected to cover. It varied by population density and geographic features.

Police departments were quick to appreciate the potential of the automobile. In 1904 the Indianapolis police department replaced its horses with automobiles. Rather than use their cars for patrol duties, the police at first used them to respond to emergencies as they were reported—much like the fire department does today. However, as the reform era progressed, administrators were eager to replace foot patrols with officers who worked out of squad cars. This was seen as beneficial for several reasons. First, it lessened the intimacy of contact between police officers and citizens, and thereby reduced opportunities for corruption. Second, police cars were seen by specialists in police management as a better way of allocating manpower. Two police officers working in a car could cover a much larger area than the same two officers could on separate foot beats. As the use of police cars became more widespread, a tactical philosophy emerged to further justify their use. O.W. Wilson formulated the concept of *preventive patrol*, according to which the police were to drive conspicuously marked cars.[31] Wilson felt that by having the police randomly patrol the city in marked cars they would generate a feeling of police omnipresence that would deter crime and reassure the public. The concept of preventive patrol also assumed that police cars could facilitate the patrolling of high-risk areas and the interdiction of crimes in progress. Interestingly, the reform procedure (preventive patrol) merely applied a new technology (automobiles) to an established procedure (assigning uniformed officers to a specific area). The automobile quickly became the keystone of police operations. As Moore et al. have noted, professional crime-fighting came to rely predominantly on three tactics: (1) motorized patrol; (2) rapid response to calls for service; and (3) retrospective investigation of crimes. However, as we will see later there are grounds to question the validity of this approach.[32]

The automobile had another profound impact on the police: it brought them into frequent and regular contact with "ordinary" citizens through traffic law enforcement. Unfortunately, this had the unintended consequence of forcing them into an adversarial relationship with ordinarily law-abiding citizens.[33] Since traffic infractions are seldom reported by the public, their enforcement is basically the application of police-invoked rules, and its intensity is more often a consequence of departmental policy than objective need.[34] As Wilson notes, "The traffic violator is, of course, the easiest offender for the patrolman to apprehend and he can be apprehended in large numbers if departmental policies require it."[35] Most citizens are well aware of this, and many resent how the police perform this function. Traffic law enforcement became an important part of the reform movement, but not without consequences that endure to the present. As Fogelson noted, "By requiring the police to act against ordinarily law-abiding citizens, the reformers unwittingly deprived the officers of an invaluable source of public support that might have alleviated their deep-seated feeling of alienation and persecution."[36]

The automobile has become a mobile office for the police. Now that patrol areas are larger than foot beats and cars contain equipment, police officers generally are expected to stay in their cars unless specific circumstances dictate otherwise. The cost of this increased mobility is a diminished contact with the public. Most patrol officers now have virtually no contact with the public other than traffic stops or encounters arising out of a request for service. The impact of the automobile on policing is a classic case study in how technology has become an engine of reform.

Communications

When most of the older American police departments were established, telegraphy was already in widespread use. Many departments used telegraph systems to connect their headquarters with precinct stations and call boxes that were strategically located throughout the city. Many cities also employed the Gamewell Communications System, by which police officers communicated with their headquarters by sending coded telegraph messages from "Gamewell boxes" located on their beats. Although telegraphy was an important communications medium, it had limitations (such as requiring knowledge of code) that made it impractical for use by beat cops. What was needed was some means of voice communication between people at different locations.[37]

This breakthrough was to come through the work of people studying improved methods of telegraphy—in particular, Alexander Graham Bell, a young Scottish professor of "vocal physiology" who had a passion for teaching the deaf. Bell was especially interested in the physiology of acoustics, through which he hoped to develop improved methods for teaching the deaf. He experimented with devices for transcribing tone vibrations electrically in hopes of developing a "speaking telegraph" that used electrified metal discs to convert sound waves into electrical impulses and vice versa. In 1875 he was granted a patent for a harmonic telegraph, a device for sending multiple messages over the same wire. Concerned over its lack of acceptance, Bell continued with his experiments. On March 10, 1876 he spoke into one of his transmitting devices saying, "Mr. Watson, come here; I want you." His assistant, Thomas A. Watson, was at a receiver in another room and heard what is now regarded as the first telephone call. A little over a year later, in July of 1877, the Bell Telephone Company was established; in 1880 it became the American Bell Telephone Company. In 1899 the American Bell Telephone Company conveyed its assets to a new central organization, the American Telephone and Telegraph Company (A, T & T), which developed the national telephone system familiar to all of us.[38]

Because the telephone is such a common part of our daily lives, it is easy to overlook; yet it is a technological development of the most profound importance. Although originally regarded as a novelty, its value was quickly realized and within a single generation, the nation was instantaneously connected by Bell's "long lines." At first, telephones were expensive to use and not readily available, especially in rural areas. However, the police in urban areas were quick to adapt telephones to their work. In some cities, police "call boxes" replaced Gamewell boxes on foot beats. The call box key became as essential to the police officer as a gun and badge. Big-city police officers were required to use call boxes to contact their headquarters at regular intervals. These boxes served several purposes. First, central police telephone operators could inform officers of things that needed to be done in their sectors. This was the origin of the police dispatcher and is the reason why an assignment is still referred to as a "call." Second, call boxes enabled police officers to contact their headquarters to report problems or request assistance. Finally, call boxes were management tools: by requiring officers to check in at periodic intervals, supervisors could be certain that the officers were not sleeping or "goofing off."

The system's utility was greatly enhanced as telephones were installed in private residences. This enabled people to call police or fire departments to report emergencies as they occurred, thereby reducing response time. The simultaneous development of the automobile and telephone (and later the radio) thus revolutionized police work. The reactive capability of the police was extended beyond anything previously imagined and an entirely new actor emerged: the anonymous complainant. By using the telephone, people could contact the police without having to reveal their identity, thus enabling them to make anonymous complaints about neighbors. This in turn facilitated the development of the police as an *order maintenance* agency as well as a *law enforcement* agency. Although the police had previously performed this role, it had been based on events they discovered themselves. The telephone extended the process by enabling private citizens to report directly.

Since 1937 citizens in the United Kingdom have been able to report an emergency by dialing "999." In 1967 a resolution was introduced in the United States Congress to establish separate nationwide emergency fire and police telephone numbers. In the following year, Huntington, Indiana became the first city to install a "911" system (followed four months later by New York City). The development of a nationwide "911" system necessitated solutions to several major technical problems, all of which have been accomplished. The number "911" was selected because "1" is the first number and "9" is next to "0" and these numbers are supposed to be easy to find even for blind people. The use of "911" has resulted in greater efficiency in getting emergency help and has helped eliminate (or at least greatly reduce) the number of emergencies that are reported to telephone company operators.[39]

Radio communications, like the telephone, are so common and important that they too are taken for granted. The radio, like the telephone, emerged around the close of the last century. The first "wireless telegraph" message, sent in 1895 by Guglielmo Marconi, only covered a distance of about one mile. The human voice was first transmitted by radio in 1906, and after the invention of the audion (forerunner of the modern vacuum tube) by Lee DeForest in 1907, "wireless telephony" became a sensation. In 1910 an Enrico Caruso performance was broadcast from the Metropolitan Opera House to the amazement of radio "hams" and ship radio operators. The first unofficial news broadcast was made by DeForest when he announced the presidential election returns of 1916. The first scheduled radio program in the United States went on the air on November 2, 1920, when Station KDKA of Pittsburgh, Pennsylvania broadcast the election returns in the presidential election. On July 2, 1921, the first sports event broadcast by radio was an on-the-air, round-by-round description (by RCA) of the Dempsey-Carpentier fight in Jersey City, New Jersey, disseminated to an estimated audience of 300,000 listeners.

In the years immediately following World War I, efforts were made to develop radio-telephone communications for mobile units (i.e., cars, trucks and trains). One of the first applications was pioneered by the Detroit Police Department in 1921 "...to be used to send broadcast descriptions of escaped criminals, license numbers of stolen automobiles and other police information."[40] The Detroit Police Department operated its radio under an amateur license and had to go through a series of license changes before eventually obtaining a limited commercial license (which required them to broadcast entertainment during regular hours, with police calls interspersed as required).[41] At first there were one-way communications by which a police dispatcher could communicate with police cars that could receive but not send messages. Detroit had considerable difficulty with its equipment and even temporarily closed down its radio room. However, with persistent efforts these problems were overcome and the police department went back on the air—permanently—on April 7, 1928.

The second police department to go on the air was Cleveland, followed soon thereafter by many others. Technology improved rapidly, and in 1939 the Federal Communications Commission authorized 29 VHF channels for police use and further defined the licensing of emergency communications. After the Connecticut State Police pioneered the use of two-way radios, their use spread throughout the country as municipal police departments recognized their value. Although two-way radios were quickly adopted by larger departments, because of their cost they did not become universal until the early 1950s. Today virtually all police departments use two-way radios and are linked by inter-city frequencies that enable them to communicate instantly with any other department in the nation.

The computer, probably the most revolutionary technological innovation in communications, arrived at the tail end of the reform period. Although computers are not in and of themselves a communications medium, they have completely altered those that are—including radios and telephones. Like earlier technological innovations, the computer has changed the environment in which the police work. It has revolutionized the flow of information and enabled law enforcement agencies to conduct highly sophisticated analyses of criminal events and personalities. Computers have revolutionized communications and dispatching systems; their application to both administration and operations has redefined the nature of police work, especially in the larger departments.[42]

Forensic Science

The application of science to legal problems is known as *forensic science*. Although science has always had a law enforcement application, it was only toward the end of the nineteenth century that scientists in a variety of disciplines developed techniques and procedures that were recognized as being of great value to law enforcement. For example, the police were especially interested in developing a reliable method for accurately identifying people (especially criminals). Prior to the turn of the century, many detectives depended on memory to recall individuals whose photographs they had studied in the "rogues gallery." In 1879 French anthropologist Alphonse Bertillon developed an identification system based on three principles: (1) the near-absolute fixity of the human bone structure from the twentieth year of age; (2) the extreme diversity of dimensions in the human skeleton, comparing one subject with another; and (3) the ease and relative precision with which certain dimensions of the skeleton can be measured on living people.[43] Bertillon developed a successful system of physical measurements that quickly became popular in the United States, Europe and South America. Although Bertillon's system (anthropometry) did identify people, it was soon displaced by fingerprinting, a technique that was easier and more reliable, and which not only identified people but also enabled the police to link offenders with crimes.

Fingerprinting was developed by several people working largely independently of one another. Dr. Henry Faulds, a Scottish physician living in Japan, became interested in "finger marks" left on pottery. He recognized the variability among these "skin furrows" and conducted research to see if they were "persistent over time." Based on his findings, he wrote a letter to *Nature* in which he said, "When bloody fingermarks or impression on clay, glass, etc., exist they may lead to the scientific identification of criminals. Already I have had experience in two such cases and found useful evidence from these marks."[44]

Although Faulds became an enthusiastic advocate of fingerprinting, he had little success in getting the police to accept his methods. In 1886, after returning from Japan, he offered to set up an experimental fingerprint office for Scotland Yard at his own expense, but his offer was rejected.[45] Fauld's work was complemented by that of William James Herschel. Herschel's career in the Indian Civil Service gave him the opportunity to study fingerprints and use them extensively for personal identification. Like Faulds, he was rebuffed by local authorities in his effort to establish fingerprinting as an official means of personal identification.

The biggest problem with fingerprints was the lack of a classification system that would enable fingerprints to be catalogued and searched. That problem was solved by Edward Richard Henry, who also spent his career with the Indian Civil Service. Henry's interest in the problem of classifying fingerprints eventually led to the establishment of a system based on five patterns: plain arches, tented arches, radial loops, ulnar loops and whorls. His system was adopted in England in 1901 and shortly thereafter was also accepted in the United States, where it is still in use. Fingerprinting revolutionized police work. It introduced science to law enforcement and in the process solved the problem of personal identification and provided a link between crime scenes and suspects.

In one of the strange quirks of fate, forensic science was advanced at the turn of the century in an unexpected way. A British physician struggling to establish his practice filled his spare time writing about a fictionalized detective. Sir Arthur Conan Doyle's first Sherlock Holmes story, *A Study in Scarlet*, appeared in 1887. Three years later he published *The Sign of the Four* and soon thereafter was able to quit medicine in favor of full-time writing. The Sherlock

Holmes stories caught the public's imagination and focused attention on a scientific approach to police work. It is ironic that Sherlock Holmes was not portrayed as a member of the police but rather as a private detective. Through his use of logic and science, Holmes consistently outperformed the police, whom Doyle portrayed as hidebound, conservative and unimaginative. The public's acceptance of Sherlock Holmes carried with it a demand for more sophisticated police work, which has been met through the application of the forensic sciences.

The FBI pioneered this effort through its crime lab, established in 1932. It is now regarded as one of the most advanced and best equipped forensic laboratories in the world. Utilizing such disciplines as ballistics, chemistry, biology and engineering, the FBI brought science to bear on crime and in the process demonstrated its value in solving crimes. Because the FBI has been willing to do lab work for local police departments at no charge (including providing expert witnesses from the laboratory to testify on their findings), they have contributed immeasurably to the professionalization of police work in general and the application of forensic science in particular. The use of forensics has revolutionized the meaning of physical evidence and produced standards of proof undreamed of during the political era of policing. Initial efforts involved the examination of evidence obtained from crime scenes, suspects or victims, and the subjection of them to rudimentary scientific analysis. One of the earliest applications was *forensic toxicology* (which deals with the identification of toxic substances, usually from body tissues and fluids). Forensic toxicology has enabled scientists to determine if a deceased person has been poisoned, and if so, what substance was responsible for the poisoning.

Forensic pathology is a specialty within medicine that explores issues related to the cause and manner of death or physical trauma. In most jurisdictions the coroner system has given way to the medical examiner system, which employs forensic pathology and biology in the investigation of death cases. The role of the pathologist is critical in death investigations, as the medical examiner is often the official who determines the "manner of death" (that is, whether a death was natural, accidental, homicidal or suicidal). By working closely with law enforcement officials, the medical examiner correlates what is known about the circumstances surrounding the death (or its discovery) with physical evidence from the victim to arrive at an opinion.

The forensic sciences include a number of disciplines, including forensic psychiatry and psychology, forensic anthropology (in which experts provide information—regarding sex, race, age, blood type and time of death—on skeletal remains), forensic odontology (which deals with identification through dental remains and bitemark evidence), questioned documents (which analyzes documents for authenticity) and criminalistics (which deals with such issues as tool mark identification, firearms analysis, explosives, trace evidence, and so on).

The application of science and technology to law enforcement has created a valuable partnership between scientists and the police, resulting in a degree of sophistication impossible to imagine in previous decades.

The technological changes discussed above are only a few of many that have had a major impact on reforming the police. Technology has changed the relationship between the police and such variables as time, space and the flow of information. It has enabled them to do more things better and faster, but it has also contributed to a certain amount of estrangement between the police and the public. This estrangement has been supported by political reforms that sought to professionalize the police and make them less susceptible to corruption and outside influence. To a large extent the police are now driven by their technology, adapting both operations and administration to the tools they use. In the process, the police have evolved dramatically from the days of the beat cop walking gas-lighted streets waiting for his work to come to him.

THE SEARCH FOR IDENTITY
IN THE POST-REFORM ERA (1968 - PRESENT)

The reform era of the police drew to a close during the turbulent decade of the 1960s. Its end is arbitrarily marked by the passage of the Omnibus Crime Control and Safe Streets Act of 1968.[46] The 1960s saw social and political upheaval on an unprecedented scale. Urban riots, political assassinations and the rise of the civil rights movement combined with the highly unpopular war in Vietnam to produce both public protest and a disenchantment with government. A distinctive "counterculture" movement was spawned, particularly among the young. That movement led to widespread questioning of government at all levels as well as a massive repudiation of traditional values.

It began on February 1, 1960, when a group of black college students entered the dining section of a downtown store in Greensboro, North Carolina. In sitting down and asking for service, they challenged the widely practiced custom of refusing lunch counter service "to seated Negroes." They were denied service and the police were called. By February 15, 1960 the protest spread to at least 15 cities in five states—marked by sporadic violence against the protesters as it grew. As the movement took hold, sympathy protests quickly spread among white colleges; by July of 1960, 11 southern states adopted desegregation policies in public accommodations. By October of that year, national chain stores reported that lunch counters in 150 stores in 112 cities had been officially desegregated.

The civil rights movement grew well beyond lunch counters. On September 6, 1960, 12 black students attended the first day of classes at the previously segregated Central High School in Little Rock, Arkansas—marking the start of serious efforts to eliminate segregation in public schools. The following year, Georgia repealed its school desegregation laws. Desegregation of public schools was not popular, however, and was met with massive resistance in many communities. As black children entered previously all-white schools, some white parents pulled their children out of public schools and enrolled them in newly established "private academies" that fell outside the reach of government. The civil rights movement was accompanied by increasingly harsh rhetoric on both sides. Episodes of violence, directed mainly against blacks, were common.

In 1962 President John F. Kennedy was assassinated in Dallas, Texas. In the following year, three civil rights workers from New York were murdered in Mississippi. The first major urban riot erupted in New York City in July of 1964 and was followed by riots in Jersey City and Philadelphia. In 1965 riots erupted in Los Angeles, Cleveland and San Francisco, and the Black Panther movement emerged. On April 4, 1968, civil rights leader Martin Luther King, Jr. was assassinated in Memphis. Race riots followed in many cities (Washington, DC was particularly hard hit). Nine months later, the war in Vietnam reached a crescendo with the grueling Tet offensive. Public disorder was rampant and the police found themselves pitted against civil rights activists, anti-war protesters and college students. They were ill-prepared to cope with either the violence or the social problems producing it.

As the social fabric appeared to be coming unraveled, President Lyndon B. Johnson established a Commission on Law Enforcement and the Administration of Justice to explore the needs of the criminal justice system. The result was the Omnibus Crime Control and Safe Streets Act of 1968, enacted "to assist State and Local governments in reducing the incidence of crime, to increase the effectiveness, fairness, and coordination of law enforcement and criminal justice systems at all levels of government." Title I of the Act established the Law Enforcement Assistance Administration within the Department of Justice. The Law Enforcement Education Program (LEEP) created financial incentives for police officers to earn college degrees. A serious effort was made to upgrade the quality of law enforcement personnel through education, training and technology.

It was painfully clear that society was changing and the old way of doing business would no longer work. The police were particularly impacted because they, like many other social institutions, were a product of their past. As the reform era ended, the police moved into a new era—one that demanded changes not just *by* the police, but *within* their ranks as well. These were changes at the most fundamental levels of their organizational and operational philosophies. The post-reform era is contemporary and will extend into the next century. The police must find ways of accommodating wider community participation, especially by minorities and women. As a civil service institution, they must develop a value system that meets the needs of the public as well as their own.

The post-reform era of policing will probably be the most difficult phase in the evolution of the police in America, for it demands that they find their proper place in a rapidly changing society.

SUMMARY

As a social institution, the police have always been a product of their times. The early police in America evolved out of English customs but were quickly modified by social and economic conditions unique to this country. They quickly became affected by the rapid urbanization of the mid-nineteenth century, evolving as municipal rather than state agencies. Because of this, American police forces historically have been the product of local pressures and urban politics. Since American police departments first emerged during the spoils era of politics, it was only natural that they came to represent political interests and influences. They were deeply influenced by the spoils system and in the process came to be dominated by political powers.

Police reform came about through the simultaneous influence of three forces. The first was the role of the courts in shaping law enforcement practices. A series of court decisions brought the Bill of Rights from the federal to the state level, and in the process revised the procedures by which the police could operate. This went a long way toward standardizing law enforcement practices and ultimately produced a more fair and equitable law enforcement environment. At the same time, the spoils era of politics was replaced by professional public administration and the rise of an administrative class. Although the police were not quick to adopt "scientific management," they were drawn into municipal reform. At first, the principle emphasis for the police was to separate themselves from politics; then it was to develop a professional style of their own. The third factor in the reform of the police was the advancement of science and technology, and the application of their methods and products to the law enforcement process. Monumental advances in transportation and communications have had a profound influence on the police. The application of science to law resulted in the development of the forensic sciences. One consequence has been a dramatic increase in the technical proficiency of the law enforcement community. The use of forensic pathologists, toxicologists, ballistics experts and other specialists has redefined how the police gather and process evidence and how they link physical components of crimes to the individuals who commit them.

Despite tremendous improvements in technology and administration, the police found themselves lost in a sea of social change toward the end of the reform era. The rise of the civil rights movement, the development of the protest movement during the Vietnam War and the fast-paced social change of the

1960s left the police somewhat out of step and behind the times. As the reform era closed, the police found themselves once again facing the need for change. They are currently attempting to deal with these requirements. The police in America remain a uniquely urban institution; as cities change, the police must change with them. The challenge of the next few decades is to see whether they can do so successfully.

DISCUSSION QUESTIONS

1. Why is police history also the history of government?

2. It was not until the emergence of secular law that policing in its most rudimentary form could emerge. Why?

3. Why was the early English constable more like a district attorney than a police officer, and what was the community's role in law enforcement?

4. When the police in England were established in 1829, they were not armed. Why was this policy established, and what are its consequences?

5. Why did the states authorize cities to establish local police departments in the last century, rather than just creating statewide police forces?

6. What was the principle function of the nineteenth-century police officer in America? How did this role differ from the role of today's police officer?

7. How did American municipal police departments become corrupted by local politicians? Was that inevitable?

8. How has judicial review shaped police reform? Should the courts have the authority to tell the police how to do their work?

9. How has the redefinition of the "due process of law" clause of the Fourteenth Amendment helped to reform police at the *local* level?

10. What is meant by the "absorption" of the Bill of Rights? What does it have to do with the police?

11. How did civil service reform at the federal level influence civil service reform at the local level?

12. Where did the field of public administration emerging around the turn of the century find its role models and inspiration?

13. How did the FBI help with the professionalization of the American police? Are they still doing so?

14. How has reform distanced the police from their communities?

15. Explain the impact of the automobile on the police.

16. On what is the concept of "preventive patrol" based? Do you think it is a valid concept? Would you suggest any alternatives?

17. What are the consequences of traffic law enforcement on the relationship between the police and the public?

18. How has the application of forensic science to law enforcement changed the police?

19. How have detectives of fiction impacted on public expectations of the "real" police?

20. Why were the police unable to cope with the social turbulence of the 1960s? Who is at fault: the police or the public?

REFERENCES

1 See, for example, Philip John Stead, ed., *Pioneers in Policing* (Montclair, NJ: Patterson Smith, 1977).

2 Barbara W. Tuchman, *A Distant Mirror: The Calamitous 14th Century* (New York: Alfred A. Knopf, 1978), 107.

3 Tuchman, *A Distant Mirror*, 107-108.

4 T.A. Critchley, *A History of Police in England and Wales*, 2nd ed. (Montclair, NJ: Patterson Smith, 1967), 5.

5 Critchley, *A History of Police in England and Wales*, 7.

6 James F. Richardson, *Urban Police in the United States* (Port Washington, NY: Kennikat Press, 1974), 7.

7 Leon Radzinowics, *A History of English Criminal Law From 1750*, Vol. II, "The Clash Between Private Initiative and Public Interest in the Enforcement of the Law" (London: Police Foundation, 1988).

8 P.A.J. Waddington, *Arming an Unarmed Police: Policy and Practice in the Metropolitan Police* (London: Police Foundation, 1988).

9 Critchley, *A History of Police in England and Wales*, 52.

[10] Critchley, *A History of Police in England and Wales*, 55.

[11] Richardson, *Urban Police in the United States*, 24.

[12] Robert M. Fogelson, *Big City Police* (Cambridge, MA: Harvard University Press, 1977), 17.

[13] Fogelson, *Big City Police*, 16-17.

[14] Fogelson, *Big City Police*, 20.

[15] Richardson, *Urban Police in the United States*, 49.

[16] The year 1914 is an arbitrary designation for the beginning of the reform era. It was the year *Weeks v. United States* (232 U.S. 383, 58 L.Ed. 652, 34 S. Ct. 341) was decided. This landmark case established the so-called "exclusionary rule" wherein evidence obtained by unreasonable search and seizure would be excluded from the federal courts.

[17] For an interesting insight into police departments at the turn of the century, see Stephen J. Brodt, Dwight W. Hoover and John D. Hewitt, "Policing Middletown: 1880-1900," *Journal of Police Science and Administration* 11:2 (June 1983), 237-242.

[18] "A Dissenting Opinion on 'Third Degree' by Chief Davis, Memphis, Tennessee, 1910," in *The Blue and the Brass: American Policing, 1890-1910*, ed. Donald C. Dilworth (Gaithersburg, MD: International Association of Chiefs of Police, 1976), 78-81.

[19] *Barron v. Baltimore,* 32 U.S. 243, 8 L. Ed. 672 (1833).

[20] *Mapp v. Ohio,* 367 U.S. 643, 81 S. Ct. 1684, 6 L. Ed. 1081 (1961).

[21] *Gideon v. Wainwright,* 372 U.S. 335, 83 S. Ct. 792, 9 L. Ed. 2d 799 (1963).

[22] *Malloy v. Hogan,* 378 U.S. 1, 84 S. Ct. 1489, 12 L. Ed. 2d 653 (1964).

[23] "Police Brutality," *Time,* 25 March 1991, 16-19.

[24] Tom Matthews, et al., "The Siege of L.A.," *Newsweek,* 11 May 1992, 30.

[25] U.S. Department of Justice, Federal Bureau of Investigation, *Crime in the United States* in *Uniform Crime Reports* (Washington, DC: U.S. Government Printing Office, 11 August 1991), 237.

[26] See especially Frederick C. Mosher, *Democracy and the Public Service* (New York: Oxford University Press, 1968).

[27] U.S. Bureau of the Census, *Historical Statistics of the United States, Colonial Times to 1970*, Bicentennial Edition, Part I. (Washington, DC: U.S. Government Printing Office, 1976). See especially Chapter A, "Population," 1-42, and Chapter C, "Social Statistics," 332-422.

[28] Woodrow Wilson, "The Study of Administration," *Political Science Quarterly* 11:1 (June 1887).

[29] George L. Kelling and Mark H. Moore, "The Evolving Strategy of Policing," *Perspectives on Policing* (November 1988), 5.

[30] Herman Goldstein, *Policing in a Free Society* (Cambridge, MA: Ballinger, 1977).

[31] Orlando W. Wilson, *Police Administration* (New York: McGraw-Hill, 1950).

[32] Mark H. Moore, Robert C. Trojanowicz and George L. Kelling, "Crime and Policing," *Perspectives on Policing* (June 1988), 1.

[33] Robert M. Fogelson, *Big-City Police* (Cambridge, MA: Harvard University Press, 1977), 115.

[34] James Q. Wilson, *Varieties of Police Behavior* (New York: Athenaeum, 1974), 48-51.

[35] Wilson, *Varieties of Police Behavior*, 48-51

[36] Fogelson, *Big-City Police*, 115.

[37] Estelle Zannes, *Police Communications: Humans and Hardware* (Santa Cruz, CA: Davis Publishing Company, Inc., 1976), see especially Chapter 1, 1-86.

[38] See, for example. H.M. Boettinger, *The Telephone Book: Bell, Watson, Vail and American Life, 1876-1983*, rev. ed. (Oshkosh, WI: Stern Publications, 1983).

[39] Zannes, *Police Communications*, 52-63.

[40] "Detroit Police Now in Touch by Radio With Whole Country," *New York Times*, 24 April 1921, II-1.

[41] Zannes, *Police Communications*, 18.

[42] For more information about police uses of computer technology, see James W. Osterburg and Richard H. Ward, *Criminal Investigation: A Method for Reconstructing the Past* (Cincinnati: Anderson Publishing Co., 1992), 443-453.

[43] Henri Souchon, "Alphonse Bertillon," in *Pioneers in Policing*, ed. Philip John Stead (Montclair, NJ: Patterson Smith, 1977), 127.

[44] John J. Cronin, "The Fingerprinters," in *Pioneers in Policing*, ed. Philip John Stead, (Montclair, NJ: Patterson Smith, 1977), 162.

[45] Cronin, "The Fingerprinters," 163.

[46] Omnibus Crime Control and Safe Streets Act, Pub. L. No. 90-351 (1968).

Photo Credit: Bill Powers, Frost Publishing Group, Ltd.

Chapter 7

THE POST-REFORM ERA

The Police in Search of an Identity

Until very recently, police staffing and operations followed a well-established, traditional pattern. Across the country, in cities large and small, the police have recruited, organized, supervised and deployed their personnel in consistently similar ways. At the same time they enjoyed widespread public acceptance and, until recently, had little reason to consider doing things differently. Most members of the community acknowledged the need for both law enforcement and order maintenance, and—seeing themselves as beneficiaries of police operations—most approved of how the police defined and performed these tasks. Police efforts to maintain institutional autonomy by distancing themselves from political influence were likewise well received by the public, even at the cost of increasing the isolation of the police from the larger community. Precisely because they met community expectations, the police were allowed to go about their business in traditional ways. In more subjective terms, those in power believed they benefitted from the police (and did not feel threatened by them), while those who *did* feel threatened lacked the power to do anything about it. Thus, as the police structured their operations with the acceptance of the community majority, those who disagreed had little choice but to adapt. Moreover, the organization and deployment of police functions were left to the police themselves to decide. Not only did police departments define their own work, they also controlled who became police officers. As an occupational group they have consisted primarily of working-class white males. Until recent times the criteria for becoming a police officer were basic: a high school diploma (not always), a minimum age requirement and a "clean" record. Although some departments also imposed physical requirements and satisfactory performance on an entrance examination, most still recruited the same kind of candidates. However, an enormous amount of social change took place between the 1970s and 1990s, and traditional ways of doing business have come under increasingly close scrutiny and criticism. As a result, the police have been forced to examine what they do, how they do it and who they hire to get it done. The consequences are a great deal more profound than most people realize. To understand this, we need to look at the three traditional roles the police perform—order maintenance, law enforcement and service—and then assess how these roles have been influenced by social change.

ORDER MAINTENANCE

The "average" community consists (for the most part) of ordinary people and institutions going about their usual business in their accustomed ways. This orderliness is underwritten by community expectations, the relatively efficient operation of the private control system and the subtle (but distinct) segregation of incompatible people and institutions. This complicated process underlies such things as zoning ordinances and residential segregation based on income.[1] It is also what separates industrial, commercial and residential land uses. This process is explained by functionalist theory, which also explains why the police function as they do as part of a larger social system: because doing so is necessary in support of the larger system. In effect, it argues that police organization and operations have developed this way because the larger society, as an integrated social system, has *required* them to do so.[2]

Although communities function within an overall context of orderliness and predictability, disorder is not uncommon. When it occurs, a variety of corrective mechanisms come into play. Since most forms of disorder are minor, their corresponding corrective mechanisms are usually informal and only mildly coercive. Corrective measures are generally proportionate to the problems they redress, and are usually administered by those who suffer the most directly from the disorderly event or action. Thus, parents discipline the misconduct of their children; schools discipline the misconduct of students; bosses discipline the misconduct of their subordinates; and so on. The scope of this relationship usually widens only when those "responsible" for disciplining the misconduct of others are absent or otherwise fail to take the necessary corrective action. For example, elementary school teachers may need to discipline young children whose misconduct is condoned by their parents when their improper behavior spills over into the classroom or playground. However, this becomes a problem when the required corrective action is beyond the authority of teachers or the school system. This is also true of other failures in the private control system.

Yet another situation exists when disorder is beyond the control of informal mechanisms. This is why some forms of "order" are imposed by public or professional regulation (and why some activities and occupations are formally licensed and regulated). Finally, serious disorder—that which is beyond the corrective ability of primary, informal or regulatory groups—must be dealt with by formal institutions created specifically for that purpose. A house on fire, for example, is a serious *public* disorder. It not only threatens the house that is burning and the people who might be inside, it also threatens nearby buildings and their occupants. Use of the fire department in such a case is not left to the discretion of the homeowner. A person whose house is on fire cannot tell the fire department to go away because he or she would rather have it burn down and collect the insurance. If necessary, an owner will be forcibly removed from the scene so the fire can be extinguished despite the objection.

The police in America were established to deal with disorder; in most communities that is still their primary role. The watchmen in the pre-police era were responsible for maintaining an orderly public environment, and their duties did not include responding to serious crimes. Victims of "real" crimes had to secure a warrant from a magistrate which was then served (for a fee) by a constable, who was an officer of the court. The concept of a single agency organized to maintain public order and enforce criminal laws was alien to the American experience. It was many years before the two functions merged into a single agency. When municipal police departments were established in the middle of the nineteenth century, law enforcement was added to the traditional watchman's duties. In so doing, they accomplished two things: (1) law enforcement became a purely *public* responsibility, and (2) law enforcement tactics were added to the inventory of alternatives available to the police in dealing with disorder. Over the years the distinction between the two has become cloudy: although a police officer can maintain order without enforcing the law, the generic activities of the police are commonly (but not always correctly) accepted as "law enforcement."

To make matters even more complicated, disorderly events are not always simple to evaluate. As James Q. Wilson noted in his classic book, *Varieties of Police Behavior*, disorder "involves a dispute over what is 'right' or 'seemly' conduct or over who is to blame for conduct that is agreed to be wrong or unseemly."[3] However, what one person thinks is disorderly may seem perfectly appropriate to someone else—or a disorder may be presumed appropriate because of the circumstances that produced it. This means that someone has to decide who (and what) is right and who (and what) is wrong. This is the central purpose of a great deal of police work. It is complicated, however, by two things: danger and discretion.

DANGER

Many disorderly events involve disputes that can be charged with emotion and accompanied by reduced inhibition. This is especially likely to be the case when alcohol or other drugs are involved. For example, the police are commonly called to intervene in domestic disputes that escalate to noisy arguments or even physical fights. As these disputes escalate in intensity, the passions of the participants can run high. If by the time the police arrive, one of the disputants (or both) has been drinking, tempers may be short and behavior far less inhibited than might normally be the case. Here, the police must decide what to do, and regardless of what course they pursue, at least one of the disputants is apt to be unhappy with the outcome. As a result, violence against the police is always a istinct possibility. In 1989 alone, 20,303 police officers were assaulted while responding to disturbance calls.[4] Although police officers are more likely to be killed while attempting to make an arrest, the likelihood of their being assaulted is much higher while responding to domestic disturbances: 32.7 percent of all assaults against police officers arose from events that started as disturbance calls.[5] Between 1978 and 1989, a total of 159 police officers were killed while responding to disturbance calls, while 413 were killed during arrest situations.[6] Nearly all police officers have confronted an unruly or abusive husband at the request of an unhappy wife, only to have either the husband, the wife or both "turn" on the police. The husband may feel victimized by the police, who seem to him to be sticking their noses into the privacy of his marriage and violating the sanctity of his home. Moreover, the wife may suddenly feel compelled to come to the aid of her husband, even though she wanted him arrested only moments before. As one Chicago police officer noted,

> The worst call in the police department is a domestic disturbance. The emotional level is just so high; it's a very volatile situation. And you walk in on the middle of it. What happens a lot is, you come in, they start siding against you. I've had a vase broken over my head in a domestic. Another time, we ended up fighting with an entire family: a husband and wife, a son, a daughter, and a grandmother. It can get real hairy.[7]

Although much of the violence witnessed by the police is not directed toward them, they are very much aware that the potential for their own harm is always present. Another Chicago police officer laconically recalled a family disturbance: "I answered a domestic one time; by the time I got there, this woman was kneeling next to her husband, holding his throat together with both hands. She had slashed his throat from ear to ear. Then she had a change of heart, I guess."[8] Given the right circumstances, the officer could have been the victim instead—and that is something all police officers know.

A great deal of their order maintenance effort places the police in conflict with individuals who either think that they are in the "right" or believe their behavior is no one else's business. It does not take long for police officers to learn that much of the danger in their work arises out of routine order maintenance activities. The randomness of this danger produces a preoccupation that becomes a central element in the police officer's "working personality."[9] Officers become so sensitive to the possibility of danger (especially to themselves) that they routinely compare people with whom they have contact with the "symbolic assailant"—a personification of traits they associate with dangerous people they have encountered. As Skolnick noted,

> The policeman, because his work requires him to be occupied continually with potential violence, develops a perceptual shorthand to identify certain kinds of people as symbolic assailants, that is, as persons who use gesture, language, and attire that the policeman has come to recognize as a prelude to violence. This does not mean that violence by the symbolic assailant is necessarily predictable. On the contrary, the policeman responds to the vague indication of danger suggested by appearance. Like the animals of the experimental psychologist, the policeman finds the threat of random damage more compelling than a predetermined and inevitable punishment.[10]

The characteristics of the "symbolic assailant" vary by geography and the nature of the community. Symbolic assailants can also include the homeless, the mentally disturbed or anyone differing from the norm. Police officers use specific visual and verbal cues as tripwires to alert them to potential danger. These "alarms" are familiar to virtually all experienced cops. This leads to characterizations of their clientele based on repeated experiences over time.

Danger to the police is omnipresent and hard to predict. As a Chicago officer recalled,

> One of the first things that's imbued upon you when you come on this job is never think this guy is gonna come peaceful. Always assume he's gonna fight like Satan. With anybody at all. When I was working on the West Side, as a matter of fact, I was standing around the desk one night, a policeman came in with a little boy in handcuffs; I estimated the little boy to be about seven. I'd never seen handcuffs on a little kid. I said, "What are you—goofy? What do you got the cuffs on the kid for?" He said, "This son of a bitch just stabbed me." He turned around, and there's a slit in his pants leg where the kid had stuck a knife in his thigh.[11]

DISCRETION [12]

Many disorderly situations encountered by the police are ambiguous; exactly who is to blame is not always clear. In addition, although many of these situations are technically violations of law, police officers know that making an arrest is not always the best remedy. The police have tremendous latitude in how they handle incidents, but in order to exercise it they must assert their authority. First they must "take control" of the situation; then they must use their authority to settle the dispute. In all cases, they must try to exercise their authority in ways that are acceptable to those most directly involved.

Since perception is subjective, how the parties in a dispute view their role is a matter of interpretation. While some people may see themselves as "victims," the police may see them in an entirely different light. Since the police must assess the *legitimacy* of a person's claim to victimization, those who are victims as a result of their own misconduct generally receive little sympathy from the police:

> Several young men had been arguing in a bar when their dispute heated up. One invited another to step outside to "settle" the bone of contention. When they got outside, the person who instigated the fight threw a punch at the other man, who subsequently beat him up. The disgruntled loser went back into the bar and called the police. When they arrived he tried to get them to arrest his "assailant." When the police figured out what had happened, they told both of them to go home or they would throw them both in jail. After the combatants agreed to go their separate ways, the police left. *(Author's field notes.)*

Individual attitudes play a major role in how the police exercise their discretionary authority. People who refuse to acknowledge police authority or who treat them with contempt are much more likely to suffer negative consequences as a result. Nowhere is this more evident than in traffic enforcement. Although traffic infractions are violations of law, their enforcement is essentially an order maintenance activity. Moreover, it is the one order maintenance activity in which the average person is most likely to come into contact with the police. Whether a person actually gets a ticket depends on many factors, but chief among them is the violator's attitude.

> When a young man was stopped for running a traffic light, the police officer asked him for his license and registration. The young man responded by asking the police officer if he didn't have anything better to do than harass honest citizens and suggested that the officer could spend his time more productively by looking for criminals. When the officer asked him why he didn't stop for

the traffic light, the young man said, "If you've seen one, you've seen them all." He got a ticket. *(Author's field notes.)*

After several people became involved in a dispute in a public park, the police were called. The responding police officer told the disputants that he would listen to what each had to say, but he was going to listen to them in turn. When one of the men in the group interrupted one of the others, the police officer told him to wait his turn. When he kept on interrupting, the officer told him if he "made one more peep," he would be arrested. The man said "peep" and the officer arrested him. When a colleague asked him later what he arrested the man for, he said "contempt of cop." *(Author's field notes.)*

Police officers, like all other people, bring personal feelings and biases to their work. When disorder or misconduct collide with strong personal feelings held by individual police officers, the exercise of their discretionary latitude is almost certain to reflect those biases. Claims of victimization between or by homosexuals, for example, are typically seen by the police as lacking merit (especially if the complaint is invoked by a citizen as opposed to being initiated by the police). People deemed to be of marginal status (including juveniles, the homeless, deviants, drunks, homosexuals and "low-lifes") historically have had difficulty in getting the police to respond to their complaints—especially when those complaints involve relatively minor order maintenance matters.

If "disorder" is defined as behavior or situations that do not match expectations, the key question is: "*whose* expectations?" If only one person (or a small number of people) is offended, the disorder is essentially a *personal* problem. If a large number of people are offended, it is a *public* problem. In either case, people who are offended by the disorder want it corrected. If the ordinary social mechanisms for dealing with disorder do not work or are not available, the police are likely to be called. The police response is part of a larger context known as *order maintenance*. How they will deal with the problem is determined by the department's policies, the perceptions of individual police officers and the nature of the disorder. In general, the goal of the police in order maintenance is not to arrest people or even to invoke the formal processes of the criminal justice system. Their goal is to fix the immediate problem to the best of their ability and then move on. Unfortunately, people who call the police on order maintenance issues may view the police role quite differently than the police do. Offended citizens may want the police to invoke formal sanctions against the offending parties and may be disappointed when the police refuse to do so. Another source of difficulty arises when the police approach order maintenance issues as law enforcement problems and invoke formal responses when they are not really necessary.

LAW ENFORCEMENT

There is considerable difference between the operational tactics of order maintenance and those of law enforcement. In the former, the police regulate conduct; in the latter, they detect crimes and arrest offenders. To be sure, order maintenance *can* result in arrests, but when it happens it is usually because the person who gets arrested refuses to submit to the authority of the police. Despite the fact that arrests may occur during the course of maintaining order, such is not usually the objective. In law enforcement, on the other hand, making arrests and taking other punitive actions *is* the goal. Even though law enforcement may be viewed as a means of maintaining order, neither its tactics nor its objectives are oriented specifically toward that goal. Law enforcement operations are guided by tactical objectives and are moderated by the substantive and due process requirements of the law rather than by a desire to facilitate the flow of community activity. In law enforcement, discretionary latitude is diminished and replaced by a more formal and legalistic approach. Police officers who see themselves as law enforcement specialists tend to place a greater emphasis on their "professional" status as agents of the law. They characteristically avoid order maintenance activities unless such activities can be converted into law enforcement issues. Thus, a police officer who approaches a domestic disturbance from the order maintenance perspective is likely to make an effort to negotiate with the disputants to resolve the immediate problem. A police officer who approaches the same dispute from the law enforcement perspective will look for a criminal event, and if one is found, will arrest the offender. Because of the differences in how the police approach order maintenance and law enforcement objectives, the latter is usually carried out by specialized units, while the former remains the domain of patrol officers. Members of the department's plainclothes or detective components are considered its law enforcement specialists. Their work typically enjoys high prestige within the department (at least higher than patrol or traffic work). However, not all law enforcement specialists are in the plainclothes segment of the department. In some departments special patrol units augment the "regular" patrol force by performing highly aggressive law enforcement tactics. For example, in response to the escalating homicide rate in Washington, DC, the Metropolitan Police Department established a Rapid Deployment Unit whose officers were "freed from much routine police work, including responding to calls about domestic disputes, purse snatchings and traffic accidents."[13]

> Each night, its troops are sent to put criminals on the defensive, and to do it with an attitude, in the parts of the city experiencing the worst gun violence. In the neighborhood where [a woman had been gunned down near the daycare center where she had dropped off her three-year-old daughter], RDU was using any excuse, including minor traffic violations, to search cars for guns. The unit's members harass drug dealers, slam suspects against walls if they try

to escape, get into brawls with suspects who challenge them, and interrogate detainees about unsolved murders.[14]

These kinds of uniformed law enforcement units are called by different names (e.g., "Tactical Patrol" or "Anti-Crime" squads), but their targets and methods are similar. They focus on specific crimes and categories of offenders and employ tactics designed to produce results. These units are usually found in the larger cities where the crime problem is serious and informal controls on public behavior range from weak to nonexistent. Although there may be mixed feelings about some of their tactics, the public generally supports the police as long as they feel "criminals" rather than "ordinary citizens" are being targeted. However, when the police use highly aggressive law enforcement tactics in circumstances that call for an order maintenance approach, public support erodes quickly. The following example illustrates the point:

> A Howard University student said she was chased, tackled, kicked and ultimately arrested by a plainclothes police officer who caught her jaywalking last week. Chandra Shealey, 19, said she heard someone yell when she was crossing Euclid Street about 7:30 p.m. She said she looked back, saw a man in a white car that had stopped and assumed it was a cab driver making a comment. Shealey, who said she had arrived from Chicago a day earlier, had just registered at Howard and was carrying $440 in cash, said she continued walking. After hearing a second yell, she turned and saw a man wearing a T-shirt running toward her. "He grabs me by the neck, throws me down on the floor and picks me up by the neck," said Shealey. "He was like 'You better shut up or I'll really give you something to complain about.'" The officer who arrested Shealey...is assigned to an undercover narcotics detail, police said. Police confirmed that Shealey was arrested and charged with a pedestrian violation and disorderly conduct.[15]

The incident described above was the second within a week (the first involved a police cadet who assaulted and arrested a businessman for jaywalking). The failure to distinguish between situations that call for order maintenance versus those that call for law enforcement can produce unfortunate and unnecessary outcomes. For example, as a man in Sheridan, Colorado was driving his wife (who was seven-months pregnant) to the hospital at 1:00 a.m., he was stopped by a police officer for going 78 mph in a 45 mph zone. The man explained his emergency and asked the police officer for an escort to the hospital. The officer refused, but agreed to follow the man's car to the hospital. However, a few minutes later the police officer stopped him again and called for an ambulance (which took about 10 minutes to arrive). After the ambulance took the pregnant woman to the hospital (where she gave birth prematurely), the police officer wrote the hapless husband a speeding ticket. By the time he got to the hospital he had missed the birth.[16] This kind of difference of perspective undoubtedly accounts for much of the conflict between the police and the public.

Law enforcement (unlike order maintenance) is aggressive and punitive. Its objectives are to identify violations of law and invoke the criminal justice process. To the extent that the public perceives the targeted violation as a *crime*, it is likely to support law enforcement tactics used by the police in dealing with it. However, when there is a difference in perspective between the public and the police, the public's support of the police diminishes. This has been the dilemma of approaching vice as a crime. For example, crimes such as recreational drug use and prostitution (as well as other so-called "victimless" crimes) are viewed by many as private matters that should be outside the reach of the law. Those who engage in these behaviors are not likely to see themselves as criminals and they resent law enforcement tactics that interfere with what they consider their privacy or personal habits. The police, on the other hand, see "victimless" crimes in an entirely different light and are willing to go against a great deal of popular sentiment to deal with them. For example, when Sarasota, Florida police arrested Paul Reubens (television personality Pee Wee Herman) for masturbating in a pornography theater, a great many people wondered why the police were in that theater to begin with. As one national newsweekly noted, "What people seemed to be searching for, in their edgy conversations and dozens of gross-but-funny jokes, was a way to think about a case that appeared to have a shortage of victims and an excess of police."[17] The police responded lamely that they do not *make* the laws—they just enforce them. They reportedly had been working on a drug case and when their leads did not pan out, decided to check out the pornography theater for sex offenders.[18]

Traffic law enforcement is another area in which the police and the public are often at odds with one another. Although traffic law enforcement is essentially an order maintenance activity, it is handled by the police as a law enforcement issue—albeit one in which they exercise a great deal of discretionary latitude. Public resentment over traffic law enforcement is largely a function of the difference in outlook between the public and the police. Much of the public sees traffic law enforcement as either a means by which the local government generates revenue or as a police activity so arbitrary and capricious that it is "unfair." The police disagree. They do not see it as a means of generating revenue (because *they* do not get the money), and they know from firsthand experience the potential tragic consequences of drivers who violate traffic laws. The police are well aware that traffic enforcement is a bone of contention. As a result, in many jurisdictions they either do not pursue it aggressively or have special units that focus on it. Where police departments *do* have "ticket quotas," their goal is not to harass the public but to have a performance measure against which police efficiency can be measured. The public, however, is much less concerned with internal police management issues than with whether they will get a ticket.

SERVICE

The police provide a variety of public services, including escorting funeral processions, issuing death (or other emergency) notifications, giving advice on crime-related matters, assisting stranded motorists, giving directions to people who are lost, looking for missing persons, and so on. People ask the police for help for various reasons—because they are available, because they are easy to contact, because they do not charge for their services, or because no one else may be available (or willing) to help. Most police departments are willing to provide these services as long as they do not detract from what they consider "real" police work—failing to realize, of course, that such services traditionally have been part of American police work.

The service function was more important during the political and reform eras than it has been since. However, both time and technology have changed communities and the police in ways that have reduced the opportunity for direct contact between the public and the police. As a result, the police have become more insular and less service-oriented. In many communities it may even be difficult to come into direct contact with them. Requests for police assistance are usually made by telephone, and call-takers screen out a great many calls for service. Sometimes they refer the caller to another agency or simply explain that personnel shortages and other demands do not permit the use of police resources for non-essential purposes.[19]

GLITCHES IN THE SYSTEM

Although it is easy to criticize the police for their tactics, doing so is both unfair and hasty. As we have already seen, communities are complex places and it is sometimes difficult to distinguish order maintenance from law enforcement. In addition, most (though certainly not all) police departments *are* responsive to community needs. The problem is that these needs may not be seen the same way by the public as by the police, and there may be substantial disagreement on how they should be met. Many public expectations contain mixed messages. An example is the wish for the police to effectively control crime without exceeding the limitations of the law. Communication between the police and the public is nearly always limited and seldom effective. Clearly, there are a number of glitches in the system that result in the police being at odds with the public. These glitches arise out of four broad considerations: (1) anxiety provoked by disorder, (2) the public's attitude toward crime, (3) public antipathy towards "criminals," and (4) concern over abuse of authority by the police.

ANXIETY PROVOKED BY DISORDER

The public does not always distinguish between *criminal* versus *disorderly* conduct; in fact, to the casual observer the two may appear to be much the same. The fear of crime, therefore, may also include personal anxiety that arises from disorderly situations. As Moore and Trojanowicz note,

> ...when citizens are asked about the things that frighten them, there is little talk about "real crimes" such as robbery, rape, and murder. More often there is talk about other signs of physical decay and social disorganization such as "junk and trash in vacant lots, boarded-up buildings, stripped and abandoned cars, bands of teenagers congregating on street corners, street prostitution, panhandling, public drinking, verbal harassment of women, open gambling and drug use, and other incivilities."[20]

In their widely cited article, "Broken Windows," Wilson and Kelling point out that "...we tend to overlook or forget another source of fear—the fear of being bothered by disorderly people. Not violent people, nor, necessarily, criminals, but disreputable or obstreperous or unpredictable people: panhandlers, drunks addicts, rowdy teenagers, prostitutes, loiterers, the mentally disturbed."[21] The title of the Wilson and Kelling article, "Broken Windows," is a metaphor for disorder and urban deterioration. Their central thesis is that if a broken window is left unrepaired, it invites further vandalism and ultimately hastens the deterioration of the whole neighborhood. The "broken windows" they refer to are various kinds of disorder. They note, for example, that "[t]he unchecked panhandler is, in effect, the first 'broken window' and that if the neighborhood cannot keep a bothersome panhandler from annoying passersby, the thief may reason, it is even less likely to call the police to identify a potential mugger or to interfere if the mugging actually takes place."[22] According to Wilson and Kelling, it comes down to a basic question:

> Should police activity on the street be shaped, in important ways, by the standards of the neighborhood rather than by the rules of the state? Over the past two decades, the shift of police from order maintenance to law enforcement has brought them increasingly under the influence of legal restrictions, provoked by media complaints and enforced by court decision and departmental orders. As a consequence, the order maintenance functions of the police are now governed by rules developed to control police relations with suspected criminals.[23]

The perception of unchecked disorder—regardless of whether it is accurate—provokes anxiety among those who come into contact with it. Indecorous conduct is referred to as a "broken window" by Wilson and Kelling. These researchers believe that the relatively recent "decriminalization" of disreputable behavior has removed "the ultimate sanction the police can employ to maintain neighborhood order," and they think this has been a mistake.[24] A large segment of the public believes the police *can* and *should* protect them from disorderly people and events. Although they do not necessarily think disorderly people should be put in jail, they want the disorderly situation "corrected." Moreover, a great many think the police ought to be the ones to do the job. When the police will not, do not or cannot do so, public disappointment or anger may result. Seldom considered is whether the police have the capability to give the public what it thinks it wants. The factors that define the overall problem are many and complicated, and the interplay of crime and disorder can lead to dissatisfaction with the police and an abandonment of one's sense of community. This is indicated by one person who moved from the city to the suburbs:

> Deciding to move to the suburbs was the most difficult decision of our marriage. For years, we had rationalized staying on.... When the tires on 28 cars...were slashed...three years ago, we chalked it up to reckless youth. When our car was stolen, we were plenty mad, but we told ourselves that it was worth staying...because of the easy access to so many cultural outlets we would not find elsewhere. When our next-door neighbor was held up at the Safeway on a Wednesday afternoon by an 8-year old boy brandishing a plastic gun, we reasoned that such a ludicrous event would never happen again. When we were assaulted in our vestibule by four hoodlums one evening, we were frightened, but we reminded ourselves of how convenient we were to work. When someone was murdered at random in our area, we decided it was silly to walk the dog after dark. Eventually, we got a car alarm and a steering wheel bar. We didn't walk to [the subway] after dark and did so with caution during the day. We gave up shopping at the local Safeway and went to the suburbs, where the stores are safer and cleaner, the prices lower and the help friendlier. We skipped going around the corner after dark for that forgotten pint of milk. We stopped answering the door after too many solicitations for money for some fabricated injury to some nonexistent child. We ignored Halloween after finding our that more than half the trick-or-treaters were adults, canvassing for trouble. We didn't even plant bulbs in our front yard after one of our neighbors was held up at gunpoint on a Sunday afternoon while doing his yard work. The iron bars we installed on our windows kept people out, but they also kept us in. Finally, reluctantly, we gave up and counted ourselves lucky that we had the means to leave....[25]

THE PUBLIC'S ATTITUDE TOWARD CRIME

Crime is very real and occurs with greater frequency than most people realize; moreover, it can have a direct impact on the quality of life in any community. In presenting crime trends as a ratio to time, the FBI reported that in 1990 there was one violent crime every 17 seconds and a property crime every two seconds. According to the FBI, "The Crime Index total rose 2 percent to 14.5

million offenses in 1990. Five- and 10-year percent changes showed the 1990 total was 10 percent above the 1986 level and 8 percent higher than in 1981."[26] More than eight out of 10 people questioned in a Gallup poll in 1989 believed that there was more crime in the United States in that current year than in the year earlier, and a majority believed drugs were the most responsible causative factor.[27] Even though the public believes crime is rising, most feel detached from the problem. For example, only 10 percent said they felt unsafe at home and only 40 percent indicated they were afraid to walk alone at night.[28] Interestingly, when asked to identify the most important problem facing the county, fewer than five percent believed it was crime.

What does this mean? Although people are aware that crime is a problem, they do not believe it touches them directly. What is even more peculiar is that the people who fear crime the most (the elderly and female segments of the population) are the least likely to be victimized.[29] This begins to make sense only upon understanding that people view both crime and its solution as being external to them and their daily lives. When people actually are victimized, that experience occurs in some kind of context. Although the victim may not like what has happened, he or she at least can understand it in terms of the context in which it occurred. Much of what is presented in the news and entertainment media is not relevant to the audience's personal experience and is therefore perceived as alien. Since these events are not grounded in personal experience, they are compartmentalized into a kind of psychological limbo. The offenders consigned to this category are the "criminals" the public dislikes so intensely. Having little direct contact with these criminals, the public readily supports the police in their law enforcement role and has little compassion for criminals.

PUBLIC ANTIPATHY TOWARD "CRIMINALS"

The news and entertainment media offer a steady diet of highly sensational crimes—some genuine, some "dramatized" and some fictitious. Newspaper accounts of serial rapists, psychopathic killers, wealthy drug lords and other unsavory characters fan public passions. Reinforcing this are the television programs and movies that dramatize these kinds of things. Such accounts present a biased perspective of crime and criminals. It is no wonder, then, that the public's perception of the problem is also biased. The criminals feared most by the public are those who are seen as differing from noncriminals in kind rather than degree. The public is quite willing to see this particular "kind" of criminal punished severely.

A Gallup poll in 1989 indicated that a majority of Americans favored making parole more difficult for persons convicted of violent crimes and supported the enactment of tougher gun control laws. A majority also favored not allowing those accused of violent crimes to be released on bail while awaiting trial.[30] Nationally, nearly three-fourths favored capital punishment for persons convicted of murder.[31] Over eight out of 10 felt the courts did not deal harshly enough with criminals, and nearly as many worried that criminals were let off too easily.[32] It would appear that when the public labels a person a criminal, it wants that person punished. But although the public wants criminals punished, it does not believe the police have the ability to protect them from violent crime. Fifty percent of the respondents in a poll asking about the extent of the police's ability to protect the public from violent crime reported "not very much" (42 percent) confidence and 8 percent indicated no confidence at all. On the other side of the coin, only 48 percent indicated either "quite a bit" (34 percent) or "a great deal" of confidence in the ability of the police to protect them from violent crime.[33] Nearly twice as many people felt that "additional money and effort should go to attacking the social and economic problems that lead to crime through better education and job training" than by "spending more money and effort...by improving law enforcement with more prisons, police and judges."[34]

ABUSE OF AUTHORITY BY THE POLICE

Even though the public is willing to acknowledge the seriousness of crime, it is unwilling to expand the authority of the police. The problem is not that the public thinks of the police as dishonest or unethical (85 percent rate the honesty and ethical standards of the police from average to very high).[35] Rather, the problem lies with the traditional reluctance of the police to include the public in the development of law enforcement strategies, differences of opinion over police tactics and, mostly, the unfortunate history of police misconduct. As Goldstein notes, "Police authority is not easily controlled. Against a history of considerable abuse, new examples of how that authority can be wrongly used always appear. It is no wonder, therefore, that a large segment of the public attaches great importance to controlling the police."[36]

Police misconduct is a reality that cannot be ignored. In fact, it has proven itself to be a persistent problem in many departments throughout the country. Police misconduct can take many forms—ranging from inconsequential acts of incivility to the commission of serious crimes. Police misconduct can be isolated to an individual or it can be spread throughout the department, i.e., be institutional in nature. In general, police misconduct falls into three categories: *mal*feasance, *mis*feasance and *non*feasance.

Malfeasance

Malfeasance is the performance by a public official of an act that is not legally justified or that is harmful or contrary to law. Police officers who commit acts of malfeasance typically do so in connection with their work, and many of these acts involve allegations of brutality or the excessive use of force. For example, a Seattle police officer assigned to investigate a traffic accident arrested a man involved in the accident. When he discovered the man was his ex-wife's new husband, he knocked him to the ground and then hit him again while transporting him to the police station.[37] The incident was witnessed by several people who reported it to the police department, and the officer was subsequently fired. This same officer, several years earlier, had been convicted of third-degree assault and fined $50 for "pistol-whipping" an Army sergeant he was trying to arrest, but at that time no action was taken against him by the police department. Complaints of brutality are hard to sort out because they usually represent two different points of view: that of the complainant and that of the police. Regardless of whether they are justified or even accurate, reports of police brutality are common. Even if they are only partially founded, their publicity gives rise to serious concern. When it does occur and is witnessed by the public, it can have a profound impact, as the following case illustrates.

> Two small boys wanted to cross a busy street late one afternoon. The first, a 12-year-old, looked both ways before running across the street. His eight-year-old brother did not watch the traffic but kept his eye on his brother instead, and when he ran into the street he was struck by a motorist and fatally injured. Police and fire units responded and began providing emergency treatment to the child. As these efforts were in progress, the child's father appeared on the scene and when he realized the victim was his youngest child he tried to get to him. A police lieutenant at the scene grabbed the man and led him away, telling him he had to stand back. The father tried again to get to his son, and was told again by the lieutenant to go away. The third time the father tried to get to the child, the lieutenant grabbed him by the shirt and told him "You better get out of here before I'm forced to hurt you." *(Author's field notes.)*

The accident occurred on a busy road in front of a major shopping center and the police lieutenant's conduct was witnessed by a large number of bystanders. The comments about the lieutenant's behavior made by some of the other witnesses are "unprintable" and his conduct probably never will be forgotten by those who witnessed it. That officer's conduct, unfortunately, is typical of police officers in his particular department (a large, county-wide police department in one of the more affluent suburbs of Washington, DC). It therefore came as no surprise to the author a couple years later when the voters resoundingly defeated a public safety referendum during a local election.

Misfeasance

Misfeasance is the wrongful and injurious exercise of lawful authority. It can take place in many ways. For example, when people are arrested on "cover charges," misfeasance is likely to be involved. In these cases an individual is arrested for resisting arrest, interfering with a law enforcement officer or for disorderly conduct. These charges are used because the arresting officer either wants to harass the victim or "cover" himself after assaulting the person to be arrested. Misfeasance also occurs when police officers use their authority to insult or humble people. Consider the following newspaper article:

> ...County Police are investigating allegations that police used excessive force on and harassed a...man and his three brothers outside [a] nightclub...late last month. Joanne McCoy told [reporters] that her husband, Thomas McCoy, Jr., 27, was speaking with his three 18-year-old brothers and several other acquaintances outside [the nightclub] on the night of Nov. 30 when five or six police officers began questioning the group. According to Joanne McCoy, one officer demanded, "Got any drugs on you? We've been watching you for two hours." The officer then told Thomas McCoy and his brothers to empty their pockets and later shoved his nightstick in Thomas McCoy's stomach, Joanne McCoy said. ...Thomas had taken his three brothers, who were visiting...to [the nightclub] on the night in question to entertain them but discovered the club did not admit anyone under 21. Thomas McCoy saw some friends outside the club and was "socializing" for about a half hour when police—who had been dispatched to a car accident in front of the club—approached them. One of Thomas McCoy's brothers, Tim McCoy, was arrested and charged with disorderly conduct after he made an obscene remark to police as he and his brothers were leaving following the questioning, according to both Joanne McCoy and police. Joanne McCoy said police threatened to throw her in jail when she went to the [police] Station to ask why her brother-in-law had been arrested.[38]

Calling minorities by racial epithets or nicknames, or using a condescending tone of voice and demeanor are mild examples of this kind of misconduct. In other cases, the police may speak to citizens in ways designed to anger them or at least irritate them, sometimes in the hope the victim will do something for which the officer feels an actual arrest would be justified. Sometimes this happens because the officer is tired, unhappy or just in a sour mood. For example, one winter evening the police were diverting traffic from a main thoroughfare onto a side street because of an accident. The accident, however, could not be seen from the point where one officer was diverting traffic. The author (on his way home) was stopped by the patrolman and brusquely told to exit on the side street. He said, "O.K.—what have you got up ahead?" The officer walked up to the author's window and said, "What's the matter, asshole, are you deaf? I said *move it!*"

Nonfeasance

Nonfeasance is the omission of some act which ought to have been performed. Again, there are many ways in which this can be done. For example, a veteran police officer in one large Texas city was widely regarded by most other members of his department as both stupid and incompetent. He was assigned to the police garage as a "liaison officer," but in fact only showed up on payday, and then only long enough to collect his paycheck and leave. This case raises interesting questions. Some would argue that the officer was guilty of malfeasance because he was stealing his pay (taking his check without working for it). Others would argue that he was actually paid not to work (as the lesser of two evils), and thus *was* doing what he was paid to do. It also might be argued that he could not be accused of failing to do his job because the department did not give him a job to do, unless it was literally just to collect his check. (This officer, incidentally, is long gone, along with most of the administrators who condoned this practice.)

More serious forms of nonfeasance occur when officers simply refuse to act in cases where their action is called for. For years the police in the South routinely disregarded crimes by blacks against other blacks. A particularly common form of nonfeasance occurs when police officers refuse to act against other officers who are clearly guilty of misconduct. Again, this can be major or minor. Police officers typically extend "professional courtesy" to other police officers caught in off-duty traffic violations. In other cases the police may refuse to act against officers involved in substantive crimes. Police departments often prefer to request the resignation of such officers, unless the crime has come to the attention of the media. Even then, police officers forced to resign because of criminal misconduct usually are allowed to resign "for personal reasons" rather than face prosecution. It is argued that this is done to avoid damaging the credibility of the department as a whole and the reputation of its "good" officers.

Police corruption is typically based on nonfeasance and has been a long-standing problem. In fact, many of the efforts during the reform era were designed to limit the possibilities of police corruption. Because of the nature of their work, police officers have unique opportunities to drift from the so-called "straight and narrow." For example, the enormous amount of money generated by the illicit narcotics industry is a continuing threat to police integrity. Police corruption may start out small and grow, or it might involve traditionally accepted behavior condoned by one's peers. Low-level corruption is easy to rationalize: accepting money to "look the other way" is easier to justify than being a direct participant in a criminal activity, and stealing money from drug dealers can be easier to explain than stealing from an "ordinary" citizen (especially if it is part of a group activity by police officers). Although police corruption is indeed a problem in the larger cities, its seriousness probably has been somewhat exaggerated. As the Knapp Commission in New York City noted in the aftermath of a major police corruption scandal,

> Corrupt policemen have been informally described as being either "grass-eaters" or "meat-eaters." The overwhelming majority of those who do take payoffs are grass-eaters, who accept gratuities and solicit five- and ten- and twenty-dollar payments from contractors, tow-truck operators, gamblers, and the like, but do not aggressively pursue corruption payments. "Meat-eaters," probably only a small percentage of the force, spend a good deal of their working hours aggressively seeking out situations they can exploit for financial gain, including gambling, narcotics, and other serious offenses which can yield payments of thousands of dollars.[39]

One of the most difficult questions in law enforcement is: who is to police the police?[40] There are few realistic mechanisms for overseeing the conduct of the police. Attempts by the public to provide supervision through civilian review boards have met with hostile rejection by most police departments. Judicial oversight of police misconduct through rulings on questionable law enforcement tactics is too far removed in time and place to provide a sense of security to the community. For the average citizen, "what they see is what they get"—and what they see does not reassure them very much. The public, therefore, remains extremely reluctant to expand the authority of the police.

THE PROFESSIONAL MODEL OF POLICING

When the police in America entered the reform era, its leaders attempted to fashion a new model by removing the police from partisan politics and by centralizing control over law enforcement personnel. Discipline and efficiency were key elements, and this is one reason why American police departments are organized and administered along paramilitary lines. In larger departments the principles of "scientific management" were adopted where they seemed to fit and the law enforcement role was given primary emphasis. Although order maintenance has remained a fundamental part of police work, it has been viewed as secondary to the law enforcement duties of the police. This *professional model* of policing was founded on organizational values that have been used to both justify and guide the organization and operations of police departments. These values include:[41]

1. Police authority is based solely in the law. Professional police organizations are committed to enforcement of the law as their primary objective.

2. Communities can provide the police with assistance in enforcing the law. Helpful communities will provide police with information to assist them (the police) in carrying out their mission.

3. Responding to citizen calls for service is the highest police priority. All calls must receive the fastest response possible.

4. Social problems and other neighborhood issues are not the concern of the police unless they threaten the breakdown of public order.

5. The police, as the experts in crime control, are the ones best suited to develop police priorities and strategies.

During the reform era police departments combined advances in technology with more stringent control over their personnel to achieve the goal of professional law enforcement. The resulting operational strategy focused on the law enforcement role and on centralized control of highly mobile uniformed officers. One of the most widely respected texts on police administration says:

> Crime results from the coexistence of the desire to commit the act and the belief that the opportunity to do so exists. When either factor is absent, criminal acts will not be committed. The presence of one factor alone, regardless of how strong it may be, will not result in crime. The elimination or reduction of these two factors, therefore, is a basic police duty. One task is to prevent or eradicate criminality in the individual; the other embraces all security measures designed to hamper or prevent criminal operations.[42]

Having stated the forgoing as the purpose of the police, the authors go on to say, "Patrol is an indispensable service that plays a leading role in the accomplishment of the police purpose."[43] Thus, the uniformed patrol function has been universally regarded as "the backbone of police service." Although it may be augmented by specialized units (e.g., traffic, plainclothes, etc.), patrol remains the principle operating activity of virtually all American police departments. Until recently most police departments put the majority of their officers in the patrol division, which was then distributed evenly among three eight-hour shifts, assigning individual officers beats of approximately the same size. In most cities now, allocation of patrol force functions is based on demand for services and other criteria.

For a long time, traditional methods of allocating police manpower were accepted largely without question, and little research was conducted to test the validity of their underlying assumptions. The police function first came under sustained, serious scrutiny in the 1960s.[44] Preliminary results were disconcerting, as it quickly became evident that there was a significant gap between traditional theory and day-to-day reality. This early work was followed by the pioneering efforts of the Kansas City (Missouri) Police Department, which conducted a series of operations-oriented research projects. The most notable of these was the Preventive Patrol Experiment. Additional research followed in short order and the results were shocking.[45] The traditional assumptions about the efficiency of patrol and the need for rapid police response to all calls were found to be seriously flawed, if not outright wrong.

The professional model saw the police service as consisting of two components: administration and operations. *Administration* consists of the management of the department and its personnel. It focuses *inward* and includes recruiting, training, deploying and controlling the members of the department. Although the leading advocates of reform were quick to embrace many of the principles of management and apply them to police administration, a great deal of police administration remained closed to outside influence. The exclusion of minorities and women from police work and reliance on a rigid paramilitary model of personnel administration are but two examples of this. Administration of the police function has traditionally rested in the hands of men who came up through the ranks and whose post-secondary education was limited to professional police courses or, more recently, to criminal justice programs at the college level. As a consequence, police administration has not benefitted as much as it should from such disciplines as operations research or management, and most of the philosophy underlying administrative decisions is based on conventional wisdom rather than empirical data.

Police operations in the professional model are essentially reactive and driven by demands for service.[46] In its most basic format, the police respond to calls for service, sort things out after they arrive, do what seems best and then return to service. Patrol units are responsible for geographic areas of coverage and are considered "out of service" when responding to calls. As a result, one of the most important goals of a patrol element is to get back in service as soon as possible so it can respond to other calls. If the call is with regard to a serious crime, the responding patrol officers almost certainly will resume their patrol after being replaced by detectives or other specialists. As a practical consequence the goal of patrol is to be available for calls and to provide the minimum essential service when responding. This means the police in the professional model tend to be *incident-driven* rather than *outcome-driven*.[47] Because of this, police departments that have invested heavily in this model tend to work in cycles—often responding to the same places for the same problems.

STRATEGIC POLICING

The formal concept of *strategic policing* grew out of the Executive Session on Policing at Harvard University's Kennedy School of Government between 1985 and 1988.[48] An extension of the professional model, strategic policing focuses on crime control by targeting law enforcement resources against specific crimes or criminals. In using this approach the police define the crime problems they want to attack and use enhanced law enforcement techniques to achieve their objectives. For example, *Selected Traffic Enforcement Programs* (STEPs) were developed to reduce injuries and fatalities resulting from intoxicated drivers. One approach was to offer police officers overtime pay to work extra hours specifically to increase DWI arrests. "Directed patrol" likewise concentrates police patrol resources in certain areas and may emphasize specific tactics (e.g., finding and apprehending armed individuals). For example, prior to New Year's Eve in 1991 the Los Angeles Police enacted its "gunfire reduction program" to "help clear the streets of people considered dangerous before the start of holiday revelry."[48] The police were concerned with people who fired weapons to celebrate the new year. Although the sweep was successful, it was not popular with everyone. As one police supervisor said, "Whenever we go into a neighborhood in large numbers to clean up the areas, people are going to get their feet stepped on. If you want to be liked, I guess you have to join the fire department."[49] Decoy operations in convenience stores, transportation systems or other high-risk locations are used strategically to catch robbers or burglars. Sting operations have been used with great success in identifying and arresting burglars, thieves and fences as well as in recovering stolen property.

Strategic policing acknowledges the importance of the public in supporting police efforts, using such techniques as "crime stoppers" or "silent witness" programs to encourage people with information on crimes to come forward. In the case of the Los Angeles program to reduce random gunfire on New Year's Eve, the department distributed 800,000 fliers and 15,000 posters in English and Spanish explaining that random shooting is a felony that could be punished by up to three years in prison. Although public support is viewed as important, strategic policing does not involve non-police participation in the *defining* of crime problems or proposed law enforcement measures. Because the police view themselves as the experts on crime, they want the public to support —rather than help determine—the substance of their efforts.

Strategic policing has been particularly useful in dealing with such non-traditional crimes as serial rapes and murders, especially where the crimes cross jurisdictional lines. The use of multi-agency task forces has proven highly effective in the resolution of these kinds of crimes. Strategic policing also has been productive in working against organized criminal enterprises such as drug networks, gangs and economic crimes. These operations usually involve multi-agency cooperation and the use of highly sophisticated electronic surveillance resources, undercover assets and computerized application of link analysis and artificial intelligence. This kind of police work calls for computer specialists, behavioral scientists with expertise in crime analysis and profiling, and police officers with training in such areas as finance and accounting.

Because of the range of specialties required, strategic policing is more practical in larger departments. However, smaller police agencies can enter in cooperative agreements by forming "metro squads" and sharing human and physical resources on problems of mutual interest. As Moore and Trojanowicz point out,

> ...in strategic policing the police response to crime becomes broader, more proactive, and more sophisticated. The range of investigative and patrol methods is expanded to include intelligence operations, undercover stings, electronic surveillance, and sophisticated forensic methods. The range of targets is enlarged to include sophisticated offenders and inchoate crimes. The key new investments involve the creation of specialized investigative capabilities and improved criminal intelligence functions.[50]

Strategic policing is an extension of the professional model. Applying sophisticated resources proactively to specific crimes, it requires little change in organizational structure and none in institutional values. It does not concern itself with order maintenance or the provision of public services, except as they serve as a side benefit to improved law enforcement. Strategic policing does not replace any of the traditional tasks performed under the professional model, but instead augments them through the application of special resources to clearly defined crime-related problems.

PROBLEM-ORIENTED POLICING

The concept of *problem-oriented policing* grew out of the work of Herman Goldstein. Unlike the professional model or strategic policing, it represents a conceptually new approach to police work.[51] Goldstein notes that in the professional model, "police officers usually deal with the most obvious, superficial manifestations of a deeper problem—not the problem itself." As a result, "the police generally are expected to deal with the disruptive, intolerable effects of a problem. That requires a response quite different from what might be involved in dealing with the underlying conditions or problem."[52] Consider, for example, patrol officers dispatched to a woman's domestic violence complaint against her husband. According to the professional model, their goal would be the resolution of that specific incident so they could return to service as quickly as possible. If they took the *order maintenance* approach, they would try to negotiate with the disputants to resolve the immediate crisis (typically by suggesting that the husband spend the night elsewhere or by threatening to arrest him if they have to return). If they took the *law enforcement* approach, they would try to determine whether an assault occurred and if one did, they would arrest the husband. In any event, their actions would be driven by the specific incident. Because the larger problem of domestic violence is viewed as beyond their charter, its underlying dynamics are, of necessity, ignored. In *strategic policing* certain patrol units may be specially designated to respond to domestic violence calls and may be specifically interested in arresting domestic assailants. Although they might be more efficient in their approach, they would be no more effective.

In problem-oriented policing the focus is not on the specific incident but rather on the problem manifested by the incident. Goldstein suggests that it makes more sense to make the problem become the unit of work than to simply commit police resources to a stream of incidents that repeat themselves because the underlying problem is never addressed. In his formulation, these issues are community problems, not just police problems. To be sure, the police have a role to play, but Goldstein believes they can develop greater effectiveness in dealing with these community problems by understanding them better and tailoring their responses to the causes of the problem. The goal of greater effectiveness can occur at five levels. The police can:[53]

1. Eliminate the problem;

2. Reduce the number of incidents the problem creates;

3. Reduce the seriousness of the incidents the problem creates;

4. Design methods for handling the incidents better; and

5. Remove the problem from police consideration.

The first step in problem-oriented policing is to study the problem thoroughly. This involves going beyond the traditional application of "criminal labels." The reason for this is that "the use of statutory labels to describe substantive problems may mask important distinctions when the ultimate objective is to develop a more appropriate response to a specific form of behavior."[54]   This process should yield a great deal of useful information and identify a number of elements in the community that share a common interest in the problem. For example, the problem of daytime residential burglaries may be related to school absenteeism, drug abuse and issues involving environmental design. The next step—the actual goal of problem-oriented policing—is to develop responses that have the "greatest potential for eliminating or reducing the specific problem."[55] The final approach will involve a wide range of community resources—each committed to making an impact on the problem—acting in concert to bring about the desired changes.

Problem-oriented policing asks a great deal of the police. It requires them to diagnose police incidents as community problems and then to integrate the community into a formulated response. It also calls for the use of crime analysis in ways that are novel for most police departments. Although it does not reject either the order maintenance or law enforcement approach, it does take a much broader perspective than the police traditionally have embraced. It does not ask the police to change their values, but it does ask them to broaden their perspective and to consider viewpoints and responsibilities held by other elements of the community.

COMMUNITY POLICING

The most recent innovation in police thinking involves a concept known as *community policing*. Unlike the professional model, strategic policing or even problem-oriented policing, community policing tries to create an effective partnership between the community and the police by emphasizing the role of a *community police officer* (CPO). The CPO works with concerned citizens at the grass-roots level. This approach does not supplement "real" police work, it becomes police work in and of itself. It embodies an effort to create "competent communities," in which the police (through CPOs) enter into partnerships with existing community institutions such as families, schools, neighborhood associations, merchant groups and others.[56] Part of this approach involves changes in the operational philosophy of the department and the means by which it allocates personnel and conducts its operations. The role of the individual police officer is substantially different in community policing, and the department as a whole must change to support that role. Since community policing is based more on attention to customer-oriented *values* than on traditional law enforcement *methods*, it represents a radical departure in the philosophy of policing. Although it continues to place an emphasis on crime control and order maintenance, community policing stresses the importance of citizen and community involvement in the total process. The requirement for a significant shift in organizational values makes it difficult and time-consuming to implement. As one authority has noted, "Police organizations...have considerable momentum. Having a strong personal commitment to the values with which they have 'grown up,' police officers will find any hint of proposed change in the police culture extremely threatening."[57] Thus, a major obstacle in implementing community policing is getting the entirety of the police department to accept the concept and change how they have been accustomed to operating. See Figure 7.1 for some comparisons between community policing and traditional policing styles.

Figure 7.1

TRADITIONAL VS. COMMUNITY POLICING
Questions and Answers

TRADITIONAL POLICING	COMMUNITY POLICING
Who are the police?	
A government agency principally responsible for law enforcement.	*Police are the public and the public are the police; the police officers are those who are paid to give full-time attention to the duties of every citizen.*
What is the relationship of the police to other service departments?	
Priorities often conflict.	*The police are one department among many responsible for improving the quality of life.*
How is police efficiency measured?	
By detection and arrest rates.	*By the absence of crime and disorder.*
What are the highest priorities?	
Crimes that are high value (e.g., bank robberies) and those involving violence.	*Whatever problems most disturb the community.*
What, specifically, do police deal with?	
Incidents.	*Citizens' problems and concerns.*
What determines the effectiveness of police?	
Response time.	*Public cooperation.*
What view do the police take of service calls?	
Deal with them only if there is no real police work to do.	*Vital function and great opportunity.*

TRADITIONAL VS. COMMUNITY POLICING
Questions and Answers

TRADITIONAL POLICING	COMMUNITY POLICING
What is police professionalism?	
Swift effective response to serious crime.	*Keeping close to the community.*
What kind of intelligence is most important?	
Crime intelligence (study of particular crimes or series of crimes).	*Criminal intelligence (information about the activities of individuals or groups).*
What is the essential nature of police accountability?	
Highly centralized; governed by rules, regulations, and policy directives; accountable to the law.	*Emphasis on local accountability to community needs.*
What is the role of the headquarters?	
To provide necessary rules and policy directives.	*To preach organizational values.*
What is the role of the press liaison department?	
To keep the "heat" off operational officers so they can get on with the job.	*To coordinate an essential channel of communications with the community.*
How do the police regard prosecutions?	
As an important goal.	*As one tool among many.*

Source: Malcolm K. Sparrow, "Implementing Community Policing," *Perspectives on Policing*, No. 9 (November 1988), 8-9.

ORIGINS OF THE CONCEPT:
THE FLINT, MICHIGAN EXPERIMENT [58]

Community policing started in Flint, Michigan. The goal at the time was not to apply a new philosophy of policing but to find a way to reach the community more effectively. The chief of police wanted to improve the department's effectiveness in neighborhoods where the relationship between the police and the community was especially poor. Flint, dependent on the automobile industry, experienced a major economic downturn during the energy crisis and afterwards when the industry went into a steep decline. The city's unemployment reached 25 percent, and by 1979 "one-fourth of Flint's citizens had moved away, leaving slightly fewer than 160,000 residents, 41.5 percent black and 56.2 percent white, in a city riddled with violent crime, racial tension, and seemingly endless recriminations about what had happened to its once-promising future." [59] Max Durbin, police chief at the time, was aware of the broader social and economic problems facing the city. He believed the police department needed a new approach if it was going to overcome the effects of these problems and serve the community effectively. After a series of unfortunate racial incidents involving the police (including a shootout between two police officers—a white male and a black female—over who was going to drive their patrol car) it became clear that *something* had to be done.

Following a series of meetings between members of the police department and interested citizens, a plan was developed that called for establishing neighborhood foot patrols in 14 neighborhoods. The goal was to get police officers out of their cars and into contact with residents in the target neighborhoods. The architects of the experiment hoped that by placing police officers on foot in the neighborhoods they would develop a better sense of what their neighborhoods wanted and needed. The experiment was funded by the Mott Foundation, which provided a $2.6 million dollar grant for three years to fund 22 foot patrol officers working out of base stations in selected neighborhoods. These foot patrols were not intended to replace regular patrol units but rather to supplement them. A major part of the experiment called for participation by neighborhood residents. Based on inputs from all participants, the initial experiment had seven goals:

1. To decrease the amount of actual or perceived criminal activity;

2. To increase the citizens' perceptions of personal safety;

3. To deliver to Flint residents a type of law enforcement consistent with community needs and the ideals of modern police practice;

4. To create a community awareness of crime problems and methods of increasing law enforcement's ability to effectively deal with actual or potential criminal activity;

5. To develop citizen volunteer action aimed at various target areas in support of (and under the direction of) the police department;

6. To eliminate citizen apathy about reporting crimes to the police; and

7. To increase protection for women, children and the aged.

Since they supplemented "regular" patrol officers, the foot patrol officers were given considerable latitude in how they approached their work; in a nutshell, they "owned" their piece of the city and were free to experiment with new ideas. Since they were not following any pre-established plan, they had to figure out what to do by trial and error. As Trojanowicz and Bucqueroux noted, "...this was the genesis of a new problem-solving approach to community problems related to crime and disorder. Freed from the patrol car and the police radio, the Flint foot officers began to make the shift from responding to incidents to focusing on addressing the underlying dynamics, without formally articulating what the philosophical shift entailed."[60] In the professional model of policing most police-citizen contacts are initiated *by people who call the police*. For the foot patrol officers in Flint, however, the police-citizen contacts had to be initiated *by the police themselves*. In order to learn what the neighborhood problems were and to define solutions for them, the officers were enjoined to approach the residents and earn their confidence. The experiment was not without its problems, but though it did have some failures it made steady progress and most of the foot patrol officers developed effective relationships within their areas. A year after it began, the experiment was extended to cover one-third of the city. Eventually the foot patrol was extended to the entire city.

Unfortunately, as the foot patrol experiment grew, the city's financial situation continued to deteriorate. Declining revenues put a serious crunch on the city's ability to fund services, and it was evident that the city could not absorb the cost of the program once the Mott Foundation grant expired. In August of 1982 the city put a referendum before the voters to increase their taxes for three years to support the foot patrol program; in effect, the vote was a referendum on the program itself. The vote passed. The same referendum was put before the voters again in 1985 and passed by an even wider margin than it did in 1982.

Even with this public support, the program was not without its detractors. In 1987 the new mayor (elected in 1984) put all Flint police officers back in their patrol cars. The following November he lost his bid for re-election. In addition to fiscal and political turmoil, the police department had six chiefs in less than five years and the foot patrol experiment was not popular with all members of the department. In 1988 the new mayor again went to the voters to see if they would increase their taxes to fund foot patrol for four years. In August of 1988, 68 percent of the voters voted "yes" and a modified version of the program was instituted. In its new form the police officers were assigned to work out of cars but were encouraged to maintain contact with the residents of their beats. What was the outcome? As Trojanowicz and Bucqueroux noted, "the research confirms that the foot patrol effort in Flint was a remarkable success. Yet the full story of what happened to foot patrol in Flint also shows how political and economic pressures can mean the operation was a success, but the patient died, though many continue to hope it will be reborn even stronger."[61]

In spite of the ultimate outcome of the Flint experiment, it became clear there was a better way to deliver police services and that involving the community was the key to positive change. The concept spread to many other cities and became a hot topic in police circles. The ten principles of the community policing process are detailed in Figure 7.2.[62]

The search for identity in the post-reform era has been difficult and frustrating for the police. Their major roles—law enforcement, order maintenance and service—call for different approaches. Some problems can be treated either as law enforcement *or* order maintenance issues. Police departments that have embraced the professional model as a means of reducing corruption and political influence have simultaneously downplayed their order maintenance and service roles, thereby estranging themselves from the public. Departments that have emphasized service or order maintenance have run the risk of being ineffective in fighting crime. Police departments have had a great deal of difficulty developing organizational values that allow them to embrace all three missions. By placing emphasis on any one, the others have suffered.

Part of the problem is tradition: police departments, like all other institutions, are reluctant to change. Over the years police departments have developed a pattern of organization and style of operation that emphasize the response to incidents and the assessment of them as "law enforcement" issues. They have not been concerned about the underlying problems reflected by those incidents. In addition, the police have been partially driven by the technologies they use, which compliment the traditional organizational style (emphasizing downward control and a measure of efficiency based on such things as response time and number of arrests). To add to the problem, most cities have changed in the last three decades in such crucial areas as racial composition, availability of public funding, land use and community expectations. It is clear that the traditional methods of policing are no longer the answer but, unfortunately, the "right" answer is yet to be revealed. Problem-oriented policing offers great promise, as does community policing, but both face serious obstacles.

Figure 7.2

TEN PRINCIPLES OF COMMUNITY POLICING

1. Community Policing is both a philosophy and an organizational strategy that allows the police and community residents to work closely together in new ways to solve the problems of crime, fear of crime, physical and social disorder, and neighborhood decay. The philosophy rests on the belief that law-abiding people in the community deserve input into the police process in exchange for their participation and support. It also rests on the belief that solutions to contemporary community problems demand freeing both people and the police to explore creative, new ways to address neighborhood concerns beyond a narrow focus on individual crime incidents.

2. Community Policing's organizational strategy first demands that everyone in the department, including both civilian and sworn personnel, must investigate ways to translate the philosophy into practice. This demands making the subtle but sophisticated shift so that everyone in the department understands the need to focus on solving community problems in creative, new ways that can include challenging and enlisting people in the process of policing themselves. Community Policing also implies a shift within the department that grants greater autonomy to line officers, which implies enhanced respect for their judgment as police professionals.

3. To implement true Community Policing, police departments must also create and develop a new breed of line officer, the Community Policing Officer (CPO), who acts as the direct link between the police and people in the community. As the department's community outreach specialists, CPOs must be freed from the isolation of the patrol car and the demands of the police radio, so they can maintain daily, direct, face-to-face contact with the people they serve in a clearly defined beat area.

4. The CPO's broad role demands routine, sustained contact with the law-abiding people in the community, so that together they can explore creative new solutions to local concerns involving crime, fear of crime, disorder, and decay, with private citizens serving as unpaid volunteers. As full-fledged law enforcement officers, CPOs respond to calls for service and make arrests, but they also go beyond this narrow focus to develop and monitor broad-based, long-term initiatives that can involve community residents in efforts to improve the overall quality of life in the area over time. As the community's ombudsmen, CPOs also link individuals and groups in the community to the public and private agencies that offer help.

5. Community Policing implies a new contract between the police and the citizens it serves, one that offers the hope of overcoming widespread apathy, at the same time it restrains any impulse to vigilantism. The new relationship, based on mutual trust, also suggests that the police serve as a catalyst, challenging people to accept their share of the responsibility for solving their own individual problems, as well as their

(5, continued)

share of the responsibility for the overall quality of life in the community. The shift to Community Policing also means a slower response time for non-emergency calls and the citizens themselves will be asked to handle more of their minor concerns, but in exchange this will free the department to work with people on developing long-term solutions for pressing community concerns.

6. Community Policing adds a vital proactive element to the traditional reactive role of the police, resulting in full-spectrum police service. As the only agency of social control open 24 hours a day, seven days a week, the police must maintain the ability to respond to immediate crises and crime incidents, but Community Policing broadens the police role so that they can make a greater impact on making changes today that hold the promise of making communities safer and more attractive places to live tomorrow.

7. Community Policing stresses exploring new ways to protect and enhance the lives of those who are most vulnerable—juveniles, the elderly, minorities, the poor, the disabled, the homeless. It both assimilates and broadens the scope of previous outreach efforts, such as Crime Prevention and Police/Community Relations Units, by involving the entire department in efforts to prevent and control crime in ways that encourage the police and law-abiding people to work together with mutual respect and accountability.

8. Community Policing promotes the judicious use of technology, but it also rests on the belief that nothing surpasses what dedicated human beings, talking and working together, can achieve. It invests trust in those who are on the front lines together on the street, relying on their combined judgment, wisdom and expertise to fashion creative new approaches to contemporary community concerns.

9. Community Policing must be a fully integrated approach that involves everyone in the department, with the CPOs as specialists in bridging the gap between the police and the people they serve. The Community Policing approach plays a crucial role internally, within the police department, by providing information and assistance about the community and its problems, and by enlisting broad-based community support for the department's overall objectives.

10. Community Policing provides decentralized, personalized police service to the community. It recognizes that the police cannot impose order on the community from outside, but that people must be encouraged to think of the police as a resource they can use in helping to solve contemporary community concerns. It is not a tactic to be applied, then abandoned, but an entirely new way of thinking about the police role in society, a philosophy that also offers a coherent and cohesive organizational plan that police departments can modify to suit their specific needs.

Source: Robert Trojanowicz and Bonnie Bucqueroux, *Community Policing: A Contemporary Perspective* (Cincinnati: Anderson Publishing Co., 1990), xiii-xv.

SUMMARY

The police are currently trying to find their way in a period of massive social, economic and technological change. As communities themselves are going through rapid change, many traditional roles and values are being challenged—including those of the police. For decades the police enjoyed widespread public support and were left alone to define both *what* they did and *how* they did it. The public was largely supportive because during the reform era the police worked hard to reduce political influence and eliminate corruption. Moreover, the existing power structure of the community was largely content with police activities and methods, and the rest of the community lacked the standing to have their complaints heard. Thus, the police system that existed perpetuated itself with public approval. It was not until the aftermath of the civil rights movement and the entry of women into previously all-male occupations that things began to change. The changing makeup of cities and the demand for greater accountability on the part of police made changes inevitable. In the post-reform era, the police are searching for a role that meets both public expectations and the need to assure public safety.

One of the major components of police work is *order maintenance*; in fact, the police in America were originally formed to deal with disorder. This continues to be one of their primary functions. Events that could be considered crimes are only a part of "disorder" in its general sense. Most disorder involves unpleasant or undesired activities. In many cases it is hard to tell who is right and who is wrong, but in any event, the police are called upon to make judgments and decisions on such matters and ultimately to resolve the disorderly situation. If the activity involves a breach of law, they have the option of invoking the criminal justice process; if not, they must negotiate, "criminalize" or abandon the problem. Disorderly situations carry a risk of danger to the police who, quite naturally, must structure their responses in ways that maximize their personal safety. This sometimes places them in conflict (if not confrontation) with the people they police. Since disorderly situations are often ambiguous, and since the police must gain control over the situation before deciding what to do about it, they are forced to assert their authority and make what often amount to arbitrary decisions. They have learned from experience how to handle most of these situations, but sometimes make poor decisions or take actions that are seen as capricious. When the police were accountable only to themselves, poor outcomes were insignificant and often unnoticed. With increasing demands for their accountability, however, police order maintenance efforts receive closer scrutiny than in the past, thereby making the job more difficult (and even riskier) for the police.

The second major role of the police is *law enforcement*. Since this role is governed by substantive and procedural law, it is much less ambiguous than order maintenance. It also calls for different tactics and value orientation. In law enforcement the police simply carry out the mandate of the law. By emphasizing this role the police can filter out a great deal of unwanted order maintenance activity. In a rigidly law enforcement-oriented department, a call that does not involve a crime results in the police removing themselves from the scene and advising the people involved to work it out among themselves or seek other professional assistance. Most police departments embrace a mixture of order maintenance and law enforcement. The patrol division of the department responds to all routine calls (most of which involve order maintenance issues), while specialized units (tactical squads and detective units) work on law enforcement issues. The biggest problems occur when order maintenance issues are handled from a law enforcement perspective, or when the police attempt to enforce the law in those "victimless" crimes in which the offender sees engagement in such activities as a private matter (and thus, none of the police department's business).

The third role played by the police is to provide *service* to members of the community. Service includes a wide array of activities, ranging from acting as funeral escorts to delivering messages. In general, the police do not object to providing these services as long as they do not interfere with what they consider to be "real" police work or consume an excessive amount of the officer's time. Most police officers accept service calls as necessary but deem them to be low-priority tasks.

The three roles—order maintenance, law enforcement and service—are often intertwined and produce expectations of the police that are sometimes contradictory or confusing. The police are expected to maintain order but not to exceed the limits of their legal authority. Difficulty between the police and the public seems to arise from four primary areas:

1. *Anxiety is provoked by disorder.* The public does not like disorderly situations and looks to the police to correct them, but the police may not have the training or authority to resolve many of these situations (such as homelessness, juvenile deliquency, domestic violence, and so on).

2. *The public has an ambivalent attitude toward crime.* When a crime involves someone they know and occurs in a context that is "understandable," the public is likely to withhold support from the police in dealing with it. If, on the other hand, crime is something separate and apart from the experience and understanding of the citizen, he or she fully expects the police not only to handle it but to take harsh measures (as long as those measures do not go *too* far).

3. *There is concern over abuse of police authority.* Unfortunately, there is a lengthy and sordid history of such problems. The fact that the public *likes* the police does not necessarily mean it *trusts* them.

Police departments are organized in various ways. The *professional model* of police work places an emphasis on fighting crime. Its measures of efficiency are response time, number of arrests made and crime rates. Police departments organized along the lines of the professional model use a command hierarchy that imposes control from the top downward. Although individual officers in these departments may have considerable discretion in how they handle calls, they have little discretion regarding department organization or functions. The professional model is organized to deliver law enforcement services and to minimize the risk of either political influence or corruption within the department. Seeing themselves as the experts on crime and disorder, the police ask for public support in accepting department decisions.

Strategic policing is an extension of the professional model in which the department concentrates specialized resources on specific crime problems. By using tactical patrol forces, multi-agency investigative teams, sophisticated technical surveillance equipment and experts in crime analysis and profiling, they focus specialized resources on tough problems. Strategic policing can be extremely effective, and in those circumstances where it is called for it is unquestionably the best response. However, it has little to do with order maintenance per se, as it is freed from service calls. Not suitable for an entire department, this model seves as a supplement to the broader patrol, traffic and investigative functions of the police.

Problem-oriented policing embodies a much different approach. It asks police officers (and departments) to analyze the problems generating the incidents to which they respond so they can work toward the resolution of the rudimentary problem. It seeks to tailor the police department's response to issues by first studying the issues and then by involving other parts of the community in the solution of them. It places less emphasis on traditional tactics and more emphasis on understanding the problem and finding the best long-term solution.

Finally, there is *community policing*, a new approach to providing police services. Community policing stresses the dynamic relationship between the public and the police, and seeks to actively involve the community in its own policing. "Community police officers" (CPOs) become facilitators of this process. They interact with their clientele on a regular, face-to-face basis by working a foot beat in a compact area. They are thus freed from the anonymity of the police car and the demands of the police radio. The underlying concept is that the community must police itself. The professional police officers are there to help citizens do this by providing information, support and a means of liaison with the rest of the governmental structure. Although community policing is a popular concept, it has a number of drawbacks. It challenges the traditional or-ganization of police bureaucracies and vests a great deal of authority in those at the bottom rather than those at the top; it is a new concept and police officers who have a deep psychological investment in traditional police methods may find it difficult to accept. It remains to be seen just how effective it will be in the more crime-ridden neighborhoods or communities. Although it is not yet a proven method, preliminary results indicate that community policing has the potential to be highly successful.

DISCUSSION QUESTIONS

1. Why has the typical American community been so willing to accept tradi-tional police methods?

2. How does functionalist theory explain why the police are organized and operate as they do?

3. To what extent should the police be involved in order maintenance, espe-cially when no actual crimes are involved?

4. Is police work actually dangerous? If not, are the police justified in the high degree of concern they express for their personal safety?

5. What is the "symbolic assailant" and is it a reasonable concept?

6. How is it that the police officer—the person with the least authority in the department—has the greatest degree of discretionary latitude?

7. What is the difference between police discretion and arbitrariness?

8. How does the law enforcement approach differ from the order maintenance approach? Is one better than the other?

9. Why is discretionary latitude diminished when police officers take a law enforcement approach to their work?

10. What happens when order maintenance problems are treated as law en-forcement issues?

11. How can the police "criminalize" an order maintenance issue? Is doing so an abuse of police authority or a good tactic?

12. Should traffic law enforcement be handled the way it is, or can you suggest a better way?

13. Is it reasonable to expect the police to perform a service role in this day and age? Defend your position.

14. Why does public disorder provoke citizen anxiety—and why should the police be the ones who have to deal with it?

15. Do we expect too much from the police in their order maintenance role?

16. Do you agree with Wilson and Kelling's thesis in "Broken Windows"? Why or why not?

17. Is the public's attitude toward crime realistic? Explain.

18. What kinds of "criminals" do the public dislike the most? Why?

19. How do you think the typical police officer is most likely to abuse his or her authority (if at all)?

20. What is the difference between misfeasance and malfeasance?

21. What are the values that underlie the professional model of policing?

22. How does strategic policing differ from the professional model of policing?

23. How does problem-oriented policing differ from community policing?

24. What is the principle utility of strategic policing (where does it do the most good)?

25. What is the focus of problem-oriented policing?

26. What is the first step in problem-oriented policing?

27. What do proponents of community policing mean when they refer to "competent communities"?

28. What are the organizational values of community policing? How do they differ from those of the professional model?

29. Who are most likely to be the biggest sources of resistance in a police department that wants to shift to community policing?

30. Can community policing work in all departments? If not, where are they least likely to succeed?

REFERENCES

[1] See, for example, Roderick D. McKenzie, *On Human Ecology* (Chicago: The University of Chicago Press, 1968), especially Chapter II, "The Local Community," 51-101.

[2] Kenneth D. Bailey, *Methods of Social Research*, 3rd ed. (New York: The Free Press, 1987), 454-456.

[3] James Q. Wilson, *Varieties of Police Behavior* (New York: Athenaeum, 1974), 16.

[4] U.S. Department of Justice, Federal Bureau of Investigation, "Law Enforcement Officers Killed and Assaulted, 1989," *FBI Uniform Crime Reports* (Washington, DC: U.S. Government Printing Office, 1990), 53.

[5] U.S. Department of Justice, Federal Bureau of Investigation, "Law Enforcement Officers Killed and Assaulted, 1989," 53.

[6] U.S. Department of Justice, Federal Bureau of Investigation, "Law Enforcement Officers Killed and Assaulted, 1987," *FBI Uniform Crime Reports* (Washington, DC: U.S. Government Printing Office, 1987), 17; and U.S. Department of Justice, Federal Bureau of Investigation, "Law Enforcement Officers Killed and Assaulted, 1989," 18.

[7] Connie Fletcher, *What Cops Know* (New York: Villard Books, 1991), 30-31.

[8] Fletcher, *What Cops Know*, 30-31.

[9] Jerome H. Skolnick, *Justice Without Trial* (New York: John Wiley & Sons, 1966), see especially 42-48.

[10] Skolnick, *Justice Without Trial*, 42-48.

[11] Fletcher, *What Cops Know*, 15.

[12] See especially, Richard E. Sykes, James C. Fox and John P. Clark, "A Socio-Legal Theory of Police Discretion," in *The Ambivalent Force: Perspective on the Police*, 2nd ed., ed. Arthur Niederhoffer and Abraham S. Blumberg (Hinsdale, IL: The Dryden Press, 1976), 171-182.

[13] Michael York and Pierre Thomas, "D.C. Police Unit Fights Crime With Attitude," *The Washington Post*, 15 December 1991, A1, A20.

[14] York and Thomas, "D.C. Police Unit Fights Crime With Attitude," A1, A20.

[15] Gabriel Escobar, "Harrowing D.C. Jaywalking Arrest Described," *The Washington Post*, 29 August 1990, D5.

[16] "Tough Stop," *Insight on the News*, 5 January 1992, 19.

[17] Charles Leerhsen, et al., "His Career Is Over: Americans Couldn't Stop Talking About His Sad Adventure," *Newsweek*, 12 August 1991, 54-55.

[18] Leerhsen, et al., "His Career Is Over," 54-55.

[19] See, for example, Michael F. Cahn ad James F. Tien, *An Alternative Approach in Police Response: Wilmington Management of Demand Program* (Washington, DC: U.S. Government Printing Office, 1981); Michael T. Farmer, ed., *Differential Police Response Strategies* (Washington, DC: Police Executive Research Forum, 1981); and J. Thomas McEwen, Edward F. Connors and Marcia T. Cohen, *Evaluation of the Differential Police Response Field Test* (Alexandria, VA: Research Management Associates, 1984).

[20] Mark H. Moore and Robert C. Trojanowicz, "Policing and the Fear of Crime," *Perspectives on Policing* (June 1988), 3.

[21] James Q. Wilson and George L. Kelling, "Broken Windows," *The Atlantic Monthly*, March 1982, 29-30.

[22] Wilson and Kelling, "Broken Windows," 34.

[23] Wilson and Kelling, "Broken Windows," 34.

[24] Wilson and Kelling, "Broken Windows," 34.

[25] Charles Z. Bach, "Driven from the District," *The Washington Post*, 22 December 1991, C8.

[26] U.S. Department of Justice, Federal Bureau of Investigation, *Uniform Crime Reports 1990* (Washington, DC: U.S. Government Printing Office, 11 August 1991), 7, 50.

[27] George Gallup, Jr., *The Gallup Report*, Report No. 285 (Princeton, NJ: The Gallup Poll, June 1989), 24.

[28] Kathleen Maguire and Timothy J. Flanagan, eds., U.S. Department of Justice, Bureau of Justice Statistics, *Sourcebook of Criminal Justice Statistics 1990* (Washington, DC: U.S. Government Printing Office, 1991), Table 2.37, "Attitudes Toward Walking Alone at Night and Safety at Home" (p. 184).

[29] See, for example, W.G. Skogan, "Public Policy and the Fear of Crime in Large American Cities," in *Public Law and Public Policy*, ed. J.S. Gardiner (New York: Praeger, 1977), 1-18.

[30] George Gallup, Jr., *The Gallup Report*, Report No. 285, 29, 30.

[31] Maguire and Flanagan, *Sourcebook of Criminal Justice Statistics 1990*, Table 2.51 "Attitudes Toward Capital Punishment for Persons Convicted of Murder" (pp. 200-201).

[32] *The Gallup Report*, Report No. 285, 28.

[33] *The Gallup Report*, Report No. 285, 27.

[34] *The Gallup Report*, Report No. 285, 31.

[35] Maguire and Flanagan, *Sourcebook of Criminal Justice Statistics 1990*, Table 2.17 "Respondents' Ratings of the Honesty and Ethical Standards of Policemen" (p. 165).

[36] Herman Goldstein, *Problem-Oriented Policing* (New York: McGraw-Hill Publishing Co., 1990), 45.

[37] Ed Cray, *The Enemy in the Streets: Police Malpractice in America* (Garden City, NY: Anchor Books, 1972), 167.

[38] Ian Zack, "Police Investigate Harassment Charges," *The Connection*, 18 December 1991, 3, 11.

[39] "An Example of Police Corruption: Knapp Commission Report on Police Corruption in New York City," in Thomas Barker and David L. Carter, *Police Deviance* (Cincinnati: Pilgrimage, A Division of Anderson Publishing Co., 1986), 28.

[40] See, for example, Kevin Krajack, "Police vs. Police," *Police Magazine*, May 1980, 6-20.

[41] Robert Wasserman and Mark H. Moore, "Values in Policing," *Perspectives on Policing* (November 1988), 4.

[42] O.W. Wilson and Roy C. McLaren, *Police Administration*, 3rd ed. (New York: McGraw-Hill Book Company, 1972), 319.

[43] Wilson and McLaren, *Police Administration*, 320.

[44] See, for example, the following classics: Egon Bittner, "The Police on Skid-Row: A Study of Peace Keeping," *American Sociological Review* 32 (1967), 699-715; Albert J. Reiss, Jr., *The Police and the Public* (New Haven, CT: Yale University Press, 1971); Jerome H. Skolnick, *Justice Without Trial: Law Enforcement in Democratic Society* (New York: John Wiley & Sons, 1966); and James Q. Wilson, *Varieties of Police Behavior: The Management of Law and Order in Eight Communities* (Cambridge, MA: Harvard University Press, 1968.)

[45] John E. Eck and William Spelman, "Who Ya Gonna Call? The Police as Problem Busters," *Crime & Delinquency* 33 (1987), 35.

[46] See especially Mark H. Moore, Robert C. Trojanowicz and George L. Kelling, "Crime and Policing," *Perspectives on Policing* (June 1988).

[47] Eck and Spelman, "Who Ya Gonna Call?," 1, 2.

[48] Leef Smith, "Los Angeles Police Sweep Aims to Curb Holiday Gunfire," *The Washington Post* , 1 January 1992, A16.

[49] Smith, "Los Angeles Police Sweep Aims to Curb Holiday Gunfire," A16.

[50] Mark H. Moore and Robert C. Trojanowicz, "Corporate Strategies for Policing," *Perspectives on Policing* (November 1988).

[51] Goldstein's proposal first appeared as "Improving Policing: A Problem-Oriented Approach," in *Crime and Delinquency* 25 (1979), 236-258. It has been systematically developed in his book, *Problem-Oriented Policing* (New York: McGraw-Hill Publishing Co., 1990).

[52] Goldstein, *Problem-Oriented Policing*, 45.

[53] Eck and Spelman, "Who Ya Gonna Call?," 5-6.

[54] Goldstein, *Problem-Oriented Policing*, 39.

[55] Goldstein, *Problem-Oriented Policing*, 44.

[56] Moore and Trojanowicz, "Corporate Strategies for Policing," 9.

[57] Malcolm K. Sparrow, "Implementing Community Policing," *Perspectives on Policing* (8 November 1988), 1.

[58] Robert C. Trojanowicz and Bonnie Bucqueroux, *Community Policing: A Contemporary Perspective* (Cincinnati: Anderson Publishing Co., 1990). See Chapter 7, "The Flint Experience," 195-228.

[59] Trojanowicz and Bucqueroux, *Community Policing*, 195-228.

[60] Trojanowicz and Bucqueroux, *Community Policing*, 203.

[61] Trojanowicz and Bucqueroux, *Community Policing*, 226.

[62] Trojanowicz and Bucqueroux, *Community Policing*, xiii-xv.

Photo Credit: Tony O'Brien, Frost Publishing Group, Ltd.

Chapter 8

THE POLICE CULTURE
AND THE CHALLENGE
OF THE TWENTY-FIRST CENTURY

So far we have looked at the police institution as it has developed over the years. However, it is more than an institution; it is also a human enterprise and for that reason it is important to understand its culture. The police culture has been nurtured by specific historical processes that are now undergoing rapid change. As a result the police as an institution is also undergoing enormous and sometimes stressful change. We have seen how cities have changed in recent decades and noted some of the pressures they must face. The same is true of police departments. The demand for change in how they recruit, who will become police officers and what is expected of the profession will almost certainly change the police culture. With increased participation of women in the labor force and the growth of ethnic and racial minorities as a larger proportionate share of the total population, white males are becoming a distinct minority in the labor force.[1] Such an eventuality would have a dramatic impact on law enforcement, which historically has been a predominantly white male occupation.

Obviously, there is a great deal of diversity among police officers—if for no other reason than the fact that there are so many of them and so many different law enforcement agencies. The typical police officer in 1991 was a white male, 33.7 years old, with 11 years of service. He had some college and worked in a department that paid an average starting salary of $22,500.[2] In 1990 there were nearly 17,000 publicly funded state and local law enforcement agencies in the United States (including 49 general purpose state police departments and an estimated 12,288 general purpose police departments, 3,100 sheriff's departments and about 1,563 special police departments).[3] Police officers work in city, county and state agencies ranging in size from just a few sworn officers to thousands of them. The "big six"—Detroit, Philadelphia, Houston, Chicago, Los Angeles and New York City—fit into the latter category, led by the New York City Police Department, which employs over 26,000.[4] In spite of an enormous diversity in department size and jurisdiction, all police officers share a great deal in common.

Who are these people? Where do they come from and why are they drawn to police work? Are police officers representative of the communities they serve, or are they a unique subset of the population? Why do they have such a unique occupational culture, and how does that culture influence their work or how they deal with the public? To what extent do selection procedures influence who becomes a police officer, and how do those decisions impact on the quality of law enforcement in the community? Not surprisingly, the answers to these questions are complex.

As we have already noted, in the last half of the nineteenth century millions of immigrants came to this country, mostly from Europe. The overwhelming majority were unlettered, unskilled and poor. Most, like the Irish who fled from famine, or the Germans and Italians who fled from poverty and political oppression, came to America in the hope of finding a better life for themselves and their families. Unfortunately, a great many of them found continued economic hardship punctuated with ethnic hostility. Although their expectations were based on optimism and hope, the reality of their new lives was shaped by limited social and economic opportunities and prejudice. Many found a cool reception in the private sector, where all too often there were more applicants than jobs. During this period the cities into which they immigrated were growing rapidly (in part because of the massive immigration) and "many newcomers sought jobs...in the fire, police, water, and sanitation departments, the courts and schools, and the other burgeoning government bureaucracies. By the end of the century thousands of first- and second-generation Americans counted on these municipal agencies for their livelihood."[5] Jobs in the police department were highly desirable. They generally paid well, did not require much (if any) literacy or education, gave the incumbents higher status in the community and sometimes offered free medical care.

Because in the big cities access to these jobs was through the political machine, "political affiliation" was the most important consideration in determining who was selected to join the police force.[6] Although politicians in some jurisdictions demanded kickbacks for passing out jobs on the police force, most political bosses "preferred evidence that the candidate and his friends or relatives had been helpful to the party in the past and could be counted on by the organization in the future."[7] Even where entry into the police was governed by civil service requirements, there were few obstacles for those who were politically connected.

> For applicants who had the machine's backing, the official requirements were no problem. Neither the medical examiners, who gave the physical tests, nor the police officials, who made the character checks, were inclined to stand in the way of an influential politician, because they too were political appointees....Hence some recruits were overweight, undersize, and [over-aged]; others were illiterate, alcoholic, and syphilitic; still others had outstanding debts and criminal records; and one Kansas City patrolman had a wooden leg. For applicants who had the organization's support, the civil service exams were no problem either....Rarely did the civil service prevent a candidate endorsed by the machine, no matter how low he scored on the tests, from being appointed to the force.[8]

As might be expected, this kind of selection process did not always produce the best police officers. According to one survey made in Chicago at the turn of the century, a great many of the police officers admitted they "spent most of their time not on the streets but in saloons, restaurants, barbershops, bowling alleys, pool halls, and bootblack stands. They were everywhere save on the beat."[9] However, the fact that so many police officers performed poorly should not come as a surprise. The primary motive for becoming a police officer during this era was economic: the job paid well and offered reasonable security. The work was not difficult and there were extra benefits, depending on the individual police officer's personal ethics and inclination for exploiting opportunity.

Police officers during the political era were drawn from the lower and lower-middle classes. As such, they brought with them the values and cultural perspectives of the uneducated and those accustomed to earning a living through manual labor. They tended to be pragmatic men who knew how tough the world really was, and they were quite prepared to meet it on its own terms. They maintained order largely through intimidation and the threat of force and did so largely with the support of the existing power structure of the community. They were loyal to their families, their ethnic community and the politicians who got them their jobs. They did not worry a great deal about the finer points of the law nor were they encouraged to do so. This generation of police officers left several important legacies that became foundations in American police culture. First, police work was clearly defined as a blue-collar occupation. Second, as a semi-skilled occupation it did not require education or much specialized training beyond what was learned on the job. This established a recruiting pattern that did not emphasize education. Finally, the police entrenched a long-standing standard of making police work the exclusive domain of white males.

During the reform era, control was slowly wrested from the political machine as reformers made serious efforts to eliminate or at least reduce corruption within the ranks of the police. The initial goal was to bring police departments under control and remove them from the influence of politicians and others. As these efforts succeeded, the professional model emerged and the police gradually (and grudgingly) became more honest and less subject to outside control. The goal then shifted to bringing individual police officers under control. As we noted previously, civil service reform played an important role in shaping municipal police departments. And as departments came under the control of civil service, the selection and promotion of police officers became less a matter of political connection and more one of merit. This enabled cities to be more selective in who they hired. Civil service reform also protected police officers from being arbitrarily fired, further reducing the dependence of the police on political bosses or a need to cultivate outside support. In order to strengthen control over police officers, reformers imposed stronger central leadership and emphasized the military model of authority and control. Entrance mandates were stiffened to include height, weight, age and—sometimes—education requirements. In addition, background checks were performed to ensure that applicants did not have criminal histories or serious character problems. Training for new police officers was established and departments insisted on more stringent record-keeping (which further fostered the notion of accountability).

Many of those who entered police work during the reform era came from police families; in fact, one writer noted that because "a preference for police work often is passed from one generation to the next within a family...[t]he handing down from father to son of police work as an occupation, contributes to the perpetuation of a common body of police values and traditions."[10] Others became police officers because they were interested in police work itself and the security offered by the job.[11] Gradually, the primary reason why people joined the police began to shift from a quest for job security to a desire to do police work.

Even though screening requirements became more rigorous, they were still limited in scope and arbitrary in nature. Although educational requirements were minimal during the reform era, physical requirements were rigid because police work was still thought of a physical labor. As late as the early 1960s about one-fourth of all law enforcement agencies did not require more than an elementary school education.[12] On the other hand, the minimum physical standards during the same time frame usually required near-perfect vision along with clearly defined weight and height standards. By the mid-1960s less than one-third of all police departments conducted any kind of emotional or psychiatric evaluation of police candidates. At most they were subjected to an interview and a background investigation.

Until very recently police officers continued to be drawn largely from working-class backgrounds, and for many of them their occupational status was an advancement over that of their fathers. A major impetus to change came in 1967 when the President's Commission on Law Enforcement and the Administration of Justice recommended that "[t]he ultimate aim of all police departments should be that all personnel with general enforcement powers have baccalaureate degrees" and that "[p]olice departments should take immediate steps to establish a minimum requirement of a baccalaureate degree for all supervisory and executive positions."[13]   To create incentives for this goal, Congress passed legislation that (among other things) created the Law Enforcement Education Program (LEEP). LEEP provided funding for curriculum and program development as well as financing for police officers to attend college. Across the country, criminal justice programs mushroomed. Their courses were soon filled with would-be police officers and others interested in the field. Fueled by this renewed interest in the police and reinforced by a steady stream of television shows and movies about police work, a broader slice of American society became interested in policing.

THE POLICE CULTURE IN THE LATE REFORM ERA

Police departments, like other complex institutions, tend to have a unique culture. This culture may vary from one police agency to the next, but most agencies share a number of common traits. This is not surprising because nearly every organization "...has an invisible quality—a certain style, a character, a way of doing things—that may be more powerful than the dictates of any one person or any formal system. Understanding the soul of the organization requires that we travel below the charts, rule books, machines and buildings into the underground world of corporate cultures."[14] Virtually any organization can be said to have an organizational culture if it has formalized ways of responding to issues, has norms and values that are shared by its members and operates in a climate that specifies how people are to be dealt with (both inside and outside the organization).

An organization's culture is sustained by a number of key elements, among the most important of which are:

1. What the organization's bosses pay attention to;

2. How the organization reacts to critical incidents or organizational crises;

3. How the organization communicates expectations to its members;

4. What the organization rewards its members for and how it does so;

5. Criteria for recruiting, selecting, promoting and removing members of the organization; and

6. The kinds of organizational ceremonies and rites that impart meaning and expectations to its members.[15]

Although people may be attracted to police work for different reasons, the majority of police officers are drawn from a pool of young males, most of whom share relatively similar social, cultural and economic backgrounds. Their similarities to one another make them a nonrepresentative segment of the larger population. This is refined by the police departments as they screen and evaluate police candidates; those who pass the initial screening and graduate from the police academy are then socialized into police work by their more experienced peers. This is a time-consuming process that requires new entrants to learn the expectations amd folklore of the department. Those who succeed eventually become members of the police culture and serve to perpetuate that culture.

The impact of the police culture is clearly stronger in some departments than in others, but its presence is felt in most police departments. What are the factors that help shape police culture? To a certain extent the culture is shaped by the personalities of those who enter the work force and remain, but it also is shaped by a combination of factors unique to police work. These factors include internal control, power, solidarity, private knowledge, alienation and cynicism, the concepts of doing good and performing well, and social and political conservatism.

INTERNAL CONTROL

Police departments are hierarchical structures; internal relationships are based largely on power and formal authority. This is reinforced by uniforms, military ranks, formal regulations and a distinctive etiquette that rests on clear lines of superordination and subordination. Many police officers are veterans of the military. Those who did serve in the lower ranks of the military experienced taking (and sometimes giving) orders, working in a highly structured environment, learning to subordinate themselves to discipline and working as a team. The police share another feature with the military: both are trained in the use of force and under certain circumstances are empowered to use it—up to and including lethal force. Just as members of the military distinguish themselves from civilians, so do police officers. Thus, the experience of being in the military is an excellent platform from which an individual can assess the desirability of working in the paramilitary environment of the police profession. Those who find the military congenial are likely to have little difficulty adapting to the police, for it operates on much the same basis. One of the first hurdles a potential police officer must surmount is adaptation to a work environment with relatively rigid patterns of authority and obligation. Individuals who are not temperamentally suited to such a setting are apt to find police work disagreeable and stressful.

Police departments further control their members through another subtle but important process. New police officers lack standing within their departments because it takes time to gain the experience by which they must "pay their dues." They must prove themselves to their more experienced peers and earn their respect and trust before being fully accepted. The police community is so insular and self-contained that rookie police officers find themselves under great pressure to meet the expectations of their seniors. This produces a high degree of conforming behavior. As new officers subordinate themselves to the expectations of their peers, they simultaneously accept the values of the police culture and become a part of it.

POWER

Police officers exercise considerable power over others in their day-to-day relationships with the community. Their wide discretionary latitude (which enables them to deal with most of the situations they encounter) also produces a psychological sense of personal power. This sense of power befits the internal dynamics that drive the police departments themselves. Police departments typically demand strict obedience to higher-ranking officers and respect for those who have been on the job for a longer period of time (or who occupy special or privileged assignments). Accepting such an obligation to officers above them in rank encourages many officers to demand similar respect from those whom they police. Not necessarily autocratic in nature, this expectation of respect from citizens is a means of establishing and maintaining the control essential for dealing with disorderly situations.

SOLIDARITY

Because of the unique nature of their working environment and the absolute need to be able to depend on one another, police officers enjoy a kind of solidarity seldom seen in other occupations. As the author was told when he was a young police officer, "the world is divided into two kinds of people: cops and those who are not." Although this institutional solidarity produces a strong sense of kinship among police officers, at the same time it fosters isolation from the rest of the community. Maintaining this solidarity in part are the consequences of the discretionary latitude exercised by the police. Such latitude means that mistakes are inevitable. All police officers make them from time to time, and they know it. Sometimes it is a matter of poor judgment; sometimes worse. Under psychological stress, pressure from above or because of intentional provocation, an officer might act inappropriately or even fail to act. Trust among police officers demands that the mistakes of individual officers be concealed by a code of silence. This mutual support against adversity arising from error protects all police officers. It is one of the foundations of the legendary secrecy of the police service.

SECRECY

Secrecy among police officers is not new. In 1930 the Wickersham Commission noted that, "It is an unwritten law in police departments that police officers must never testify against their brother officers."[16] Although police officers generally respect the law, they above all know how unrealistic its enforcement or administration can be. The pressure to cut corners or stretch the rules can be great and sometimes it is felt that the ends justify the means.

Case Example: The police were called to a jewelry store, where a young clerk said an expensive ring had been stolen. She said a customer, whom she knew, came in and asked to see a tray of rings. When she placed the tray in front of him he began to examine several of the rings. Her attention was temporarily diverted by another customer, and when she returned the individual with the tray of rings thanked her and left. As she was putting the tray up she noticed one of the rings was missing. She did not see him take the ring but was certain that he had. She told the police she was going to have to make good the loss and could not afford to do so. Based on her identification of the man the police were able to determine where he lived and went to visit him. When he answered the door, one of the officers told him that he understood the man had found something and wanted to get it back to its rightful owner. The officer told the man he would be happy to take it back for him. When the man told the officer he didn't know what he was talking about, the officer told him he had about 30 seconds to get the ring or he'd "pound his ass into the ground and find it himself." The man suddenly recalled finding a ring and retrieved it for the officer, who took it back to the store. No one was arrested and no offense report was made. *(Author's field notes.)*

Case Example: During the early morning hours on a slow shift, a police officer felt sleepy and wanted to do something to wake up. He decided to stop the next car he saw, which he did. After stopping the car the officer approached the driver and immediately became suspicious because of the driver's demeanor. He ordered him out of the car and while his partner watched him he searched the car. After finding a 9mm automatic pistol under the front seat he opened the trunk where he found a quantity of drugs. In making their report the two officers said the car had been driving in an erratic manner and they stopped it based on their suspicion the driver was intoxicated. They also agreed to say the pistol was open to view on the floorboard and that the driver had consented to a search of his trunk. The driver subsequently pleaded guilty on a negotiated plea. *(Author's field notes.)*

Police work can be fast-paced and emotionally charged. Decisions made at the spur of the moment might seem inappropriate when examined later. For that reason police officers are tolerant of the decisions made by their peers. An officer who consistently exercises poor judgment may be shunned by peers, but is not likely to be reported unless the conduct immediately threatens the peers' safety. New police officers—"rookies"—can be problematic for experienced police officers because they may not yet understand how the code of silence works or why. Part of their indoctrination (noted above under "Internal Control") includes telling them to keep their mouths shut and their eyes and ears open—and then observing them to see if they will.

Secrecy also keeps police officers from sharing what they learn at work with "outsiders." Since those outside the police environment cannot relate to police work or its decision-making processes, it is considered better not to talk about work with them. This is exacerbated by the solidarity of the profession and the fact that many officers decline to maintain social contact with the non-police community. Finally, because police work is intrusive, officers see things few others ever do, and this "private knowledge" may not be appropriate to share outside police circles.

PRIVATE KNOWLEDGE

Police officers are routinely admitted into the most private aspects of other people's lives. They enter their homes, hear their secrets and often decide what will be done to whom. They see life as it seldom is seen outside police work and this knowledge carries an implicit obligation of confidentiality. During the course of their duties police officers learn a great deal about people, businesses and institutions. Although they are free to pass this information on to other police officers, it is not apt to be shared with those outside of the police profession. Interestingly, police officers routinely ask other police officers for information with the full expectation that whatever is known will be shared while at the same time withholding information from other police officers. This includes the identities of informants, details of undercover or covert operations, and information pertaining to certain kinds of confidential investigations.

ALIENATION AND CYNICISM

As Niederhoffer and Niederhoffer noted, "To become a police officer is to become a citizen of a different world that exists in another dimension from our own, but in the same time and place."[17] Police officers soon learn not to share their experiences. Moreover, working on rotating shifts or in parts of the community where they cannot or would not live further estranges them from the non-police community. The solidarity and secrecy that define the police culture isolate them from their non-police peers in all but the most superficial ways. They are thereby more socially isolated and dependent on the department.

Another consequence of engaging in police work is learning that just about everyone lies. Some lie outright, others lie by omission and yet others just put "a little twist" on what they tell the police. People who read about police activities in the paper seldom realize that what is reported is almost always incomplete or inaccurate.   Because police officers see a great many so-called "responsible" citizens engaged in irresponsible activities (ranging from theft to sexual misconduct), after a while their initial amazement is replaced by cynicism. As they come to realize that all is not as it appears, police officers turn further inward. Gradually they come to see themselves as "the thin blue line" that separates society from savages.

The alienation felt by many police officers is partly defensive and partly offensive. Just as it enables them to cope with disappointment and rejection, it also provides a solution of sorts by supporting the alternative reality of police solidarity. In addition, over time police officers grow weary of violence, misconduct and conflict. They then experience a sense of alienation that feeds and exacerbates the cynicism.[18] The cynical attitude assumed by many police officers results in a "loss of faith in people, of enthusiasm for the higher ideals of police work and of pride and integrity."[19] The cynicism in turn reinforces the alienation, convincing police that only other police officers can be trusted. Sometimes such prejudice extends even to believing that only certain *types* of police officers can be trusted—just the kind with which they work, whether they be patrol officers, detectives or whatever.

DOING GOOD AND PERFORMING WELL

By doing their job well, police officers also "do good"; that is, by performing their duties with efficiency they provide a benefit to others. They are involved in countless human dramas, which, although small in scale, are still extremely important to those whom the police help. The more proficient a police officer becomes at police work, the more the officer is able to help others. Thus, "performing well" and "doing good" are closely linked. The skills police officers develop as they gain experience can be quite extraordinary. For example, as police officers learn to "read" the streets, they develop an ability to ascertain what is out of place, what is different and even simply what is going on. As one Chicago police officer pointed out, "We see things that you would never see. And if you did see it, you wouldn't know what you were seeing." When this particular officer was taking a college course in deviant psychology, his class had to walk around downtown for an hour and report to the professor and the class on what they had seen. He said:

> So here we are, a gaggle of maybe twenty-three people walking around the Loop. We get back, the girls were saying, "Did you see the dresses in the windows of Saks?" The guys were saying, "Did you notice how congested the traffic was?" And then it came my turn. And I said, "Well, did anybody see the guy that was fighting with his girlfriend and he was gonna jump off the bridge into the river?" And the prof says, "I didn't see that." I said, "My gosh, they were no further than five feet from you." And I said, "Did you see that one guy that was trying to get his hand in the woman's purse?" He said, "I didn't see that!" He thought I was making it up. I said, "No. That's what I saw. I'm sure that's not what you saw." Nobody saw it. Not a soul. And here was this guy, we walked right past him, standing on one of the stanchions of the Wacker Avenue Bridge, and he was telling this girl he was gonna jump in the river and kill himself. And she was telling him not to. A few seconds later, he came down off the stanchion and they walked off. And you couldn't have missed it, I didn't think. Apparently, you could—twenty-two of them didn't see it. Seeing what's really going on—that's what they used to call "street eyes."[20]

Police work brings law enforcement officers into regular contact with people who need help—and the police *do* help them, sometimes by listening to their complaints, at other times by saving their lives. Their order maintenance role forces them to be problem-solvers. Most of the problems they encounter are "people problems," and in resolving those problems the police provide a very real benefit to their clients. Sometimes they help in ways that no one else can. Consider the following (actual) events from the perspective of the person who benefited from what the police did:

> **Case Example:** A woman was driving with her two-year-old daughter in the car. The child had a piece of candy lodged in her throat. When the mother noticed the child was not breathing she pulled her car over, but did not know what else to do. She saw a police car approaching from the opposite direction and jumped out of her car and flagged him down. When she told the police officer what was wrong, he radioed for a fire department ambulance and ran to the car. By this time the child was unconscious and blue. He performed the Heimlich maneuver, which dislodged the candy. By the time the ambulance arrived the child was conscious and the crisis was over. *(Author's field notes.)*

Case Example: During the early evening hours an off-duty police officer noticed a man outside a shopping mall who looked suspicious, so he decided to watch him for a few minutes. As a young woman walked past the man she looked at him and clutched her purse under her arm. The man noticed this and followed her into the parking lot. As he caught up with her and grabbed her purse, the police officer was right behind him. He said, "what do you think you're doing?" The man snarled back, "mess with me, asshole, and you'll find out." The police officer drew his weapon and arrested the man. (*Author's field notes.*)

Case Example: A man and his estranged wife were in the process of getting a divorce. When she came to his apartment one Sunday to pick up their children he strangled her and had a friend dump the body along a rural road. The killer collected a substantial insurance payment and obtained custody of their two children. It took the detectives three years to get the evidence they needed, and they arrested the killer. During the entire time they maintained contact with the slain woman's mother, keeping her informed on the status of the case. After the killer was convicted and sentenced to life in prison, the victim's mother got custody of the children. She said the only thing that enabled her to endure the long ordeal was the compassion and kindness extended to her by the police. (*Author's field notes.*)

Police officers intervene in the lives of others in ways that make a major difference. They "serve and protect" even when their efforts go unappreciated. They know that in a sense they *are* the thin blue line. Their social and political views are shaped by their background and refined by their work. They have typically been conservative in both.

SOCIAL AND POLITICAL CONSERVATISM

In 1965 one scholar noted: "Conservatism, in every form, fits tidily into the police scheme of things. The very nature of the police task with its emphasis on regulation and control is conservative. This conservatism affects attitudes toward politics, social custom, education, and the rearing of the young. From the very outset of a police officer's career, the pressure toward conformity is extremely intense."[21] Although times have changed a great deal since then, the basic point is still valid. For the most part, the police are still conservative, though as a group they are becoming more "middle-of-the-road."[22] They are still drawn from essentially the same strata of society and face the same pressures as their predecessors. In addition, the disorder, violence and criminal misconduct they see causes them to place a premium on orderliness and lawful conduct. To maintain order and enforce the law, they must at least tacitly support the social system the law seeks to maintain. In the long run this forces the police to represent the status quo and shapes their political perspective.

POLICE RECRUITING: GETTING THE BEST IN OR KEEPING THE WORST OUT?

The very characteristics that define the police culture create a grave risk that the wrong kinds of people will be attracted to the work. People with psychological deficiencies may be particularly attracted to police work because of the authority it gives them (a significant proportion of complaints against police officers are based on abuse of authority). The brutal, cruel and emotionally impaired are also attracted to police work because it provides them ample opportunity to act out their violent fantasies (25 percent of the police applicants in one sample were rejected on psychiatric grounds because they were classified as borderline psychotic, inadequate personalities, schizoid personalities or paranoid).[23] A large body of research shows that many people are drawn to police work for reasons that serve their personal pathologies rather than the needs of the public. As far back as 1968 an analysis of Chicago police applicants revealed that 20.7 percent of the candidates screened by department psychologists were diagnosed as having an incapacitating mental illness. This included people diagnosed as neurotic, psychotic or as suffering from chronic brain syndrome. The analysis also found them to represent almost 10 percent of the total applicant population.[24]

Police selection must therefore deal with two questions: who should be allowed in and who should be kept out? Prior to the reform era this was not much of a problem. Since police departments could set their own standards, they focused their requirements on the applicant's physical strength, degree of agility and reputation. In addition, reform-era police departments concerned with reducing corruption naturally concentrated on hiring applicants who had "clean" records—in the hope that the absence of obvious dishonesty in a candidate's past would be a good predictor of future honesty on the job. Minorities and females were largely ignored and education played almost no role in the selection of police officers. Since the 1960s three independent but related factors changed the picture: (1) the rapid growth of civil liability in police performance, (2) the civil rights movement, and (3) the advent of higher education for police.

CIVIL LIABILITY

In 1871 Congress passed legislation creating federal jurisdiction for claims of deprivation of federally secured rights "under color of" state law.[25] This statute provides as follows:

> Every person who, under color of any statute, ordinance, regulation, custom, or usage of any State of Territory, subjects, or causes to be subjected, any citizen of the United States or any other person within the jurisdiction thereof to the deprivation of any rights, privileges, or immunities secured by the Constitution and laws, shall be liable to the party injured in an action at law, suit in equity, or other proper proceeding for redress....

This law was passed in the aftermath of the Civil War because of the inability or unwillingness of local authorities in the Southern states to deal with the activities of the Ku Klux Klan.[26] It is important to note that this law is *civil* rather than *criminal* in nature; it established cause of action in cases arising from an abridgement of rights by individuals acting "under color of any statute, ordinance, regulation, custom, or usage...." For many years "state officers" (including police officers) who violated their authority were not included within the scope of the law. However, in 1945 the Supreme Court held in *Screws v. United States* that a sheriff who beat a black prisoner to death acted "under color," and Justice Douglas defined "under color" of law as meaning "under the pretense" of law.[27] This meant that law enforcement officers who engaged in misconduct during the performance of their duties were liable as individuals for their "official" actions.

In 1961 the Supreme Court considered a case in which 13 Chicago police officers broke into a home without a warrant, forced the residents out of bed at gunpoint and made them stand naked while the police searched their house. Moreover, during the search they were also subjected to verbal and physical abuse. One of them was taken to the police station, held for 10 hours and then released without being charged. The residents sued, alleging that the police conducted an illegal search under color of law. The lower courts found for the police, but the Supreme Court held for the plaintiffs; however, the Supreme Court also held that municipalities were immune from liability under Section 1983.[28] By granting municipalities absolute immunity, the Supreme Court in effect affirmed that the police acted on their own and that the cities that employed them were not responsible for the misconduct of individual police officers. Because of the Supreme Court's ruling, cities had no financial incentive to deal with the problem.

The immunity enjoyed by municipalities came to an end in an unlikely case. In 1971 a group of pregnant women employed by the Board of Education and the Department of Social Services in New York City sought redress because they were forced to take unpaid leave before their condition physically required them to do so. They sought injunctive relief to keep from being forced to take leave and back pay for the period of leave they had been forced to take. The Supreme Court reversed its previous position, stating that their analysis of the legislative history of the Civil Rights Act of 1871 "compels the conclusion that Congress did intend municipalities and other local government units to be included among those persons to whom Section 1983 applies. Local governing bodies, therefore, can be sued directly under Section 1983...."[29]

Since members of virtually all criminal justice agencies—especially the police—act "under color of state law," abuse of their authority is subject to redress under Section 1983. Moreover, the units of government they work for may be sued for injunctive, declaratory or monetary relief.[30] As might be expected, liability lawsuits against police departments mushroomed in response and cities have been forced to pay many millions of dollars in damages. Thus far, lawsuits have concentrated in the areas of illegal search and seizure, false arrest, false testimony, police brutality, wrongful death and off-duty conduct in which an officer's actions are misrepresented as "official" police activity.[31] Police departments also have been found liable under Section 1983 for other forms of negligence, including the failure to weed out employees who are unfit for their work, failure to provide adequate supervision and failure to provide adequate training.[32] A result has been the development of the theory of *vicarious liability*, in which supervisors and managers can be held liable for the conduct of their subordinates. Thus, the failure to adequately train and supervise can be defined as an act of omission that renders supervisory police officials and their departments liable for the conduct of their subordinates.

Hiring and promotion issues have become particularly important areas of civil liability. For example, tests used to screen prospective employees must be job-related, valid, free from any "inherent bias," properly administered and properly graded. Failure in any of these respects is a legitimate basis for a lawsuit under Section 1983.[33] Because of this, the threat of adverse actions under civil liability has placed a major responsibility on state and local governments, as well as individual police departments, in ways never previously contemplated. Police departments have lost the prerogative of hiring, training and supervising as they please and have been forced to either meet rigorous standards or face expensive lawsuits.

CIVIL RIGHTS

Until the 1970s black officers were a rarity in most police departments. In 1940 they comprised only about 1 percent of the police population and by 1984 had risen to only about 8 percent. Many of the departments that hired black police officers limited both their activities and promotion prospects. In some cities they were forbidden to detain or arrest whites, barred from operating police cars or restricted to policing black neighborhoods.[34] This changed in the aftermath of the urban unrest of the 1960s, which was followed by civil rights legislation that brought about substantial changes in the recruiting and hiring of black police officers. The Civil Rights Act of 1964 prohibited discrimination on the basis of race, color, religion, sex or national origin. Although it applied to private employers, labor unions and employment agencies engaged in any industry affecting commerce and employing 25 or more employees, it did not extend the same requirement to *public* employment. As a result many police departments continued to follow many of their traditional hiring practices, even though those practices continued to restrict the number of blacks and women who could enter police ranks. The most important limitation on police personnel practices was Section 1983. However, in the 1960s the issue of civil liability in personnel practices had not yet reached significant proportions.

The Civil Rights Act of 1964 was incomplete in its coverage and difficult to enforce [the Equal Employment Opportunity Commission (EEOC), which was created by Title VII of the Civil Rights Act of 1964, is the primary enforcement arm of the federal government with regard to employment discrimination]. In its early years the EEOC was largely ineffective because it had no powers of enforcement or prosecution. It could do little more than investigate complaints and reach findings. Although it could (and did) encourage people with legitimate complaints to file lawsuits in the federal courts, the process was time-consuming and expensive. After passage of the Civil Rights Act of 1964, most employers stopped discriminating directly on the basis of race, but many instituted or maintained indirect personnel criteria that had the same effect (i.e., education requirements, the use of seniority systems, hiring or advancement on the basis of test scores, and disqualification based on a prior arrest record). Police departments (and their municipal governments) should have seen the handwriting on the wall as early as 1971 in the landmark case of *Griggs v. Duke Power Company*, in which the Supreme Court held that under the Civil Rights Act "practices, procedures, or tests neutral on their face, and even neutral in terms of intent, cannot be maintained if they operate to 'freeze' the status quo of prior discriminatory employment practices."[35] However, state and local governments did not heed the warning and in 1972 Title VII amended the Civil Rights Act to include public employment, thereby forcing local governments to reassess their hiring practices. In 1972 Congress also gave the EEOC the authority to bring lawsuits in certain instances, thereby strengthening its enforcement abilities. To deal with the problem of indirect discrimination in personnel practices, the EEOC issued its *Uniform Guidelines on Employee Selection Procedures* in 1978. These guidelines prohibited the use of standards that had an adverse impact on a disproportionate number of minorities—even when the standards appeared to be racially neutral. The guidelines provided that any hiring practice having such an "adverse impact" on minorities (including women and racial groups) was illegal unless the employer could demonstrate that it was justified by business necessity. The concept of *adverse impact* was subsequently interpreted by the courts to include recruiting, testing or promotional practices that fail to include members of minority groups or women in numbers equivalent to their representation in the local labor force.[36]

The EEOC guidelines issued in 1978 applied to police departments. The goal was not so much to force police departments to hire women or blacks as it was to remove artificial employment barriers that served to discriminate against them. The full impact of *Griggs v. Duke Power Company* was brought to bear on police departments when they learned that "Congress directed the thrust of the [Civil Rights] Act to the consequences of employment practices, not simply the motivation."[37] As a result, police recruiting and promotion practices changed dramatically.

In 1989 the Supreme Court overruled the *Griggs* decision, holding that regardless of how strong the proof of discriminatory effect, employers were no longer required to prove that its practices were based on business necessity. In *Wards Cove Packing Co. v. Atonio* the court ruled that those who believe they have been discriminated against must prove that the employer has no justification for its discriminatory practices, thus shifting the burden from the defendant to the plaintiff. The Civil Rights Act of 1991 was designed to overturn nine Supreme Court decisions that made it more difficult for workers to initiate and win job discrimination suits. Its primary target was *Wards Cove v. Atonio*. The main thrust of the bill was that hiring and promotion requirements should be related to job performance; again the burden was placed on the *employer* to justify practices that resulted in indirect discrimination. It also gave the right to sue for monetary awards and damages (a right previously limited to victims of racial discrimination) to victims of intentional discrimination based on sex, religion, national origin or disability.

The last three decades have produced unprecedented change in American society. These changes have touched virtually every community and institution in the country. We have already seen that the combined effects of technological, social, economic and legal changes have had a profound impact on the police. Although police departments have had to respond to these changes, many have not embraced the challenge with open arms, and many have actively resisted them. This is particularly evident with regard to the challenge of bringing women and minorities into police work.

Until the 1960s discrimination in employment was blatant and direct. As a result, police departments remained essentially white male institutions. Far from being static organizations engaged in self-serving traditions, police departments have been in a continuous state of evolution. The task of bringing the police from what they were in the political era to where they are today is a story of great progress and achievement (although both have been uneven in many respects). In the 65 years from the turn of the century, through the passage of the Civil Rights Act of 1964, the police made tremendous advances in almost every respect. That they had remained essentially white male institutions was the result of a combination of history and public policy. After passage of the Act, public policy changed and the white male historical legacy became a liability. Although simple on the surface, the problem's solution has proven to be profoundly difficult. The first issue was how the police were going to make themselves representative of the community. The solution seemed to lie in removing barriers to employment. This meant that standards that had been used for a long time had to be carefully examined and sometimes completely scrapped. It also meant that the selection policy of focusing on hiring *in* the best candidates had to be modified in favor of selecting the unfit *out* of the police work force pool. The second issue, equally difficult, was the requirement that the police not only abandon a whole range of discriminatory practices, but also overcome the results of past discrimination. In other words, they had to fix what was broken and play "catch-up" at the same time.

The vehicle for meeting these objectives was (and is) affirmative action. Affirmative action requires employers to first take positive steps to overcome the effects of past discrimination and then develop plans to achieve equality in employment opportunity. Thus, the police had to draw women and minorities to the profession as well as ensure their fair and unimpeded access to all levels of the department. Police recruiting and promotion practices had to change. Opportunities that either never existed before or had been extremely limited needed to be facilitated. Since this was done at the expense of the traditions and values of the police culture, the change was painful for many. In many cases changes occurred only because police departments were threatened with lawsuits or other court action. Many affirmative action plans have been imposed on police departments by the courts and have not represented the wishes of the majority of the officers. For example, as the 1980s came to a close, nearly two-thirds of the 50 largest police departments reported that they were (or had been) operating under an affirmative action plan during the past five years; 23 of these plans were court-ordered and only seven were voluntary.[38]

It was noted in an earlier chapter that public policies virtually always have unintended consequences. Affirmative action is no exception. Although affirmative action plans deal with one problem and are intended to enrich the quality of the police department as a whole, they also can generate organizational trauma. By instigating the aggressive recruitment, training and promotion of minorities and women, they have created tension in departments whose members do not see the absence of minorities and women as a problem—or even as the result of intentional discrimination. Moreover, these plans have been viewed by many as a serious wrong in and of themselves because they run counter to long-cherished beliefs about the importance of merit and seniority. Conflicts over affirmative action plans can divide and polarize a police agency, especially when affirmative action criteria seem to have more to do with race and gender than with ability or fundamental fairness.[39] Illustrating this is the situation of the police department in Dallas, Texas, which has a policy requiring that 25 percent of all promotions go to blacks and 10 percent to Hispanics. In 1990, 24 white lieutenants filed a reverse discrimination suit claiming that, based on this policy, they were passed over for promotion to the rank of captain in favor of the highest ranking blacks and Hispanics. In 1980 the North Carolina Highway Patrol avoided a lawsuit by entering into a consent decree in which they agreed to fill half of their trooper vacancies with blacks and 25 percent with women until the composition of the patrol consisted of blacks and females in the same proportion as the state's labor force.[40] Other jurisdictions have implemented plans that establish quotas (usually referred to as "goals") and set timetables that circumvent traditional hiring and promotion practices, effectively limiting the participation of white males in the pool of eligible candidates competing for police jobs (or promotions within them). For example, in 1991 an agreement was reached between the Coalition of Black Maryland State Troopers and the state that contained a five-year timetable for increasing the number of blacks in ranks through First Sergeant to 22 percent. The Maryland Troopers Association, which represents the majority of the Maryland State Police, challenged the settlement saying that it violates other trooper's rights by requiring black promotions.[41] The Michigan State Police also entered a consent decree that established lower test scores for minority applicants and set lower standards for promoting minorities and women to supervisory positions. Bitter conflict followed within the agency.

Two assumptions behind the concept of affirmative action were that standards would not be lowered and reverse discrimination would not be allowed. The theoretical objective of affirmative action was for departments to identify and recruit minority candidates who met the same basic standards as whites. It assumed that if two candidates were equally qualified, consideration would be given to the minority candidate. However, as Carter and Sapp point out,

> The reactive procedures have typically addressed the letter of affirmative action without addressing the spirit of the concept. It appears that many administrators (and not just police administrators) assumed that qualified minority candidates simply could not be found. Therefore, in order to meet demographic parity demands, qualifying criteria (e.g., background, education, traffic records, etc.) and test scores for minority and non-minority applicants were sometimes different. The effect of these practices has been to increase tensions between majority and minority officers as well as to breed the concept of "reverse discrimination."[42]

The greatest increase in the percentage of black police officers has taken place in cities with black mayors and police chiefs—especially in cities that entered into affirmative action consent decrees.[43] Police departments that either cannot or will not select the best qualified people for its police officers could be condemned to be staffed and managed by those who are marginally qualified. If so, will those departments slowly stagnate and become like the police departments of an earlier era but different in their racial, gender or ethnic composition? This may very well be the major challenge to the police of the next century.

HIGHER EDUCATION

We have already noted that in 1967 President Johnson's crime commission recommended the baccalaureate degree as the minimum standard for employment in law enforcement, and that in 1968 the federal government established the Law Enforcement Education Program to help bring that goal to reality. Because of the financial incentives provided under the Law Enforcement Education Program, criminal justice and law enforcement degree programs quickly became a major growth area in higher education. Police departments cooperated in a variety of ways: in some cities by establishing incentive pay for higher education; in others by increasing the minimum educational requirements for employment. The initial thrust was for in-service police officers to return to school. After criminal justice programs became established, large numbers of non-police students took the courses; some majored in criminal justice and subsequently sought employment in the criminal justice system. In the rush to create criminal justice degree programs, little careful thought was given to curriculum or faculty credentials. Many of the programs left themselves open to criticism.[44] Even so, criminal justice programs became (and remain) popular in many colleges. Degree programs are offered from the associate to the doctorate level.

What is the impact of a college education on police officers? In an early assessment by Trojanowicz and Nicholson, a number of differences were noted between police officers with and without college educations. Those who did not attend college preferred to follow schedules and daily routines; they were quicker to act aggressively against people who acted hostile toward them; they considered themselves more "practical" as opposed to imaginative; they preferred working with their supervisors to working alone and preferred having their supervisors make decisions for them; and finally, they placed a high premium on the values of the police culture. On the other hand, police officers with a college education were more willing to experiment and try new ideas; they preferred assuming a leadership role and liked supervising others; they were more methodical in processing information and reaching decisions; they enjoyed excitement and variety in their work; and finally, they were less inclined to define themselves in terms of the traditional police culture.[45] Subsequent research has indicated consistently that police officers with a college education perform better than those without one.

However, certain unanticipated consequences resulted from making criminal justice a college discipline. First, students who major in criminal justice programs understandably wish to be hired in the field after they graduate. It is possible that, as a result, larger numbers of young people from middle-class backgrounds are seeking entry into police work, thereby disrupting the traditional blue-collar, working-class population of the police profession. These college-educated, middle-class people bring with them a different set of expectations and experiences, all of which tend to challenge the traditional police culture. They tend to be less conservative, more flexible and less interested in traditional forms of authority. A second negative consequence is that by establishing post-secondary education requirements, police departments automatically limit access to jobs, thereby creating an adverse impact and bringing higher education for police officers into conflict with EEOC guidelines. As Carter and Sapp point out, "The push for increased education for police came at almost the same time that concern for civil rights and equal opportunity for all Americans became a national priority. An obstacle was the concern that requiring a college education for entry into policing might be discriminatory."[46] At the basis of this argument is the contention that historically minorities have had disproportionately lower access to higher education and would therefore be excluded from police work if a college degree became a requirement. This argument is not without merit: in 1984 the total college enrollment of blacks (at all levels) was 8.8 percent.[47]

The question came down to the issue raised in *Griggs v. Duke Power Company*: Do requirements for college education constitute an artificial barrier that discriminates against minorities, or does it have a "valid business necessity" in police work? This was the key issue in *Davis v. Dallas*, in which the plaintiff challenged the Dallas Police Department, claiming the requirement of 45 college semester hours was discriminatory.[48] The court found in *Davis* that since policing was a professional occupation requiring an unusual degree of risk, and since it also embodied a unique public responsibility, the department's "educational requirement bears a manifest relationship to the position of police officer" that offsets its otherwise discriminatory effects.[49]

How have the courts found higher education to be related to police work? In reviewing the case law on the subject, Carter and Sapp answer the question by noting:

> The essence of these cases points to the fact that the courts have continually taken notice of the important responsibility to public safety inherent in certain occupations such as the transportation industry and health occupations. It can

clearly be argued that the responsibilities of police officers to apprehend criminals, decide whether to use deadly force, operate a police vehicle under emergency conditions, and make decisions affecting citizens' constitutional rights [are matters] of public risk and responsibility...Thus, the need and legal justification for a college requirement can be established.[50]

But what happens when the need for education comes into conflict with the requirement to increase minority representation on the department? Minority representation in police departments tends to be low, and many police departments have come under court order to increase the number of minorities on the force and to promote those who are already employed. In some departments this has resulted in lower entrance requirements for minorities and women or in preferential promotion policies for those already in the department. The use of racial quotas as a means of reversing the effects of past discrimination has been upheld by the Supreme Court.[51] As the stated purpose of affirmative action has been to recruit and promote *qualified* minorities, affirmative action calls for extending the benefit to the minority member in those cases where both applicants are equally qualified. Unfortunately, some departments have succumbed to pressure by lowering standards and establishing quotas. This has culminated in the escalation of animosity between black and white police officers due to a feeling on the part of white members that *they* are becoming victims of "reverse discrimination."

The conflict between EEOC goals, affirmative action programs and the goal of increased higher education for police officers has generally dampened the drive for higher educational achievement for police officers. Although police departments are willing to concede that college-educated officers might be better in the long run, they often feel that requiring a degree may actually call for overqualified candidates while turning away others who might be able to do a satisfactory job. Some reformers have been skeptical of requiring police officers to have a college degree. Wilson, for example, objected on the grounds that a college-educated police force would not be representative of its community, which consists primarily of people who do not go to college. He also argued that the police should serve as a "ladder" for middle-class blacks, and that blacks would have great difficulty entering the police service if a college degree were required. Finally, he objected to making a college degree an entrance requirement based on the belief that anyone with a solid tenth-grade education should have no difficulty with police training and would be able to understand departmental regulations.[52] What is the bottom line? As Benner noted,

> The goal of selecting competent police officers while avoiding discrimination has proven to be an arduous task. The effort to develop "valid" selection procedures is foundering in a quagmire of technical psychometric complexities. These complexities are exacerbated by a more fundamental problem. That is

the lack of consensus over what constitutes a "good" police officer. Without this consensus, technical "validity" is irrelevant. The situation is analogous to building something before deciding exactly what the "something" is supposed to do. In terms of "building" better police officers, the problem is that it is difficult to obtain consensus on what it (the police officer) should and should not do or should and should not be. This fundamental problem exists, partly, because of the formal role police have in society and, partly, because of the conflict with the public which is inherent in that role.[53]

Even though the issue of higher education for police officers remains entangled in controversy, the police have made major progress since the 1920s, when only two out of three police officers finished grade school, one out of 10 graduated from high school and one out of five scored high enough on intelligence tests to handle their duties.[54] The combined impact of civil liability, civil rights and higher education significantly changed the hiring pool from which police officers are selected. The process has been traumatic for tradition-oriented police departments and the consequences will almost certainly be far-reaching. As departments change, their culture also changes; by the twenty-first century we will probably see a police system that is substantially different from what we have had in the past. In 1989 the average education was 13.6 years for male police officers and 14.6 years for female police officers; moreover, 72 percent of blacks and 73 percent of Hispanics who enter police work have some college (compared with 66 percent of whites).[55] Police departments, especially the larger and more affluent ones, are clearly moving in the direction of hiring more educated officers.

WOMEN IN POLICE WORK

Historically, women have been excluded from mainstream police work. Their participation was limited to support activities and offenses involving women and children. For generations they were commonly referred to as police "matrons," reflecting their primary role of managing the custody of females who had been arrested. Police work during the political era was a male occupation and its functions were at complete variance from what was expected of women at that time. During that period police work was physical, autocratic and tough. Viewed in the context of the times, women were not thought to have the strength or cultural disposition to perform traditional police duties, and the public would have almost certainly rejected them if they tried. Women were deemed to be unsuited for police work as it was practiced in the early years. In addition, it was widely believed that society had a duty to protect women and that exposing them to the "underside" of life was inappropriate.

In spite of the cultural limitations of the time, women were indeed needed in police work. Their roles, however, were narrowly defined and were in effect "a logical extension of the hearth with a role function congruent with the conventional view of women as mothers, guardians of children, and protectors of public morals."[56] Since it was felt that women and female juveniles in custody could not be supervised by males, there was an obvious need for female police matrons. The first police matron was hired by the New York City Police Department in 1845, the year after that department was established as a full-service police department. In time the role of women expanded slightly but was still oriented toward dealing with other women and crimes committed against them. Women who entered police work were typically social workers; both their duties and enforcement powers were largely limited to work involving juvenile delinquents, female criminals, victims of sex crimes and runaway children.[57] Although female participation gradually widened, the duties of policewomen remained outside the traditional police functions of patrol, traffic and general detective work. Women were used as quasi-social workers and the departments that hired them not only maintained separate entrance requirements for women, but also limited the number who could be hired. The larger departments had the greatest number of female officers. Most consolidated them into a "women's bureau," which kept them isolated within the department, away from traditional police work.

The long-term impact of the reform movement altered the nature of police work so that it gradually became more legalistic and less confrontational. As departments evolved into modern agencies shaped by law and technology, and as police officers became more middle-class and educated, the occupational environment changed. The lessening of emphasis on physical force and agility changed the restrictive requirements for police officers and the job gradually became appropriate for a larger segment of the population—including women. Although the civil rights movement was essentially oriented toward the needs of blacks, it sparked a comparable movement among other minorities and women. As reformers sought to eliminate or reduce the barriers that kept women from entering certain occupations (and receiving equal pay when they were hired), it became inevitable that female participation in police work would expand to include the full range of traditional law enforcement. The major barrier was patrol, which had always been the exclusive preserve of male officers. That barrier was broken in 1968 when two female police officers in Indianapolis were assigned to patrol duty. Shortly thereafter, other departments followed suit and began to integrate their female officers into all aspects of police work.

Progress was extremely slow at first. In a study conducted for the Police Foundation in 1972, Milton found that women remained primarily in clerical or juvenile work and still were required to have special training or college degrees. The number of women in many departments remained limited to a small percentage of the total number of sworn officers.[58]   However, when Congress amended Title VII of the Civil Rights Act of 1964 to include public employers, the legal framework for change was set. Finally, the Crime Control Act of 1973 banned sex discrimination by police agencies receiving federal aid. In addition, police departments with 50 or more employees that received $25,000 or more in federal grants were required to implement equal opportunity programs for women.[59]

Studies show that generally women have performed patrol duties as competently as their male counterparts.[60] Female police officers also are regarded as competent by the public. There has been little public outcry against the use of women in all aspects of police work. However, their participation in traditional police work has met with tremendous resistance by rank-and-file male police officers. Female police officers have been forced to deal with a unique problem: in order for them to gain acceptance within their departments, they have been expected to accept the norms of a police culture which essentially rejects them in the first place. Part of the problem has been the expectation that they must act with authority and decisiveness while remaining "feminine" at the same time. According to Berg and Budnick, women who entered police work in the late 1960s and the 1970s often gave into the pressure and sacrificed their femininity in order to be accepted by their peers.[61] Women have had to work hard to overcome the view by many male officers that females are too emotional, irrational and illogical to effectively engage in street policing.[62] Research indicates that male police officers view women in general and female police officers in much the same way, but that female officers view themselves differently from how they view other women.[63] Although female police officers do not reject their status as women, they seem to see themselves as a special class of female.

The reasons given by women for selecting a police career do not differ significantly from the reasons given by men. Both are apparently attracted by work that provides both job security and an opportunity to help people. Interestingly, however, a study by Meagher and Yentes found that although males and females are attracted to police work for the same reasons, both men and women are more likely to (incorrectly) think men are attracted to it because of the power and authority associated with being a police officer.[64] In spite of misgivings by many male officers and misconceptions by both male and female officers, women are participating in police work to a greater extent than ever before. How their presence will alter the police culture remains to be seen; it is certain to have an impact. It is important to remember that police work has changed over the years and that it will continue to do so. It is shaped not only by the community but by its own members. Police departments are no longer the exclusive domain of white males, nor is it likely that such a day will ever return. An interesting question is not how police work will change the women who come into it, but rather how those women will change police work.[65]

POLICE WORK AND STRESS

Stress can be defined as mental, emotional or physical tension. Because stress is a normal part of life, people adapt to it through a variety of coping mechanisms. However, when stress is abnormal or prolonged, the usual coping mechanisms may not be adequate. Long-term or severe stress can result in physical problems such as high blood pressure, cardiovascular disease, chronic headaches and gastric ulcers. It also can lead to serious emotional infirmities, such as clinical depression, substance abuse, violent aggression and even suicide.[66] Perhaps it helps to understand *stress* as pressure and *strain* as the result of that pressure. Most systems can adapt easily to limited pressure; however, when at some point the pressure becomes too great or lasts too long, strain results. When unrelieved strain crosses the limits of toleration, the system breaks down. This is true of people just as it is of physical objects. However, people "break" in both physical and emotional ways. Although crippling stress can result from a single, overwhelming traumatic incident (e.g., killing a suspect or having one's partner killed in the line of duty), such occurrences are relatively rare. Moreover, most police departments understand the need to deal with them and are appropriately prepared. It is the routine stressors experienced by most police officers that tend to create the most significant problems. This day-to-day stress accumulates over time. There is seldom any one thing that accounts for it; rather, it results from a combination of stressors that occur over a long period.

Police officers may not realize that the tumultuous nature of their work, the profound influence of the police culture and the organization and administration of their departments are sources of considerable stress. To complicate matters further, some inappropriate reactions to stress may be viewed as "macho" behavior rather than being seen as symptoms of an officer's inability to cope. For example, a police officer may pathologically vent frustration through unwarranted aggression against suspects or violators and on people who are powerless to retaliate. Sexual promiscuity may be another inappropriate means of reacting to stress. Substance abuse, particularly alcoholism, is yet another common outcome. The stress experienced by police officers falls into several overlapping categories. By looking at them separately we can see how various aspects of the occupation can have a stressful impact on individual officers.

OPERATIONAL STRESS

The nature of a police officer's duties can produce considerable stress, especially when they are performed over a long period of time. Unlike the kind of work portrayed on television, real police work is often tedious and uneventful. Patrol officers often spend long hours simply driving around waiting for a call or looking for something out of the ordinary. This boredom is punctuated by periods of activity, some of which can be intense, frightening or highly emotional. Going from a state of inactivity to an emergency call (complete with lights, siren and a confrontation with a serious accident or crime) can be extremely intense.[67] Dealing with death, injury or victimization also can be stressful—especially when children are involved. Moreover, many of the people that police officers deal with are dishonest, distasteful or hostile, and dealing with them can be unpleasant.

Since the police provide round-the-clock service, most departments schedule the duty hours of patrol officers on rotating shifts. Undergoing shift changes can be stressful, especially when the changes are made on a short-term schedule (e.g., on a weekly basis). Officers are forced to adjust their personal, family and social schedules accordingly. The stress associated with shift changes is frequently compounded by poor dietary habits, lack of exercise and long hours spent in traffic. Finally, the fear of death or injury is a very real occupational stressor to police officers. Their job holds both actual and imagined dangers, ranging from coming into contact with HIV-infected blood to being assaulted or even killed.

ORGANIZATIONAL STRESS

The way police departments are staffed, organized and administered contributes to stress. Police officers have relatively little to say about the administrative policies and procedures of their departments, despite the fact that many of those policies can produce stress. One study indicated that the most frequently reported sources of stress among police officers fell into this category. They included concerns over such things as equitable treatment from upper management, anxiety over advancement and assignments, ambiguous policies and rules, fear of internal reviews and investigations, paperwork and peer pressure.[68]

Police officers in most departments are told that they are to be police officers 24 hours a day. As such they are required to carry their weapons at all times. This kind of organizational policy often turns out to be a mistake, as people need to "get away from" their work and its pressures. Expecting police officers to carry their weapons off-duty can lead to particularly unwholesome (and stressful) circumstances, especially when off-duty officers who are tired, intoxicated or out-of-uniform pull their weapons to intervene in dangerous situations.

Police departments commonly regulate the lives of their members by controlling off-duty employment, imposing residency requirements, intervening in lifestyle issues and restricting travel. Indeed, police officers frequently see themselves as having fewer rights than the criminals they are expected to arrest, and they often resent the autocratic way they are treated by their own departments—especially in matters involving infractions of police department policy.[69] Additional organizational stressors include inadequate supervision, a lack of administrative support and a failure to recognize high quality work. In addition, the advent of affirmative action programs and court-supervised consent decrees has initiated a perception of diminished career development opportunity that has become an increasingly important source of stress among police officers. (This stress is, of course, compounded by any accompanying polarization of a department.)

SYSTEM STRESS

Not all of the stress police officers experience comes from their dealings with the community and the police department. Much of it also comes from other parts of the criminal justice system. Having to deal with lawyers (e.g., testifying in court) can be stressful. As Goolkasian, Geddes and DeJong note,

> Several stressors from the criminal justice system and society at large have also been identified. Lack of consideration by the courts in scheduling police officers for court appearances is an often-cited source of stress for officers. Court appearances often interfere with officers' work assignments, their personal time, and even their sleeping schedules. Turf battles and lack of cooperation among individual law enforcement agencies, court decisions that curtail individual officers' discretion or restrict the role of law enforcement, the perceived leniency of the courts, and the premature release of offenders on bail or parole are also frequently-cited stressors.[70]

PERSONAL STRESS

Also stress-producing are individual factors that, though related to police work, are outside of its immediate scope. The police officer's family, for example, can act as a stressor. As the Niederhoffers noted, "...all police families—happy or unhappy—are like one another, patterned by the lathe of the police occupation. They dwell in the shadow of the job. The rhythm of their life is metered by the ringing of the telephone and the implacable schedule of the duty chart. Police department imperatives supersede the most cherished family occasions; fundamental family relations take second place."[71] Being the spouse of a police officer is difficult, and it is not made easier by the department. Like military dependents, police spouses live in the shadow of their spouse's work but are not a part of it. The stress that police work imposes on the family can become cyclic—with unhappy families placing further pressure on the police officers. The safety of the police officer is a concern shared by both officers and spouses. Because there is little that can be done to reassure a spouse, tension remains. As noted earlier, police officers tend to be socially isolated, mixing primarily with other police officers and their families. Since many of them feel the effects of taking their job home, the pressures remain even when they socialize. The fact that they are likely to have to work during birthdays, anniversaries and other events does not help the situation.

When stress is extreme or lasts too long, the most common responses are "burnout," behavioral changes and emotional reactions. These responses, which are usually gradual (and thus hard to link to any specific stressor), are often overlooked as symptoms of excessive stress and usually are either punished or ignored. "Burnout" occurs when a police officer feels emotionally depleted by the job and is no longer able to cope with its pressures. This is likely to show up first in the form of emotional hardening and indifference to others.[72] Other symptoms include a drop in energy level, lowered resistance to illness, increased pessimism, diminished sense of humor, social withdrawal and an increase in physical complaints.[73]

Prolonged stress that goes beyond an officer's ability to cope can lead to grossly impaired performance, misconduct, divorce, suicide or alcoholism. In recognition of the problems associated with stress, many departments have developed employee assistance programs to help impaired officers deal with their reactions to stress. However, the highly stressful nature of police work is likely to increase in the future. In large cities streets are getting meaner, police budgets tighter, and operational and personnel issues more complex. Police officers, who confront the stressors that all citizens face (e.g., taxes, mortgage payments, tuition, in-laws, etc.), also must deal with unique stressors that cannot be fully understood by the remainder of the community.

SUMMARY

The police in America have evolved as a distinctive culture because of the unique context in which they function. This culture is the outgrowth of historical, administrative and operational factors that have shaped the police service over the years, which in turn shapes the individuals who become police officers. The process began in the nineteenth century when fledgling police departments were staffed by working-class men (often immigrants from Europe) who took the job because it required little skill and provided job security. As the reform movement reshaped the police profession, entry into police work continued to represent a secure blue-collar occupation, attracting working-class men, particularly from police families. For years the prime emphasis was placed on recruiting white males on the basis of their physical prowess; education and training received minimal emphasis. As the reform movement wrested police departments from the control of politicians, the departments sought to gain greater control over individual officers by centralizing authority and emphasizing a strict military style of organization. This linear progression of police recruiting and socialization resulted in the development of a police culture based on internal control, power, solidarity, secrecy and private knowledge. In the long run the culture generates both alienation and cynicism on the part of police officers. In addition, it fosters both social and political conservatism among its members.

The traditional police culture has been challenged by major changes in three areas. The first charge was the development of *civil liability*, whereby both police officers and the jurisdictions hiring them can be held liable for misconduct. This produced a level of accountability previously unknown to cities and had a major impact on supervision, training and operational conduct. The second area of change was in the advancement of *civil rights*. Police departments discriminated against minorities and women for so long that the process became institutional in most departments. It was only after the passage of the Civil Rights Act of 1964 (and its amendments) that local governments dropped their barriers to employment and advancement. Equal opportunity was achieved in part through affirmative action plans and consent decrees that expanded participation by minorities and women, but the processes themselves produced enormous stress within the police profession. Finally, the advent of higher education for police officers began to lure college-educated people to police work, resulting in the advancement of police work as a middle-class occupation. Although a conflict developed between the goal of higher education for police and the requirements of civil rights legislation, the mandating of higher education standards for police officers has been accepted by the courts as a proper business necessity, and has contributed to the advancing status of police officers.

One of the most significant challenges to the traditional police culture has been the entry of women into police work. For generations women were denied entry into police work. The few who became police officers were limited in both their duties and their opportunities for advancement. Historically, female police officers have been assigned to women's bureaus in order to deal with female offenders, juveniles and females in custody. Only since the late 1960s have women been allowed to participate in traditional policing duties. As they continue to grow in number and advance in rank, they will almost certainly reshape the police culture that excluded them for so many decades. The results of this are likely to become evident as the American police enter the twenty-first century.

The final component of the police culture is the stress unique to the occupation. The stress experienced by police officers arises from operational considerations, organizational issues and stressors within the criminal justice system as a whole. All of these factors impact on the personal life of police officers, and stress resulting from family tension can feed back into the operating environment to create a vicious cycle.

DISCUSSION QUESTIONS

1. What was the impact of immigration on the development of nineteenth-century American police departments?

2. How did the leaders of the reform movement bring police officers under effective control? What have been the long-term consequences?

3. Why was selecting police officers on the basis of merit an important issue during the reform movement? Did it have any unintended negative consequences?

4. Why do police departments continue to place such heavy emphasis on internal control? Do you think there is a "better way"?

5. Very few police officers have been military officers. Do you think this has had any consequences on how police executives who are military veterans run their departments?

6. What is the relationship between power and the police culture? Do you think the concept has been given too much emphasis?

7. What are the factors that support police solidarity? Is it healthy or counterproductive? Why?

8. Secrecy has been an integral part of the police culture for generations. Should departments try to change it, keep it or modify how it works?

9. What is the private knowledge police officers obtain through their work? What *realistic* obligations does (or should) it impose on them?

10. Why do police officers become alienated from the rest of the community? Is the process inevitable?

11. Do you think the police *really* "do good" in their work, or is that just how they see it?

12. Why have the police been socially and politically conservative? Will new recruiting practices change that? Would the police benefit from becoming more liberal in their social and political perspectives?

13. Does police recruiting in fact get the best *in* or does it only keep the worst *out*? What should it do?

14. How has the development of civil liability shaped police performance? Do you think it is a valid concept?

15. Should the current generation of police officers be held accountable for the discriminatory practices of their predecessors?

16. What does the concept of "adverse impact" mean, and how does it apply to the selection of police officers?

17. Are affirmative action plans the best way to correct historic patterns of discrimination in police departments? If not, what is?

18. Should the police be forced to hire on the basis of quotas?

19. How has the philosophy of affirmative action been subverted? What are the consequences of this?

20. Do you think police officers should have a college diploma? Why? What are the advantages and disadvantages of requiring a college education for police officers?

21. How do you think the presence of women in police work will change the profession in the coming years?

22. Are women subject to any special pressures or demands when they enter police work? How would you deal with those problems if you were in charge?

23. Is stress in police work inevitable? Why or why not?

24. Some researchers have reported that organizational factors are more stressful to police officers than operational factors. Why?

25. How do the various stress factors in a police officer's life interact with one another? Can anything be done to reduce its impact?

REFERENCES

1 Deidre Martin and Mark Levine, "The Changing Work Force in the 1990s and Beyond," *Law Enforcement Technology* 18:3 (March 1991), 36-41.

2 "The Typical Police Officer," *Law Enforcement Technology* 18:10 (October 1991), 32.

3 Brian A. Reaves, "State and Local Police Departments, 1990," *Bureau of Justice Statistics Bulletin* (February 1992); see also U.S. Department of Justice (Federal Bureau of Investigation), *Crime in the United States: Uniform Crime Reports, 1990* (Washington, DC: U.S. Government Printing Office, 11 August 1991), 237.

4 Antony Pate and Edwin E. Hamilton, *The Big Six* (Washington, DC: The Police Foundation, 1991), 49.

5 Robert M. Fogelson, *Big-City Police* (Cambridge, MA: Harvard University Press, 1977), 18.

6 Fogelson, *Big-City Police*, 27.

7 Fogelson, *Big-City Police*, 27.

8 Fogelson, *Big-City Police*, 28.

9 Fogelson, *Big-City Police*, 31.

10 Harlan Hahn, "A Profile of Urban Police," *Law and Contemporary Problems* 36 (Autumn 1971), 449-466.

11 See, for example, David J. Bordua, *The Police: Six Sociological Essays* (New York: John Wiley and Sons, 1967); specifically, note 1 at page 193 in McNamara, "Uncertainties in Police Work: The Relevance of Police Recruits' Backgrounds and Training."

12 George W. O'Connor, *Survey of Selection Methods* (Washington, DC: International Association of Chiefs of Police, 1962), Table 15.

13 President's Commission on Law Enforcement and Administration of Justice, Nicholas deB. Katzenbach, Chair, *The Challenge of Crime in a Free Society* (Washington, DC: U.S. Government Printing Office, 1967), 109, 110.

14 R.H. Killman, "Corporate Culture," *Psychology Today* (April 1985), 2.

15 Don Hellriegel, John W. Slocum, Jr., and Richard W. Woodman, *Organizational Behavior*, 5th ed. (St. Paul: West Publishing Co., 1989), 307-310.

16 U.S. National Committee in Law Observance and Enforcement, *Report on the Police* (Washington, DC: U.S. Government Printing Office, 1930), 48.

[17] Arthur Niederhoffer and Elaine Niederhoffer, *The Police Family* (Lexington, MA: Lexington Books, D.C. Heath and Company, 1978), 1.

[18] Arthur Niederhoffer, "A Study of Police Cynicism" (Doctoral dissertation submitted to New York University, 1963.)

[19] Arthur Niederhoffer, *Behind the Shield: The Police in Urban Society* (Garden City, NY: Doubleday, 1967), 67.

[20] Connie Fletcher, *What Cops Know* (New York: Villard Books, 1991), 17-18.

[21] Jacob Chwast, "Value Conflicts in Law Enforcement," *Crime and Delinquency*, 11 (April 1965), 151-161.

[22] John G. Stratton, *Police Passages* (Manhattan Beach, CA: Glennon Publishing Co., 1984), 28-29.

[23] James H. Shaw, "Effectiveness of the MMPI in Differentiating Ideal from Undesirable Police Officer Applicants," in James T. Reese and Harvey A. Goldstein, *Psychological Services for Law Enforcement* (Washington, DC: Federal Bureau of Investigation, December 1986), 91.

[24] Clifton Rhead, Arnold Abrams, Harry Trosman and Philip Margolis, "The Psychological Assessment of Police Candidates," *American Journal of Psychiatry* 124:11 (May 1968), 1575-1580. For further enlightenment on the subject of police deviance, see Thomas Barker and David L. Carter, *Police Deviance*, 2nd ed. (Cincinnati: Anderson Publishing Co., 1991).

[25] Title 42, United States Code, Section 1983.

[26] H.E. Barrineau, III, *Civil Liability in Criminal Justice* (Cincinnati: Anderson Publishing Co., 1987), 7.

[27] Barrineau, *Civil Liability in Criminal Justice*, 8; see also *Screws v. United States*, 325 U.S. 91 (1945).

[28] *Monroe v. Pape*, 365 U.S. 167, 82 S. Ct. 473 (1961).

[29] *Monell v. Department of Social Services*, 436 U.S. 658, 98 S. Ct. 2018 (1978).

[30] Barrineau, *Civil Liability in Criminal Justice*, 29.

[31] Barrineau, *Civil Liability in Criminal Justice*, 35.

[32] See, for example, *Peters v. Bellinger*, 159 N.E.2d 528 (Ill. App. 1959); *Marusa v. District of Columbia*, 484 F.2d 828 (D.C. Cir. 1973) and *Owens v. Haas*, 601 F.2d 1224 (1979).

[33] Barrineau, *Civil Liability in Criminal Justice*, 67.

[34] Gerald David Jaynes and Robin M. Williams, Jr., eds., *A Common Destiny: Blacks and American Society* (Washington, DC: Committee on the Status of Black Americans, Commission on Behavioral and Social Sciences and Education, National Research Council, National Academy Press, 1989), 489.

[35] *Griggs v. Duke Power Company*, 401 U.S. 424, 91 S. Ct. 849 (1971).

[36] Alan W. Benner, "Psychological Screening of Police Applicants," in James T. Reese and Harvey A. Goldstein, eds., *Psychological Services for Law Enforcement* (Quantico, VA: FBI Academy, December 1986), 11-12.

[37] *Griggs v. Power Duke Company* (1971).

[38] Samuel Walker, *Employment of Black and Hispanic Police Officers 1983-1988: A Follow-Up Study* (Omaha, NE: Urban Research, University of Nebraska, 1989).

[39] Harry W. More, *Special Topics in Policing* (Cincinnati Anderson Publishing Co., 1992), 154.

[40] Cited in More, *Special Topics in Policing*, 147.

[41] "Black Troopers Settle Bias Suit," *The Washington Post*, 5 January 1991, B5.

[42] David L. Carter and Allen D. Sapp, *Police Education and Minority Recruitment: The Impact of a College Requirement* (Washington, DC: Police Executive Research Forum), 20.

[43] Gerald D. Jaynes amd Robin M. Williams, *A Common Destiny: Blacks and American Society*, 491.

[44] See, for example, Lawrence W. Sherman and the National Advisory Commission on Higher Education for Police Officers, *The Quality of Police Education* (Washington, DC: Josey-Bass, 1978).

[45] Robert C. Trojanowicz and T.G. Nicholson, "A Comparison of Behavioral Styles of College Graduate Police Officers vs. Noncollege-going Police Officers," *Police Chief* 43: 8 (1976), 56-59, cited in Charles D. Spielberger, *Police Selection and Evaluation* (Washington: Hemisphere Publishing Co., 1979), 118.

[46] Carter and Sapp, *Police Education and Minority Recruitment*, 4.

[47] Carter and Sapp, *Police Education and Minority Recruitment*, 5.

[48] *Davis v. Dallas*, 777 F.2d 205 (5th Cir. 1985).

[49] *Davis v. Dallas* (at 211), cited in Carter and Sapp, *Police Education and Minority Recruitment*, 15.

[50] Carter and Sapp, *Police Education and Minority Recruitment*, 18, 19.

[51] See, for example, *United States v. Paradise*, 480 U.S. 149, 107 S. Ct. 1053, 94 L. Ed. 2d 203 (1987).

[52] Jerry Wilson, letter to *The Washington Post*, 19 December 1970. See also, Jerry Wilson, *Police Report* (Boston, 1975), 142.

[53] Benner "Psychological Screening of Police Applicants," 12.

[54] Fogelson, *Big-City Police*, 102.

[55] David L. Carter, Allen D. Sapp and Darrel W. Stephens, *The State of Police Education: Policy Direction for the 21st Century* (Washington, DC: Police Executive Research Forum, 1989).

[56] Lesli Kay Lord, "A Comparison of Male and Female Peace Officers' Sterotypic Perceptions of Women and Women Peace Officers," *Journal of Police Science and Administration* 14:2 (1986), 84.

[57] Peter Horne, *Women in Law Enforcement* (Springfield, IL: Charles C Thomas, 1980), 20.

[58] Catherine Milton, "Women in Policing," in *Police and Law Enforcement, 1973-1974* (New York: AMS Press, Inc., 1975).

[59] Daniel J. Bell, "Policewomen: Myths and Reality," *Journal of Police Science and Administration* 10:1 (1982), 112-120.

[60] See, for example, P. Block and D. Anderson, *Police on Parole: Final Report* (Washington, DC: The Police Foundation, 1974) and Lawrence Sherman, "Evaluation of Policewomen on Patrol in a Suburban Police Department," *Journal of Police Science and Administration* 3 (1075), 434-438.

[61] Bruce L. Berg and Kimberly J. Budnick, "Defeminization of Women in Law Enforcement: A New Twist in the Traditional Police Personality," *Journal of Police Science and Administration* 14:4 (1986), 314-319.

[62] Lord, "A Comparison of Male and Female Peace Officers' Sterotypic Perceptions of Women and Women Peace Officers," 85.

[63] Lord, "A Comparison of Male and Female Peace Officers' Sterotypic Perceptions of Women and Women Peace Officers," 89.

[64] M. Steven Meagher and Nancy A. Yentes, "Choosing a Career in Policing: A Comparison of Male and Female Perceptions." *Journal of Police Science and Administration* 14:4 (1986), 320-327.

[65] For further information on women and police work, see Donna C. Hale, "Women in Policing," In *What Works in Policing? Operations and Administration Examined*, ed. G.W. Cordner and D.C. Hale (Cincinnati: Anderson Publishing Co., 1992), 125-142.

[66] Gail A. Goolkasian, Ronald W. Geddes and William DeJong, *Coping With Police Stress* (Washington, DC: National Institute of Justice, June 1985), 1.

[67] B. Westmoreland and B.D. Haddock. "Code '3' Driving: Psychological and Physiological Stress Effects," *Law and Order* 37:11 (November 1989), 29-31.

68 J.P. Crank and M. Caldero, "Production of Occupational Stress in Medium-Sized Police Agencies: A Survey of Line Officers in Eight Municipal Departments," *Journal of Criminal Justice* 19:4 (1991), 339-349.

69 Harold E. Russell and Alan Beigel, *Understanding Human Behavior for Effective Police Work*, 2nd ed. (New York: Basic Books, 1982), 339-349.

70 Goolkasian et al., *Coping With Police Stress*, 5.

71 Niederhoffer and Niederhoffer, *The Police Family*, 1.

72 L.B. Johnson, "Job Strain Among Police Officers: Gender Comparisons," *Police Studies* 14:1 (Spring 1991), 12-16.

73 Robert L. Veniga and James Spradley, *How To Cope With Job Burnout* (Englewood Cliffs, NJ: Prentice Hall, 1981), 31-40.

Photo Credit: Bill Powers, Frost Publishing Group, Ltd.

. *Chapter 9*

LAWYERS

Prosecutors and Defenders

We have seen that the community handles problems of individual misconduct in a stepwise fashion, going from the purely informal methods of the private control system to the more structured tactics of the public control system. We have also seen that the police, though technically part of the public control system, sometimes function informally as part of the private control system through their order-maintenance role. When the police shift from order maintenance to law enforcement, the process becomes substantially more formal and impersonal—especially in cases that are moved into the next phase of the criminal justice system, i.e., sent forward for possible prosecution in the courts.

When cases go from the police to the prosecutor they are placed in the hands of attorneys. From that point forward, what happens is determined almost exclusively by lawyers. In theory, the case becomes a battle between prosecutors and defense attorneys, an adversarial process in which counsel for both sides grapple with one another on substantive and procedural legal grounds. Unfortunately, actual practice often falls short of theory, and a great many criminal defendants are processed through the system like so much "chow," as Tom Wolfe referred to them in *The Bonfire of the Vanities*.[1]

GROWTH OF THE LEGAL PROFESSION IN AMERICA

The legal profession did not get off to a particularly distinguished start in America.[2] Colonial lawyers as a whole were poorly trained, unskilled and of little benefit to the ordinary person. Even the landed gentry and businessmen viewed them as a threat. In short, lawyers were seen by most of the community as having little to offer but much to gain—usually at someone else's expense. The rapid growth of mercantile capitalism in both Europe and the American colonies produced a need for contracts, commercial instruments, deeds and other legal documents too complex for a layperson to prepare. Since understanding and preparing these documents (and ushering them through the legal system) came to be beyond the ability of the average layperson, by the end of the seventeenth century non-lawyers were prohibited from practicing law.[3]

During the eighteenth century colonial courts became more formal and legalistic. This development meant that the lawyers representing cases before them had to be properly trained. This need for legal competence resulted in the establishment of formal law programs in the fledgling American universities.

The slowly emerging prestige of the legal profession was dealt a serious setback by the American Revolution. Lawyers, whether educated in the Colonies or in the English Inns of Court, were trained in English common law, and were therefore associated with the earlier English hegemony over the colonies. This association added to their unpopularity, as did some of the nature and circumstances of their work (for example, a primary task was bill collecting). In addition, they were criticized for refusing to work without an advance retainer.[4] During this period, the courts too were unpopular, intensifying the low status of lawyers.[5]

As the nation recovered from the war and the effects of the Industrial Revolution began to be felt, the fortunes of lawyers rose both literally and figuratively. The legal profession made inroads into the commercial-mercantile community and the practice of corporate law emerged as a prestigious occupation. Even so, the legal profession remained splintered because from 1800 to 1860 lawyers could be admitted to the bar in two ways: they could take the bar exam after completing a formal course of study leading to a law degree, or they could take it after serving an apprenticeship (without going to law school). During this period many states opened up the practice of law by abolishing educational requirements and reducing (or eliminating) the length and quality of professional training.[6] The subsequent influx of unethical or dishonest practitioners undermined the reputations of honest lawyers and had a negative impact on the profession's status overall.

After the Civil War, the more competent lawyers gravitated toward the rapidly expanding industrial and business sectors. This brought about significant changes in the profession; perhaps the most important were movements toward spending less time in court and more time advising clients, and away from practicing general law in favor of specialization.[7] Lawyers continued to find lucrative opportunities in the corporate setting, and as a result a great deal of legal practice was not advocate-oriented but rather took the form of legal consulting to and on behalf of businesses.

The practice of criminal law was not generally an attractive option to the aspiring lawyer. Even a successful criminal practice did not confer the kind of monetary or social benefits that came with a comparably successful corporate practice. Criminal advocacy therefore remained low in quality and unevenly distributed, resulting in an emphasis on law over justice. The period between the Civil War and World War I was an era of great industrial and technological growth. Empires were built and great strides in American finance were made. Corporate lawyers played a major role in this process by guiding businesses through legal difficulties and influencing the legislative process. During this period, legal services for the public were minimal at best. Some lawyers seemed to be motivated more by high fees than by professional ethics. Moreover, the legal profession imposed few realistic controls on its members.

Starting in the late 1800s the law firm began to emerge as an important part of the legal community. Some firms made it a point to employ politically and socially connected specialists who were well-positioned to serve the business and financial communities. The subsequent high degree of specialization further divided the legal community. In addition, the negative reputation of business during the era of the "robber barons"* also biased public opinion against the legal profession, which was seen by many to be amoral—driven solely by power and self-interest. The solo practitioner was regarded as marginal within the profession. Although the status of the legal profession rose as its members gained power, the reputation of individual lawyers declined. A license to practice law seemed to many to be a license to steal.

Gradually, the quality of legal education and standards for admission to the bar improved. With the advent of the New Deal reforms of the 1930s, the government began to take a more active interest in the common citizen. An increasing public awareness of individual rights, a growing sophistication of government regulatory agencies and a reform movement within the legal profession itself produced a profession which, although far from ideal, became increasingly responsive to public needs. Although criminal lawyers are still held in low regard by many, the profession as a whole is beginning to develop some measure of respectability.

---

* The term *robber baron* is commonly applied to the industrialists of the latter nineteenth century who achieved enormous wealth by exploiting the environment, corrupting legislative bodies and advancing their business interests through unethical means.

The historically low status of the legal profession has not been confined to American lawyers; it is a sentiment of ancient vintage in other countries as well. This was evidenced in Shakespeare's *King Henry VI* when Dick the butcher (who advocates turning England over to the commoner) cries out, "The first thing we do, let's kill all the lawyers!"[8]   Other critics include the satirist Jonathan Swift and the novelist Charles Dickens (whose novel *Bleak House* is a bitter, scathing attack on the English legal system).[9]   In spite of steady improvement, public opinion of the legal system remains low.[10]   The public's opinion is not without justification: on National Law Day (May 1) in 1990, an organization advocating legal reform issued a "report card" rating the legal systems of the District of Columbia and the 50 states.   Only two states (California and Washington) received an overall grade of C; five (Minnesota, Oregon, Massachusetts, Michigan and Hawaii) received D averages; and all the rest failed.[11]   As one writer noted, "Almost everyone these days has had some experience with a lawyer, and it's usually unhappy and results in a large bill."[12]

There are a great many lawyers in the United States: 281 lawyers per 100,000 population in the United States, as compared to 11 per 100,000 in Japan, 82 in England and 111 in Germany.   Proportionately, the United States has 26 times the number of lawyers as Japan.   From 1972 to 1991 the number of lawyers grew five times faster than the entire United States population and twice as fast as the number of total jobs.   In 1991 partners in law firms nationwide averaged $168,000 in annual income (those in New York and Los Angeles more commonly earn over a million dollars a year).   Lawyers contribute significantly to the total cost of our legal system, estimated in 1991 as being something on the order of $300 billion a year.   For example, it has been estimated that nearly half the $40 billion cost of the 1991 Clean Air Act will go to lawyers.[13]

There is a rigid class hierarchy among lawyers that is reflected in their educational backgrounds, the kinds of firms for which they work and the nature of the duties they perform.

PROSECUTORS

Prosecution is an active intervention by the state into the life of an individual offender, based on the belief that because he or she has violated the law such government intervention is necessary.   Intervention can be motivated by a desire to protect society from a menace to public safety or order, or possibly by a wish to help the offender (whether or not the offender wants to be helped).   Sometimes prosecution is based on a desire to make an example of the offender (i.e., to deter others from behaving in a particular manner) or as a means of punishment that affirms the moral position of the state against criminal behavior in general (and that offender's behavior in particular).   Some more practical reasons exist as well.   A prosecutor may wish to build an impressive string of convictions in order to have a solid record of achievement to point to when running for higher elective office, or pursue a case based on the belief that some cases "look good" when prosecuted, regardless of their meaning to the offender, the victim or society.

Prosecution is a process involving a variety of separate people and decisions. The simple fact that a person committed a crime and got caught is by no means a guarantee that the person will be prosecuted. In many cases chances are high that the offender will not be prosecuted at all. To understand this process, it is necessary to look at the primary actors, the roles they play and the means by which their roles are performed.

WHO PROSECUTES?

Accusing a person of a crime is one thing; *charging* them with one is another matter. The police accuse, but the prosecutor charges. The specific prosecutive agency that charges an offender is a function of two factors: the crime itself and the jurisdiction of the court that will try the case. Crimes can be violations of city or county ordinances or violations of state or federal laws. In some instances one crime may violate both state and federal laws, in which case both jurisdictions may prosecute. Jurisdiction is the authority of a court to hear a case. If a crime violates state law, it must be tried in a state court. If it violates a municipal ordinance, it must be tried in a city court. The seriousness of a crime also determines jurisdiction. Some courts are limited as to the seriousness of the cases they may try, and all courts have geographic limitations (e.g., a crime committed in Virginia may not be tried in a Maryland court).

Incorporated cities prosecute violations of their local ordinances in municipal courts (sometimes called corporation or police courts). Municipal courts deal with offenses against the city that, because of the geographic limitation of its ordinances, cannot be tried in state courts. These cases typically involve minor misdemeanors such as the unlawful burning of trash or selling without a license. These trials are usually informal and are not attended by a prosecutor; the accused is simply obliged to appear in court to either plead guilty or offer a case for the defense. Such prosecutions are almost always initiated by a summons.

Most states are divided into judicial districts, which vary in size according to population. Some judicial districts serve only a county or a single municipality; others serve multi-county areas. Usually there are two types of criminal courts within these judicial districts. The lower court (often called the district court) hears misdemeanors, such as traffic offenses, simple assaults and check fraud cases. These cases involve violations of state law, and this level of prosecution represents state action rather than city or county action (even though the offense may have been committed and tried within the same city). The second level of court within a judicial district is the court of general jurisdiction (frequently called the circuit court). This court is empowered to try all cases up to and including capital crimes.[14]

Included in a judicial district is the office of the district attorney. The district attorney is an elected state officer whose job is to prosecute state cases within the district. A prosecutor's job can range from supervision of a large staff and heavy caseload to acting as the sole prosecutor within a district with a private law practice on the side. There are 8,000 state and local prosecution agencies headed by county prosecutors and district attorneys. Most are small offices with only one or two assistants and a low volume of actual criminal cases.

At the federal level, the chief prosecutor is the United States Attorney General. However, the country is divided into federal judicial districts, each of which has its own courts and prosecutor. The "local" federal prosecutor of each district is the United States District Attorney (usually called the U.S. Attorney), who may have a staff of several assistants.

WHERE DO PROSECUTORS GET THEIR CASES?

In general, prosecutors get their cases from law enforcement agencies. An individual may contact a prosecutor directly and make a complaint, but in most cases the prosecutor will refer the person to the proper law enforcement agency. In cases where the prosecutor has reason to suspect that such a referral would not be advisable (as in cases involving dishonesty or corruption on the part of the law enforcement agency itself), the allegation can be investigated by the prosecutor's staff. In most cases, however, the primary input to the prosecutor's office is the output of the law enforcement agency that serves it. The size of a community can play a major role in how the prosecutor manages complaints. In small communities, individuals may come directly to the prosecutor with complaints concerning borderline issues such as domestic relations matters or check fraud cases. Because prosecutors normally do not want to take these cases to court, most of them are willing to settle the conflict informally in their offices.

In larger cities the prosecutor plays a more formal and structured role. The primary prosecutorial task is management of the office. There is usually little time for the prosecutor to take a personal interest in minor matters. Thus, in larger communities, the prosecutor tends to receive cases from official agencies rather than from private individuals—typically from the police department and sheriff's office. Crimes against state law that take place inside incorporated cities are handled primarily by local police departments. Crimes against state law that take place in the unincorporated areas of the county are serviced by the sheriff's department or the county police, depending on the part of the country. A number of states employ state police and state bureaus of investigation. These agencies usually confine their activities to complex statewide cases or serious crimes committed where local law enforcement personnel lack the resources to deal with the problem. Offenses against federal laws are investigated by federal law enforcement agencies, such as the Federal Bureau of Investigation, United States Secret Service, Drug Enforcement Administration, and so on. Thus, each jurisdiction (federal, state and local) has its own law enforcement or investigative agencies, its own prosecutor and its own courts. Although prosecutors may work very closely with law enforcement agencies, they usually do not direct those agencies to investigate certain crimes. Some prosecutors, however, inform law enforcement agencies that they will not prosecute cases unless certain criteria—such as minimum dollar values in thefts or minimum drug quantities in narcotics cases—are met.[15]

The basic tasks of a prosecutor are to screen criminal accusations and bring those with prosecutive merit before the proper court for adjudication. The prosecutor's overall goal is to recommend dispositions that are in the best interests of society; this can range from dropping the case to bringing it before the courts for prosecution. Cases are disposed of by the most appropriate (or convenient) means at each step along the way.

Screening

The prosecutor determines whether a case will be accepted for prosecution. Even though the goals of the police and the prosecutor may be compatible, not all cases presented by police to prosecutor are accepted; in fact, there is a significant rejection rate by prosecutors. For example, in Washington, DC in 1988, "[o]ne in four arrests...did not last out the first day in the system. Prosecutors—judging the crime unimportant, the evidence insufficient or the 'probable cause' for arrest to be poor—simply dropped those cases before they got started, refusing to bring charges before a judge."[16] Many cases rejected by the prosecutor involve problems that are outside the control of the police, including such things as a lack of credibility on the part of a witness or a witness's refusal to testify. Some problems, such as the failure to obtain sufficient physical evidence, result from inadequate police work. At issue in part is the type of case and the way the police became involved in it in the first place. For example, in cases where the police are called by an identified complainant and where physical evidence is legally available, any problems that emerge at a later date are likely to result from matters largely out of the control of the police. On the other hand, in cases initiated by the police (e.g., vice and narcotics cases), there is a greater likelihood of the case being rejected because of procedural errors such as lack of probable cause in making the arrest or the performance of an illegal search.

A prosecutor may initially accept a case from the police but later decide that it should be dropped. The right to do this (technically known as a *nolle prosequi*, or "nol pros") is at the prosecutor's discretion. This is a power that Newman calls, "[o]ne of the broadest, most powerful examples of discretionary authority in the entire criminal justice system."[17] See Figures 9.1 and 9.2.

Figure 9.1

PROSECUTORS' REASONS TO REFUSE

Some of the 62 reasons given by the U.S. Attorney's Office for declining to pursue a criminal case included the following:

— No corroboration of evidence

— Insufficient link between defendant and crime, such as finding marijuana under the defendant's car

— Essential witness doesn't show up or appears unfit for trial

— Witness privilege against testifying, such as marital privilege, Fifth Amendment right against self-incrimination

— Witness story confused or garbled, unrealistic, implausible, disbelieved

— Witness personal credibility questionable: damaging conduct, insufficiencies in ability to observe, such as weak eyes, mental incompetence

— Violates letter, not spirit, of law

— Offense of trivial or insignificant nature

— Good defense, such as alibi, entrapment, self-defense

— Case moot: defendant dies, statute of limitations runs out

— Defendant's personal characteristics, such as history, record, age, circumstances, remorse

— No probable cause for arrest

— Inadmissible confession or statement

— Private remedy taken: restitution made, defendant warned off

— Plead immunity in return for testimony

Source: Barton Gellman, *The Washington Post,* 8 June 1989.

Figure 9.2

CASES DECLINED

In Washington, D.C. some criminal charges are routinely declined for prosecution. If the offender has no criminal convictions or pending charges, they are highly unlikely to be charged with:

— Possession of drug paraphernalia

— Possession of marijuana (less than five bags)

— Possession of numbers slips

— Simple assault of a relative or acquaintance

— Aggravated assault if there are no serious injuries and the victim came out even

— Shoplifting less than $10

— Car theft if the offender had the key, was a passenger, or if the vehicle was a rental car

---

Source: Barton Gellman, *The Washington Post,* 8 June 1989.

Diversion

Many cases clearly require *some* action—but not necessarily criminal prosecution. These cases can be removed from the formal system and diverted into channels better suited to handling the problem. *Diversion* takes place after an offender has been arrested but before he or she is brought to court and charged with the crime. By using a diversionary program the prosecutor "suspends" criminal action by placing the offender in a program that deals with the problem well enough to merit dropping the criminal charges. The philosophy behind diversion is both humane and pragmatic. On the humane side, it identifies people who have a greater need for treatment than they do for prosecution and spares the offender the social and economic hardship of a criminal prosecution. On the pragmatic side, it reduces congestion in the courts, eases the prosecutor's caseload and saves the state money. Because it attempts to deal with the problems that lead to criminal activity initially, it reduces the likelihood of recidivism.

Most diversionary projects place the offender in a program for a set period of time ranging from a few months to a year. If the offender cooperates and avoids re-arrest during this period the prosecution dismisses the original criminal charges as a reward. Diversion programs take minimum-risk cases off of overloaded court dockets and place them in the hands of intervention agencies.

Diversion and *intervention* are not the same thing. Although the terms are often used interchangeably, they represent different concepts. Diversion is based on the traditional discretionary authority of the prosecutor or the court. Its primary function is case screening and its objectives are to conserve criminal justice resources for cases requiring close supervision and to remove defendants who may not require a full criminal disposition.[18] The purpose of intervention, on the other hand, is rehabilitation. It identifies defendants in need of treatment and provides the treatment they need. It is an attempt to provide an effective alternative to normal criminal or juvenile justice system processing.[19] In practice, although most programs provide both services, the prosecutor *diverts*, while rehabilitation programs *intervene*.

A serious problem with diversion projects is their evaluation. It is difficult to say how effective a program really is if it only takes low-risk offenders; however, it is clear that a great many people charged with crimes can and should be dealt with by some means other than a criminal prosecution. Diversion programs can be an excellent way to apply community resources through counseling, conflict resolution and community-based treatment programs. However, the use of diversion is not without some substantial problems. Because diversion programs operate on the implicit assumption that the accused is guilty, an offender who wants to take advantage of a diversion program is expected to acknowledge guilt and show cooperation and contrition. Some offenders may feel coerced to go along with a diversion program as the lesser of two evils, in order to avoid criminal prosecution and the possibility of a harsh sentence. This shift from a presumption of innocence to a presumption of guilt causes an offender who fails in a diversion program to run the risk of more vigorous prosecution than might otherwise have been the case. Perhaps the most serious shortcoming of diversion programs is that they are sometimes used more for the convenience of the criminal justice system than for the benefit of the offender. Diversion projects allow prosecutors and courts to reduce their workload and give them added flexibility in how they can approach certain cases. Although convenience and flexibility are desirable, they should not be the primary goals of diversion.

Another drawback of diversion programs is the risk that they may deny equal treatment to similar offenders. The decision to select an accused for diversion has the potential for being arbitrary unless safeguards are established to assure fundamental fairness in selection procedures. And because diversion programs select those most likely to succeed, time and resources may be wasted on the people least likely to get into trouble again anyway. This is related to the problem of evaluation. Because most diversion projects are operated informally, they are seldom evaluated; thus, gaps have been left in our knowledge of what works and what does not.

Charging

Charging represents the decision to invoke the criminal justice process. This step involves deciding exactly what crime an offender will be officially charged with, what indictments will be sought and what plea negotiations will be initiated. According to Miller, the decision to file charges against an offender involves three major questions: (1) Is there sufficient evidence to show probable cause that the defendant is guilty of a crime?; (2) Is prosecution of the offense in the public interest?; and (3) What specific crime should the suspect be charged with?[20]

Regarding the first question, the National Advisory Commission on Criminal Justice Standards and Goals stated in 1972 that "[a]n individual should be screened out of the criminal justice system if there is not a reasonable likelihood that the evidence admissible against him would be sufficient to obtain a conviction and sustain it on appeal."[21] This remains as true today as it was then. Although the commission did not define "reasonable likelihood," it said that "where the need is high (e.g., the defendant is clearly dangerous and preventive detention is essential, or the crime is such that convictions are valuable for deterrent purposes) a prosecutor would be justified in proceeding with formal action even though the probability of a conviction was low."[22] In some instances this process turns into a game of chicken: the prosecutor may bluff the accused (or the defense counsel) into thinking the case against the defendant is good enough to go to trial, in the hope that the defense will negotiate in order to escape the outcome. Much of this is a function of the prosecutor's personality, the political climate and the workload borne. An aggressive prosecutor in a conservative community with a manageable caseload is likely to routinely charge offenders whose cases might be dropped in neighboring jurisdictions.[23]

The second issue—whether or not prosecution is in the public interest—can play a controlling role even when a crime is serious. For example, should a prosecutor go after an elderly man who kills his terminally ill wife because she was in great pain? What about the man who entered a Chicago hospital at gunpoint and held doctors and nurses at bay so he could disconnect the life support systems from his brain-dead child? What about the Louisiana father of a sexually abused child who shot his child's molester as police led him down an airport corridor after extraditing him from Texas?

If the most important decision for a prosecutor is whether or not to charge in the first place, the second most important decision is to decide exactly what charge to apply. This decision is based on a multitude of factors, including the:

1. Strength of the case, based on the availability of witnesses and evidence;

2. Degree of cooperativeness on the part of the offender (that is, willingness to "bargain");

3. Complexity of the case;

4. Defense attorney's theory of defense and the tactics most likely to be employed;

5. Notoriety of the case;

6. Dangerousness of the accused;

7. Prosecutor's workload;

8. Congestion of the court's docket;

9. Anticipated cost of a trial (in both time and money);

10. The prosecutor's own charging policies;

11. Likelihood of a conviction;

12. Availability and appropriateness of diversion programs.

Part of the process is a function of the chief prosecutor's goals, either political or personal. For instance, some prosecutors concentrate on drug-related crimes, while others are more interested in prosecuting white-collar or so-called "career" criminals. In deciding how to charge an offender, the rule of thumb is that an accused will be charged with the most serious crime for which the prosecutor thinks there is a good chance of winning a conviction. However, it is important to remember that most serious crimes include other, less serious crimes within them. For example, burglary "contains" the lesser offense of criminal trespass; depending on the wording of the state's laws, it might also include housebreaking. All murders encompass the crime of manslaughter, and rape includes various forms of assault. A prosecutor, in examining all the circumstances of a given case, may conclude that it would be easier and more certain to obtain a conviction on one of these lesser included offenses. In one city a baby was brought into the emergency room of the county hospital by its parents. The infant, less than one year old, was dead. Examination of the body clearly indicated that although it was malnourished and showed signs of other injuries, the baby died as a result of a severe scalding. Although the parents claimed the death was an accident, the doctors, the police and the district attorney were certain the child had been intentionally scalded by its stepfather. However, the prosecutor believed that the best chance for a conviction would be in charging the stepfather with negligent manslaughter rather than murder, and this he did.

Charging Decisions and Plea Bargaining

Plea bargaining is one of the most important considerations in making a charging decision. In the plea bargaining process the offender "accepts" guilt on a charge in return for some consideration.

In populous jurisdictions prosecutors tend to have a heavy caseload. Even though some cases may be "nol prossed" and others diverted, a substantial number remain to be brought before the courts. If each of these cases went to trial, the courts would become bogged down very quickly. As former Supreme Court Chief Justice Warren Burger pointed out, "[a] reduction from 90 percent to 80 percent in guilty pleas requires the assignment of twice the judicial manpower and facilities—judges, court reporters, bailiffs, clerks, jurors and courtrooms. A reduction to 70 percent trebles this demand."[24] The solution has been to make deals.When an accused agrees to plead guilty, the courts are spared the time, cost and inconvenience of trying them. Some people plead guilty because the evidence against them is strong and they have no reasonable defense. The prosecutor, of course, chooses whether or not to be flexible. The convenience of the prosecutor then can be traded for some benefit to the offender—either in the form of a reduced charge or a promise to recommend leniency in sentencing. Some people plead guilty as part of a "negotiated outcome" in which both the charge and the sentence are determined before the accused ever walks into the courtroom.

The course of the plea bargaining process often boils down to each side's perception of its chances of winning. If the prosecutor thinks there is a likelihood of getting a conviction on the highest possible charge in a serious case, he or she is not likely to be inclined to bargain on the charge (though perhaps on recommended sentence). On the other hand, if the prosecutor thinks there is a weak case for the most serious charge, a reduction in the charge may be exchanged in return for a guilty plea.

When a defense lawyer believes there is an excellent case for the defense there may be no need to bargain at all. It is possible, though, that a defense lawyer, despite having a weak case, will demand a jury trial for a client in the hope that the district attorney will bargain for a reduction to avoid the aggravation of going to trial. This is most often done in cases that do not involve major property loss or physical injury. A guide used by many prosecutors is that they will accept a guilty plea only if the offender will get a sentence close to what the prosecutor believes could have been secured by trial anyway. Thus, in the final analysis, an offender is usually charged with the most serious charge for which the prosecutor thinks a conviction can be obtained without actually having to go to trial. The charge or sentence is usually the least the defense attorney believes can be obtained by bargaining the case. In general, the procedure of plea bargaining is not reviewable by higher courts. Moreover, the agreement reached by the prosecutor and the defendant is not binding on the court before which the plea is entered. A prosecutor may make a deal with a defendant who agrees to plead guilty in return for the prosecutor's recommendation of a minimum sentence, only to have the judge impose the maximum sentence anyway. In such a case, the offender has no grounds for appeal.

Informations and Indictments

In some jurisdictions, an *information*—a formal document accusing the offender of a crime—is filed after the prosecutor determines the charge that will be applied. The information becomes the basis for arraignment and trial. In the case of misdemeanors, the information process almost exclusively takes the form of a summons or complaint. The traffic ticket you receive for running a stop sign is actually an information document accusing you of a minor crime. On the basis of that ticket, you must appear in court, enter your plea (arraign yourself) and answer to the allegation—unless you avoid the process by paying the ticket.

In many jurisdictions (including the federal courts), serious crimes are sent to a grand jury composed of local citizens—usually between 16 and 23 in number—that sits for a specified period of time (a term) to hear all "presentments" that come before it. The purpose of the grand jury is to decide whether there is sufficient cause to warrant bringing the case to trial. If the grand jury believes there is, it returns a *true bill* or *indictment*. If it finds insufficient cause, it returns a *no bill* (in which case the prosecutor normally drops the case).

An indictment is not evidence of guilt; it only means there is enough reason (probable cause) to suspect guilt and that the accused should be compelled to answer to the state's formal accusation in court. Grand jury proceedings are closed. The person accused of a crime has no right to offer evidence before it or be present during its deliberations. The fact that a grand jury returns a no bill does not mean the accused has been declared innocent. It is legal for the prosecutor to take the same case before a subsequent grand jury to secure an indictment. However, usually a prosecutor will only do this when new evidence that strengthens the original accusation is uncovered. Grand juries are not bound to render findings based on purely legal grounds, but most do.

The prosecutor, though an attorney for the state, must also act as a manager. It is the prosecutor's responsibility to ensure that the citizens of the jurisdiction get the best service for their tax dollar. In more active jurisdictions the prosecutor's office may be overwhelmed with pending cases. This can produce inefficiency, allowing minor offenders to undergo prosecution while more serious offenders escape it. Delays in docketing cases before the courts can result in the loss of the essential elements of a successful prosecution (e.g., testimony of witnesses).

PROSECUTION AS PUBLIC ENTERPRISE

Although justice is a collective good, prosecution is a public business that deals with specific individuals. As a business, it has a job to do: to dispose of the cases it receives. The techniques of diversion programs, plea bargaining and trials are theoretically carried out in such a way that the "efforts of the prosecutor and the court are directed toward fairness and justice."[25] As a matter of practical reality, however, prosecutors are "part lawyer, part bureaucrat, and part politician."[26] The work of the prosecutor is sometimes less concerned with fairness and justice than with other considerations.

As with the police, the quality of a prosecutor's output is difficult to measure—especially in light of the fact that criminal convictions are not always the best way to deal with a crime. How then is a prosecutor's effectiveness to be measured?Blumberg argues that "the occupational role of the prosecutor is characterized by five major functions in our system of criminal justice: (1) collection agent; (2) dispenser of justice; (3) power-broker-fixer, (4) political 'enforcer'; and (5) overseer of the police."[27] This is a valuable perspective, for it clearly illustrates how prosecution as a public enterprise serves a number of constituencies, each of which evaluates performance in a different way. Blumberg's perspective clearly recognizes the complexity of the prosecutor's role.

As Collection Agent

Blumberg points out that "one of the most important services that a prosecutor's office renders, especially in smaller communities, is as an agency to collect and disburse debts which arise in a variety of legal contexts."[28] Most of these situations are clear-cut: bad checks, child support payments that have fallen in arrears and some cases of fraud or embezzlement.

As Dispenser of Justice

Statutes are impersonal, whereas the cases that come before a prosecutor for charging decisions are very real human situations as well as legal problems. Moreover, not all crimes that violate a given statute are equal. Silberman has noted, for example, that "by and large prosecutors distinguish between 'real crimes'—crimes committed by strangers—and 'junk' (or 'garbage') cases, i.e., those which grow out of a dispute between people who know one another."[29] The prosecutor sorts out the meaning of a given case, looks at it in light of its own merits and then decides which direction to take with the case. In this respect the prosecutor is acting as a judge—a dispenser of justice. The choices range from dismissing the charges to pursuing them in a "no-holds-barred" courtroom battle seeking the maximum punishment.

As Power-Broker-Fixer

Blumberg says the "power-broker-fixer" role is performed by prosecutors from time to time, involving cases in which "a defendant is being prosecuted for reasons or purposes other than, or extraneous to, underlying factors of guilt in a crime."[30] Probably the most frequent motive for such an action is publicity. As elected officials, prosecutors must maintain a certain amount of visibility. One of the best ways of doing this is by "cashing in" on certain crimes, especially those which have already captured the public's attention. Prosecutors sometimes engage in what amounts to malicious prosecution—even if there is reason to doubt the guilt of the offender.[31]

As Political Enforcer

The district attorney is part of what is often called "the courthouse gang," which consists of such elected officials as the sheriff, the district attorney and judges. Not only do these people play specific roles within the criminal justice system, they also represent a great deal of political power within the community. Sometimes this power is used to dispense "patronage" jobs or to keep a tight reign on local politics.

As Overseer of the Police

In evaluating a criminal case, a prosecutor evaluates the work of the police officers who prepared the case. Under ideal circumstances, the prosecutor will actively assist the police in the preparation of a case. This is more likely to occur when there is a strong chance that the case will result in a trial.[32] In a sense the prosecutor oversees the criminal case preparation of the police—through both charging decisions and decisions of whether to prosecute. If the police wish to secure criminal convictions in the cases they prepare, they must see to it that their cases are consistent with the expectations of the prosecutor.[33]

Although there are exceptions, most experienced police officers are basically familiar with the laws they enforce. When they make an arrest, they usually know the elements of the crimes for which it is made. In preparing their cases for presentation to the prosecutor, the police tend to be quite confident about what they have. Many are equally certain about what they expect from the prosecutor. However, in some cases the prosecutor's charging decisions vary significantly from what the police expect. Under such circumstances, the police have no power to change matters. Officers sometimes complain that prosecutors are critical of the quality of cases sent forward by the police, but that they rarely offer any helpful suggestions. Traditionally, there has been a mild degree of animosity between police and prosecutors, with allegations proffered on both sides. For example, one prosecutor in Washington, DC said, "The level of [police] training is abysmal. You've got illiterate renditions of what the facts should be ..... On certain charges [like assault on a police officer] they come in here with their attitude. A lot of the stuff they bring us is crap. The person shouldn't have been arrested. You can preach Supreme Court cases to them until you're blue in the face and they don't care. They have instincts and they're right, this guy's dirty."[34] A police officer offered this opinion: "It's the class thing. Police officers, they think, are sort of loutish types, aren't all that intelligent—and this from lawyers who have gone to high school and college and have probably never really been scared in their lives, except if they took the wrong mogul on a ski slope...."[35]

The relationship between the prosecutor and the police is actually part of a larger "exchange system" in which the participants share an overlapping interest and often collaborate to achieve their respective goals. The prosecutor generally is dependant on the police for both cases and evidence, and due to a lack of resources to investigate cases, is dependent on the output of the police department. However, the prosecutor can effectively "oversee" the police through the power to return cases to them and by refusing to approve arrest warrants. Even though prosecutors and police officers may view one another's role with skepticism or even hostility, they must still work out a system of accommodations that enables both institutions to function. They do so through a variety of tactics. For example, a prosecutor cited by Cole said the following about the police: "You have to keep them on their toes, otherwise they get lazy. If they aren't doing their job, send the case back and then leak the situation to the newspapers."[36]

CHARGING DECISIONS
AND COMMUNITY EXPECTATIONS

The average citizen is not trained in the complexities of substantive or procedural law, but most know that doing certain things constitutes committing a crime and that the law sets punishments for the commission of crimes. It is reasonable for people to expect those who commit crimes to be punished for them. Indeed, ample evidence indicates that the general public is not tolerant of crime. Many citizens seem concerned that too many criminals are "getting off on technicalities." They attribute this problem not to the police but to the courts. Unfortunately, most citizens do not realize that there is a significant difference between *factual guilt* and *legal guilt*. Factual guilt acknowledges that a suspect committed an illegal act. Legal guilt is the proper, procedural establishment of the person's guilt in a court of law. Even if factual guilt is not disputed, the state must establish legal guilt. For example, if insanity is a defense, legal guilt cannot attach to a crime committed by a person judged to be insane. In some cases legal guilt cannot be established because evidence in support of the case is either non-existent or was obtained improperly and therefore suppressed. In this situation, the prosecutor must either charge the offender with whatever charges it can prove, or the case must be dismissed.

THE PROSECUTOR AS PRIVATE ENTREPRENEUR

Prosecutors, whether elected (district attorneys) or appointed (assistant district attorneys), are responsible for building their own careers. New assistant prosecutors are usually recent law school graduates just entering the legal profession. Many entry-level assistant prosecutors have little (if any) trial experience. Often, young graduates of lesser-known law schools start their legal careers in the prosecutor's office so they can gain experience and recognition. There are a number of reasons why this is a good idea. Although salaries are not high, they are usually adequate. It also gives young attorneys experience in dealing with criminal cases and quickly orients them to the general practice of criminal law in the community. They learn how the prosecutorial process works and gain valuable trial experience by prosecuting cases. They learn about the administration of dockets, participate in plea bargaining with defense attorneys and are provided the opportunity to increase their visibility in the local legal community. Other attorneys, who may be defending or otherwise representing clients, deal with them and have the opportunity to see how they work. A favorable reputation among local attorneys eventually can result in a job offer from a law firm—particularly one that needs an attorney with recent experience in criminal cases.

Once elected, a district attorney has ample opportunity to develop an image with the public and become involved with the local political infrastructure. The average tenure of office for all elected prosecutors is one and a half terms.[37] Many prosecutors go on to seek higher political office—a judgeship, a seat in Congress or some other public position. In order to do so they must achieve name recognition and a public reputation.

DEFENSE LAWYERS

Many kinds of lawyers—tax attorneys, corporation counsel, patent attorneys and other kinds of legal specialists—would be lost if they had to act as defense counsel in a criminal court. It is the unique environment of lawyers who work in *criminal* practice. Defense lawyers are part of a larger community of legal professionals who work within the criminal justice system, including judges, prosecutors, the police, public defenders, various kinds of paraprofessionals, and others. To function effectively in this environment, the defense lawyer must maintain cooperative relationships with other officials.[38] It is not unusual for the members of this legal community to be on a first-name basis with one another. Ties may be so close that jailers, police officers, bailiffs or other officials recommend certain lawyers to newly arrested defendants.[39] In addition, judges (often motivated by a desire to develop political allies or to repay political or personal debts) may favor some defense lawyers over others, especially when selecting counsel to be paid at public expense. The defense lawyer, though technically an officer of the court, must function in a highly complex and competitive environment dominated by people who may have both political power and strong personalties. To operate effectively in this environment, the defense lawyer must master this situation. Bargaining and compromise are favored tactics of defense attorneys; the negotiations that lead to a guilty plea exemplify this process.

Some defendants in criminal cases are extremely critical of their lawyers, especially in the case of public defenders.[40] Unsuccessful defendants often blame their attorneys for losing their cases (sometimes with justification). In addition to suffering the public's ambivalence toward lawyers in general, defense lawyers are considered by many to be at the bottom of the legal profession's class structure. Despite the fact that some defense lawyers earn excellent incomes and a few have gained some fame among the general public (e.g., F. Lee Bailey and Percy Foreman), the prestige of the defense lawyer does not match that of the corporate lawyer or most other specialists within the legal profession. It is debatable whether this lack of prestige stems from the somewhat unsavory nature of their practice, the flamboyant style of some defense lawyers or the lack of social standing of most of the people they defend.

DEFENDER OF CLIENT VS. OFFICER OF THE COURT: THE CONFLICT

The American legal system is based on the duty and obligation of the contending lawyers to represent their client's cases to the best of their ability.* Lawyers are expected to present every scrap of evidence, find favorable legal precedents and argue the merits of their client's case as persuasively as possible. The logic of the adversary system holds that all possible evidence will emerge if both sides of the case are given optimal presentation, and that the judge or jury will thus be able to discern the truth and render justice.[41] The adversary system places an important responsibility upon the lawyer who defends individuals accused of a crime. At least in theory, the defense counsel is the only one looking out for the interests of the defendant. Consequently, the defense attorney makes a major contribution to achieving justice within the adversarial system.

In addition to being an advocate for clients, the defense lawyer is also an officer of the court.[42] Consequently, it is the defense lawyer's duty to assist the court in seeing that justice is done. This duty requires that only truthful statements be made and only true and accurate evidence be presented to the court. The lawyer technically has a dual obligation to both the client and the court. The type of problems that ensue are illustrated in the following hypothetical case.

A. Mugger is charged with robbery. He has been convicted of several prior crimes, some involving violence and others involving only property offenses. Mugger has admitted his guilt to his lawyer, D. Fender. Strong corroborating evidence exists as well. In spite of this, Fender knows that she can obtain an acquittal based on the fact that the police illegally obtained evidence against Mugger. Barring the unlikely possibility that Mugger does not wish to be acquitted, Fender is obligated by professional ethics and the logic of the adversary system to obtain Mugger's acquittal. If Fender finds such an outcome repugnant to her personal morals, professional ethics dictate that she seek to be relieved as Mugger's counsel. The prevailing view, as mandated by legal ethics, finds no conflict between Fender's duty to Mugger and her obligation to the court.

---

* The "client" in the case of the prosecutor is the people—society as a whole, whereas the defense lawyer is obliged to represent the person accused of the crime.

Some people contend that a lawyer in such a situation has an obligation to the public interest that supersedes the duty to the offender, and that consequently the lawyer should not seek the client's acquittal.[43] Some members of the public would accept this view as well, and would consider Fender's action toward Mugger's acquittal to be contrary to the public interest. However, such a contention is in direct opposition to the logic and ethics of the adversary system—a system misunderstood by much of the public.

Another factor also presents a dilemma of considerable proportions. The close working relationships necessary for effective representation of a defense lawyer's clients may also be used to the detriment of those represented. Prosecutors and judges might make demands of the defense attorney that are detrimental to the client. Such demands might include an expectation on the part of a judge that the attorney engage in plea bargaining, question witnesses expeditiously or otherwise speed up the process. Obviously, as an integral part of the judicial bureaucracy, a defense lawyer would have to regard these expectations seriously. There is ample opportunity for a conflict of interest between judge and defense attorney. Judges are concerned with the regular movement of the cases that come before them. Once created, a logjam is difficult to break, yet a reasonably quick disposition of a criminal case is crucial to most concepts of American justice. An inability to move cases and keep the docket up-to-date can negatively influence the evaluation of a judge's performance. Once again this illustrates the phenomenon of instruments that have become institutions, with a logic of their own, separate from the reasons why they were created in the first place.

The prompt handling of cases is a legitimate concern of the trial judge. The most expeditious way to move cases is to encourage the use of plea bargaining; negotiated cases consume a relatively small amount of time and there is little risk of reversal. Without a preponderance of guilty pleas, many criminal courts would be unable to function; the "assembly-line justice" characteristic of so many American courts would grind to a stop. Consequently, it is understandable why a trial judge would exert either overt or subtle pressure to encourage guilty pleas or communicate a desire that time-consuming motions and pleadings be curtailed or expedited.

Such a dependence on the system is greater for public defenders who are employed by the state. It is particularly heightened for those who are appointed by the very judges before whom they practice.[44] Countering the judge's expectations could jeopardize the defender's source of livelihood. Professional ethics and the logic of the adversary system demand that the greatest possible effort be made on behalf of the client, yet this same effort can harm relationships with the judge and the prosecutor—relationships crucial to continued effectiveness in the criminal court. Of course, different attorneys respond to this dilemma in different ways. Complete adherence to the norms of the judicial-prosecutorial establishment is one possibility. A middle ground of occasional adherence and occasional circumspect defiance is another. Outright rejection of these norms is also a possible response.[45] Each defense lawyer must find a unique mix of responses and develop a means of coping with the dilemma. The wide diversity of defense styles encountered in the criminal courts is one result of this phenomenon.[46]

HOW DO DEFENSE LAWYERS DEFEND THEIR CLIENTS?

The tactics and strategies employed by defense lawyers vary greatly depending on: the seriousness of the charge; the resources available for the defense; the laws, customs and practices of the jurisdiction; the type of client defended; the lawyer's relationships with the appropriate criminal justice personnel; and the overall nature of the case. A well-designed strategy for one case could be a very poor strategy for another case. Moreover, similar cases in different jurisdictions might require completely different defensive strategies.

Defense lawyers try to have their cases decided in the most beneficial form and arena. They attempt to avoid biased or unfavorable judges by requesting a change of judge when the law so allows. By the same token, they may try to move the trial to a more favorable geographic location. This is likely when pretrial publicity would be prejudicial to the case if it were to be heard in the area. In addition, when selecting jurors in a contested case (the process of voir dire), defense lawyers strive to pick jurors who are likely to be favorably inclined toward the defendant.

The very cumbersome judicial machinery is often vulnerable to defense lawyers who utilize its inefficiencies to their own benefit. Numerous postponements (known as continuances) may ultimately result in the failure of a key witness to appear and a consequent dismissal of the prosecution for lack of evidence. Jury trials may be requested as a possible delaying tactic. The more ineffective the judicial process in an area, the easier it is for a case to "fall between the cracks" of the system. Many defense attorneys play these inefficiencies with consummate skill—especially with misdemeanors and less serious felonies. Run-of-the-mill cases can often be disposed of through these tactics, while notorious cases—especially those with considerable public interest—are much less amenable to these kinds of procedural attacks.

The standard tactics and strategies employed by defense attorneys are similar to those employed by all attorneys. Their clients are portrayed as favorably as possible. Glowing descriptions of defendants are common, and redeeming characteristics are extolled. On the other hand, witnesses testifying against the defendant may be subjected to intensely critical interrogation in which every silence, pause, lie, inconsistency—basically any conceivable weakness in testimony—will be used to attempt to discredit the witness in the eyes of the judge and jury. The prosecution employs these same tactics.

The demeanor, appearance, attitude and criminal record of the defendant may significantly influence a defense attorney's strategy. An individual who is resentful and contemptuous of authority and who can be provoked easily makes a poor witness. The prosecution can bait them on cross-examination and accentuate their resentment and contempt for authority. Unusual or eccentric dress also can produce an unfavorable reaction. If a defendant is likely to make a poor impression, the defense lawyer will usually try to keep him or her off the stand (the prosecution cannot call to the stand a defendant who has not been placed there first by the defense). Any witness who makes a bad impression can substantially weaken a defense lawyer's case. Utilizing a witness or defendant who keeps emotion under control and shows respect in the courtroom can strengthen a case by making a favorable impression on the judge and the jurors. The characteristics of the defendant and the witnesses are vitally important in developing the defensive strategy in a criminal case.

TO BARGAIN OR TO FIGHT: THE DEFENSE LAWYER'S STRATEGIC DILEMMA

It is widely believed that, frequently, judges mete out more severe punishments to defendants who elect to stand trial rather than accept terms under a negotiated plea. Although there is some evidence to support such an assumption of a "jury trial penalty,"[47] there are questions concerning the extent to which it actually exists and the kinds of cases in which it is likely to arise.[48] It is probably impossible to know for certain whether the failure to plead is a factor in sentencing—and whether this is an incentive to engage in plea bargaining—but it is a possibility that clearly deserves attention.

Plea bargaining is a common means of disposing of criminal cases and is part of the "exchange system" mentioned earlier. There are many incentives that support the practice, not the least of which is the willingness of courts to accept plea bargains in order to keep dockets moving. Defense attorneys use them for two basic reasons. The first is to gain *some* benefit, however small, for clients whose prospects are otherwise bleak. The second (and less noble) reason is that plea bargaining enables the rapid processing of a number of low-paying clients, thereby allowing attorneys to earn by virtue of volume what they would be unable to make from individual clients.[49] Contrary to conventional wisdom, however, plea bargaining does not always result in leniency for the defendant—nor is that always the goal. Leniency is most likely to occur in cases concerning less serious offenses, and as the seriousness of the crime increases, the benefits to be derived from pleading guilty decrease. Moreover, some defendants plead guilty because they have nothing upon which to base a defense and feel that they have no possibility of escaping conviction.

Additional incentives include the tremendous expenses of a trial. If a defendant is unable to post a bail bond and is awaiting trial in the county jail, a bargained plea could mean an end to an unpleasant incarceration in jail, with either a probated sentence or commitment to a more tolerable prison. A plea bargain also translates to a quick resolution of the prosecution and an end to uncertainty; the accused need no longer wonder what will take place.

An illustration of the strong pressure to plea bargain is found in the United States Supreme Court case of *Bordenkircher v. Hayes*.[50] The defendant, Paul Lewis Hayes, was charged with uttering a false instrument in the amount of $88.30. In Kentucky, where the offense took place, the sentence for this crime was two to 10 years in prison. During a plea bargaining session the prosecutor agreed to recommend a five-year prison sentence if Hayes would agree to plead guilty. The prosecutor said that if Hayes refused to plead guilty and did not save the court the inconvenience and necessity of conducting a trial, he would ask the grand jury to indict him under the Kentucky Habitual Criminal Act. Hayes did not plead guilty, and true to his word, the prosecutor obtained an indictment charging him with violating the Habitual Criminal Act. At the subsequent trial Hayes was found guilty on the charge of uttering a forged instrument. In a separate hearing, based on two prior felonies, he was also found guilty of violating the Habitual Criminal Act. Hayes was sentenced to a life term in a Kentucky penitentiary.

The Supreme Court upheld the conviction, stating that this was a valid exercise of prosecutorial discretion. In explaining its decision, the court stated that

> ...in the "give and take" of plea bargaining, there is no such element of punishment or retaliation so long as the accused is free to accept or reject the prosecutor's offer. Plea bargaining flows from "the mutuality of advantage" to defendants and prosecutors, each with his own reasons for wanting to avoid trial. Defendants advised by competent counsel and protected by other procedural safeguards are presumptively capable of intelligent choice in response to prosecutorial persuasion, and unlikely to be driven to false self-condemnation...

> While confronting a defendant with the risk of more severe punishment clearly may have a "discouraging effect on the defendant's assertion of his trial rights, the imposition of these difficult choices [is] an inevitable"—and permissible—attribute of any legitimate system which tolerates and encourages the negotiation of pleas...

> It follows that, by tolerating and encouraging the negotiation of pleas, this Court has necessarily accepted as constitutionally legitimate the simple reality that the prosecutor's interest at the bargaining table is to persuade the defendant to forego his right to plead not guilty.[51]

Most defendants face strong pressure by the criminal justice system to participate in plea bargaining. The inducements favoring plea bargaining are so strong that the decision of whether to plea bargain is perhaps the most significant decision for the defense lawyer and client. The majority of defendants find this pressure too strong and go ahead with the plea bargain,[52] meaning that in a great many cases the defense lawyer does not fight for an acquittal at all but rather negotiates for the best possible "guilty" outcome. Whether this represents justice has been hotly debated.

DEFENSE OF THE POOR

A cursory visit to any criminal court or county jail will quickly convince the observer that the majority of criminal defendants are poor—most so poor that they cannot retain their own counsel. Although represented by counsel at public expense, the quality of their representation is often inferior to that received by defendants who can afford their own attorneys. Consequently, the poor often receive an inferior brand of justice.[53] Poverty is a central problem for the criminal justice system and a major impediment to the realization of equal justice for all.

The stark realization of the gap between the ideal of equal justice and reality of unequal justice—and the greater concern with human rights that has evolved over the last 50 years—have inspired a family of Supreme Court cases demanding that all criminal defendants be represented by counsel. The first of these cases, *Powell v. Alabama*, held that in capital cases poor, illiterate and young defendants were entitled to a lawyer supplied by the state.[54] This limited decision grew out of the controversial case in which nine young black men were charged in the Alabama courts with raping two white women. Throughout the proceedings there was a hostile mob, which at one point threatened to lynch the young men. They were indicted on March 31, 1931, and their trial was set for six days later, on April 6. After confusion over the appointment of the defense counsel, an alcohol-impaired Tennessee lawyer by the name of Steven Roddy represented the defendants, even though he had not had any preparation time and only a 30-minute interview with the youths prior to commencement of the trial. The defendants were quickly convicted. The Supreme Court later overturned the conviction, holding that the Due Process Clause of the Fourteenth Amendment required that the right to counsel be offered, in capital cases, to defendants in state courts who were poor, young and illiterate.

A significant broadening of the *Powell* rule took place with *Gideon v. Wainwright* in 1963.[55] Gideon was charged with breaking into a pool hall. Upon arraignment Gideon stated that he was unable to pay for a lawyer and asked that one be appointed for him. He was told by the Florida district judge that the Fourteenth Amendment Due Process clause required only that defendants in state courts be supplied counsel in capital cases when the defendants were poor, illiterate and young (the *Powell* rule). Denied legal counsel, Gideon represented himself and was convicted. His handwritten appeal to the United State Supreme Court was accepted; in its opinion the Court substantially broadened the right to counsel by applying it to all defendants accused of a felony who were too poor to afford their own lawyer.

The *Gideon* case was further expanded by *Argersinger v. Hamlin* (1972).[56] Hamlin was convicted of a misdemeanor and sentenced to 60 days in jail. As in the *Gideon* case, Hamlin was not offered the right to counsel because the requirements of the Fourteenth Amendment did not extend the right to counsel to cases such as his. In *Argersinger* the Supreme Court extended the right to counsel to every person accused of a crime carrying the possibility of even a one-day jail sentence. With this decision, the Court completed the long process of providing the right to counsel to every defendant too poor to afford a lawyer.

These cases forced state and county judicial systems to develop mechanisms for providing attorneys for the poor. Under the assigned counsel system, judges appoint lawyers selected from a pool of interested attorneys to represent the poor on a case-by-case basis. This method probably is most effective when the lawyers are compensated at a scale approximating a private attorney's fee and when the selected lawyers have experience with substantial numbers of criminal cases. Public defender systems are the second basic means of providing counsel for the poor. A public defender is a public official charged with the task of defending the poor. Frequently a full-time public servant, the public defender may head an office of several lawyers, paraprofessionals, investigators, clerks and secretaries. Offices for populous urban areas may have more than 50 attorneys.

As McIntyre has noted, "Public defenders are social anomalies. They are paid by the state to befriend those whom the state believes are its enemies and to question—and wherever possible, to thwart—the prosecution of those whom the state suspects are criminals."[57] It would be a mistake to look upon the public defenders as either second-rate lawyers or bureaucratic functionaries paid by the state, for they serve an extremely important purpose: they protect the legitimacy of the courts; their job is not to destroy the law but to fulfill it.[58] Unfortunately, public defenders operate under a public and professional stigma. They are professionally stigmatized in general because they practice *criminal* law and in particular because they operate in the "shadow" of the trial bar. As McIntyre noted, "Because the public defender's office exists in the shadows and avoids negotiating legitimacy with the broader society, it denies its incumbents the shelter that legitimate institutions can offer workers."[59] The public stigma is a function of public defenders being tainted by their clientele, in addition to being seen as less effective—and more interested in making deals—than attorneys who defend paying clients.[60]

Defendants who are convicted are likely to complain about the quality of the defense they receive at the hands of public defenders. However, their complaints need to be kept in perspective: many of them had little upon which to base a defense and sometimes it is easier for them to blame the defender than to accept responsibility for their own actions. The feeling that they received an inadequate defense may also be based on the limited amount of time they may have spent with a public defender. Private lawyers *do* spend more time with their clients,[61] but the fact that more time is spent with a client does not necessarily mean that the quality of the defense is any better. In fact, spending more time with a client may have more psychological value than legal value.

Public defender offices are most effective when they are adequately funded, have reasonable caseloads and endure little political influence. They function best when defense counsel is independent of the trial judge and support services such as investigators are available. Naturally, the system needs to be effectively administered.[62] If a system lacks one or more of these criteria—or possesses some other fault—inadequate representation for their clients can result. Heavy caseloads can severely limit the amount of time that can be spent per case, resulting in a lack of adequate preparation or unprofessional performance. Too many cases, too much work and a constant "parade" of new defendants can result in disillusioned, cynical and "burned out" public defenders.[63]

LAWYERS AND NON-LAWYERS: A CONFLICT OF EXPECTATIONS

There is more to the adversary nature of criminal justice than the demeanor of lawyers in the courtroom. The police (official initiators of action against an accused) tend to have a low opinion of defense lawyers, whom they see as trying to undo their work. The reason is simple: the police see the consequences of crimes in the most direct ways. They deal with victims who have been beaten, murdered, robbed or raped, and see the agony and loss. They also see offenders in their "natural environment" and therefore know from firsthand experience the tragic nature of crime and criminals. They see wrongs being committed and feel such wrongs deserve to be redressed. They often see the tactics of defense lawyers as a means to thwart—rather than serve—the ends of justice. As a result of plea bargaining and the peculiarities of the trial process, many police officers become embittered toward lawyers and cynical toward the courts.

Consider, for example, the case of the police officer who tried to arrest a suspect who broke the officer's arm in an attack with a baseball bat. The officer secured a warrant charging the suspect with the felony of aggravated assault on a police officer, resulting in grievous bodily harm. The prosecutor, in a routine move, reduced the case to two misdemeanors: simple assault and possession of a prohibited weapon. The suspect, who pleaded not guilty, will be represented at trial by a public defender. The prosecutor will have to prove exactly the same legal "elements" that would be required if the case had been filed as a felony; the difference is that, if convicted, the suspect would get one year in jail instead of 10 years in prison. As one police officer noted, "All these high-priced snobby lawyers—whether they be prosecutors, defense lawyers or judges—are nothing but clerks, because if it weren't for police officers they would have nothing to do."[64]

One of the most disturbing aspects of the criminal justice system is that justice *is* for sale in many cases. Yet criminal law is only one area of law practice. This raises the interesting question of just what do lawyers practice?Unlike most workers, lawyers do not increase the value of a natural resource through their labors, nor do they produce a "thing of value," like a pair of shoes, a clipboard or an automobile, which can be sold in an open competitive marketplace. Lawyers do not have a tangible product, unless you are willing to accept legal forms and other pieces of paper as tangible products. What lawyers do is enable clients to avail themselves of legal rights: to form corporations, dissolve marriages, transfer property, obtain patents, raise defenses in criminal proceedings, and so on.

This perspective on lawyers is certainly not new, nor is it without critics. Adam Smith, the founder of modern economics, in his classic *Wealth of Nations*, distinguished between productive and unproductive labor. The former produces a "value" (as in the manufacture of a product); the latter, although useful, adds nothing to value per se. In this latter group Smith included, "menial servants, ...the sovereign, ...with all the officers both of justice and war, ...the whole army and navy," and also "churchmen, lawyers, physicians, men of letters of all kinds; players, buffoons, musicians, opera singers...etc."[65]

Since the rights enjoyed by all citizens are set forth in (and described by) laws, and since the procedures for obtaining them are essentially *legal* procedures, lawyers sell their services as guides, expediters, facilitators and advocates. Through them, clients are able to obtain the benefits and rights to which they are entitled. All of this is done, of course, for a fee. Lawyers also tend to gravitate toward settings where laws are made and administered. Lawyers are well represented in legislatures, as they are in many administrative and political positions across the branches of government. In a very real sense, lawyers make the laws, administer and interpret them, and act as paid gatekeepers—admitting only those outsiders who can pay for their services.

This operates to the advantage of lawyers. In all probability the general public would grant its approval if it felt that the lawyers met the social obligations clearly set forth in the attorneys' canon of ethics. All too often, however, this does not appear to be the case.[66] The public is painfully aware that the highly paid principals in the Watergate scandal were lawyers. The public saw how Vice President Spiro Agnew bargained his way through his legal problems, and how neither money nor influence was spared on behalf of kidnapped heiress Patty Hearst. It has become clear that sometimes money is the main thing that differentiates among the many standards of justice.

Everyone who retains a lawyer expects the same thing to a certain extent; regardless of which side they are on, they want their lawyer to do a good job in representing their interests. The criminal defendant expects and deserves to be adequately represented. The defense lawyer should ascertain whether the police or other officials acted properly during apprehension, questioning and the gathering of evidence, and should follow every proper legal procedure available for the defense of the client. The question is whether it is "fair," for instance, for a lawyer to argue that a chronic drunk driver should retain a drivers license based solely on the grounds that the driver is a merchant and church member? Is this not placing the life of the client and the lives of others in danger? Although it is reasonable to argue that the defense lawyer has an obligation to see that a client's rights are protected, does that also imply an obligation to seek the acquittal of a person who is both obviously guilty and dangerous? These issues fuel heated discussion among both legal theorists and the public.

VICTIMS OF CRIME

Although many people in the community believe that in criminal cases the victim is represented by the prosecutor and has the right to expect redress for harm suffered, this is not the case. The injured party is not the victim; society as a whole is the victim. The prosecutor thus represents the entire community, not the person who was harmed. Because many victims fail to understand this, they feel the system does not care about them, often attributing this indifference to either malice or incompetence. However, the reason some prosecutors may seem not to care about the victim is because tending to the victim is not their job.

Some changes have been implemented to make the roles of both victims and witnesses less traumatic and unpleasant. These changes, long overdue in light of the central role played by victims and witnesses in the administration of justice, have the potential to greatly enhance the quality of the relationship between the community and the criminal justice system. They also provide expanded opportunities for the community to involve itself directly in the justice process.

A number of jurisdictions have established programs to help victims of serious crime.[67] Actual agencies of government (such as the prosecutor's office or the courts themselves) make compensations to victims of certain kinds of crimes. Private or quasi-public agencies likewise have begun to provide valuable services to victims, including such things as rape counseling and victim assistance.

Witness assistance programs, usually operated by the prosecutor's office, seek to educate witnesses with regard to what will be expected of them and how the trial process works. In some cases the prosecutor can reduce the number of appearances a witness must make or shorten the waiting time prior to testimony. Some jurisdictions have experimented with providing transportation for witnesses who would otherwise have difficulty getting to and from court. These basic considerations contribute to a more positive feeling on the part of those who must participate in the criminal justice process.

The use of community resources in assisting witnesses and victims is in the best interests of all parties. From the perspective of the prosecutor, it enhances the likelihood that witnesses will appear and provide the testimony vital to the case. For the victim, it is a means of restoring the equilibrium that was lost when the crime was committed and for reducing the sense of shock, loss and self-destruction. For the community, it is a means of providing support and care, thereby fostering more positive feelings toward the government.

Even if a government agency (e.g., the police or prosecutor) is limited in what it can do for victims, it can still play a valuable role by encouraging groups within the community to operate victim and witness assistance programs. In fact, it is the government's responsibility to educate the public regarding how it can secure the benefits of such programs. By bringing data on needs and opportunities before interested groups, the criminal justice system not only serves its own purposes but brings the community into closer involvement with its own criminal justice-related problems.[68]

Victims and witnesses who have been handled with a lack of sensitivity and care often walk away from the courts disappointed or disgusted. Moreover, they may not know that what they expect of lawyers may not be what lawyers expect of themselves. Legal conflicts are like mazes that are defined by law and procedure rather than by abstract concepts of justice or people's feelings. In an adversary system, a defense lawyer is required to advocate the client's case. In addition, the defense realizes that the prosecution has some powerful tools at its disposal, including the police and other investigative resources, and that their own strength lies in its understanding of the law and the means of its administration. This essentially healthy process is corrupted only when either side fails to meet its obligations, i.e., when prosecutors fail to prosecute or defenders fail to defend. The problem with the negotiated plea is that it waters down the adversary process and can reduce the effectiveness of counsel for each side down to the level of a legal clerk. The negotiated plea can deny both the offender and society as a whole the fruits of justice. It also encourages careless treatment of those who have been victimized and those who must come forward to testify.

SUMMARY

Crimes forwarded by the police for prosecution are processed almost exclusively by lawyers—prosecuting attorneys, defense lawyers and judges—who apply legal rules and customs to individual cases. In theory, this is supposed to culminate in an *adversarial process* in which prosecution and defense counsel battle one another before a jury of the accused's peers. Reality, however, often falls short of this ideal.

Lawyers are members of a profession that is highly stratified within its own ranks. Those who work in the criminal arena are seldom at the top of the hierarchy. Criminal lawyers for the state are called *prosecutors*. It is their job to bring criminal cases before the courts for adjudication. Prosecutors must make a number of important decisions as to how any given case will be handled; this is part of the *screening* process. They may decline to prosecute a case for a variety of reasons. In busy jurisdictions many minor cases are dropped simply to expedite the processing of more important cases. Other cases may be *diverted* by being channeled into some other program, thereby helping the offender deal with the causal problem while reducing the burden on the courts. In other instances the prosecutor may accept *intervention* by a treatment agency as an alternative to criminal prosecution. Both diversion and intervention screen out cases by providing an alternative to prosecution. They thereby reduce clutter in the courts and offer help to those who need it and appear to be good risks.

One of the most important decisions made by a prosecutor is the specific crime with which an accused will be charged. Charging decisions are based on two key issues: (1) the kind and quality of evidence available to the prosecutor, and (2) the question of what charge would best serve the public interest. Other factors, such as the notoriety of the case, the cost of prosecuting it and the prosecutor's workload, also play a role in charging decisions. A great many cases are "negotiated" by the prosecutor and the defendant (or defense counsel). This generally involves an agreement to plead guilty in return for a specified consideration, such as being charged with the lesser crime, getting probation instead of "hard time," and so on.

Prosecutors play a variety of roles in the criminal justice system, some of which are only indirectly related to the prosecution of crimes. In some cases they act as collection agents, using the threat of prosecution as a tactic; in other instances, they essentially adjudicate cases by deciding how to handle them. Prosecutors are elected officials who belong to the political infrastructure. As such, they must be mindful of the political sentiments of the community in how they handle their caseload. In addition, because prosecutors oversee the work of the police by deciding which cases will be prosecuted, they are often at odds with the police.

Defense lawyers—whether they are private attorneys hired by an accused or public defenders whose job is to provide criminal defense—are officers of the court as well as representatives of their clients' interests. This dual obligation sometimes places them in a difficult position. Defense lawyers work in a legal environment in which they are dependent to a certain extent on the goodwill of prosecutors and judges. A great deal of the style of a defense lawyer is determined by how he or she handles this problem. These differences in style account for much of the diversity in the defense bar. Defense lawyers must use the weaknesses of the legal system to their clients' advantage. Characteristically, they make the best possible use of the plea bargaining system.

Although most people charged with crimes are poor, legal advocacy for the poor historically has been insufficient. A series of Supreme Court cases extended important rights to the indigent, including the right to a defense lawyer. This resulted in a public defense system that provides attorneys to defendants too poor to hire private counsel. Often underfunded and overworked, public defenders are frequently under great pressure to negotiate rather than litigate. Although the individual lawyers involved may be talented, the public defense *system* is often strained to a point where it provides minimal services for its clients.

There is a great deal of conflict among the participants in the criminal justice system. The police are often frustrated with prosecutors and defense lawyers, often seeing them as using the legal arena to play games without regard to the victims of crime or the importance of the police function. Prosecutors, in turn, are often frustrated with the police, criticizing how they handle their investigations and questioning the quality of the cases forwarded for prosecution. The public often sees the lawyers in the system as manipulators who use the political environment and criminal justice system without serious regard for the public good. Compounding citizen frustration is confusion over the distinction between *factual guilt* and *legal guilt* and the generally poor treatment witnesses receive at the hands of the courts.

DISCUSSION QUESTIONS

1. How has the development of the legal profession in America influenced the kind of lawyers who work in criminal practice?

2. Do we have too many lawyers in this country? Why or why not?

3. Should prosecutors have the unrestricted right to "nol pros" a case?

4. How does *jurisdiction* influence who prosecutes a criminal case?

5. Can a crime that violates both federal and state law be prosecuted in both federal and state courts without violating the accused's constitutional right against double jeopardy?

6. What are some of the main reasons that would lead a prosecutor to screen a case "out" without taking it to court?

7. What is the difference between *diversion* and *intervention*?

8. Are diversion programs fair? If not, why?

9. Under what constraints must a prosecutor work in coming to a charging decision?

10. How does the concept of "lesser included offenses" influence a charging decision?

11. What would happen if plea bargaining was abolished? Do you think our criminal justice system is improving or getting worse?

12. What is the difference between an information and an indictment?

13. How does the prosecutor act as a "dispenser of justice"?

14. What could be done to improve the relationship between the prosecutor and the police?

15. Does the political role of the prosecutor unduly influence decision-making?

16. Is it realistic to consider defense lawyers as officers of the court? Why or why not?

17. Are the tactics used by defense lawyers in the public interest?

18. Do you think defense lawyers are too quick to cut deals on behalf of their clients? If so, does this represent "justice denied"?

19. How has the defense of the poor changed during the present century? Do you support these changes?

20. Is the public's perception of the role of prosecutors and defense lawyers realistic? If not, does it make any difference?

21. Since the state represents the people in a criminal prosecution and the defense lawyer represents the defendant, who represents the victim?

22. What can prosecutors do to assist witnesses?

23. Do you think victim compensation programs are worthwhile?

REFERENCES

1   Tom Wolf, *The Bonfire of the Vanities* (New York: Farrar, Straus, Giroux, 1987), 40.

2   Gregg Barak, *In Defense of Whom? A Critique of Criminal Justice Reform* (Cincinnati: Anderson Publishing Co., 1980), 27-51.

3   Roscoe Pound, *The Lawyer from Antiquity to Modern Times* (St. Paul: West Publishing Company, 1953), 136.

4   Barak, *In Defense of Whom?*, 33.

5   Esther L. Brown, *Lawyers and the Promotion of Justice* (New York: Russell Sage Foundation, 1938), 11-12.

6   Barak, *In Defense of Whom?*, 37.

7   Barak, *In Defense of Whom?*, 37.

8   William Shakespeare, *King Henry VI*, Part II, Act IV, Scene 2, Line 86.

9   Jonathan Swift, *Gulliver's Travels*, in Walter F. Murphy and C. Herman Pritchett, *Courts, Judges and Politics* (New York: Random House, 1961), 129-131.

10 See, for example, "Respondents' Ratings of the Honesty and Ethical Standards of Various Occupations," in George Gallup, Jr., *The Gallup Poll* (May 22, 1991), 3, 4.

11 William Smart, "Legal Report Cards," *The Washington Post*, 8 May 1990, B5.

12 Ken Ringle, "Wit of Habeas Corpus: Throwing the Books at the Barristers," *The Washington Post*, 30 August 1989, B2.

13 Ken Adelman, "Lawyers in a Defensive Crouch," *The Washington Post*, 7 February 1992, F3.

14 See National Center for State Courts, *State Court Caseload Statistics Annual Report 1988* (Williamsburg, VA: National Center for State Courts, 1990).

15 See Brian Forst, *Improving Police-Prosecutor Coordination: A Research Agenda* (Washington, DC: Institute for Law and Social Research, 1981).

16 Barton Gellman, "In the District, Justice vs. Management," *The Washington Post*, 8 June 1989, C1, C11.

17 Donald J. Newman, *Introduction to Criminal Justice* (New Haven: Yale University Press, 1972).

18 Joan Mullen, *The Dilemma of Diversion* (Washington, DC: U.S. Government Printing Office, 1975), 6.

19 Mullen, *The Dilemma of Diversion*, 56.

[20] Frank W. Miller, *Prosecution: The Decision to Charge a Suspect With a Crime* (Boston: Little, Brown and Company, 1969).

[21] National Advisory Commission on Criminal Justice Standards and Goals, Russell W. Peterson, Chair, *Courts* (Washington, DC: U.S. Government Printing Office, 1973), 20.

[22] National Advisory Commission on Criminal Justice Standards and Goals, *Courts*, 20.

[23] See especially Stuart Schiengold and Lynne Gressett, "Policy, Politics and the Criminal Courts," *American Bar Foundation Research Journal* 2/3 (1987), 461-505.

[24] Chief Justice Warren Burger, "Address at the American Bar Association Annual Convention," *The New York Times*, 11 August 1979, 24.

[25] Harold J. Grilliot, *Introduction to Law and the Legal System*, 2nd ed. (Boston: Houghton, Mifflin Co., 1979), 315.

[26] James P. Levine, Michael C. Musheno and Dennis J. Palumbo, *Criminal Justice: A Public Policy Approach* (New York: Harcourt, Brace Jovanovich, Inc., 1980), 202.

[27] Abraham S. Blumberg, *Criminal Justice: Issues and Ironies*, 2nd ed. (New York: New Viewpoints, 1979), 133-139.

[28] Blumberg, *Criminal Justice: Issues and Ironies*, 133-139.

[29] Charles E. Silberman, *Criminal Violence, Criminal Justice* (New York: Vintage Books, 1978), 358-359.

[30] Blumberg, *Criminal Justice: Issues and Ironies*, 136.

[31] See especially the cases of Bruno Hauptmann, who was executed for killing Charles Lindbergh's baby, Anthony Scaduto, "Bruno Hauptmann Was Innocent," *New York Magazine*, 22 November 1976, 59-76; Clay Shaw, the man relentlessly pursued by New Orleans District Attorney James Garrison for complicity in the assassination of John F. Kennedy (*Shaw v. Garrison*, 467 F.2d 113 (1972)); and the "Scottsboro Boys," nine black youths accused of raping two white girls in the absence of any corroborating evidence (*Powell v. Alabama*, 287 U.S. 45 (1932)).

[32] Forst, *Improving Police-Prosecutor Coordination: A Research Agenda.*

[33] For both good and bad examples of how this relationship works, see Vincent Bugliosi, with Curt Gentry, *Helter Skelter* (New York: Bantam Books, 1975), which describes the behind-the-scenes efforts in the notorious Manson murder trial in Los Angeles.

[34] Gellman, "In the District, Justice vs. Management," C11.

[35] Gellman, "In the District, Justice vs. Management," C11.

[36] George F. Cole, "The Decision to Prosecute," *Law and Society Review* 4 (1970), 331-343. This is an excellent analysis of a prosecutor's office as an "exchange system."

[37] James Eisenstein, *Politician and the Legal Process* (New York: Harper and Row, 1973), 20-25.

[38] Abraham S. Blumberg, "The Practice of Law as a Confidence Game: Organizational Cooptation of a Profession," *Law and Society Review* (June 1967), 20.

[39] Samuel Dash, "Cracks in the Foundation of Criminal Justice," in John A. Robertson, ed., *Rough Justice* (Boston: Little, Brown and Co., 1974), 249-250.

[40] Jonathan D. Casper, *American Criminal Justice: The Defendant's Perspective* (Englewood Cliffs, NJ: Prentice Hall, Inc., 1971), 109-110.

[41] Jerome Frank, *Courts on Trial* (New York: Athenaeum, 1971), 80-81.

[42] American Bar Association, *Legal Ethics* (Chicago: American Bar Association, 1980).

[43] Howard James, *Crisis in the Courts* (New York: David McKay Co., 1971), 95.

[44] Norman G. Kittel, "Trial Judges Should Not Appoint Counsel for the Indigent," *The Legal Aid Briefcase* (June 1967), 171-181.

[45] See, for example, the role played by the defense counsel in Joseph Wambaugh, *The Onion Field* (New York: Delacourte Press, 1973).

[46] See also Malcolm Feeley, "Two Models of the Criminal Justice System: An Organizational Perspective," *Law and Society Review* 7 (1973), 407, and Michael Lichtenstein, "Public Defenders: Dimensions of Cooperation," *Justice Systems Journal* (1984), 102.

[47] Raymond J. Nimmer, "The Influence of the Defendant's Plea on Judicial Determination of Sentence," *Yale Law Journal* (December 1956), 207-208.

[48] See, for example, Douglas Smith, "The Plea Bargaining Controversy," *The Journal of Criminal Law and Criminology* 77 (1986), 949-968; David Brereton and Jonathan Casper, "Does it Pay to Plead Guilty? Differential Sentencing and the Functioning of the Criminal Courts," *Law and Society Review* 16 (1981/82); James Eisenstein and Herbert Jacob, *Felony Justice: An Organizational Analysis of the Criminal Courts* (Boston: Little, Brown, 1977); and Jonathan Casper, *American Criminal Justice: The Defendant's Perspective* (Englewood Cliffs, NJ: Prentice Hall, 1972).

[49] George F. Cole, "The Decision to Prosecute," *Law and Society Review* 4 (1970), 321-342, see especially 337-340.

[50] *Bordenkircher v. Hayes*, 434 U.S. 357, 98 S. Ct. 663, 54 L. Ed. 2d 604 (1978).

[51] *Bordenkircher v. Hayes*.

[52] Lee Silverstein, *Defense of the Poor in Criminal Cases in American State Courts* (Chicago: American Bar Foundation, 1965), Vol. I, 92-94.

[53] Norman G. Kittel, "Defense of the Poor: A Study in Public Parsimony and Private Property," *Indiana Law Journal* (Fall 1969), 110-112; National Legal Aid and Defender Association, *The Other Side of Justice* (Chicago: National Legal Aid and Defender Association, 1973), 36, 77, 78.

[54] *Powell v. Alabama*, 287 U.S. 45, 53 S. Ct. 55, 77 L. Ed. 158 (1932).

[55] *Gideon v. Wainwright,* 372 U.S. 335 (1963).

[56] *Argersinger v. Hamlin,* 407 U.S. 25, 92 S. Ct. 2006, 32 L. Ed. 2d 530 (1972).

[57] Lisa J. McIntyre, *The Public Defender: The Practice of Law in the Shadows of Repute* (Chicago: The University of Chicago Press, 1982), 1.

[58] McIntyre, *The Public Defender,* 142. See also Jerome H. Skolnick, "Social Control in the Adversary System," *Conflict Resolution* XI (1967), 52-70.

[59] McIntyre, *The Public Defender,* 135.

[60] D.C. Dahlin, "Towards a Theory of the Public Defender's Place in the Legal System," *South Dakota Law Review* 99 (1974), 87-120.

[61] Casper, *Criminal Courts: The Defendant's Perspective,* 36.

[62] Kittel, "Defense of the Poor: A Study in Public Parsimony and Private Property," 110-112.

[63] Peter Goldman and Don Holt, "How Justice Works: The People v. Donald Payne," *Newsweek,* 8 March 1971, 28-32.

[64] Gellman, "In the District, Justice vs. Management," C11 .

[65] Adam Smith, "An Inquiry Into the Nature and Causes of the Wealth of Nations," in John Fred Bell, *A History of Economic Thought* (New York: The Ronald Press Co., 1953), 179.

[66] See, for example, Mary Collins, "The Wrong Side of the Lawyers," *The Washington Post,* 26 January 1992, C1, C4.

[67] See, for example, Joseph Garofalo and L. Paul Sutton, *Compensating Victims of Violent Crime: Potential Costs and Coverage of a National Program.* Applications of the National Crime Survey Victimization and Attitude Data, Analytic Report SD-VAD-5: National Criminal Justice Information and Statistics Service, Law Enforcement Assistance Administration (Washington, DC: U.S. Government Printing Office, 1977); see also "Restitution Programs Are Likely Candidates for Expansion," *Crime Control Digest* 15:28 (1981).

[68] For an interesting perspective on victim participation in sentencing, see Edna Erez and Pamela Tontodonato, "The Effect of Victim Participation in Sentencing on Sentence Outcome," *Criminology* 28 (1990), 451-473.

Photo Credit: Bill Powers, Frost Publishing Group, Ltd.

Chapter 10

THE COURTS

The inevitability of conflict renders *conflict resolution* one of society's most important tasks. The socialization process provides informal rules and procedures for conflict resolution, which vary according to one's social status and cultural values. As long as the conflict is simple and involves people who know one another, resolution is usually a matter of negotiation among the concerned parties. When conflict involves major issues, is highly complex or occurs between people who are unable or unwilling to negotiate, the problem may require a formal means of resolution. In the United States the formal institution for the resolution of conflict is the court system.

There are many kinds of courts, designed to deal with a wide range of conflicts. The courts do not simply listen to a conflict and render an arbitrary decision. They are a forum for hearing disputes and rendering judgments in light of existing legal concepts. Conflicts are resolved on the basis of existing legal norms. The court weighs the facts and issues and renders a judgment consistent with these. Legal conflicts generally arise over disputes involving rights and duties. A *right* is "a legal capacity to act or to demand action or forbearance on the part of another."[1] As Schantz has noted,

> If a right is a legal capacity to act—what is an act? Used in this sense, an act is a voluntary physical movement of a human being. But a right can also be the ability to demand action or forbearance on the part of another. A forbearance is a consciously willed absence of physical movement. And a forbear-

ance can be a very valuable thing. If you have the ability—the right—to prevent someone from doing a certain thing, say for instance, from selling a piece of land to anyone else but you, it can be worth a great deal of money to you.[2]

A *duty*, on the other hand, is a legal obligation to either act or to refrain from acting. When a right is vested in one person or group, there is always a corresponding duty on the part of some other person or group.[3] The conflicts that come before the courts invariably deal with some failure concerning rights or duties. These rights and duties fall into specific areas or categories and constitute the major facets of the practice of law. An individual conflict will fall into one or more commonly accepted legal areas or categories which include (but are not limited to):

Administrative law	Environmental law
Admiralty	International law
Agency—Partnership	Labor law
Antitrust law	Land use law
Civil rights law	Oil and gas law
Commercial law	Products liability law
Constitutional law	Property law
Contract law	Remedies
Corporation law	Tax law
Criminal law	Tort law
Domestic relations	Wills, trusts and estate law

Within each of these areas there is a large body of decided cases, rules and remedies defining the legal norms that must be applied to any give case. An individual involved in a serious conflict can ask the proper court (that is, one that hears cases dealing with that particular kind of problem) to determine what rights and duties operate in the case and what remedies are available. In order for a court to hear a case, it must first have jurisdiction, which is defined as "the power or authority of a court to determine the merits of a dispute and to grant relief."[4] A court has jurisdiction only when it has such power over both the subject matter of a case and the people who are the parties to the case. Some courts are permitted to hear a wide variety of cases; others have very limited jurisdictions and hear cases of only one kind (e.g., traffic or domestic relations courts). This text focuses on courts with jurisdiction in criminal and juvenile cases. Any "civil" jurisdiction these courts may have will not be discussed.

THE CRIMINAL COURTS

A crime is a conflict between the state and an offender. The state is regarded as the victim, even if only a single individual actually "suffered" as a result of the crime. Criminal law sets forth certain rights and duties. For example, all citizens have the right to be safe and secure in their homes and persons, and all citizens have the duty to respect that right. To break into another person's home for purposes of committing an unlawful act violates both rights and duties and thus results in a conflict between the offender and the state. Criminal courts accept accusations from prosecutors and hear the facts of the case. The law pertaining to that particular offense is then reviewed and the appropriate remedy issued.

There are 51 major court systems in the United States. Each state has its own court system, as does the federal government. The courts are created either by constitutional provision or legislative enactment. Within a given system there are essentially two kinds of courts: trial and appellate. Trial courts hear cases, determine facts by applying the appropriate legal rules and grant remedies for those disputes. A trial court *cannot* initiate a case on its own because it wishes to consider some legal issue, nor may it decide purely theoretical controversies. Cases that come before the courts must involve real disputes and the parties involved must have "standing" before the court, i.e., their dispute must meet criteria for appearing before the court). This means that only the people who are harmed have the right to bring a case before a court. As a representative of the state, the prosecutor has standing in all criminal cases because the state is considered the victim of all crimes.

Trial courts resolve the conflicts that come before them by having the opposing parties present their respective arguments through attorneys. Each attorney argues on points of law as they apply to the case and presents evidence (in the forms of physical objects and the testimony of witnesses). These arguments may be presented before a jury or judge who makes the final decision. Participants are guided by a comprehensive set of legal procedures that define the conduct of the trial.

Appellate courts do not try cases, but instead review cases that have already been tried in order to determine whether there were any errors in the way the trial court handled them. Appellate courts determine whether the trial court acted in accordance with the legal rules that govern it. No new arguments or evidence may be introduced, and the specific facts of the case (i.e., the crime that was committed) are not considered. Upon finding that the state erred, an appellate court may choose to vacate the remedy granted by the trial court. For example, if an appeal in a criminal case is based on the contention that an accused was convicted on the strength of an illegally obtained confession, the appellate court would rule that the trial court erred in permitting the confession to be entered into evidence and would reverse the findings of the trial court. Notice, however, that the appellate court does not say the defendant did not commit the crime; it only says the trial court made a serious error by admitting inadmissible evidence, and because of that error, a conviction cannot be sustained.

CRIMINAL JURISDICTION OF STATE TRIAL COURTS

Each state has the right to create its own system of courts. Although all state court systems are similar, there are differences among them. Trial courts typically exist at two levels. Those at the lower level are courts of *limited jurisdiction*. They have original jurisdiction over misdemeanors and are limited in the remedies they can apply (e.g., they have maximum fines and terms of imprisonment). They are not courts of record, meaning that transcripts of their proceedings are not usually kept, although the disposition of each case is recorded.

These lower-level courts are very busy, for the majority of cases that come before the criminal courts are heard in courts of limited jurisdiction. Although these courts do not try felony cases, they may accept "first appearances" of persons arrested for serious crimes. People arrested for felonies have the right to be brought before a magistrate so they can be informed of the charges being brought against them and of their legal rights. It is at this stage that bail is usually set.

The higher-level trial courts are courts of *general jurisdiction*. They have original jurisdiction over serious crimes, i.e., felonies. They also may have appellate jurisdiction over the lower trial courts. Thus, a person convicted by a lower court for some misdemeanor can appeal the case to a higher trial court for a hearing *de novo* (literally, a new hearing). This is not an appeal in the sense that the actions of the lower court are reviewed; it is simply a new trial. Because these superior courts are courts of record, a transcript of their proceedings is usually kept. Such courts have the power to impose the maximum sentences allowed by the state, including the death sentence.

STATE APPELLATE COURTS

Each state has at least one appellate court. In most states the highest appellate court is called the supreme court of that state. Some states have an intermediate appellate court, usually called the court of criminal appeals. These tribunals differ from trial courts in that they have more than one judge (who are usually called "justices"). Depending on the particular state, appellate courts have between three and nine justices. These courts review the actions of the trial courts to see if any errors of law occurred. These errors can involve such things as:

- Depriving a defendant of his Constitutional rights

- Violating the rules of evidence

- Accepting guilty pleas not properly given

- Admitting into evidence an illegally obtained confession

- Improper jury charging by the trial judge

- Allowing a racially biased jury to be impaneled

- Failing to make clear the possible consequences of a guilty plea (despite any sentencing promises made by the prosecutor to the defendant)

- Passing an unlawful sentence.[5]

The appellate courts serve as a powerful check on both the trial courts and the police, for there are many possible grounds upon which a convicted offender may appeal. As Robin notes,

> Almost anything that could have reasonably prevented the defendant from receiving a fair hearing and sentence may become the basis of an appeal: police entrapment; unfavorable pretrial publicity; holding the trial where the entire community is openly hostile to the defendant; racial composition of the jury; failure to give indigents state supported counsel; sentencing the defendant without a presentence report; not permitting the trial to be held in a different county from where the crime occurred (failure to order a change of venue); unethical or illegal conduct by the prosecutor; having a defendant appear in court for trial while still wearing jail clothing, and so on.[6]

The roles of trial and appellate courts are fundamentally different. Trial courts consider issues of *fact*, whereas appellate courts consider issues of *law*. These issues of law arise "because a litigant has asked the trial judge to do something. In response, the judge either acts or declines to act in accordance with the request. If the aggrieved party believes that the judge has acted wrongly, he may appeal."[7] Through these appellate decisions the body of "rules" that govern judges' decisions and trial procedures are constantly modified and shaped to fit the times. When a court of appeals finds that the trial court did commit an error, it remands the case back to the trial court for a retrial or some other action; a court of appeals does not and cannot acquit a defendant. After a case is remanded back to the trial court the defendant may or may not be retried.   If certain items of evidence are suppressed based on the ruling of the court of appeals, the state may feel it no long has a strong enough case to support a retrial. In this event the defendant will go free—even though not found to be "not guilty." This simply means the trial court did not successfully convict the offender. It is important to remember that at no point is the accused ever found innocent: one is either found guilty or acquitted, or the case is dismissed.

JUDGES

The central figure in any courtroom is the judge. As the President's Crime Commission noted in 1967, "The quality of justice depends in large measure on the quality of judges."[8] Judges have a vast amount of authority that they can exercise at different points in the legal process. The most visible and direct role of a judge is to supervise criminal trials. The judge is continuously faced with issues and conflicts during a trial: questions on the admissibility of evidence, the relevance of testimony offered by witnesses, the techniques used by lawyers in questioning witnesses, and so on. In a sense, the judge is the gatekeeper of information in a criminal trial; the way such issues are handled sets the tone for the trial.

How a judge rules on issues raised during a trial and the messages conveyed nonverbally create the flavor of a courtroom very quickly. All other participants must accommodate themselves to the kind of court thus "created." The judge can also control verdicts; in about half of the cases that go to trial, the defendant waives a jury and is tried by the judge alone.[9] Finally, the judge exercises tremendous power in sentencing convicted criminals. Judges impose fines, incarcerate people in jails or prisons, suspend sentences and otherwise control the future of the convicted.

Most Americans appear to respect the judiciary. Judges—especially those who sit on appellate or supreme courts—generally are granted considerable prestige.[10] Many judges fully deserve this respect; some great jurists (e.g., Oliver Wendell Holmes, Learned Hand and Benjamin Cardozo) have left an indelible mark on the quality of justice in the United States. Unfortunately, there are other kinds of judges as well, and they are the ones who have produced a great volume of community concern. As one writer noted, "There are bigots on the bench and arrogant martinets. There are the dull-witted, the narrow-minded, the harsh, and the lazy. There are those who are merely weak, mediocre, the 'gray mice' of the judiciary. And there are the callous and insensitive, judges whose exposure to human pride and folly has encrusted their own humanity."[11]

Judges are not interchangeable; there are different "levels" of judgeships and each level tends to represent different backgrounds and perspectives toward judicial functions. Judges at the lowest levels—those who sit in the state trial courts—often include non-lawyers (in states where this is permitted) and lawyers with less-than-prestigious educational backgrounds. At this level we find many of the municipal court judges, magistrates, justices of the peace and other judges in courts of limited jurisdiction.[12] Although some of them may eventually move up to higher levels within the judiciary, most do not.

Judges at the "middle" level typically sit on the courts of general jurisdiction and the intermediate appellate courts. A judgeship at this level is often considered both a reward and a promotion for loyalty, service and efficiency. Many of these judges are selected by the governor of their state and approved by the legislature or some other body.[13] According to Blumberg, "Recruitment at this level is likely to be from among lower level judges who not only have served the party well but have shown astuteness and imagination."[14]

The "upper-level" judges are apt to come from prominent families and are more likely to have attended first-rate law schools. They are also likely to have been partners in prestigious law firms and may even have held political office. As Blumberg points out, however, "Although many upper level judges have distinguished themselves as legal scholars, having published in the legal journals and in other scholarly journals, for the most part they are politically well-connected and sophisticated in the vagaries of political life. Often they are simply possessed of great personal wealth and political influence and are otherwise prosaic and pedestrian."[15] The strong role of politics in the selection of judges is not hard to discern and has been particularly evident in the selection of members of the United States Supreme Court.[16]

On June 26, 1987 Justice Lewis F. Powell retired from the Supreme Court. On July 1, 1987 Robert H. Bork was nominated to replace him. Bork's nomination was quickly embroiled in controversy as liberal Senate members waged a determined campaign to block his nomination. The Senate Judiciary Committee rejected his nomination with a 9-5 vote on October 6, 1987; his nomination was rejected by the full Senate on October 23 by a 58-42 vote.[17] In 1990 Justice William J. Brennan announced his retirement from the Supreme Court. David H. Souter was nominated to take his place. Liberal and conservative political communities again engaged in spirited debate, but Souter was confirmed. In 1991 Justice Thurgood Marshall's retirement was announced.

On July 1 President George Bush nominated Clarence Thomas to replace Marshall. Thomas, a black jurist who had been openly critical of civil rights leaders and affirmative action programs, was quickly opposed by Senators Edward Kennedy and Howard Metzenbaum. Again, a heated political battle ensued. This one took a particularly ugly turn when a black, female law professor from Oklahoma alleged that Thomas had sexually harassed her several years earlier when she worked for him at the Equal Employment Opportunity Commission. Thomas was ultimately confirmed, but the spectacle of his hearings generated considerable public dismay. Beneath much of the rhetoric were unspoken but clearly understood political agendas.

THE SELECTION OF JUDGES

In theory, there are four ways a person may obtain a judgeship: (1) appointment, (2) election on non-partisan ballot, (3) election on partisan ballot, and (4) merit selection. In the case of appointment, the person is appointed by the governor or by the legislature, and the appointment is then confirmed by the legislature or an executive council. The second method, used in some states, is election on a non-partisan ballot. Although not identified by party on the ballot, the candidate is usually nominated by a particular political party. A third method is for judges to be elected on a partisan ballot. Where this is done, the primary election is usually the real contest because many of these states are dominated by one of the major parties. The fourth and final method involves the merit selection of judges. Sometimes called the "Missouri Plan" (because it was first adopted in that state in 1940), this system allows the governor to select a person from a list of names submitted by a merit selection committee, and after appointment, this person runs without opposition on a retention ballot, in essence placing confirmation of the appointment in the hands of the voters.

The process of becoming a judge involves many factors. Three of the most important ones are the individual's legal education, work background and politics. Such variables inevitably impact on the values, perceptions and judicial orientations of most judges. Although citizens tend to assume that judges are value-neutral and objective, and respect them accordingly, they are often perplexed at how judges manage their courts and handle the cases that come before them. Few realize that judges, like the police, have a degree of autonomy which for all practical purposes places them above accountability.

Consider the following actual event: An 18-year-old girl in a southeastern city received a traffic ticket for running a red light. She was convicted in district court and appealed her case to the superior court where she was scheduled for a trial *de novo*. She was supposed to appear at 9:30 in the morning on her court date. Although she arrived at the appropriate parking lot with time to spare, the lot was so full so that she had to drive to a parking garage about four blocks away, where she had to park on the top floor. By the time she made it to the court it was 9:35. A few minutes later a bailiff asked what her name was, and when she told him the bailiff said, "Honey, we have orders to put you in jail." He explained that her case had been called at the start of court and when she did not appear, the judge ordered her to be taken into custody. The startled young lady was removed from the courtroom and placed in a holding cell. Later, she was handcuffed and led to the county jail where she was placed in another cell—this time with two other women. "I have never been in a place that smelled so bad," she later declared. "The toilet looked like it hadn't been cleaned in three years. There was toilet paper on the floor and the dirt on the floor must have been an inch thick." The men in a nearby holding cell used vulgar and abusive language, much of it directed at the three women in the women's cell. After about 45 minutes she was taken to the main cell block where she was placed in a cell by herself. Four hours later she was removed from her cell and handcuffed to a man; both of them were taken to the courthouse (the man had been charged with shooting a police officer). Back in the courtroom an official advised her that if she accepted the lower court's guilty verdict in her case, there would be no record of her having been incarcerated for failure to appear. She reluctantly agreed, and after paying her fine she was released. The district attorney later said, "What happened may have been a little unusual, but the judge has a right to do it. It just happened that on this day the judge came into the courtroom at 9:30 and only about half the docket was there and he was peeved. On this particular day there were just too many who didn't show up on time and he ordered them arrested." The judge was later contacted in Florida where he was vacationing, but he could not recall the case.[18]

Many people do not realize that in a criminal case (as in any other legal contest) the courts simply apply legal rules and remedies to the case. Judges and courts concern themselves for the most part with the law rather than with people, personal problems or even "common sense." For example, a Texas case involved a man who had been convicted of murdering two police officers and had been sentenced to death. Evidence was subsequently obtained that strongly supported his claim of innocence. His lawyers filed a petition for habeas corpus in federal court three days before his scheduled execution; however, a three-judge appellate panel ruled that his innocence "was irrelevant as a matter of law." The judges stated that unless conviction resulted from a violation of his constitutional rights (such as the prosecutor hiding favorable evidence), the federal court had no business interfering in the state's criminal justice system. Texas law allows those convicted of crimes to come forward with new evidence but they must do so within 30 days of sentencing—not three days before they are supposed to be executed. In this particular case the defendant had to depend on clemency by the governor because the courts at both the state and federal levels could not accept proof of his innocence as a justifiable grounds for preventing his execution.[19]

Few judges have ever been police officers and even fewer have been street criminals. Very few come from the backgrounds of the people whom they judge and very seldom do they actually witness the types of incidents that bring defendants into the courtroom. Even legal education does little to acquaint them with such issues as poverty, ignorance, alienation or deviance. Judges can and do command respect under penalty of law, but they rarely operate in the same context as the people who come to them for judgment. Jackson captured this in the following anecdote:

In Washington Family Court, a black mother tries to explain to the white judge that her delinquent thirteen-year-old son is not a bad child. "He just resents somethin', y' know? He wants to be recognized." The judge looks up from the forms he is filling out, asks two or three questions, and orders the boy to a detention center. The mother collapses in sobs, hugging her son. "I love you, I'm so sorry," she cries. "You're breaking my heart. I don't want nothin' to happen to you, I don't want you to go nowhere. Oh, I'm so sorry." Her son begins to cry too, and the sound of their heavy sobs fills the small courtroom. The lawyers and social workers stare at the wall, while the judge continues to fill out forms. "What's the date of that report?" he asks a social worker. Finally he can no longer ignore the weeping mother and son. "I want to tell you a story, James," he says. "I had a young security guard come up to me the other day when I was parking my car. He said I had put him in the detention center once for delinquency. He said he learned a lot, got a good education, and now he was a guard. You've got a lot of good in you, James. You'll do okay if you cooperate...."[20]

COURT ADMINISTRATION

Courts are complex institutions that do more than just conduct trials.[21] The focus on the trial role of the courts diverts attention from less dramatic functions, such as their routine administration. Courts are bureaucratic government agencies: they keep records, have support personnel, require budgets and perform all the administrative tasks necessary to schedule, process and dispose of their business. The inability to effectively manage the courts ultimately produces an important result: delay. Delay in the courts can result in a series of interlocking problems. For example, after some time has passed witnesses may no longer be available or their memories may become clouded, and defendants may be forced to suffer continuing hardship (especially if incarcerated while awaiting trial). In addition, delay produces pressure to clear the dockets, which then becomes a goal in its own right, often leading to dispositions by dismissal or through plea negotiations. Court delays ultimately reduce the deterrent effect of prosecution and cause public confidence in the courts to diminish. In 1971 Howard James cited eight reasons for delay in the courts: (1) an acute shortage of judges, (2) too few courtrooms, (3) lazy judges, (4) procrastinating lawyers, (5) the use of "expert witnesses" who confuse jurors and cause delays, (6) lax legislatures, and (8) "cat and dog" cases (i.e., minor cases that consume more time than they are worth).[22] To many, these problems do not seem to have diminished since then.

There has been a growing reform movement in the courts for many years. This movement started in 1906 when Roscoe Pound recommended that states consolidate their courts into one unified system having two branches—trial and appellate. This concept, known as *court unification*, is designed to establish both uniformity in court operations and efficiency in administration. One of the themes of court unification is the establishment of centralized supervision of both judicial and non-judicial personnel. Ideally, this would allow courts in one part of the state to use judges from another area in the case of illness or some other reason for absence. It also would regularize procedures across the system, assuring uniform treatment of citizens and effectiveness of operations.

There are, of course, other facets to the reform of court management. Personnel problems are important because there must be judges to hear cases; court stenographers to transcribe proceedings; administrators to manage dockets, purchase supplies, administer other support personnel and handle finances; bailiffs to provide security; and probation officers to supervise probationers and prepare investigations and reports. Adequate facilities must be maintained, including courtrooms, judge's chambers, law libraries and record storage facilities. The flow of cases has to be carefully monitored and jurors must be managed. All of this is part of court administration.

In recent years there has been a movement in the direction of hiring professionally trained court administrators to handle court administration tasks, thus freeing judges to concentrate on matters of law. The introduction of electronic data processing has facilitated this process and shows great promise for the future. Professional administrators have taken on a great deal of the burden of court management and it appears that they will become increasingly important. Although some judges have resisted these improvements for the sake of tradition, such resistance is being overcome.

New ways of reducing delay in the courts appear to have significant potential. They include using volunteers, enhancing the use of automation, improving the role of judges and maximizing human resources.[23] Experts are learning that trial court delay is not inevitable and that the courts most effective in reducing delay share a number of characteristics: strong leadership, clear goals, timely and accurate information about caseloads, effective communications mechanisms and the use of a few relatively simple case management techniques.[24] Courts are also actively exploring ways of using technology to expedite their work. One especially promising avenue lies in closer cooperation between the private sector and the courts, particularly in data automation.[25]

Data automation is playing an increasingly important role in case management. For example, each U.S. Attorney's office has a local caseload and debt collection management system that can be used to produce a variety of local reports. These reports are used for such management purposes as monitoring the office's workload and making case assignments. Local procedures are established to make sure timely and accurate information is provided to docket personnel. In addition, the JURIS legal research system offers U.S. Attorney's offices the ability to conduct instant searches of cases, statutes and digests by means of a computer terminal.[26] The application of this kind of technology offers great promise in the management of court systems.

BAIL OR JAIL?

The awesome power of the courts and judges starts well before a person actually comes to trial. After being arrested (especially in the case of felonies), a person is brought before a judge who formally explains the nature of the charge and the arrestee's rights. At this time the judge may do one of the following things:

1. Release the accused on the person's own recognizance (based on a promise to appear in court when such presence is required);

2. Release the accused to the custody of another person, usually a relative, who is then responsible for seeing to it that the accused appears in court;

3. Require the accused to post a cash bond, which is forfeited upon failure to appear (this is most often done in traffic and other misdemeanor cases);

4. Require a surety bond in a certain amount of money, which is usually purchased from a bail bondsman at 10 percent of the face value;

5. Require the accused to post a cash bond, which amounts to a percentage of the full bail; if the person appears in court when required, most of the cash bond is returned, but if the person fails to appear, the cash bond is forfeited and the person becomes liable for the remainder of the bail originally set;

6. Deny bail altogether and order the accused to be placed in jail under preventive detention. This is usually only done in capital crimes or when the offender is likely to flee.

The right to bail is written into the Eighth Amendment to the Constitution, which specifies that, "excessive bail shall not be required." However, the issue of whether there is an absolute right to bail has never been fully resolved by the courts; the most common interpretation is that the Constitution does not grant an absolute right to bail, but rather provides protection against *excessive* bail. (This is a limitation on the federal courts and does not necessarily apply to state courts.) The courts have held that neither the Eighth Amendment nor the Fourteenth Amendment require that everyone charged with a state offense must be given liberty on bail pending trial.

The Eighth Amendment to the Constitution provides that "extensive bail shall not be required," leading some to believe that bail is a constitutionally protected right. In historical perspective, it is interesting to note that the bail clause was taken with very little change from the English Bill of Rights Act, where it was not construed to confer the right to bail in all cases. It provided, simply, that bail was not to be excessive in those cases where it has been deemed proper to grant bail. When this clause was carried over into the United States' Bill of Rights, nothing was said or implied to indicate any different concept.[27] In *United States v. Salerno* the Supreme Court held that the Bail Reform Act of 1984 was constitutional and that the denial of bail under the Act was proper, as was the provision concerning preventive detention. As such, there is no absolute right to bail in the Eighth Amendment. Bail *may* be provided in criminal cases, and if it is, it must not be excessive. It also may be denied if there are reasonable grounds to believe the accused will flee or interfere with the judicial process, or if there is reason to believe that the accused will be a threat to the safety of the community.[28] In a nutshell, bail may not be used as punishment for dangerous people, but it may be used to prevent danger to the community, which is a legitimate regulatory goal.

Bail, simply put, "is a procedure for releasing arrested persons on financial or other conditions to ensure their return for trial."[29] In a sense it is judicial ransom that gives the state a financial hold over the accused to assure cooperation with the courts.[30] Bail deals with a very real problem: people accused of serious crimes may wish to run away rather than face the consequences of their actions in court. One of the major problems of the bail system, however, is that it places a disproportionate burden on the poor. If a person cannot afford bail or if a bail bond agent refuses to "go his bail," the accused goes to jail to await trial (often at great expense to both the accused and the state). The following actual cases illustrate this problem:

> Item: A man was jailed on a serious charge on Christmas Eve. He could not afford bail and spent 101 days in jail until a hearing was held. At that time the complainant admitted the charges were false.

> Item: A man could not raise $300 bail. He spent 54 days in jail waiting for trial on a traffic offense, for which he could have been sentenced to no more than five days in jail if convicted.

> Item: A man spent two months in jail before his trial, at which he was acquitted. During the time he was in jail he lost his job and his car, and his family was split up. He did not find another job for four months.[31]

Not only can bail abuse bring hardship to the defendant, it can cost the state a great deal of money. Persons held in custody represent a cost to the state: they must be fed and housed; their loss of income while out of work results in a loss of tax revenue to the state; and in some cases, the defendant's family may be forced to go on welfare. There have also been cases of unsavory relationships between bail bond agents and judges (or other officials) in which judges set high bail so the agent can get a higher fee. As Jackson notes,

> Bail procedures, often scandalous in themselves, present yet another opportunity for covert lining of the judicial pocket. Judge Louis W. Kizas of Chicago attracted more attention than he wanted when he released two men charged with armed robbery on their own recognizance. The subsequent investigation turned up evidence that Kizas had repeatedly granted low bail for a price. Suddenly afflicted with poor health, Judge Kizas resigned before a scheduled hearing by the Illinois Courts commission in 1967. Two years later he pleaded guilty to criminal charges of official misconduct and was fined $15,000.

> In 1972 a Los Angeles grand jury accused three judges of signing blank prisoner-release orders and dispensing them to favored bail bondsmen. The bondsmen, who bought and sold the orders among themselves, were then free to set bail at whatever figure they chose—or negotiated. A prosecutor said that one presigned release order was used to bail a suspected Mafia member out of jail for $1,000 when arresting officers recommended bail of $100,000.[32]

In some cases bail is intentionally set so high that the defendant cannot make the bond. One reason for doing this is to avoid the negative publicity that is generated when someone alleged to be a serious offender is turned loose pending trial. Another reason for setting high bail is to give the prosecution a bargaining chip in plea negotiations. In this case, if an accused is willing to plead guilty to a lesser charge, the prosecutor may be willing to recommend a reduction in bail, thus allowing the individual to get out of jail. In fact, the amount of the bail is usually more closely related to the seriousness of the charge than to any evidence that the defendant might flee. It is difficult to separate the two factors because the more serious the charge, the more severe the penalty and the more incentive an accused has to flee.

In 1961 Louis Schweitzer became concerned over the fact that an individual could sit in jail for a year or more in New York—despite being innocent—simply because he or she lacked the money to pay a bail bond agent. Schweitzer created the Vera Foundation (now called the Vera Institute of Justice), which subsequently developed a project aimed at screening defendants to see how many were sufficiently good risks to warrant a release on their own recognizance. Staff members used four key factors in making their assessments:

(1) residential stability; (2) employment history; (3) presence of family contacts in the area; and (4) the defendant's prior record. Each of these factors was scored according to a system of points, and if the accused got a score of five or higher, the staff would recommend that an ROR (release on one's own recognizance) be granted. Project members felt that a defendant with sufficient "roots in the community" would be a good risk. This program, known as the Manhattan Bail Project, proved successful. Between October 16, 1961 and April 8, 1964, staff members screened 10,000 eligible offenders and recommended that 4,000 be released on their own recognizance. The courts accepted 2,195 of these recommendations; of that number, only 15 defendants failed to appear in court.[33]

The Vera project was successful and saved the city so much money that it was widely copied, but in most jurisdictions the bail system continues to operate much as it has in the past. Scandals continue to appear in the papers from time to time—and bail continues to be used for purposes other than that for which it was originally intended. As Levine noted, "If the purpose of bail is to ensure appearance in court, 'ransoming' defendants makes little sense because it usually is unnecessary and is no guarantee anyway when the stakes of the trial are greater than the loss of bail money. But other purposes like crime prevention, public reassurance, and pretrial punishment of the guilty as well as the innocent prevail. Justice and due process come out the losers."[34]

An interesting sidelight of this problem is that much of the community *expects* criminals to be put in jail, and the distinction between pretrial confinement and incarceration as part of sentence is often lost. Some people become indignant when a person accused of a serious crime is let out of jail to await trial; indeed, a large proportion of the general public believe the courts are too lenient in dealing with criminals.[35] Because the complexity of law and criminal procedure is unclear to many people, they become disturbed at the thought of a "criminal" *not* being in jail. Conventional wisdom holds that the police put criminals in jail, and in recent years people have begun to voice concern that the courts are letting them out. This contradiction between public expectations and the legal obligations of the courts has produced a growing mistrust on the part of many. Although some of what the general public expects of the courts is unrealistic, the courts seem to have made little effort to educate the public or speak to their concerns. A reason for this is that the courts are—in their narrowest interpretation—answerable to the *law*, not to the *people*. If people do not like the way the law works, they must address their concerns to their legislators, not to the courts. However, one can speculate that many people either do not know this or feel that the legislators themselves are unresponsive to public wishes. The American public's long history of distrust of authority tends to manifest itself more in complaining about government (including legal processes) than in actually trying to change it.

JURIES

Silberman reminds us that "[c]riminal courts are multipurpose institutions, charged with protecting society against criminals and with protecting the innocent individual against the coercive power of the state."[36] At the very heart of the process is the jury trial. The function of a jury trial is to determine the guilt or innocence of the accused by (1) analyzing the facts presented through the testimony of the witnesses and (2) applying the law of the case as it is explained by the trial judge. The jury system has been both praised and criticized, yet it remains one of the most fundamental elements of our legal system. Although a case is argued by lawyers and presided over by a judge, in a jury trial, it is a jury of common people that renders the ultimate decision.

Jury trials are a vanishing species, however. Most people convicted of crimes plead guilty, usually in consideration for some benefit, and most of the remainder are tried by a judge and do not have a jury trial.[37] In all probability, not more than about 2 percent of all criminal cases actually come before a jury. According to a carefully controlled survey, no more than 32 percent of adult Americans have ever been called for jury duty and only 16 percent of those polled ever actually served on one.[38] The mere existence of the right to a trial by jury serves as the final legitimization of the due-process model of justice.[39] Even though seldom used, jury trials underscore the highest ideals of American judicial practice. The irony is that juries are not always rational in either their composition or their decisions.

JURORS AND JURY SELECTION

There are about 3,000 courts using juries in the United States, requiring an annual total of about 20 million jurors.[40] The principal aim of a jury trial is to provide the accused with a fair and impartial hearing. Theoretically, the jurors sought will objectively and fairly weigh the evidence presented before them. They should not be prejudiced either for or against the defendant, nor may the circumstances of their selection contain any built-in bias that could affect the outcome of the trial. This is the ideal; the reality of what happens often falls short.

Jurors are picked from pools of prospective jurors known as *venires*. The persons on venires are called *veniremen*. The venire consists of people whose names have been selected from such sources as voter registration lists, driver registration lists, local census rolls and even city directories. One of the basic tasks in creating a venire is to get a good cross-sample of the community as a whole. This is not always easy to do, for there are a great many "hidden" people in any community—e.g., those who do not register to vote (or who cannot because of alien status), those whose names do not appear on driver registration lists, etc. Randomly selecting names from voter registration lists has been accepted as the best means of getting a cross-section of the community, provided there has not been a systematic exclusion of blacks or other groups from voter registration.[41] Even at that, venires tend to over-represent whites, males, middle-aged people, the middle class and the moderately educated. At the same time, they tend to under-represent the young, the elderly, minorities and women.[42] As this has been the outcome of using voter registration lists, many jurisdictions have begun to use multiple-source lists.

The next step in the jury selection process, the selection of prospective jurors for a specific case, is extremely important. This is done through a process known as *voir dire* (meaning "to tell the truth") in which jurors are questioned to determine their suitability for serving on the jury. Many lawyers believe a case can be won or lost on voir dire. The prospective jurors are called from the jury pool and proceed to the court, where they are questioned by either the judge, the lawyers or both. Voir dire might start with the judge asking all of the prospective jurors whether they have an interest in the case or know any of the parties involved—or other questions that would reveal a possible conflict of interest. The more significant questioning, however, commences on individual voir dire, where jurors are examined first by the prosecutor and then by the defense counsel.

Lawyers on both sides try to learn as much as they can about the prospective jurors, including their attitudes, prejudices and backgrounds. In subtle ways, a lawyer begins to build a case through the examination of prospective jurors. Instead of trying to find a fair and unbiased juror, the attorney often looks for one who will be biased in the "proper" direction and who will view things as the lawyer would like to have them seen.

In recent years this has produced some interesting approaches to jury selection. One case that received widespread publicity illustrates many of these points. It involved a black female by the name of Joan Little.[43] Little had been in jail in Beaufort County, North Carolina awaiting appeal on a conviction for burglary. She and her brother had been arrested for stealing $850 from two mobile homes; her brother received a suspended sentence through a plea bargain, but she was sentenced to prison. She was unable to post her $15,000 bond and remained in the Beaufort County jail awaiting her appeal. On August 27, 1974 she killed a 62-year-old, white night jail guard by stabbing him to death with an ice pick and fled from the jail. Little surrendered later and claimed the guard had forced her to have oral sex with him by threatening her with the ice pick. She claimed that when he dropped the ice pick, she grabbed it and stabbed him, and then fled. There was some evidence to support her claim. The guard's shoes were found outside the cell; he was nude from the waist down and had semen on his leg. Joan Little was indicted for first-degree murder.

The case was taken up by the Southern Poverty Law Center and some women's groups. About $350,000 was raised for her defense. Her attorney, Jerry Paul, used part of the money to conduct a survey in the Beaufort County area, which revealed a high degree of racial prejudice and a widespread belief that Little had used sex to lure the jailer into her cell so she could make her escape. They also found blacks, women and young people under-represented on venire lists. Based on all this information they secured a change of venue, moving the trial to Raleigh (the state capital). Additional money was spent in Raleigh to ascertain whether the jury pool was representative of the entire community and to construct psychological profiles of jurors who would be sympathetic to Little. On voir dire, prospective jurors were questioned about such things as their occupation, income, political views and attitudes toward blacks, law enforcement officers, capital punishment and rape. Paul used a team of five lawyers to comb the evidence and hired three social psychologists, a "body language" expert and three statisticians. During voir dire the prospective jurors were intensively questioned in an effort to find jurors who would be sympathetic with the defense's case.

Little's "scientifically selected" jury deliberated for one hour and 18 minutes before acquitting her (in spite of the fact that she had previously had sexual contact with the deceased). Jerry Paul confidently stated after the trial, "given enough money, I can buy justice. I can win any case in the country, given enough money."[44] Similar jury selection techniques have been used in other cases. Such techniques can be highly successful, as was indicated in the Joan Little case.

Challenges are the basic tools used by attorneys in voir dire. There are two kinds: *challenges for cause* and *peremptory challenges*. A challenge for cause is used to remove an unacceptable juror when there is reason to believe that he or she would not be impartial (e.g., an admitted prejudice against blacks, prejudging the case, or an objection to capital punishment). An attorney who thinks that a prospective juror should be challenged for cause makes a recommendation to the court. Peremptory challenges, on the other hand, do not require any basis. A limited number are automatically granted. The defense usually has more peremptory challenges than the prosecution. Lawyers on both sides are very careful in using their peremptory challenges and often save them for jurors about whom they have strong hunches or on whom they were overruled on challenges for cause.[45]

A juror who has been successfully challenged goes back to the jury room to await being called for voir dire in another case. After the careful and rigorous screening of prospective jurors the trial is ready to begin. In many jurisdictions jeopardy attaches when the jury is sworn: it is at that point that the trial per se actually begins.

PROBLEMS ASSOCIATED WITH JURY TRIALS

Numerous commentators have pointed out flaws in the jury system. One complaint is that jury trials produce congestion of the court's calendar and result in delay. This is a valid criticism, for jury trials indeed take longer than trials heard by a judge alone. In a major case, jury selection alone can be a lengthy and difficult process. For example, a well-publicized or "political" case can have a jury selection process that takes weeks or even months. In cases that use expert witnesses, such as psychiatrists or other specialists who can vary in their interpretation of events, the trial may stretch out even longer.

Another problem with jury trials is their cost; they can be quite expensive. The average juror pay is $10 per day, amounting to about $200 million per year, although the cost to society based on the average pay is estimated to be about three times this amount, or $600 million per year.[46] Additional costs can be incurred in the actual prosecution of the case and in some jurisdictions in the provision of meals for jurors. The longer a trial, the more expensive it is and the more resources it consumes. In states where there is no public defender system, private attorneys may be appointed by the court at public expense to defend the accused. The fees paid to these attorneys can add up to a considerable amount of money. Although these issues are not unique to jury trials, they can be (and often are) exaggerated by them.

A third problem of the system is juror ignorance. The jury has been described as a group of 12 people of average ignorance, yet some of the cases heard by juries involve highly sophisticated and subtle points of evidence and law. Jurors are not allowed to take notes during a trial, nor are they permitted to ask questions, slow testimony down or compel additional evidence to be presented. Some people believe that it stretches the limits of credibility to expect 12 common people to grasp the complexities involved in a difficult case. Others lament that jurors tend to make decisions based on their own subjective feelings. In a famous study done at the University of Chicago Law School, judges who presided over 3,591 jury trials across the country indicated they would have convicted in 19 percent of the cases where the jury acquitted and would have acquitted in 3 percent of the cases where the jury convicted.[47] This small difference between jury verdicts and what legal experts would have done may indicate that it is unfair to criticize juries because of the presumed ignorance of their members.

Another common problem with jury trials is that many people are reluctant to serve on juries. For some people, it would translate to financial hardship. For others, such as doctors and dentists, it would create considerable inconvenience to many other people. Some people who might make fine jurors (e.g., lawyers, police officers, medical personnel, pharmacists, legislators, clergymen, fire fighters, educators) are routinely exempted from jury duty. Between the people who cannot serve and the people who do not wish to, a great deal of talent is lost to the jury system. Even when well-qualified jurors are available to serve, one side or the other may remove them with a peremptory challenge. Scientists, engineers, college professors and others presumed to have strong analytic skills are especially likely to be rejected.

The use of 12-person juries has been criticized as unnecessary. Actually, a 12-member jury is as much an accident of history as anything else. In medieval times a person accused of a crime might have taken an oath attesting to his or her innocence. Accused persons could earn acquittal if they were able to gain the support of enough "oath-helpers" or *compurgators*. In medieval England the required number of compurgators was 12. As the jury system developed, the compurgators became jurors, whose role shifted from testifying in behalf of the accused to hearing evidence about the matter.

A series of Supreme Court decisions, beginning with *Duncan v. Louisiana* in 1968, defined requirements as to jury size and unanimity. In *Duncan v. Louisiana* the Court held that, because trial by jury in serious criminal cases is "fundamental to the American scheme of justice" and essential to the due process of law, the Fourteenth Amendment guarantees a state criminal defendant the right to a jury trial in any case which, if tried in a federal court, would require a jury under the Sixth Amendment.[48] Just two terms later the Supreme Court held in *Williams v. Florida* that the constitutional guarantee of a trial by jury did not require a state to provide the accused with a jury of 12 members, and that Florida did not violate the rights of criminal defendants by using juries comprised of only six people.[49] In this case Williams was convicted of robbery by a six-person jury and was sentenced to life in prison. He appealed his conviction on the grounds that he had been denied his Sixth and Fourteenth Amendment rights to a trial by jury. In ruling that his rights had not been violated, the Court said that the touchstone should be whether the group is large enough to promote group deliberation free from outside attempts at intimidation, and whether it provides a fair possibility of obtaining a representative cross section of the community.

In *Ballew v. Georgia* the Court held that conviction by a unanimous five-person jury in a trial for a nonpetty offense deprived an accused of the right to a trial by jury.[50] Thus, the Court has established that the Constitution permits juries of fewer than 12 members, but that it requires at least six. In terms of non-unanimous verdicts, in *Apodaco v. Oregon*, the Court upheld a state statute providing that only 10 members of a 12-person jury needed to concur to render a verdict in certain non-capital cases.[51] Finally, in *Burch v. Louisiana* the Court ruled that conviction by a unanimous six-person jury in a state criminal trial for a nonpetty offense violates the accused's right to trial by jury that is guaranteed by the Sixth and Fourteenth Amendments.[52] Thus, a state court may use juries of fewer than 12 (but not less than six) persons, and they may render non-unanimous verdicts, except for juries of six members, which must be unanimous.

Two decades ago the National Advisory Commission on Criminal Justice Standards and Goals agreed with the use of smaller juries, stating that it believed that juries of fewer than 12 members are capable of holding group deliberation on the issue of guilt, resisting outside influences and providing a fair possibility of obtaining a representative cross-section of the community; however, the Commission felt that fewer than six persons on a jury would be unsound.[53] Time proved them correct. These changes have the potential for considerable benefit to the courts. For example, in some instances hung juries might no longer result in a mistrial. Also a corrupt juror could no longer determine the outcome of a trial by holding out for an acquittal. It might also shorten trial time by reducing the amount of effort that goes into the voir dire examination, because each juror as an individual member of the jury would no longer be as important. On the other side of the argument, juries could simply bypass the one or two jurors who hold out and perhaps ought to be heard. Time undoubtedly will tell what impact non-unanimous juries will have.

THE COURTS AND SENTENCING

Upon being convicted, through either a guilty plea or a jury verdict, a defendant is sentenced when the court pronounces its judgment and awards a punishment. A judge usually imposes the sentence, and there may be some limitations on the sentences that can be imposed. For one thing, sentences for crimes are determined by the legislature. When the state deems an act a crime it also sets the limits of punishment that may be inflicted; judges must sentence within the limits authorized by the law. In some states the law is open-ended and permits *indeterminate sentencing* for felonies. In its most basic form, this is a sentence that sends a person to prison wherein the length of incarceration is determined by the state's parole board rather than the judge. Thus, a person may be sentenced to prison for an indeterminate period ranging from one year to life, but the actual date of release is determined by the parole board on the basis of the progress made toward rehabilitation. Indeterminate sentencing was developed for the purpose of confining offenders for just as long as it takes to "straighten them out." Most states that use the indeterminate sentence use a modified form of it. For example, a person may be sentenced to a term of imprisonment of not less than four years nor more than eight years. In this case the offender must serve the minimum sentence, but may be paroled if found to exhibit behavior that merits release at the end of four years. At most, the offender would be kept for the full eight years. This modified indeterminate sentence protects the offender from the possibility of being kept in prison for an excessive period of time while still giving the state leverage.

The opposite of the indeterminate sentence is the *determinate sentence* (or *flat sentence*). In this case the offender is sentenced to a specific term of imprisonment; there is no minimum and no maximum. Where flat sentencing is used, parole is typically eliminated; however, inmates can reduce their sentences through "good time," which is time taken off a sentence in exchange for good behavior. Good time is calculated according to fixed formulas. A similar concept is involved in *mandatory minimum sentences*, which provide (in certain crimes) that a person convicted must spend a fixed minimum amount of time in confinement. This approach is used as a punitive means of dealing with certain kinds of crimes (e.g., those involving firearms or drugs).

One of the most widely used sentencing techniques involves the *probated sentence*. In this situation the convicted person is sentenced to a term of imprisonment, but the actual imposition of the sentence is suspended so long as the offender abides by conditions set by the court. If these conditions are violated, the offender may be sent to prison for the full term of the sentence. This approach is used frequently for first offenders and for those who can demonstrate a likelihood for community-based rehabilitation. Probation is not necessarily "getting off the hook," as many people think; it is a sentence in its own right and can be used very effectively to the benefit of both the offender and the community. Probation is a widely used practice; during 1990 a total of 2,670,234 adult offenders were serving probated sentences, a gain of 5.9 percent over the previous year's count.[54]

There are many variations on these basic sentencing schemes, each grounded in some set of correctional objectives.[55] However, sentencing as it is practiced in this country has focused a great deal of public disapproval on the courts in general and on judges in particular. One frequently hears references made to "getting away with murder" and descriptions of "our disastrous court system." People hear about cases like that of Joseph Morse and they worry as much about the courts as they do about Morse:

> When he was eighteen, Joseph Bernard Morse picked up a large rock and bashed in his mother's head. Then he beat his invalid sister to death with a baseball bat. All this happened in San Diego, in 1962. In 1964, while he was serving a life sentence for killing his mother, Morse murdered a fellow inmate by strangling him with a garrote improvised from twine. For this murder, Morse was given a life sentence. Last year (1977) after many sessions with Morse, a psychological tester concluded that the prisoner's potential for violence was low, provided everything went his way. More recently, a psychiatrist reported that Morse is "antisocial" but that he should nevertheless be paroled and watched to see what happens.[56]

Morse indeed received significant sentences for his crimes and it is not the courts that will release him if he is released. The public, however, often holds the courts responsible for such outcomes, even though the defendant may have received the most severe sentence the court could impose.

There are a number of problems associated with sentencing. One is the inconsistency of sentences, especially for what appear to be the same or similar crimes. Perhaps the key element in sentencing is not the crime but the judge—at least in some of these cases.[57] Judges, after all, have biases and personal feelings that may be difficult to shed when sentencing offenders. In fact, some judges worry quite a bit about the sentences they give, often feeling both pressured and isolated. As one judge said, "Who can a judge talk to about these things? There's nobody. Other judges don't help—they can give you advice, but then they're wounded if you don't take it. No one can help you."[58]

Some judges are tough on everyone; some are tough only in certain kinds of cases; others are consistently lenient. There are judges who do not seem to care one way or another and may base their sentences on how they feel at the moment or on the recommendations of the prosecutor or the defender. The high degree of inconsistency that results is referred to as *sentencing disparity*. Judicial decision-making is not the sole reason for sentencing disparity, however. A major role is played by the process of plea bargaining itself. Since most sentences are based on negotiated pleas, the role of the judge in sentence disparity may be somewhat overemphasized. In plea bargaining a charge may be reduced—or a sentence set in advance—in return for a guilty plea. Seen in this light, the disparity in sentences may be an illusion, as in such cases different defendants are *not* being given different sentences for the same crime; in reality, their actual crimes may be quite different and there may be other reasons for the sentences that are imposed.

Another problem in sentencing is naivete on the part of many judges with regard to the actual consequences of prison sentences. Howard James pointedly noted, "As I toured the country, I was told that when judges pass sentence, they often do not realize what a prison sentence means to the man convicted."[59] Instead, "decisions are sometimes...based on the judge's reaction to the way a man is dressed, his age, the length of his hair, the color of his skin, his nationality, or even his religion."[60] Few judges ever visit the prisons to which they send people. Many spend an entire career on the bench without ever seeing the inside of a prison.

One of the most serious problems of sentencing, as perceived by the pubic, is *leniency*. Virtually all available survey data indicate that the public would like to see more stringent sentencing practices. A Wisconsin judge, for example, sentenced a 15-year-old defendant to one year on probation for raping a woman, noting that the boy's behavior was a normal reaction in an era of see-through blouses and permissive sexuality. In a subsequent recall election (based on this case) the judge was removed from the bench. Many people are appalled at the fact that perpetrators of serious crimes sometimes receive either light or probated sentences—and are sometimes allowed to avoid prison altogether.

Repeat offenders frighten the public because they symbolize the violent stranger who is at the core of the public's fear of crime. Interestingly, many of the same people are much less inclined to severity when the offender is a friend or relative. When that is the case, they are more likely to feel that the best response would be a probated sentence requiring psychological treatment or other help. Public opinion concerning sentencing seems based in part on a general fear of crime, especially violent crimes committed by strangers. Many people feel that if the "strangers" who commit the violent crimes are given lengthy sentences, the threat of crime will be reduced.

The public's perception of the leniency of sentences is not always accurate; most criminals are in fact caught and punished at some time or another, and many so-called "light" sentences are actually much heavier than the public realizes.[61] In all likelihood public indignation over light sentencing is reinforced by sensational cases that are not necessarily representative. Charles Peters, in considering the problem of public safety and criminal sentencing, offered the following comment:

> To me the justification for prison is not deterrence or rehabilitation. It is the punishment of the guilty and the protection of society. If you've ever visited a prison, you know that six months is adequate for just about any crime. The only justification for longer sentences—all of which qualify as cruel and unusual—should be to protect the rest of us. This means locking up the violent, sane or insane, until they have ceased to be violent, but for all nonviolent crime six months should be the standard sentence.[62]

The sentiment expressed by Peters seems to reflect a basic concern of many people: the wish to be safe from violent crime and to punish those who commit them. It is not likely, however, that many people would go along with his concept of six-month sentences, despite what merit the proposal may have. However, the public might be responsive to a more consistent pattern of sentencing in criminal cases. This may account for the growing popularity of flat sentences, but it remains unclear how a uniform flat sentencing policy would affect the plea bargaining process. It could result in a greater number of litigated trials and possibly even more acquittals.

One method of dealing with sentencing problems is through the use of *presentence investigations and reports*. These reports, usually prepared by a probation officer, are detailed case histories of the offender's social, criminal and educational background. They also contain recommendations concerning the type of punishment that is likely to produce the greatest benefit. Presentencing reports are provided to the court in the hope that the sentencing decision made will be consistent with the prisoner's needs as well as those of society. The use of presentence investigations is mandatory in some jurisdictions and discretionary in others.

THE COURTS AND COMMUNITY SENTIMENT

One of the key problems of courts is that in spite of the fact that they are public institutions, they are isolated from the community. Although the courts technically are answerable to the law, ultimately they must be responsive to the community. They must serve not only those who actually use them, but the community as a whole. In 1973 the National Advisory Commission on Criminal Justice Standards and Goals suggested that one way to attain this goal was to have court administrators establish a forum combining the efforts of members of the community who are interested in judicial administration.[63] This idea, though commendable, has little to do with the "average" person in the community. It would be beneficial to introduce some form of law-focused education into the curricula of elementary and secondary schools. This could possibly give citizens a better and more basic understanding of what the courts are and what they can and cannot do.

The problems of the courts require immediate and direct attention in order for there to be a better relationship between courts and the community. Public dissatisfaction with the courts can foster a disrespect for the entire criminal justice system and its processes; therefore, efforts must be undertaken to reduce public dissatisfaction. The American Bar Association (through its Subcommittee on Unjust Criticism of the Bench, Courts and Community Committee) has recognized this problem and offered guidelines for dealing with it. They propose a model program to deal with reporting errors as well as inaccurate or unjust criticism of judges, courts and/or the administration of justice. Their plan calls for making information available to the news media, encouraging broad dissemination of information to the public about noteworthy achievements and improvements within the justice system—and generally seeking a better understanding within the community of the legal system and the role of lawyers and judges.[64]

There are a number of specific areas in which substantial efforts are needed. Public knowledge is certainly one of them. For example, in one survey it was discovered that fully one-half of the American public (including 31 percent of college graduates) does not understand or appreciate the legal concept of "innocent until proven guilty."[65] This may not be surprising in light of the fact that 54 percent of the public says it gets its information about the courts from television news.[66] Moreover, court facilities are inadequate, with much of the physical space occupied by courts being either deficient or deteriorated. This is basically a funding problem that must be dealt with by state and local governments, yet in a period of increasing fiscal austerity it seems unlikely that many major improvements in this area will be forthcoming.

The court's treatment of witnesses is another area contributing to strained feelings within the community. Witnesses are seldom adequately compensated for their time, much less for the actual expenses they incur. In addition, many court systems treat witnesses in an off-hand and disinterested manner. Witnesses are simply told to show up and wait until they are called, without knowing when, or even if, they will be called upon to testify. Most courthouses do not have facilities for witnesses. It might help to inform them of what is going on and when they are likely to be called, and to provide them with a reasonably pleasant setting in which prosecution and defense witnesses can wait separately. This kind of courtesy could go a long way toward easing the unpleasantness of serving as a witness. Much the same thing can be said of jurors. They too should be provided with adequate waiting rooms while they are held in the jury pool awaiting call for voir dire.

Another major deficiency in the courts' relationship with the community is the lack of information services in the courthouse itself.[67] As one report noted,

> Participating in the criminal justice process, whether by witness, juror, or defendant, often is a confusing and traumatic experience that leaves the participants with an unfavorable impression of the system. Defendants and witnesses may experience difficulty locating the site of the trials at which they are to appear. No provision generally is made for answering basic questions concerning rights and responsibilities of participants, or the meaning of various parts of the process. Consequently, jurors, witnesses, and defendants may fail to exercise rights they otherwise would, or may come away from contact with a criminal case with an erroneous impression of the system.[68]

These deficiencies seem to reflect a general insensitivity on the part of the courts toward virtually all who come before them, regardless of why they are there. Like so many other government agencies, the courts have evolved from instruments into institutions, and have come to serve the needs of lawyers and judges more than the interests of justice.

SUMMARY

One of the functions of social organization is to manage conflict resolution; this is done by both formal and informal means. The courts provide a formal means for resolving conflicts between the individual and the state (i.e., crimes). The courts deal with crimes in an effort to restore social harmony and resolve these conflicts according to established legal rules that regulate rights and duties. When conflicts come before the courts, the respective rights and duties of the opposing parties are examined in light of existing legal principles. The courts then provide the remedies allowed by law. All courts have jurisdictions that define the nature of the conflicts that may be brought before them. The criminal courts operate at two levels: trial and appellate. Trial courts hear disputes of fact and apply appropriate remedies; appellate courts review the actions of the trial courts.

The central figure in any court is the judge, who has wide latitude in how the court conducts business. Although most judges are competent and hardworking, some are not—and it is the latter who inspire a great deal of the criticism levied against the courts. Once judges are on the bench it is very difficult to remove them or nullify their effects on the quality of justice. A possible reason for the large number of inadequate judges is the means by which they are selected. In many states (and at the federal level) judges are selected because of their political connections as well as their merit.

Another problem of the courts is in their administration. Because courts are also bureaucratic agencies, they suffer from the basic problems of organization and administration common to virtually all bureaucracies. Recent efforts in court reform, especially court unification and the hiring of professional administrators, has helped to correct some of these problems, but ingrained tradition has proven difficult to overcome.

A serious problem of the courts is the issue of bail. Bail is the posting of money or other sureties in support of a defendant's promise to appear at trial. The poor often cannot afford bail and must remain in jail until after their trial. This is not always accidental, as courts may set bail so high that a defendant cannot raise the money to get out (even though this is not the purpose of bail). Again, this is a problem that has been addressed through bail reform, but more effort is needed before the problem can be resolved.

Trial juries also have been the subject of considerable controversy, in spite of the fact that a relatively small proportion of cases ever result in jury trials (which tend to be expensive, time-consuming and unpredictable in their outcome). However, in spite of its shortcomings, the jury trial still remains the hallmark of our legal system. Two Supreme Court decisions have created a potential for the significant modification of jury utilization. One was the decision to allow six-member juries in felony cases; the other was the decision to allow courts to accept non-unanimous verdicts. However, it is still too early to tell just how much influence these decisions will have on the overall quality of the administration of justice.

Considerable controversy has surrounded the issue of sentencing, especially the disparity of sentences awarded for the same or similar crimes. This problem may result more from the nature of plea bargaining than from actual decision-making by the courts. The public is also concerned over what it perceives as judicial lenience in sentencing. This perceived lenience may be more speculative than real (in spite of some widely publicized examples of leniency) and may be based on the public's fear of violent, stranger-to-stranger crimes. The truth is that most criminals are caught and most of them do receive active sentences, yet the idea of lenient sentencing remains a focal point of public dissatisfaction with the courts.

Finally, there is a major need for courts and their administrators to concern themselves with the relationship between the courts and the community, especially in the treatment of jurors, witnesses and defendants. Better facilities, information services and basic consideration might go a long way toward improving the relationship between the courts and the public. In addition, law-focused education in the schools would give citizens a better understanding of the courts and the community's responsibilities toward them.

DISCUSSION QUESTIONS

1. How do the roles of trial and appellate courts differ?

2. Do judges have too much power and too little accountability?

3. Do you think class and status differences between judges and lawyers on the one hand and most criminal defendants on the other make a difference in how people are treated by the courts?

4. How can differences in a judge's legal education and work background make a difference in performance on the bench?

5. What effects can delay in the courts have on public opinion toward the criminal justice system?

6. Do you think it is fair for bail bond agents to possess the powers that they do? How can their actions harm the reputation of the criminal justice system?

7. Does the use of psychological profiles in jury selection defeat the interests of justice—or is it an effective way for a defense lawyer to secure justice for the defendant?

8. The public seems to think criminal sentences are too lenient. What would happen, in your opinion, if criminal sentences were increased? Is public sentiment the best guide to follow in these matters?

9. People who receive probated sentences are often regarded as having "gotten away with" their crime. Is this a realistic assessment? Should the victim have a say in the sentencing process?

10. Does sentencing disparity bring into question the credibility of sentencing, or does it merely reflect the diversity of our courts?

11. What is the difference between an *indeterminate sentence* and a *flat sentence*?

12. Do you think some sentences should be "enhanced" if the defendant committed the crime with a firearm or if certain other specific conditions can be demonstrated?

13. Does plea bargaining interfere with the ability of the courts to impose appropriate sentences?

14. How do you think the public could be given a more accurate understanding of the roles and limitations of the courts?

15. Do you think the courts make an honest effort to consider the safety of the public or community sentiment in how they process cases and pass out sentences?

16. Do you think that television provides an accurate perspective of the courts or that it distorts the public's knowledge of such matters?

17. How can data automation reduce delay in the courts? Why would courts be reluctant to use data automation systems?

18. Should there be limitations on how much money can be spent by the defense in a criminal case?

19. Why do trial lawyers want biased jurors? Is this fair?

20. Do you think there should be minimum education standards for serving on a jury?

REFERENCES

1 William T. Schantz, *The American Legal Environment: Individuals, Their Business, and Their Governments* (St. Paul: West Publishing Co., 1976), 122.

2 Schantz, *The American Legal Environment*, 122.

3 Schantz, *The American Legal Environment*, 122.

4 Harold J. Grilliot, *Introduction to Law and the Legal System*, 2nd ed. (Boston: Houghton Mifflin Company, 1979), 49.

5 Gerald D. Robin, *Introduction to the Criminal Justice System: Principles, Procedures, Practice* (New York: Harper and Row Publishers, 1980), 174.

6 Robin, *Introduction to the Criminal Justice System*, 174.

7 William Chambliss and Robert B. Seidman, *Law, Order and Power* (Reading, MA: Addison-Wesley Publishing Co., 1971), 76.

8 President's Commission on Law Enforcement and the Administration of Justice, Nicholas deB. Katzenback, Chair, *Task Force Report: The Courts* (Washington, DC: U.S. Government Printing Office, 1967), 65.

9 James P. Levine, Michael C. Musheno and Dennis J Palumbo, *Criminal Justice: A Public Policy Process* (New York: Harcourt Brace Jovanovich, 1980), 263.

10 Abraham S. Blumberg, *Criminal Justice: Issues and Ironies*, 2nd ed. (New York: New Viewpoints, 1979), 247-267.

11 Donald Dale Jackson, *Judges: An Inside View of the Agonies and Excesses of an American Elite* (New York: Atheneum, 1974), 10.

12 Blumberg, *Criminal Justice*, 250.

13 Blumberg, *Criminal Justice*, 258.

14 Blumberg, *Criminal Justice*, 258.

15 Blumberg, *Criminal Justice*, 251.

16 Harold Spaeth, *Supreme Court Decision Making: Explaining and Prediction.* (San Francisco: Freeman and Company, 1976), see especially Chapters 4 and 5; and Lawrence Baum, *The Supreme Court*, 4th ed. (Washington, DC: CQ Press, 1992), especially Chapters 2 and 4.

17 For a fascinating discussion of this event and the politics behind it, see Robert H. Bork, *The Tempting of America* (New York: The Free Press, 1990).

18 *Greensboro Record*, 25 March 1980, B1, B2.

19 Ruth Marcus, "Execution Stalled in 11th-Hour Claim of Innocence," *The Washington Post*, 25 February 1992, A3.

20 Jackson, *Judges*, 4-5.

21 Charles E. Silberman, *Criminal Violence, Criminal Justice* (Nee York: Vintage Books, 1978), 375.

22 Howard James, *Crisis in the Courts* (New York: David McKay Company, 1971).

23 Sidney C. Snellenburg, "New Approaches to Reducing Court Delay and Congestion," *State Court Journal* 13:3 (Summer 1989), 19-23.

[24] Barry Mahoney, *Changing Times in Trial Courts* (Williamsburg, VA: National Center for State Courts, 1988), 6.

[25] Keith L. Bumsted, "Courts and the Private Sector," National Center for State Courts (September 1988).

[26] U.S. Department of Justice, *United States Attorney's Manual* (Washington, DC: Executive Office for United States Attorneys, 1 October 1988). See especially Chapter 7, "Information Management."

[27] *Carlson v. Landon*, 342 U.S. 524 (1952) at 545-546.

[28] *United States v. Salerno et al.* (on certiorari to the United States Court of Appeals for the Second Circuit), 481 U.S. 739 (1987).

[29] President's Commission on Law Enforcement and the Administration of Justice, *The Courts*, 37.

[30] Ronald Goldfarb, *Ransom: A Critique of the American Bail System* (New York: Harper and Row Publishers, 1965).

[31] President's Commission on Law Enforcement and the Administration of Justice, *The Courts*, 38.

[32] Jackson, *Judges*, 144-145. For further discussion of the bail problem, see James, *Crisis in the Courts*, especially Chapter VII, "Jail or Bail," 112-125; John E. Conklin and Dermot Meagher, "The Percentage Deposit Bail System: An Alternative to the Professional Bondsman," *Journal of Criminal Justice* (Winter 1973).

[33] Robin, *Introduction to the Criminal Justice System*, 204.

[34] Levine et al., *Criminal Justice: A Public Policy Approach*, 281.

[35] Kathleen Maguire and Timothy J. Flanagan, *Sourcebook of Criminal Justice Statistics 1990* (Washington, DC: U.S. Department of Justice, Office of Justice Programs, Bureau of Justice Statistics, 1991); see especially Table 2.42, "Attitudes Toward the Courts' Treatment of Criminals," 191.

[36] Silberman, *Criminal Violence, Criminal Justice*, 402.

[37] In *Duncan v. Louisiana*, 391 U.S. 145 (1968), the Supreme Court ruled that the constitutional right to a trial applies only to crimes that carry a possible penalty of more than six months in jail; this eliminates quite a few minor misdemeanors and may therefor preclude many cases from qualifying for jury trials.

[38] Frank A. Bennack, Jr., "The American Public, The Media and the Judicial System," (transcript of an address presented at the National Conference of Metropolitan Courts, San Antonio, TX, October 21, 1983), 7.

[39] Chambliss and Siedman, *Law, Order and Power*, 443. For a general history of the jury trial, see Lloyd E. Moore, *The Jury: Tool of Kings, Palladium of Liberty*, 2nd ed. (Cincinnati: Anderson Publishing Co., 1988).

[40] National Institute for Law Enforcement and Criminal Justice, *A Guide to Jury System Management* (Washington, DC: U.S. Government Printing Office, 1975), 1-3.

[41] *Swain v. Alabama*, 380 U.S. 202 (1965).

[42] Haywood Alker, Carl Hosticha and Michael Mitchell, "Jury Selection as a Biased Social Process," *Law and Society Review* (Fall 1976), 9-41.

[43] James Reston, Jr., *The Innocence of Joan Little: A Southern Mystery* (New York: Time Books, 1977).

[44] Wayne King, "Joan Little's Lawyer Scorns Legal System and Says He 'Bought' Her Acquittal," *New York Times*, 20 October 1975, 23.

[45] See Rita Simon and Prentice Marshall, "The Jury System," in Stuart Nagel, ed., *The Rights of the Accused in Law and Action* (Beverly Hills, CA: Sage, 1972).

[46] National Institute, *A Guide to Jury System Management*, 1-3 .

[47] Harry Kalven and Hans Zeisel, *The American Jury* (Boston: Little, Brown, 1966), 58.

[48] *Duncan v. Louisiana*, 391 U.S. 145 (1968) at 149, 158-159.

[49] *Williams v. Florida*, 399 U.S. 78, 86 (1970).

[50] *Ballew v. Georgia*, 435 U.S. 223 (1978).

[51] *Apodaca v. Oregon*, 406 U.S. 404 (1972). See also *Johnson v. Louisiana*, 406 U.S. 356 (1972), in which the Supreme Court stated, "In our view, disagreement of three jurors does not alone establish reasonable doubt, particularly with such a heavy majority of the jury, after having considered the dissenters' views, remains convinced of guilt That rational men disagree is not itself equivalent to a failure by the State, nor does it indicate infidelity to the reasonable doubt standard."

[52] *Burch et al. v. Louisiana*, 441 U.S. 130 (1979).

[53] National Advisory Commission on Criminal Justice Standards and Goals, Russell W. Peterson, Chair, *Courts* (Washington, DC: U.S. Government Printing Office, 1973), 101.

[54] Louis Jankowski, "Probation and Parole," *Bureau of Justice Statistics Bulletin* (November 1991), 1.

[55] See especially Michael Serrill, "Determinate Sentencing: History, Theory, Debate," *Correctional Magazine*, September 1977.

[56] Nicholas Scoppetta, "Getting Away With Murder: Our Disastrous Court System," *The Saturday Review*, 10 June 1978, 11.

[57] See Marvin E. Frankel, *Criminal Sentences: Law Without Order* (New York: Hill and Wang, 1973).

[58] Jackson, *Judges*, 201.

[59] James, *Crisis in the Courts*, 148.

[60] James, *Crisis in the Courts*, 147.

[61] Silberman, *Criminal Violence, Criminal Justice*.

[62] Charles Peters, "Tilting at Windmills," *The Washington Post*, 1 June 1980), D2.

[63] National Advisory Commission, *Courts*, 191.

[64] American Bar Association, Subcommittee on Unjust Criticism of the Bench, Courts and Community Committee, "Unjust Criticism of Judges," no date or place of publication.

[65] Bennack, "The American Public, The Media and the Judicial System", 5.

[66] Bennack, "The American Public, The Media and the Judicial System", 6.

[67] National Advisory Commission, *Courts*, 194.

[68] National Advisory Commission, *Courts*, 194.

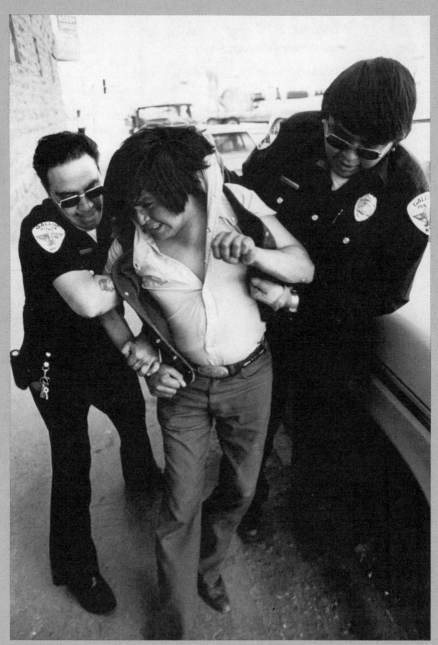

Photo Credit: Tony O'Brien, Frost Publishing Group, Ltd.

Chapter 11

JUVENILE JUSTICE

The status of children today is quite different from what it has been for most of recorded history. Until the present century, inadequate prenatal care, high infant mortality and death resulting from childhood diseases converged to dramatically reduce the odds of a child being born healthy and living to adulthood. Throughout most of recorded history children were regarded as little more than another set of mouths to feed; scant regard was given to their emotional or physical well-being. This was especially so after the onset of the Industrial Revolution, when children as young as four were employed in the English textile industry.[1] The Industrial Revolution did not set a new precedent, however, as child labor had long been taken for granted on farms and in domestic industry. In fact, universal education was frowned upon in eighteenth-century England because it was seen as producing too many scholars and not enough laborers. Orphanages and poorhouses were especially eager to place children, some as young as five years old, in mills and factories in order to avoid the cost of having to care for them. In some instances these "charitable" institutions stipulated that employers were to take one "idiot" for every 20 other children.[2] These children labored under extreme hardship, worked 12 to 14 hours a day for negligible wages and were subjected to constant abuse. Young boys and girls were hired out to farmers, coal mine operators and industrial plants, where they received no education or time to play. Many of them were used in extremely hazardous occupations where they were considered expendable. For example, because of their small size, little boys were used to clean chimneys. They were dropped down the top of the chimney and once inside scrubbed the flue with a brush. Because the bricks were often hot, most of these children suffered severe burns to their hands and legs. If a boy became wedged in the chimney, "...his ascent was hastened by lighting straw beneath him and thus driving him up. Death often resulted. Orthodox opinion saw nothing inhuman in this."[3] Efforts to prohibit this practice in Edinburgh in 1819 were blocked because "...humanity is a modern invention; and there are many chimneys in old houses that cannot be swept in any other manner."[4] It took over 100 years to produce the legislation in England and America that finally abolished child labor.

Although laws *protecting* children were few and largely ineffective, criminal laws were used to vigorously *prosecute* them. For example, in 1833 Nicolas White, a boy of nine, was charged with breaking a window and stealing paint worth two pennies. He was tried at the Old Bailey* and sentenced to be hanged. Although his sentence was commuted, that of another child was not: 13-year-old John Bell was hanged for an equally petty offense two years earlier. One witness at a trial where several young boys were condemned to be hanged wrote, "Never did I see boys cry so." Another contemporary writer reported that he saw "a cartload of young girls, in dresses of various colours, on their way to be hanged at Tyburn Tree."[5] When legal reforms were proposed in the early nineteenth century they were bitterly opposed by lawyers on the grounds that they would encourage crime.

The English legal system historically held that children under the age of seven could not formulate the intent necessary to commit a crime and therefore could not be charged with a crime.[6] Children from seven to 13 were also presumed to be incapable of formulating the intent required to commit a crime, but that presumption could be rebutted upon proof that the child could tell right from wrong. Children 14 years of age and older were considered adults because it was assumed they were mature enough to determine right from wrong. As a result, children aged 14 and older (and those from seven to 13 who were proven capable of distinguishing right from wrong) were tried as adults and often received the same punishments.

Because American criminal law is based on the same presumptions, a great many American children above the age of 14 have been prosecuted as adults. However, there is evidence that, due to the severity of adult punishments, judges and juries in the last century were sometimes reluctant to convict children lest

---

* The Old Bailey is an ancient criminal court that previously adjoined the Newgate Prison in London, England. It is officially known as the Central Criminal Court, even though it is still called "Old Bailey." The term *bailey* originally referred to the area between a fortification's inner walls and its outer walls. "Old Bailey" was one of London's original baileys.

they be punished as adults. Many children were acquitted as a result.[7] Incarcerated children frequently intermingled with adult felons in jails and prisons. In 1869 when the Illinois Board of State Commissioners of Public Charities inspected 78 jails they found that of the 511 inmates, 98 (or 19 percent) were children under the age of 16.[8]

EVOLUTION OF THE JUVENILE JUSTICE SYSTEM

The current juvenile justice system evolved in response to three separate legal needs and three broad categories of remedy. The three areas of legal need are child welfare (which deals with abused, neglected or dependent children), status offenses (an area that lies somewhere between delinquency and parental fitness) and criminal offenses by minors. The only point these areas have in common is the age of the child.[9] The three broad categories of remedy are private intervention, civil law and criminal law.

CHILD WELFARE

During the Puritan era children were considered to be property (in fact, most of the laws and regulations aimed at them also applied to servants).[10] The child in Puritan times was not considered innocent but rather was deemed to be an evil creature whose sin could only be repressed by discipline.[11] The harsh economic realities of nineteenth-century urban America did little to help the plight of children. We have noted that children as young as four and five years of age were forced into mills and factories where they were paid scant wages while having their childhood (and sometimes their health or even their lives) taken from them. Then (as now) some children were abandoned, neglected or even criminally victimized. There was a distinct need for some kind of system to look after the interests of these children. Private charities were not always the answer; indeed, they were often part of the problem, and in any event had limited legal authority. Children who were physically, emotionally or sexually abused by their own families or others needed legal advocates to look after their interests and assure their protection.

STATUS OFFENSES

Childhood—especially adolescence—is a turbulent time and some children fail to conform to society's expectations. Driven by rebelliousness and a wish for personal autonomy, some children act in ways that produce social disapproval. Much juvenile misconduct is not necessarily criminal in nature but can endanger their moral, social or physical well-being. Truancy, promiscuity, substance abuse, incorrigibility and running away from home are regarded as problems when they involve children. Although adults are generally free to "mess up their lives" if they wish, children are not given the same latitude. Juvenile misconduct that falls below a distinctly criminal threshold draws its importance from the status of the offender; therefore, non-criminal offenses by juveniles are usually referred to as *status offenses*. Society has a compelling interest in addressing these behaviors and it is questionable whether the criminal courts are the proper venue for doing so. As a result, society needs a juvenile system that regulates the conduct of some children, especially those who are unwilling to heed the counsel of their parents, teachers or other adults

Status offenses have been recognized throughout most of American history; in fact, the first status offense law in America was the Massachusetts Stubborn Child Law passed in 1646, which remained on the books in revised form for over 300 years. This law prescribed harsh punishment for juveniles over 16 who were disobedient toward their parents, for rude or disorderly children and for children who profaned the sabbath.[12] Most of the early legislation concerning children was oriented toward children 16 years of age or older who were physically and emotionally mature enough to threaten family stability by declaring their independence, thus depriving their families of their labor and productivity. Time has changed society's attitude toward children but not its wish to control their behavior. Non-criminal misconduct by juveniles remains an important consideration within the juvenile justice system. As we will see, the concept has been difficult to deal with.

CRIMINAL OFFENSES

Juveniles can and do commit crimes. In some instances their crimes are petty. Acts of vandalism and shoplifting are generally regarded as a common part of growing up, especially when committed by young children. On the other hand, some juveniles commit adult crimes that seem to be well beyond the excuse of immaturity. The direct involvement of children in serious crimes, both as offenders and victims, requires a legal system that recognizes the seriousness of their misconduct but also holds out hope for rehabilitation. Since there is little to be gained and much to be lost by writing youthful criminals off as lost causes, it is important to segregate youthful offenders from adult criminals. Some juvenile offenders, however (especially those at the upper end of the juvenile age range) may warrant treatment as adults. The system must have some means for deciding who will be kept within the juvenile justice system and who will be passed on to the criminal justice system.

REMEDIES

Historically, three categories of remedy have been available: private intervention, civil law and criminal law. Private intervention has been the preferred remedy for dealing with children. In earlier generations this was undertaken by public and private charities, including societies founded for the express purpose of caring for the needy. In modern times it has been joined by the profession of social work and various youth advocacy groups. However, institutions that provide private intervention are limited in what they can do, both in terms of their authority and their resources. Moreover, private resources cannot compel action of any kind and are forced to rely on the willingness of others to cooperate with them.

Although civil law offers greater flexibility, the common law traditions of England and the United States offer little precedent for dealing specifically with the problems of juveniles. A large part of traditional civil law focused on private disputes, most often involving rights and duties regarding the possession, use and disposition of property. The welfare of children was seldom considered, and criminal acts committed by children were seen as the proper business of the criminal courts. In order for civil law to support a juvenile justice system, either a new legal philosophy had to be developed or an old one modified to meet the need. The answer was found in the already existing legal doctrine of *parens patriae* (literally, "father of his country"). In England the *parens patriae* is the sovereign, i.e., the King; in America it is the state. The concept refers to sovereign guardianship over those who are disabled. The doctrine was extended from the insane and incompetent to minors and was first used in a juvenile issue in 1838 in *Ex parte Cruse*.[13] Since then it has become the legal standard for actions involving children.

Some students of the situation contend that criminal law is not an appropriate remedy for children in need of protection, nor is it the best vehicle for dealing with status offenses. Even when it is the appropriate remedy for juveniles who commit criminal acts, these cases must be examined in light of the crime and the age of the child. Much of the impetus behind the development of a juvenile justice system has been based on the wish to remove children from the control of the *criminal justice system.*

THE BEGINNINGS OF JUVENILE JUSTICE: THE 1800s

The nineteenth century was a period of almost continuous change and turbulence in the United States. It was in many respects the adolescence of our nation. During the first 60 years the economy was based on agriculture; these decades saw the taming of the frontier, the rise of the industrial state and finally a terrible civil war. During the reconstruction era (roughly from the end of the

Civil War to the beginning of World War I) the United States emerged as a modern industrial power. As the industrial cities of the north came into their own, the issue of adolescent misbehavior became a growing concern.[14] The advent of compulsory education also played a role. As Ferdinand has noted, "Just as children who were beyond parental control and roamed the city at night could not be ignored, so too children who disrupted school or truanted needed to be held in check."[15] He further noted that "...as compulsory education and industrialization swept America's cities in the 19th century, they produced a growing troop of wayward, incorrigible children who resisted in one fashion or another the efforts of society to shape them for adulthood."[16]

During this period of industrialization, immigration and rapid urban growth the cities were characterized by disrupted families, overcrowding, poverty, slums, alcoholism and spiraling levels of vice and crime. These conditions spurred social reformers who were concerned with improving the overall quality of urban life. Many of them had great faith in the ability of the developing social sciences to help children and at the same time eradicate the social blight that was producing so many problems in the cities.[17] Part of the social reform movement during the nineteenth century therefore focused on trying to humanize the treatment of children by the criminal courts. The doctrine of *parens patriae* fit hand-in-glove with their efforts.

However, long before the juvenile civil courts matured, steps were taken to segregate juveniles from adults in correctional institutions. A separate correctional institution for juveniles, the New York House of Refuge, was established in New York City in 1824 to rescue children of the poor (both criminal and vagrant) and to provide them with care and discipline in the hope of preventing them from becoming adult criminals.[18] Similar institutions were subsequently founded in Philadelphia and Boston. For children who were brought before the courts, separate trials, dockets and records for juveniles were created in Massachusetts in 1872, in New York in 1892 and in Rhode Island in 1898. These developments set the stage for what would ultimately become exclusively juvenile courts.

Even though many juvenile cases were handled by the criminal courts, an increasingly large number were filed in civil courts. This process quickly added a major burden to the civil courts, as juvenile cases had to compete with all the other normal business of the courts. Although this brought juveniles under the doctrine of *parens patriae*, the process was not entirely effective. For one thing, children accused of serious crimes were still processed by the criminal courts, and civil court judges did not necessarily have the training (or interest) required for dealing effectively with children. As a result, they relied heavily on outside agencies for assistance—thus perpetuating the influence of private and charitable institutions on juvenile justice.

THE INTERMEDIATE ERA:
FROM CHICAGO TO *IN RE GAULT* (1899-1967)

Reform enthusiasm peaked when the Illinois legislature created the first juvenile court in Chicago in 1899. The new juvenile court was given jurisdiction over all juvenile cases, including serious criminal offenders, status offenders, and neglected and dependent children.[19] This was an important move for several reasons. First, it strengthened the concept of *parens patriae*; second, it gave legal sanction to the stratification of society by age; and finally, for the first time it located responsibility for official action in a unique legal body for children.[20] Since its mission was care and rehabilitation, it was given broad latitude unrestrained by the procedural safeguards given to adults.[21] From Illinois, juvenile courts spread rapidly. By 1920, 30 states had established juvenile courts and by 1945 every state had them. The juvenile justice system that emerged was *treatment-driven* rather than *law-driven*. The court process during this period functioned as a non-adversarial process conducted away from public view.

From the outset the purposes and objectives of the juvenile court differed substantially from those of the criminal court. Rather than placing blame, finding guilt and punishing offenders, juvenile court was intended to be nonjudgmental. The emphasis was to be on helping children overcome paternal neglect and unwholesome environments through extensive help from the social sciences. An analogy frequently used in describing the juvenile court was that the court (or judge) was a kindly father expressing concern for his wayward child. As a result, the juvenile court process differed substantially from that of the criminal courts.[22] Juvenile court records were confidential and state law generally allowed juvenile court judges to exclude the public. Instead of sitting behind a bench, the judge often sat behind a table or desk, and the hearings were usually informal in nature. Since the main objective was to diagnose and treat, the process was deemed to be non-adversarial. As a result, the use of lawyers was discouraged. Instead, probation officers were assigned to the court to investigate delinquent acts or conditions of dependency and/or neglect—as well as the child's background—and to report their findings to the judge. Psychologists, psychiatrists, social workers and other social scientists were attracted to the juvenile court in professional, consultant or volunteer capacities. These objectives, procedures and characteristics—although somewhat altered over the years—characterized the majority of the juvenile courts during this era.

THE JUVENILE COURT PROCESS

The juvenile court's jurisdiction includes cases of dependency, neglect and delinquency. The terms *dependency* and *neglect* are often used synonymously. *Dependent* youths are sent to the juvenile court because there is no other place to send them. *Neglected* children are those who have been abandoned or mistreated by their parents or caretakers, including children whose parents fail to provide an adequate home environment. Juvenile courts also deal with allegations of delinquency, i.e., acts that would be crimes if committed by adults. Delinquency also includes the violation of rules and regulations that apply specifically to children, including curfew violations, truancy and the use of alcohol, drugs and tobacco. Finally, juvenile courts exercise jurisdiction over children deemed by parents or other authorities to be uncontrollable, incorrigible, runaway or otherwise in need of special supervision. Juvenile courts have jurisdiction over children up to a specified maximum age (usually 18).[23] If the offender is over the maximum age for juveniles, the criminal courts have jurisdiction, and will be treated as an adult. A number of states, however, have "youthful offender" provisions that let them extend special consideration to offenders up to the age of 21. Although the juvenile justice process varies widely from state to state, it follows a general pattern along the lines of the steps described below.[24]

REFERRAL

A juvenile first comes into contact with the juvenile justice process after being referred to the court by another party. Most referrals are made by the police.[25] We have already noted that the police exercise a great deal of discretion and have a wide variety of options available to them. This is especially the case with juveniles. Police may choose to admonish them and then let them go, or they may warn them, release them and follow up on the incident with an official report. An additional method of handling juveniles, sometimes called a *station adjustment*, is to take them to the police station, call their parents and warn all of them of the future consequences of additional misconduct. In the past some watchman-style police departments placed them under a kind of informal "probation" by the police department, but this is seldom done anymore. Another alternative is to refer the juvenile to a mental health clinic, drug or alcohol abuse agency, youth service bureau, Big Brothers program, the YMCA, a local youth center or some other social service agency. In the 1930s and 1940s many police departments sponsored a police athletic league or a police boy's club to help provide alternatives for wayward children. Such agencies, however, have largely fallen from favor. For example, although the Washington, DC Police

Department established its Metropolitan Boys and Girls Club in 1934 to combat juvenile delinquency, such clubs are becoming increasingly rare By exercising discretion in these ways, the police diverted children from juvenile court. When this kind of informal diversion was deemed inappropriate, the police took the juvenile either to the police station or to a juvenile detention facility where the child would then be released to the parents. At that time both youth and parents would be directed to appear in court. The police also have the option of placing the juvenile offender in jail or a juvenile detention facility and referring the case to the juvenile court.

In all probability, most encounters between the police and juveniles take place on the street and are settled by informal means. Only a relatively small number are referred to a juvenile court. Referrals usually occur if the juvenile commits a particularly serious crime, if he or she is a danger to society or if specific guidance or treatment is needed (and the family is unable to provide it). Some police departments (especially larger ones) have a youth division. In this situation all cases involving juveniles are routinely turned over to youth officers who then decide on the best course of action. The decision to refer a juvenile to court is based on a number of factors, including the seriousness of the offense, the attitude of the child, community sentiment, the offender's prior record and age, and departmental polices. In general, most law enforcement agencies prefer to avoid referring a case to juvenile court if there is any other reasonable alternative.[26]

School administrators, welfare case workers and citizens who have complaints also may refer cases to the juvenile court. Every once in a while parents or other members of the family may ask the court to discipline or even assume complete responsibility for the child. Parents who do this often plead that they can no longer control the child or that they no longer wish to exercise their parental responsibilities. These children are then considered to be "persons in need of supervision" and may become wards of the juvenile court. In some cases they may be taken out of their family setting and placed under the direct control of the state.

INTAKE

After a juvenile is referred to court, a preliminary screening known as *intake* is performed by the probation department of the juvenile court. In larger courts, intake may be carried out by a special section of the probation department. At the intake proceeding an intake officer determines whether the juvenile should be released to parents with a warning or if the matter should be referred to the juvenile court.[27] The inquiry may be a very limited and abbreviated process, or it may involve an extensive study of the child's misconduct and social history. Depending upon personal judgment, the strength of the case and the seriousness of the offense, the intake officer may choose to dismiss the matter, refer the youth to another agency or place the child on an informal probation. When the latter course is chosen, the proceeding might involve an informal hearing before the judge, at which time the act is discussed and the child is admonished to change the behavior. Many juvenile cases are handled in this manner. As a final course of action, the intake officer may recommend that a formal juvenile court petition be filed. This is the equivalent of filing a criminal charge. If a court referral is decided upon, the intake officer must make a decision concerning detention pending the judicial hearing. In most states, law provides for the release of the child to the parents or some other suitable caretaker unless the juvenile is deemed to be such a severe threat to the community that detention is appropriate. In a minority of states and in the federal system, juveniles have the right to bail.[28] About a quarter of the cases result in detention of the juvenile prior to disposition of their cases.[29]

PETITION

When a court petition is filed, the prosecutor of the juvenile court reviews the recommendation and report of the intake officer. At this time the prosecutor may dismiss the case if doing so is deemed to be in the best interests of all parties. If the allegations are found to be sufficiently serious to warrant court action, documents are filed to begin the adjudication process. If the circumstances are appropriate, a prosecutor may recommend waiver.

WAIVER

When the juvenile court officially assumes jurisdiction, a decision concerning *waiver* to criminal court must be made. Waiver is the process by which the juvenile's case is transferred to criminal court where he or she can be tried as an adult. A juvenile who loses the protection of the juvenile court through waiver can be tried as an adult and may receive the same punishment as an adult. Waiver can take place only when the grounds for delinquency are acts that would constitute a crime if committed by an adult. In addition, the child must be at or above the minimum age at which a child can be convicted of a crime (in most states the age is 18).

ADJUDICATION

If a petition is filed with the juvenile court and a decision is made to retain jurisdiction (that is, not to waive the case to the criminal courts) then the court must decide what it will do. The judge may reject the allegations and release the juvenile, or withhold adjudication on the condition that the juvenile participate in a diversion program. If the allegations are sustained, the court may find the child to be delinquent, dependent or in need of supervision. Although the process is generally informal, in some cases it is not. When the juvenile (usually through an attorney) contests the action, a *contested hearing* is held. Contested hearings are held before the juvenile court judge. In such cases an actual prosecutor is likely to be present.[30] At contested hearings witnesses may be sworn and cross-examined by the juvenile (again, usually through a lawyer). These hearings can be short—20 to 30 minutes—or can take several hours. The length is usually dependent on the number of witnesses, the complexity of the case and the seriousness of the offense. Because prosecutors and defense attorneys have shown themselves unable to reach a mutually satisfactory resolution of the matter prior to the formal hearing, these hearings are the most adversarial aspect of what is otherwise a largely non-adversarial process.

Lawyers representing juveniles in these cases often see their role as being distinctly different from what it would be in a criminal court. Most lawyers in juvenile courts believe it is their duty to assist the court in helping the child rather than to aggressively seek acquittal—especially when they believe the juvenile is guilty and in need of some kind of treatment.[31] These lawyers typically have cooperative relationships with juvenile court professionals and subscribe to the ideals of the court. Consequently, they plead the great majority of juveniles guilty, vigorously contest few cases and frequently negotiate settlements. While a minority of lawyers representing juveniles conduct themselves as they would in a contested criminal case, the prevailing mode of operations is non-adversarial and inquisitorial; the parties usually act in the interest of getting to the truth of the case rather than engaging in a winner-take-all courtroom battle.[32]

DISPOSITION

If the juvenile is found delinquent after a contested hearing or admits to the allegation of delinquency, a *disposition* hearing will follow. At this hearing the judge tries to find out why the youth committed the delinquent acts and attempts to discover remedies that will correct the errant behavior. The court is usually aided by a report written by the probation officer that deals with the child's social background and psychological makeup. The report, known as the *social history report*, includes recommended dispositions. Probation officers, social workers, psychologists and welfare caseworkers may contribute professional opinions concerning the most appropriate disposition in a given case. Often the child's parents and relatives—and even the child—will present their respective views as to the best resolution of the matter. All of these opinions are then taken into consideration by the judge.

Like many decisionmakers in the juvenile justice system, the judge has a wide variety of alternatives from which to choose; however, this range is either constricted or expanded by the extent of the social services or institutional facilities available in the area. A judge who deems an act to be of limited gravity and does not consider the youth a serious threat to society may proffer a stern warning and place the child on unsupervised probation or assign a probation officer to provide limited supervision. An alternative is to give the juvenile a sentence but then suspend it for a period of time; if no new crimes are committed by the end of this period, the court removes the finding of delinquency from the records and closes the matter. When the law so allows, a fine might be levied or the juvenile ordered to perform certain kinds of community service as a condition of probation. Repainting or repairing structures that have been vandalized or removing trash from parks and playgrounds are typical community service tasks required.

When a judge believes that an act is serious and the juvenile is a threat to either self or others (but not sufficiently dangerous to require actual confinement), the juvenile can be placed under closely supervised probation. The terms of this kind of probation include a specific plan of action designed to improve the juvenile's behavior and may include a referral to a social service agency, public mental health clinic or private psychologist. Like the previous alternative, the disposition may include a fine, compensatory labor or community service.

The most serious cases result in more structured and confined placements. If a halfway house or private institution suitable for the particular youth is available, the judge may arrange for commitment to that kind of institution. Otherwise, the child might be committed either to a state youth correctional authority or to a particular training or reform school. The frequency with which juvenile court judges commit juveniles to a state institution may depend on their faith in these kinds of places. Most courts place the majority of youths on probation. Only a small proportion are ever committed to a state institution.

In many states juveniles committed to a state institution are first sent to a diagnostic and testing center. After being evaluated the juvenile is assigned to the most appropriate institution or granted the most appropriate placement within a given institution. Except for the least populous states, which may have only one or two juvenile institutions, most states have a number of institutions, including reform schools, ranches, forestry camps, halfway houses and group homes that range from maximum- to minimum-security facilities. With the exception of some innovative programs, juvenile institutions are often characterized by an aura of brutality and hostility (usually at the hands of other inmates),[33] staff coercion and harassment—all of which tend to produce youths who are more delinquent when they are released than they were when they entered. This is aggravated by the process of secondary deviance, a process by which many of these juveniles are essentially rejected by the communities to which they return. Incarceration in a juvenile facility frequently paves the way for subsequent stays in other juvenile institutions and adult prisons.

JUVENILE JUSTICE SINCE *IN RE GAULT* (1967 AND BEYOND)

Over time, policy-makers, professionals in the field and the general public became increasingly concerned that the juvenile justice system neither adequately diagnosed nor cured delinquency, that juvenile court judges were sometimes tyrannical rather than solicitous and caring, and that reform schools frequently did not reform.[34] As a consequence of the tremendous disparity between the promise and the performance of the juvenile justice system, several movements developed in the hope of strengthening, reforming or changing the system. These moves were summarized as the "Four Ds"—due process, decriminalization, diversion and deinstitutionalization. The most important was due process. A single case—*In re Gault*—led the reform movement in this area.

DUE PROCESS

During the reform movement the juvenile court's original goal of individual diagnosis and treatment, which basically follows the medical model, came under sharp attack. The optimistic belief that social scientists could cure delinquents was seriously questioned in light of many attempts that resulted in failure. The psychological basis for the medical model was attacked on the grounds that it failed to consider the deterministic pressures of the social environment that influence (and perhaps even encourage) juveniles to violate legal norms and that seek to adjust juvenile behavior to the existing social environment.[35] The system was also bitterly attacked for the harsh and often unfair way it dealt with juveniles (and disproportionately with the poor) and with the assertion that it ultimately delivered them into the criminal justice system.[36] These attacks were not levied on the basic precepts of the criminal justice system, but rather on its outcomes.

The juvenile justice movement discouraged lawyers from practicing in juvenile court. Adversarial proceedings were seen as an impediment to the court's central tasks of diagnosing the delinquent and prescribing appropriate cures, and protecting dependent or neglected children. As a result, the majority of juveniles were not represented by lawyers. Because of the absence of lawyers in juvenile court, the judge assumed a virtually omnipotent role, performing the normal functions of both judge and defense attorney.* One result was that the juvenile justice process gradually became more inquisitorial than adversarial. Many observers believed that the lack of checks and balances on juvenile court judges resulted in arbitrary and capricious treatment of large numbers of juveniles. Instead of "loving concern and care," many judges seemed to impose their own personal brands of morality on recalcitrant juveniles.[37]

The United States Supreme Court first extended limited due process guarantees to juveniles in 1966 when it heard *Kent v. United States.* In *Kent* the Court said:

> There is much evidence that some juvenile courts, including that of the District of Columbia, lack the personnel, facilities, and techniques to perform adequately as representatives of the State in a *parens patriae* capacity, at least with respect to children charged with law violation. There is evidence, in fact, that there may be grounds for concern that the child receives the worst of both worlds: that he gets neither the protections accorded to adults nor the solicitous care and regenerative treatment postulated for children.[38]

Kent v. United States was significant because it extended the first due process guarantees to juveniles by invalidating a waiver in which the accused was transferred to the criminal courts without a statement of reasons, a hearing or assistance of counsel. *Kent* was followed in short order by another case, perhaps the most significant juvenile justice case ever to be heard by the United States Supreme Court: *In re Gault.*[39] A petition alleging delinquency was filed in the Gila County (Arizona) Juvenile Court against Gerald Gault, a 15-year-old, alleging that he made obscene telephone calls to one Mrs. Cook. The petition was not served upon, given to or even shown to Gerald Gault or his parents at any time. Notice of hearing was cursory, and neither Gerald nor his parents were told that they were entitled to representation by counsel. The complaining witness, Cook, was not present at the hearing. As a result she was not subject to cross-examination. Prior to the hearing Cook spoke to the probation officer over the phone and told him Gerald Gault made obscene telephone calls to her. Gerald Gault and his parents were not told that they had a right to confront and

---

* Since juvenile court proceedings are not considered criminal cases, and since juvenile hearings are not trials, their results are not generally subject to review by appellate courts. This could be construed as an open invitation to abuse.

cross-examine her or any other witnesses, nor were they told that Gerald did not have to testify or make a statement at the hearing. Finally, they were not warned of the possible consequences of his making a statement.

At the conclusion of his hearing, Gerald Gault was found to be a delinquent and was committed to a state industrial school for an undetermined term not to exceed six years. While reviewing the essential role of due process of law in the American legal system and the failure of the juvenile justice system to provide such procedural due process, the Supreme Court stated:

> Accordingly, the highest motives and most enlightened impulses led to a peculiar system for juveniles, unknown to our law in any comparable context. The constitutional and theoretical basis for this peculiar system is—to say the least—debatable. And in practice...the results have not been entirely satisfactory. Juvenile court history has again demonstrated that unbridled discretion, however benevolently motivated, is frequently a poor substitute for principle and procedure. In 1937 Dean Pound wrote: "The powers of the Star Chamber were a trifle in comparison with those of our juvenile courts...." The absence of substantive standards has not necessarily meant that children have received careful, compassionate, individualized treatment. The absence of procedural rules based upon constitutional principle has not always produced fair, efficient, and effective procedures. Departures from established principles of due process have frequently resulted not in enlightened procedure, but in arbitrariness. The Chairman of the Pennsylvania Council of Juvenile Court Judges has recently observed: "Unfortunately, loose procedures, high-handed methods and crowded court calendars, either singly or in combination, all too often, have resulted in depriving some juveniles of fundamental rights that have resulted in a denial of due process."[40]

Failure to observe the fundamental requirements of due process resulted in instances that could have been avoided—instances of unfairness to individuals, inadequate (or inaccurate) findings of fact and unfortunate prescriptions of remedy. Due process of law is the primary and indispensable foundation of individual freedom. It is the basic and essential part of the social contract that defines the rights of—and limits the state's power over—the individual. As Justice Felix Frankfurter once pointed out, the history of American freedom is in no small measure the history of procedure. The procedural rules fashioned from the foundation of due process are instruments for distilling and evaluating the conflicts presented by life (and by our adversarial methods). It is these instruments of due process that are supposed to enhance the possibility that truth will emerge from the confrontation of opposing versions and conflicting data. The Supreme Court concluded its decision in *Gault* by holding that due process requires that juveniles alleged to be delinquent are entitled to a number of important rights. The courts have since continued to expand on these rights, and have thereby defined the specific parameters of juvenile justice as it is administered by the juvenile courts.

Waiver

In *Kent v. United States* the Supreme Court held that the juvenile judge must provide a hearing on waiver and state the reasons sufficient to prove that a full inquiry has taken place.[41] Generally, those waived are juveniles accused of serious crimes of violence such as murder, rape or robbery. Juveniles who are not amenable to juvenile court protection or treatment (usually because of repeated prior adjudications of delinquency) may also be waived. Usually waiver is a discretionary act of the juvenile court judge, except in crimes such as first-degree murder, which in some states *must* be transferred to the criminal courts. Waiver hearings probably occur in less than 1 percent of the cases that pass through the juvenile court, but they take up a disproportionate amount of time and resources.[42] Waiver has become an important issue in juvenile justice because of the increase in both the frequency and violence of juvenile crimes. As a result, between 1978 and 1982 more than 40 state legislatures amended their juvenile codes to simplify and expedite the transfer of juveniles to criminal courts for trial as adults. In addition, some states gave the prosecutor concurrent jurisdiction, significantly expanding the discretion of that office. Thus, under some circumstances the prosecutor can assume jurisdiction in a case involving juveniles without having the case waived by a juvenile court.[43] Since *In re Gault*, waiver hearings have been used with greater frequency on juveniles in the upper age ranges (15-17) in order to get them into the jurisdiction of the criminal courts. The trend appears to be closely associated with the public's disenchantment with rehabilitation and growing support for the "just deserts" philosophy of punishment. Even so, successful waivers do not necessarily result in more severe penalties.[44]

Notice

According to the Supreme Court's holding, a juvenile is entitled to notice of the specific allegations being made after the filing of a petition alleging delinquency but prior to the initial hearing.[45] The Court believed the issue of notice was sufficiently important to make this explicit holding: "Process of law requires notice of the sort we have described—that is, notice which would be deemed constitutionally adequate in a civil or criminal proceeding. It does not allow a hearing to be held in which a youth's freedom and his parent's right to his custody are at stake without giving them timely notice, in advance of the hearing, of the specific issues that they must meet."[46] In other words, both juvenile and parents must be told what is happening and why.

Right to Counsel

In addressing the issue of right to counsel, the Supreme Court said, "We conclude that the due process clause of the Fourteenth Amendment requires that in respect of proceedings to determine delinquency which may result in commitment to an institution in which the juvenile's freedom is curtailed, the child and his parents must be notified of the child's right to be represented by counsel retained by them, or if they are unable to afford counsel, that counsel will be appointed to represent the child."[47] The exercise of this right reintroduces an adversarial element into the proceedings and limits the arbitrary authority of the judge; at a minimum, it gives the youth some input through an appropriate legal representative. Although the Supreme Court was emphatic on a juvenile's right to counsel, in the years since *In re Gault* the Court's mandate remains largely unrealized. In many states fewer than half the juveniles adjudicated as delinquents receive legal counsel. This is probably due to a combination of factors. For example, non-urban areas typically do not have a public defender service (or have ones that are inadequately staffed) and parents are often reluctant, unable or unwilling to obtain counsel at their own expense. This situation is compounded by a judicial readiness to waive the juvenile's right to counsel in order to ease the court's dockets. Finally, there is a great deal of hostility to the advocacy role in juvenile courts based on their traditional treatment-oriented philosophy.[48] As one researcher noted, "Whatever the reason and despite *In re Gault's* promise of counsel, many juveniles facing potentially coercive state action never see a lawyer, waive their right to counsel without consulting with an attorney or appreciating the legal consequences of relinquishing counsel, and face the prosecutorial power of the state alone and unaided."[49]

Self-Incrimination

In a similar note, the Supreme Court also held that "the constitutional privilege against self-incrimination is as applicable in the case of juveniles as it is with respect to adults."[50] The articulation of this right was very important because actions against juveniles were not considered criminal actions until the *In re Gault* case. Therefore, the safeguards built into the criminal justice system were ignored. This finding meant that the same basic rights an adult offender has against self-incrimination also apply to children.

Cross-Examination and Confrontation

Prior to *In re Gault* the juvenile court process was simple and informal. In most instances the juvenile and the parents met with the judge and discussed the issue that brought the child before the court. Witnesses were not usually present and the juvenile had little opportunity to confront accusers. Because of the clear abuse in the *Gault* case, the Supreme Court stated, "We now hold that, absent a valid confession, a determination of delinquency and an order of commitment to a state institution cannot be sustained in the absence of sworn testimony subjected to the opportunity for cross-examination in accordance with our law and constitutional requirements."[51]   This means that a child cannot be adjudged delinquent solely on the unsworn testimony of witnesses, and that evidence presented by witnesses must be subject to cross-examination. It would not be possible to adjudge Gault a delinquent on the basis of what Cook told the probation officer over the phone. She would have to appear in court, offer her testimony under oath and be subject to cross-examination.

In re Gault sent reverberations throughout the entire juvenile justice system, for in essence it re-wrote the rules. Predictions of disaster were echoed throughout the land, and some local authorities were convinced that the Court had gone too far. Empirical studies of compliance with *Gault* have shown that some juvenile court judges have refused to heed its requirements and some choose to observe only a few of them.[52] Other judges have complied with *Gault* in a manner designed to minimize its impact. Where there *has* been substantial compliance, one result has been an increase in legal representation of juveniles. The presence of these lawyers, however, has brought about only modest change. Rather than transforming juvenile courts into adversary-oriented tribunals, attorneys appear to have been co-opted into accepting the values of the original juvenile justice system. As a result, the system has emerged from the challenge of *Gault* with its basic values intact, although modified in theory (if not always in fact) to incorporate due process rights.

The overall trend in juvenile courts since *In re Gault* has been to make procedures more formal with the unintended consequence of strengthening their punitive element. This trend has been fed by an increasing focus on violent juvenile offenders and a growing desire to move violent crimes committed by juveniles into the criminal courts.[53] Since *Gault* most states have passed legislation to simplify the procedures and eased the criteria for waiving juvenile cases to the criminal courts. In addition, with a more active role for attorneys in juvenile court, the process itself has become more *law-driven* and less *treatment-driven*. Thus, at least in urban areas, the juvenile courts have come to more closely resemble the criminal courts. In addition, the courts have begun to impose sentences that were seldom seen before *Gault*, including restitution, community service and fines.[54] In comparing the juvenile and criminal justice systems, Dawson notes:

> We apply similar rules for both arrests of adults and for taking children into custody and for custodial interrogation. Identical rules for searches and pre-trial identification apply. There is pervasive plea bargaining in both seasons, only we are more likely to acknowledge it openly in the criminal system than the juvenile. The government is required to prove its case beyond a reasonable doubt in both systems and exclusionary rules apply with equal force. The guilt/innocence phase of court proceedings are separated from the sentencing phase in both systems, with the broad judicial discretion historically associated with the juvenile system now largely confined to the sentencing phase, as has long been true in the criminal system."[55]

The only constitutional right extended to adults but not to juveniles is the right to a jury trial. Although some states allow jury trials for juveniles as a matter of state law, the requirement to do so has not been imposed by the Supreme Court.[56]

Incarceration

Every year thousands of juveniles are taken into custody by the police; for example, on February 15, 1989 a total of 56,123 juveniles were held in confinement.[57] Although most of them are released to their parents, some are held to await court action. In the past juveniles who were held for further action were placed in adult jails, but the placement of juveniles in these jails has been an emotional issue for many years.[58] During 1982, 99,709 minors were held in adult confinement facilities throughout the state of California. The placement of juveniles in adult jails can have tragic consequences. Nationwide, juveniles commit suicide in adult jails at a rate eight times higher than when they are held in juvenile detention facilities and four times higher than in the general population.[59] For example,

> Kathy Sue Robbins, a 15-year-old girl, was booked into the Glenn County jail in August of 1983 for the offense of running away from home. She was frightened and depressed in this setting, and at her court hearing begged the judge to send her home. The judge refused, indicating the jail was an appropriate place for this young woman to cool her heels for a few days. She was returned to jail, where she hanged herself.[60]

One reason why juveniles were confined in adult jails is because there often were no other places to put them. The process of getting juveniles out of adult jails (and keeping them out in the first place) has been long and complex. Early legal efforts used the writ of habeas corpus to get individual juveniles out of jail. The key case was *White v. Reid*, which was decided in November of 1954. Isaac White, a 16-year-old boy, had been sentenced to the National Training School for Boys in 1952 for auto theft. He was paroled in 1953. Six months later he was arrested for murder, but the charges were dismissed. In spite of this, White was held in the Washington, DC jail for violating his juvenile court parole and his lawyers filed a writ of habeas corpus. The court held that since the proceedings of the juvenile court are not criminal, juveniles held under the District of Columbia Juvenile Court Act could only be confined to places where training and care could be provided, and that the Washington, DC jail was not such a place.[61]

In the 1960s the effort shifted from an individual habeas corpus action to a civil rights-oriented approach in which the constitutionality of incarcerating juveniles in adult jails was challenged on the grounds that it denied their rights under the Fourteenth Amendment (due process). Many of the cases brought before the courts argued that the conditions to which juveniles were subjected violated their due process rights, especially since many of the juveniles were confined for status offenses.[62] The courts showed a willingness to accept this argument, and in one landmark case held that confinement of a child in an adult jail, pending adjudication of the charges against the child, violated due process rights.[63] In 1974 Congress passed the Juvenile Justice and Delinquency Prevention Act, which among other things prohibited the placement of juveniles in any confinement facility where they would have sight or sound contact with adult inmates. It also prohibited the jailing of neglected children or status offenders. In addition, the Act created the Office of Juvenile Justice and Delinquency Prevention (OJJDP) within the Department of Justice. In 1980 an amendment to the Act required that states remove all juveniles from adult lockups.

Finally, there has been a major movement at the state and local levels to prohibit placing juveniles in adult jails. This movement has been supported by the National Sheriffs' Association, the National Association of Appellate Court Judges, the National Association of Counties, the American Jail Association and the National Parents and Teachers Association. In 1984 California became the first state to outlaw the use of adult jails for the confinement of minors and set limits on the detention of juveniles in adult jails or police stations. A number of other states are considering similar legislation, and it is clear that in the future local governments may have to develop alternatives to placing juveniles in jails.

DIVERSION

A historic part of the juvenile justice system has consisted of private institutions of a charitable or religious nature. Such institutions have provided an alternative to "corrections" through rehabilitation programs and even out-of-home placement. The widespread use of diversion has been based largely on the availability of such private resources. It also results from a recognition that the use of custodial institutions (and the ensuing labeling process) runs the risk of further alienating juveniles—and of ultimately delivering them to the criminal justice system when they come of age. Consequently, alternative ways of handling juvenile cases have been developed and their use widely encouraged. For example, "Choice" is a diversion program in Baltimore, Maryland run by young adults willing to spend a year or more supervising troubled youths who live in some of the city's most blighted neighborhoods. The volunteers are on call 24 hours a day and make daily contact with children assigned to them by public agencies; in fact, they make contact with their charges three to five times a day.[64] "Choice" is an intensive program devoted to the well-being of children. It has received wide acclaim and has proven to be a genuine boon to the juvenile justice system in Baltimore.[65] Juveniles who engage in delinquent activities, especially those of a less serious nature, are routinely sent to a diversion service that in turn refers them to some kind of treatment, counseling or relief agency. This is technically a voluntary process, although refusal to take part might result in a reconsideration of the decision not to proceed more formally in juvenile court.

Diversion programs, often called youth service bureaus, have been established in many parts of the country. In 1973 the National Advisory Commission on Criminal Justice Standards and Goals formally recommended that youth service bureaus be established to divert juveniles from the justice system.[66] There is some irony to the fact that systems have been established to divert juveniles from the juvenile justice system, which was itself established to divert them from the criminal justice system. Diversion programs comprise a very large proportion of juvenile justice "outcomes." In 1991, for example, out of a total of 96,910 minors under the control of juvenile courts, 51,753 (or 53%) were in nonresidential programs.[67]

The use of diversion seems to recognize that the juvenile justice system doles out far more punishment than treatment, and that often the best interests of the child and society are better served when the matter is taken out of the court's hands altogether. A child who is placed in a program where problems can be diagnosed and treated may be more likely to fare well. In spite of the "soft" language of the juvenile courts, juvenile proceedings are still essentially legal matters; like adult courts, the most that juvenile courts have to offer is a variation in punishment. If the child's problem requires something other than punishment (even though the state does not like to refer to its juvenile treatment programs by that name), it will not usually be forthcoming unless it is provided by some agency outside the courts.

Many of the diversion projects throughout the United States have been quite successful. The chief problem they face is in the screening of juveniles so that only those who are likely to benefit from treatment will be admitted. Juveniles with a history of serious crimes, especially crimes of violence, are not usually welcome in these programs. There are relatively few diversion or treatment programs that can provide the kind of intensive psychological or psychiatric treatment needed by such juveniles. Many of the juveniles accused of those kinds of crimes are discharged to the criminal justice system and tried as adults—especially if they are on the legal borderline with respect to age.

DECRIMINALIZATION

Status offenses have been a matter of considerable concern and criticism over the years. Status offenses, as previously noted, are grounds for delinquency based on acts that would not be crimes if they were committed by an adult. Examples include truancy, running away from home, curfew violations and some sexual misconduct. Sometimes included under the general category of *incorrigibility* and at other times spelled out as separate grounds for delinquency are some of the more purely moralistic offenses, such as smoking, swearing or drinking alcoholic beverages and other forms of substance abuse.

Contemporary values are no longer in accord with some of the more blatantly moralistic grounds for juvenile delinquency. Also, the realization that the juvenile justice system has not been able to diagnose and correct delinquency has caused many professionals in the area to re-examine the validity and value of using these behaviors as the basis for assigning the label "delinquent." As a result there has been a major trend away from using status offenses against young people. A national commission has recommended the deletion of truancy as a ground for delinquency.[68] The board of directors of the National Council on Crime and Delinquency (among other groups) has advocated the removal of *all* status offenses from the juvenile codes.[69] As a result of the trend toward decriminalization, many states have revised their juvenile codes. Some have limited their codes to such basic grounds as the commission of a crime, habitual truancy or incorrigibility. For example, in Pennsylvania the juvenile courts no longer have jurisdiction over status offenders, and in California status offenders are referred to the juvenile court only as a last resort. However, in the Midwest in the late 1980s status offenses were still the most common type of case handled by the juvenile courts.[70] More liberal attitudes towards the consumption of alcohol and the use of recreational drugs also have shortened the reach of the juvenile courts.

For over 20 years there has been a concerted effort to "deinstitutionalize" status offenders, that is, to remove noncriminal juvenile offenders from secure detention and correctional facilities and treat them through community-based resources. This effort was a major part of the 1974 Juvenile Justice and Delinquency Prevention Act and has been a guiding force in juvenile justice policy since the 1970s. Federal funding has been used as an incentive to encourage states to deinstitutionalize status offenders and to encourage local jurisdictions to establish community-based alternatives for dealing with status offenders.[71]

DEINSTITUTIONALIZATION

Deinstitutionalization, another contemporary trend, stems from the belief that many juveniles emerge from correctional institutions more delinquent than when they entered. Incarceration frequently paves the way for subsequent confinement in other juvenile institutions and adult prisons by producing youths who become both dependent and "institutionalized." Indeed, many adult felons are "graduates" of juvenile correctional institutions. Unfortunately, reality has fallen short of the theory behind juvenile correctional institutions. Strong criticism has been raised against the practice of committing youths to juvenile correctional institutions. The number of juveniles in state custody is not small: as of January 1, 1991, a total of 36,852 juveniles were confined in state and local residential correctional facilities. This amounts to 38 percent of all juveniles under the control of juvenile courts.[72]

Some of these institutions have been plagued with serious problems, including ineffectiveness. For example, the District of Columbia maintains a minimum-security youth detention center at Cedar Knoll (near Laurel, Maryland) where security is so lax that 177 inmates escaped between January of 1990 and March of 1992. According to one report, "What they run away from is a place so neglected, run-down and failing in its primary mission to rehabilitate delinquent boys that a D.C. Superior Court judge ordered the city to shut it down more than five years ago."[73] In 1973 the National Advisory Commission on Criminal Justice Standards and Goals recommended that no more training schools be built and that existing schools be phased out.[74] In spite of this recommendation, in 1991 there were still 130 such facilities, housing over 23,000 juveniles.[75]

In some states deinstitutionalization has resulted from legislative acts that permit the sending of fewer juveniles (or fewer categories of youths, e.g., dependent or neglected children) to such institutions. Other states have chosen to close institutions or limit their use. In the early 1970s Massachusetts replaced its large training schools with a network of smaller programs for violent and serious offenders and began to use community programs for the majority of their other juvenile offenders. Thus far, the Massachusetts Department of Youth Services has been highly effective in its approach and has become a model for other jurisdictions.[76] In virtually all states there is some evidence that juvenile court judges have lost their faith in these institutions. The trend, however, is not universal; some states (including California, Illinois, Ohio and Texas) are making greater use of such facilities than others.

THE "LEAST DISRUPTIVE ALTERNATIVE" APPROACH

The foregoing trends (particularly deinstitutionalization) are complemented by the move toward community-based facilities.[77] Prompting this move was the lack of success of correctional institutions and the isolation from family and community that is fostered by their typically remote locations. Community-based facilities are usually small in size, specialized in nature and operated by private organizations or local governments. They may include nonresidential treatment centers, residential facilities, foster homes or local juvenile detention centers.

Disillusionment with the inefficacy of the juvenile justice system also has encouraged the development of an attitude approach known as the *least disruptive alternative*.[78] Supporters of this approach believe the juvenile justice system has counter-productive results, and that many juveniles will stop being delinquent *without* intervention by the juvenile justice system. As a result, they favor as little disruption of their lives as possible, consistent with the need to protect society and the child, and recommend the absolute minimum amount of intervention into the life of the child. It might be argued that these reform measures are designed to enable the juvenile justice system to achieve its objectives without running counter to the juvenile court's values of protection, compassion and individualized treatment. The point is to make these values attainable. For example, due process and its concomitant fairness may produce a child who is more amenable to treatment. Diversion, decriminalization, deinstitutionalization and community-based alternatives are all attempts to bring the system into accord with contemporary values and to enable it to adapt to the challenges which confront it.

JUVENILE JUSTICE:
THE COMMON VIEW

There are many views of juvenile justice. The preceding paragraphs largely concern the legal dimension of juvenile justice and point out the major legal/philosophical problems involved in dealing with youth crime. A less legalistic and more common view reflects the opinion of a large segment of the American public.[79] This view sees uncontrolled young people intent on destroying both themselves and their society. Based on highly publicized cases that appear in the news and entertainment media, as well as on the fear of crime, this view tends to define juvenile delinquents as violent offenders who remain outside the control of the courts—either criminal or juvenile. Although there are such people, they actually represent a very small proportion of the juvenile court's caseload, and by the time they mature in their misconduct, they have "aged out" of the juvenile justice system and are dealt with by the criminal courts. Moreover, when juveniles do commit serious crimes of violence, they are usually *not* dealt with leniently:

ITEM: One Christmas Eve a 17-year-old boy left a party with his date, a girl with whom he was casually acquainted. After leaving the party, he raped her, beat her to death with a tire iron and set her body on fire with gasoline. He was found the next day in near zero-degree weather, still obviously under the influence of drugs. He was sentenced to life in prison.

ITEM: A 16-year-old Texas youth who had been in an argument with another youth cut his opponent's spinal column with a linoleum knife, permanently paralyzing the victim. He said he did it on purpose, that he wanted to hurt the victim "bad." He was held in a juvenile detention facility until he was 17 and then tried on the felony charge of maiming. He was convicted and sentenced to 20 years in the state prison.

As is often the case in the criminal justice system, the question of class and status plays an important role in outcomes. There is broad agreement that minority youth are overrepresented at all stages of the juvenile justice system as compared to their numbers in the general population (which is probably at least partially explained by the disproportionate involvement of minority juveniles in serious and violent crimes). In fact, race is probably the single best predictor of arrest, incarceration and release—even when the influences of other variables are accounted for.[80] For example, in 1982 black males represented about 14 percent of all males under the jurisdiction of the juvenile courts but 39 percent of all incarcerated male juveniles (see Table 11.1).

Table 11.1

Juveniles Under State Control in Agency-Operated Residential Facilities (as of January 1, 1991)

Race/Ethnicity	Number	Percent
Black	15,796	43%
White	11,878	32%
Hispanic	5,576	15%
Other	3,602	10%
Total	36,852	100%

Source: George M. Camp and Camille Graham Camp, *The Corrections Yearbook 1991* (South Salem, NY: Criminal Justice Institute, 1991), 7-8.

It is very difficult to say just what is fair and what is not; however, it is clear that many factors influence how a juvenile will be treated in any given case. What is clear is that many juveniles are involved in serious misconduct and it is difficult to match problems with the appropriate remedies.

Many people concerned with controlling crime point to the often appalling crimes of violence committed by juveniles, the massive vandalism of both private and public property, the terrorizing of elderly people by juveniles and increased gang violence as evidence that the juvenile justice system should control crime.[81] Adherents of this *crime control model* view the rehabilitative attempts of juvenile courts as a failure and argue that the juvenile justice system shelters, permits and even encourages youths to commit criminal acts that they know to be wrong.[82] Those who subscribe to the crime control model feel that juvenile offenders should be quickly punished and isolated from the law-abiding community rather than "coddled" (which they see as strengthening their deviant behavior). Proponents have great faith in the philosophy that punishment will change juvenile behavior and thus they favor the isolation of juvenile offenders in county jails, detention centers, training schools and local correctional facilities. Because of demands for control of juvenile crime, some courts have set bail, broadened the grounds for waiver to criminal court and instituted mandatory sentencing laws. Unlike due process, diversion, decriminalization and community-based facilities, such practices run directly counter to traditional juvenile court values. Rather than helping to realize the ideal of individualized and compassionate treatment, crime control model practices strengthen already existing tendencies toward the bureaucratic processing similar to that used in the criminal justice system. Adherents of the crime control model, both within and outside the juvenile justice system, gained strength during the 1970s and 1980s and have been influential in the growing punishment orientation against older juveniles (especially those accused of crimes of violence). This has caused the juvenile justice system to lose some of its distinctiveness and become more like the criminal justice system.

This crime control movement seems to have been fed by the apparent failure of treatment programs, whereby rehabilitation appears to have been more an ideal than a reality. During the 1960s a great deal of federal and private money was spent on delinquency prevention programs in such places as New York, Illinois, Michigan, Massachusetts, California and Utah. When evaluated, few of these programs were found to have had any positive impact and some were found to be counterproductive.[83] Although some efforts have been successful and a great deal has been learned, a widespread sentiment has arisen holding that treatment (whether in a correctional institution or within community-based programs) is not effective in reducing delinquency.[84] It now seems likely that at least part of the reason for the failure of these programs was due to underfunding and the short-term approach many of them took. Also, since treatment programs are so closely linked to diversion, the juvenile courts have not had much influence over the programs themselves.

The resurgence of violence by youth gangs and reports of drug-related violent crimes by juveniles has alarmed the public and fed its fear. Media reports of recreational homicides, drive-by shootings, guns being brought into the schools and other serious events have aroused public concern—a concern that seems to be taking the form of an increasingly punitive attitude towards delinquent juveniles. However, it is worth noting that only about 6 percent of the juvenile court's total delinquency caseload involves violent crimes; of these, aggravated assault accounted for one-half, robbery for over one-third, violent sex offenses for just over 10 percent and criminal homicide for only 2 percent.[85]

JUVENILE JUSTICE:
AN ALTERNATIVE VIEW

It is tempting to be swayed by the newsworthy crimes committed by delinquents. Very seldom do we have the chance to look behind delinquent acts to examine what has really happened. We often find young criminals who have gone through incredible hardships. The juvenile courts constantly see tragedy that many people would find incomprehensible: children who are abused, neglected, frightened and/or emotionally disturbed—many of whom are unwanted. Schools and social service agencies often express concern about the "problem" of such children while showing remarkable indifference to the children themselves. Most of these problems end up being dealt with by the juvenile justice system.

> Example: After six-year-old Emily reported that her father sexually abused both her and her 10-year-old sister while their mother cooked dinner, she was placed in foster care. Three years earlier, after high levels of lead were found in her blood her parents resisted health department efforts to rid their home of the metal and court papers described their house as filthy, unsanitary and insect-infested. Three years later inspectors found insects crawling in a bowl of soup, trash containers overflowing, food spoiling on a table, bare and broken mattresses, and pornographic pictures strewn on the floor of the house. Her younger brother's medical reports indicate he may have suffered anal penetration.[86]

It is little wonder that some neglected and abused children lash back violently at society. Products of an inadequate (or in some cases, nonexistent) private control system and a public control system that is not yet ready to receive them, such juveniles break forth on society in violence and fury. The absence of love, warmth, affection and positive human contact can take a toll on the human organism. Usually, the first inkling we have of this is when these children bring their problems to school; unfortunately, most schools are either unable or unwilling to deal with these problems. Ultimately they come before the juvenile courts, and although they are often able to deal effectively with some of the less serious cases, they are not consistent even in this respect.

JUVENILE JUSTICE AND THE COMMUNITY

The problems built into our juvenile justice system present a seemingly endless series of dilemmas. Criminal acts committed by juveniles are usually not prosecuted as such so that (hopefully) the juvenile can be redeemed, yet the juvenile justice system frequently has been unable to provide the kinds of remedies that are needed. It would seem that more often than not, nothing is done: the child remains at liberty to "age out" into the criminal justice system. When the state does intervene, it often does so for offenses that are either not criminal in their own right or which are peculiar to children. How does all this affect community attitudes? In the absence of empirical data, the answer to such a question must remain speculative; however, there is good reason to believe that many citizens are unhappy with the ineffectiveness of the juvenile justice system and public displeasure is likely to focus on the criminal justice system as a whole.

The police are well aware of the restrictions imposed on them in dealing with juvenile cases, and juvenile courts themselves realize that there is little that can be done. Perhaps an effective approach would be to seek greater community involvement in the juvenile justice system. If the misconduct of many juveniles represents hostility based on underlying unhappiness or frustration, then dealing with the underlying problem should eliminate much of the misconduct. There are two problems with this approach, however. The first is diagnosis and the second is patience. In considering diagnosis, it may be difficult and time-consuming to find out exactly why a given juvenile behaves in a disruptive fashion; it is apt to require time and money that may not be available. As for patience, many people and groups simply do not have much of it. Those who work with an offender need their efforts reinforced by appropriate responses on the part of the offender; when such reinforcement is not forthcoming, frustration gives rise to aggression and the helping relationship is likely to end. Although this is only natural, it means that those children who need the most help may also be the ones least likely to get it.

In the final analysis, people want "closure" for their problems—a solution. In many cases, they would rather have a bad solution than no solution at all. When community members see problems with juveniles (especially when the juveniles differ significantly from them on variables such as race and class), they are apt to be open to "solutions" that they would not find appropriate in cases closer to home. It is easier to see juveniles from "the other side of the town" waived to the criminal courts or sent to juvenile detention facilities. Perhaps this is the legacy of our once widely held view that crime is the domain of the "dangerous class" or perhaps it simply represents indifference to those who differ from us.

Perhaps much of the problem with juveniles is that the youth culture, which is constantly changing, tends to be so different from that of adults. As a result, many adults measure the behavior of young people against an inappropriate or outdated set of standards. When compounded by cultural differences, the resulting perceptions can be even more at variance. Some adults place responsibility on the children to prove themselves worthy of being "legitimate" members of society rather than accepting the view that adult society should be charged with shaping the child into a responsible adult. It might also be the case that the community has placed too many expectations on schools and too few on the family, and when failure results, both the child and the criminal justice system get blamed.

The institution of the family itself has undergone major change during the past generation. Some of these changes almost certainly correlate with the problem of delinquency. For example, the proportion of one-parent families increased from 12.9 percent of all families with children in 1970 to 27.3 in 1988. In addition, families headed by a single parent (usually the mother) made up 21.7 percent of white families with children in 1988, compared with 59.4 percent of black families with children and 33.6 percent of Hispanic families with children. Single-parent families are much more likely to be poor: the average family income in 1988 for children under 18 living with their single mother was only $11,989, compared with $23,919 for those living with their father only and $40,067 for those living with both parents. Many of the children in single female-headed households are born out of wedlock; in fact, childbearing for unmarried women has reached the highest level ever recorded in the United States. Rates stand at 80.9 per 1,000 unmarried black women and 23.2 per 1,000 unmarried white women between the ages of 15 and 44.[87]

SUMMARY

The status of children has changed considerably over time, and it has only been within recent generations that society has made a significant effort to consider their emotional and developmental needs and to incorporate those needs into a separate justice system. Juvenile justice in America grew out of earlier English practices in which children above the age of seven were treated as adults if they were formally accused of a crime. This was part of a system that ultimately led social reformers to seek better ways of dealing with children in need of protection, accused of criminal acts or guilty of status offenses. At first, confined children were simply segregated from adult offenders, but by the end of the nineteenth century an alternative juvenile justice system began to emerge. This alternative system parallels the criminal justice system, but is based on a non-punitive, non-adversarial approach to juvenile offenders in which the court seeks to act as an interested parent on behalf of the child. Its goal is not to punish, but rather to set the child "on the right track." The juvenile justice system was designed to be informal, supportive and dedicated to salvaging youths who had gotten into trouble. Many feel, however, that this alternative system has fallen short of its lofty goals.

In terms of its processes, the juvenile offender (or the dependent or neglected child) comes to the attention of the juvenile court through an intake process that can be initiated by the police, school authorities or even parents. The merits of a child's case are examined and efforts are made to dispose of the case with the least possible intervention into the child's life as long as it is consistent with the child's needs and those of the community. If the matter is serious, the juvenile court must consider whether to waive the case directly to the criminal courts. If it retains jurisdiction, a formal hearing may be held. The youth is not "convicted" in the conventional case, but may be adjudged "delinquent." In that case, the court must determine whether the child should be released back into the community under some kind of supervision or placed under state custody in some kind of residential facility.

The juvenile justice system came under considerable criticism because in many instances the juvenile received neither the due process afforded adult offenders nor the solicitous care intended by the founders of the system. As a result of the Supreme Court's decision in *In re Gault*, procedural safeguards were introduced into the juvenile justice system, but their application has been erratic. One effect of these safeguards has been the conversion of juvenile court cases into more adversarial hearings. Most lawyers who represent youths, however, tend to be less aggressive on behalf of their clients than they would be in criminal cases.

The primary thrust in juvenile justice in the 1980s has been away from charging juveniles with status offenses. The movement has been characterized by the four "Ds"—due process, diversion, decriminalization and deinstitutionalization. The basic problem in juvenile justice is the same as that of the criminal justice system: the conflict between the due process and crime control models. In the former, the rights of the accused are paramount, whereas the safety of society is most important in the latter. Juvenile justice is a complex and difficult area; attempting to design remedies around age offers little guidance, and many of the problems are actually social and psychological maladies for which legal remedies are wholly inappropriate.

DISCUSSION QUESTIONS

1. Why have children historically been held in such low regard? Has this really changed?

2. Should the same courts have jurisdiction over delinquency, dependency and status offenses? If not, how should these areas be handled?

3. What is the difference between a crime, an act of delinquency and a status offense?

4. How did the use of the doctrine of *parens patriae* develop? Why is it important to the juvenile justice system?

5. How does the juvenile justice process differ from the criminal justice process? Are these real differences, or differences in name only?

6. How does a "person in need of supervision" differ from a "delinquent"?

7. In some states children below the age of waiver are held in juvenile facilities until they reach the proper age and are then transferred to adult criminal courts. Is this fair? Why or why not?

8. What was the significance of *In re Gault*? Has the juvenile justice system lived up to its requirements?

9. Do you think the increasing "formalization" of juvenile courts will ultimately erode their basic philosophy and leave them more like the criminal courts?

10. Why might it sometimes be advisable to incarcerate juveniles in adult jails?

11. How has the focus on removing juveniles from adult jails evolved over the years?

12. How does diversion in the juvenile justice system work? Is it a realistic alternative to incarceration?

13. How has public opinion on status offenses changed since the 1970s? What impact has this had on the juvenile justice system?

14. Should juveniles who commit serious crimes of violence be handled as adults?

15. Are there any differences in representation by race or ethnic group in the juvenile justice process? If so, what accounts for these differences?

16. Is the trend toward deinstitutionalization likely to have any impact on how serious violators are handled? If so, what will that impact be?

17. Do you think the average community is realistic in its understanding and expectations of the juvenile justice system?

18. How does the crime control model of justice influence public expectations of the juvenile justice system? Is this fair?

19. Is the changing youth culture also changing the public's expectations of the juvenile justice system? Do you think we are more liberal in what we are willing to tolerate from juveniles?

20. What is the future of juvenile justice?

REFERENCES

1 Will Durant and Ariel Durant, *The Story of Civilization*, Part VIII: "The Age of Louis XIV" (New York: Simon and Schuster, 1963), 257.

2 Will Durant and Ariel Durant, *The Story of Civilization*, Part X: "Rousseau and Revolution" (New York: Simon and Schuster, 1967), 678.

3 L.A. Parry, *The History of Torture in England* (Montclair, NJ: Patterson Smith, 1975), 17.

4 *The Edinburgh Review* (1819), cited in Parry, *The History of Torture in England*, 17.

5 L.A. Parry, *The History of Torture in England*, 15.

6 Wayne R. LaFave and Austin W. Scott, Jr., *Handbook on Criminal Law* (St. Paul: West Publishing Co., 1972), 351-352.

7 Anthony Platt, *The Child Savers* (Chicago: University of Chicago Press, 1969), 202.

8 Mark Soler, "Litigation on Behalf of Children in Adult Jails," *Crime and Delinquency* 34: 2 (April 1988), 190-208.

9 Charles P. Smith, David J. Berkman, Warren M. Fraser and John Sutton, U.S. Department of Justice, Office of Juvenile Justice and Delinquency Prevention, *Reports of the National Juvenile Justice Assessment Centers* (Washington, DC: U.S. Government Printing Office, April 1980), 26.

10 Lawrence R. Widman, "The Massachusetts Stubborn Child Law: Law and Order in the Home," *Family Law Quarterly* 6:1 (1972), 33-58.

11 Lee E. Teitelbaum and Aidan R. Gough, *Beyond Control: Status Offenders in the Juvenile Court* (Cambridge, MA: Ballinger Publishing Company, 1977); see especially, Lee E. Teitelbaum and Leslie J. Harris, "Some Historical Perspectives on Governmental Regulation of Children and Parents," 1-44.

12 Smith et al., *Reports of the National Juvenile Justice Assessment Centers*, 6.

13 *Ex parte Crouse*, 4 Whart. 9 (Pa. 1838).

14 Theodore N. Ferdinand, "Juvenile Delinquency or Juvenile Justice: Which Came First?," *Criminology* 27 (1989), 79-106.

15 Theodore N. Ferdinand, "History Overtakes the Juvenile Justice System," *Crime and Delinquency* 37:2 (1991), 186-203.

16 Ferdinand, "History Overtakes the Juvenile Justice System," 206.

17 Some scholars assert that the juvenile justice movement was an attempt by the middle class to impose its values on immigrants and the poor. See Anthony Platt, "The Rise of the Child Saving Movement: A Study in Social Policy and Correctional Reform," *The Annals of the American Academy of Political and Social Science* 381 (January 1969), 21-38.

[18] Society for the Reformation of Juvenile Delinquents, "The Founding of the New York House of Refuge," in Paul Lerman, *Delinquency and Social Policy* (New York: Praeger Press, 1970), 12-14.

[19] Ferdinand, "History Overtakes the Juvenile Justice System," 209.

[20] LaMar T. Empey, "The Social Construction of Childhood Delinquency and Social Reform," in Malcolm Klein, ed., *The Juvenile Justice System* (Beverly Hills: Sage Publications, 1976), 47.

[21] Robert O. Dawson, "The Future of Juvenile Justice: Is It Time to Abolish the System?" *The Journal of Criminal Law and Criminology* 81:1 (Spring 1990), 136-155.

[22] For two accounts of early juvenile court procedure, see Julian W. Mack, "The Juvenile Court," *Harvard Law Review* 23:104; and Harvey H. Baker, "Procedure of the Boston Juvenile Court," *The Survey* 23:643, as reprinted in Frederick L. Faust and Paul J. Brantigham, eds., *Juvenile Justice Philosophy* (St. Paul: West Publishing Co., 1974), 150-169.

[23] LeFave and Scott, *Handbook on Criminal Law*, 354.

[24] See also "The In's and Out's of the Juvenile Justice Process," in U.S. Department of Justice, National Institute for Juvenile Justice and Delinquency Prevention, *Facts About Youth and Delinquency: A Citizen's Guide to Juvenile Justice* (Washington, DC: U.S. Government Printing Office, November 1982).

[25] For a treatment of the police-juvenile relationship, see Robert W. Kobetz and Betty W. Bosorge, *Juvenile Justice Administration* (Gaithersburg, MD: International Association of Chiefs of Police, 1973).

[26] See, for example, John T. Whitehead and Steven P. Lab, *Juvenile Justice: An Introduction* (Cincinnati: Anderson Publishing Co., 1990), particularly Chapter 7, "The Police and Juveniles," 211-241.

[27] National Institute of Justice, "The In's and Out's of the Juvenile Justice Process."

[28] For more on the right to bail bond in the federal system, see *Durst v. United States*, 434 U.S. 542, 98 S. Ct. 849, 55 L. Ed. 2d 14 (1978).

[29] Howard N. Snyder et al., U.S. Department of Justice, Office of Juvenile Justice and Delinquency Prevention, *Juvenile Court Statistics 1987* (Washington, DC: U.S. Government Printing Office, 1973), 17.

[30] M. Marvin Finkelstem, et al., *Prosecution in the Juvenile Courts: Guideline for the Future* (Washington, DC: U.S. Government Printing Office, 1973), 17.

[31] The juvenile court continues to be strongly influenced by the doctrine of *parens patriae*. For example, challenges to state juvenile laws on the basis of equal protection have not been successful (see, for example, *Martarella v. Kelley*, 349 F. Supp. 575 (S.D.N.Y. 1972) and *In re Blakes*, 4 Ill. App. 3d 567, 281 N.E.2d 454 (1972).

[32] W.V. Stapleton and L.A. Teitelbaum, *In Defense of Youth: A Study of the Role of Counsel in American Juvenile Courts.* (New York: Russell Sage Foundation), 1972.

[33] Clemens Bartollas, Stuart J. Miller and Simon Dinitz, *Juvenile Victimization: The Institutional Paradox* (New York: Halsted Press, A Sage Publication, 1976).

[34] See, for example, Paul Tappan, "Treatment Without Trial," *Social Problems* 24 (1946), 306-311.

[35] Robert W. Balch, "The Medical Model of Delinquency," *Crime and Delinquency* (April 1975), 116-117; Michael H. Longley, "The Juvenile Court and Individualized Treatment," *Crime and Delinquency* (January 1972), 81-82; Martin T. Silver, "The New York City Family Court: A Law Guardian's Overview," *Crime and Delinquency* (January 1972), 96.

[36] See, for example, Lisa Aversa Richette, *The Throw Away Children* (New York: Dell Publishing Co., 1970).

[37] Martin T. Silver, "The New York City Family Court: A Law Guardian's Overview," 95.

[38] *Kent v. United States*, 383 U.S. 541, 86 S. Ct. 1045, 16 L. Ed. 2d 84 (1966).

[39] *In re Gault*, 387 U.S. 1, 87 S. Ct. 1428, 18 L. Ed. 2d 527 (1967) at 21. For a strong argument that procedural due process rights should apply to dependent-neglect proceedings, see Diane M. Faber, "Dependent-Neglect Proceedings: A Case for Procedural Due Process," *Duquesne Law Review* (1971), 651-664.

[40] *In re Gault*, 17-21.

[41] *Kent v. United States*.

[42] Dawson, "The Future of Juvenile Justice," 143.

[43] See especially Jeffrey Fagan and Elizabeth Piper Deschenes, "Determinants of Judicial Waiver Decisions for Violent Juvenile Offenders," *Journal of Criminal Law and Criminology* 81:2 (1990), 314-347.

[44] Dean J. Champion, "Teenage Felons and Waiver Hearings: Some Recent Trends," *Crime and Delinquency* 35:4 (1989), 577-585.

[45] *In re Gault*.

[46] *In re Gault*, 33-34.

[47] *In re Gault*, 41.

[48] Barry C. Feld, "*In re Gault* Revisited: A Cross-State Comparison of Right to Counsel in Juvenile Court," *Crime and Delinquency* 34:4 (1988), 393-424.

[49] Feld, "*In re Gault* Revisited," 395.

[50] *In re Gault*, 55.

[51] *In re Gault*, 57.

[52] Norman G. Kittel, "Juvenile Justice—Twelve Years After *Gault*," Paper presented to the Academy of Criminal Justice Sciences, Cincinnati, OH, March 14-16, 1979.

[53] Jeffrey Fagan and Elizabeth Piper Deschenes, "Determinants of Judicial Waiver Decisions for Violent Juvenile Offenders," 32.

[54] Dawson, "The Future of Juvenile Justice," 138. See also Anne Larason Schneider and Jean Shumway Warner, U.S. Department of Justice, Office of Juvenile Justice and Delinquency Prevention, *National Trends in Juvenile Restitution Programming* (Washington, DC: U.S. Government Printing Office, July 1989).

[55] Dawson, "The Future of Juvenile Justice," 139-140.

[56] See *McKeiver v. Pennsylvania*, 403 U.S. 528 (1971).

[57] Barbara Allen-Hagen, U.S. Department of Justice, Office of Juvenile Justice and Delinquency Prevention, *Children in Custody 1989* (Washington, DC: U.S. Government Printing Office, January 1991), 1.

[58] See, for example, Children's Defense Fund, *Children in Adult Jails* (Washington, DC: Research Project, 1976) and R.C. Sarri, *Under Lock and Key: Juveniles in Jails and Detention* (Ann Arbor, MI: University of Michigan, National Assessment of Juvenile Corrections, 1974).

[59] Robert W. Sweet, Jr., "Juvenile Jailing: Federal Compliance," *American Jails* (March/April 1991), 93.

[60] *Robbins v. Glenn County*, No. CIVS-85-0675 RAR (U.S.D.C., E.D. Calif., 1986). Cited in Mark Soler, "Litigation on Behalf of Children in Adult Jails," *Crime and Delinquency* 34:2 (April 1988), 190-208.

[61] Soler, "Litigation on Behalf of Children in Adult Jails."

[62] Soler, "Litigation on Behalf of Children in Adult Jails," 193-197.

[63] *D.B. v. Tewksbury*, 545 F. Supp. 896 (D. Or. 1982)

[64] George F. Will, "God Don't Make Junk," *The Washington Post*, 29 March 1992, C7.

[65] See Michael Riley, "Corridors of Agony," *Time*, 27 January 1992, 48-55.

[66] Donald R. Cressey and Robert A. McDermot, *Diversion From the Juvenile Justice System* (Washington, DC: U.S. Government Printing Office, 1973), 70-81.

[67] George M. Camp and Camille Graham Camp, *The Corrections Yearbook 1991* (South Salem, NY: Criminal Justice Institute, 1991), 3.

[68] National Advisory Commission, *Community Crime Prevention* (Washington, DC: U.S. Government Printing Office, 1973), 70-81.

[69] National Council on Crime and Delinquency (Board of Directors), "Jurisdiction Over Status Offenses Should Be Removed From the Juvenile Court," *Crime and Delinquency* (April 1975), 97-99; President's Commission on Law Enforcement and Administration of Justice, *The Challenge of Crime in a Free Society* (Washington, DC: U.S. Government Printing Office, 1969), 55-89.

[70] Feld, "*In re Gault* Revisited," 400.

[71] Verne L. Speirs, "Assessing the Effects of the Deinstitutionalization of Status Offenders," *Juvenile Justice Bulletin* (January 1989).

[72] Camp and Camp, *The Corrections Yearbook 1991*, 4-5.

[73] Keith Harriston, "Calamity of Cedar Knoll," *The Washington Post*, 30 March 1992, D1, D5.

[74] National Advisory Commission on Criminal Justice Standards and Goals, *Corrections* (Washington DC: U.S. Government Printing Office, 1973), 360.

[75] Camp and Camp, *The Corrections Yearbook 1991*, 27-30.

[76] Barry Krisberg, James Austin and Patricia A. Steele, *Unlocking Juvenile Corrections: Evaluation the Massachusetts Department of Youth Services*, 2 vols. (San Francisco: National Council on Crime and Delinquency, 1989).

[77] Andrew Rutherford and Osman Bengur, *National Evaluation Program of Community-Based Alternatives to Juvenile Incarceration* (Washington, DC: U.S. Government Printing Office, 1976).

[78] Edwin M. Schur, *Radical Non-Intervention: Rethinking the Delinquency Problem* (Englewood Cliffs, NJ: Prentice-Hall, 1973).

[79] See, for example, P.D. McAnany, D. Thompson and D. Fogel, eds., *Probation and Justice: Reconsideration of Mission* (Cambridge, MA: Oelgeschlager, Gunn and Hain, 1984), especially 65-99. See also Paul Gendreau and Robert R. Ross, "Revivification of Rehabilitation: Evidence From the 1980s" *Justice Quarterly* 4 (1987), 349-407.

[80] Barry Krisberg, Ira Schwartz, Gideon Fishman, Avi Eisikovits and Edna Guttman, "The Incarceration of Minority Youth," University of Minnesota, Center for the Study of Youth: Policy of the Hubert H. Humphrey Institute of Public Affairs, May 1986, 3.

[81] Walter B. Miller, *Violence by Youth Gangs and Youth Groups as a Crime Problem in Major American Cities* (Washington, DC: U.S. Government Printing Office, 1975). See also Ronald Huff, "Youth Gangs and Public Policy," *Crime and Delinquency* 35:4 (1989), 524-537.

[82] The basic crime control model is set forth by Herbert Packer, *The Limits of Criminal Sanctions* (Palo Alto, CA: Stanford University Press, 1968), 149-173.

[83] Ferdinand, "History Overtakes the Juvenile Justice System," 212-215.

[84] Robert Martinson, "What Works: Questions and Answers About Prison Reform," *Public Interest* 32 (1974), 22-54.

[85] Verne L. Speirs, "The Juvenile Court's Response to Violent Crime," *Juvenile Justice Bulletin* (January 1989).

[86] Riley, "Corridors of Agony," 51.

[87] Spencer Rich, "A Generation Alters Notion of U.S. Family," *The Washington Post*, 5 September 1989, A12.

Photo Credit: Tony O'Brien, Frost Publishing Group, Ltd.

Chapter 12

CORRECTIONS

Concepts and Contexts

The concept of "corrections" has evolved slowly and painfully over the ages. Most of what we take for granted today is a far cry from what was accepted in past generations. Corrections began as personal vengeance, and was gradually taken over: first by the victim's family, then by the community, then by the church and finally by the state. The concept of corrections almost always has embodied various forms of physical punishment and monetary compensation. Physical punishment, which grew out of the goal of vengeance, eventually receded in favor of fines and confinement. In recent years society shifted its focus from *punishment* to *prevention through rehabilitation*. Even though the philosophy of corrections has changed over time, its previous goals and values remain imbedded in current practices.

As Parry has noted, "Uncivilized man was by nature a cruel animal. His environment compelled him to be brutal and unscrupulous. If he wished to survive in the struggle for existence it was impossible for him to be anything else. As civilization progressed, man became perhaps less brutal, but many centuries were to pass before even the worst of the cruel tendencies of the human race became subdued."[1] In ancient society, wrongs committed against an individual were redressed either by the victim or by relatives of the victim. Vengeance was both a necessity for survival and a matter of honor, especially since ancient societies had few formal means for dealing with interpersonal conflicts. These so-called "blood feuds" could be complicated; for example, in ancient England they involved all kinsmen to the sixth cousin.[2] Since communities were small and isolated, and intermarriage among families was the rule rather than the exception, a blood feud could result in great confusion over who was obligated to whom over what.

Blood feuds were a personal matter; this meant that retribution had to be initiated either by the injured party or blood relatives. In fact, the concept of "casting the first stone" refers to the ancient obligation of the injured party to throw the first stone in the execution of a death penalty. However, since vengeance invited more of the same and could quickly get out of hand, it was essential for ancient communities to limit and regulate blood feuds lest the entire community eventually became embroiled in an endless conflict. For this reason the severity of revenge in blood feuds was offset by the use of compensations. In some cases those accused of harming others could avoid death or physical punishment by compensating the victim or the victim's family. Eventually, two forces took vengeance out of the hands of the individual and placed it with the government. One was the influence of Christianity; the other was feudalism (and the eventual development of the nation state).

THE INFLUENCE OF CHRISTIANITY

Christianity embodies a system of ethics that includes the Ten Commandments (absorbed from Judaism through the Old Testament), scriptural teachings on the human being's "fall from grace" and subsequent redemption through Christ. Christianity established and nurtured systems of sin, virtue, punishment and penance. It was (and is) a highly systematic theology that organizes belief across class lines and (like all religions) requires the acceptance of certain dogma. Within three centuries after its founding, Christianity overcame opposition by secular leaders and produced a complex network of clergy, churches and even administrative districts (known as episcopates) presided over by senior church officials (bishops). Well before the medieval period, Christianity became *the* common denominator in community life. It regulated custom and united the community by defining the role between humankind and a Creator, and the obligations between fellow human beings. As the influence of Christianity grew, the church accumulated enormous power. It used its power by taking on many of the processes of government and ruled as a theocracy, sharing its power with secular nobles.

After the fall of Rome in 426 A.D., Europe entered what is now known as the "Dark Ages." During this period the principle agents of social control were the Catholic church and local kings. The two institutions shared a sometimes uneasy truce in how they jointly regulated society. Of the two, the church was the more important because it provided broad unifying themes for society as a whole and because its organizational structure was transnational. The church was the final word on matters of morality and ethics. As Bodenheimer pointed out, "In the Middle Ages all Christians shared one common concept of the universe: that which had been laid down in the New Testament and in the teachings of the fathers of the Church. Legal philosophy, like all other branches of sciences and thinking, was dominated by the church and its doctrines."[3] Christianity defined wrongs as *sins*, thereby providing a classification of misconduct. This was important because it elevated wrongs from purely interpersonal issues to a "higher" moral context. Thus, a person not only harmed the victim upon committing a wrong against another, but also committed a sin that jeopardized his or her redemption and offended the church. The use of personal vengeance to redress these wrongs was gradually wrested from the individual as both the church and the state replaced the injured party as the victim in a crime.

THE RISE OF FEUDALISM

Before the Norman invasion in 1066 the British Isles were divided into small kingdoms presided over by local nobles who provided secular rule largely according to their own wishes. Although customs in these local kingdoms were similar, they were not part of any larger formal fabric other than through the control imposed by the church. After William conquered England in 1066 he changed the structure of English society by imposing a feudal framework on the noble families. He did this by establishing a hierarchy of tenants and subtenants for the entire country, with himself at the apex. Local nobles were allowed to govern their fiefdoms under royal charter; in turn, they granted their tenants the right to use land in return for rents and services. Local lords administered justice within their jurisdictions through manorial courts (known as *moots*). Crimes could be redressed through physical punishment as well as compensation, but the lord became the recipient of the compensation because crimes within his jurisdiction were seen as depriving him of his subjects or their services. The right to impose fines ultimately became an important source of revenue for nobles. However, some crimes were also defined as breaches of the "king's peace," thereby giving the crown an economic interest in their outcome. The relationship between local lords and the king was often strained over who had the right to income based on certain crimes. As McDougall pointed out,

A tension thus existed between the king and the lord over the scope of their power or to put it more bluntly, their relative capacity to raise revenue from the community. The power to set the value of the holdings subject to the king's levy and to reap the benefit of judicial proceedings were significant, especially as the king sought additional revenue to fight wars. State officials led by the sheriff at the county level, and the system of royal courts nationally, played a major role in asserting state interests over the manors. The lord, on the other hand, controlled the land and the tenant farmers on that land. The organization of local production, definition of rents and the proceeds from the major court, the hallmote, all were crucial to his income.[4]

The king established the *curia regis* (king's court) to help him deal with matters of government. He also appointed deputies (judges) to travel throughout the country on his behalf to resolve disputes and, more importantly, to make sure all the revenues due the crown were paid. The king also used a system of inquests to protect his economic interests. This consisted of officials who traveled throughout the kingdom to inquire into circumstances on behalf of the Crown. Community representatives were required to attend these inquests, report on crimes and administrative matters, and answer any questions put to them. As part of this process the justices heard testimony under oath and dispensed justice in the name of the Crown, levying fines or setting fees as they felt appropriate or as accepted by custom.

The relationship between church and state remained close in criminal matters. In practice the church defined moral wrongs (which were frequently regarded as both sins and crimes) and the secular state exacted punishment for both. In the process the concept of individual vengeance was replaced by the imposition of fines and punishments by both the church and the state. Thus, "by the time Anglo-Saxon England emerged from her dark ages and laws began to appear on record, revenge and the blood feud had given way to a complex form of involuntary compensation for criminal acts, including the payment of money to a slain man's kindred."[5] Although the use of compensations eased the physical harshness of vengeance, it had an extremely important unintended consequence: it created an economic interest in the outcome of justice. In short, there was money to be made in the prosecution of criminals and this "opportunity" became a powerful incentive to both the church and the state.

The relationship between the church and the state, especially with respect to crimes and punishment, became an important issue after the Norman invasion. From the time of William the Conqueror it was generally agreed that religious issues were to be heard in ecclesiastical courts. However, the Church continued to expand its grasp over civil processes until the reign of Henry II, who formulated the Constitutions of Clarendon in 1164 to regulate relations between church and state. This marked the beginning of the separation of church and state and the serious empowerment of secular government. Afterwards the "king's peace" became the cornerstone of English criminal justice. Acts that disturbed the "king's peace" were crimes against the state and could be punished as such. This process resulted in the development of a law-based society in which personal vengeance gave way to state-imposed punishment.

AN EVOLVING PHILOSOPHY

At first it was difficult to distinguish between judgment and punishment because the means for discovering the truth of an allegation were often violent or even fatal. For example, in the pre-law days of England *trials by battle* or *ordeal* were popular methods for resolving a complaint. Trial by ordeal was legalized in England by William I and was a cross between religious ritual and secular torture. It was based on an appeal to God to reveal the truth in an allegation. In a typical trial by ordeal, after elaborate religious ceremony

> ...the accused was taken to the boiling vessel, his arms wrapped in numerous linen bandages. At the bottom of the vessel was a stone and if he could snatch this away from the vessel, in the cloud of smoke and steam arising from it, without injury to himself, the first act of the ordeal was over. Three days were allowed to elapse, when the bandages were taken off and the arm exposed. If it were unsinged he was declared innocent, if there were any trace of scalding, he was guilty and suffered such punishment as was awarded.[6]

Although trial by ordeal was abolished in 1219, other cruelties were employed to resolve allegations, thereby giving rise to the use of torture to coerce confessions. Interestingly, torture was employed by the state primarily in cases of treason and by the church in cases of suspected heresy. Torture to extract confessions for ordinary crimes was never authorized and was even forbidden by the common law. When employed, it was carried out under orders of the king as a royal prerogative superior to the common law. Not surprisingly, early forms of punishment were harsh; burning at the stake, beheading, hanging, being thrown from a height and being "broken on the wheel" were common in England and continental Europe. Even lesser punishments were often cruel in the extreme. For example, during the reign of Henry I one punishment for stealing was to shave the head of the thief, pour boiling pitch on the scalp and then cover it with feathers. Other minor offenders had their ears cut off, their noses split, hands amputated, and so on. In time most crimes in England came to be regarded as felonies for which the death sentence could be inflicted. By the end of the eighteenth century the law of England inflicted capital punishment for over 220 crimes; "stealing property of the value of five shillings, picking pockets, robbing a rabbit warren and similar minor offences, all entailed the death penalty."[7]

Crimes designated as capital offenses mushroomed in England between 1688 and 1815. The term "Bloody Code" traditionally refers to the English legal system during this period.[8] Two factors seem to have been behind this movement. First, there was no formal system of police and the threat of execution was depended upon to deter crimes. Second, the "proliferation of capital statutes [was]...explicable in terms of lobbying by special interests to impose the death penalty for threats against their particular form of property."[9] Ironically, even though the number of capital crimes grew rapidly, the rate of executions remained low. Although a great many people were convicted and sentenced to death, the actual proportion who were hanged was much less. One result was that the number of crimes for which a person could be executed (about 200) was often greater than the actual number of people executed in a given year. This is not to say that there were few executions, only that the actual application of the death sentence fell far below its potential.

Executions were public spectacles that routinely drew large crowds. As McLynn noted,

> The brazen theatricality of public hangings seemed to excite popular blood lust. Here, if anywhere, the "crowd" became the "mob." Pugnacious, aggressive, combative, and abusive, the onlookers struggled and jostled for pride of place by the gallows. If barriers were erected, they were soon swept away by the press of the crowd. Spectators often suffered broken limbs and had their teeth knocked out. Some were crushed to death. This risk was especially acute for women and children. (It was thought particularly instructive for young children to witness hangings. Often they were taken home and beaten afterwards lest they forget the awful example).[10]

Particularly notorious criminals had the additional disgrace of being "anatomized" (i.e., their bodies delivered to medical schools to be cut up). This was based on a belief that eternal life after death could be denied the victim by making resurrection of the body impossible. The brutality of public executions was not enough for some who wanted even harsher punishments. For example, one treatise recommended the following:

> Trials should take place immediately after arrest; those found guilty should be kept in solitary confinement on bread and water; hanging should follow as soon as possible after the trial; the condemned should be hanged in prison uniform. If all this did not sufficiently cow the criminal classes, they should be hanged in chains or starved to death. These bloodthirsty proposals were supplemented by advocacy of the French punishment of being broken on the wheel. Whipping criminals to death, hanging them in chains, and starving them to death continued to be popularly peddled options in the first half of the century. Knowing the popular horror of surgical dissection, some strongly pushed this as the most efficacious form of aggravated death penalty. Others advocated castration as a penalty for non-capital crimes and death by rabies for capital ones. The idea was that the condemned man would be deliberately

subjected to the bite of a mad dog, so as to induce the most painful death. Medical science would also benefit from the inspection of cadavers dispatched this way.[11]

A large proportion of those sentenced to death were spared execution by receiving some other form of punishment instead. Branding and whipping were common forms of corporal punishment. The pillory was also common but was not as humane as one might think. People locked into the stocks were often abused and even killed by the public. It was a favored punishment for homosexuals or those accused of sex crimes. To be pilloried for homosexuality could easily amount to a death sentence, as mobs were particularly hostile to them.

One of the most interesting (and ultimately significant) secondary punishments for those who were spared the gallows was *transportation,* i.e., exile in indentured servitude. The most popular dumping ground for these people was America. During the first half of the eighteenth century about 30,000 convicts were shipped to America as indentured servants. After the American Revolution it was no longer possible to send convicts to the United States so the British started sending them to Australia. Many of today's leading Australian families lay proud claim to being descendants of transported convicts. The use of transportation was important for another (more subtle) reason as well: it marked the beginning of dealing with criminals by *sending them away.* The utilization of these secondary punishments enabled England to maintain its severe death penalties without actually having to carry them out. In practice, execution of the death penalty was restricted for the most part to traditional capital cases such as murder, highway robbery, burglary, horse-theft and gang crimes.

The predecessor of the prison was the English *bridewell* or house of corrections. Bridewells were first established during the reign of Queen Elizabeth I (1558-1603) to house and "correct" vagrants, beggars, gypsies and the homeless. Unemployed men were forced into the bridewells, which then contracted them out in enforced labor. Because the concept did not function very well, the use of bridewells was discontinued (although such institutions reappeared intermittently over the years). The concept of penitentiaries, however, slowly gained popularity. In 1779 Parliament passed the Penitential Act, an idea that received considerable support because imprisonment was much less severe than execution, branding, whipping or transportation, and was easy to impose. "Magistrates sitting in summary session without a jury could hand down sentences of imprisonment for vagrancy, desertion of family, bastardy, minor trade embezzlement by workers, minor game offenses, and for a host of crimes where customary practice clashed with property rights: the theft of turnips and other field produce, the taking of firewood from private premises, etc."[12] After 1800 imprisonment began to replace other forms of punishment for non-capital crimes.

AMERICAN PRISONS AND THE DEATH PENALTY

Prisons in America emerged at least in part as an alternative to capital punishment. The death penalty is an ancient practice that has been exercised in nearly all parts of the world. Several things explain why the death penalty has been so widely used. First, it is quick and easy (or at least was until modern times). Second, it solves the most immediate problem (i.e., offenders who are executed never repeat their crimes). Finally, until recently, life was considered "cheap." Death, humankind's constant companion, was not as feared in the past as it is today, perhaps because it was never very far away. High infant mortality rates claimed a large proportion of newborn babies; diseases that are easily cured or controlled today took a heavy toll before the era of modern medicine and hygiene; and public health disasters like the plague claimed millions of lives (and were so catastrophic that when they swept through Europe many thought the world had actually come to an end).[13] The average person's life span was about half of what it is today and the world was seen as a fearful place in which any number of uncontrollable events could take the lives of rich and poor alike. In this context, the death penalty did not seem such a terrible thing; in a sense, it could be viewed almost as an extension of normality.[14]

Perhaps it was not the death penalty per se that came to disturb people so much as the number of crimes for which it could be applied. As noted above, in eighteenth century England there were over 200 crimes for which a person could be executed. However, during the eighteenth century Western society went through a period of intellectual change referred to as the Age of Enlightenment. New ideas in science and the humanities emerged and gave rise to new political institutions, and the self-perception of humankind began to change. Montesquieu stated that harsh punishments served to undermine morality, while Jeremy Bentham (1748-1832) argued that a utilitarian position be applied to the administration of justice. Cesare Beccaria electrified society with his classic essay *On Crimes and Punishment*, published in 1764. He set forth the radical notions that the prevention of crime was more important than its punishment and that the certainty of punishment was a better deterrent to crime than its severity. He also urged the use of imprisonment as a punishment for crimes as opposed to the brutal death sentences that were common in his day. His concern about potential backlash to his work was so great that he published it anonymously, but his reasoned and compassionate ideas instead fell on fertile ground and were echoed throughout Europe. This marked a turning point in how to deal with offenders.[15]

Between 1608 (when George Kendall was executed in Virginia) and 1991, over 14,500 executions were carried out in the United States.[16] From the first execution in 1608 to the beginning of the twentieth century, approximately 97 percent of all lawful executions in the United States were carried out under *local* authority. This trend reversed during the twentieth century, when 72 percent of executions were carried out under state authority. (The majority of executions that were carried out under local authority in this century took place in the 1930s.) Capital punishment has thus become a state responsibility rather than a local responsibility; when carried out it generally takes place in the state prison.

Capital punishment tends to be a highly emotional issue. It has been attacked on a multitude of grounds, including arguments that it is ethically repugnant, that it is cruel and unusual punishment, that it discriminates against blacks and the economically disadvantaged, and that it does not deter crime.[17] Questions involving capital punishment have been brought before the courts almost continuously since the 1960s, and for decades the death penalty has been a matter of close scrutiny by the Supreme Court. The 1972 Supreme Court decisions in *Furman v. Georgia*, *Jackson v. Georgia* and *Branch v. Texas* illustrate the complexity of the issue.[18] Defendants in all three cases were under sentence of death (Furman for murder and the other two for rape). Although there was a five-member majority, the court rendered nine separate opinions. The majority did not find capital punishment to be cruel and unusual in and of itself, but did find that the way it was imposed on the three defendants was cruel and unusual. They further held that since capital punishment was so seldom imposed, it was no longer a deterrent to crime, and that it was imposed in a discriminatory fashion. Justices Marshall and Brennan argued that the death penalty itself was totally impermissible.[19] Justice Marshall wrote, "It is also evident that the burden of capital punishment falls upon the poor, the ignorant, and the underprivileged members of society. It is the poor, and the members of minority groups who are least able to voice their complaints against capital punishment."[20] The effect of *Furman* was sweeping; it invalidated the capital punishment statutes of 41 states and the federal government, thereby commuting the death sentences of over 600 inmates. *Furman* established guidelines that had to be followed if a state's capital punishment statute was to be permissible; specifically, the new statutes must:

- Have the support of a substantial majority of the people in that state,
- Provide statutory guidance and direction so that the decision to use the death penalty will not be made by a jury or judge arbitrarily or capriciously. To do this, the statute must provide that the sentencing authority (jury or judge):

  Find the existence of a statutory aggravating circumstance before the death penalty may be imposed; and

  Be allowed to consider mitigating circumstances before imposing the death penalty.

- The new statute must be made applicable only to the most severe crimes, and not to those crimes where the sentence of death would be grossly disproportionate and excessive punishment.[21]

The Model Penal Code proposed a series of standards that conform to the requirements of *Furman* and illustrate the current demands for a death penalty. Aggravating circumstances under the Model Penal Code include:

a.   The murder was committed by a convict under sentence of imprisonment.

b.   The defendant was previously convicted of another murder or of a felony involving the use or threat of violence to the person.

c.   At the time the murder was committed the defendant also committed another murder.

d.   The defendant knowingly created a great risk of death to many persons.

e.   The murder was committed while the defendant was engaged or was an accomplice in the commission of, or an attempt to commit, or flight after committing or attempting to commit robbery, rape or deviate sexual intercourse by force or threat of force, arson, burglary or kidnapping.

f.   The murder was committed for the purpose of avoiding or preventing a lawful arrest or effecting an escape from lawful custody.

g.   The murder was committed for pecuniary gain.

h.   The murder was especially heinous, atrocious or cruel, manifesting exceptional depravity.

The Model Penal Code also proposes a list of mitigating circumstances that should be considered in a potential capital case, including:

a.   The defendant has no significant history of prior criminal activity.

b.   The murder was committed while the defendant was under the influence of extreme mental or emotional disturbance.

c.   The victim was a participant in the defendant's homicidal conduct or consented to the homicidal act.

d.   The murder was committed under circumstances that the defendant believed to provide a moral justification or extenuation for the conduct.

e. The defendant was an accomplice in a murder committed by another person and participation in the homicidal act was relatively minor.

f. The defendant acted under duress or under the domination of another person.

g. At the time of the murder, the capacity of the defendant to appreciate the criminality of the conduct or to conform the conduct to the requirements of law was impaired as a result of mental disease or defect or intoxication.

h. The youth of the defendant at the time of the crime.

After *Furman* a number of states revised their capital punishment statutes to conform to the requirements set by the Supreme Court. In 1990, 36 states and the federal government had capital punishment laws and well over 2,000 people waited on death row, all convicted of murder.[22] There are five methods of execution in the United States: lethal injection (21 states), electrocution (13 states), lethal gas (6 states), hanging (3 states) and firing squad (2 states). Nine states authorize more than one method of execution (generally at the election of the condemned prisoner or based on the date of sentencing), which means that death by firing squad and death by hanging are options rather than mandatory forms of execution in the states that allow them. Lethal injection and electrocution are the preferred methods of execution in the United States.

After capital punishment resumed in the aftermath of *Furman*, it was used with increased frequency. From 1977 through 1990 a total of 143 people were executed in 16 states. Not all of those sentenced to death are executed: 1,335 were "removed" for reasons other than execution. Some were re-sentenced; others were retried or had their sentence commuted. In America a sentence to death is by no means an assurance of its reality.[23]

THE FRAGMENTATION OF CORRECTIONS

Corrections is not centrally administered within any given jurisdiction, nor do all of its practices fall within the purview of the same (or even a single) agency. In a nutshell, the term *corrections* refers to what is done with people convicted of crimes. Sending them to prison or some other residential facility is only one possibility. In some cases the courts see fit to allow offenders to remain at large within the community with certain restrictions placed on them. Corrections in America consists of three components: probation, prisons and parole. Each component serves a different purpose; collectively they define the correctional process.

PROBATION

Probation amounts to *constructive custody*; that is, the person, although at large in the community, is still under the direct control and supervision of the state. This departure from incarceration upon conviction has its roots in a number of earlier practices. One example is the doctrine of "benefit of clergy," which began in the twelfth century and was based on the claim that clerics should be exempt from the civil courts and should answer to ecclesiastical courts alone (where they tended to receive much lighter treatment). The test of being a "cleric" consisted of being able to read the opening words of the 51st Psalm (*Have mercy upon me, O God, according to thy loving kindness; according unto the multitude of thy tender mercies blot out my transgression*). This was known as the "neck verse" because a person successful in claiming benefit of clergy through recitation of the verse could avoid being hanged. The practice was later extended to the layperson as well, and it was an important means of moderating the severity of the criminal law. Benefit of clergy was abolished by statute in 1827.

The first use of probation in the United States came about through the efforts of John Augustus, a Boston shoemaker. In 1841 Augustus, a spectator in the Boston Police Court, interceded on behalf of a man charged with being a common drunk. Augustus asked the judge to release the man to his custody, which the judge agreed to do. When the man returned to court three weeks later, the judge was so impressed with his improvement that he only fined him one cent. For the next 18 years Augustus took almost 2,000 defendants from the court and worked with them. In 1878 Massachusetts passed the first probation law, formally creating a practice that rapidly spread throughout the nation.

Probation consists of four basic elements: (1) the suspension of a sentence, (2) the creation of a status, (3) the imposition of conditions, and (4) supervision.[24] Probation is considered appropriate when its use does not jeopardize the safety of the community and when it is believed that incarceration is not in the offender's best interests. A person convicted and given probation receives a prison sentence, but has its actual execution suspended on the contingency that certain conditions are met. The individual is placed under the supervision of a probation officer (who is an officer of the court) and is required to report to the officer on a regular basis. An offender who satisfies the terms of the probation is discharged from the sentence. Theoretically, the conditions of a probation sentence should be carefully tailored to meet the needs of both society and the offender. The conditions should be performable and the courts should have adequate staff and resources to monitor progress and ensure that the conditions are being met. Conditions might include requiring the offender to maintain steady employment, avoid ex-convicts, pay restitution to victims, refrain from changing one's address or marrying without consent of the court, support one's spouse and children, and/or keep regular meetings with the probation officer. Some states require probationers to pay the court a fee to offset the administrative cost of its services to the probationer. Probation saves the state a considerable sum of money and gives the offender a chance to modify inappropriate behavior without suffering a loss of liberty.

Two major problems with probation are (1) that it sometimes is arbitrarily imposed and (2) that probationers frequently receive inadequate supervision.[25] With respect to the first point, many people receive probation as the result of a negotiated pleas in which the offender agrees to plead guilty in return for a probated sentence. Although this may be a proper trade-off in some cases, in others it amounts to a free ride. As to the second point, some probation officers have such heavy caseloads that it is impossible for them to give each probationer the proper attention. Some officers simply instruct their probationers to visit them at regular intervals, at which time they question them on how they are doing but never follow up to see whether the probationer is telling the truth. When properly administered, however, probation can be one of the most cost-effective and beneficial components of the correctional system.

Probation probably constitutes the largest constituency of the correctional process. During 1990 state and federal agencies reported that 2,670,234 adult offenders were on probation, a 5.9 percent gain over the previous year's count.[26] Of the more than 4.3 million people under correctional supervision in 1990, about 61.4 percent were on probation and at large in the community, making probation the most commonly imposed form of correctional supervision. In assessing the successfulness of this approach, the results are mixed. In one Justice Department report 62 percent of probationers in a three-year follow-up study (1986-1989) were either arrested for a new felony or charged with violating the conditions of their supervision. The overall estimate of 62 percent consisted of 30 percent who had both a subsequent felony arrest and a disciplinary hearing, 13 percent who had just an arrest and 19 percent who had only a hearing.[27] When probation department files and individual rap sheets were examined in conjunction with one another, it appeared that 43 percent of probationers within the state were arrested for a felony—a rate that would have been higher had out-of-state arrests been included. Moreover, although there was a tendency for offenders to repeat the crimes for which they had originally been arrested, the vast majority of arrested probationers were not rearrested for the same offenses for which they were serving probation.[28]

Probation agencies operate within constraints that often seriously limit their effectiveness. For example, staff shortages are the leading complaint of probation agencies, followed by coordination problems within the larger criminal justice system, institutional overcrowding and a lack of understanding by the public. They also report increased supervision needs as a serious problem.[29] This last point is especially important, because probation officials report that they are not keeping pace with the number of offenders they must supervise and that the offenders' needs are greater than they have been in the past.

CONFINEMENT

In most cases where probation is not indicated, the offender is sentenced to an "active" term of confinement. Oddly enough, prisons are "the least important segment of the correctional system, in terms of the number of 'clients' under its control."[30] People in confinement are held in either jails or prisons (see Chapter 13 for a more detailed discussion of this issue). The smallest proportion of them are in prisons.

Since prisoners are not equal in terms of dangerousness or custodial requirements, it is necessary to segregate them accordingly. Although prison systems vary a great deal from one state to the next, most maintain different facilities for different classes of offenders. In many prisons the first step in the confinement process is the screening of new prisoners to see just where they should be placed within the system. The reception process starts when the inmate is delivered to the prison's admitting unit, which receives them from the sentencing courts. At this time a copy of the court's commitment, signed by the sentencing judge and impressed with the court's official seal, also is delivered. At the time of admission, the prisoner is given a thorough physical examination and is photographed and fingerprinted.

After being admitted, the prisoner is processed and placed within the system by classification personnel. Where the inmate will be housed is normally based on age, sex, type of offense, length of sentence, degree of custodial risk presented and the requirements of the correctional institution itself. Part of the decision-making process includes administering psychological tests that ultimately become part of the offender's prison file (or "jacket"). While this screening and classification is in progress, the inmate is indoctrinated into the prison world. This process is designed to coordinate the custody level, work assignment, housing needs and rehabilitation requirements of the offender so that placement in the institution will result in both the greatest benefit and the least harm to all parties concerned.

The classification procedure can be divided into four steps: *referral, assignment, implementation* and *evaluation*. *Referral*, the first step, is a formal recommendation that provides the rationale for the offender's institutional status. The second step is the classification authority's decision (subject to review) regarding *assignment*, based on relevant background information, the referral itself, departmental needs and the offender's interests. The classification committee prepares reports providing the necessary instruction and reasons for the assignment. The third step is the *implementation* of the classification decision with respect to custody, work, housing and program activities. The fourth step is the *evaluation* of the offender's performance and progress. This evaluative information is collected and utilized in future referrals, classification decisions and assignment implementations.

There are essentially two types of classifications: *initial classification* and *periodic review*. The initial classification usually occurs within two or three weeks after the offender is admitted to the prison. This process includes pychometric tests, behavioral observations, the collection of background information, community resources reports, estimation of the offender's degree of dangerousness and escape potential, and the development of correctional recommendations. The results of this detailed intake screening are transmitted to the correctional unit to which the inmate is assigned.

The second major type of classification, *periodic review* (or reclassification), consists of any action that reviews or changes the inmates' status after the initial classification. This may occur for any number of reasons, such as custody review, program review, reassignment or work release.

PAROLE

The overwhelming majority of people who leave prisons do so early; most of them are released on parole before they have served their maximum term.[31] Although the majority of offenders discharged from state prisons are released on some kind of conditional release, the proportion released on parole changed significantly since the late 1970s. For example, in 1977 nearly 73 percent of the inmates released from state prisons were released as a result of parole board decisions, but by 1989 only 41 percent were.[32] Parole has been defined as "release from confinement after serving part of the sentence; conditional release from prison under the supervision of a parole officer, who has the authority to recommend a return to prison if the conditions of parole...are violated,"[33] and as "supervised suspension of the execution of a convict's sentence and release from prison, conditional upon his continued compliance with the terms of parole."[34]

Parole is similar to probation, except that in parole the offender is actually incarcerated before being granted freedom. In both probation and parole, the offender is technically under state control and must abide by certain conditions. If those conditions are violated, the offender may be placed in confinement again. Parole, however, is generally classified at higher supervision levels than probation cases, thereby requiring more intensive staffing and more community resources such as halfway houses and pre-release centers. Probation is always granted by the sentencing court, whereas parole is granted by an administrative decision either by the correctional institution itself or by a state parole board.

A distinction must be made between parole (which is also known as *conditional* or *discretional release*) and *mandatory release*. Inmates on parole are released subject to certain conditions at the discretion of a board or commission.

They must meet the general conditions that are imposed on all inmates released on parole and may also be subject to certain specific conditions applied to their individual cases. Parolees are released under continued supervision, i.e., their progress is monitored to ensure that they abide by the conditions imposed on them. If they fail to meet those conditions, parole can be revoked and they may be returned to prison to complete their sentences in confinement.

Mandatory release is somewhat different. It is not based on the decision of a parole board or commission. In mandatory release circumstances, correctional authorities determine a release date by subtracting time off for good behavior in prison. In recent years, discretionary release has dropped while mandatory release has increased about fivefold.[35]

The use of parole was pioneered at the Elmira, New York Reformatory, which confined inmates under indeterminate sentences. In that program, a person who exhibited satisfactory behavior could be released for a parole term, during which there was a requirement to report to a sponsor who kept abreast of the offender's conduct. The system proved satisfactory and was soon adopted in all major prison systems in the United States.

Parole is not without its complications. Parole authorities must concern themselves with the degree of risk to the public posed by the release of the offender. They also must be sensitive to public sentiment for or against certain prisoners, consider their own subjective impressions of whether the offender has "done enough time," and decide whether additional confinement would be harmful or beneficial. None of these questions are easy to answer.

In 1990 a total of 531,407 adults were on parole; in fact, in that year an estimated one of every 43 adults in the United States was under some form of correctional control; one out of every 24 men was under such supervision.[36] According to the United States Justice Department, more than 85 percent of those released from prison receive supervision in the community. This presents an interesting irony: although corrections is regarded as a *state* function, the bulk of its processes are carried out at the *community* level.

CORRECTIONS AS A COLLECTIVE GOOD

For corrections to be a collective good, it must provide some indivisible benefit; that is, it must achieve a positive end that benefits society as a whole. What then are the benefits of corrections? There are several, and they have been individually and collectively used as the justification for maintaining the American system of corrections.

DETERRENCE

One social benefit of corrections is that the entire process—in all of its many forms—is believed to act as a deterrent to crime. It is presumed to do this at two levels: (1) *general* deterrence (which assumes that the punishment of at least some offenders is effective in preventing others from following in their footsteps) and (2) *specific* deterrence (which assumes that the individual offender, if punished enough, will not repeat the misbehavior). The concept of deterrence is based on the idea of "free will," which argues that people are capable of making their own choices for good or ill. This position was taken by Bentham, a contemporary of Beccaria.[37] Bentham's assumption was that humankind is rational and would consciously choose pleasure over pain. He suggested that the pain resulting from criminal acts (via punishment) would offset any pleasure the criminal might have realized from an offense.

The issue of deterrence, however, is very complex and to a certain extent poorly understood. Although punishment does deter some kinds of behavior, the relationship becomes unwieldy when the concept of crime is linked to certain behaviors that penal measures are designed to punish. For one thing, some deviant "criminal" behavior is irrational and the threat of punishment has little or no effect on it. The use of punishment as a deterrent presumes a rationality on the part of the actor that is not always the case. In some cases misbehavior is virtually forced on people through the process of secondary deviance, and there are many whose value structure has taught them that their behavior is normatively correct. Indeed, this is one of the major problems of a pluralistic society. Schafer recognized this when he noted that the "law is the formal expression of the value system of the prevailing social power." He went on to say that, "The law is coercive and negative, but it is also positive in that it affirms the values of the ruling social power. As such it is not always concerned with reality: not what is but what should be is its central concern."[38] If people behave in ways that they believe are proper given their circumstances, it is unlikely that they will be deterred by the general prospect of being punished for that behavior.

Efforts to test the actual deterrent effect of punishment, including both its certainty and its severity, have met with mixed results.[39] How an individual *perceives* the likelihood of punishment may be more important than the actual deterrent effects of the punishment itself. Unfortunately, research into deterrence perception has likewise produced ambiguous results. As Paternoster has noted,

> Perceptual deterrence researchers and proponents of the deterrence doctrine should also begin to prepare themselves for possible bad news. No matter how sophisticated the study or how valiant the effort, very little relationship may exist between people's estimates of the certainty and severity of punishment and their behavior. Deterrence theory assumes that even if people do not

perceive accurately the objective certainty and severity of punishment, at least they are motivated rationally by their perceptions of those risks. Perhaps not; it may not be in the nature of the beast to be so rational.[40]

A good case in point is speeding. Countless drivers have installed radar detectors and citizen-band radios to help them circumvent the speed limit by avoiding the police. The desire to avoid punishment can be dealt with quite effectively by simply avoiding the people who can punish you rather than by avoiding the behavior that can be punished. In some cases going to jail or prison is simply accepted as the cost of doing business. For example, one group has asserted that young, black males in the District of Columbia are imprisoned at such a high rate that getting locked up has become a "rite of passage" in the District (they noted that on any given day in 1991, about 42 percent of the black men between 18 and 35 years of age in the District of Columbia were incarcerated, on probation, on parole, awaiting trial or being sought on an arrest warrant).[41]

Even in the case of serious crimes, the probability of punishment is relatively low. Many crimes are never reported to the police, and each level of the criminal justice system screens out many offenders.[42] Although punishment can and does deter crime, it is important to ask the following questions *for each crime*: What kind of punishment is the best deterrent for this crime? Under what circumstances and by what means is it best applied? What is the relative probability that a given form of punishment in fact will be imposed on someone who commits the particular crime for which it would be most appropriate? These unanswered questions are part of the challenge of the future of corrections.

INCAPACITATION

One way to achieve the collective good of *public safety* is to incapacitate those who harm or victimize others. It would seem logical that criminals who cannot be deterred can at least be incapacitated by locking them up, and conventional wisdom holds that imprisonment is an effective means of incapacitating criminals. There are two kinds of incapacitation: *collective* and *selective*. Collective incapacitation represents the so-called "just deserts" philosophy and is based on traditional offense-based sentencing policies. It links specific periods of confinement with correspondingly specific crimes and sentences are applied without respect to individual differences (although an offender's prior record may play a role in sentencing policy). It is fair because it does not discriminate: everyone gets essentially the same treatment. Collective incapacitation strategies try to reduce crime by interrupting the offender's criminal career. Unfortunately, research indicates that "collective incapacitation strategies involving greater use of imprisonment reduce crimes only modestly but increase prison populations substantially."[43]

Selective incapacitation strategies, on the other hand, target offenders who are likely to commit high rates of serious crimes. This perspective is based on the observation that although lots of people commit a *few* crimes, only a small proportion of people commit *many* crimes.[44] Selective incapacitation therefore calls for the enhanced use of prison terms for those most likely to commit higher rates of serious crimes, while it reduces confinement for those who present a lesser risk. The problem, of course, is identifying those most likely to commit a high rate of serious offenses. As Visher notes,

> In many ways, selective incapacitation is distinct from the traditional objectives of criminal sanctions: retribution, deterrence, rehabilitation and general (collective) incapacitation. The most important difference is that sentencing within a selective incapacitation strategy punishes an offender on the basis of the possibility of crimes not yet committed rather than solely because of the gravity of the current crime. The traditional just-deserts philosophy of imposing sanctions for criminal acts emphasizes uniformity in sanctions among offenders convicted of similar offense and severity of sanction proportional to the seriousness of the offense. Selective incapacitation encourages different sentences for the same offense to take account of differences in anticipated future crimes among offenders.[45]

Researchers have been plagued with problems in accurately predicting who is most likely to commit a high volume of serious offenses in the future. There is also the ethical issue of punishing people for what they might do in the future as opposed to for what they have done in the past. Even though selective incapacitation has considerable appeal at first blush, it is fraught with complexities and pitfalls. Selective incapacitation may have merit, but it is probably most effective when combined with a variety of crime control strategies.

REHABILITATION

The goal of rehabilitation serves the collective good of *social harmony*; it not only restores the equilibrium disturbed by the criminal's behavior, but also renders the offender socially productive. In principle, rehabilitation is an ideal solution to the problem of crime and is a goal that has long been sought by the criminal justice system. To appreciate the concept of rehabilitation in relation to confinement, it is important to distinguish between philosophy and practice., As a philosophy, rehabilitation is a liberal perspective that evolved in opposition to punishment as a preferred means of dealing with incarcerated offenders. It calls upon government to develop programs that can provide the means to improve the lives of its citizens. Moreover, there is a fundamental assumption in liberalism that crime is caused by the structural conditions of society rather than by the individual's' calculation that crime pays. The long-term remedy for the crime problem, then, is fundamental social change. Short-term programs, favored by liberals, tend to focus on improving the situation of the offender as well as on reducing crime.[46]

This perspective stands in contrast to the conservative outlook, which emphasizes order maintenance and crime control, and favors protecting society more than reforming criminals.

The goals and philosophy of rehabilitation are alive and well, and Cullen and Gilbert offer four reasons why liberals "should reaffirm and not reject the correctional ideology of rehabilitation":

1. Rehabilitation is the only justification of criminal sanctioning that obligates the state to care for an offender's needs or welfare;

2. The ideology of rehabilitation provides an important rationale for opposing the conservative's assumption that increased repression will reduce crime;

3. Rehabilitation still receives considerable support as a major goal of the correctional system; and

4. Rehabilitation has historically been an important motive underlying reform efforts that have increased the humanity of the correctional system.[47]

An interesting attack on liberal objectives of correctional rehabilitation was articulated by James Q. Wilson. He maintained that rehabilitation has not had a significant impact on recidivism and does not deal with the root causes of crime (i.e., those found in the community). Wilson instead argued for a "sober view of man and his institutions that would permit reasonable things to be accomplished, foolish things abandoned and utopian things forgotten."[48] There is, and will continue to be, considerable debate on the philosophical merits of liberal versus conservative approaches to correctional rehabilitation

Correctional rehabilitation is also *practice*; that is, specific programs run within correctional settings are designed to "restore" the offender to society as a productive non-violator. There has been considerable controversy over whether rehabilitation works.[49] In a widely cited article published in 1974, Martinson reported the results of extensive research on the effectiveness of rehabilitation programs in correctional facilities. After examining 231 treatment studies conducted from 1945 to 1967 he said, "with few and isolated exceptions, the rehabilitation efforts that have been reported so far have no appreciable effect on recidivism."[50] Martinson's conclusion was widely echoed and cited as proof of the failure of rehabilitation. However, five years later he did an about-face and reported that there were many examples of successful rehabilitation efforts.[51]

Perhaps the concept of correctional rehabilitation makes more sense when viewed as part of the total institutional management of inmates. In fact, it might be instructive to view rehabilitation as part of the larger process of providing prisoners with basic services and preparing them for eventual release while supporting the prison's custodial function.[52] Thus, institutional rehabilitation can include such diverse efforts as therapy programs (e.g., for psychological problems and substance abuse), educational programs (ranging from GED to graduate degree programs) and vocational training designed to enable an inmate to make the transition into the free world labor force.

RETRIBUTION

Retribution is vengeance, pure and simple. It is the concept that, as Packer has said, the "morally derelict" deserve to be punished.[53] Retribution is an ancient concept and one of the most enduring. It goes back to the Roman law, *lex talionis** and is an inescapable component of our correctional philosophy. Retribution represents the "setting right" of a wrong. As such it can be considered a collective good, for without retribution, what would be the purpose of good behavior? The state has reason to impose retribution: if it were left to the injured party to inflict, then some crimes would go unpunished because of the inability of the victim to act against the offender. In other cases, the retribution wrought by the victim would transcend the crime for which it was being administered. This is based on the difficulty people have in viewing acts against them in an objective light. Thus, *lex talionis* not only cries out for "an eye for an eye," it also says, "and nothing more!" The state regulates retribution through laws that define crimes and set punishments.

The state has both the right and the obligation to exact vengeance on those convicted of crimes, especially serious crimes, and in recent decades public opinion has alternated between the desire to rehabilitate criminals and the compulsion to punish them—although the two goals are not necessarily contradictory. To a certain extent these goals mirror the debate on crime control vs. due process.[54] The desire to punish criminals has been tempered by a corresponding effort to make sure that punishments are reasonable and that they focus on the crime more than the criminal. Sometimes called the *just deserts* or *justice*

---

* *Lex talionis* is the law of retaliation calling for punishment that corresponds to the harm that has been done; that is, "an eye for an eye and a tooth for a tooth."

model, this approach argues that the severity of punishment must be commensurate with the crime. The rationale behind it is:

> The severity of the penalty carries implications of degree of reprobation: the sterner the punishment, the greater that implicit blame: sending someone away for several years connotes that he is more to be condemned than does jailing him for a few months or putting him on probation. In [setting] penalties, therefore, the crime should be sufficiently serious to merit the implicit reprobation....Where an offender convicted of a minor offense is punished severely, the blame which so drastic a penalty ordinarily carries will attach to him—and unjustly so, in view of the not-so-very-wrongful character of the offense... [Conversely] imposing only a slight penalty for a serious offense treats the offender as less blameworthy than he deserves.[55]

Thus, to satisfy the requirement of justice the penalty must be determined by the offense, not the offender. This means that retribution must be scaled, with the more serious sentences applied to the most serious crimes. The justice model contains a number of key assumptions, including the following:[56]

1. For justice to be possible, all sentences must be "determinate" or "flat."

2. The principle of just deserts and not that of individualized treatment should regulate the sanction an offender receives.

3. Sentences should be legislatively fixed and narrow in range

4. Compared to current sentencing practices, the lengths of prison terms should be substantially reduced.

5. The discretion exercised by judges should be severely restricted.

6. Parole-release should be abolished.

7. Voluntary rehabilitation programs should be supported and expanded.

8. All inmates should reside in a just and humane environment.

The fragmentation of corrections reflects the variety of philosophies on the subject. The wish to alter an offender's behavior by controlling him—but without running the risk of making it worse—underlies the goals of probation. The wish to protect the public from predators is a major part of the rationale behind confinement (incapacitation). The wish to take revenge on criminals represents the ancient goal of punishment and historically has been one of the major goals of imprisonment (retribution). All of these approaches are used to support the collective goods of social harmony, justice (equality under the law), political and economic stability, and the ability of citizens to be secure in their homes, persons and possessions. The system seeks to achieve these through a variety of means, each of which is an instrument that has become an institution. These institutions, often highly fragmented and poorly coordinated, are all part of an ancient heritage that has been shaped over hundreds of years and continues to be molded by contemporary hopes, fears and expectations.

DILEMMAS IN IDEOLOGY: PUNISH, CONTROL OR TREAT?

The most immediate concern of correctional facilities is security. But once inmates are secure, what is to be done with them? Many think that, ideally, they should be rehabilitated. In addition, many believe that they should be used for institutional purposes (that is, many of the internal housekeeping functions of prisons could be performed by prisoners). Almost everyone agrees that prisoners who require medical, dental or psychiatric services should receive them. Finally, some feel that prisons are places of punishment and that prisoners should be punished accordingly.

Just what prisons *ought* to do has become a controversial issue.[57] It has been exacerbated by reports that rehabilitation does not work and the development of a more punishment-oriented philosophy on the part of the public. Ernst Van den Haag, one of the principal architects of the so-called *punishment model* of corrections, tersely noted that laws "threaten, or promise, punishment for crimes. Society has obligated itself by threatening. It owes the carrying out of its threats. Society pays its debts by punishing the offender, however unwilling he is to accept payment."[58] This idea seems to have found receptive listeners; indeed, there are many who fully agree with Wilson, who said, "Wicked people exist. Nothing avails except to set them apart from innocent people."[59]

Prisons are a contradiction of ideologies. They attempt to do a number of things at the same time, and they do them with minimal public support, inadequate manpower, antiquated physical plants and sometimes no clear sense of purpose other than to ensure that inmates do not get out until the state officially releases them. Few, if any, of the actors involved have any realistic ability to change the system, and the matter is becoming ever more complex and difficult as a result of increasing litigation on behalf of prisoners' rights.

The bottom line is that corrections treats, rehabilitates and punishes with varying degrees of public support. This is characteristic of the relationship between the public and the criminal justice system: all too often it gets what it asks for, but finds that that is not really what it wants or needs. The system is then blamed for the defective product it produces. Perhaps corrections would be able to eliminate or reduce this ideological conflict if it worked backwards from the outcomes desired rather than starting with established means and then asking for specific outcomes. First, the criminal justice system needs to find out what kinds of rehabilitation are possible or practical. After answering this, the correctional system should determine just what kind of setting or design is most likely to produce a rehabilitated offender, and then build its facilities accordingly. If punishment is the goal, then the criminal justice system needs to find out what kinds of punishments are most appropriate. Perhaps what each state should have is a *department of punishments* in addition to a department of corrections, each to perform its own functions in the most cost-effective and sensible manner possible.

COMMUNITY CORRECTIONS

The overwhelming majority of people under control of the criminal justice system are at liberty within the community; only a small proportion are confined to jail or prison at any given time.[60] As Duffee and McGarrell point out, "Changes in sentencing practice, changes in prison policy, and changes in probation and parole supervision have blurred considerably what may once have been a clear line between community and non-community corrections."[61] They go on to point out that community corrections is a fuzzy concept. Its lack of clarity rests in part on the fact that it is not a systematically orchestrated effort but instead consists of a wide array of different approaches, policies and political considerations. According to Duffee and McGarrell, community corrections falls under three broad headings: community-*run* corrections, community-*placed* corrections and community-*based* corrections.[62]

COMMUNITY-RUN CORRECTIONS

This approach includes programs controlled by and within the community where the offense took place. The crime, the judgment and the offender disposition all take place in the same community and employ that community's resources. Such programs include local diversion programs, some kinds of probation and local incarceration (or a combination of all three).

COMMUNITY-PLACED CORRECTIONS

This category also includes correctional programs carried out within the community, but is distinguished from community-run programs in that program impetus, policy formulation and resource generation are non-local. Federal probation programs are a good example, as are state-administered probation and parole programs (like the program operation by the California Youth Authority and the halfway houses operated by the Pennsylvania Bureau of Corrections). These programs operate at the local level but are part of a larger system. Their goals are also different from community-run corrections. Community-placed corrections tend to be oriented more toward the offender, whereas community-run correctional programs tend to be more interested in maintaining order within the community.

COMMUNITY-BASED CORRECTIONS

These programs are usually some combination of community-run and community-placed programs. For example, they may be funded by the state or federal governments but operated and administered at the local level (with their policies formulated within the community). An example would include county work-release programs subsidized on a contract basis by the Federal Bureau of Prisons. Community-based corrections offers the prospect of innovation by making outside support available at the local level, especially in support of "new" programs or technologies.

COMMUNITY PROGRAMS

Community corrections programs are specific efforts carried out at the local level. They are used to avoid, supplement or follow confinement and all are oriented toward re-integrating the offender into the community as a productive member of society. These programs are extremely diverse in nature, frequently serve different clienteles and may be called upon at different points in the processing of the offender. We have already seen how diversion is used prior to formal adjudication (after arrest but before trial). It avoids criminal prosecution by allowing the offender to voluntarily participate in a community-based program that resolves the problem that led to the arrest in the first place. Programs that enable offenders to come to grips with problems involving domestic violence or substance abuse fall into this category. Most community corrections programs, however, come into play after the offender has been convicted. Probation and parole have already been mentioned and are good examples of community corrections programs. The programs listed below are examples of corrections programs often employed at the community level.

Fines and Restitution

Monetary fines are neither new nor unusual, as most of us know from paying traffic tickets. Although fines are used extensively in both courts of limited and general jurisdiction, they are used with greater frequency in the lower courts.[63] The use of monetary fines has a number of pros and cons. On the positive side, they can be an effective means of punishment and can be used to deprive offenders of the fruits of their crimes. The amounts of fines can be adjusted to meet the ability of the defendant to pay, and fines are financially self-sustaining (that is, they are not an economic burden to the courts). On the other hand, fines do not incapacitate offenders and thereby leave the community at continued risk, and they may be used with disproportionate impact on the poor. Fines are often used in conjunction with other sentencing strategies, including restitution, victim compensation and recovery of court costs. Thus, fines may be used to punish offenders while simultaneously recovering cost to victims and the criminal justice system.

Temporary Release

People who are actually incarcerated are economically unproductive and expensive to support. Temporary release programs acknowledge the propriety of confinement while enabling offenders to function on a limited basis within the community. In effect, it is a compromise between incarceration and release. *Work release* programs enable offenders to remain employed during the day but require them to remain incarcerated during non-work hours. The working inmate can thereby support a family, pay taxes and meet financial restitution requirements that are often set as part of the program. *Study release* programs enable the offender to temporarily leave confinement to attend school or vocational training programs. Like offenders on work release, the people in these programs must return to confinement when not actively involved in the study program. Finally, *furloughs* may be granted to incarcerated individuals that allow them to go back into the community for short periods of time for specific reasons (e.g., to attend a funeral, look for a job or find support for upcoming release).

Halfway Houses

Halfway houses are residential facilities used by inmates as part of a graduated release program. As Stojkovic and Lovell note, "Placement of offenders in such facilities is most often combined with probation (halfway in) or parole or other early release (halfway out)."[64] Inmates placed in halfway houses are typically expected to hold a job (or be looking for work) and to participate in treatment or rehabilitation programs such as counseling or substance abuse.

Halfway houses have been used for many years and are becoming an even more important component of corrections as prison crowding increases. Limited research comparing halfway houses with probation alone on the basis of social adjustment and subsequent conviction for new offense suggests that both approaches are equally effective—especially if halfway house placement is based on the needs of the offender.[65] One problem with halfway houses has been the issue of public acceptance. The public must not only accept the philosophy and goals of halfway houses, but also must be willing to accept them as physical institutions. The establishment of halfway houses sometimes runs into the "NIMBY" ("not in my back yard") objection. Public acceptance of community corrections may not come easy, but an effective, well-run community corrections program requires a variety of options and willing public support.[66]

House Arrest

A novel and promising development in community-based corrections is *house arrest*, in which convicted offenders are ordered to remain in their own homes. These "inmates" are normally allowed to leave home to go to work, to get medical treatment or for other court-approved reasons. They also may be ordered to perform community service and/or pay a supervision fee to offset the cost of their participation in the program. Their home confinement is monitored either through intensive probation supervision or through electronic monitoring. House arrest has a number of advantages. First, it is not only less expensive than incarceration, it also saves money in indirect ways. Taxes—and perhaps even restitution—can be paid because the offender is required to work. Working offenders can support their families, thus saving the state the cost of welfare. In addition, house arrest enables the inmate to avoid the corrupting influence of actual imprisonment. Finally, it reduces jail and prison crowding, while giving the state the flexibility of being able to put the offender in prison very quickly if the terms of the house arrest are violated.

House arrest is not without its potential problems. For one thing, it might be applied to people who would not normally have been incarceration-bound (who would probably have been assigned to routine probation). In the opposite vein, it might be used on people for whom a jail sentence might be a good idea, thereby undercutting the retributive value of some incarceration. Finally, there is the danger that house arrest will not be applied equally. Because it assumes both that the inmate has a house in which to be confined and that he or she has the ability to work, those at the bottom of the socioeconomic ladder may not be eligible.[67]

Closely related to house arrest is the issue of electronic monitoring. This is a technology that applies telemetry to determine whether an offender is at the proper place at the proper time.[68] Although first used to track animals, this technology was applied to the monitoring of criminals in 1984. Since then it has gained steady acceptance as a form of intermediate punishment. There are two types of monitors: *continuously signaling devices* and *programmed contact devices*. *Continuously signaling devices* constantly monitor the presence of an offender at a particular location (electronically monitored house arrest—i.e.,

EMHA—fits into this category); *programmed contact devices*, contact the offender periodically to verify his or her presence. Both are surveillance devices keyed to specific individuals.

At its outset, electronic monitoring was used primarily to monitor probationers. It has since been expanded to include post-incarceration offenders and those sentenced to community corrections programs. In some cases it is used on individuals before they are brought to trial or between their trial and their sentencing. At present, the majority of offenders under electronic monitoring have been convicted of property offenses, drug crimes, major traffic offenses and (to a lesser extent) crimes against the person. When all factors are considered, monitoring appears to be increasing disproportionately among young offenders (particularly females).[69] The majority of these programs charge the inmates a fee to offset the cost of the monitors. Even though the technique is effective, there is a point beyond which it appears to become counterproductive: according to a Justice Department survey, "somewhere between 60 and 120 days is about as much as anyone can take of monitoring."[70] Even so, the research also suggests that monitoring might be useful for longer than the average current term of 79 days.

Electronic monitoring programs are not without their glitches. In one example, Washington, DC police arrested a man with 80 bags of crack cocaine who was missing the "non-removable" transmitter he was supposed to be wearing while awaiting trial on a murder charge as part of the house arrest program.[71] Also, the electronic monitors do not necessarily keep offenders from committing crimes within the home (e.g., selling or using drugs). There is a great deal of concern among advocates of electronic monitoring that its occasional failures can threaten the entire program. The key may rest in reserving electronic monitoring for the kinds of people most likely to benefit from the program.

SUMMARY

Corrections in America is the most recent phase of an evolutionary process reaching back into antiquity. In ancient society individuals redressed wrongs through personal revenge, and in time vengeance became the responsibility of the victim's blood relatives. Blood feuds involving extensive family networks entailed the possibility of counter-vengeance. The use of compensations soon arose and was used to supplement and sometimes replace physical vengeance. The onset of Christianity played a major role in reshaping humankind's concepts of right and wrong by shifting responsibility for revenge away from individual victims and their families. It thereby established a stabilizing influence in Western society. As secular governments gained power and influence in the

Middle Ages, they vied with the church for the right to impose vengeance on offenders. Although physical punishments (death and corporal punishment) continued to be used, secular government established a claim for compensation in crimes committed against individuals. This was accomplished through the creation of the "king's peace," which when violated gave the crown the right of redress (including the right to levy fines in some cases). This is the process by which the claim of victimization was removed from the injured party and placed with the state, a concept fundamental to our system of criminal justice. In the process, however, it ended the right of individual vengeance and placed the burden of corrections on the state.

After the state assumed the right to impose corrections, the individual offender was typically "corrected" by being executed or maimed and/or by having to pay a fine (or forfeiture) to the crown. The death penalty was popular because of its public entertainment value and was considered a means of crime prevention. Although in England capital punishment could be administered for a staggering number of reasons, its actual application fell short of its potential because a large proportion of the executions were reduced to secondary forms of punishment. The capital punishment laws in England during the years of its "bloody code" were a response to economic conditions; they represented an effort to safeguard economic interests more than a substantive interest in controlling crime.

One method of dealing with the homeless and unemployed in England was through the establishment of *bridewells* (or workhouses) that confined the vagrant and the indigent. Once in a bridewell, an individual was expected to support oneself by working; often the person's labor was contracted out involuntarily. Although the bridewell did not succeed, it gave rise to the idea of confining petty criminals as an alternative means of punishing them. Thus, the concept of penitentiaries as places of punishment took hold and was further supported by a growing public dissatisfaction with public executions, maiming and deportation.

The penitentiary movement received support in this country during the late colonial period. Ultimately it evolved into our current system of prisons. Capital punishment, which carried over in America as a form of punishment for serious crimes, came under attack from many quarters on the grounds that it is immoral, cruel and unusual, and unfair in its application. Its use has been closely scrutinized by the Supreme Court and in 1972 the capital punishment statutes of virtually all the states and the federal government were annulled by the Supreme Court in *Furman v. Georgia*. Since then, however, capital punishment was reinstituted by 36 states and the federal government, though limited by rigorous tests designed to ensure that it be used only in the most serious of crimes and then only when there are aggravating circumstances that are not offset by mitigating factors.

Corrections in America is fragmented into *probation, confinement* and *parole*. *Probation* involves the imposition of a sentence along with a suspension of that sentence on the contingency that certain conditions are met by the offender. Although at liberty, an offender on probation is under the supervision of the court. Failure to meet the terms of the probation can result in revocation of probation and imprisonment of the offender. Shortcomings of probation include the existence of heavy caseloads that may preclude effective supervision and a surplus of people who receive probation based on plea bargains rather than on the best interests of society and offender. Offenders in *confinement* are sentenced to active terms in a jail or prison. They represent the smallest proportion of people under correctional control, and most of them eventually return to the community. The third form of correctional control, *parole*, is a conditional freedom granted to an offender who has served part of a sentence. It releases the offender from confinement on certain conditions.

As a collective good, corrections serves a number of objectives. It is presumed to be a deterrent to crime; it incapacitates the criminal; it provides a possibility for rehabilitation; and it is a regulated form of state-imposed retribution. Unfortunately, these goals often contradict one another. By virtue of its administration, corrections often constitutes a conflict of ideologies. Its effectiveness can be limited by deficiencies in public support, adequate resources and a clear sense of purpose.

Although prisons are operated by the state, the bulk of correctional effort takes place at the community level. The concept of *community corrections* is becoming increasingly important in the overall correctional process. It includes three components: *community-run corrections, community-placed corrections* and *community-based corrections. Community-run corrections* involves programs that are locally run and responsive to local policy and community needs. *Community-placed corrections* take place at the local level but respond to policies and goals set outside of the local community. *Community-based corrections* combine elements of the other two and usually involve a partnership between the local community and either the state or federal government. Community programs are comprised of such efforts as restitution and fines, temporary release, halfway houses and house arrest.

House arrest (by which offenders are sentenced to confinement in their own homes) is perhaps the newest and most controversial effort in corrections. Offenders are allowed to leave for work or other court-approved purposes but are otherwise restricted to their homes. In some instances they are monitored by electronic devices to make sure that they are complying with their sentence. Although electronically monitored house arrest (EMHA) is not foolproof, it offers considerable promise for the control of certain offenders and precludes having to deny complete freedom or spend large sums of money for confinement.

DISCUSSION QUESTIONS

1. Is vengeance a valid motive for determining how a person should be punished for a crime? Defend your position.

2. Why was participation in blood feuds in ancient times limited to blood relatives and not relatives by marriage?

3. How did the definition of crimes as sins influence how they would be treated in medieval times?

4. With respect to the right to punish people for crimes, what was the relationship between local nobles and the King in medieval England?

5. Why did England impose the death sentence on so many trivial offenses during the years of the "bloody code"?

6. Is there any relationship between the practice of *transportation* and the subsequent development of penitentiaries?

7. Define the relationship between bridewells, workhouses and penitentiaries.

8. What two sets of factors (as required by *Furman v. Georgia*) must a state's death penalty statute take into consideration in capital cases? Do you think these requirements are realistic and fair?

9. It has been argued that the death sentence falls at a disproportionate rate on blacks. What might this mean?

10. Do you think getting a probated sentence for a crime amounts to getting a free ride? Why or why not?

11. How do negotiated sentences work against the concept of probation?

12. Specify the probation system's biggest problems. Can they be fixed?

13. How does parole differ from probation?

14. What is the difference between conditional release from prison and parole?

15. Do you think general deterrence (i.e., punishing someone to keep others from committing the same offense) is fair?

16. If an offender thinks illegal conduct is appropriate, does the goal of deterrence make sense?

17. Is rehabilitation consistent with confinement?

18. In what ways are society's various correctional objectives in conflict with one another? Give an example.

19. Contrast community-run corrections with community-placed corrections.

20. Is electronically monitored house arrest (EMHA) a sensible approach to offender management?

21. What are the principle weaknesses of EMHA?

22. How are the community's correctional needs likely to change in the future?

23. How should a community go about developing a consensus on how local punishment should be carried out—or should they?

24. How does the fragmentation of corrections hurt its overall goals?

25. In your opinion, what is the single greatest problem in corrections?

REFERENCES

[1] L.A. Parry, *The History of Torture in England* (Montclair, NJ: Patterson Smith, 1975), 15.

[2] Michael J. Cook, *The Court and You* (London: Oyez Publishing Limited, 1976), 20.

[3] Edgar Bodenheimer, *Jurisprudence: The Philosophy and Method of the Law* (Cambridge, MA: Harvard University Press, 1962), 21.

[4] Allan K. McDougall, "The Police Mandate: An Historical Perspective," *Canadian Police College Journal* 12:1 (1988), 23.

[5] Herbert A. Johnson, *History of Criminal Justice* (Cincinnati: Anderson Publishing Co., 1988), 46.

[6] Parry, *The History of Torture in England*, 89.

[7] Parry, *The History of Torture in England*, 15.

[8] Frank McLynn, *Crime and Punishment in Eighteenth-Century England* (London: Routledge, 1989), xi.

[9] McLynn, *Crime and Punishment in Eighteenth-Century England*, xv.

[10] McLynn, *Crime and Punishment in Eighteenth-Century England*, 267.

[11] McLynn, *Crime and Punishment in Eighteenth-Century England*, 272.

[12] McLynn, *Crime and Punishment in Eighteenth-Century England*, 297.

[13] Barbara W. Tuchman, *A Distant Mirror: The Calamitous 14th Century* (New York: Alfred A. Knopf, 1978), 96-131.

[14] See Albrecht Keller, ed., *A Hangman's Diary, Being the Journal of Master Franz Schmidt, Public Executioner of Nuremberg, 1573-1617*, trans., C.V Calvert and A.W. Gruner (Montclair, NJ: Patterson Smith, 1973).

[15] Beccaria's motives have not gone unquestioned; see, for example, "Inventing Criminology: The 'Science of Man' in Cesare Beccaria's *Del Delitti E Delli Pene* (1764)," *Criminology* 29:4 (November 1991), 777-820.

[16] Robert M. Bohm, ed., *The Death Penalty in America: Current Research* (Cincinnati: Anderson Publishing Co., 1991); see especially Victoria Schneider and John Ortiz Smykla, "A Summary Analysis of Executions in the Unite States, 1608-1987: The Espy File," 1-19.

[17] See, for example, D.D. Hook and K. Lothat, *Death in the Balance: The Debate Over Capital Punishment* (Lexington, MA: D.C. Heath and Company, 1989); U.S. General Accounting Office, *Death Penalty Sentencing: Research Indicates Pattern of Racial Disparities* (Government Accounting Office Report GAO/T-GGD-90-37, 1990); Information Aids, Inc., *Capital Punishment: Cruel or Unusual?* (Plano, TX: Information Aids, Inc., 1988); T. Sorell, *Moral Theory and Capital Punishment* (Oxford, England: Basil Blackwell & Mott, Ltd., 1987); and D.C. Baldus, G.G. Woodworth and M.C.A. Pulaski, *Equal Justice and the Death Penalty* (Boston: Northeastern University Center for Applied Social Research, 1990).

[18] *Furman v. Georgia*, 408 U.S. 238, 92 S. Ct. 2726 (1972).

[19] Thomas J. Gardner and Victor Manian, *Criminal Law*, 2nd ed. (St. Paul: West Publishing Company, 1980), 167.

[20] *Furman v. Georgia*, 408 U.S. at 366, 92 S. Ct. at 2791.

[21] Gardner and Manian, *Criminal Law*, 168.

[22] Lawrence A. Greenfeld, "Capital Punishment 1990," *Bureau of Justice Statistics Bulletin* (September 1991).

[23] Greenfeld, "Capital Punishment 1990."

[24] Louis P. Carney, *Probation and Parole: Legal and Social Dimensions* (New York: McGraw Hill Book Company, 1977), 84.

[25] See especially Comptroller General of the United States. "State and County Probation: Systems in Crisis," May 27, 1976.

[26] Louis Jankowski, "Probation and Parole 1990," *Bureau of Justice Statistics Bulletin* (November 1991), 1.

[27] Patrick A. Langan and Mark A. Cunniff, "Recidivism of Felons on Probation, 1986-1989," *Bureau of Justice Statistics Bulletin* (February 1992), 3.

[28] Langan and Cunniff, "Recidivism of Felons on Probation, 1986-1989," 6.

[29] Randall Guynes, "Difficult Clients, Large Caseloads Plague Probation, Parole Agencies," *National Institute of Justice: Research in Action* (August 1988).

[30] Lawrence F. Travis, III, Martin D. Schwartz and Todd R. Clear, *Corrections: An Issues Approach*, 2nd ed. (Cincinnati: Anderson Publishing Co., 1983), 30.

[31] Lawrence A. Greenfeld, *Prisons and Prisoners in the United States* (Washington, DC: Bureau of Justice Statistics, April 1992), see especially XIV.

[32] Greenfeld, *Prisons and Prisoners in the United States*, XIV. In 1989 an additional 30 percent were released under supervised mandatory release and nearly 11 percent were released to cope with prison crowding.

[33] William P. Statsky, *Legal Thesaurus/Dictionary* (St. Paul: West Publishing Company, 1985).

[34] Wesley Gilmer, Jr., *The Law Dictionary*, 6th ed. (Cincinnati: Anderson Publishing Co., 1986).

[35] Bureau of Justice Statistics, *Probation and Parole 1988* (Washington, DC: United States Department of Justice, May 1989), 4.

[36] Louis Jankowski, "Probation and Parole 1990," 1.

[37] Coleman Phillipson, *Three Criminal Law Reformers: Beccaria, Bentham, and Romily* (Montclair, NJ: Patterson Smith, 1970); see also Hermann Mannheim, ed., *Pioneers in Criminology* (Chicago: Quadrangle Books, 1960).

[38] Stephen Shafer, *Theories in Criminology* (New York: Random House, 1969), 17.

[39] Raymond Paternoster, "The Deterrent Effect of the Perceived Certainty and Severity of Punishment: A Review of the Evidence and Issues," *Justice Quarterly* 4 (June 1987), 173-217.

[40] Paternoster, "The Deterrent Effect of the Perceived Certainty and Severity of Punishment," 214.

[41] Keith Harriston, "Going to Jail is 'Rite of Passage' for Many D.C. Men, Report Says," *The Washington Post*, 18 April 1992, B3.

[42] See Philip H. Ennis, "Crimes, Victims, and the Police," *Transaction* 4 (June 1967), 36-44.

[43] Christy A. Visher, "Incapacitation and Crime Control: 'Does a 'Lock 'Em Up' Strategy Reduce Crime?" *Justice Quarterly* 4 (December 1987), 517.

[44] See, for example, Jan M. Chaiken and M.R. Chaiken, *Varieties of Criminal Behavior*, RAND Report R-2814-NIJ. (Santa Monica, CA: The RAND Corporation, 1982).

[45] Visher, "Incapacitation and Crime Control," 524.

[46] Francis T. Cullen and Karen E. Gilbert, *Reaffirming Rehabilitation* (Cincinnati: Anderson Publishing Co., 1982), 38.

[47] Cullen and Gilbert, *Reaffirming Rehabilitation*, 246-263.

[48] James Q. Wilson, *Thinking About Crime* (New York: Random House, 1975), 222-223.

[49] For an excellent review of the literature, see Paul Gendreau and Robert R. Ross, "Revivication of Rehabilitation: Evidence From the 1980s," *Justice Quarterly* 4 (September 1987), 349-407.

[50] Robert Martinson, "What Works? Questions and Answers About Prison Reform, " *Public Interest* (Spring 1974), 22-54 (cited at 25). Martinson was not without his critics. See, for example, Ted Palmer "Martinson Revisited," *Journal of Research in Crime and Delinquency* 12 (1975), 133-152.

[51] Robert Martinson, "New Findings, New Views: A Note of Caution Regarding Sentencing Reform," *Hofstra Law Review* 7 (1979), 242-258.

[52] Paul S. Embert and David B. Kalinich, *Behind Walls: Correctional Institutions and Facilities: A Many-Faceted Phenomena* (Salem, WI: Sheffield Publishing, 1988).

[53] Herbert L. Packer, "The Justification of Punishment," in Rudolph J. Gerber and Patrick D. McAnany, *Contemporary Punishment: Views, Explanations and Justification* (Notre Dame, IN: University of Notre Dame Press, 1972), 183.

[54] See especially Herbert L. Packer, "Two Models of Criminal Justice," *University of Pennsylvania Law Review* 113 (November 1964), 1-68.

[55] Andrew von Hirsh, *Doing Justice: The Choice of Punishments* (New York: Hill and Wang, 1976), 71-73.

[56] Cullen and Gilbert, *Reaffirming Rehabilitation,* 127-131.

[57] For an interesting look at some of the dilemmas involved in corrections, see Peter J. Benekos and Alida V. Merlo, eds., *Corrections: Dilemmas and Directions* (Cincinnati: Anderson Publishing Co., 1992).

[58] Ernst van den Haag, *Punishing Criminals* (New York: Basic Books, 1975), 15.

[59] Wilson, *Thinking About Crime,* 209.

[60] Louis Jankowski, "Probation and Parole 1990." *Bureau of Justice Statistics Bulletin* (November 1991).

[61] David E. Duffee and Edmund F. McGarrell, *Community Corrections: A Community Field Approach* (Cincinnati: Anderson Publishing Co., 1990), 2.

[62] Duffee and McGarrell, *Community Corrections,* 30-36.

[63] Sally T. Hillsman, Barry Mahoney, George F. Cole and Bernard Auchter, "Fines as Criminal Sanctions," *National Institute of Justice Research Brief* (September 1987), 2.

[64] Stan Stojkovic and Rock Lovell, *Corrections: An Introduction.* (Cincinnati: Anderson Publishing Co., 1992), 553.

[65] Edward J. Latessa and Lawrence F. Travis, III, "Halfway House or Probation: A Comparison of Alternative Dispositions." *Journal of Crime and Justice* XIV (1991), 53-75.

[66] Walter L. Barkdull, "Probation: Call It Control and Mean It," in Travis, Schwartz and Clear, *Corrections: An Issues Approach,* see especially 157-158.

[67] Joan Petersilia, "House Arrest," *National Institute of Justice Crime File Study Guide* (1988).

[68] Annesley K. Schmidt, "Electronic Monitors—Realistically, What Can Be Expected?" *Federal Probation* LV:2 (June 1991), 47-53.

[69] Marc Renzema and David B. Skelton, "Use of Electronic Monitoring in the United States: 1989 Update," *National Institute of Justice Reports,* No. 222 (November/December 1990), 3.

[70] Renzema and Skelton, "Use of Electronic Monitoring in the United States: 1989 Update," 4.

[71] Tracy Thompson, "Electronically Monitored House Arrest Far From Perfect," *The Washington Post,* 10 December 1990, D1, D7.

Photo Credit: Tony O'Brien, Frost Publishing Group, Ltd.

Chapter 13

CORRECTIONS

Jails and Prisons

On any given day a large number of people are in confinement. This incarceration ranges from people held in temporary confinement to those serving long-term sentences. Just as their reasons for confinement vary, so do the kinds of facilities in which they are held. The involuntary confinement of people suspected or convicted of crimes falls under the umbrella of corrections. We noted in Chapter 12 that corrections is an extremely complex field because it serves a number of different purposes, has conflicting goals and is fragmented throughout all levels of government. This chapter focuses on the specific kinds of institutions in which people are confined and the respective problems of those institutions.

Simply stated, confinement facilities are divided into two broad categories: *jails* and *prisons*. Prisons are used for housing convicted felons who received active sentences lasting more than a year. Prisons are run by states or the federal government. Jails, on the other hand, are run at the municipal or county level. About half the people in county jails are unconvicted inmates either awaiting trial or temporarily confined pending some kind of conditional release. Most of the remainder are serving time (usually less than a year) for minor offenses. Some jail inmates have not been convicted of any crime, but are held briefly for minor offenses (such as driving while intoxicated, disorderly conduct or shoplifting). Most are released within a few hours, usually either after sobering up or posting a bond.

JAILS

On an average day in 1990 over 408,000 people were in jail; during the year there were nearly 20 million jail admissions and releases.[1] As might be suspected, jails are used to confine "such diverse groups as those persons awaiting trial, inmates serving misdemeanor sentences, suspected mental patients, alleged parole violators, felony prisoners in transit, and chronic drunkenness offenders in the process of 'drying out.'"[2] Some people find themselves in jail for peculiar reasons. For instance, a woman in Dale City, Virginia "was handcuffed, fingerprinted, strip-searched, forced to dress in a baggy orange jumpsuit and locked in solitude behind a steel jail-house door. For five days and nights, she cried and paced around the cell, eating only one boiled egg and taking an occasional sip of juice. Her crime? Failing to pay a $780 court-ordered fee to the court-appointed lawyer who had represented her children in [her] custody case against her husband...."[3]

The first official jail was approved by the Assize of Clarendon in 1166 during the reign of Henry II. Its purpose was to provide a place where suspected offenders could be detained until they were brought to trial.[4] The task of operating the jail (spelled "gaol" at that time) fell to the sheriff. This is why most county jails in America are administered by the sheriff's department. In general, American jails have not been places of punishment per se. As noted in Chapter 12, in the early years of the Republic punishment for most crimes was either capital or corporal. Capital punishment meant the death of the offender and corporal punishment involved physical and psychological abuse (including branding, maiming, public humiliation and the use of stocks or dunking stool).[5]

In the late 1600s two major developments changed the course of corrections in America. In 1682, the so-called *Great Law* was enacted in Pennsylvania under the leadership of William Penn. This resulted in the establishment of prisons in which confinement itself was used as a form of punishment. This reform reduced the number of crimes that were considered punishable by death or maiming. The idea of using incarceration as a punishment filtered down to the local jails, and punishments for less serious offenses were gradually written into law providing short-term detention in local jails. The second major development, which came in the latter part of the 1600s, was the emergence of the "workhouse," which was based on the English bridewell. These facilities were originally designed for the unemployed and grew out of "poor laws" that defined vagrancy and made idleness a crime. Before long they were also used to house petty thieves, prostitutes and drunks as well. Eventually, county jails took on many of the functions of the workhouse. Ultimately, they emerged as places of confinement for persons awaiting trial or considered to be public nuisances (such as drunks, the mentally ill and others), as well as for those convicted of minor crimes.[6]

The *calaboose* or small-town jail is something of an American tradition. The term itself probably comes from the Spanish *calabozo*, which means "dungeon." Calabooses were used to lock up drunks until they became sober. If room was available, transients were often allowed to spend the night without being charged with either a crime or a fee for the night's lodging.[7] They also were used to confine people who had been accused of crimes until the time they could be transported to a bigger jail.[8]

Two important points explain many of the problems that surround local jails. The first is that jails are local institutions, usually run as a part of the police department or sheriff's office. The second point is that jails are places of short-term confinement. Taken together, these two factors create the backdrop against which jails are administered.

JAILS AS LOCAL AGENCIES

Most jails are part of *local* government, and until very recent times there were no uniform or national standards regulating their construction, use or administration. Thus, alcoholics, the mentally ill, petty offenders and hardened criminals have been indiscriminately mixed in most jails with little regard for crowding or classification. As a part of local government, jails depend on city councils or county commissions for funding—and in the past local governments typically have not been generous in spending money on them. (The author recalls one Texas county that fed its jail inmates a stew made from "road kills" until the court ordered them to provide "real food" to the inmates.) Moreover, since the jail is normally part of a larger law enforcement agency, it is forced into an *allocational conflict* with the remainder of its host agency. Jails historically have been a low-priority item among police chiefs and sheriffs. In fact, law enforcement executives tend to view jails "as a sideline to their crime-fighting activities."[9] Because of this, and since many law enforcement officials are not especially sympathetic toward those whom they incarcerate, local jails often are operated as inexpensively as possible.

JAILS AS TEMPORARY HOLDING FACILITIES

Unlike prisons, which deal with long-term inmates, jails confine their prisoners for relatively short periods of time—in many instances for only a matter of hours. Their primary emphasis is therefore on *security* and *custodial conve-*

nience. Security measures are employed to keep inmates from escaping, hurting or killing themselves or others, as well as to maintain order within the jail. Upon admission prisoners must surrender any objects they could use to hurt themselves or others and give up any valuables for which other inmates might hurt them. After their possessions are impounded, prisoners are photographed and fingerprinted. In many jails prisoners are clothed in special uniforms so they can be easily distinguished from non-prisoners (as well as for reasons of sanitation).

Security is maintained by locking prisoners in cells. This keeps them away from one another (most of the time) and prevents them from escaping. It also allows a small number of jailers to control a large number of prisoners. A typical jail includes "prisoner-proof" toilets and other equipment that discourage inmate misuse. Showers and other lavatory facilities usually are restricted to a common area. Visitors are restricted and items brought to prisoners (when they are allowed at all) are closely inspected for contraband such as drugs, weapons or tools. Lights are left on and people come and go at all hours of the day.

Such security measures can be degrading and dehumanizing. Prisoners are forced to give up not only their freedom and possessions but their privacy as well. Because of the custodial restrictions imposed in most jails, the atmosphere is oppressive and depressing. Since jails are places of short-term confinement, few administrators feel the need to provide libraries, recreational facilities or routine health care services. Although some jails have good food, most do not; in many of them prisoners are fed only twice a day. The general sentiment appears to maintain that prisoners can tolerate prevailing jail conditions because they will not be there very long anyway.

Since the turnover in jails is relatively rapid, it is difficult to implement programs that might benefit inmates. This fact alone works against the establishment of educational or training programs. Shortages in professional support staff clinch the situation. Although jails deal with immediate health care problems (especially if they are urgent), chronic health problems are generally ignored.

As a result of all of this, jails tend to be distasteful places. Richard Velde, former head of the now defunct Law Enforcement Assistance Administration, referred to them as "festering sores in the criminal justice system," and said that they are "...without question, brutal, filthy cesspools of crime—institutions which serve to brutalize and embitter men, to prevent them from returning to a useful role in society."[10] The problems are the product of circumstances beyond any one person's control. Police chiefs and sheriffs usually have higher priorities, and antiquated facilities cost too much to replace or renovate (especially during times of serious budgetary restrictions). Prisoners themselves often damage or destroy facilities, and jail administrators often are loathe to replace non-essentials destroyed by them. There are very few options.

Although informed citizens may be appalled by the conditions in jails, the average person probably does not know anything about them—and does not care to know more.[11] A large part of the public feels that people in jail are treated exactly as they should be. The "just deserts" movement that sprang up in the 1970s and 1980s supported the belief that one does not go to jail for "being good" and that people ought to be punished for their misbehavior. When prisoners are afforded decent treatment or are given some small modicum of consideration, cries of "coddling criminals" and allegations of "turning jails into country clubs" quickly emerge. Of course, most people never see the inside of a jail and have no concept of what they are expecting others to tolerate. Because of the need for security and institutional convenience, jails are an invisible component of the criminal justice system, and because they are hidden from view, the public is not able to make accurate judgments about them.

The nation's jails are plagued with problems. Crowding and staffing are the most important of these. According to the United States Justice Department, when a jail exceeds 105 percent of capacity its ability to assign cells for effective management is effectively eliminated.[12] Crowding is common, especially in the larger jails. It has come about as a result of higher arrest rates, an increase in jail sentences for those convicted of driving while intoxicated, the deinstitutionalization of mental patients, the increased use of jails to confine sentenced felons and the use of jails to hold prisoners for state correctional departments. Some of these problems have little to do with jail management, and some of the proposed solutions (e.g., expanded pretrial release programs, weekend sentences and home detention) require cooperation from the courts.[13]

Low salaries, a limited opportunity for advancement and a poor image of jail work all contribute to difficulties in recruiting and retaining staff members. Training also is a matter of increasing concern to jail managers—especially with regard to stress management, the handling of special problem inmates, liability issues, interpersonal relations, crisis intervention, management and techniques for handling prisoners with AIDS.[14] Staffing problems are also affected by the shortage of medical and mental health services. In a national survey of approximately 2,500 jail managers from a sample of 375 counties nationwide, the United States Justice Department determined that:[15]

- Over half the country's jails hold more inmates than their rated capacity,

- More than one-third (38 percent) are under court order for unconstitutional conditions of confinement,

- Almost 70 percent say they operate with a shortage of correctional officers,

- At least 40 percent report shortages of space for both classification needs in housing and inmate program needs, and

- Over 50 percent report shortages of space for booking and intake areas and for visitation (including lawyer consultation).

Because of successful litigation by jail inmates, jail managers have been forced to deal with problems that were previously ignored. Under the sponsorship of the American Correctional Association, the Commission on Accreditation for Corrections was organized to develop standards for jails.[16] Although these standards are not mandatory, they serve as an effective guideline for jail managers. As one author has noted,

> Jails have for too long been relatively closed institutions in many states. Closed institutions tend to fall into practices not necessarily constitutional. Rather than a grand jury investigation or a legislative inquiry every 5 years, state and local legislators, county officials, judges, bar associations, and other community groups would do well to monitor jail conditions on a regular basis, and to press for comprehensive reform.[17]

PRISONS

Prisons are state and federal institutions that exist for the confinement of people convicted of serious crimes. They are normally used for the incarceration of those sentenced to more than one year of "active" time. They are long-term custodial institutions and can take a variety of forms ranging from fortress-like buildings to farms or factories. If people are sent to prisons for the purpose of having their liberty restricted, then the basic mission of these facilities is custody. However, most have developed programs of various types that support the correctional philosophy of the institution. The potential conflict between the goal of custody and such programs is of profound importance in facilities where other efforts must take a backseat to custody.

We noted above that one of the leading figures in the New World was William Penn, founder of Pennsylvania, whose "Great Law" was enacted in 1682. This was a humane code—well ahead of its time—that provided for a house of corrections where punishment would replace executions. Prisoners were sentenced to hard labor, and the only capital crime was premeditated murder. Although the Great Law was repealed in 1718 after Penn's death, the seeds of reform had been sown. In the latter part of the eighteenth century, when the United States found itself in the position of trying to figure out how to deal with people convicted of crimes, the founding fathers were well acquainted with the new ideas produced by the Enlightenment. In 1776 the first American Penitentiary Act was passed; however, its implementation was delayed by the American Revolution.[18] After the war some Philadelphia Quakers managed to secure legislation, making a wing of Philadelphia's Walnut Street Jail a penitentiary to house felons who were not under sentence of death. It was to be used exclusively for the "correction" of convicted felons.[19]

After the turn of the century, prisons sprang up in many states: in Kentucky and Virginia in 1800, in Massachusetts in 1805, in Vermont in 1809, in Maryland and New Hampshire in 1812, in Ohio in 1816 and in Georgia in 1817. In the beginning there was conflict over how prisons should manage their inmates. In the "Pennsylvania System" inmates at the Eastern State Penitentiary were kept in solitary confinement completely isolated from one another. The prisoners engaged in solitary labor under the supervision of prison officials. The Pennsylvania reformers were convinced that if the prisoners were first subjected to enforced idleness and then given work, they would be grateful and the work would instill good habits and discipline in them. From time to time outside visitors would come to the prison to provide inmates with instruction in religion and morality. The advocates of the Pennsylvania System believed that, as a result of having time to dwell on their misdeeds, convicts would become penitent and ultimately emerge as morally reformed, useful members of society.

A competing model, the "Auburn System," was based on the way prisoners were managed in the New York Penitentiary at Auburn. Here convicts were confined in solitary cells, but—unlike in the Pennsylvania System—dined and worked together. Despite dining and working in "congregate" areas, prisoners were not allowed to communicate with one another. Discipline was extremely harsh; a prisoner who committed an infraction was quickly and severely punished. Elam Lynds, the warden of Auburn (and later of Sing-Sing Prison) believed that all convicts were cowards who could not be reformed until their spirits were broken. In keeping with this, he beat them with cat-o-nine tails, a whip with barbs of metal in leather strips that gouged flesh out of those being beaten.[20]

Although the Pennsylvania System was popular, it was expensive to build and operate. The Auburn System, on the other hand, was able to produce more goods by using congregate labor. Ultimately, the Auburn System prevailed and throughout the nineteenth century new prisons were based on the Auburn model. At this time convicts who went to prison faced a world of grinding humiliation, beatings, enforced idleness and pointless labor, and a daily regimen almost incomprehensible by today's standards.

Though contemporary prisons descended from the Auburn System, most are a far cry from their predecessors. They are no longer seen as places where people are send to be punished and have their spirits broken, but rather as custodial institutions where a number of competing concerns must be managed. Thus, inmate custody and institutional security must be considered in designing programs to provide inmate care and welfare. Work programs must be orchestrated within the confines of sound fiscal management and the institution's overall general administration. The legal rights of prisoners must be protected, while prisoners—some of whom are quite dangerous—must be properly managed. All of this requires enormous skill and costs a great deal of money. Many of the same challenges found in the "free" world are complicated by enforced confinement. Examples include ethnic and racial divisions, potentially divisive inmate social structures; public health issues (including AIDS); inmate violence and criminal misconduct within prisons themselves.

Another part of the problem is the enormous cost most states have invested in their prison systems. It is difficult to change something that has been done for so long in order to start doing something else. As a part of state government, most prisons tend to evidence a bureaucratic inertia. A state prison system represents a great deal more than just the warehousing of inmates. It also involves the employment of many people whose livelihood depends on their continued operation. In states where the prison system runs large farms and factories, the institutions represent an economic asset to the state. Because money-conscious state legislators have been reluctant to tinker with this asset, most changes have been imposed by the courts rather than by legislatures. Finally, significant changes in the prison system would require large cash outlays. This appears to be something that neither politicians nor the public is willing to tolerate.

Corrections is an umbrella term that covers a wide range of concepts and activities, including community supervision of criminal offenders and the actual incarceration of persons accused or convicted of crimes. A major component of the criminal justice system (despite its relatively low visibility), its importance is highlighted by the existence of approximately 456,000 state and local adult correctional personnel, of which about 378,438 work in correctional institutions and about 63,893 work in probation, parole and pardon agencies.[21] This system is responsible for controlling over one quarter of a million people—not including approximately 158,000 others who are confined in local jails on any given day, who are at liberty within their communities on suspended or probated sentences, or who are on parole from prison. The cost of this effort is staggering: in 1988 corrections in the United States cost $19,118,734,000; 94 percent of this was accounted for by state and local correctional activities.[22]

In its *Task Force Report on Prisons*, the President's Commission on Law Enforcement and the Administration of Justice noted that, "When the Quakers built the famous Western State Penitentiary in 1829, they understood that plant and program planning should be hand-in-glove, and they built their institution at Cherry Hill to fit their program, even though the result was America's most costly public building of its day." The report went on to note that, "Much of today's institutional programming is circumscribed by outmoded architecture, or by prisons built with only economy, isolation or security in mind. The result, in many instances, is that the program fits the structure, rather than the other way around."[23] That was a quarter of a century ago, but the basic principle remains the same: function is often driven by form, and the physical nature of an institution is likely to have a major impact on the kinds of programs that can be carried out within the institution.

Prisons built before the present century were harsh places, and this is clearly reflected in their architecture. The programs within them were likewise harsh, as is quickly seen in how prisoners were managed and treated. Not only were prisoners commonly forced to wear striped prison suits, in some states inmates were forced to have shaved heads. (In the case of the Maryland penitentiary in the 1830s, half the head was shaved.)[24] Historically, prisons have been classed according to security level; each of the three major categories has distinctive features.[25]

MAXIMUM-SECURITY PRISONS [26]

From 1830 to 1900 most prisons in the United States were built to ensure security. Characterized by high walls, rigid control over inmate movement, cage-like cells, "sweat shops," a bare minimum of recreational space and little else, these prisons kept convicts *in* and the public *out*—and that was basically all that was expected of them. Many were constructed so well that they have lasted up to the present; in fact, 56 of them are still in use, although some have been remodeled and expanded. At present there are 79 maximum-security prisons in the United States; they confine about 13 percent of all prison inmates.[27]

Any attempt to describe the "typical" maximum-security prison runs the risk of being overly simplistic. One was constructed almost two centuries ago; another was opened in 1991. The largest confines more than 4,000 inmates; another, fewer than 60. Some contain massive undifferentiated cell blocks, each caging as many as 500 inmates or more; others are built in small modules housing fewer than 16. The industries in some are archaic "sweat shops," whereas others have large, modern factories. Many provide no inside recreation space with only a minimum of outdoor space, while others have excellent gyms, recreation yards and auditoriums. Some are as dark, dingy and depressing as dungeons, while others are well-lighted and sunny. In one, the early warning system consists of cow bells strung along chicken wire atop a masonry wall, while in others closed-circuit television and electronic sensors are used to monitor corridors and fences.

Maximum-security prisons are geared to provide the fullest possible supervision, control and surveillance of inmates. Their physical design and program choices optimize security. Buildings and policies restrict the inmate's movement and minimize individual control over the environment. All other considerations, such as individual or social needs, must conform with security requirements. Trustworthiness on the part of the inmate is not anticipated; in fact, the opposite is taken for granted. Technology has brought much to the design and construction of these institutions, and the development of custodial tools has far outpaced the development of skill in using rapport with inmates to maintain security or control. Modern maximum-security institutions generally embody the correctional philosophy of retribution.

This kind of prison typically is surrounded by a masonry wall or double fence with manned gun towers. Electronic sensors and strategically placed lights impose continuous surveillance and control. Inside the institution the need for security dictates that convicts live in cells rather than rooms. Doors, which might afford privacy, are replaced by grills of tool-resistant steel. Toilets are open to view and showers are taken under supervision.

The control so diligently sought in these facilities is not limited to structural considerations. All activity is weighed in terms of its relationship to security, including how meals are served. Prisoners often sit on fixed, backless stools and eat without knives and forks at tables that have no salt, pepper or other condiments. Visits by outsiders are rigidly controlled; relatives must communicate with inmates by telephone and can see them only through double layers of glass. All contacts take place under the watchful eye of guards, and searches precede and follow visits.

Internal movement is limited by the strategic placement of bars and grills that specifically define where inmates can go. Areas of inmate concentration or possible illegal activity are monitored by either correctional officers, closed-circuit television or both. "Blind spots" are avoided in the design of the prisons. Places for privacy or small group activity are structurally (if not operationally) precluded. As a consequence, maximum-security institutions are characterized by high-perimeter security and operational regulations that curtail movement and maximize control over the inmates.

MEDIUM-SECURITY PRISONS [28]

Since the early years of this century prison officials have explored alternatives to maximum-security prisons. Developments in the behavioral sciences, the increasing importance of education, the dominance of the work ethic and changes in technology have led to modified treatment methods. At the same time, the use of probation and parole has increased. Institutions were established to handle special inmate populations. Prisons began to utilize psychological and sociological knowledge and skills to classify prisoners. Pretrial holding centers were separated from those facilities holding convicted felons. Finally, different levels of security (maximum, medium and minimum) were developed. Much of the major correctional construction in the past 50 years has been of medium-security institutions. About 41 percent of all inmates are held in the nation's 277 medium-security prisons.[29]

Today medium-security institutions embody most of the ideals and goals of the early correctional reformers. It is in these facilities that the most intensive correctional or rehabilitative efforts are attempted. Inmates are exposed to a variety of programs intended to help them become useful members of society, but security remains a predominant consideration. In a medium-security prison internal security is usually maintained by locks, bars and concrete walls; by a clear separation of activities; by highly defined movement paths both indoors and outdoors; by schedules and "head counts"; and by sightline supervision and the use of electronic surveillance. Housing areas, medical and dental treatment rooms, recreational and entertainment facilities, counseling offices, vocational training and industrial shops, administrative offices and maintenance facilities generally are clearly separated; occasionally they are located in individual fenced-in compounds. A complex series of barred gates with sally ports and guard posts controls the flow of traffic from one area to another. Central control stations keep track of movement at all times. Circulation is restricted to specified corridors or outdoor walks, with certain spaces and movement paths designated as off-limits. Closed-circuit television and alarm networks are widely used; locked steel doors predominate; and bars (or concrete substitutes) line corridors, surround control points and cross all external windows (and even some internal windows).

Housing units in medium-security prisons vary from crowded dormitories to private rooms. Dormitories may house as many as 80 prisoners or as few as 16. Some individual cells have grilled fronts and doors. The variation found in the maximum-security prisons is also seen in medium-security prisons, but is not so extreme—possibly because the inmates in medium-security prisons are considered to be less of a security risk than those in maximum-security prisons.

New approaches have been employed in the construction of medium-security prisons. Some campus-like facilities have been designed that largely eliminate the cramped oppressiveness of most confinement facilities. Widely separated buildings are connected by meandering pathways, and modulated ground surfaces are designed to reduce monotony. Attractive residences house small groups of inmates in single rooms. Schools, vocational education buildings, gymnasiums and athletic fields compare favorably with those found at community colleges, yet external security is provided by double cyclone fences and internal security enforced by unobtrusive building design. All of this protects the public from the inmates and the inmates from one another.

MINIMUM-SECURITY PRISONS [30]

The facilities in this category are diverse but generally have one feature in common. Because they are relatively open, custody is a function of *classification* rather than prison architecture and security hardware. Minimum-security institutions range from large drug rehabilitation centers to small farm, road and forestry camps. Most facilities were created to serve the economic needs of society and only incidentally the correctional needs of offenders. Cotton is picked, lumber is cut, livestock is raised, roads are built, forest fires are fought, and parks and government buildings are maintained. Most seem to feel that these are all legitimate tasks for offenders who are a minimal threat to themselves or others. Moreover, open prisons serve therapeutic purposes by removing offenders from the stifling environment of more remote prisons, separating the young and unsophisticated from the predatory and substituting controls based on trust for the bars found in other types of prisons.

Minimum-security prisons do, however, have some important deficiencies. They seldom provide educational or service resources other than work. Moreover, their predominantly rural location and the nature of the labor performed by inmates bear little relationship to the work skills required for the urban life to which most inmates will return. In fact, prisoners in these institutions are separated from the "real" world to which they had been accustomed almost as completely as they would have been in a maximum-security prison.

THE POWER SETTING OF PRISONS

As Jacobs pointed out, "Prisons do not exist in a vacuum: they are part of a political, social, economic and moral order."[31] Correctional facilities, like all other social institutions, must function within the context of the larger society. It is the larger society that sets the outer limits that define the role and scope of all public agencies. As one writer (Carney) has observed, "correctional programs must pass the test of compatibility with public sentiment. That test is administered by the representatives of the people in their legislative role."[32] He goes on to say that politicians are sensitive to public opinion, and if "an unenlightened public calls for an unenlightened correctional measure, the politicians will be strongly influenced by the sentiment of the public."[33]

As an agency of government, corrections operates in a power setting different from that of the other elements of the criminal justice system. Like the courts, corrections is largely invisible. What little most people know about corrections comes from what they see through the news and entertainment media and what they learn through conventional wisdom. Since they do not have access to corrections, people base their sentiments on what is available to them; for the most part that consists of press reports of notorious criminal cases. Because notorious cases by their nature deal with offenders whose crimes are particularly repugnant—e.g., mass murders, serial killings, etc.—they are not likely to generate sympathy. The effects on public sentiment extend from those exceptionally abhorrent kinds of prisoners to the more conventional inmates who make up the bulk of prison populations.

Low visibility is compounded by the fact that prisons are state agencies despite the fact that they serve the needs of local communities. Local communities tend to see prison problems as the responsibility of the state. In the final analysis, public opinion concerning corrections seems to fall somewhere between indifference and hostility. This means that the improvement of corrections (which costs money) is likely to have very low priority in most states, even where prison problems are clearly identified and solutions urgently needed. Cost is a very important issue in corrections; in 1991 it cost $15.4 billion to operate the 52 correctional systems in the United States (which does not include another $2.6 billion reported by 42 agencies for capital expenditures). The amount spent by individual states varies tremendously; in 1991 California spent the most (more than 3.6 billion) and North Dakota spent the least (10.5 million). The average cost per inmate in 1990 was $48.07 per day.[34]

The "sovereign" of a prison is its warden. The training and experience levels of wardens vary widely. As chief administrator of a place of confinement, a warden has remarkably little flexibility. Wardens are responsible for the administration of a large and expensive physical plant; they must provide custody to a population of unwilling tenants (all of whom have been convicted of crimes); they must supervise budgets over which they have little direct control; and they must manage the daily lives and careers of correctional officers whose average entry salary was $17,923 in 1991.[35] On top of all this, they have been second-guessed by the courts on a variety of constitutional issues. Many have had their authority seriously eroded by court-appointed masters. Wardens cannot select their "clients"; they have difficulty attracting and retaining qualified personnel; and many are forced into operational and administrative changes that they are powerless to control. There are few executives in any line of work who labor under more difficult conditions.

Historically, corrections has had no rivals; as state agencies they have been responsible for their own functions. There are many instances of correctional agencies contracting out some of their functions (or, as the case may be, the labor of their inmates), but the contractors utilized did not compete with the state for the correctional mandate. "The history of private-sector corrections is unrelievedly bleak, a well-documented tale of inmate abuse and political corruption. In many instances, private contractors worked inmates to death, beat or killed them for minor rule infractions, or failed to provide them with the quantity and quality of life's necessities...specified in often meticulously drafted contracts."[36] As more stringent limitations were placed on the use of convict labor, corrections became almost exclusively a state function and has come under increasing criticism for its overall performance, prompting calls for change and reform. Since the 1960s "practitioners, activists, policy-makers, and scholars have been searching for ways to relieve America's ailing correctional complex."[37]

In the 1980s a movement was initiated to reinvolve the private sector. Proposals were made to give the private sector a significant role in the administration, finance and construction of facilities and programs. The notion of privatizing prisons replaced the earlier concept of contracting prison labor out to private firms. In 1985 the Corrections Corporation of America tried to obtain a contract to run the Tennessee prison system. Although unsuccessful in their bid, the concept generated great interest at both the state and federal levels. By 1987 three states passed laws permitting privately operated state correctional facilities. So far, the greatest influence of privatization has been in the delivery of selected correctional services rather than the complete operation of correctional systems. This includes contracting out such functions as medical and mental health programs, institutional food services, community treatment center operations and prison construction, and providing such inmate services as remedial education, drug treatment, education, vocational training and counseling.[38]

The privatization of corrections is a complex undertaking, and a number of issues remain to be resolved.[39] From a political point of view, there is concern over converting a *public* obligation into one that is *private*. How this would impact on correctional philosophy remains to be seen. Would the public goal of rehabilitation be replaced by a private goal of profit, and are these two goals compatible? Would private correctional systems skim off the best inmate prospects and leave the most troublesome to the state? From an *administrative* perspective, can private prisons provide the same service at comparable levels of quality? Many observers contend that since private prisons would be free of civil service requirements and the cumbersome administrative procedures commonly associated with government operations, the quality of their services are likely to be superior—at least in the short run.[40] The question of accountability also has been raised. There is concern that the potential loss of control by state government might diminish the accountability of private correctional agencies and that this could invite abuses. If corrections is contracted out, the state would remain responsible, even though they might not have immediate control of functions placed in the hands of private correctional contractors. From a *legal* perspective, states wishing to expand the scope of private corrections contractors may have to revise their laws to deal with such issues as liability, security (including use of force), labor relations (including the right of contractor employees to strike), and so on.[41]

Even though state correctional agencies do not have any *functional* rivals, they have a great many *allocational* rivals. This is where the influence of the public (via legislatures) becomes important. If public lobby groups can successfully exert pressure on legislators to support other interests, then prisons will surely lose; indeed history has shown this to be the case. One of the reasons many prisons operate the way they do could be to reduce their dependence on state legislatures. Prison labor either generates revenues for the institution or enables them to reduce cost (e.g., by producing many of their own consumables). The ability of prisons to maintain economic self-sufficiency has been seriously curtailed by court-mandated reform. This has placed a much greater burden on the already-strapped state legislatures.

It is hard to say who the direct beneficiaries of corrections are. Most inmates would probably argue that they do not benefit from corrections. Neither does the public see itself as a direct beneficiary. In fact, it generally does not even see itself as an indirect beneficiary; most citizens seem to view prisons as necessary but unfortunate economic liabilities. The most direct beneficiaries of the corrections system are those who earn their livelihood from it. The absence of a large and clearly identified body of external direct beneficiaries is one of the major reasons why corrections has such difficulty getting the funding it needs to improve its resources and programs.

PRISON INDUSTRIES

On the other hand, there are many who perceive themselves as *sufferers*. Prisoners see themselves as sufferers, as do guards and other correctional workers who must contend with low pay, long hours and public indifference—not to mention danger and distasteful working conditions. The public, too, sees itself as an indirect sufferer as a result of having to pay for the upkeep of prisons and prisoners. Even commercial interests see themselves as sufferers as a result of the productivity of prison industries. In fact, free-world commercial interests have been instrumental in securing restrictive legislation *against* prison labor. Prison industries that might otherwise keep inmates employed in the production of goods have been harshly attacked by private business. As the American labor movement gained momentum at the beginning of the century, it saw the use of contract prison labor as a threat. It thus began an opposition that reached its peak during the Great Depression of the 1930s.

Two federal laws sealed the fate of prison industries. The first was the Hawes-Cooper Act (1929), which made prison products subject to the laws of the states into which they were shipped. Many states followed this with the passage of laws prohibiting the open sale of prison-manufactured goods. The second federal law was the Ashurst-Sumners Act (1935), which stopped the interstate shipment of prison products. Prison industries, which might have been highly beneficial to both inmates and states, have been restricted by commercial interests that see themselves as direct sufferers of corrections when economic competition is involved.

There are some significant advantages to prison industries. They can teach inmates work skills, generate revenues and promote productivity among inmates who would otherwise be forced into idleness.[42] As a result, some states have re-examined their position on prison industries, many of them replacing the restrictive legislation that barred the private sector from using prison labor. In addition, in 1984 federal legislation was amended to allow the limited entry of prison industry into interstate commerce.[43] There are six models for private sector involvement in prison industries:[44]

1. The Employer Model: In this arrangement the private sector owns and operates a business that uses inmate labor to produce goods or services. The business has control of the hiring, firing and supervision of the inmate labor force. An example includes Best Western's telephone reservation center, which is located inside the Arizona Correctional Institution for Women in Phoenix. Best Western hires female convicts as reservation agents and pays them at the same rate as free-world reservation agents.

2. The Investor Model: In these industries the private sector provides the capital to fund a business operated by a state correctional agency but otherwise has no role in the actual operation of the business. For example, the Wahlers Company, a Phoenix-based manufacturer of office furniture, has invested in a furniture plant that is owned and operated by ARCOR (Arizona Correctional Industries) and located at the Arizona Correctional Facility at Perryville. Wahlers provided the plant's equipment in exchange for a share of the financial returns; ARCOR built the plant. The products are marketed in both the state-use and open markets within Arizona.

3. The Customer Model: In this arrangement the private sector buys the product of a business operated by a state correctional agency but plays no direct role in the administration or management of the prison industry. An example is the Utah Printing and Graphics Shop, which employs 30 workers in the State Prison at Draper, is operated by Utah Correctional Industries and sells to both the public and private sectors (over 40 percent to the private sector).

4. The Manager Model: In this arrangement the prison industry is owned by the state but managed by a private enterprise. An example was implemented in the 1970s by the Connecticut Department of Corrections, when it contracted with the Hartford Economic Development Corporation to manage the state's correctional industry program. Although the contract was not renewed at the end of its initial period, the reasons were not related to the merits of the model.

5. The Joint Venture Model: In this model the private sector manages or helps manage a business in which it has jointly invested along with a correctional agency. There are no current examples of this model although such enterprises could become a reality in the near future.

6. The Controlling Customer Model: In this model the private sector is the dominant customer of a business it either owns or has helped to capitalize—and which it may help to operate. The electrical/mechanical assembly shop operated by Minnesota Correctional Industries in the State Prison at Stillwater employs 100 male prisoners in the assembly of disk drives and wiring harnesses for Magnetic Peripherals, Inc., a subsidiary of Control Data Corporation. Control Data Corporation is the sole customer of this industry.

Outside of these limited economic relationships, corrections has few allies. Even those who work in other components of the criminal justice system do not identify with corrections. Corrections, unfortunately, stands very much alone and isolated as a public agency.

CORRECTIONS AND THE COURTS

Most Americans have a strong and abiding belief in the rule of law. This has been honored for generations, in theory if not in actual practice. In the past the law has been applied unevenly in the criminal justice system, leading to periodic pressure for reform. This has been particularly evident in the post-conviction treatment of criminals. After being convicted an offender's fate was quite often left to the arbitrary decisions of others. This was true in the sentencing phase, in the discretion exercised by prison administrators over the inmate and ultimately in the authority of parole boards. Until the 1960s the courts were reluctant to intervene in matters pertaining to prisons. This position is commonly referred to as the *"hands-off" doctrine.* For generations the courts maintained the belief that complaints raised by prisoners dealt with privileges rather than rights. The courts also believed that correctional administrators knew what they were doing and that the techniques employed were routine and proper considering the nature of the clientele with whom they had to deal. Few judges ever visited prisons and most assumed corrections was a world of its own with no need for intervention.

Traditionally, a person convicted of a crime and sent to prison was deemed to have lost all rights. For all practical purposes the prisoner became a ward of the state and was allowed only those rights granted by correctional authorities. The granting or withholding of rights was believed to be a proper part of the correctional process.[45] However, in 1941 the courts held that prison inmates have a right to reasonable access to the courts;[46] and in 1944 the courts further held that a "prisoner retains all the rights of an ordinary citizen except those expressly or by necessary implication taken from him by law."[47] Administrative convenience was no longer accepted as a valid basis for denying a prisoner fundamental rights, and correctional administrators were told, among other things, to run their programs with clearly enunciated policies and to establish fair procedures for the resolution of grievances.[48] Even though the courts were willing to affirm fundamental rights of prisoners, they continued to take a hands-off policy with respect to how prisons were run. "It was only when the complaints began to detail conditions so crass, so gross, as to shock the minds of all decent people that the courts became involved."[49] For example, in a lawsuit against the Arkansas prison system, the plaintiff stated that he and seven other inmates had been harnessed to a plow and forced to pull it for 12.5 hours. He told the court that if they slowed down, they were whipped and beaten.[50] In a letter smuggled out of the same prison unit, another inmate said, "We are worked from sunup until sundown at times in rain, cold, snow, until we are soaking wet or half frozen. Like human machines we are talked about, humiliated, beaten, half fed, and when we complain we are told we were sentenced to hard labor and there is nothing illegal in what they are doing."[51]

The courts' abandonment of their traditional hands-off policy was virtually assured in 1964 after the Supreme Court held that inmates could bring lawsuits against prison authorities under Section 1983 of Title 42 of the United States Code.[52] Prisoners may use this provision to attack conditions of confinement, but not to challenge the fact or length of their sentences. This ruling opened the floodgates and in the next two decades prisoner litigation increased dramatically.[53] During the 1960s prisoner cases filed under Section 1983 exposed the conditions that were then prevalent in many prisons. As a result, federal district courts began to inquire into correctional policies and actions of administrators, and to declare them unconstitutional under various provisions of the Bill of Rights—most frequently the First, Eighth, and Fourteenth Amendments.[54]

Other disciplines, represented by the American Bar Association, the American Medical Association and others, also took an interest in prison reform. The American Law Institute drafted the Model Penal Code, which stimulated widespread recodification of the substantive criminal law at both federal and state levels. The American Bar Association embarked on an ambitious series of programs to involve lawyers in correctional issues, both within institutions and in the local community. As a result, some lawyers began to inquire into correctional policies and the actions of prison officials by filing the kinds of prisoner cases previously barred by the courts.

It became increasingly clear that many correctional methods were both harsh and extreme. The courts therefore began to examine correctional practices in light of constitutional law. The *de facto* immunity from constitutional requirements enjoyed by prisons for so many years came to an end when their abuses were brought before the courts. The Constitution does not exempt prisoners from its protection, and an increasing number of offenders asked the courts for relief on constitutional grounds. The courts quickly abandoned their hands-off policy and became a driving force in prison reform.

The abundance of cases brought before the federal courts successfully used the Constitution to challenge long-standing correctional practices and abuses. The First Amendment's protection of freedom of religion and expression was extended to correctional settings. The Fifth and Fourteenth Amendments' due process clauses were used to protect prisoners' religious freedoms, provide access to communication and impose orderly procedures on disciplinary hearings and classification systems. The Eighth Amendment's prohibition of cruel and unusual punishment was invoked to place limits on crowding and to order changes in the delivery of medical and food services and recreational opportunities.

The constitutional issue most frequently addressed in cases filed by prisoners is the Eighth Amendment ban on "cruel and unusual punishment."   The leading case in this area (a landmark prison reform case) was *Holt v. Sarver*, in which the Federal Court of Appeals declared the entire Arkansas prison system to be in violation of the Eighth Amendment because of the violence, unsanitary living conditions, inadequate medical facilities and lack of rehabilitation programs that were characteristic of the system.[55] Likewise, in *Jackson v. Hendrick*, the court ruled that deficiencies in living, health, overcrowding and program conditions rendered Philadelphia's three-facility penal system cruel, inhumane and unconstitutional.[56] Such decisions have placed an enormous burden on the facilities involved as well as on their state governments. In examining the role of prisons in Eighth Amendment cases, the Supreme Court's standard for determining whether the prison violated the Eighth Amendment was whether the state's polices constituted cruel and unusual punishment when considered in light of the "totality of the circumstances."[57] However, in 1991 the Supreme Court ruled that under an objective analysis the standard for review is whether the state policies or actions by correctional officers constitute "deliberate indifference" to constitutional rights.[58] The courts have increasingly accepted the position that prisoners are sent to prison *as* punishment, not *for* punishment.

Nevertheless, the realities of having to keep a large number of people in forced confinement continues to present many difficulties. In the past, prisons attempted to control inmates by placing severe restrictions that were gradually released as inmates demonstrated that they deserved better treatment. This brought prisons into conflict with prisoners' perceptions of their rights. There are two basic problems. First, to acknowledge prisoners' rights in practice, correctional administrators must relinquish the almost unlimited power they have traditionally held (and many administrators believe they need such authority to manage prisons effectively). Second, it is sometimes hard to tell where individual rights of prisoners come into legitimate conflict with the administration and operation of a prison. It has fallen largely to the courts to find answers to these complex problems.

Exemplifying this dynamic is the situation concerning prisoners' religious freedom with regard to diet. Some religious groups, such as the Black Muslims, have argued that because their religious dietary restrictions (e.g., no pork) have not been taken into consideration, prisons have denied them freedom of religion.[59] After they petitioned to have menus altered to accommodate religious requirements, the court directed that it be done. Custodial institutions with large inmate populations traditionally have depended on an economy of scale for efficiency of operation. This means, for example, that food service was undertaken for the institution as a whole and involved fixed menus which, although nutritious, allowed limited variety. Although menu changes can be implemented for certain groups, such a move imposes an additional burden on the institutions and can generate hostility among other inmates.

Some prison administrators have been less than enthusiastic over lawsuits that they see as interfering with established procedures. In some cases they have refused to comply with court orders. For example, in 1973 an inmate suit was brought against the Georgia State Prison at Reidsville. A subsequent report found that the prison violated 22 standards for the civil rights and well-being of prisoners, including poor living conditions in the solitary confinement and administrative segregation cells, improper use of force by guards, and racial discrimination in cell and job assignments. The warden refused to comply with court's orders and was replaced.[60]

We have already noted that the role of the courts is to determine whether a plaintiff is entitled to relief. If the courts find that someone is entitled to relief, they specify the relief to be granted and, when necessary, ensure that it is granted. This is as true in cases involving institutions as it is in those involving individuals.[61] In forcing the outcome of these prison cases the courts have used court monitoring under continuing jurisdiction. This approach often places the prison (or even the entire state prison system) under court supervision until it complies with the standards set by the court. In some instances this involves the formulation of plans, the setting of deadlines, the appointment of neutral monitors and periodic review by the trial judge. In other cases the management plan is implemented by a court-appointed special master who in effect takes over administration of the prison (or correctional system, as was the case in Texas under *Ruiz v. Estelle*, in which the entire corrections system of Texas was subjected to a comprehensive court order requiring fundamental changes in virtually every aspect of the system). Known under a variety of titles (e.g., "monitors," "ombudsmen," "compliance officers"), these special masters are agents of the court appointed under Rule 53 of the Federal Rules of Civil Procedure.[62] Such court orders have been used to impose significant changes in the structure of correctional institutions, the policies by which prisons are governed and administered, and the delivery of specific services within institutions.[63] Since the advent of the court-enforced prison reform movement, the majority of the nation's prison systems have been under court orders. The impact of the courts on corrections is so widespread that it has become a matter of serious controversy and debate.[64]

As a result of these changes, convicted offenders remain firmly within the constitutional and legislative protection of the legal system. There seems to have been a recognition of the irony involved in using a system that is itself unresponsive to law for training lawbreakers to obey the law. The alternatives before the courts in most cases involving correctional practices are choices between constitutional principle and correctional expediency, or between an institution that runs smoothly and one that actually helps the offender. In exercising their proper function as supervisors of the criminal justice system, the courts have upset practices that have stifled correctional progress for years.

After nearly 15 years of hearing prisoner lawsuits, in 1979 the Supreme Court handed down its ruling in *Bell v. Wolfish*.[65] This case challenged the constitutionality of "double bunking" (placing two or more inmates in cells intended for one). In a 6-3 decision the court held that jail management should be left to corrections personnel. This was followed in 1981 by *Rhodes v. Chapman*, in which the Supreme Court held that double bunking is not cruel and unusual punishment. Justice Powell stated that, "the Constitution does not mandate comfortable prisons."[66] These rulings seem to indicate a movement back in the direction of a "hands-off" policy. Though perhaps they may no longer play a strong activist role, courts are likely to continue monitoring correctional decisions and practices. The nature of the judicial process dictates that this supervision will be done on a case-by-case basis. Although some court rulings have made the administration of correctional programs much more difficult, they also have made them more responsive to law.

PRISON RIOTS

When the public focuses its attention on prisons, it is usually because of a riot or other major disturbance. The first American prison riot occurred in 1774. To date there have been approximately 300 major prison disturbances. Prison riots in the last century were relatively infrequent and in considering why, Allen and Simonsen noted that, "presumably inmates were either too tired to riot or control was too strict."[67] During the present century riots have been not only more frequent, but increasingly violent.[68] There was a wave of riots between 1929 and 1932, and from 1950 to 1966 over 100 riots or other major disturbances struck American prisons. Riots appear to have been based on a fairly consistent set of causes including inadequate financial support, substandard personnel, enforced idleness, lack of professional leadership or professional programs, excessive size and overcrowding of the institutions, political domination and motivation of prison managers, and unwise sentencing and parole practices.[69]

In their study of prison riots Hartung and Floch concluded that there are essentially two types of prison riots. The first, which they labeled "brutal riots," arise from such traditional causes as poor, insufficient or contaminated food; inadequate or unsanitary housing; sadistic brutality by prison officials; or some combination of these things.[70] They attribute the overwhelming majority of past prison riots to these root causes. They called the second kind of prison riot the "collective riot" and attributed its causes to "mainly...a combination of certain penal advances and the nature of the maximum custody prison." They asserted:

[The collective riot] stems directly from the specific nature of the prisoner community, and is a good illustration of what can happen when the collective social forces of a community are not integrated into collective goals for the community. This type of riot appears to have been the result primarily of the following combination of sociological and social psychological components:

1. The nature of the maximum custody prison.

2. The aggregation of different types of inmates within one prison.

3. The destruction of semi-official, informal inmate self-government by new administration.[71]

Hartung and Floch presented their analysis in the mid-1950s and many of its basic tenets have been echoed by other writers. Bowker took a slightly different approach in his analysis of prison riots (though it does not contradict Hartung and Floch). He classified prison violence as *instrumental* and *expressive*. He wrote that instrumental violence "has the general goal of garnering power and status for the aggressor. The power sought may be over individuals in the aggressor's immediate social environment or it may be broad political power and influence..." He described expressive violence as "nonrational in that it has no goals with respect to the external environment. Its only goal is tension reduction, and that internal goal is not necessarily consciously felt."[72] The interplay between these two kinds of violence is often expressed in prison riots. Bowker offers an interesting observation on the aftermath of these riots: "Once the emotional energy that fueled the riot has been spent, prisoners begin to rationally consider their situation. How can they put the best face on what they have done? They usually do so by formulating a series of complaints and demands, calculated to have some appeal to the media and the general population-at-large."[73] This is done by presenting the usual inmate grievances. The question of whether grievances precipitate riots or are used to justify them is probably something of a "what came first, the chicken or the egg?" argument. Riots and grievances are clearly linked, and there is a relative consistency over time between both prisoner complaints and the riots.

Garson, writing in 1972, examined the use of force versus restraint in prison riots.[74] He noted that "the 1952 series of prison riots was preceded by a revival of prison reform..."; this is a condition required by Hartung and Floch for a collective riot.[75] "Brutal riots" have come about at least in part as a result of traditional inmate grievances. For example, the Oklahoma State Penitentiary at McAlester was severely damaged in July of 1973 after angry inmates took it over and set it on fire. They took hostages and sought as a condition of their release the formation of an inmate council to represent inmates in dealing with the administration. They also sought immediate access to United States Justice Department attorneys (and lawyers from the American Civil Liberties Union) and the suspension of a long-time prison employee whom the inmates claimed hated prisoners.[76]

One of America's most widely reported prison riots took place at Attica Prison in New York between September 9 and 13, 1971. In that riot 11 guards and 23 convicts were killed. The convicts had prepared a lengthy list of traditional grievances, most of which the administration subsequently agreed to accept. The Attica riot, however, was only the bloodiest of a series of riots that took place within a three-year period. During the 1960s and 1970s riots occurred in prisons all around the country—from Florida to Oregon to California to North Carolina—resulting in substantial destruction and loss of life.[77]

One of the most violent brutal riots in recent decades took place at the Penitentiary of New Mexico at Santa Fe on February 2, 1980. During that riot 33 inmates were murdered and about 200 others were beaten and raped—all by other inmates. The extreme violence by prisoners against other prisoners was a unique feature of this riot.[78] Some victims were tortured first and then mutilated. Some were killed when others threw gasoline into their locked cells and burned them alive. One prisoner (who had been convicted of raping and murdering two young girls and their mother) received especially harsh treatment: "inmates reportedly dragged him out of his protective custody cell and turned a blow torch on him. As he screamed with pain, they first burned off his genitals, and then moved the torch up his body to his face and burned his eyes out."[79]

RACIAL AND ETHNIC TENSION

In addition to the usual complaints (e.g., overcrowding, the desire for better food, the need for educational and recreational programs, a lack of work, inadequate grievance procedures, and so on), a new and volatile problem is emerging.

Many of the young, urban blacks who enter prisons see themselves as "political prisoners" rather than criminals.[80] The identification along racial or ethnic lines is certainly not limited to blacks; it is also common among Hispanics and whites. Thus, many of the racial tensions that exist in the cities have been magnified by the conditions of confinement in prison. Racial tensions produce conflict not just between inmates and staff, but among inmates as well. Police crackdowns on violent gangs in major cities have sent many of their members to prison. This has not necessarily disintegrated the gangs; instead it moved them to the prisons, where they continue their violent activities.[81]

As Stojkovic and Lovell note, "the composition of the inmate population was shifting in prisons across the country. Attica was no exception. With the influx of a greater number of Puerto Rican, Chicano and black prisoners, the traditionally white-controlled prisoner society was changing. Furthermore, many of these inmates were more politically conscious and powerless in mainstream society. With changes in the inmate population and the 'political consciousness' of these inmates rising, expectations about how the prison was to be run were in a state of flux."[82] This changing makeup of the prison population took place during a period when significant legal reforms in the area of prisoner rights challenged the traditional means by which prisons had been managed. Conservative prison officials, reluctant to change the way things had been in the past, quickly found themselves out of touch with the expectations (and demands) of prisoners, thus setting the stage for a new generation of prison violence.[83]

OVERCROWDING

Racial tension is compounded by overcrowding. Overcrowding is regarded by many as "one of the most critical problems facing the contemporary American criminal justice system."[84] The *number* of people in prison tripled between 1970 and 1985 and the *rate* of incarceration more than doubled. There are several reasons for this. As one writer noted, during the 1970s "[b]oth liberals and conservatives embraced the just-deserts, or justice, model of punishment, and the late 1970s and early 1980s saw a wave of reforms put into action to provide a public policy articulation of this new approach."[85] The increased use of determinate sentences was part of this "get tough" attitude. This resulted in increased sentences for many crimes, thereby keeping more inmates in prison for longer periods of time. In addition, rapid growth of the high-risk segment of the population (males between 18 and 24) increased the base from which offenders have traditionally been drawn. Finally, the rise of the urban drug problem created an extensive network of criminal enterprise in the inner cities, thus adding to the pool of potential prisoners accessible to local communities taking a hard-line approach to the suppression of their drug problems. One unintended consequence is that despite significant building programs, 41 states are now under court order because of overcrowding. This pressure from the courts has itself produced some unintended outcomes in the policy arena. For example, the Florida legislature enacted an emergency release provision that provided for automatic release of inmates when the prison population approached the court-mandated cap.[86]

When the capacity of a prison exceeds its capacity (based on one prisoner per cell), the ability of the staff to manage prisoners is seriously degraded.[87] As crowding increases, space normally used for other purposes (such as recreation) must be converted to dormitory use. Inmate amenities are thereby reduced. As crowding increases, boredom and conflict likewise increase, and the growing number of violent incidents necessitates more rigorous control measures. This has a negative impact on staff morale, inmate attitudes and diminishes control overall.

Prison populations are not only crowded; they contain factions that are extremely hostile to one another. Maximum-security prisons (where most of the riots take place) contain many people who have used, suffered or witnessed violence before coming to prison. When they experience racial or ethnic conflict in prison, they cannot go back to their respective parts of town, but are forced to remain physically close to one another, engendering "feelings of intense discomfort and hatred."[88] Many of these inmates—especially those in maximum-security prisons—are difficult to manage because they have nothing to lose; many believe violence is the only way they can manage or control their personal environment.

CONTROL

One of the most basic questions in prisons is, "Who runs this place?" The problems stemming from prison control issues are closely related to prisoners' rights and inmate violence. Control is easiest when it is harshest. In order to impose maximum control over inmates, the prison staff must exercise brutal tactics (including physical violence) on prisoners. Clearly, such control is neither desirable on ethical grounds nor defensible on legal grounds. The question then becomes one of how much control the state can (or is willing to) relinquish before it loses control? Court-ordered reforms have stripped prisons of their ability to impose traditional controls, but in the process have contributed to the unmanageability of inmate populations. Inmates themselves may choose not to exercise their rights in a responsible manner. It is a continuation of the dilemma of the entire criminal justice system: middle-class standards of behavior often are applied to groups who either will not or cannot accept them.

The collective riot described by Hartung and Floch is a product of the control dilemma and also illustrates the rapidly changing nature of maximum-security institutions. One of the major factors mentioned was "destruction of semi-official, informal inmate self-government by a new administration."[89] They went on to note that the prison population is classified into two broad categories of inmates: overtly aggressive individuals and covertly passive individuals. The first category presents the most problems; if given an opportunity, these prisoners will seize leadership of the inmate community. This leadership has been tacitly recognized in many prisons in the past, and these "leaders" have had their power enhanced by being given jobs as inmate-assistants and inmate-clerks (assisting important staff officials or overseeing important functions). Administrators have been willing to informally share power with such leaders in return for a "quiet" prison. This process allowed the creation of an informal inmate government. As Hartung and Floch pointed out:

> In return for being allowed to operate the prison semi-officially, the inmate leaders relieved the warden of the burden of discipline. If there was an individual prisoner who grumbled too much and too openly, he was "taken care of" by his leaders. If news of group discontent reached the warden, he suggested that the inmate leaders "knew what to do" and they did it. They wanted no trouble that would endanger their positions. Thus the prison floated on an even keel for years, with no serious disturbance.[90]

Reform efforts since the 1940s deprived the more aggressive and ambitious inmates of the leadership. Many riots seem to take place after the displacement of inmate leaders. This has been coupled with an increase in prisoners' rights and the granting of new liberties to inmates. Sanford Bates, former Federal Commissioner of Prisons, recognized this problem:

> ...[D]isturbances were in many cases accompanied by the capture of hostages or prison employees by the rioters, and on reflection it can thus be understood that they were literally made possible by the greater liberties accorded to our inmates. If we were willing to return to the rigid program of separate confinement without liberties, we could prevent them![91]

Inmate control of prisons is changing, and "prisoners are less willing to exercise a controlling effect over other inmates, which is accompanied by an increasing toleration of the use of violence on the part of fellow inmates."[92] Thus, as correction reform (imposed by the courts) limits the extent of control the state can impose on inmates, the prisoners themselves are becoming less willing to work for a stable prison environment. A third problem is the rapid increase of gang, racial and ethnic separation within prisons.

As prison populations continue to divide along racial, ethnic or gang lines they present correctional administrators with some of the most difficult problems in the history of American corrections. Some of these inmates espoused radical, revolutionary or extremist ideologies before coming into prison and have found fertile grounds for fanning existing hatred since arriving in prison. This was evident in the Attica riot, for example, when some black prisoners demanded asylum and safe passage "to some nonimperialist country" and were granted meetings with figures identified with the "new left."[93] The fragmentation of inmates into political cliques, especially those that are antagonistic to conventional ideologies, makes attempts at rehabilitation difficult. Rehabilitation by its very nature requires acceptance of conventional cultural values in the first place.[94]

Places of incarceration are closely tied to communities: they receive their "inputs" (inmates) from the community and send their "outputs" (parolees and released inmates) back into them. As part of the formal control system, they deal with people whose conduct is unacceptable to the community. Ideally, jails and prisons play a positive role in improving the conduct of prisoners by making them less likely to commit new crimes. Failing that, they incapacitate them—at least for a period of time. Their challenge is daunting and must be carried out under difficult circumstances with limited resources.

Overcrowding and mandatory sentencing policies have begun to play a role in who is confined and for what crimes. This can change the character of confinement facilities by altering the demographic makeup of inmates. It also screens inmate populations in ways that force local communities to deal with more offenders without ready recourse to imprisonment. In other words, communities are likely to come under increasing pressure to deal with a broader range of offenders through community-based corrections. Should this prove to be the case, and should communities be effective in their efforts, two interesting things are likely to happen. First, communities may become more responsive to their own needs, amd in the process probably improve their effectiveness in dealing with many of these offenders. If this happens, a second (unanticipated) outcome is likely to occur: jails and prisons will be used for a narrower and much more difficult range of inmates: those who are ineligible for community treatment by virtue of the seriousness or extent of their crimes. If prison populations shift in this direction, results could include an increased difficulty in inmate management and a greater emphasis on security, all to the likely detriment of rehabilitation. Although all of this remains to be seen, it is important to remember that what happens in the community has a direct influence on correctional institutions—and vice versa.

SUMMARY

Corrections contains two categories of confinement settings: jails and prisons. Jails are places of short-term confinement used to hold people awaiting disposition of their cases or who are serving short sentences for misdemeanors. Until recent years they were administered by local authorities and were not high-priority items on the local budget. Even after the adoption of standards—and in spite of intervention by the courts—jails remain plagued with problems. The most serious problem facing local jails is overcrowding, followed by a lack of inmate resources. These problems are compounded by difficulties in finding adequate jail staffs, a pursuit that is hampered by low salaries and limited opportunities for advancement.

Prisons, on the other hand, are places of long-term confinement and come under the authority of state rather than local government. They evolved as part of a reform that reacted against the harsh capital and corporal punishments that were typical until the Age of Enlightenment. American prisons developed out of the so-called *Auburn Model*, which enforced both idleness and pointless labor and managed inmate populations under conditions unimaginable by modern standards. Prisons are divided among three basic patterns, based on their respective security needs: *maximum, medium* and *minimum*. The management of inmates is largely a function of how they are classified. The overriding factor has been (and remains) security.

Historically, prisons have been part of the invisible segment of the criminal justice system. They usually have been isolated from local communities and administered largely according to the wishes of prison administrators. This is changing, however, as states consider the privatization of prisons. A number of models are currently being explored that might ultimately bring prisons and prison labor into more direct contact with the free world.

The biggest impetus behind reform in corrections has come through the courts. After accepting prisoner cases on constitutional issues, they became highly activist in their rulings and abandoned their traditional hands-off policy. The courts have restructured much of the way American prisons function. This has not been a painless process; in fact, most state prison systems had to be brought under court order to secure compliance. As a consequence, the administration of prisons, and even entire corrections systems, is now much more responsive to law than at any earlier point in American history, and most of the major abuses within prisons have been banned.

In spite of these changes (or perhaps even because of them), prison riots have been a serious problem. Prison riots have been attributable to a variety of causes, but are clearly related to the nature of maximum-security prisons, the attitudes of the inmates contained within them and changes in how inmates are controlled or governed. Riots have been described as either *instrumental* (initiated to achieve some explicit purpose or goal) or *expressive* (serving only to reduce tension). Key issues in prison riots include overcrowding, poor food, lack of work, inadequate recreation and educational resources, and so on. However, in recent years the situation has been complicated by the presence of politically alienated extremists and prisoners who identify along ethnic lines. As the population of prisons grows to include more serious and violent offenders as well as the politically disaffected, prison management becomes more difficult. The court-mandated reforms, while meeting the requirements of law, have added to the strain. Jails and prisons remain a troubled and complicated part of the American criminal justice system.

DISCUSSION QUESTIONS

1. How do police jails differ from county jails?

2. What influence did poor laws and vagrancy statutes have on the development of jails?

3. Why is it significant that jails are part of local government? Why should that make any difference in how they are run?

4. How can jail administrators overcome the problems associated with jails as places of temporary confinement?

5. What are the main staffing problems in jails? What level of government should be responsible for correcting those problems?

6. Since prisons are state agencies, what obligation (if any) does local government have toward them?

7. Is it true that the primary mission of prisons is custody? Defend you position.

8. How did the Pennsylvania and Auburn models of prisons differ? Why did the Auburn model win out in the long run?

9. Which of the three approaches to relieving prison overcrowding (building more prisons, diverting people from them, shortening sentences) do you prefer? Why?

10. If a federal court orders a state to reduce its prison population to the level of its capacity, what factors should be taken into account in determining which prisoners to release?

11. Do you think prisons are effective in reducing crime? How would you go about determining this?

12. Do you think stricter punishment is a good way to reduce crime? What are the possible consequences of stricter punishment?

13. Should a judge's sentencing decisions be influenced by how crowded prisons are?

14. Is it ethical to contract out corrections to private companies that operate them for profit?

15. Why does the public generally not see itself as a beneficiary of its state prison system?

16. Should prison-made products be free to compete in an open economic marketplace, or are restrictions on prison labor valid? Defend your position.

17. Which model of private-sector involvement in prison industries do you think is the best for all parties? Which is the least desirable?

18. Why did the courts maintain a hands-off attitude toward corrections for so long? Should they return to that position?

19. How did the courts use the Constitution to enforce prison reform? Was their approach proper, or was it an illegitimate extension of judicial authority?

20. Why do you think Title 42, Section 1983 of the U.S. Code does not allow prisoners to challenge the length of their sentences?

21. Does the liberalization of prisons contribute to unrest within them? If so, why? Is it worth it?

22. How does the need for economies of scale influence the kind and quality of services given to prison inmates? Is this a reasonable way to do business?

23. In appointing special masters to oversee a state prison system, have federal judges extended their authority? Do you think they should use that approach? Defend your position.

24. Serious prison riots seem to be a phenomenon of the present century. Why?

25. What is the difference between an instrumental riot and an expressive riot?

26. What was the most unique feature of the Santa Fe riot in which 33 inmates were murdered?

27. What is the impact of racial and ethnic cleavages in prisons? What can prison administrators do about it?

28. How have inmates controlled prisons in the past? Do you think this was a good idea?

29. What kind of relationship (if any) should exist between local communities and state prisons?

30. What should be the goals of prison? Can prisons actually achieve those goals?

REFERENCES

[1] James J. Stephan and Louis W. Jankowski, "Jail Inmates, 1990," *Bureau of Justice Statistics Bulletin* (June 1991), 1.

[2] Neal Shover, *A Sociology of American Corrections* (Homewood, IL: The Dorsey Press, 1979), 141.

[3] Avis Thomas-Lester, "I Will Never Forget Being Locked Up Like a Criminal," *The Washington Post*, 27 January 1991, B1, B2.

[4] Harry E. Allen and Clifford E. Simonsen, *Corrections in America: An Introduction* (Encino, CA: Glencoe Publishing Co., Inc., 1978), 441.

[5] For a discussion on early punishments, see Alice Morse Earle, *Curious Punishments of Bygone Days* (Montclair, NJ: Patterson Smith, 1969).

[6] For an excellent discussion on the origins of jails, see Linda L. Zupan, *Jails: Reform and the New Generation Philosophy* (Cincinnati: Anderson Publishing Co., 1991), especially 9-23.

[7] In the early 1960s, when the author was a college student, he worked for the local fire department and lived in the Central Fire Station. Drifters would frequently come into the fire station and ask for directions to the jail where they anticipated getting a free night's lodging.

[8] For an interesting discussion of the small town jail, see Louis A. Guyon and Helen Fay Green, "Calaboose: Small Town Lockup," *Federal Probation* LIV:2 (June 1990), 58-62.

[9] Gerald D. Robin, *Introduction to the Criminal Justice System: Principles, Procedures Practices* (New York: Harper and Row, 1980), 441.

[10] Cited in Allen and Simonsen, *Corrections in America*, 441.

[11] See, for example, Nicholas L. Demos, "The Future Jail: A Professionally Managed Corrections Center That Controls Its Population," *Federal Probation* XLVIII:1 (March 1984), 35-39.

[12] Randall Guynes, "Nations Jail Managers Assess Their Problems," *National Institute of Justice: Research In Action* (August 1988).

[13] Zupan, *Jails*, 44-47.

[14] Guynes, "Nations Jail Managers Assess Their Problems," 4-5.

[15] Guynes, "Nations Jail Managers Assess Their Problems."

[16] See *Manual of Standards for Adult Local Detention Facilities* (Rockville, MD: Commission on Accreditation for Corrections).

[17] Nicholas L. Demos, "The Future Jail," *Federal Probation* XLVIII:1 (March 1984), 35-39.

[18] Allen and Simonsen, *Corrections in America*, 29.

[19] Allen and Simonsen, *Corrections in America*, 29.

[20] Blake McKelvey, *American Prisons: A History of Good Intentions* (reprint, Montclair, NJ: Patterson Smith, 1977).

[21] Kathleen Maguire and Timothy J. Flanagan, eds., U.S. Department of Justice, Bureau of Justice Statistics, *Sourcebook of Criminal Justice Statistics 1990* (Washington, DC: U.S. Government Printing Office, 1991), Table 1.18, "State and Local Corrections Full-Time Equivalent Employment," 30-34.

[22] Maguire and Flanagan, *Sourcebook of Criminal Justice Statistics 1990*, Tables 1.1 "Justice System Expenditures," (p. 2) and 1.7 "Direct Expenditure for State and Local Corrections Activities," (p. 7).

[23] President's Commission on Law Enforcement and the Administration of Justice, *Task Force Report: Corrections*. (Washington, DC: U.S. Government Printing Office, 1967), 179.

[24] Paul W. Keve, *Corrections* (New York: John Wiley and Sons, Inc., 1981), 82.

[25] The description of types of prisons in this chapter is adapted from the National Advisory Commission on Criminal Justice Standards and Goals Report, *Corrections* (Washington, DC: U.S. Government Printing Office, 1973), 343-345.

[26] National Advisory Commission on Criminal Justice Standards and Goals, *Corrections*, 343-345.

[27] George M. Camp and Camille Graham Camp, *The Corrections Yearbook 1991* (South Salem, NY: Criminal Justice Institute, 1991), 33-34.

[28] National Advisory Commission on Criminal Justice Standards and Goals, *Corrections*, 343-345.

[29] Camp and Camp, *The Corrections Yearbook 1991*, 33-34.

[30] National Advisory Commission on Criminal Justice Standards and Goals, *Corrections*, 343-345.

[31] James B. Jacobs, "Macrosociology and Imprisonment," in David F. Greenburg, ed., *Corrections and Punishment* (Beverly Hills, CA: Sage Publishing Co., 1977), 89-107.

[32] Louis P. Carney, *Corrections: Treatment and Philosophy* (Englewood Cliffs, NJ: Prentice-Hall, Inc., 1980), 102.

[33] Carney, *Corrections: Treatment and Philosophy*, 102.

[34] Camp and Camp, *The Corrections Yearbook 1991*, 48-50.

[35] Camp and Camp, *The Corrections Yearbook 1991*, 78-79.

[36] John J. DiIulio, Jr., "Private Prisons," *National Institute of Justice Crime File* (1988), 3.

[37] DiIulio, "Private Prisons."

[38] DiIulio, "Private Prisons."

[39] See also David K. Burright, "Privatization of Prisons, Fad or Future?" *FBI Law Enforcement Bulletin* 59:2 (February 1990), 1-4.

[40] Joan Mullen, "Corrections and the Private Sector," *National Institute of Justice Research Brief* (March 1985), 6.

[41] See also Judith C. Hackett, Harry P. Hatry, Robert B. Levinson, Joan Allen, Keon Chi and Edward D. Feigenbaum, "Contracting for the Operation of Prisons and Jails," *National Institute of Justcie Research Brief* (June 1987).

[42] George E. Sexton, Franklin C. Farrow and Barbara J. Auerbach, "The Private Sector Prison Industries," *National Institute of Justice Research Brief* (August 1985), 2.

[43] This legislation was contained in the Justice Assistance Act of 1984 (Public Law 93-473, Section 819), which authorized up to 20 projects to sell goods via interstate commerce providing certain safeguards were imposed.

[44] This information is extracted with minor modification from Sexton, Farrow and Auerbach, "The Private Sector and Prison Industries," 2-3.

[45] See also Alvin J. Bronstein, "Prisoners and Their Endangered Rights," *Prison Journal* 65 (1985), 3-17.

[46] *Ex parte Hull*, 312 U.S. 546 (1941).

[47] *Coffin v. Reichard*, 143 F.2d 443 (6th Cir. 1944), *cert. denied*, 325 U.S. 887 (1945).

[48] National Advisory Commission on Criminal Justice Standards and Goals, *Corrections*, 19.

[49] Richard G. Singer, "Prisoners' Rights Litigation: A Look at the Past Decade, and a Look at the Coming Decade," *Federal Probation* XLIV:4 (December 1980), 3-11.

[50] Robert Pearlman, "The Whip Pays Off," *The Nation*, 26 December 1966, 701.

[51] Pearlman, "The Whip Pays Off," 702.

[52] *Cooper v. Pate*, 378 U.S. 546 (1964).

[53] Dean J. Champion, "Some Recent Trends in Civil Litigation by Federal and State Prison Inmates," *Federal Probation* LII:3 (1988), 43-47.

[54] Candace McCoy, "The Impact of Section 1983 Litigation on Policymaking in Corrections," *Federal Probation* XLV:4 (December 1981), 17-23.

[55] *Holt v. Sarver*, 309 F. Supp. 362 (E.D. Ark. 1970), *aff'd*, 442 F.2d 304 (8th Cir. 1971). This case launched an avalanche of similar lawsuits. See, for example, *Thompson v. Enomoto*, No. 79-1630 (N.D. Ca. 1980), *aff'd*, 679 F.2d 1115 (5th Cir. 1982), *cert. denied*, 460 U.S. 1042 (1983); *Grubbs v. Bradley*, 552 F. Supp. 1052 (M.D. Tenn. 1982); *Pugh v. Locke*, 406 F. Supp. 318 (M.D. Ala. 1976); and *Jones v. Wittenberg*, 323 F. Supp. 93 (N.D. Ohio 1971).

[56] *Jackson v. Hendrick*, 40 U.S.L.W. 2710 (1972).

[57] *Rhodes v. Chapman*, 452 U.S. 337 (1981).

[58] *Wilson v. Seiter*, 501 U.S. ——, 111 S. Ct. 2321, 115 L. Ed. 2d 271 (1991). See also Larry D. Woods' editorial on the *Hudson v. McMillian* decision (60 U.S.L.W. 4151), "Supreme Court Interprets Eighth Amendment to Include Non-Serious Injury Over Justice Thomas' Dissent, *CJ Update* XX:3 (Spring 1992), 2.

[59] *Barnett v. Rogers*, 410 F.2d 995, 1001 (D.C. Cir. 1969).

[60] "Georgia Is Struggling to Comply with Reidsville Court Order," *Corrections Magazine* (June 1980), 4.

[61] See, for example, Morris E. Lasker, "Judicial Supervision of Institutional Reform," *Criminal Justice Ethics* 5:1 (Winter/Spring 1986), 2, 79-80.

[62] Irving Kaufman, "Masters in Federal Courts: Rule 53," *Columbia Law Review* (1958), 452; see also Vincent Nathan, "The Use of Masters in Institutional Reform Litigation," *University of Toledo Law Review* (1979), 419.

[63] John J. DiIulio, Jr., *Courts, Corrections and the Constitution* (New York: Oxford University Press, 1990); see especially Malcolm M. Feeley and Roger A. Hanson, "The Impact of Judicial Intervention on Prisons and Jails: A Framework for Analysis and a Review of the Literature," 12-45.

[64] The National Prison Project, *Status Report: The Courts and Prisons* (Washington, DC: American Civil Liberties Union, December 1, 1988). For more on the courts' impact on corrections, consult Rolando del Carmen et al., *Briefs of Leading Cases in Corrections* (Cincinnati: Anderson Publishing Co., 1993).

[65] *Bell v. Wolfish*, 441 U.S. 520 (1979).

[66] *Rhodes v. Chapman*, 452 U.S. 337 (1981).

[67] Harry E. Allen and Clifford E. Simonsen, *Corrections in America: An Introduction*, 2nd ed. (Encino, CA: Glencoe Publishing Co.,1978), 59.

[68] Israel L. Barak-Glantz, "The Anatomy of Another Prison Riot," in Michael Braswell, Steven Dillingham and Reid Montgomery, Jr., *Prison Violence in America* (Cincinnati: Anderson Publishing Co., 1985), 47-71.

[69] Allen and Simonsen, *Corrections in America*, 59.

[70] Frank E. Hartung and Maurice Floch, "A Social-Psychological Analysis of Prison Riots: An Hypothesis," *Journal of Criminal Law, Criminology and Police Science* 47 (May-June 1956), 51.

[71] Hartung and Floch, "A Social-Psychological Analysis of Prison Riots," 52.

[72] Lee H. Bowker, "An Essay on Prison Violence," in Braswell at al., *Prison Violence in America*, 7-17.

[73] Bowker, "An Essay on Prison Violence," 14.

[74] G. David Garson, "Force Versus Restraint in Prison Riots," *Crime and Delinquency* (October 1972), 411-421.

75 Garson, "Force Versus Restraint in Prison Riots," *Crime and Delinquency*, 414.

76 "Rioters Seek Amnesty, New Inmate Panel," *Oklahoma City Times*, 28 July 1973, 1.

77 "A Mounting Wave of Violence," *U.S. News and World Report*, 27 September 1971, 20.

78 See especially Sue Mahan, "An 'Orgy of Brutality' at Attica and the 'Killing Ground' at Santa Fe: A Comparison of Prison Riots," in Braswell et al., *Prison Violence in America*, 74-87.

79 Michael S. Serrill and Peter Katel, "The Anatomy of a Riot," *Corrections Magazine* (June 1980), 12-13.

80 Bert Useem and Peter Kimball, *States of Siege: U.S. Prisons Riots, 1971-1986* (New York: Oxford University Press, 1989).

81 Kevin Krajick, "At Statesville, The Calm is Tense," *Corrections Magazine* (June 1980): 109; see also "The Menace of the Gangs," same issue, 11-14.

82 Stojkovic and Lovell, *Corrections: An Introduction*, 334.

83 Useem and Kimball, *States of Siege*, 24-25.

84 Fred Holbert and Jack E. Call, "The Perspective of State Correctional Officials on Prison Overcrowding: Causes, Court Orders and Solutions," *Federal Probation* LIII:1 (March 1989), 25-32.

85 Alexis M. Durham III, "Then and Now: The Fruits of Late 20th Century Penal Reform," *Federal Probation* (September 1991), 28-36.

86 See *Law Enforcement News*, 3 March 1990, 8.

87 Alfred Blumstein, "Prison Crowding," *National Institute of Justice Crime File*, undated.

88 Braswell et al., *Prison Violence in America*, viii.

89 Hartung and Floch, "A Social-Psychological Analysis of Prison Riots: An Hypothesis."

90 Hartung and Floch, "A Social-Psychological Analysis of Prison Riots: An Hypothesis," 54.

91 Sanford Bates, "Penal Institutions," *National Probation and Parole Journal* (October 1957), 370.

92 Barak-Glantz, "The Anatomy of Another Prison Riot," 56.

93 Jack Waugh, "Prisons Fuel Radical Politics," *Christian Science Monitor*, 14 September 1971, 1.

94 See also Erika S. Fairchild, "Politicalization of the Criminal Offender: Prisoner Perceptions of Crime and Politics," *Criminology* (1977), 287-318; and Ronald Berkman, *Opening the Gates: The Rise of the Prisoners' Movement* (Lexington, MA: Lexington Books, 1979).

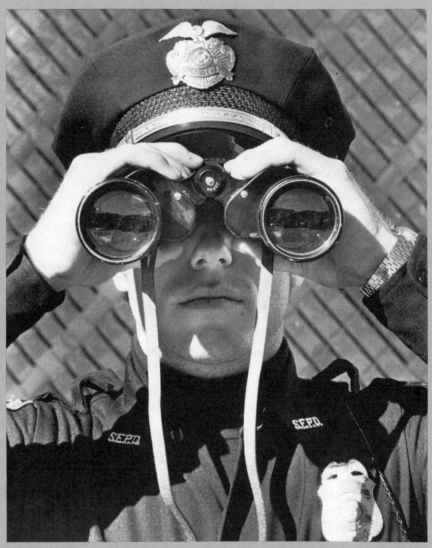

Photo Credit: Tony O'Brien, Frost Publishing Group, Ltd.

Chapter 14

THE FUTURE

Many people see the future as an extension of the present—as nothing more than a point on a time-line.[1] It is easy to understand this perspective because most changes are subtle and seem like part of the seamless flow of ordinary events. Because of this, major changes occur all the time but their importance is masked by their subtlety. Consider the first flight by the Wright brothers at Kitty Hawk, North Carolina on December 17, 1903. Although Orville Wright flew their primitive airplane only 120 feet, it was a momentous event. Even so, few people were aware at the time that the two bicycle builders from Dayton had opened the era of aviation, and no one could have anticipated the ultimate impact of that first, hesitant flight on an isolated sand dune.

Significant change takes place through two complementary processes: conceptual revolutions and technological advances. To understand the former, it is important to remember that we are guided by certain social realities. Society has various acceptable ways of interpreting reality, which seem to provide answers to important questions and are consistent with contemporary knowledge. These widely accepted theories (or *paradigms*) can be social, scientific, theological or intellectual. With the passage of time, however, new information accumulates that is at variance with the existing model or that cannot be explained. These non-conforming bits and pieces (*anomalies*) are treated as curios or artifacts. This is why a new finding that is incongruent with existing knowledge is usually dismissed by the experts. A sudden advance in knowledge—either

449

through a new discovery or the development of a more comprehensive theory—can result in a new model that not only provides answers to old questions, but accounts for anomalies as well. New theories render the old ones obsolete and, because they attack the conventional way of thinking, may be bitterly resisted by experts committed to the old paradigm. One such conceptual revolution was the shift from Ptolemaic to Copernican cosmology.

Ptolemy (127-151 A.D.) was a Greek mathematician/astronomer who claimed the earth was the center of the universe and that it remained in a fixed position while the heavens rotated about it on a daily basis. This theory explained the arrangement of the heavens for almost 1,200 years. It became an article of faith and had a profound influence on life as an integral part of both religion and science. Even though there were anomalies it could not explain, the Ptolemaic system of cosmology remained unquestioned until the sixteenth century when the Polish astronomer Nicolaus Copernicus (after finding many inconsistencies and errors in it) suggested an alternative hypothesis. Copernicus suggested that the sun was the center of the universe and that the planets, including the earth, rotated around the sun. This concept was revolutionary in every sense of the word, for it completely changed the popular perception of the universe and the human being's role within the scheme of things. Until then the concepts of "heaven and earth" were fervently believed; Copernicus' theory defined the earth as a planet like the others in the solar system, replacing the idea of heaven with the concept of space. This was such an affront to the theology of the time that Copernicus was extremely cautious about publishing his theory; people had been declared heretics and burned at the stake for far less. Thomas Kuhn has developed a theory about the structure of scientific revolutions. He relates the advancement of humankind to these kinds of major changes in theory; changes that have dramatically altered the nature and quality of life.[2]

The second way the future is significantly altered is through the discovery of revolutionary processes or technologies. Although these kinds of advances do not generally alter *theory*, they do change *practice*. The "discovery" of agriculture, for example, revolutionized social history. It led to the domestication of animals, the establishment of permanent settlements, a new division of labor and the creation of new social arrangements. Another example is the Industrial Revolution, which produced the factory system, industrialism, labor mechanization, the development of the modern nation-state and mercantile capitalism. Each of these changes followed the development of new technologies and processes. Consider the inventions of Thomas Alva Edison—especially the phonograph, the moving picture camera and a system for economically operating incandescent light. On September 4, 1882 Edison opened his first commercial power plant for generating electricity in New York City. It served 85 customers and about 400 electric lamps. When Edison died 49 years later (on October 18, 1931) President Herbert Hoover wanted all the lights in America turned off for two minutes in Edison's honor. Doing so was neither practical nor possible, for the "Wizard of Menlo Park" had truly changed the entire world with his advances in technology.

During the second half of the twentieth century advances in electronics, communications, data processing, fiber optics and other fields of technology have led us into a "Third Wave," which has likewise radically altered both physical and social reality.[3] The full impact of this revolution is only now beginning to be felt by large numbers of people. The future promises even more change; in fact, the next 100 years will probably see more change than has occurred in all of recorded history, most of it arising from new technologies.

Although we can surmise that the future will be different from the present, just as the present differs from the past, we do not know exactly what the future holds. Some prophesy doom.[4] Heilbronner, for example, gloomily noted that, "The outlook for man, I believe, is painful, difficult, perhaps desperate, and the hope that can be held out for his future prospect seems to be very slim indeed....the answer to whether we can conceive of the future other than as a continuation of darkness, cruelty, and disorder of the past seems to me to be no; and to whether worse impends, yes."[5] On the other hand, advances in nearly every field of human endeavor seem to hold the tantalizing prospect for solving some of our oldest and most serious problems. Farming the oceans, for example, may offer an alternative to starvation—a threat which has already become a reality for millions in parts of Africa and Southwest Asia. The discovery and employment of alternative energy sources that do not consume the already dwindling supplies of non-renewable fossil fuels is another prospect that may become a reality in the near future. Advances in chemistry, biology and medicine could cure cancer and heart disease and thereby prolong life for millions. Discoveries in space technology, fiber optics and cell biology likewise have vast potential for reshaping the future for the better. As Toffler noted,

> Just as the second wave combined coal, steel, electricity, and rail transport to produce automobiles and a thousand other life-transforming products, the real impact of the new changes will not be felt until we reach the stage of combining the new technologies—linking computers, electronics, new materials from outer space and the oceans, with genetics, and all of these in turn, with the new energy base. Bringing these elements together will release a flood of innovation unlike any seen before in human history.[6]

Technology also provides the means for humankind's own annihilation. Moreover, our collective environmental folly and longstanding lack of respect for the fragile biosphere upon which we all depend have potentially catastrophic outcomes—depletion of the ozone layer, deforestation, desertification, pollution, etc. It is possible that the positive application of technology will not be employed quickly enough to solve some of these problems. In addition to widespread famine and disease in much of the world, AIDS has the potential for becoming an apocalyptic specter beyond imagination. Given a more efficient vector and increasingly pathogenic mutations, it is possible that the HIV virus could spread death around the globe with an impact as great as that of the Black Death of the Middle Ages.

Although it is impossible to forecast just how technology will be used, it is obvious that it can work for good or ill. It is thus, as our very existence hangs in the balance, that we move into the twenty-first century.

THE FUTURE OF JUSTICE

As technology changes, social relationships change as well; however, even though technology and political institutions may change, it is likely that human nature will not. Conflict, as a continuing by-product of human interaction, will need to be resolved, order maintained and human affairs regulated. Some of these changes will probably influence how justice will be defined and the means by which it will be administered.

MORALITY

Plato, in *The Republic*, saw justice as consisting of a harmonious relationship among the various components of the social organism; that is, he saw justice as being *integrative*. As Bodenheimer notes, "...justice is concerned with the fitness of a group order or social system for the task of accomplishing its essential objectives. The aim of justice is to coordinate the diversified efforts and activities of members of the community and to allocate rights, powers, and duties among them in a manner which will satisfy the reasonable needs and aspirations of individuals and at the same time promote maximum productive effort and social cohesion."[7]

Justice, however, must be more than integrative; many feel it must also take ethical and moral questions into account. Moral values are always in a state of flux, and by the time public policy has come to terms with shifts in moral or ethical values, they have usually shifted yet again. Justice, at least as it is publicly administered, tends to be hypocritical because it is based on ideals rather than realities, and the actual administration of government policy (including justice) often falls considerably short of those ideals. This gives rise to criticism of the government and its agents, who are seen as practicing one thing while preaching another. Thus, the administration of justice will nearly always be something of a contradiction of terms.

Predicting moral trends is much more difficult than predicting technological trends. Although we can be certain that morality will change, and that doing so will have an influence on the criminal justice system, we cannot be sure how, when or why these shifts will take place. Even as morals change, approaches to the changes will produce conflict among those who hold differing perspectives. Advocates probably will try to use law and political machinery to support their positions, and morality will likely continue to be expressed in terms of power (especially political power). Thus, these issues will remain a source of community conflict. The battle over abortion rights is a clear example of this process.

The real problem with moral conflicts is not that they involve issues upon which reasonable people may disagree, but that they become issues that polarize groups within the same community. When this happens the focus of attention shifts from the moral issue under debate to the nature of the groups in conflict, pitting one against the other. This process underlies much of the racial and religious conflict we have seen in our own lifetimes. The prolonged conflicts in Northern Ireland and the Middle East clearly illustrate this phenomenon. There is a distinct possibility that such conflict could arise in the United States as racial, ethnic and gender-based interest groups battle with one another for power and the right to decide a variety of social and economic issues.

For centuries religion has shaped values and produced at least a rough consensus among members of the community. This is no longer the case. Religion is now fragmented into scores of denominations and sects, most of which disagree with one another on a variety of issues. As a result, religion has lost much of its power to regulate community life and individual conduct. Since religion is a major component of the private control system, its loss of influence has diminished the overall ability of the private control system to regulate individual behavior.

THE LAW

The ability of the criminal justice system to act is firmly grounded in laws that define crimes, establish procedures and provide sanctions. Changes in the law therefore produce a corresponding (but not necessarily *equal*) change in how the criminal justice system works. These changes fall into two categories: *substantive* and *procedural*. Substantive changes involve basic definitions of crimes. In the future some old crimes will be eliminated and new ones will be added. For example drunkenness, vagrancy and gambling have all been decriminalized in varying degrees, and this has had a direct impact on how the police structure both their law enforcement and order-maintenance roles. In all probability, the state will continue this process by moving away from legislating morality except in cases where doing so is necessary for the protection of minors or where it can be shown that an actual harm will befall the victim. Sexual practices among consenting adults and perhaps even the recreational use of some drugs may be decriminalized in the future.

New crimes will emerge, and there may be a temptation to expand the kinds of things that can be considered criminal. For example in recent years we have seen the rise of so-called "hate crimes." These are wrongful acts in which the defendant's conduct has been motivated by hatred, bias or prejudice based on the actual or perceived race, color, religion, national origin, ethnicity, gender or sexual orientation of another individual or group. This represents a significant trend. Conventional crimes speak to overt acts (e.g., assaults, theft, vandalism, job and housing discrimination, and so on) but not to the *motive* behind them. Indeed, historically motive has been considered irrelevant in crimes; *intent* was focused upon instead. Adding motive to the definition of crime creates the potential for widening the scope of police investigations to include examining the beliefs of suspects. Hate crimes run the risk of taking this even a step further by making bias itself a crime, thus regulating opinion. The Hate Crimes Sentencing Enhancement Act of 1992 required the United States Sentencing Commission to "enhance" (increase) the sentence of people convicted of hate crimes. As Hentoff noted, "Anyone convicted of having been somehow driven by bigotry to commit a federal crime in this category would get more years in the slammer than someone who committed the same crime with nothing on his or her mind but the proceeds."[8] Bias may be reprehensible, but to make it a crime is risky indeed. It is but a small step from punishing someone for an actual harm resulting from actions based on bias to punishing the bias itself.

If future crimes include acts against the environment, it will require modification of our concepts of harm, wrong and responsibility, and will change the arena in which the criminal justice system works, who its clients are and what it will be expected to accomplish. As the definitions of substantive crimes change, corresponding changes in the laws defining civil wrongs and criminal procedure are likely to take place as well.

TECHNOLOGY

The future of the criminal justice system cannot be considered apart from the future of technology, because it will be forced to respond to technological changes. While advances in technology will create new jobs and modify old ones, they also will help open up opportunities for both traditional and new crimes. As the criminal justice system adapts, employment within the system will call for increased levels of technical competence. Although this should result in the improved delivery of services, it will have great impact on the profession because these skill and knowledge requirements will limit the selection of recruits to the criminal justice system.

Improved technologies—particularly in communications and the information and decision sciences—are also apt to increase both the efficiency and the effectiveness of the criminal justice system. The reduction of human resource requirements and simultaneous enhancement of the quality of outputs should enable the criminal justice system to do more things, better and more quickly, with fewer people. These same technologies might also provide dramatic improvements in such areas as criminal surveillance, crime-scene and evidence processing, and the prediction of crimes. The way these changes force the various elements of the criminal justice system to integrate their efforts more effectively will ultimately revitalize the entire criminal justice system.

DEMOGRAPHY

How and where people distribute themselves in the future is likely to be different. The major population shift away from the cities that started in the 1960s will probably continue. Results of the 1990 census indicate that this process continues in full swing. An especially important trend in the demography of the cities is the "doughnut complex" in which the "hole" is the decaying central city and the "doughnut" is the growing and prosperous suburban and exurban ring. This phenomenon was clearly identified by Sternlieb and Hughes in 1980.[9]

Three developments are taking place. First, the central cities are shrinking; those who *can* leave are doing so. Second, non-metropolitan areas are experiencing rapid growth. Third, there is a demographic shift toward the direction of the Sun Belt—with large numbers of people moving from northeastern and north central states to southwestern and western states. The long-term impact of these trends will be staggering. For one thing, the role of the central cities is changing dramatically and will continue to do so. When the cities were centers of commerce and industry, they attracted many workers, especially those in blue-collar and service occupations. The cities have now become centers of dependency, places where the unemployed, sick, elderly and poor congregate to have their needs met through public support. As the middle class leaves the city the remaining tax base is reduced and few stabilizing influences are left behind. The results are serious: "the greater reality is the city of the poor, with from a fourth (Boston) to a seventh (New York) of the population on welfare, with staggering crime rates and truancy levels (vastly understated by the official reports) that make a mockery of the traditional role of public education as an influence for homogeneity and a route upward for the urban young."[10]

The loss of industry, the flight of the upper and middle classes to the suburbs, the concentration of the poor in unsafe and unhealthy environments and the increased demands for public services have created major financial and administrative problems for cities. The long-term consequences of this situation are hard to assess; however, one should not overlook the prospect of urban terrorism as inner-city youths become increasingly isolated, alienated and hostile. The riots in Los Angeles in May of 1992 showed clear evidence of this problem.[11] Increased drug activity, the spiraling use of firearms and the emergence of a cynical underclass have changed the face of the inner cities. Increasingly, suburban residents have even abandoned going into the cities for shopping or entertainment.[12] Unless the cycle of poverty and dependency can be broken, it seems likely that as the inner cities become smaller in population, they will become much more volatile—and almost certainly will become breeding grounds for serious violence.

Part of the changing demography includes the alteration of family arrangements. The traditional "nuclear family," composed of the breadwinning father, the housekeeping mother and two children, is largely a thing of the past. This kind of family is already a distinct minority of family arrangements, competing with a wide range of alternative family styles. Alternatives include the single (never married) parent; dyads composed of one parent and one or more children in which the other parent has left through death, divorce or abandonment; homosexual marriages (sometimes with adopted children); solo adult relationships; and so on. These and many other kinds of family arrangements are already common, but it remains to be seen how they will create, modify or assign meaning to social values and even the law itself. The future promises to provide enormous variety in living arrangements. This will affect not only basic family law, but an even broader scope of social policy. The criminal justice system will have to adapt to this and whatever problems accompany it.

America also is becoming more ethnically diverse. According to the 1990 census, 19.9 million people now living in the United States (or about 8 percent of the population) are foreign-born.[13] Never before have so many immigrants lived in the United States, and these newer immigrants differ from previous waves of immigrants in that the population is more Asian and Hispanic than European in origin. Absorbing this quantity of immigrants is not likely to be easy; for example, right now nearly 32 million people living in America do not speak English at home, and more than 40 percent of all foreign-born immigrants say they do not speak English very well.[14] This has very real consequences. For example, almost three-quarters of the residents of Miami, Florida do not speak English at home. Other cities (most notably Los Angeles, Chicago, New York and Washington, DC) are feeling the impact of large numbers of foreign-born and non-English speaking immigrants. As minority populations continue to expand, new and more frustrating problems will emerge—including the need to alter public education to meet the needs of children for whom English is a second language and who have been reared in cultures with different traditions and values. In the past, the primary social animosity was between whites and blacks. This has been added to by animosity between Asians and blacks, Hispanics and whites, and to a certain extent, each racial or ethnic group against every other one. In addition, we are also faced with conflict based on gender and sexual orientation. Diversity seems to have ceased to be integrative and instead become a zero-sum game in which each group competes for the largest possible slice of the "power pie" at the expense of all other groups. Such battles, fought from the courts to the streets, are likely to continue into the next century—perhaps with even greater intensity. If the lack of consensus among various ethnic and special interest groups persists, the struggle for power may be fought at the polls, perhaps producing a political gridlock that could, in turn, intensify tensions and further divide the community.

Another significant demographic change looming on the horizon is the decline of the middle class. In 1969 approximately 71 percent of all households lived on middle income, but by 1989 that figure had dropped to 63 percent (during the same period the proportion of households reporting high income went from almost 11 percent to almost 15 percent). The median household income, another important index, has also shown a disturbing change. The median household income is the point at which half earn more and half earn less. Although the median income continues to increase, it is doing so at about one-fifth the rate it did during the 1950s and 1960s. Although the average household income is relatively stagnant, it is clear that indeed the rich *are* getting richer as the poor are getting poorer.[15]

In addition, with a decline in the availability of moderately priced housing, increases in housing costs have outpaced income. This has forced the poor into blighted areas that take a larger share of their income than in the past (among the poor, about 56 percent spend over half their income on housing alone). All of this suggests an inevitable outcome: in the near future the disadvantaged will be crowded together in dense environments from which they will have fewer opportunities to escape.[16]

COMMUNITY EXPECTATIONS

In the future, urban populations may expect or demand more services from local government, including the criminal justice system. Such expectations are likely to exceed the capabilities of local governments, which will have to operate within their budgets at a time when revenues are likely to be in more dire straits than they are at present. This means that difficult choices will have to be made. Since much of what is done within the criminal justice system is labor-intensive, and since salaries are the major source of public expenditures, the number of people the cities can afford to hire will be limited by the amount of money available. The bottom line is that not all interests within the community will be served, and those that are served will probably be provided at levels below what the public wants. This will most likely lead to dissatisfaction accompanied by complaints of discrimination.

The trend of diminished federal funding for state and local governments is likely to continue, especially as momentum for a balanced federal budget increases. This could be compounded by the continued decline of heavy industry, high levels of unemployment (especially among the poorly educated) and increased demands for major social service programs (especially publicly supported health care).

The most crucial problem facing the city of the future will be the management of scarce resources, and virtually all criminal justice agencies will have to compete for funding in this increasingly competitive economic environment. Various segments of the community may demand that their interests be given priority, and even though each may be valid in its own right, not all of these interests are compatible. For example, the goal of increasing minority and female representation in the criminal justice work force has proven to be a divisive and bitter issue when the correction of past wrongs involves the creation of new ones. The extreme polarization of the issue may preclude an amicable resolution of the problem in the foreseeable future.

The competing demands of crime control and due process are also bound to continue to fan public passions. An increasingly large segment of the public appears to have grown weary of what it believes to be an arbitrary, capricious and ineffective criminal justice system that they see as favoring criminals over victims. Countered by another segment of the population that believes individual liberties can only be secured through rigid procedural safeguards that limit what the criminal justice system can do, the enormous gap between "factual" and "legal" guilt will continue to pit liberals and conservatives against one another.

THE CRIMINAL JUSTICE SYSTEM: THINGS TO WORRY ABOUT

There are no guarantees that everything will work out. Unanticipated problems continue to crop up, many of which seem to defy solution. For example, although the computer boom of the 1970s and 1980s produced incredible new communications and data processing capabilities, it also introduced an entirely new kind of "illiteracy" (adding people who cannot use computers to those who cannot read or write).

A number of potential pitfalls could prevent the criminal justice system from adapting to the changes of the future. The issues presented below are a contentious sample. Even offering them for discussion will raise a lot of controversy, but they can be ignored only at great peril.

THE POLICE

The police are faced with enormous internal and external problems. Unfortunately, their ability (and willingness) to solve these problems by themselves is seriously limited. The police have become caught up in a web spun by their own historical development along with external pressures imposed on them by legislatures, courts and community sentiment.

Selection

The selection of police officers is rapidly becoming more a process of social engineering than an effort to recruit the most capable candidates. Affirmative action was designed to give an edge to minorities who were as qualified as the officers already employed; however, in many departments the principle of affirmative action has been abandoned in favor of numeric or percentage hiring quotas. Many police departments have avoided the cost and effort involved in developing honest and well-administered affirmative action programs. Others have done so to avoid having to deal with lawsuits and consent decrees, while others do it because the courts have ordered them to do so. If police departments continue to recruit by merely screening the worst *out* rather than by selecting the best *in*, they are bound to become lackluster institutions staffed by mediocre officers. Lowering the levels of expectation becomes a self-fulfilling prophecy that not only guarantees mediocrity but makes it a virtue.

Promotion

The promotion of police officers, especially in the larger cities, is following the same pattern. It is based increasingly on attempts to remedy past racial and gender discrimination and to increase the participation of minorities and women in the higher ranks. However, if this goal is accomplished by focusing on race and gender rather than on qualifications, it will ultimately be counterproductive and expensive. Because leadership drives an organization, who is selected (and how so) will have a major impact on department morale, the quality of leadership at the top and the quality of performance at the bottom. Any promotion practice that violates fundamental fairness will demoralize those not promoted and stigmatize those who are. If their ability to lead is compromised by the unwillingness of subordinates to follow, the task of leadership will become monumentally difficult. The advancement of less qualified supervisors and leaders will lower the overall quality of the police and fan the embers of internal strife within departments.

Deployment

We have seen how contemporary police work has grown out of a long so-cial and political tradition. How valid are those traditions? How well do they answer today's problems? Do we still need to have the bulk of the police force performing patrol in marked cars? Should the investigative function pay more attention to the social and behavioral sciences, or should it retain its strong orientation toward legal definitions of behavior? Do police know what their communities expect of them, and are they willing to modify their operations to meet those expectations? These are critical questions that receive little attention in many departments. Since the demise of the federal government's Law Enforcement Assistance Administration (and the end of the Law Enforcement Education Program) in 1981, there has been little quality research on the police function in either academic or operational environments.

Administration

Historically, police departments have been administered by men who have come up through the ranks. Socialized into the culture of police work, these people are typically oriented more toward operations than toward management. As a consequence, they have been notoriously poor administrators because their background does not include specific training in public policy formulation, pub-lic finance and budgeting, public personnel administration, management or the nature of complex organizations. Indeed, some feel that most of the problems facing the police are a direct result of a past history of inadequate administra-tion. This is compounded by the fact that there are few if any checks or bal-ances on police administrators. In a very practical sense, senior police execu-tives do not answer to anyone.

The police of the twenty-first century may end up re-establishing their working-class status by failing to move beyond their current limitations. Should this be the case, the police will find themselves growing further apart from their communities and perhaps even supplemented or replaced by private police. The police cannot remain apart from the larger community or continue to define their work in terms of their own agendas. The police of the next century need leader-ship that assesses their role in light of community expectations and the limita-tions under which they operate. Community policing offers one way out of this dilemma, but requires attitudes and skills not yet embraced by the average po-lice administrator.

THE COURTS

The prosecution and defense functions are almost solely the domain of lawyers (the only part of the criminal justice system dominated by this group). Sometimes charges are dropped, modified, ignored or negotiated just for the sake of keeping the dockets moving or to feed personal and institutional goals. One hope for the future is to streamline the process by moving away from traditional litigation and into other forms of conflict resolution or offense adjudication. This concept is known as *participator justice* and involves such devices as mediation and arbitration as alternatives to the adversarial system currently employed in civil and criminal cases. However, this could meet major resistance because it would require changes in legislation. Lawyers are not only the people who benefit most from the inefficiencies of the system, they are the practitioners of the adversary system and controllers of the legislative process. The question is whether the profession can rise far enough above self-interest to provide substantial benefit to the public.

CORRECTIONS

Whether corrections is a failure is a mystery. We do know that it is very expensive and strangely detached from reality. We measure crimes by whether they are felonies or misdemeanors, but there are no clear standards by which we assess them in terms of their actual harm to society. By the same token, we assess criminals by the legal infractions for which they are convicted, not by what they have actually done or by measuring its impact on the community. Many offenders pass through the system. Although some abandon criminality, it is not known whether they would have done so anyway. (A large proportion of offenders do seem to "age out" and become law-abiding, with or without the system's help.) The processing of criminals largely ignores the long-term consequences of their crimes on society.

At some point the criminal justice system will have to separate the concepts of punishment and rehabilitation. Prisons must confine serious predators to protect the public, and a system of punishments must be implemented to deal with the remainder of the criminal population. Ideally, the punishments should "fit" the crime without making the problem worse. Finally, we must find ways of curbing violent and destructive behavior.

It is possible that some future society will be willing to consider chemical or surgical methods for taming these kinds of violent criminals. The potential for using such methods is evident in the consideration of RO15-5413, a drug (first tested by a Swiss pharmaceutical firm) that was found to sober up heavily intoxicated rats within two minutes after its administration. If administered before alcohol consumption, the rats did not get drunk. If it was taken over time, the rats lost interest in alcohol altogether. Because this drug may have the same effect on humans, it could be used to combat alcohol abuse and may even reduce some of the crime arising from alcohol abuse.[17]

Will we learn from our mistakes? Will communities of the future be willing and able to overcome the narrow fetters of bias, greed and stupidity? Only time will tell. Remarkable improvements have taken place in the criminal justice system since the late 1950s, but it is evident that our society learns quite slowly—fighting change and resisting the new while embracing what is convenient or personally satisfying. As the Byzantine emperor Justinian (483-565 A.D.) said, "Justice is the earnest and constant will to render to every man his due. The precepts of the law are these: to live honorably, to injure no other man, to render to every man his due."[18] Doing so is the challenge of the twenty-first century.

DISCUSSION QUESTIONS

1. Why is it so hard to recognize the importance of major changes?

2. What do you think will demand the greatest attention in the next quarter century: regional, national or global issues?

3. Moral questions deal with basic beliefs of what is right and wrong. If this is so, why do they change?

4. Can any community accept a range of acceptable moral and ethical beliefs that regulate human behavior? Why or why not?

5. To what extent should the justice system enforce morality? Should morality even be enforced at all?

6. Why is public policy with regard to private morality inevitably hypocritical?

7. The author contends that religion is no longer an integrative force in the community. Do you agree? Does it actually make any difference whether it is?

8. What kinds of new crimes do you think technology will "create" in the future? How will this impact on the criminal justice system?

9. At what point does the use of law to "protect" the public actually become harmful instead? Are there any safeguards to protect against that happening?

10. Will police officers in the future have to be better educated and smarter than they are today? If so, how will that impact on their recruitment?

11. What will become of the large cities during the next 25 years? Is it inevitable?

12. How will public education change in our urban areas? Why will this happen, and what could be the consequences?

13. Do you think urban terrorism is a realistic prospect for the future? If it is, how will the police control it?

14. Will changes in family arrangements change either the criminal or civil law? What do you predict, and what are your reasons?

15. The large influx of Asians and Hispanics is changing the demography of many cities. How do you think they will mix with the blacks and whites who are already there? Do you see any potential problems?

16. Do we have a permanent "underclass" in our cities? If so, what does this mean? Is it a problem?

17. Will competing factions within the community be able to mediate their demands for services? If not, what will happen?

18. The author contends that the management of scarce resources will be one of the biggest challenges of the future. Do you agree with this contention? Defend your position.

19. Do you think the police will be as slow to change in the future as they have been in the past? What factors influence how fast and how effectively the police change?

20. What are the likely future consequences of today's methods for selecting and promoting police officers?

21. Should we retain the "adversary system" in resolving criminal and civil issues? Suggest some practical alternatives.

22. How would you recommend changing corrections in the future?

23. Will the criminal justice system of the future be shaped by external events or will the system itself bring about change? What is the difference between the two concepts?

24. What problems do you predict for the future?

25. Do you view the future of criminal justice optimistically or pessimistically? Defend your position.

REFERENCES

1 Alvin Toffler, *The Third Wave* (New York: William Morrow and Company, Inc., 1980), see especially Chapter 11, "The New Synthesis."

2 Thomas S. Kuhn, *Structure of Scientific Revolutions*, 2nd ed., Foundation of the Unity of Science Series, vol. 2, no. 2 (Chicago: University of Chicago Press, 1970).

3 Toffler, *The Third Wave*.

4 See, for example, L.S. Stavrianos, *The Promises of the Coming Dark Ages* (San Francisco: W.H. Freeman and Company, 1976) and Robert L. Heilbronner, A*n Inquiry Into the Human Prospect* (New York: W.W. Norton and Company), 22.

5 Heilbronner, *An Inquiry Into the Human Prospect*, 22.

6 Toffler, *The Third Wave*, 164.

7 Edgar Bodenheimer, *Jurisprudence: The Philosophy and Method of the Law* (Cambridge, MA: Harvard University Press, 1962), 177.

8 Nat Hentoff, "Punishing People for What You Think They Thought," *The Washington Post*, 30 May 1992, A21.

9 George Sternlieb and James W. Hughes, "The Changing Demography of the Central City, " *Scientific American* 243 (August 1980), 48-53.

10 Sternlieb and Hughes, "The Changing Demography of the Central City, " 53.

11 See David H. Hackworth, "The Was No Riot, It Was a Revolt," *Newsweek*, 25 May 1992, 33.

12 See also Barbara Vobejda, "Urban Recovery Impeded by Changes of Past Three Decades," *The Washington Post*, 8 May 1992, A1-A11.

13 U.S. Bureau of the Census, *Statistical Abstract of the United States: 1992*, 112th ed. (Washington, DC: U.S. Government Printing Office, 1992).

14 Barbara Vobejda, "A Nation in Transition," *The Washington Post*, 29 May 1992, A1-A19.

15 Vobejda, "A Nation in Transition," A19.

16 Vobejda, "A Nation in Transition," A19.

17 Gene Stephens, "Drugs and Crime," *The Futurist* 26:3 (May-June 1992), 19-22.

18 Peter Birks and Grant McLeod, [Justinian's] *Institutes* (Ithaca, NY: Cornell University Press, 1987).

SUBJECT INDEX

NAME INDEX

TABLE OF CASES

In re Blakes, 4 Ill. App. 3d 576, 281 N.E.2d 454 (1972).

In re Gault, 387 U.S. 1, 87 S. Ct. 1428, 18 L. Ed. 2d 527 (1967).

Jackson v. Hendrick, 40 U.S.L.W. 2710 (1972).

Johnson v. Louisiana, 406 U.S. 356 (1972).

Jones v. Wittenberg, 323 F. Supp. 93 (N.D. Ohio 1971).

Kent v. United States, 383 U.S. 541, 86 S. Ct. 1045, 16 L. Ed 2d (1966).

Malloy v. Hogan, 378 U.S. 1, 84 S. Ct. 1489, 12 L. Ed. 2d 653 (1964).

Mapp v. Ohio, 367 U.S. 643, 81 S. Ct. 1684, 6 L. Ed. 1801 (1961).

Marusa v. District of Columbia, 484 F.2d 828 (D.C. Cir. 1973).

Martarella v. Kelley, 349 F. Supp. 575 (S.D.N.Y. 1972).

McKeiver v. Pennsylvania, 403 U.S. 528 (1971).

Monell v. Department of Social Services, 436 U.S. 658, 98 S. Ct. 2018 (1978).

Monroe v. Pape, 365 U.S. 167, 82 S. Ct. 473 (1961).

Owens v. Haas, 601 F.2d 1224 (2d Cir. 1979).

Peters v. Bellinger, 159 N.E.2d 528 (Ill. App. 1959).

Powell v. Alabama, 287 U.S. 45, 53 S. Ct. 55, 77 L. Ed. 158 (1932).

Pugh v. Locke, 406 F. Supp. 318 (M.D. Ala. 1976).

Rhodes v. Chapman, 452 U.S. 337 (1981).

Robbins v. Glenn County, No. CIVS-85-0675 RAR (E.D. Cal. 1986).

School Board of Nassau County v. Arline, 55 U.S.L.W. 4245 (1987).

Swain v. Alabama, 380 U.S. 202 (1965).

Thompson v. Enomoto, No. 79-1630 (N.D. Cal. 1980), *aff'd*, 679 F.2d 1115 (5th Cir. 1982), *cert. denied*, 460 U.S. 1042 (1983).

United States v. Paradise, 480 U.S. 149, 107 S. Ct. 1053, 94 L. Ed. 2d 203 (1987).

United States v. Salerno et al. (on certiorari to the U.S. Court of Appeals, 2d Circuit), 481 U.S. 739 (1987).

Weeks v. United States, 232 U.S. 383, 34 S. Ct. 341, 58 L. Ed. 652 (1914).

Williams v. Florida, 399 U.S. 78, 86 (1970).

Wilson v. Seiter, 501 U.S. ——, 111 S. Ct. 2321, 115 L. Ed. 2d 271 (1991).